HUMAN RESOURCE MANAGEMENT

LAWRENCE A. KLATT
ROBERT G. MURDICK
FREDERICK E. SCHUSTER

Florida Atlantic University

Charles E. Merrill Publishing Company
A Bell & Howell Company
Columbus Toronto London Sydney

Dedicated to Dean Gary A. Luing, whose support and encouragement made this book possible.

Published by
Charles E. Merrill Publishing Company
A Bell & Howell Company
Columbus, Ohio 43216

This book was set in Zapf Book.
Text Design: Cynthia Brunk
Cover Illustration: Dave Mankins
Cover Design: Cathy Watterson
Production Coordination: Tracey E. Dils

Part 1 photo courtesy of Nationwide Insurance; Part II photo courtesy of Lanier Business Products; Part III photo courtesy of Eastman Kodak Company; Part IV photo courtesy of ROLM Corporation, Santa Clara, California; Part V photo courtesy of American Federation of Labor and Congress of Industrial Organizations; Part VI photo courtesy of Hewlett Packard Company.

Copyright © 1985 by Bell & Howell Company. All rights reserved. No part of this book may be reproduced in any form, electronic or mechanical, including photocopy, recording, or any information storage and retrieval system, without permission in writing from the publisher.

Library of Congress Catalog Card Number: 84–62637
International Standard Book Number: 0-675-20331-7
Printed in the United States of America
1 2 3 4 5 6 7 8 9 10—89 88 87 86 85

PREFACE

This text offers both theory and hands-on applications to provide balanced, practical coverage of human resources management. It is designed for a comprehensive, introductory course in personnel/human resource management, serving the needs of majors who need a broad outlook and nonmajors who need awareness of opportunities in the field. We hope to prepare students for the modern workplace. We look at management both philosophically and managerially as a systems process in which the workers' and company's goals are achieved together. As such every business has objectives that must be met efficiently by responsible management. We stress personnel and human resource management issues within a systems approach. Our view is that appreciation of systems principles leads to more effective achievement of objectives, including worker satisfaction, than does intuitive nonsystematic management.

In our integrated approach, we explore all the perspectives: rational, behavioral, functional, diagnostic, and applied. In addition to covering traditional topics, we move on in scope to acknowledge the tremendous changes that have occurred in the field of human resource management. We discuss social and legal changes involving women, the elderly, and minorities; health and safety issues and the quality of work life; mid-life career changing; and how computers and research impact this field. We think line managers have the primary responsibility to use human resources well, but we also recognize the advisory function of the personnel department as an agent of change. Our approach considers traditional topics but always relates them to management's responsibility.

Throughout the text's six parts there are features to aid study:

- "Spotlights"—brief sketches of managers' on-the-job experiences
- Case studies—real-life problems on the job
- Charts, graphs, tables—visually reinforce key concepts

PREFACE

- Chapter outlines and objectives—goals for learning
- Bibliography—springboard for assignments and discussion

We have forged this text and our ideas with the help of many people. In particular we wish to thank the editorial staff at Charles E. Merrill Publishing Company, especially Steven Smith, Tracey Dils, and Kathleen Nevils. The authors also wish to thank Elaine Klatt, Emily Murdick, and Elizabeth Schuster for their patience and support during this lengthy project.

In addition, the authors are indebted to the following people who reviewed various stages of the manuscript. We certainly do not claim that our views necessarily represent their views—but they have helped us shape our thoughts more clearly:

Jarold Abbott,
Florida Atlantic University
Kermit Davis,
Auburn University
Thomas Dougherty,
University of Missouri
Lucy Gulielmino,
Florida Atlantic University
Paul Gulielmino,
Florida Atlantic University
Durward Hofler,
Northeastern Illinois University
George Munchus III,
University of Alabama

Robert Paul,
Kansas State University
Tom Urban,
Arco Oil & Gas Company
Elizabeth Wesman,
Syracuse University
Leon A. Klatt, Michigan Employment Security Commission
John M. Larsen,
The University of Tennessee
Wayne Wilson,
Cameron University

Lawrence A. Klatt
Robert G. Murdick
Fred E. Schuster

CONTENTS

PART I
THE SETTING

1

HUMAN RESOURCES IN THE BUSINESS SYSTEM 2

Productivity and the Quality of Work Life 4
From Personnel Administration to Human Resource Management 5
Social and Legal Changes Influencing HR Management 9
Conditions of Employment 13
Labor-Management Relations 16
Changes in the Economy and Problems of Productivity 18
Changing Work Force 20
P/HR Department 25
Professionalization in the P/HR Field 35
Integrated Approach to Managing the P/HR Function 38

2

THE LEGAL ENVIRONMENT FOR HUMAN RESOURCE MANAGEMENT 46

Public Policy and Human Resource Management 49
Equal Employment Opportunity (EEO) 50
Affirmative Action 55
Uniform Guidelines on Employee Selection Procedures 61
Government's Role in Employee Safety and Health 62
Legal Influences on Compensation and Benefits 64
Legal Influences on Labor Relations 65
Implications of Public Policy for Human Resource Management 66

3

ORGANIZATIONAL BEHAVIOR 74

Formal and Informal Organization 76
Emergent Behavior Subsystem 79
Required Behavior and Sentiments 81
The Individual Worker 83
Work Groups and Other Worker Associations 86
Implications of Worker Similarities and Differences 89

PART I Case Studies 94

Case Study: Little Things Mean a Lot 94
Case Study: Action and Reaction 96
Case Study: Order Processing 97

PART II
PLANNING AND STAFFING

4

PLANNING FOR HUMAN RESOURCES 100

Advantages of Human Resource Planning 103
Integrated Business and Human Resource Planning 104
The Human Resource Planning Process 106
The Planning Approach to Determining Manpower Requirements 109
Forecasting Manpower Requirements 117
Forecasting Manpower Supply 120

5

WORK DESIGN AND JOB ANALYSIS 128

Work Design and Organizational Output 133
Hierarchy of Work 135
General Approach to Job Design 136
Classical Design of Jobs 137
Expectancy Model of Job Design 138
Job Characteristics Model of Job Design 139
Major Job Design Factors from Research 141
Job Design and Class of Work 146
Documentation of Job Design 146
Job Analysis Overview 149

Major Steps in Job Analysis 150
Job Analysis Techniques 151
Job Redesign 161

RECRUITMENT 168

The Recruitment Process 171
Constraints on Recruitment 173
Internal Recruitment 177
External Recruitment 181
Alternatives to Recruiting 190
Evaluation of Recruitment Programs 190

7

SELECTION 196

Selecting Human Resources 199
Determining Validity and Reliability for Selection Techniques 201
The Selection Process 203
Assessment Centers 217
Legal Influences on the Staffing Process 217
Selection Strategies 220
Evaluation of the Selection Process 221

PART II Case Studies 227

Case Study: Company Growth and Good Ole Boys (and Girls) 227
Case Study: Management Resource Planning: Keys to Success 228
Case Study: KMS Industries 230

PART III
DEVELOPMENT

MOTIVATION AND LEADERSHIP FOR PRODUCTIVITY 234

Productivity 239
Motivation 242
Leadership 250
Quality Circles: Application of Motivation/Leadership Theory 259

9

ORGANIZATION DEVELOPMENT 268

What Is Organization Development (OD)? 271
Three Main Approaches to OD 275
Conducting An Effective OD Program 277
The Impact of OD 290

10

DEVELOPING COMMUNICATIONS 298

Roles of Communication in the HR System 302
Responsibilities of the HR Manager for Development of
    Communications 303
Line Managers and the Human Resource Department 304
Development of Formal Communication Systems 305
Development of Informal Communication Systems 312
Models of Communication 320
Objectives of Manager-Subordinate Communication 322
Guides for Improving Communication with Employees 324

11

INDIVIDUAL TRAINING AND DEVELOPMENT 334

The Systems View 337
Determining T & D Needs 340
Long-Range T & D Objectives and Policies for HR Management 342
Organizing for T & D 345
Identifying and Selecting T & D Methods and Techniques 345
Developing the T & D Programs 351
Implementing the T & D Program 355
Conducting the Teaching Activities 363
Evaluating the T & D System 364
Modification and Maintenance 369
The T & D Information System 369
The Computerized T & D Management System 370

12

CAREER MANAGEMENT 376

Reasons for Interest in Career Management 379
What is a Career? 380

Career Management 381
Career Planning 383
Career Development 394

PART III Case Studies 402

Case Study: NTEL, Inc. 402
Case Study: Transforming the Transformer Company 403
Case Study: A Question of Training 404
Case Study: The Case of Anne Greblad 406

PART IV
MEASURING AND REWARDING

13
APPRAISING PERFORMANCE 408

Role of Performance Appraisal 411
Approaches to Appraisal 413
Current Practice in Performance Appraisal 428
Current Status of the Appraisal Process 435
Conclusions and Recommendations 435
Legal Considerations in Performance Appraisal 436
Relating Performance Appraisal to Rewarding 438
Step-By-Step Implementation Procedure for a Performance Appraisal System 439

14
COMPENSATION AND BENEFITS 453

Role of the Reward System 458
The Extrinsic Reward System 462
The Intrinsic Reward System 464
Requirements of An Effective Reward System 466
Forms of Compensation 468
Noncash Benefits 474
Recent Trends in Compensation and Benefits 478

15
ADMINISTERING THE COMPENSATION PROGRAM 484

Developing the Compensation Strategy 488
Governmental Influences on Compensation 489

Legal Constraints on Compensation Policy   491
Impact of Labor Market Conditions   492
Impact of a Union   493
Procedure for Developing the Compensation System   493
Job Evaluation   497
Executive Compensation   502
Implementing a Flexible System   502
Administration of Compensation and Benefits   506

PART IV   Case Studies   515

Case Study: A Matter of Money   515
Case Study: Delta Corporation   517
Case Study: Marco, Incorporated   518
Case Study: The Old Order Changeth   524

PART V
EMPLOYEE RELATIONS

16
LABOR-MANAGEMENT RELATIONS   528

Nature of Labor-Management Relations   531
The Legal Framework for Labor-Management Relations   538
The Unionization Process   541
The Impact of Labor-Management Relations on the HR System   546

17
COLLECTIVE BARGAINING   554

Structure and Strategy of Bargaining Relationships   558
Negotiating the Contract   559
Administering the Contract   569
Current Developments   573

18
QUALITY OF WORK LIFE AND EMPLOYEE MAINTENANCE   580

QWL—What and Why   583
Specific Issues in QWL   585
QWL and Maintenance Concepts   592

Implementation of Employee Maintenance and Service Programs 594
QWL and Productivity 606

PART V Case Studies 610

Case Study: How Much Better Must a Junior Employee Be to Win a Bid Over a Senior Man? 610
Case Study: Can You Bar Employees from Discussing Their Salaries Among Themselves? 610
Case Study: Certified Health Care Delivery Systems (A) 611

PART VI
ANALYSIS AND CONTROL OF PERSONNEL ACTIVITIES

19

THE HUMAN RESOURCE MANAGEMENT SYSTEM AND THE COMPUTER 620

What *Is* a System? 623
Environment and Subsystems 626
Advantages of the Systems Perspective 627
Dimensions of a System: Operations and Information 629
Developing and Installing the HR Management System 630
Computer-Based HR Management Information System 635
Role of the Computer in Modern HR Management Systems 647

20

HUMAN RESOURCE MANAGEMENT CONTROL, PROBLEM DIAGNOSIS, AND RESEARCH 652

Systems View of HR Control 655
Types of Control Systems 658
Systems View of Organizational Control 662
Developing the HR Control System 663
Diagnosis 676
Human Resource Research 679

PART VI Case Studies 690

Case Study: Fast Food—Slow Control 690
Case Study: Improving a Computerized HR Information System 690
Case Study: A Problem of Research Methodology 692
Case Study: Computer and Telecommunications Technology, Inc. 692

Appendix A
IMPORTANT ORGANIZATIONS IN PERSONNEL MANAGEMENT   695

Appendix B
IMPORTANT PERIODICALS FOR MANAGEMENT OF HUMAN RESOURCES   698

GLOSSARY   700

INDEX   711

I The Setting

Human Resources in the Business System

CHAPTER OUTLINE

Productivity and the Quality of Work Life

From Personnel Administration to Human Resource Management

Nature of Personnel/Human Resource Management □ Past Development of P/HR Management □ Future Fundamental Trends □ Changing Role of Human Resource Specialists

Social and Legal Changes Influencing HR Management

Women at Work □ Discrimination at Work □ Drug Abuse, Alcoholism, Handicapped Workers, and Ex-Convicts □ Demography and the Energy Shortage □ Aging Work Force □ Sexuality in the Office

Conditions of Employment

Time □ Compensation □ Impact of the Computer □ Objectivity in Selecting, Promoting, Compensating □ Health and Safety □ Quality of Life

Labor–Management Relations

Union Membership □ Labor Issues □ Collective Bargaining Process

Changes in the Economy and Problems of Productivity

Decline in the Rate of Productivity Gains □ Increasing Attention to Productivity

Changing Work Force

Education □ Value Systems □ Work Ethic and Productivity □ Shift to Knowledge Workers □ Midlife Career Changing □ Underqualified Workers

P/HR Department

Goals □ Functions of the P/HR Management System □ Organization of the P/HR Function □ Careers in P/HR

Professionalization in the P/HR Field

Integrated Approach to Managing the P/HR Function

OBJECTIVES

1. Describe the development of the field of human resource management
2. Describe the effect of social and legal changes on human resource management
3. Identify major factors of work life
4. Describe the principal *factors* of labor management relations and productivity
5. Describe trends in the work force
6. Identify career opportunities in the personnel/human resource field

SPOTLIGHT:
Edward R. Toth, Jr.

Edward R. Toth, Jr., is Vice President of Operations for RMI Company, Niles, Ohio, and is responsible for all production, maintenance, quality control, engineering, and construction activities. After graduating with a Bachelor of Science degree in chemical engineering from Case Institute of Technology, he served in various production management and engineering positions with National Distillers & Chemical Co.

RMI Company is a major producer of titanium metal sponge and mill products with six manufacturing facilities employing approximately 2,000 people.

Comments by Edward R. Toth, Jr.

It is commonplace for practitioners in the art of management to say, "people are a company's greatest asset." All too often, however, today's manager is preoccupied with achieving technological excellence at the expense of concern for the very employees who must use this technology to manufacture products that face a stiff test in the marketplace.

A careful distinction must be made. We believe people are a company's greatest asset *only* if treated and motivated properly. We also feel that motivation of a work force is the major factor in achieving profit goals and increased productivity.

To create a highly productive and motivated work force, basic needs must be fulfilled for each employee, from the chief executive officer to the janitor. While there exists no consensus on what constitutes the basic needs of employees, there are five obvious, fundamental needs:

- ☐ Wages sufficient to enable a person to enjoy a standard of living perceived to be fair and equitable;
- ☐ Security derived from the knowledge that a job will exist for as long as the employee wishes to work and can perform his or her duties properly;
- ☐ Recognition of the individual's importance and vital contribution to the company's team effort;
- ☐ Pride in oneself, one's work, the company, and the greater community of which the individual is a part.

4 THE SETTING

For over six decades, the American Management Association has sought the answer to the question "What makes managers competent?" On the basis of its most recent research, the AMA answered this question by identifying 18 generic competencies in four clusters:

1. Goal and action management: a focus on efficiency, orientation, proactivity, and diagnostic use of concepts
2. Direction of subordinates: an ability to give directions, to obtain compliance, to develop others, and free-and-easy communication
3. Human resource management: an ability to have positive expectations about others and realistic views of oneself, to build coalitions to accomplish tasks, and to stimulate cooperation
4. Leadership: an ability to express confidence and be decisive, to identify new concepts, and to understand cause-and-effect relationships.[1]

It is important to note that, to some extent, *all four clusters relate to human resource management.* Further, according to Norrell, a human resource service firm, labor and the cost of personnel administration account for 75 percent of every business dollar. That's why now, more than ever, business views the Human Resource Manager as a member of the corporate decision-making team.

PRODUCTIVITY AND THE QUALITY OF WORK LIFE

Increased productivity is the means by which all stakeholders in business, particularly owners and employees, can improve their lot. *Productivity* is measured by the ratio of output to input and the *quality* of the output. Increasing productivity can not best be achieved by workers speeding up beyond a comfortable rate, but by better management planning and worker participation in task improvement. Worker and management cooperation can also bring about better *quality of work life (QWL)* just as better QWL tends to increase productivity.

We have been living up to now in a world in which we could waste material resources. The continual development of technology has kept increasing production but has disguised increasing waste. Suddenly we are finding that by following this route our resources will no longer continue to meet society's needs. We must start managing our human resources significantly more effectively. If workers, for example, were motivated to the extent that players on a winning football team are, a mind-staggering increase in output and quality would be possible. We are not referring here only to the millions of individual contributors—we are including managers at *all* levels of the organization.

FROM PERSONNEL ADMINISTRATION TO HUMAN RESOURCE MANAGEMENT

Nature of Personnel/Human Resource Management

Human resources consist of all employees, both workers and managers, of the organization. The term "human resource management" covers all activities by both line managers and the "personnel department" that deal with them. The term *personnel/human resource (P/HR) management* comprises the managerial activities involved in planning for recruiting, staffing, training, developing, rewarding, utilizing, and maintaining human resources. The organization may be private or public, small and simple, or large and complex. All managers perform the above functions to some degree. At the same time, in our complex world, all require the assistance and advice of staff specialists with highly developed skills in the personnel/human resource field.

The personnel department as it has existed in most firms up to and through the 1970s will no longer exist in the rest of the century in any but the smallest organizations. The staff specialists in human resources will take on a radically different role. While line managers will continue to have the direct responsibility for management of human resources, they will need to rely much more heavily on staff expertise for both broad long-range proposals and specialized technical advice. The managers in the P/HR organization will, therefore, impact company strategy. *P/HR specialists*, each with his or her own special skills, will also be required to clarify ever more complex technical problems in their individual disciplines such as recruiting, training, wage and salary administration, benefits administration, and industrial relations.

In the 1980s and beyond, the staff specialists will spend less time on routine maintenance functions such as record keeping and standard reports because of the computer revolution. P/HR specialists will be called upon more as a source of expert advice and counsel by busy line managers. And possibly even more importantly, they will be developing options for policies to protect the company against heavy losses in the future. The day of the "washed-up" line manager moving into the position of P/HR manager will no longer be affordable.

Past Development of P/HR Management

The meaning of human resource management must be considered in terms of historical development. P/HR management today is not the same as it was in 1900, say, nor will it be the same in the year 2000. Knowledge, philosophy, values, and technology continue to evolve as Exhibit 1–1 illustrates. Six threads intertwine in the development of P/HR management in this exhibit:

- ☐ Management technology
- ☐ Organizational behavior
- ☐ Personnel theory

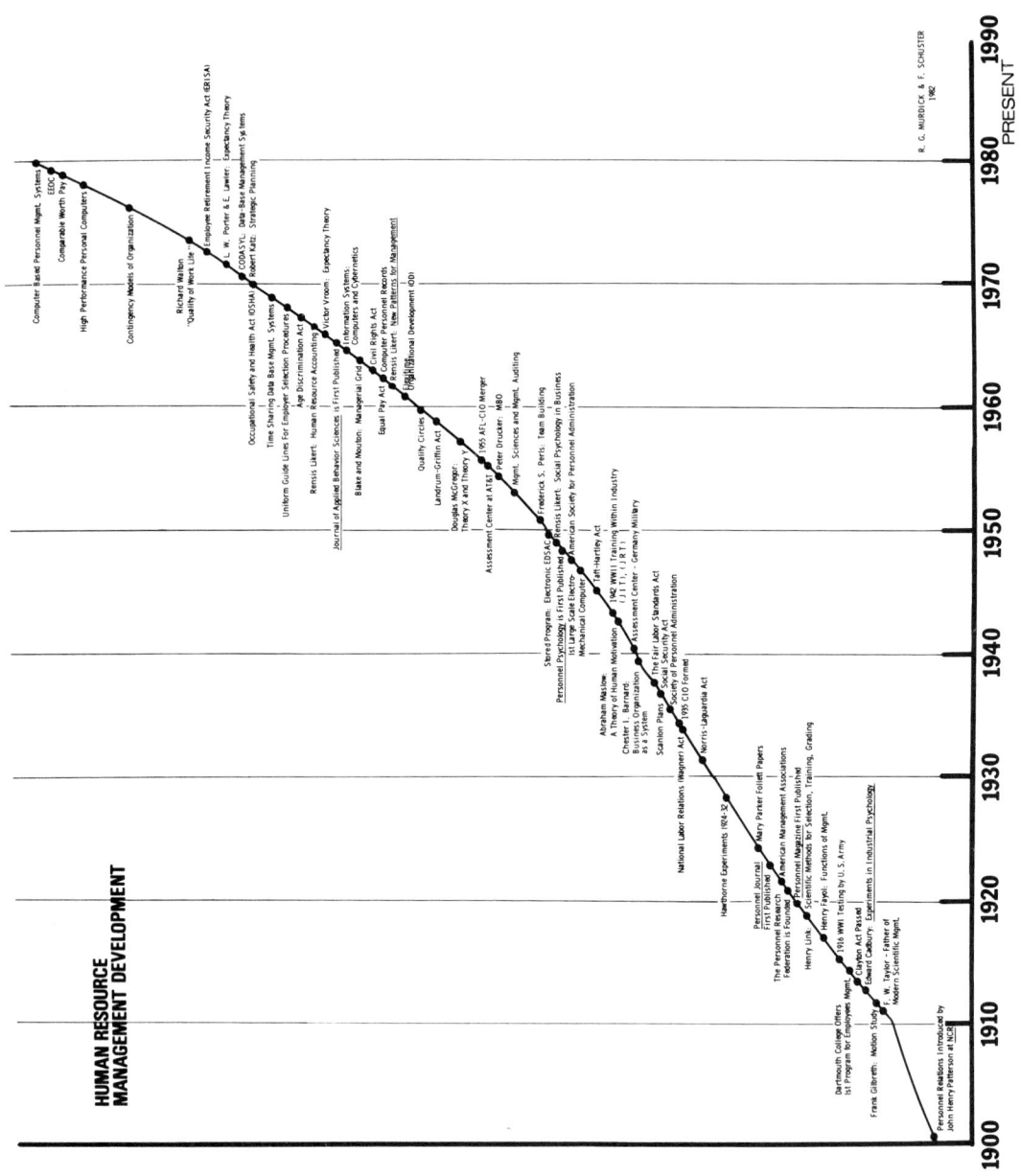

EXHIBIT 1–1
Development of P/HR knowledge and practice; an index of growth.

- ☐ Union growth and maturation
- ☐ Legal requirements
- ☐ Computer technology

The growth in company size and complexity from the early 20th century to the present has changed the environment and importance of personnel work. In the beginning, the personnel person (not manager) simply processed people for hiring and maintained simple records for each employee. The state-of-the-art Vice President of P/HR now participates in corporate strategic planning.

The present concept of P/HR management is that it plays a role in corporate manpower policy and planning; the attraction, recruiting, and selection of people matched to designed jobs; development of human resources; development of appraisal and reward systems; and negotiating, reporting, and controlling human resource problems. Environmental changes continue to affect the scope and role of human resource management.

Future Fundamental Trends

"The past is prologue to the future," and there are six fundamental trends that we believe will increase the importance of the P/HR function:

1. The increasing realization of top management that in an era of declining productivity human resources *really* are the organization's most important asset. Top management will expect human resources specialists to be more anticipatory in solving the real management problems of the company, and will come to expect a more meaningful *bottom-line* contribution from them.
2. Severe pressure on the economy springing from declining productivity in the United States, coexistent with rapidly increasing productivity in Japan, West Germany, and other competing economies.
3. Radical social changes in the American culture that have led to a new set of values among the American work force. Altered family structure, increased drug use, and upward mobility of working women are examples.
4. The rising expectations of members of the work force with regard to the possibilities for satisfying higher-level (self-fulfillment) needs as well as lower-level (subsistence) needs at the workplace. Coupled with this are an increasing resistance to the role of authority and an increasing desire for participation in decision making, control over job factors, and a voice in how the organization is run.
5. Increasing legislation and court decisions affecting every aspect of the worker on, and perhaps off, the job. Some areas affected are wages, working conditions, and recruitment.
6. The development of the computer, which will doubtless surpass the imagination of any of us in the years ahead. Robots operating assembly lines were once science fiction. In the same way, the scenario of the future may be computers replacing middle managers so that only supervisors and top managers remain.

Changing Role of Human Resource Specialists

Because of the changes in management philosophy and the environment discussed above, we foresee the following radical changes in the role of specialists in human resource management:

1. These specialists will tend less and less to be individuals who spend their entire careers in human resource management. An increasing proportion of human resource specialists will be managers who spend a part of their career assigned to the specialized function of managing human resources. Often these slots will be seen as key development assignments for high-potential executives who are being groomed for top management positions—the result of the modern view that human resource management is an integral function of line management and, therefore, an important training step for high general management positions. The P/HR management function will be looked upon increasingly as a profit center in the organization, that can generate incremental profit. Thus, it will require some of the best executive talent that the organization can obtain. Although this phenomenon will occur much more extensively over the next 25 years, there is evidence that such a trend has already developed. In the early 1980s more and more organizations began promoting their top personnel executives to general management positions. At the same time, more up-and-coming "fast trackers" began to receive development assignments in human resource management. We have only begun to see the tip of the iceberg; what is now worthy of comment will be commonplace by the year 2000. By then, we believe, it will be no more unusual for the Vice President of Human Resources to become a company president than it would be for the Vice President of Marketing, the Vice President of Production, or the Vice President of Finance.

2. As the human resource department takes on its new role as internal consultant to line management, some specialists will also take on the role of staff behavioral scientists. Their key duties will include bringing the latest ideas from research and theory in the behavioral sciences to the organization and translating those ideas for line executives in practical, operational terms. The P/HR department will be charged with introducing the latest scientific techniques for effectively managing human resources, just as the research and development department is charged with bringing the latest developments of technology into the organization. The human resources management specialist will be viewed, therefore, as a member of the total management team, as an internal consultant to all levels of management, and as a source of expertise.

3. Because both of the above developments call for vastly greater skills (both general management skills and technical skills in the behavioral sciences), human resource specialists will be better educated and more experienced than they typically are at present. Advanced degrees in general

management such as the MBA or Ph.D., supported by computer systems and behavioral skills, will become commonplace.

4. Vastly increased attention will be paid to fitting the various subfunctions of human resource management to organizational objectives. A systems view will require that the organization's overall objectives (especially profit objectives) be the starting point for the development of all strategies for the management of human resources; the only purpose of the subfunctions of human resource management will be to serve the achievement of overall organizational objectives and strategy.

5. Certain subfunctions of human resource management will receive proportionately greater emphasis during the last 15 years of the 20th century. Among the functions that we see growing dramatically in importance are organization development, work force planning, compensation planning and administration, and Management By Objectives (MBO). The logic behind this increased demand is that they have the greatest potential for contributing to increased profits. At the same time, much less attention will be paid to routine record keeping, lower-level training unrelated to organizational objectives, and employee services.

6. Finally, underlying all of the above changes will be a new approach to managing human resources. Called the contingency approach, it departs from the assumption that all people have the same needs and expectations and that they can therefore be managed in the same way. Rather, it assumes that people are quite different in terms of the needs that motivate them, the managerial styles and policies to which they will respond, and the kinds of organizational environments in which they can be most effective. The organization will adapt to fit its many workers as individuals rather than fitting individuals to the organization. This will be done to obtain the maximum response from each individual.

SOCIAL AND LEGAL CHANGES INFLUENCING HR MANAGEMENT

Women at Work

The proportion of women in the labor force will rise to almost 50 percent by 1990, but women will constitute less than 15 percent of managers. Currently, they hold lower-paying positions in business, the result of traditional patterns of *sex discrimination* in business, among other reasons. As marriages become equalized relationships, more women will be able to engage in lifetime careers. In addition, the number of women attending colleges of business administration will increase greatly over the next ten years. As the pool of competent people increases, the quality and productivity of the work force will tend to increase significantly.[2]

Organization development programs directed at changing the attitudes of both men and women are a possible response by management.

Managements may also establish day-care centers at the plant to relieve the stress on both husband and wife with regard to the care of preschool children.

Discrimination at Work

Most objective measures indicate that blacks have made steady gains during the past decade in terms of income, promotion and employment opportunities, and skills.[3] At the same time, a great many career opportunities are now being opened to women, and all but the subtle discriminatory barriers are disappearing. Thus, although equal employment opportunities for women and minority groups will remain important problems, more emphasis will shift to discrimination based on age.

We can expect the state and federal regulatory agencies to change their emphasis from a preoccupation with overt discrimination to correcting the more deep-rooted practices that have perpetuated inequality. This will mean more challenges to the traditional selection, promotion, and lay-off methods of all organizations. It will also mean more action from the regulatory agencies to require individual firms to establish specific goals and quotas for certain age groups, females, and members of minority groups. This, in turn, will result in growing resentment among the white males who are bypassed for employment and/or promotion. Lawsuits and charges of reverse discrimination can be expected.

Unless human resource departments devise ways of increasing job opportunities for minority, female, and older workers, they will face challenges to their traditional selection, training, and promotion practices. At the same time, all human resource managers must devise ways of handling the resentment that will develop among those employees who are negatively affected by these new antidiscrimination policies.

Drug Abuse, Alcoholism, Handicapped Workers, and Ex-Convicts

Today a number of small groups or organizations are concerned with rehabilitating people who have special employment problems. These people are drug abusers (including alcoholics), handicapped workers, and ex-convicts. The National Alcohol Council estimates that 6 percent of the nation's work force suffers from some kind of alcohol or drug abuse problem and that another 4 percent suffers from some kind of physical or mental disorder that affects job performance. There are over 10 million "troubled" workers. The cost to business is *10 billion* dollars annually.

The percentage of alcoholics is likely to remain about the same. On the other hand, our country has become more health-conscious, and the social use of alcohol may decline slightly. Further, as programs improve, abusers may be rehabilitated at an earlier stage. Offsetting this decrease will be the growing number of people who turn to alcohol for relief from the declining quality of life.

Drugs may be classified as sedative-hypnotic, psychedelic, central nervous system stimulant, and narcotic. With ever-increasing tension and competition for jobs, the first group, tranquilizers, and the third group, "pep pills," will probably become more common. The use of narcotics, however, which receives so much attention due to its visible impact on individual behavior, may start to decrease in the next few years. This is because the large number of hard-drug addicts who acquired their habits in Vietnam are turning increasingly to sedative-hypnotic drugs. Organized crime law enforcement agencies may also hold down the distribution of narcotics.

Some companies, notably Kemper Insurance Company, have long-standing alcoholic rehabilitation programs. Kemper currently also has a program to aid former drug addicts. Such programs generally consist of sensitizing all managers to these problems, early detection, professional help, and indicating company concern for the welfare of the individual. It is made clear to the worker (or manager) that the responsibility for cure, and job retention, lies with him or her. Agencies such as the National Institute of Alcohol Abuse and Alcoholism provide assistance to companies in starting such programs.

A much smaller group of people now receiving concentrated attention by government and business are the physically handicapped. New regulations have recently been issued by the Labor Department under Section 503 of the Vocational Rehabilitation Act of 1973 to spur the employment of handicapped workers.

A serious problem exists with regard to ex-convicts. Generally, they have a difficult time finding employment despite the government agencies that provide assistance. Companies that do have programs do not seek publicity. Companies do not show such past history in the individual's personnel record in order to protect the worker.

It will be advantageous for business if companies take the initiative in developing programs for the rehabilitation and employment of such problem workers. If they do not, we expect that laws will be strengthened and government regulations issued to *require* expanded affirmative action and constant reporting in these areas.

Demography and the Energy Shortage

Our population has grown rapidly in the past but will continue to grow at a slower rate. People have spread out from the center of cities. The automobile has become a necessary means for getting to work, and a crisis is now in the offing. The general public is having difficulty understanding that a serious energy shortage could develop at any time due to a cutoff of foreign petroleum or that in the next 25 years diminished reserves of petroleum will change our lives tremendously.

To cope with these problems, work force planning and site location should be closely related. Large companies may be able to establish themselves centrally to residential communities. If heavy industry can clean itself up, avoid pollution, and increase the beautification of plants, it may be able to locate near residential areas. In the meantime, however, companies may have to become involved with local governments in developing mass transit from city to plants.

Aging Work Force

The population of the United States will be aging as we move into the 21st century: There will be fewer people in the 15–29-year age group and more in the prime working-age group of 30–59 (Exhibit 1–2). Through the 1980s, therefore, the number of workers in the prime working ages will increase dramatically.

Currently most companies have a mandatory retirement age, often overruled for chief executive officers. Retirement at age 70 is required in most companies, although the optional retirement age may vary from 62 to 70 years of age. In the future, pressure will develop to do away with mandatory retirement age limits.

Increasingly enforced, the Age Discrimination in Employment Act covers private employers of 20 or more people and public and labor organizations. It protects people between the ages of 40 and 70. We can expect greater government pressure to prevent age discrimination.

Human resource managers will be critical in developing criteria to differentiate between adequate and inadequate job performance. Companies cannot afford to retain slow, senile workers, but they also cannot afford to lose alert, intelligent, and highly experienced people because of age barriers and prejudices.

Sexuality in the Office

Two unrelated phenomena that are now becoming apparent are *sexual harassment* and the existence of homosexuals in business.

Women in business have long been forced to bear up quietly under physical and verbal indignities; less frequently, men have been subjected to

EXHIBIT 1–2
U.S. population estimates (millions).

Age Group	1970	1980	1990	2000
15–19	21.0	20.6	16.8	19.7
20–24	20.2	20.9	17.9	16.9
25–29	17.9	18.9	20.2	16.5
30–39	28.8	31.2	40.2	38.4
40–49	22.7	22.7	31.2	39.1
50–59	23.1	23.1	21.8	30.0
60–69	18.0	18.5	20.4	19.3

Source: Bureau of Census (Series P-25).

such coercion. Complaints may be filed under federal laws, as well as under state laws in some areas, but few do, because such cases are difficult to prove.

With women's rights and growing awareness of women on how to effectively handle sexual harassment, such treatment will decline somewhat. On the other hand, as more women rise to positions of power, males may find themselves facing the same type of harassment.

Management will have to stop closing its eyes to such practices, and policies must be formulated in writing. Serious action, including the careful investigation of complaints and protection for the victims, must be instituted. Penalties and sanctions should be levied against offenders.

As for homosexuality, studies have produced conflicting results about its prevalence. For example, Richard Zoglin estimated the percentage of gay managers to range from 10 percent to 20 percent.[4] Many homosexuals fear that they may lose their jobs or be barred from promotion, and frequently live double lives with wives and children. Research on homosexual women in industry is essentially nonexistent.[5]

As sexual identities and roles become more open, however, society may come to accept the presence of homosexuals so that such persons will have less to fear. As long as their behavior does not influence accepted work roles, homosexuals will no longer need to suffer the tensions of secrecy and potential blackmail.

CONDITIONS OF EMPLOYMENT

Time

Reduction in time spent on the job will continue to be the trend. In 1910, the average employee worked 54 hours per week. Today, the five-day, 40-hour workweek is standard. In New York City, the workday is generally 9 A.M. to 5 P.M. In some isolated industries, such as rubber, the workweek ranges from 32 to 35 hours.

Because we will be able to satisfy the majority of society's material needs with fewer and fewer workers, it is likely that the workweek will be further reduced within the next 10 years. The alternative could be permanently high unemployment. In addition, as women achieve equality with men, it is possible that workweeks will be shortened so that more people can be employed and husbands and wives may spend more time together.

Probably increasing in the next decade will be "flexitime," an innovation more common in Europe but receiving considerable attention in the United States and Canada. Flexitime allows each employee to work the required number of hours within a range of time. It is built around a central core of hours during the middle of the business day, when all employees are expected to be present. Starting and quitting times are set by workers to meet their own needs. For example, nightowls might come to work at

10 A.M., take a shorter lunch break, and work extra time at the end of the normal day. Other employees might like to take a longer lunch break, and perhaps squeeze in a few sets of tennis; they would start earlier and finish later than the normal hours. Although complex administrative problems may increase, employee cooperation to date has surprised many opponents of flexitime.

As more workers get more time off, however, their desire for goods and services will increase, and boredom will become a problem for many. Therefore, we anticipate that moonlighting (holding down two jobs) will increase. The restraining forces will be the severe competition for most jobs. However, skilled workers and managers will not find this a great obstacle.

At the executive level, leaves of absence for professional development purposes are being tried by larger companies. The executive may work for the federal government or return to school for an advanced degree. Shorter leaves of several months are granted so that executives can attend advanced management programs. Such sabbaticals broaden and recharge the individual.

The human resource manager must guide the company to develop policies that will encourage such flexibility, assure fairness to individuals, and work to the mutual advantage of the person and the company.

Compensation

Because compensation comes in so many forms, the human resource manager of the future faces a great challenge. Many forms of compensation may provide greater rewards to the employee than they cost the company. A highly paid executive, for example, may perceive several days off per month or a long vacation as more valuable than a raise that costs the company the same amount. Christmas or vacation bonuses may have more impact than does the equivalent in salary spread throughout the year. On the other hand, the company may pay out large amounts in salary and fringe benefits that fail to be perceived as great rewards by employees.

The concept of cafeteria-style benefits and flexible compensation, in which compensation is tailored to each employee's desires, may expand in the future. For example, an older worker might prefer to give up a birthday as a paid holiday in exchange for more health insurance. Younger employees might like "maternity leaves" for new fathers. An infinite number of combinations is possible, given a sophisticated benefit structure. Because of the complexity of such policies, the human resource staff will need to become deeply involved in this task.

Impact of the Computer

The impact that the computer will have on business operations in the next 10 years is beyond the imagination of most people. The present rate of increase in computer miniaturization, speed, and storage capacity has already revolutionized the organization and processes within companies.

Managers will become systems oriented and will participate as partners with systems designers. The master–servant relationship of today's hierarchical organization will fade considerably as people play out their roles in systems when a large proportion of decisions will be programmed. The HR *computer-based information system* will be a fact of life.

The development of special-purpose and general-purpose process computers for the factory will relieve humans of much of the dull routine of monitoring automatic machines.

The human resources manager should be looking forward to the need for hiring and training systems designers, people with a broad knowledge of various areas of business. Fewer unskilled workers will be required, and jobs will demand more creativity.

Objectivity in Selecting, Promoting, Compensating

Over the years sophisticated tools for selecting, promoting, and compensating employees have been developed. Many companies are not aware of these tools, and many more don't use them, preferring the less objective bases of friendships or political arrangements within the organization.

In the future, however, civil rights laws and the need for increased productivity will lead to the adoption of more scientific approaches to selecting and rewarding personnel. It will be essential to fit people better to jobs and to fit better people to the better jobs. With the increased education of managers and the development of the systems approach to managing, the incompetent manager or marginal worker will soon be uncovered. This is because management by objectives and the evaluation of performance against established objectives will be increasingly applied as measurement tools.

Health and Safety

Much has been accomplished in providing a safe workplace for the employee. Unfortunately, however, the rise in the frequency of work injuries that began in the 1960s has not been reversed. Although most Fortune 500 firms now have excellent accident prevention and safety engineering programs, many small and medium-sized employers are facing a rising accident rate.

The *Occupational Safety and Health Act* (OSHA) of 1970 was passed in order to make the working environment safer. Both employees and employers will need to learn of the intent and the procedures of the new regulations, which are still undergoing modification. Public employees, once considered outside the purview of such laws, are now covered. Members of the human resource department will become the in-house experts on safety and occupational health.

The impact of the employee's job upon mental health is just becoming recognized. There is growing awareness by some corporate managements that they have a stake in the "whole person," not just in the employee's physical being. This awareness will lead to such things as corporate alcoholic and drug abuse programs. Accordingly, organization-wide programs of information and education concerning the dimensions of these problems need to be established. Provision must also be made for professional services, and supervisors and managers at all levels must be given training so that they can carry out their responsibilities under such programs.

Quality of Life

It is generally conceded that the quality of life has been deteriorating. Inflation, pollution, overpopulation, crime, and the stress due to the complexity of modern life are all contributing factors. Instead of the rugged individualist, we find the nervous citizen who views the employer as arbiter of his or her fate.[6] Workers will face increasing frustration and resentment over unfulfilled expectations about life outside the workplace.

Although the human resource specialist and management are limited in their power to reduce most frustrations off the job, they can seek more ways to reduce frustrations on the job. Possible responses include making greater efforts toward job enrichment, devoting greater attention to the encouragement and recognition of each individual, and arranging work tasks to bring about more social interaction on the job.

LABOR–MANAGEMENT RELATIONS

Union Membership

A *labor union* is an organization of workers formed to further the social and economic interests of its members. During recent years, union membership has been decreasing despite the growth of the total labor force.[7] Many projections suggest that it will continue to decline for three reasons:

1. Management has grown more sophisticated in its treatment of workers.
2. "Smokestack" industries are declining, and "enlightened" high-tech industries provide better treatment of workers as individuals.
3. Unions now lag instead of lead in their understanding of today's workers. That is, the increase in white-collar jobs and female employees, more educated workers, higher standard of living, and better personnel practices will lead to the near extinction of unions over the next few decades.

Some experts, however, see union growth as being on the verge of a tremendous leap forward as teachers and professors, police officers, government employees, nurses, and other professionals and paraprofessionals begin to organize. In view of the changes discussed above, this prediction of growth appears unlikely.

The recession of the early 1980s, combined with continuing intensive foreign competition, has left a lasting impression on union leaders and members. They have seen even the largest companies close to bankruptcy and retrenching permanently and drastically. Labor–management cooperation in the search for increased productivity appears now to make sense. Flexible work rules will revolutionize the present archaic system and these include: eliminating unneeded jobs, allowing management more flexibility in scheduling, eliminating overtime pay, and restricting the use of seniority in filling job vacancies.

Labor Issues

The labor unions themselves are likely to face increased internal conflict and strife as younger members and leaders challenge older leaders and members. The younger workers, with different values and more education, are likely to be more demanding and to be concerned with different issues. For example, pension programs, which have been gaining since the 1950s, will decline in importance, and other benefits, such as company-financed training programs, will be emphasized. New union members will be less interested in seniority for job upgrading, and instead will push for programs that will allow them to adjust to change and to upgrade themselves. Unions will also put more pressure on management to enrich jobs and to give more attention to social issues, such as ecology.

A trend is developing toward fewer but larger labor unions, whose broader structure results in more financial and political power. This facilitates union-organizing activities. The development of broad-base unions will also reduce jurisdictional disputes among unions and make them more adaptive to technological change. We may also see the Auto Workers and the Teamsters reaffiliate with the AFL–CIO (American Federation of Labor–Congress of Industrial Organizations).[8] If this occurs, the labor movement will have even more political clout. Thus, as the federal government increases its control over employment matters, the AFL-CIO, with its added strength, will expand its political activity in order to obtain favorable labor laws and regulations.

Collective Bargaining Process

It is well known that in the past the *collective bargaining process* has often been marked by prolonged and violent strikes as well as other forms of hostile behavior. In more recent times, labor relations have improved considerably—an overwhelming number of contracts have been settled without stalemates and strikes. When strikes have taken place, however, incidents of violence have decreased significantly. Furthermore, instead of resorting to open warfare in order to settle disputes over the interpretation of existing contracts, unions and management have reached equitable settlements through the grievance and arbitration procedures.

Regardless of what may be said to the press during contract negotiations, there is growing evidence that a feeling of mutual respect and trust exists between many union officials and management. In addition, more and more companies have changed their emphasis from "breaking" the union to seeing how to get along with it on a day-to-day basis.

At the same time, unions are recognizing that, since no business firm is an island, future wage and benefit increases hinge on productivity increases. We will probably be hearing more about productivity bargaining, and unions will probably be urging their members to find new ways to increase output to ward off foreign competition. Increasingly, union leaders will realize that in the last analysis the future of employees depends upon the economic survival and the prosperity of the business.

It is unlikely that the lawmakers will pass any restrictions on free collective bargaining, such as compulsory arbitration. Although conflict and disruption will still occur, management and the unions are likely to voluntarily agree to have third parties resolve such incidents. At the same time, more private and public organizations will hire qualified professional staffs to handle the technical aspects of union–management relations, such as contract negotiations. These human resource specialists will also play an important role in advising and training line managers on labor relations matters.

CHANGES IN THE ECONOMY AND PROBLEMS OF PRODUCTIVITY

In the early 1970s a number of simultaneous profound changes in the business environment called unprecedented attention to the importance of the human resource management function. These environmental pressures included a major recession for the entire United States, vastly increased foreign competition in many of America's traditionally strong markets (including such high-technology areas as electronics and computers), and a halt for the first time in the steady rise of productivity per worker-hour. These three environmental pressures were interrelated and tended to reinforce one another, but they were also to some extent independent.

Although these environmental forces all seemed to hit at once, the pressures had been building for years. Furthermore, these forces will continue to push industry in essentially the same direction for at least the next 20 years. They will continue to play an important role in calling attention to and increasing the importance of the human resource management function for the remainder of the 20th century.

Decline in the Rate of Productivity Gains

A serious slippage in the rate of increase in productivity per worker-hour began in the mid-1960s—a decline to about 3 percent per year. Although this was lower than the historical average in the United States, and far lower than that of any of the rapidly industrializing competing nations such as Japan and West Germany, the 3 percent figure was generally viewed at the time as a problem to be solved rather than as an impending disaster.

Toward the end of the 60s, however, the rate of increase slowed even more, and it was near zero by 1973. It again fell sharply in 1974, resulting in an unprecedented *decline* in productivity per worker-hour. Although the severity of the decline may have been due *in part* to the severe recession under way in 1974, the long-range trend makes it obvious that declining productivity is a long-term problem.

Increasing Attention to Productivity

In several states productivity commissions have been created to encourage the joint participation of management and labor to improve the quality of work. One of the early states to set up such a joint productivity commission was Ohio. C. Jackson Grayson established and now operates the nonprofit American Productivity Center (Houston, Texas), which conducts research and provides information services on productivity (Exhibit 1-3).

Although the 1974-1975 and 1981-1983 recessions seem to have contributed to the decrease in worker-hour productivity, the long-term downward trend appears to have more fundamental causes. A number of studies, such as the 1973 Department of Health, Education, and Welfare Special Task Force study *Work in America*, edited by Elliot Richardson, and a 1976 report of the American Assembly Seminar conducted by Columbia University, have pointed to the quality of working life and the lack of fundamental satisfaction in jobs as the underlying causes of the productivity problem.

Both reports concluded that major changes are taking place in American life that present both a threat and an opportunity in relation to industrial productivity. The consensus of both reports was that a major part of the solution to this problem must lie in a massive attempt to restructure and improve the quality of working life and to give workers increasing opportunities to satisfy such higher-level needs as recognition, participation, autonomy, responsibility, and self-development.

Some data are now available on early experimental attempts—including job enrichment—to improve productivity through improving the quality of work life. Among the organizations whose efforts appear to be having significant success are General Motors, Ford, Travelers Insurance, Texas Instruments, American Telephone and Telegraph, Kaiser Aluminum, Xerox, and Motorola.

Aside from human factors, the rapid advance of the robotics technology is also leading to noteworthy increases in productivity. In some plants (e.g., General Motors and General Electric), robotic equipment permits an entire plant to be operated with only a half-dozen workers. Such structured changes will provide considerable challenges for companies and for the country as a whole in minimizing unemployment.

EXHIBIT 1-3
American Productivity Center's policy statement, based on its declared mission: to improve productivity and quality of work life in the United States.

Operating Policy:	The American Productivity Center works to:
	Serve as a major national resource for productivity and quality of work life knowledge and information.
	Operate without bias toward business, labor, government and academia to promote cooperation within these sectors and maintain their support.
	Continue to be supported by contributions and remain non-profit, allowing the Center financial flexibility to engage in non-revenue generating activities to promote productivity and quality of work life.
	Continue to acquire, develop and add to the existing knowledge on productivity and quality of work life issues by working in an advisory and action/research capacity with a diverse group of organizations.
	Maintain its broad view of productivity and quality of work life improvement.
	Actively disseminate the knowledge the Center acquires as a result of its research and field experiences.
	Continue to support and cooperate with other organizations committed to productivity and quality of work life improvement.

Source: American Productivity Center, Houston, Texas. Reprinted by permission.

CHANGING WORK FORCE

Education

It is widely recognized that the culture and the social order of the United States have undergone radical changes during the decade of the 1960s and the early 1970s. These widespread changes have been documented in an earlier section of this chapter. Not surprisingly, since the work force is merely a portion of the total society, these changes in the society at large have been reflected in changes among the work force.

Since more people in our society are graduating from high school, going to college, and receiving advanced degrees every year, the work force is made up increasingly of highly educated and sophisticated employees. An increasing number of professional employees are receiving advanced degrees. Equally important is the fact that more first-level supervisors have college degrees and that most blue-collar workers just joining the work force have high school diplomas or some college. Moreover, the work force is becoming more sophisticated because of its exposure to the media.

This change in attitude has clearly been reflected in the work force. Workers, particularly the young, are increasingly inclined to challenge management's judgment, increasingly cynical about the decisions made by superiors, and increasingly resistant to authority. Whether we are referring to executives, middle and first-line managers, or blue-collar workers, it is generally true that the "organization man" of the 50s has given way to the "assertive employee" of the 80s.

This change represents more an opportunity than a threat to management, if the change can be properly understood and defined. We say it is an opportunity because higher-quality human resources are potentially more productive human resources if they can be directed toward the organization's purpose. Managers will need to consult more with employees on decisions that affect the employees' activities.

Value Systems

One of the complexities of managing human resources over the next 25 years will be dealing with a work force with a more rapidly changing *value system*. By and large, younger workers have reflected the changed values of society at large more quickly. As compared to older workers, they are more distrustful of authority and more cynical, and they expect more satisfaction of higher-level needs from their work. Older workers tend to reflect the more traditional values of society and are therefore more inclined to be "organization men," to accept authority, and to seek primarily the satisfaction of lower-level needs at work.

A specific research study done by Altinus and Tersine supports this statement.[9] The study investigated the job satisfaction level of young blue-collar workers. The perceptions and satisfactions of the young were quite different from those of their older counterparts. The younger workers were found to rank significantly lower in satisfaction with the work itself and in total work satisfaction. The study also concluded that younger workers tend to try to meet higher-level needs on the job, whereas older workers consider social factors on the job more important.

Thus, one complication for the human resource manager of the 1980s will be the need to deal with the different values and motivations of different segments of the work force. This is, of course, only another example of the need for the contingency approach to management policy and practice, which will be incorporated throughout this book.

Work Ethic and Productivity

One cause of the drop in worker-hour productivity in recent years (discussed in an earlier section of this chapter) may well be that jobs and human resource management practices have not kept pace with the changing values and expectations of the work force. For example, in *Work in*

America, Elliot Richardson concludes that "the design of jobs appears to be lagging markedly behind the considerable gains in educational attainments of the work force, and the elevation in credentials required of the worker has not been accompanied by an elevation in the content of work. If anything, it is more routine and bureaucratized, leaving less to the imagination and control of the worker."[10]

An important change in the values of the work force during the 1970s has been a general decline in the work ethic. There was a time when most people in our culture believed that work was inherently good and took great pride in their work. They felt that work had meaning and value in its own right. This cultural belief has sometimes been referred to as the Protestant ethic, and it has been said to have originated in the Puritan notion that work represents an opportunity to earn salvation and that success symbolizes the attainment of salvation.

It has been suggested by some that the loss of pride in work is due to increases in size of organizations, remoteness of the end product, and specialization of work. We believe that this is true because size, depersonalization of organizations, remoteness of the end product, and growing specialization of work all lead to lowered opportunities to satisfy higher-level needs at work. The result of these trends has been to reduce motivation and, therefore, productivity. The only solution is to change the design of jobs so that there is a real opportunity to obtain a sense of accomplishment and pride from the work itself.

On the basis of 40 years of work before getting his doctor's degree in sociology, Robert Schrank suggests that people often retain interest in undesirable jobs because of amenities. For nonmanagers and nonprofessionals, outside activities are often the center of life. The freedom to work at one's own pace, to arrive late at work or go home early, to shop during lunch hour, and to get paid by the week or month provide satisfactions on "crummy" jobs.[11] According to National Opinion Research Center and Survey Research Center Surveys, a high percentage of workers (80–95%), except teenagers, actually are satisfied with their work.[12] The challenge for the P/HR manager is to increase the degree of satisfaction, if this is the case.

Shift to Knowledge Workers

Another important change that is having significant impact on management strategy is the shifting balance between manual workers and knowledge workers. During the early 1950s the U.S. economy passed a significant milestone when manual workers were outnumbered for the very first time in any society by *knowledge workers*, whose work depends on mental skills rather than physical skills and whose productivity is directly related to formal education.

Constantly changing events and progress in the technological and social environments call for shifts in types of skills and numbers of peoples with such skills. In Exhibit 1–4, we see a forecast of the numbers of people employed in various occupations for 1990 compared with the actual number of jobs in the same categories in 1980.

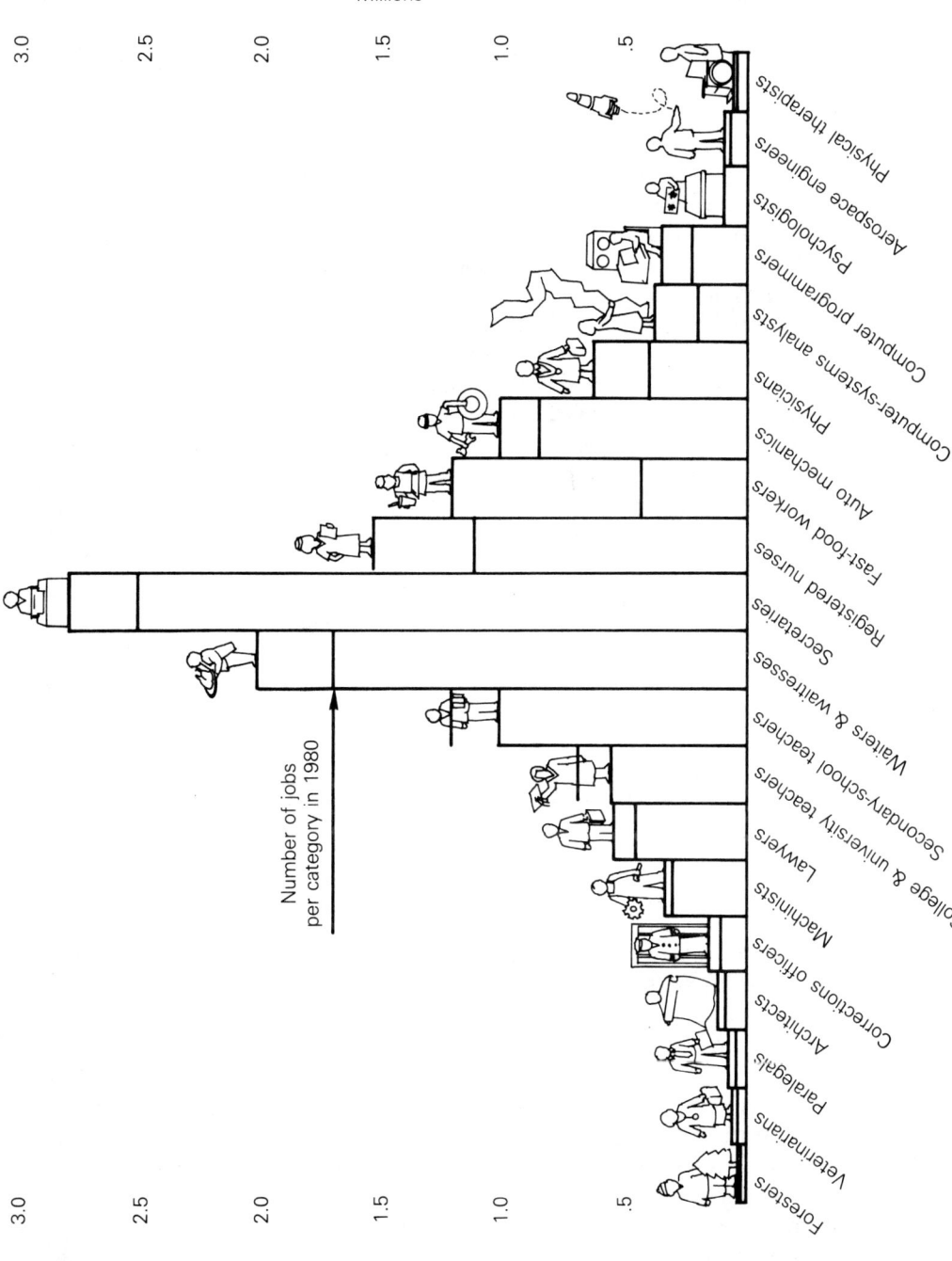

EXHIBIT 1-4
Forecasted shifts in types of skills and workers needed in 1990 compared with actual jobs in 1980.

Source: From Jeremy Main, "Work Won't Be the Same Again," *Fortune*, June 28, 1982, p. 61. Lonni Sue Johnson for *Fortune* Magazine.

There is a growing tendency for workers to identify primarily with their profession or occupation rather than with their employer. As the level of training increases, it seems to follow naturally that workers begin to identify themselves as members of a particular professional or occupational group. They become more loyal to the norms and values of that professional or occupational group than to their individual employers.

This identification has at least two immediate results. First of all, the work force is more mobile, due in part to the weakening of the ties with a particular employer. Another result is what Herbert Meyer refers to as the increased tendency toward "whistle blowing." Meyer means by this the tendency of both the worker and the executive to call public attention to the actions of the employer when they feel that these actions violate their professional or ethical standards.[13] Although this phenomenon has received relatively little attention, we believe that it may well represent a "sleeper" in terms of its future significance to management. The increased tendency of members of the work force to look for, to find, and then to publicize errors of judgment or violations of law underscores dramatically the importance of making absolutely certain that everything the organization does in managing its human resources is in accordance with regulations.

Midlife Career Changing

Related to all of the above changes is the increasing frequency of midlife career changes. It is becoming common for both managers and blue-collar workers to make dramatic shifts in their career patterns. Executives enter the priesthood; engineers and scientists go into small businesses unrelated to their technical training; and blue-collar workers leave their trade to go to college and begin a new professional career. Undoubtedly, the increased frequency of midlife career changes is due to a number of underlying factors already discussed, including increased affluence, increased education and sophistication, and increased awareness of higher-level needs.

The increased acceptance of such career changes combined with the greater knowledge requirements of most occupations has led to the rapid development of a new view of education as a lifetime pursuit. The rapid development of company-sponsored training and development programs, the increased attendance of both blue-collar and managerial workers in part-time college courses while employed, and the pursuit of advanced degrees in the evening by experienced executives, all attest to the dramatic change in the attitude of the work force toward lifetime education. Education is going to be an expensive investment for most companies—expensive in terms of the provision of educational opportunities as well as expensive in terms of worker time.

We predict that this trend will increase in intensity. By the end of the 1980s, most members of the work force will no longer make a distinction between education and their employment. Virtually all members of the work force (from the blue-collar level on up to the chief executive) will simply take it for granted that they will go to school part time while they are working. Moreover, we believe that self-education through individual reading programs will grow in significance.

This points to the need for human resource management specialists who will pay increased attention to the development of formal programs and quality materials for individual education. Programs may consist of increased opportunities for in-company training as well as university programs outside the company.

We believe that finding a viable strategy for providing increased lifetime education opportunities will be an inevitable requirement for companies that wish to be competitive and to attract the best people. But it will also make imperative the development of a parallel strategy to reduce turnover, since turnover will increasingly represent the loss of an investment.

Underqualified Workers

A report of the American Assembly Seminar sponsored by Columbia University in May 1976 to consider "Manpower Goals for American Democracy" strongly reflected the growing conviction that employment is a right of all members of our society (whether or not prequalified) and that the provision of employment opportunities to unqualified individuals is a social obligation of employers.

Among the many far-reaching proposals for extending employment opportunities to people currently considered unemployable, this report called for programs to encourage employers in both the private and public sector to employ and train "underqualified" members of the work force, with the training to be partly subsidized by government. The conclusions of this assembly reflect a new assumption that employers are obligated to utilize all elements of the potential work force, not merely the most employable. This view will represent a major challenge to human resource managers, who may be called upon to devise programs to satisfy these new demands.

P/HR DEPARTMENT

Goals

From about 1946 through the 1960s, personnel management grew by clustering old and sometimes new services. Recruiting, training, wage and salary administration, and benefits administration were established as units under the personnel manager. During the 1970s, however, the goals of the personnel department were broadened to focus on the concept of human resource management. The goals of the new P/HR function became the acquisition, development, and maintenance of the work force. Although these are still considered the operating goals, the P/HR department has now broadened its goals to include:

1. Increase productivity of human resources
2. Improve quality of work life
3. Assure compliance with new legislation.

As a result of these new goals, there is now greater emphasis on three managerial activities:

1. Setting standards and objectives that are determined to be desirable for functional activities
2. Establishing methods of measurement so that progress can be measured against standards
3. Controlling by bringing performance into line with standards and objectives.

Functions of the P/HR Management System

We may view the P/HR department as a *system* aiding line management to work on environmental "inputs" and employees (an input in the form of labor) to achieve the goals discussed above, or "outputs." In Exhibit 1–5, we have shown the inputs, major functions, and outputs as blocks in a flow chart. These three major "chunks" are:

☐ *Inputs*
　Business
　Environmental factors
☐ *Major functions*
　Human resource planning
　Organization planning
　Staffing
　Human resource inventory maintenance
　Modifying the work environment
　Individual development
　Measuring organizational and individual performance
　Appraising performance
　Analyzing performance so that corrective action may be taken
☐ *Outputs*
　Productivity of the organization
　Adaptation to the environment
　Individual's feeling of satisfaction with work life
　Compliance reports required by law for Equal Employment Opportunity (EEO), Affirmative Action, Employee Retirement Income and Security Act, etc.

Not all companies carry out all of the activities shown in Exhibit 1–5. In addition, some activities are carried out only at the corporate level or only at the business or plant level. From Exhibit 1–6 we may get an idea of the degree to which major activities are carried out in American businesses by the P/HR department. It is interesting to note that 18 percent of the respondent companies did not have labor relations as an activity. This may be because there were no unions in the businesses or because top management and legal representatives played the major roles.

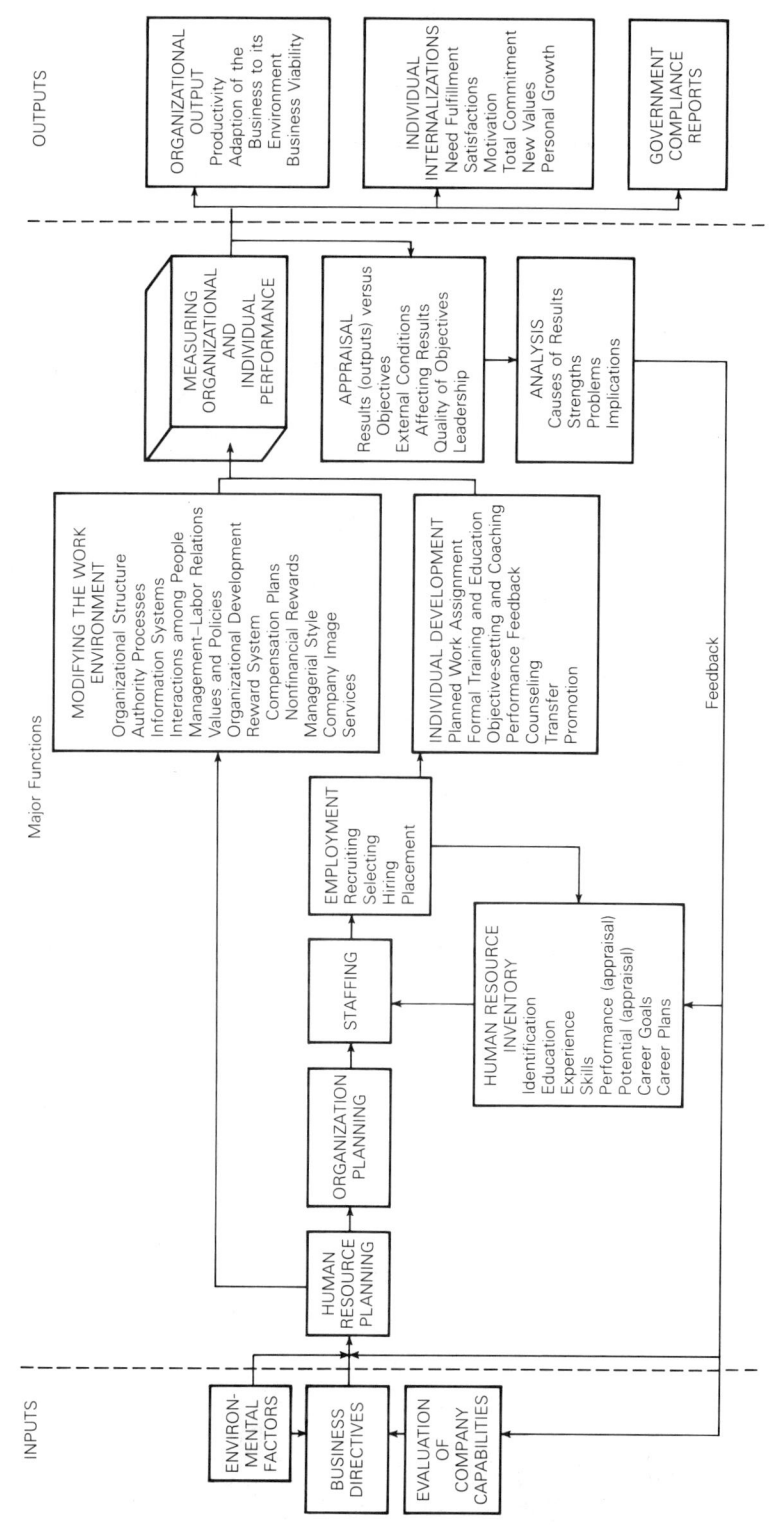

EXHIBIT 1-5
Human resource management system.

EXHIBIT 1–6
Personnel activities emerging as "major" since 1965 in 673 companies.

		Percentage of Companies					
			In Which Activity Is "Major"			In Which Activity Became "Major" since 1965	
	Companies with Activity	At Corporate Level	At Intermediate Level	At Plant or Branch Level	At Corporate Level	At Intermediate Level	At Plant or Branch Level
Labor relations	82	54	21	18	21	6	4
Contract negotiations	67	59	17	10	12	4	3
Grievance handling	84	28	21	28	6	5	1
Recruitment, selection, and employment	96	64	25	19	18	4	2
Of managers	95	53	22	8	4	3	1
Of nonsupervisory employees	93	32	25	30	7	3	4
Of sales representatives	77	23	24	8	4	3	1
Equal employment opportunity	97	66	26	19	66	26	19
Compensation	91	67	18	10	37	6	5
Of managers	95	57	17	5	24	4	2
Of senior management	87	49	6	1	21	2	1
Of nonsupervisory employees	94	39	22	20	13	4	4
Of sales representatives	79	28	21	6	7	3	2
Benefits	95	64	16	12	36	6	4
Occupational safety and health	93	47	21	21	47	21	21
Safety	90	31	21	25	18	9	11
Medical programs	88	36	17	16	12	5	4
Industrial hygiene	80	24	14	18	15	8	9
Monitoring compliance	93	42	20	16	42	20	16
Communications	85	44	14	10	17	4	2
Employee publications	85	36	12	7	10	4	3
Employee attitude surveys	71	26	9	5	7	3	2
Planning and research	83	44	9	3	20	3	1
Organization development	83	41	9	2	25	4	1
Organization charts and structure	84	36	11	3	13	2	1
Labor force forecasting and planning	86	40	15	6	28	6	3
Human resource accounting	61	23	8	3	15	3	1
Human productivity analysis	58	18	8	6	11	3	2
Training and development	90	58	20	11	35	7	4
Of managers, professionals, supervisors	92	48	19	6	29	6	3
Of sales representatives	74	19	20	6	7	3	1
Of nonsupervisory employees	87	25	22	24	12	4	4
Of disadvantaged persons	70	19	14	15	13	6	7
Employee services	80	30	15	15	6	2	1
Recreation	78	19	12	17	3	1	1
Food service	75	16	11	17	2	1	1
Security	81	20	12	21	9	4	3
Community relations	83	31	13	12	18	1	4
Public relations or public affairs	81	30	10	7	11	2	1

Source: Allen R. Janger, *The Personnel Function: Changing Objectives and Organization.* New York: The Conference Board, 1977, p. 40. Reprinted with permission.

Organization of the P/HR Function

Organization of the P/HR function varies by size of company, emphasis on various personnel activities, and degree of centralization of the P/HR function in large decentralized companies. A small, single plant or business or a decentralized subsidiary of a large company may be organized as shown in Exhibit 1–7. The smaller the company, the more likely that several of the functions shown may be combined. In addition, a labor relations specialist may be located in the P/HR department. In fact, in some companies, the entire P/HR department is headed by a Manager–Industrial Relations.

In large corporations that are subdivided into a hierarchy of groups, divisions, and businesses, there is likely to be a corporate P/HR staff. Then there is a P/HR manager for each lower level in the hierarchy. The corporate staff may have very limited or very broad responsibility according to three alternatives:

1. Small corporate staff acts in advisory capacity to top management and to P/HR managers at the lower level
2. Small- to medium-size staff establishes policies for the entire company and insures compliance

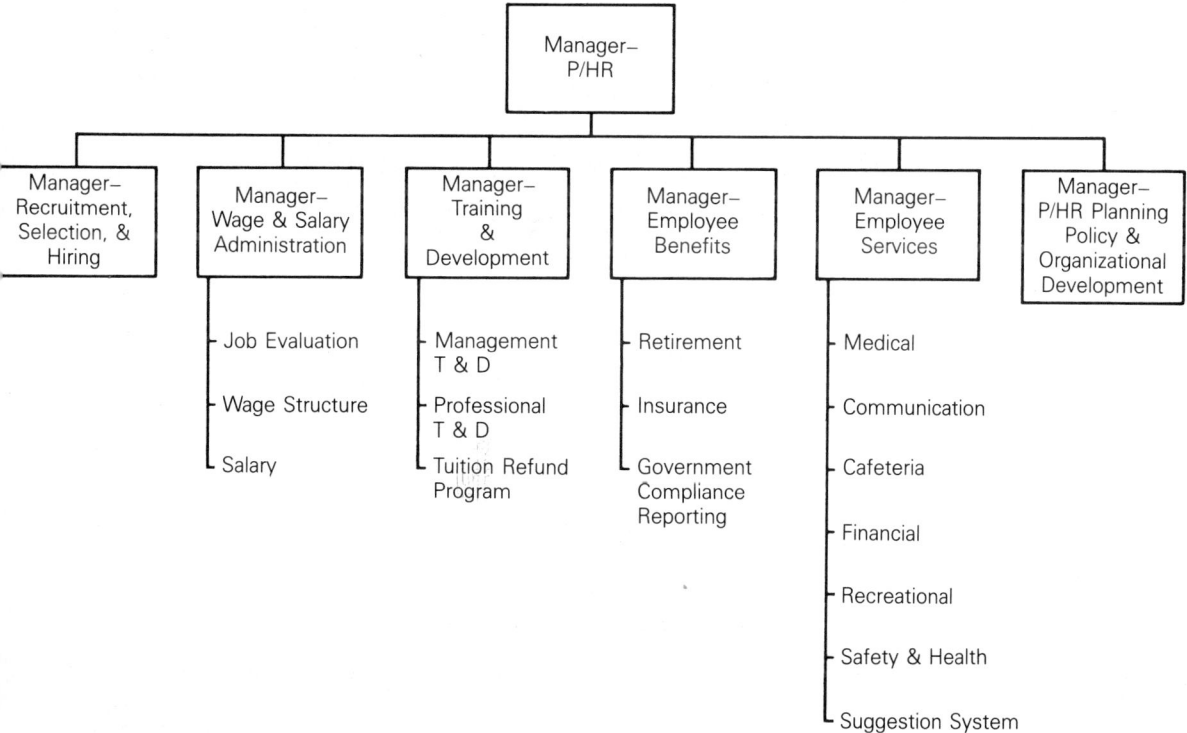

EXHIBIT 1–7
Organization of P/HR department for a single plant, small company, or decentralized subsidiary of a large company.

EXHIBIT 1–8 *Source:* Union Camp Annual Report, 1980.

Unlocking Employee Potential

As the company gets larger, the task of meshing division human resource requirements with corporate human resource needs becomes more difficult. So does the job of relating total human resource planning to long range goals. In 1980, we made that activity an even higher priority to be certain we are utilizing our people most efficiently. Our efforts assure that we are identifying talented people within our organization and providing opportunities for their development, as well as insuring an adequate supply of trained personnel to support our strategic plans for growth.

Assessing the company's long-range human resource needs is a joint endeavor of corporate and divisional Industrial Relations managers.

   3. Large corporate staff carries out P/HR for the company as a whole. Small staffs at each of the lower levels in the company hierarchy primarily assist management with implementation of corporate level requirements. See Exhibit 1–8.

P/HR department staffing ratios (personnel employees as a percent of total employees) tend to vary as a function of sales volume, number of employees, and organization structure. In Exhibit 1–9 we see how such factors relate to the number of P/HR employees in a company. Note that smaller independent organizations have significantly lower staffing ratios than large multilayer company organizations.

EXHIBIT 1-9
A) Personnel Department staffing ratios according to sales volume of company.
B) Personnel Department staffing ratios by number of employees of company.
C) Personnel Department staffing ratios compared for various structures (AMA).

Personnel Department staffing ratios according to sales volume of company.

Sales Volume ($000,000)	Refined Staffing Ratio
Under 25	.77
25–49	.67
50–99	.67
100–499	.72
500–999	1.19
Over 1,000	1.00

A)

Personnel Department staffing ratios by number of employees of company.

Number of Employees	Frequency	Refined Staffing Ratio
100–499	53	.97
500–999	91	.69
1,000–2,499	110	.63
2,500–4,999	41	.77
5,000–9,999	20	.82
1000+	15	1.04
Total	N = 330	

B)

Personnel Department staffing ratios compared for various structures (AMA Survey).

Organizational Unit	Refined Staffing Ratio	% of Survey Respondents
Conglomerate-holding	.82	3.8
Group or division	.87	26.8
Subsidiary	.72	36.8
Independent	.61	32.6

C)

Source: Reprinted by permission of the publisher, from *The Personnel Department: Its Staffing and Budgeting* by Oscar S. Ornati, Edward J. Giblin, and Richard E. Floersch, pp. 29 and 30. © 1982 AMA Research and Information Service, American Management Association, New York. All rights reserved.

According to various studies, the P/HR field provides one of the fastest-growing opportunities for careers in the U.S.[14] In 1977 the College Placement Council projected an increase in P/HR professionals to 427,000 by 1985. Not only will there be many opportunities in the field, but career growth and salaries will be attractive. Salaries for some listed open positions in 1982 are given in Exhibit 1–10. For the career-oriented student, these should be encouraging.

EXHIBIT 1-10
Selected openings in P/HR, 1982.

Position	Industry	Location	Salary
Senior VP			
	Retail	East	240,000
	Financial Services	Northeast	125,000
	Electronics	Northeast	100,000 +
	Banking	East	100,000
	Insurance	Northeast	100,000
Vice President			
	Energy	Southeast	165,000
	Office Products	Midwest	150,000
	Utility	Midwest	110,000
	Banking	East	100,000
	Medical Products	Midwest	100,000
	Consumer Products	Northeast	95,000
	Consumer Products	Midwest	90,000
	Insurance	Northeast	90,000
	Energy	Northeast	80,000
	Manufacturing	Midwest	80,000
	Food Service	East	75,000
	Insurance	West	75,000
	Manufacturing	West	65,000
	Health Care	Midwest	60,000
	Building Materials	Midwest	60,000
	Hotel	East	55,000
Compensation	Banking	Southeast	55,000
Recruiting	Banking	Southeast	55,000
Director			
	Manufacturing	Midwest	125,000
	Retail	Midwest	100,000
International	Consumer Goods	Northeast	90,000 +
	Technology	West	90,000
Compensation	Packaging	Northeast	90,000
	Food	West	85,000
Compensation	Communications	Southeast	80,000
	Food	West	80,000
	Equipment	Southeast	75,000
Employee Rel.	Computer	Northeast	65,000
	Paper	East	65,000
Employee Rel.	Medical Products	West	60,000
	Food	East	60,000
Compensation	Metals	Northeast	60,000
Man. Development	Service	Northeast	55,000
Training	Manufacturing	East	55,000
	Electronics	Midwest	50,000 +
Compensation	Electronics	Northeast	50,000
	Machine Tools	East	50,000
Manager			
	Manufacturing	East	95,000
	Manufacturing	Canada	65,000
	Petroleum	Southwest	65,000
	Rubber	East	60,000
Employee Rel.	Food	Northeast	60,000
Benefits	Insurance	East	55,000
	Transportation	Southwest	55,000
Compensation	Food	Southwest	54,000
	Transportation	Southwest	50,000
	Insurance	West	50,000
Development	Chemical	Northeast	50,000
Training	Technology	West	50,000

Source: "Executive Jobs: A 'Down' Market," *Dun's Business Month,* November 1982, p. 97. Reprinted with the special permission of Dun's Business Month (formerly Dun's Review), November 1982, Copyright 1982, Dun & Bradstreet Publications.

In the past, the "personnel clerk" was the only person dealing with personnel matters. As personnel activities expanded, people with lengthy and specialized training were required to perform the varied functions. Still, the personnel manager's position was frequently filled with a line manager who wanted semiretirement (or whom management wanted out of the way). Now P/HR management is seen by top management as an important function for profitability. Modern P/HR managers are trained to be profit-oriented as well as specialists in human resource management. Exhibit 1–11 is an example of a position description for a vice-president of human resources.

Careers in P/HR

People who work in the P/HR organization deal with both sensitive information and the lives and careers of other workers. Many companies are, therefore, very careful in selecting employees for this work. Psychological tests of candidates and psychological analysis of those selected may be required.

College graduates with a major in human resource management are well prepared for entry jobs as specialists. If they enter employment with the company in some other function and advance to supervisor or manager, they can be much more effective when they enter P/HR work. There is no substitute for line experience in gaining empathy with, and understanding of, workers' and managers' problems.

Others with less formal preparation in P/HR may also enter the field (Exhibit 1–12), but it is expected that they will continue developing their skills with additional formal training in the subject area. In addition, all functional specialists may be rotated through the various specialties during their early years of employment. This prepares them for management positions or aids them in selecting a career specialty.

The management P/HR ladder is usually clearly defined in most companies. However, functional specialists appear at different levels within companies and with varied degrees of responsibility. For example, a labor negotiator at the plant level may be paid more than a training director at the corporate level. This is because labor relations is such a complex, sensitive area where a single mistaken action may cost a company thousands of dollars.

In some companies, P/HR organization is very stable and promotions are slow. In such a case, a career-oriented individual should be on the lookout for openings with other companies at a higher level. This can result in broader experience, more rapid career development, and fresher challenges. As an alternative, the P/HR worker may shift within the same company to other staff administration positions and then back to P/HR management. Again, this presents an opportunity for growth while waiting for a higher-level opening in the P/HR organization.

EXHIBIT 1–11
Position description for a P/HR Vice President.

ORGANIZATION	LEVITZ FURNITURE CORPORATION	
SUBJECT Position Guide Vice President-Personnel	**DATE ISSUED:** 12/80 **APPROVED BY:** R.M.E.	**ORGANIZATION** Personnel

I. Broad Function

Responsible for developing, establishing and administering a personnel program for the Company which is consistent with its short- and long-range business objectives. Also responsible for developing and directing a standard procedure program for all functions in the Company.

II. Reporting Relationship

Reports directly to the President and Chief Executive Officer. Keeps him informed of the Personnel Division's activities and plans and receives guidance regarding overall corporate policy.

III. Duties and Responsibilities

A. Develops objectives for the Personnel Division based upon analysis of company requirements in the areas of compensation, benefits, manpower planning and development, medical services, management development and training, organization planning, EEO, employment and management records.

B. Directs the development and maintenance of a corporate standards procedures program for all functions of the business.

C. Reviews and analyzes the performance of the Personnel Division against objectives; initiates changes where required to achieve the highest level of performance.

D. Coordinates the activities of the Personnel Division with other operating and staff components in the development and implementation of policies, programs and practices.

E. Integrates the staff activities of the Personnel Division for the achievement of efficiency, timeliness and coordination of its various functions.

F. Directs the development and maintenance of company-wide wage and salary programs to assure the competitive and equitable compensation of associates.

G. Directs the development and maintenance of a total training and development program based upon the needs of associates and the Company.

H. Directs the development and maintenance of a competitive employee benefits program for the Company.

I. Directs an analysis of the organization structure, relationships, titling and responsibilities, and promotes the development and use of company-wide organization planning, corporate policies and counseling services.

J. Directs the development and maintenance of an effective management development program for the Company to provide manpower of the necessary quality and quantity at the time and place required.

K. Directs the development and maintenance of a medical program to provide adequate standards, services and facilities to fill the needs of associates and the Company.

L. Directs the development and maintenance of recruitment and employment programs to attract, select, and assign competent personnel within the Company.

M. Originates policies, programs and practices which will provide a complete personnel program throughout the Company.

(EXHIBIT 1–11, *continued*)

N. Keeps abreast of current industry practices, government regulations and new developments in order to keep company policies, programs and practices up-to-date and competitive.

O. Directs the selection, training, development and compensation of associates within the Personnel Division; defines responsibilities, establishes standards of performance and appraises results.

P. Directs the development of effective associate communication programs and materials and guides other divisions in their use.

Q. Works with managers responsible for associate relations and labor relations to assist them in dealing with associate morale problems, grievance handling, and providing other personnel services as required.

R. Works with other staff officers as well as the C.E.O. on corporate policy formulation as well as the implementation of personnel policies and programs.

IV. Experience and Knowledge Requirements

The position requires thorough knowledge of all personnel functions including personnel administration, training, compensation, benefits, organization planning and EEO, as well as general knowledge of branch and group operations.

The required technical and practical knowledge may be acquired through a college degree plus eight to ten years of management and personnel administration experience.

V. Accountability Factors

In appraising the performance of the Vice President–Personnel, the President will consider the following factors:

A. The extent to which the overall personnel needs are met in terms of selection, manpower development, training, benefit administration, policy formulation, compensation, standard procedures, and general personnel administration.

B. The ability to work with other staff managers in achieving company objectives.

C. The ability to develop and administer a competitive compensation program.

D. The extent to which the manpower development program satisfies the manpower needs of the corporation.

E. The degree to which the Company benefit programs meet the Company's goals in respect to competitiveness and cost.

F. The extent to which he is able to provide corporate officers with guidance and assistance in developing a corporate policy and organization program.

Courtesy of Levitz Furniture Corporation

PROFESSIONALIZATION IN THE P/HR FIELD

What is a *professional*, and should P/HR be established as a profession? If so, should only managers be admitted to the profession or should specialists such as training directors be included? Where do we stand today on this topic?

A few of the best-known professions today are engineering, elementary-school teaching, law, accounting, and medicine. What are the common

THE SETTING

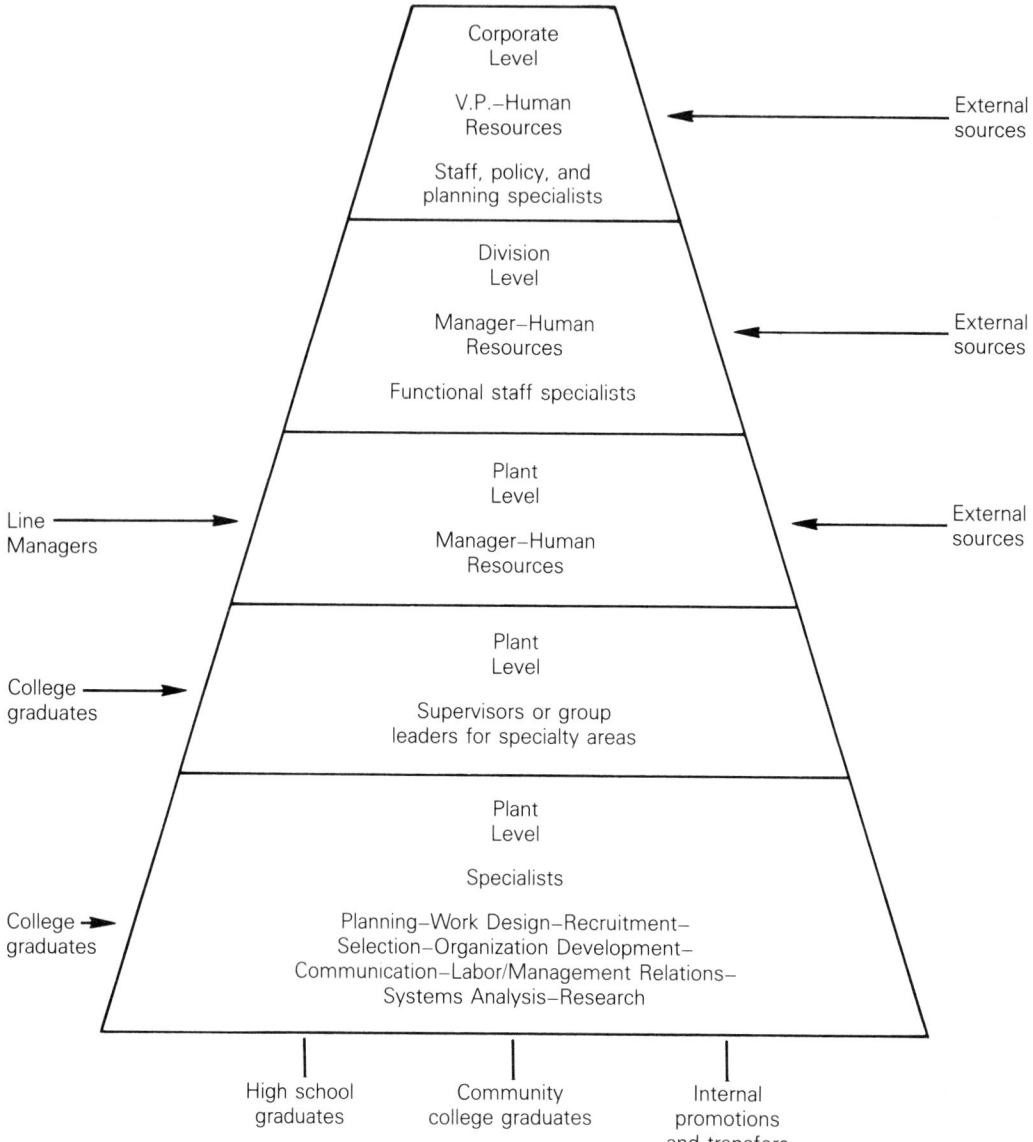

EXHIBIT 1-12
P/HR career paths.

elements of these professions that distinguish them from "professional baseball players" or "professional managers"? There are many criteria, as shown in Exhibit 1-13, but one in particular stands out—members of the profession must be licensed by a governmental body for the purpose of protecting the public.

EXHIBIT 1-13
Criteria for a profession.

1) Professional work requires knowledge obtained through advanced study in a field of science or learning customarily acquired by a prolonged *formal* course of *specialized* study as distinguished from *general* academic education and from an apprenticeship.
2) Professional work requires consistent exercise of discretion, judgment, and personal responsibility in its performance.
3) A profession must be regulated by a national-level association of its members which
   a. Establishes minimum levels of skill and knowledge.
   b. Establishes standards of ethical practice to guide the relations of members with each other, the client, and the public.
   c. Standardizes terminology.
   d. Sets policies and standard practices and procedures to be followed in appropriate cases.
   e. Publishes the official journal for the profession.
   f. Promotes the advancement of the science and art of the profession.
4) An in-training or internship period is required before professional status is achieved.
5) Practitioners are expected to extend the knowledge upon which the profession is based.
6) Practitioners make their knowledge and contributions freely available to others in the profession and take responsibility for assisting and developing the newer and younger members of the profession.
7) Members are required by law to be licensed in order to practice the profession.
8) The professional man maintains at all times an attitude towards his work and society characterized as follows:
   a. A social consciousness, a desire to contribute *to* rather than simply benefit *from* civilization; a resolve to place the public welfare above other considerations.
   b. The continued acquisition of special skills on a high intellectual plane, generally evaluated by means of self-imposed standards of excellence.
   c. A sense of trusteeship—personal responsibility to protect the employer's interest.
   d. Individual initiative and acceptance of individual responsibility, both of the highest order.
   e. A right to expect and receive adequate financial recognition.

Source: Robert G. Murdick, "The Meaning of Management As a Profession," S.A.M. *Advanced Management Journal*, April 1960 (New York: Society for Advancement of Management, a division of American Management Associations, 1960), pp. 13–14.

The growing importance of the P/HR function in all organizations has led to a movement designed to increase the professionalism of individuals employed in the P/HR department. For example, the *American Society for Personnel Administration (ASPA)* has set up the Personnel Accreditation Institute (PAI) as an independent, nonprofit, educational organization to offer the P/HR practitioner the opportunity to be accredited as a specialist in a functional area such as employment or training and development, or in a generalist category, which includes multiple specialties.

For instance, in the specialist group, the basic level is Accredited Personnel Specialist, and the advanced level is Accredited Personnel Diplomate. In the generalist category, the basic level designation is Accredited Personnel Manager and the advanced level is Accredited Executive in Personnel.[15] You don't have to be an ASPA member to be accredited, nor do you have to be accredited to be an ASPA member.

The basic goals of ASPA include improving and maintaining standards of excellence in the field of P/HR. Membership in ASPA, which exceeds 30,000, ranges from specialists to division personnel managers, to corporate vice presidents of P/HR. There are also student chapters of ASPA on college campuses throughout the country.

Other associations that promote professionalism in the field of P/HR include the Academy of Management, the American Society of Training Directors, the American Management Associations, the International Personnel Management Association, and the American Compensation Association. Most of these organizations hold national and regional meetings to discuss research findings and latest developments in the area of P/HR. In addition, most conduct seminars and publish journals that contain new developments and methods for dealing with P/HR problems.

The American Compensation Association (ACA) has an accreditation program similar to the ASPA's program, whereby compensation specialists can become accredited. The organization has a membership exceeding four thousand professionals who are responsible for the establishment or administration of compensation policies and practices. Similarly, the American Society for Training and Development is comprised of over 15,000 members who are involved in the training and development of personnel.

INTEGRATED APPROACH TO MANAGING THE P/HR FUNCTION

The management of human resources in an organization brings together three disciplines: (1) Management theory and processes; (2) organizational behavior and development; and (3) personnel administration.

Management theory deals primarily with planning, organizing, and controlling the resources of the organization to achieve the basic mission of the organization. *Organizational behavior and development* is concerned with the study of people's behavior in organized groups and methods for improving their performance and satisfactions. *Personnel administration* (used interchangeably with personnel management, personnel/human resource management, and P/HR management) is the staff function that facilitates the most effective use of people in the organization to achieve organizational and individual goals. The P/HR function is a supporting service for managers throughout the company or other such agency. We shall use the term P/HR management throughout this book.

P/HR management may be studied from a number of perspectives:

1. Process approach: What activities must be carried out to fulfill the P/HR management mission?
2. Behavioral approach: How do people behave and how can we shape the behavior of people in organizations?
3. Research approach: What does research show us as the ways that P/HR are or should be managed?
4. Diagnostic approach: From a model of organizational behavior, how do we diagnose symptoms to determine the underlying problems? What is wrong and how can we fix it?
5. Information systems approach: What is the flow of information that links together all activities of the P/HR function?

6. Contingency approach: What factors influence decisions and actions and to what extent?

It is apparent that all of these approaches contribute important ideas to the P/HR staff activities. Our approach in this book is to utilize all available approaches by taking a systems approach. In a systems approach we start by specifying the objectives (the P/HR organization). Next we structure the system based on activities that the system must perform to achieve systems objectives. Then we must define relationships and information flows among parts of the system. This step involves studying the behavior of individuals and groups within the system. Finally, we wish to control system performance through information systems and diagnostic procedures.

In the systems approach, it is important to present a framework of the system that integrates the parts (we have shown this framework in Exhibit 1–5). Six advantages of the systems approach for the study of P/HR management are:

1. It requires a clear definition of the total business, the total HR system, and the total P/HR organization and functions as well as the objectives of each of these systems. HR consists of all employees, and P/HR consists of employees working in personnel.
2. It offers a natural, straightforward method of analysis, design, and problem diagnosis by permitting division into subsystems and components.
3. It shows the interrelations among the components of the human resource system.
4. It relates the human resource system to its environment in terms of the inputs and outputs, and their effects upon the system. It then relates the P/HR staff activity to the total human resource system.
5. It permits the study of managers, individual workers, and groups as systems, based upon the extensive research going on in the area of motivation and organizational behavior.
6. It permits examination of the division of work between line managers and the manager of P/HR in terms of total system objectives and trade-offs to optimize the achievement of those objectives.

Human resources represent a subsystem of the business that dominates all other subsystems of the business. The reason is obvious—humans design and control all other systems (Exhibit 1–14). Thus, in terms of people, in terms of the functioning of the firm, and in terms of society, we would certainly agree that people at work are very important.

In the systems approach, we try to look at the total picture. The objectives of the total company determine, in turn, the objectives of each part of the company. Resources within the company must be distributed to enhance total company performance, not just a suborganization. Finally, we must modify the business system continuously to adapt the system to the

EXHIBIT 1–14
The human resource system influences all other systems in a business.

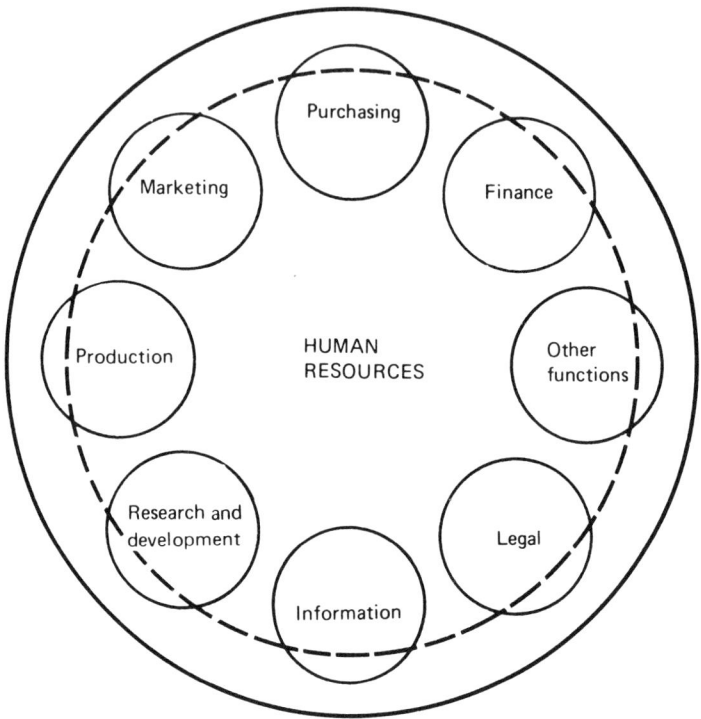

The human resource subsystem controls all other subsystems in a business

environment of (1) customers, (2) competitors, (3) the economy, (4) political change, (5) legal change, (6) cultural change, and (7) social change.

Our approach in this book is to blend all perspectives and to deal with some separately as well. The systems concept includes the environment of the HR system, the process, the behavior of the human elements, and the information flow that ties the elements together. We have devoted special sections to develop this framework. At the same time, from a practical viewpoint, the process of human resource management is what leads to achievement of business system goals. The principal progression of the central part of the book will take you through the P/HR management process. Both research and practice are treated within the systems and behavioral framework. The legal constraints and requirements are also woven in after an early treatment from a general perspective.

Diagnosis is the analysis of problems in the management of human resources, research is an aid to solution, and control is the means for anticipating and preventing problems. The general methods are given in a separate chapter.

The computer-based information system is becoming so important to the management of human resources that Chapter 19, The Human Resource Management System and the Computer, is included to describe this new technical decision-assisting and control system.

We hope that by applying an integrated model (system) to the P/HR management activities and by presenting guides to practice that you can begin to prepare for managing P/HR functions with breadth, understanding, and effectiveness.

SUMMARY

This chapter is itself a summary of the issues of human resource management today. Human resource management is a focal point for general business management in its search for increased productivity.

The need for a special personnel/human resource department arose as firms increased in size, as the underpinnings of P/HR management grew more complex, and as increased productivity became more vital. Line managers could no longer be experts in so many fields as management technology, organizational behavior, personnel theory, labor relations, legal changes in personnel, and computer technology. They required supporting expertise to make P/HR decisions.

Important changes and new developments have been occurring in such personnel-related areas as:

1. Social and legal changes involving women at work, discrimination, quality of life, problem workers, and aged workers
2. Conditions of employment involving compensation and work time, the computer, selection and promotion, and health and safety
3. Labor–management relations
4. Changes in the economy and problems of productivity
5. The changing work force as affected by education, new value systems, the shift to knowledge workers from production workers, midlife career changes, and unemployment of underqualified workers

The functions of the P/HR department are discussed and are reflected in the position guide for a manager of P/HR. The organization of the P/HR department is discussed and related to careers in the field. Growing professionalization of the field is also related to careers in the field.

Finally, the integrated, or systems approach to the P/HR field is touched on. In this book we will tie together various topics in the field in order to give you an integrated idea of what human resource management *is*—and *should* be.

KEY CONCEPTS

Productivity	OSHA
QWL	Labor union
P/HR management	Collective bargaining
P/HR specialist	Value system
Sex discrimination	Knowledge worker
Sexual harassment	Diagnosis
Conditions of employment	System
Compensation	Professional
Computer-based information system	ASPA

NOTES

1. Norman R. Horton, "Memo for Management," *Management Review*, October 1982.
2. "Women Hold Few Top Federal Jobs," *Miami Herald*, July 26, 1976.
3. See, for example, Janice Niepert Hedges and Earl F. Mellor, "Weekly and Hourly Earnings of U.S. Workers, 1967–1978," *Monthly Labor Review*, August 1979, p. 31.
4. Richard Zoglin, "The Homosexual Executive," *MBA*, July–August 1974.
5. Lesbianism in the general population is discussed in Shere Hite, *The Hite Report* (New York: Macmillan, 1976).
6. "Americans Fearful They've Lost Control of Life, Survey Says," *Miami Herald*, April 3, 1974. See also surveys conducted in 1968 and 1973 by Daniel Yankelovich, Inc., for the Institute of Life Insurance.
7. See, for example, *Monthly Labor Review*, April 1983, p. 38.
8. Victor Riesel, "Presser Sets Teamsters on High-Road Course," *Miami Herald*, April 25, 1983, p. 19A.
9. Cyrus Altinus and Richard Tersine, "Chronological Age and Job Satisfaction: The Young Blue Collar Worker," *Academy of Management Journal*, March 1973.
10. Special Task Force to the Secretary of Health, Education, and Welfare, *Work in America* (Elliot Richardson, Ed.) (Cambridge, Mass.: M.I.T. Press, 1973).
11. Robert Schrank, *Ten Thousand Working Days* (Cambridge, Mass.: M.I.T. Press, 1978).
12. See Grover Starling, *The Changing Environment of Business* (Boston: Kent, 1980, p. 479), for a tabulation of sex, race, and age.
13. Herbert E. Meyer, "Personnel Directors Are the New Corporate Heroes," *Fortune*, February 1976.
14. Roy R. Van Cleve, "Human Resources Administration: Curriculum for a Profession," *Personnel Administrator*, March 1982, p. 61.

15. Personnel/Human Resources Division, Academy of Management, *News*, March 1983, Vol. VI, Issue 2.

REVIEW AND DISCUSSION QUESTIONS

1. a. Give examples of America's wasted resources. b. Do you think we waste human resources? Discuss.
2. What are the dimensions of productivity?
3. a. What are six major factors that have been important in the development of HR management? b. Can you think of other possibly important factors that may affect the future direction of HR management? Discuss.
4. Why has growth of productivity declined in recent years?
5. a. What are the goals of the P/HR department? Discuss. b. What are major functions of a P/HR department? Discuss.
6. How is the role of business in society related to the objectives of HR management in a particular business?
7. Bring to class an organization chart for the P/HR department obtained from some local company or from an article; discuss it in terms of size of company, manufacturing or service performed, and functions performed.
8. Discuss how the study of HR management is beneficial for a career as specialist, manager, or a P/HR employee.
9. Should P/HR be established as a profession? Justify your answer.
10. "Business has only one objective—to make the maximum profit for the owners." Discuss this statement in terms of possible objectives of business and P/HR management.
11. a. What is a system? b. In what ways may a business be considered a system? c. How can the human resource system be both a "system" and a "subsystem" of a business?
12. Does the true systems approach to studying human resources in business neglect the behavioral variables? Discuss.
13. "Managing human resources is the job of the personnel department." Discuss.

BIBLIOGRAPHY

Bohlander, George W., Harold C. White, and Michael N. Wolfe. "The Three Faces of Personnel." *Personnel*, July–August, 1983.

Byham, William C. "Applying a Systems Approach to Personnel Activities." *Training and Development Journal*, December 1981, January 1982, February 1982.

Cascio, Wayne F., and Elias M. Awad. *Human Resources Management: An Information Approach*. Reston, Va.: Reston Publishing, 1981.

Desatnick, Robert L. *The Expanding Role of the Human Resources Manager.* New York: AMACOM, 1979.

Deutsch, Arnold. *The Human Resources Revolution: Communicate or Litigate.* New York: McGraw-Hill, 1979.

Devanna, Mary Anne, Charles Fombrun, and Noel Tichy. "Human Resources Management: A Strategic Perspective." *Organizational Dynamics*, Winter 1981.

Dubrin, Andrew J. *Personnel and Human Resource Management.* New York: D. Van Nostrand, 1981.

Glinow, Mary Ann, Michael J. Driver, and Kenneth Brousseau. "The Design of a Career-Oriented Human Resource System." *Academy of Management Review*, January 1983.

Harris, Marvin. "Why It's Not the Same Old America." *Psychology Today*, August 1981.

The Human Connection: Making Organizations Work. Scarsdale, N.Y.: Work in America Institute, 1982/1983.

Janger, Allen R. *The Personnel Function: Changing Objectives and Organization.* New York: The Conference Board, 1977.

Main, Jeremy. "Work Won't Be the Same Again." *Fortune*, June 28, 1982.

Manpower Goals for American Democracy. Report of the American Assembly Seminar, Columbia University; New York, 1976.

Murdick, Robert G. "The Meaning of Management As a Profession." *Advanced Management*, April 1960.

"The New Industrial Relations." *Business Week*, May 11, 1981.

Olson, Lawrence. "The Changing Labor Market in the 80s." *Financial Executive*, October 1982.

Ornati, Oscar S., Edward J. Giblin, and Richard R. Floersch. *The Personnel Department: Its Staffing and Budgeting.* New York: AMA Research and Information Service, 1982.

"Personnel Widens Its Franchise." *Business Week*, February 26, 1979.

Personick, Valerie A. "The Outlook on Industry Output and Employment through 1990." *Monthly Labor Review*, August 1981.

"Respecting Emloyee Privacy." *Business Week*, January 11, 1982.

Robbins, Stephen P. *Personnel: The Management of Human Resources.* (2nd ed.). Englewood Cliffs, N.J.: Prentice-Hall, 1982.

Ross, Joyce. "A Definition of Human Resources Management." *Personnel Journal*, October 1981.

Special Task Force to the Secretary of Health, Education and Welfare. *Work in America.* Cambridge, Mass.: M.I.T. Press, 1973.

"Tomorrow's Jobs." *Occupational Outlook Handbook.* (1978–1979 ed.). Washington D.C.: U.S. Department of Labor.

Walker, James W. *Human Resource Planning.* New York: McGraw-Hill, 1980.

Wangler, Lawrence A. "The Intensification of the Personnel Role." *Personnel Journal*, February 1979.

White, Harold C., and Michael N. Wolfe. "Industrial Management Views Personnel Administration." *Industrial Management*, March–April, 1981.

The Legal Environment For Human Resource Management

CHAPTER OUTLINE

Public Policy and Human Resource Management
Emerging Role for the Government in the 1930s □ Accelerated Role for the Government in the 1960s and 70s

Equal Employment Opportunity (EEO)
Federal Equal Employment Opportunity Laws □ State and Local EEO Laws □ Executive Orders

Affirmative Action
Developing an Affirmative Action Program (AAP) □ Reverse Discrimination

Uniform Guidelines on Employee Selection Procedures

Government's Role in Employee Safety and Health
Occupational Safety and Health Act of 1970 (OSHA) □ Workers' Compensation Laws

Legal Influences on Compensation and Benefits

Legal Influences on Labor Relations

Implications of Public Policy for Human Resource Management

OBJECTIVES

1. Describe how public policy on the management of human resources, reflected in laws and regulations, has changed since the 1930s
2. Outline the major laws, regulations, and court cases that currently affect human resource policies and practices in a firm
3. Discuss what is meant by equal employment opportunity (EEO) laws and how they affect employment decisions
4. Develop an effective affirmative action program (AAP)
5. Describe how public policy affects all aspects of human resource management

SPOTLIGHT:
Howard Barron

Howard P. Barron is Personnel Manager for Siemens Communication Systems, Inc. He is responsible for all human resource management activities for the Telephone Division (U.S.), the International Development Division, and the Siemens Leasing Company. He has sixteen years of personnel/management and independent consulting experience for such firms as Burroughs Corporation, City Stores, Inc., ARA Inc., Orlando Regional Medical Center, Honeywell, and Martin Marietta. He has been an adjunct professor at several universities.

While his background involves all areas of human resources, he is viewed as a leader in utilizing management information systems within the decision making framework of human resource management.

Comments by Howard Barron

How often we have heard, "Government should stay out of business." Many people believe that government regulations and laws will eventually destroy the free-enterprise system. There have been, however, socioeconomic conditions existing in the past that seemed to require laws or at least some enforceable regulations before private business, in the eyes of society, would do "right" by their employees. Some examples of such conditions have been child labor, race and sex discrimination, and unfair working conditions. Certainly, whether any one of us as an individual has difficulty accepting the premises of any of these conditions, we must admit that the overwhelming societal pressure that generates legislation on these issues cannot be ignored.

We need to know that there is some very basic human behavior that is affected when laws are established. A law or regulation in itself does not change people's behavior toward one another. Rather, what is initially established is a degree of tolerance. Next, there is a level of acceptance and only much later comes respect and understanding.

These same behaviors are apparent in the business world. The legal environment's effect on human resource management has in the past followed the same behavioral set. First, tolerance—"We have to hire these people because the law is forcing us to do so." Next comes, with time and exposure, acceptance—"She has actually turned out to be a good salesperson." Finally come the *respect* and *understanding* that, in general, it was a terrible waste in the past not to realize the full human potential of all people.

Hopefully, enough time, experience, and social learning have taken place for those who will be the human resource management professionals in the immediate future to allow us to operate at the "respect" and "understanding" level of human behavior. We will find that when such an environment exists there will be far less pressure for regulation or law from city, state, or federal governments.

It behooves us in our roles as influencers of management policy and practice to apply the law in the operation of our businesses with the most positive thought processes. After all, we have learned from past experience that in nearly every instance, what the law forces us to do relative to our employees is what good, sound management would be doing without the law.

PUBLIC POLICY AND HUMAN RESOURCE MANAGEMENT

Before the 1930s there existed very little public regulation of organizations with regard to personnel/human resource policies and practices. Public opinion, at least as reflected in the absence of laws and regulations, seemed to favor simply allowing the company and individual employees to work out any employment arrangement that was acceptable to both parties. In fact, courts even took a negative view of labor unions, which were viewed as restraining the natural competition that would take place between whatever the employer and individual worker agreed upon.

While some states did pass several laws such as those dealing with child labor, as early as the 1800s, the prevailing attitude was to let the forces of a free market determine all conditions of employment. This meant that employers could hire, fire, and promote whomever they desired and pay at whatever level the market would accept.

Emerging Role for the Government in the 1930s

During the 1930s, however, a significant change took place in public opinion. With almost one out of every four in the work force unemployed during the Great Depression, the public, through a series of laws, became much more involved in employment conditions.

The American people wanted a quick solution to revive the economy and to get the unemployed back to work. To accomplish this, the Roosevelt administration successfully pushed through Congress a series of laws that changed the relationship between government and business. Suddenly, the government was heavily involved in employment and labor relations activities of private firms. Laws were passed regulating the minimum wages that a firm could pay as well as the maximum number of hours that an employee could work before overtime would have to be paid. Similarly, for the first time, employers were taxed in order to pay unemployment and retirement benefits to employees. As we shall see in Chapter 16, Labor–Management Relations, the 1930s also marked the passage of the Wagner Act, which encouraged unionization and required an employer to bargain with the union in good faith over wages, hours, and working conditions.

Accelerated Role for the Government in the 1960s and 70s

It was later during the 1960s and 1970s, however, that legislation and governmental regulations were passed that dramatically affected the management of human resources. The government's role in employment decisions was significantly accelerated—major laws and amendments to existing laws were designed to eliminate discrimination based on sex, age, race, color, physical or mental handicap, religion, or national origin. Other recent laws have affected every firm's policies on health and safety, retirement, and pensions.

Some of the constraints on human resource management have come not through legislation, but as a result of *executive orders* issued during the Kennedy and Johnson administrations. Issued to private and public organizations doing business with the federal government, for example, were executive orders designed to establish *affirmative action* programs. These programs are intended to increase the number of minorities and females employed at all levels in the organization.

Back in the 1970s, Thomas H. Patten, Jr., noted:

> From a situation of virtual *laissez-faire* at the turn of the century, government has since come forth with factory inspection, unfair labor practices decisions, wage and hour suits, affirmative action compliance reviews, and detailed occupational health and safety standards and investigations. The harried personnel manager is thus likely to feel very put upon as he is saddled with reports and reviews, and to hope wistfully that he might instead someday ride away from it all into the wide open spaces and breathe the free air of *laissez-faire* once again. Alas, the likelihood of . . . this is ever so slight as we see our society moving more and more into a smothering strait jacket of legalisms and red tape.[1]

In this chapter we will survey the major laws, regulations, and court cases in order to see how they currently affect human resource policies and practices in the organization. Emphasis will be placed on equal employment laws. No challenge to managers in the 1980s is likely to be as important, or as potentially expensive, as meeting the responsibilities of maintaining an organization free of discrimination.

EQUAL EMPLOYMENT OPPORTUNITY (EEO)

Equal Employment Opportunity (EEO) laws refer to a number of federal, state, and local acts designed to provide equal treatment and employment opportunities for members of certain protected groups. These acts prohibit any discrimination based on race, religion, national origin, sex, or age. Certain laws also prohibit, under special circumstances, discrimination against the handicapped and Vietnam veterans.

Federal Equal Employment Opportunity Laws

The major federal EEO laws include Title VII of the 1964 Civil Rights Act, the Age Discrimination in Employment Act, Equal Pay Act, Vocational Rehabilitation Act, and the Vietnam Era Veterans Readjustment Act. Let us consider how they affect human resource policies and practices.

Title VII of the 1964 Civil Rights Act Title VII is one of the most prominent and probably most important EEO law. It prohibits discrimination due to race, color, religion, sex, or national origin, in any term, condition, or privilege of employment, except in relatively rare instances when a bona fide occupational qualification is permitted (for example, requiring males to play the role of males in theater productions). Enforcement of Title VII is carried out by the Equal Employment Opportunity Commission (EEOC). A decision of the EEOC may be appealed in the federal courts.

Title VII was amended in 1972 to strengthen the power and jurisdiction of the EEOC. As amended, Title VII now covers:

1. All private employers of 15 or more persons
2. All public and private educational institutions
3. State and local governments
4. Public and private employment agencies
5. Labor unions with 15 or more members

The ambiguous provisions of the act, however, give substantial leeway to the agencies who enforce the law. Furthermore, regulations resulting from interpretations have changed as membership of the agencies change. As a result, the government and employers have had to turn periodically to the courts to clarify EEOC's position that when the law speaks about equal opportunity it refers to more than not discriminating in employment decisions. Equality of *results* rather than *intent* is used to determine if an employer is in compliance with the law.

Five groups of employees are protected under Title VII. These are women, blacks, Hispanics, American Indians, and Asian-Pacific Islanders.

Equal Pay Act of 1963 Traditionally, because the male worker was viewed as head of the household and women merely supplemental wage earners, men frequently received higher pay than women for the same job.[2] The Equal Pay Act now requires an employer to pay equal wages for equal work unless there is a difference in seniority or performance levels. (The controversial issue of comparable worth will be discussed in Chapter 15.)

In 1970 the Supreme Court in *Schultz v. Wheaton Glass Company* ruled that jobs do not have to be identical; rather, equal wages must be paid for substantially similar work.[3] To be more exact, jobs are considered equal when both men and women work at the same place and the job demands substantially the same skill, effort, and responsibility. Many states have similar equal pay laws.

It should be noted, however, that an employer *can* pay men and women differently in the same job if they do so solely on the basis of merit or performance or seniority. Since courts have wide discretion under this act, back-pay awards have been granted in some cases to thousands of employees. For example, in the *Wheaton Glass Company* case, a federal court found the company guilty of violating the act and ordered Wheaton to pay $900,000 in back pay and interest to 2,000 women employees.

Age Discrimination in Employment Act The Age Discrimination in Employment Act, passed in 1967 and amended in 1978, protects persons between the ages of 40 and 70 from discrimination in any area of employment because of age. To date, while the act has not received much attention from regulatory agencies, it is likely that the older worker and employment practices will be a major issue in the 1980s. This is a reasonable prediction in view of the growing number of older workers in the labor force.

One effect of the law is to force organizations to develop and properly use performance appraisal systems to justify any personnel decisions taken against employees who are between 40 and 70. If management, for example, is to lay off employees, it can do so on the basis of poor performance or less seniority, but age cannot be the deciding factor (e.g., "Let's let old Charlie go—he's close to retirement anyway").

Vocational Rehabilitation Act According to the Vocational Rehabilitation Act of 1973, employers with government contracts of $2,500 or more must have approved affirmative action plans for the handicapped. In a sense, this act is the civil rights act for the handicapped. Together with subsequent regulations it prohibits discrimination against physically or mentally handicapped persons who, with reasonable accommodation, can perform successfully on the job.

While similar to the Civil Rights Act, the Vocational Rehabilitation Act does have some important differences. Most importantly, the employer of the handicapped must take steps to reasonably accommodate the worker so that he or she can do the job that otherwise could not be performed. Examples of such *reasonable accommodation* might include installing elevators to all floors, constructing ramps for wheelchairs, and redesigning jobs and training programs to fit the particular needs of the handicapped.

According to the act, the employer must make reasonable accommodations unless the employer "can demonstrate that the accommodation would pose an *undue hardship* on the operation of its program."[4] At this time, the courts and agencies are struggling to determine when reasonable accommodation becomes an undue hardship. Business necessity and financial costs are among the factors considered.

It should be noted that the act does not obligate an employer to hire persons who are unable to perform or who are less skilled than others. The act protects only "qualified handicapped individuals" who are capable of performing a particular job with "reasonable accommodation."

Vietnam Era Veterans Readjustment Act In order to help Vietnam War veterans who had particular difficulty in securing jobs when they returned to this country, the Vietnam Era Veterans Readjustment Act was passed in 1974. The act requires all organizations holding government contracts of $10,000 or more to hire and promote veterans of the Vietnam era. Along with the equal employment opportunity requirement, firms covered by the law must list all suitable job openings with the appropriate local employment service office, which will then give priority on referrals to Vietnam-era veterans. The Veterans' Employment Service of the Department of Labor is charged with enforcement of the law.

State and Local EEO Laws

Most states and many cities have anti-discrimination laws, often referred to as *fair employment practices*. While 45 states have such statutes, coverage and administrative and substantive provisions vary widely. Similarly, about 70 cities, some in states in which there is no state fair employment practice law, have such statutes. Most of these laws specify unfair employment practices, procedures, and enforcement powers. Most states vest enforcement powers for these laws in a state fair employment practice commission. These commissions are normally found in the executive branch of the state government.

In almost all cases, compliance with the federal laws results in compliance with state and local fair employment practices. Whenever there are inconsistencies between federal requirements and state or local requirements, the federal law takes precedence. While the state and local EEO laws are similar to the federal laws, it is important for the human resource specialist to be aware of them for a couple of reasons. For one thing, the state or local laws often extend coverage to firms exempted by the federal laws. Thus, a firm not covered by the federal law may find it is covered by a state law that may have even more stringent restrictions. Secondly, when the EEOC receives discrimination charges, it *defers* them for a limited time period to the appropriate state or local agencies with comparable jurisdiction and enforcement sanctions. If satisfactory remedies are not achieved, charges revert to EEOC for resolution.

Executive Orders

Many executive orders and actions have been issued over the years that require employers having federal contracts to be nondiscriminatory. The Office of Federal Contract Compliance (OFCC) in the Labor Department was established to enforce nondiscrimination among firms having federal contracts or subcontracts. Under Executive Order 11246 (1965), for example, the Secretary of Labor was given the power to:

1. Publish the names of noncomplying contractors or unions;
2. Recommend action to the EEOC or the Justice Department to compel compliance; and
3. Cancel the contract of a noncomplying contractor.

What is an executive order? An executive order is not a law and does not have as wide an impact as do federal laws such as the Equal Pay Act. Nor does an executive order generally affect as wide a range of employees as do most major employment laws. Executive orders (also known as presidential orders) are directives from the president aimed at federal government agencies and organizations having contracts with the federal government. See Exhibit 2–1 for a listing of employers covered and types of employment prohibited by major EEO laws and executive orders.

EXHIBIT 2–1
Major antidiscrimination laws and orders.

Federal Laws and Executive Orders	Type of Employment Discrimination Prohibited	Employers Covered
Equal Pay Act of 1963	Sex differences in pay for substantially equal work	Private employers
Executive Order 11141 (1964)	Age discrimination	Federal contractors and subcontractors
Title VII of the 1964 Civil Rights Act	Discrimination based on race, color, religion, sex, or national origin	Employers receiving federal financial assistance
Title VII of the 1964 Civil Rights Act, as amended in 1972 by the Equal Employment Act	Discrimination or segregation based on race, color, religion, sex, or national origin	Private employers with 15 or more employees; federal, state, and local governments; unions and apprenticeship committees; employment agencies; educational institutions
Executive Orders 11246 and 11375 (1965)	Discrimination based on race, color, religion, sex, or national origin (affirmative action required)	Federal contractors and subcontractors
Age Discrimination in Employment Act of 1967 as amended in 1978	Age discrimination against those between the ages of 40 and 70	Private employers with 20 or more employees; unions with 25 or more members; employment agencies; apprenticeship and training programs
Executive Order 11478 (1969)	Discrimination based on race, color, religion, sex, national origin, political affiliation, marital status, or physical handicap	Federal government
Vocational Rehabilitation Act of 1973; Executive Order No. 11914 (1974)	Discrimination based on physical or mental handicap (affirmative action required)	Federal contractors; federal government
Vietnam-Era Veterans Readjustment Act of 1974	Discrimination against disabled veterans and Vietnam-era veterans (affirmative action required)	Federal contractors; federal government

State Laws	Type of Employment Discrimination Prohibited	Employers Covered
State fair employment practices laws	Similar to federal laws	Varies by state

Executive Order 11246 (1965) We have seen in the section on EEO laws that employers are only required to *obey* them, that is, to provide an equal opportunity to protected groups. Title VII, for example, does not require an employer to take positive steps, or to act affirmatively, toward protected groups.

By Executive Order 11246, however, President Lyndon B. Johnson created what is known today as *affirmative action*. Since 1965 this order, which has been amended several times by later presidents, requires that organizations covered by the particular order take specific positive steps to improve the employment opportunity for certain protected groups. Thus, covered employers must *actively* seek, employ, promote, and train minorities and women who are underrepresented at all levels in the organization.

AFFIRMATIVE ACTION

As suggested by the above discussion of EEO laws and executive orders, there is an important difference between nondiscrimination and affirmative action with regard to human resource management. We can avoid discrimination by carefully and systematically examining all of our employment policies and practices to be sure that they do not work to the detriment of any person on grounds of color, race, religion, sex, age, handicap, or national origin. Affirmative action, on the other hand, goes far beyond ensuring "neutrality" in employment policies and practices with regard to certain groups. Thus, affirmative action is a positive set of activities taken by an employer to increase the employment, upgrading, and retention of members of protected groups.

The premise of the affirmative action concept is that unless positive steps are undertaken to overcome the effects of unintentional discrimination, neutrality in employment practices will tend to perpetuate the status quo indefinitely. Therefore, an affirmative action plan is a written, systematic program with goals and timetables for increasing the representation of protected class members in those areas where they have been underutilized. An organization may establish an affirmative action plan for one of three reasons:

1. *Court decree:* Frequently, when an employer loses a discrimination suit, the court will impose an affirmative action plan in addition to other remedies. For example, in one of the earliest and costliest battles involving the EEOC and American Telephone and Telegraph Company, the court, after more than two years of litigation, in 1973 required AT&T to pay $15 million to thousands of employees alleged to have suffered from discriminatory practices; to pay an additional estimated $50,000,000 in annual payments for promotion and wage adjustments to minority and female em-

ployees; and to develop an affirmative action plan. Other requirements included:

- Specific hiring and promotion targets, including goals to significantly increase utilization of women and minorities in every job category.
- Goals for employing males in previously all-female jobs.
- Women and minorities in nonmanagement jobs will be allowed to compete for craft jobs based on their qualifications and seniority.
- Assessment of all female college graduates hired since 1965 to determine interest and potential for higher-level jobs.

2. *Executive order:* If a firm has over $50,000 in federal contracts or subcontracts, and over 50 employees, it must have a written affirmative action plan. Without such a plan, the Office of Federal Contract Compliance Programs (OFCCP) has the power to cancel the contract(s).

3. *Voluntary compliance:* Since a discrimination suit can be very costly, an affirmative action plan makes good business sense. While it will not guarantee that the employer will not be charged with discrimination by an individual employee, a sound program reduces the likelihood of a potentially costly class-action suit such as the AT&T case. More importantly, exclusion of a group of workers such as women limits the recruiting pool from which qualified candidates can be selected. Thus, sound human resource management suggests taking positive steps to seek out and place qualified individuals who may be underutilized at all levels in the organization.

Developing an Affirmative Action Program (AAP)

An affirmative action plan is more than a formal document written by someone in the personnel/human resource department. It must begin with a commitment on the part of top management and end with a system to monitor and evaluate progress in each aspect of the program. Each program is unique in that it should be designed to fit the particular needs of each individual employer. At the same time, the EEOC has suggested several basic steps for an employer to follow when developing an effective affirmative action program. These steps, which are summarized in Exhibit 2–2, include:

1. *Issue EEO policy and affirmative action commitment.* Since many firms already have a nondiscrimination policy (although it may not be explicitly stated), an affirmative action program can be viewed, not as a new policy, but as a continuation of an existing one with a new emphasis and stronger commitment. Thus, a written policy, endorsed by one of the top executives of the company, is essential.
2. *Appoint a top official to be the director.* In many organizations the vice president of personnel/human resources is assigned the authority and responsibility for directing and implementing the AAP. In some organizations the EEO officer, who is responsible for the AAP, is given the title of Special Assistant to the President. In a very

EXHIBIT 2-2
Basic steps to develop an effective affirmative action program.

1. Issue written EEO policy and affirmative action commitment.
2. Appoint a top official with responsibility and authority to direct and implement the program.
3. Publicize the policy internally and externally.
4. Survey present minority and female employment by department and job classification.
5. Develop *goals* and *timetables* to improve utilization of minorities, males and females in each area where underutilization has been identified.
6. Develop and implement specific programs to achieve goals.
7. Establish internal audit and reporting systems to monitor progress.
8. Develop supportive in-house and community programs.

large firm, each division or geographic location may have an EEO coordinator who is responsible for the AAP at the local level and is directly responsible to the corporate EEO officer.

3. *Publicize the AAP.* The AAP must be publicized both internally and externally. Internally, managers at all levels must be persuaded of the importance of the program and the commitment it will take from each individual manager and not just the personnel/human resource department. Some firms publish the nonstatistical part of the AAP in the company newsletter or in a special booklet, which is given to all employees. Continuous reinforcement is necessary through such means or progress reports and discussion at staff meetings.

   Externally, the AAP should be publicized to potential sources of recruitment. Schools, colleges, employment agencies, and community groups should be made aware of your policy.

4. *Survey your present workforce.* The company workforce must be analyzed to identify the number and percentages of females and minorities by department and job classification. Next, data must be compared to the labor market from which the firm attracts workers. (This labor market information can be obtained from the local State Employment Office.) If fewer minorities or women are in a particular job classification than would be found in the relevant labor market, *underutilization* exists for that job classification. For example, if only 2 percent of blacks are among skilled workers while the local labor market shows 15 percent, underutilization exists. *Concentration* is the opposite of underutilization. For example, if 90 percent of the females in the organization are found in sales positions, a figure disproportionate to labor market figures, concentration exists. If either underutilization or concentration exists, management must

develop goals and timetables to correct this practice. Use of forms such as the EEO-1 form, shown in Exhibit 2–3, can be helpful in doing the workforce analysis and subsequent goal setting.

5. *Develop goals and timetables.* Goals and timetables must be realistic, and they must be attainable without discriminating against those in the majority. A goal may be qualitative as well as quantitative. To illustrate, if a company has lost a large number of minority employees due to turnover, a goal might include effective orientation and motivation of new employees as well as an evaluation of training and career-planning programs for new employees by a given date.

6. *Develop and implement specific programs.* At the heart of the affirmative action program is the need to develop and implement specific measures. All human resource policies and practices must be reviewed to identify barriers to EEO. Then, the necessary changes must be made to increase employment and advancement opportunities for the group found to be underutilized. For example, past reliance on employee referrals as the primary recruiting method may have perpetuated the same group of workers. This may be rectified by enlarging the recruiting sources (e.g., going out to schools, advertising, etc.).

   Similarly, the P/HR specialist may find that all females are concentrated in dead-end clerical jobs. Here we might set up job rotation programs that increase breadth of experience and supervisory training, thereby augmenting their skills and enabling some to move into management positions.

7. *Establish a system of controls.* Like all programs, an AAP needs a control system to monitor and evaluate its progress. The director of the program will need periodic benchmarks to evaluate the degree to which the program is on target. Evaluations, in turn, may lead to new goals and timetables based on the needs of the program. In some situations, the overall program may have satisfactory results but certain locations or occupations may have difficulties.

Reverse Discrimination

When an organization gives preferential treatment to a member of a protected group over an equally qualified (or more qualified) candidate who is not a member of a protected group, a charge of "reverse discrimination" is likely to take place. Thus, if a firm bypasses a more qualified white male to give the promotion to a less qualified Hispanic male, a dilemma is created. On the one hand, the firm may be committed to an AAP that calls for more Hispanics at higher levels in the organization. On the other hand, to bypass the white worker goes against sound human resource management practice, which calls for selecting the most qualified candidate for a job. Further-

EXHIBIT 2-3
EEO-1 form.

EEO category	All			Minorities										Percent of total		Availability Percent		Under-utilization (yes) or (no)		Ultimate goals				12-month goals												Backup goals	
				Male				Female												Minority		Female		Projection			Job openings			Goals							
	Total	Male	Female	Black	Hispanic	Asian-Amer. Pac. Isl.	Amer. Ind./ Alas. Nat.	Black	Hispanic	Asian-Amer. Pac. Isl.	Amer. Ind./ Alas. Nat.	Min.	Fem.	Min.	Fem.	Min.	Fem.	No. %	Date	No. %	Date	Attr.	Expan.	Total	From within	New hire	Total	Prom.	New hire	Date	Prom.	New hire	Date	H/G %	FEM. %

more, bypassing the more qualified candidate may lead to frustration, tensions, employee turnover, and lower morale among workers, as suggested by at least one study.[5]

The legal status of "reverse discrimination" is not entirely clear, although two landmark court cases have dealt with the issue. In the celebrated *Bakke* v. *Regents of the University of California* (1978) case, Bakke, a white male, applied to the University of California at Davis Medical School and was denied admission even though he had scored higher on the admissions criteria than minority candidates who were admitted. Bakke felt he suffered "discrimination in reverse" and sued for admission. The university had established a "special admissions" procedure in which a set number of places was reserved for minorities even though they were less qualified.

In a 5 to 4 decision, the Supreme Court ruled that Bakke should be admitted but that admission plans that consider race as a factor are not illegal. Four justices agreed with Bakke; four others felt that racial preference was justified. The ninth, Justice Powell, found against quotas as such, since they provide absolute preference for one race without giving any weight to the relative merits of other candidates. On the other hand, he said that race could be considered *one* of the relevant factors in admission decisions.

The ruling left many unanswered questions, such as *how much* weight could be given to race. Similarly, while an employer may be ordered by a court to establish certain quotas in order to eliminate racial imbalances, the question arises whether an employer can voluntarily introduce quotas. In 1979, the Supreme Court partially answered this question in the case of *United Steelworkers* v. *Weber*. In this case, Kaiser Aluminum and a union, the United Steelworkers, entered into an agreement whereby 50 percent of the openings in a craft training program were reserved for blacks. Weber, a white steelworker, sued when he was denied admission to the training program even though he had more seniority than some black workers admitted to it.

The United States Supreme Court ruled that since the AAP that gave blacks a preference was *voluntarily* agreed to by the company and union, it did not violate Title VII provisions. A key portion of the decision noted that the preferential treatment did not require discharging white workers and replacing them with black workers, and that the plan was a *temporary* measure used to eliminate racial inequality.

Thus, while the Weber case did provide further guidance, it did not entirely settle the "reverse discrimination" problem. For example, one may ask what constitutes a voluntary (and legal) program of reverse discrimination as opposed to one where government pressure is illegally exerted? For instance, may a nonunion employer unilaterally impose a temporary quota system for hiring or selecting someone for a training program? Clarification will come only as more "reverse discrimination" cases make their way through the courts.[6]

UNIFORM GUIDELINES ON EMPLOYEE SELECTION PROCEDURES

During the 1960s and 1970s, several federal agencies were issuing separate, often conflicting guidelines for employment practices. Even the organization with the best of intentions was likely to find itself violating one agency's regulations while attempting to comply with another agency.

Finally, in 1978, as a result of severe pressure from private industry, the Uniform Guidelines on Employee Selection Procedures were adopted by four federal agencies: the EEOC, the Office of Federal Contract Compliance, the Department of Justice, and the Office of Personnel Management. These guidelines provide a framework used to determine if federal laws on discrimination are being adhered to by an employer. It is strongly advised that the human resource manager read the guidelines and become familiar with the basic principles.

While the guidelines affect virtually all phases of human resource management, an important section of the guidelines deals with what is known as "adverse impact." Accordingly, the use of any selection procedure that has an adverse impact in the hiring, promotion, or other employment opportunities of members of any race, sex, or ethnic group is considered to be *discriminatory* unless the procedure has been validated in accordance with the guidelines. (We will consider the concept of validity in Chapter 7, Selection.) According to the guidelines, adverse impact occurs when there is a substantial underrepresentation of protected group members. Underrepresentation is measured by the *Four-fifths Rule*, which states that discrimination generally occurs if the selection rate for any protected group is less than 80 percent of the selection rate of majority groups. Also referred to as the *80 Percent Rule* or the *Bottom-Line Criterion*, the rule would work in the following manner: If, for example, a company hires 50 percent of all white male applicants who apply in a particular job category, then it must hire at least 40 percent (80 percent × 50 percent) of all blacks who apply and 40 percent of all women and other protected groups. A firm does not need to meet the Four-fifths Rule, however, if it can demonstrate that the selection procedures being used are *job-related* (i.e., either related to successful performance on the job or to a bona fide occupational qualification). The organization can prove job relatedness by showing that the predictors used in the selection procedure have certain kinds of validity (see Chapter 7, Selection).

In 1980 the Equal Employment Opportunity Commission (EEOC) issued guidelines that define sexual harassment. For example, it is a violation of Title VII of the Civil Rights Act to give an employment benefit to a recipient of sexual advances; a person who is denied the benefit is a victim of discrimination. (See Exhibit 2–4.)

Now that we have examined EEO and affirmative action, let us turn our attention to legal influences on other areas of human resource manage-

EXHIBIT 2-4

Woman Spurns Advances, Wins Discrimination Suit: Company Found Liable for Supervisor's Sexual Demands

A woman who did not get a promotion was a sex discrimination victim because her supervisor gave the job to another woman with whom he was having an affair, a federal district court in Delaware ruled.

A Title VII Violation

The ruling is one of the first which involves the Equal Employment Opportunity Commission's (EEOC) sexual harassment guideline, which states that it is a violation of Title VII to give an employment benefit to a recipient of sexual advances and that any person who is denied the benefit is a discrimination victim.

While the case, *Toscano* v *Ninno,* DDE, 8/31/83, No. 82-315-WKS, is much different from usual sexual harassment claims, the court said the fact that the supervisor's promotion decision was based on the granting of sexual favors—a condition which was not imposed on men—brings the case within the EEOC's Title VII boundaries. The EEOC guideline the court used to support its ruling that the unsuccessful applicant had a sex bias claim reads: "Where employment opportunities or benefits are granted because of an individual's submission to the employer's requests for sexual favors, the employer may be held liable for unlawful sex discrimination against other persons who were qualified for, but denied that employment opportunity or benefit."

The woman who had applied for but did not get the position in question did not try to establish her claim by showing that she had refused her superior's request for sexual favors and then was denied the promotion because of her refusal. Instead, she showed proof of the supervisor's affair with the promoted employee to support her claim that granting sexual favors was a condition of getting the promotion.

The company was held liable for the discrimination, the court said, though none of the supervisor's superiors knew he made the promotion on the basis of sexual favors. Employer knowledge is not a prerequisite to finding liability under Title VII, the court ruled, pointing out that traditional principles holding an employer responsible for its employees' actions make the employer liable in this case.

The firm also failed to take appropriate "remedial action" to deal with the situation, the court found, once it received notice of the supervisor's actions.

Source: From *Resource,* American Society for Personnel Administration, November 1983, p. 9.

ment. To begin with, we will discuss the increasing role of the government in protecting the employee's safety and health.

GOVERNMENT'S ROLE IN EMPLOYEE SAFETY AND HEALTH

About one out of every 11 workers is injured on the job each year. In 1978 there were 4,760 job-related deaths in firms with over 10 employees.[7] There are also about 400,000 new incidences of occupational diseases and as many as 100,000 workers who die as a result of these diseases on an average yearly basis. According to the National Safety Council, the estimated annual cost of these occupational accidents is $20 billion, and about $15 billion for the occupational diseases.

Occupational safety and health is, therefore, one of today's most significant areas of public policy, and one can see the need for laws and regulations to protect the worker. Prior to 1970, only state laws and regulations existed to protect the worker from occupational accidents and diseases. In

1970, Congress passed the controversial Occupational Safety and Health Act (OSHA), which has significantly affected management's role in employee protection.

Occupational Safety and Health Act of 1970 (OSHA)

The purpose of OSHA was to assure "so far as possible that every man and woman in the nation has a safe and healthful working condition." Passed in 1970 after three years of bitter debate and extensive lobbying by unions and employees, OSHA was supported by proponents who felt that state programs were too diverse, incomplete, and lacking in authority for enforcement.

While there are many requirements under OSHA, the three that affect most employers are:

1. Meeting safety standards
2. Submitting to OSHA inspections
3. Keeping records and reporting accidents and illnesses

Criticism of OSHA has centered on either the setting of many trivial standards or cost considerations. For example, an owner of a small business was told by an OSHA inspector that he was required to install separate men's and women's restrooms for his employees. "The owner had but one employee"—his wife.[8] On the other hand, studies have shown decreases in accidents in many industries since OSHA came into existence. One study of the meat-packing industry, one of OSHA's target industries, reported a 30 percent drop in meat-packing accidents.[9] The most common criticism of OSHA is that it is too costly. For example, the cost of complying with one OSHA requirement, the 90-decibel noise-level standard, was estimated at $13 billion.[10]

The difficulty in evaluating OSHA is that most attempts at measuring the results of the act use a cost–benefit analysis that expresses impact objectively in dollar terms alone. Since many benefits are difficult to quantify, the results of such attempts at measurement tend to give a negative view of OSHA. Advocates, however, are quick to point out that this cost-versus-benefits approach to evaluating the act overlooks such important things as (1) productivity gains from those who would have otherwise been injured, or (2) greater enjoyment of life by employees who now work in a healthier environment.[11]

Workers' Compensation Laws

All states have laws requiring compensation to workers for certain injuries. While all laws are somewhat different, they must meet certain federal standards. Essentially, workers' compensation laws require that the employer obtain insurance to compensate an employee for the expense incurred from a work-related injury. The employer, who pays the entire cost, may either obtain the insurance through a private carrier or, in some states, may participate in a state fund.

Since premium rates are based on loss experience, the improvement of safety conditions can lead to lower insurance costs as accidents decline. In addition, the laws require certain accident reports, which promote study of accident causes with the intent of reducing preventable accidents.

The state workers' compensation laws, like OSHA, deal with employee health and safety. However, two major differences exist:

1. Workers' compensation laws are intended to compensate for injuries and illnesses already received. OSHA, which provides no compensation and is preventative by design, is intended to remove hazardous conditions that lead to injuries and illnesses.
2. Workers' compensation laws use insurance premiums as incentives to get employers to improve job safety and health. OSHA is much more comprehensive and uses a system of standards, inspections, citations, and financial penalties.[12]

It should be noted that employees receive workers' compensation in a job-related injury regardless of whose fault an accident is. While workers' compensation plans originally provided only for physical injury, they have been expanded in many states to cover emotional impairments resulting from physical injury. In addition, emotional illnesses caused by job-induced stress or anxiety may be covered in a number of states.

> An employee who became drunk at an office party fell and injured himself. A court rules that since the party was sponsored by the employer and employees were "expected" to attend, the company must pay the worker's compensation claim.

Workers' compensation laws have received mixed reviews. While they have improved the system for delivering compensation to victims of work-related injuries, they have fallen short in other areas. Most notably, they have been criticized as not motivating employers to institute health and safety improvements. In many cases, it is simply less expensive to pay a higher insurance premium resulting from an injury than to spend the money for capital improvements to make a safer work environment.[13] Shortcomings such as this played an important role in leading to the passage of OSHA.

LEGAL INFLUENCES ON COMPENSATION AND BENEFITS

Human resource management in the areas of wages, hours, and benefits has been influenced by government regulations as far back as the early 1930s. In

1931, the *Davis Bacon Act* was passed to require firms working on public projects under federal contracts to pay the prevailing local wage rate. The *Walsh-Healey Act* of 1936 extended similar minimum wage standards to firms that furnished materials, supplies, or equipment to the federal government in excess of $10,000.

In 1938, a far-reaching and complex human resource–related law, the *Fair Labor Standards Act* (also known as the *Wage and Hour Law*), was passed. The law requires payment of certain minimum wages by firms involved in interstate commerce as well as time-and-a-half wages for work over 40 hours per week. Also included in the act are restrictions on the employment of children. It is interesting to note that when the act was passed in 1938, the minimum wage was 25 cents per hour. Congress has repeatedly amended the act to where in 1982 the minimum was $3.35 per hour.

A more recent law dealing with employee benefits has had a tremendous impact on pension and retirement programs. In the past, many private pension plans were badly managed and, as a result, when it came time for the employee to retire, adequate funds were not always available. Another not-uncommon hardship was caused by the design of most plans, which required employees to be with the organization for at least ten years before they gained a permanent right (referred to as *vesting*) to their benefits. In addition, the employees were often required to stay with the company until retirement age. Thus, if an employee was discharged before retirement age, he or she lost the pension benefits even though the vested period was met.

To correct these and other problems, the *Employee Retirement Income Security Act* of 1974 (ERISA) was passed. Now all private firms with retirement programs must meet federally imposed standards. While no company *must* have a retirement plan, the act requires that if one does exist:

1. A range of conditions must be met to ensure that the plan is actuarially sound.
2. Benefits must become vested with the employee after a stated period of time.
3. The plan must be administered in a prudent manner.

LEGAL INFLUENCES ON LABOR RELATIONS

Public policy, as reflected in federal laws, has influenced labor relations since the 1930s. The most important of the federal laws dealing with labor relations are summarized in Exhibit 2–5.

Discussion of all these laws is beyond the scope of this book. Chapter 16, dealing with Labor–Management Relations, however, will discuss major provisions of the laws that most significantly influence human resource

EXHIBIT 2–5
Major legal influences on labor relations.

Federal Laws	Basic Provisions
Norris-LaGuardia Act (1935)	Prohibits courts from issuing injunctions against nonviolent union activities; outlaws contracts forbidding union activities.
National Labor Relations (Wagner) Act as amended (1935)	Gives employees right to form or join labor organizations (or to refuse to), to bargain collectively through their representatives, and to engage in other concerted activities such as strikes, picketing, and boycotts; prohibits certain unfair labor practices by the employer and the union.
Labor–Management Relations (Taft-Hartley) Act, as amended (1947)	Amended Wagner Act; permits states to pass laws prohibiting compulsory union membership; set up methods to deal with strikes affecting national health and safety.
Labor–Management Reporting and Disclosure (Landrum-Griffin) Act (1959)	Amended Taft-Hartley Act and Wagner Act; guarantees individual rights of union members in dealing with their union; requires financial disclosures by unions.

management. At this point, we should note that the various laws dealing with labor relations:

1. Permit workers to engage in union activities without fear of prosecution or retaliation from management
2. Allow workers to organize and bargain collectively with management
3. Limit the rights of management in dealing with individual workers with regard to wages, hours, and conditions of employment
4. Limit the rights of unions

IMPLICATIONS OF PUBLIC POLICY FOR HUMAN RESOURCE MANAGEMENT

We have seen that public policy affects *all* aspects of human resource management. Laws, regulations, and executive orders, especially during the past 20 years, have created a heavily regulated environment for the human resource system.

Exhibit 2–6 presents a regulatory model developed by James Ledvinka that helps us to see how social and political problems relate to management responses and decisions. That is, regulations come about as a result of laws passed to solve social and political problems. These laws give government agencies the power to take the regulatory actions that result in management responses. The courts oversee this process by settling disputes between the involved parties.

Since many of the newer agencies were created to solve social problems, not industry problems, the agencies do not develop intimate concern

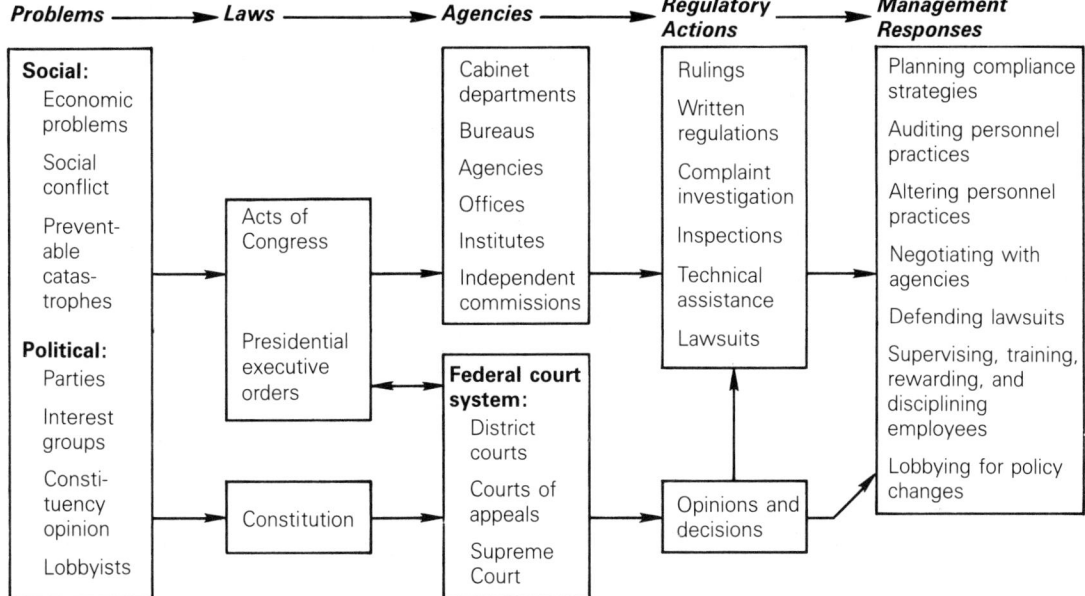

EXHIBIT 2-6
The regulatory model.
Source: From James Ledvinka, *Federal Regulation of Personnel and Human Resource Management* (Boston: Kent Publishing Company, 1982), p. 10. © 1982 by Wadsworth, Inc. Reprinted by permission of Kent Publishing Company, a division of Wadsworth, Inc.

with the overall well-being of any one company.[14] Thus, we are likely to have expensive and costly reporting requirements with similar information requested in a different format from two different agencies. For example, one large company reported that the paper work for its affirmative action case took thousands of hours to compile and weighed 65 pounds. A recent year-long study by the Senate Committee on Labor and Human Resources to evaluate the effectiveness of the Office of Federal Contract Compliance Programs (OFCCP) found excessive paper work and many inequities to frequently result from lack of flexibility by OFCCP specialists. A graphic illustration of one of the horror stories uncovered during the study is presented in Exhibit 2-7.

At the same time, failure to comply with the various regulations and laws can be extremely costly to a firm. For example, Exhibit 2-8 shows the cost of several back-pay decisions resulting from discrimination suits.

All of this regulation means a more important role for personnel/human resource specialists who, in most organizations, have become the in-house experts on EEO, OSHA, ERISA, and other laws and regulations affecting human resource management. As such, the specialist must keep abreast of changes in the laws and requirements. Accordingly, he or she must maintain proper records.

EXHIBIT 2–7
An OFCCP audit.

> Monthly reports that consider hours worked instead of number of individuals on the payroll created a nightmare for at least one employer. An OFCCP audit of Gaghan Plumbing Company, Alexandria, Va., in April, 1979, showed that in February minority employment had dropped to 18 percent of the hours worked. The figure was supposed to be 25 percent of Gaghan Plumbing's work force of five.
>
> "The one minority member we had was married in February and elected to take seven days off to go on his honeymoon," Alma Gaghan, the company's head, told the Senate committee. "Those seven days represented 56 working hours on the job site." If the man had been at work, the percentage would have been 26.6, better than the required 25.
>
> Gaghan asked the OFCCP specialist why he had not allowed for the employee's time off; she was told she should have hired another minority member to replace him.
>
> If she had, she would have faced another problem: She would not have been permitted to lay off the second minority employee when the first returned. She was informed she would have had to fire a nonminority employee, regardless of seniority.
>
> Gaghan, who told the Senate committee that she is "of Filipino-Mexican-Spanish origin" and has "no prejudice against other minorities and certainly not against women," said that to try to justify her position, she made an appointment at an OFCCP office—and showed up, even though she was suffering from pneumonia.
>
> The government employee she was to see did not show up, and no one else would talk with her. The next day Gaghan was hospitalized, and soon after she gave up her business.

Source: Mary Tuthill, "The Job Ahead on Equal Employment Regulations," *Nation's Business,* July 1982, p. 54.

Organization-wide programs of information and education concerning the dimensions of these problems need to be established. Supervisors and managers at all levels must be given training in order to enable them to carry out their responsibilities under these programs. No line manager can successfully understand and carry out an organization's human resource policies without an understanding of the public policies underlying their practice.

The area of EEO is likely to have the greatest impact on human resource policies and practices for all firms. For example, the EEOC has said that an employer needs to review its *entire* employment system to identify barriers to EEO. The specific areas mentioned as needing review and action include:

1. Recruitment: all personnel procedures
2. Selection process: job requirements, job descriptions, standards

EXHIBIT 2–8
Selected discrimination settlements.

Total Amount ($)	No. of Employees Affected	Employer	Issue(s)	Action by
55,000,000	15,000	AT&T	Equal pay—management personnel	EEOC, Department of Labor
30,900,000	40,048	9 steel companies	Race—job assignments	EEOC, Department of Labor
24,100,000	1,800	Northwest Airlines	Sex—stewardess pay	Private suit
10,000,000/year		Bank of America	Sex—hiring, promotion	Private suit
2,750,000	160	Standard Oil of California	Age	Indeterminate
900,000	2,000	Wheaton Glass	Equal pay	Private suit
600,000		Corning Glass	Sex—day/night shifts	Department of Labor/Women's groups
375,000	210	Rutgers University	Sex	EEOC
350,000	137	Eastex, Inc.	Sex—race	Justice Department
319,000		Jersey Central P & L	Race	EEOC
210,000	172	Iowa State University	Sex	Department of Labor
87,000	2	Malden (Mass.) School Committee	Sex—pregnancy	Massachusetts Commission against Discrimination
55,000	13	Boston Redevelopment Agency	Sex	Massachusetts Commission against Discrimination
43,000	79	Carborundum Company	Equal pay	Department of Labor
22,000	1	Ford Motor Company	Race—job assignment	Private suit
10,000	1	City of Chicago	Pregnancy leave	Private suit
9,000	1	AVCO Financial	Sex—"girl" reference	New York State Human Rights Commission

and procedures, pre-employment inquiries, application forms, testing, interviewing
3. Upward mobility system: assignments, job progressions, transfers, seniority, promotions, training
4. Wages and salary structure
5. Benefits and conditions of employment
6. Layoff, recall, termination, demotion, discharge, disciplinary action
7. Union contract provisions affecting the above.[15]

Since the cost of noncompliance with government regulations has become so costly, personnel/human resource departments in most organizations must monitor the practices of line managers and place constraints on managers involving most employment decisions. For example, final approval for all selection and promotion decisions may be required by the personnel/human resource department.

SUMMARY

At one time public policy favored allowing an employer and individual employee to work out any employment arrangement that was acceptable to both parties. Today, almost every human resource policy and practice is influenced by the government in the form of laws, executive orders, regulatory agencies, and court decisions.

While we have emphasized the areas of equal employment opportunity and affirmative action in this chapter, we have also surveyed the government's role in employee protection, compensation and benefits, and labor–management relations. We have seen how these laws and regulations are influencing human resource management and increasing the role of the personnel/human resource department in the organization.

A number of the major laws surveyed in this chapter will be referred to again in future sections of the book. For example, in Chapters 6 and 7, Recruitment and Selection, we shall see some specific applications of government regulations involving recruiting, testing, and interviewing. Similarly, Chapter 16, Labor–Management Relations, will include a discussion of how the major labor laws have limited the rights of management and labor, and so on.

Now that we have a basic understanding of the legal environment and how it influences human resource management, we shall examine in the next chapter, the behavioral system.

KEY CONCEPTS

Affirmative action

Equal Employment Opportunity (EEO)

Reasonable accommodation

Fair employment practices

Reverse discrimination

OSHA

ERISA

REVIEW AND DISCUSSION QUESTIONS

1. Trace the development of the government's increasing role in human resource management.
2. What is meant by equal employment opportunity laws?
3. What are the implications of the Civil Rights Act for human resource management?
4. How does minimum wage legislation affect an organization's employment practices?
5. In what ways has government involvement in employment decisions increased the importance of the human resource department in an organization?
6. EEO laws do not require that a firm hire an unqualified worker. Discuss.
7. How does an executive order differ from a law?
8. Is there a difference between "not discriminating" and affirmative action with regard to human resource management?
9. Outline the basic steps for an employer to follow when developing an effective affirmative action program.
10. In what basic way(s) does OSHA differ from workers' compensation laws in attempting to reduce job-related injury?
11. Do you agree with the statement that public policy affects *all* aspects of human resource management? Explain your position.

NOTES

1. Thomas H. Patten, Jr., "Personnel Management in the 1970's: The End of Laissez-Faire," *Human Resources Management*, Fall 1973, p. 7.
2. Gary D. Brown, "How Type of Employment Affects Earnings Difference by Sex," *Monthly Labor Review*, July 1976, p. 25–30.
3. *Shultz* v. *Wheaton Glass Company. 9 Fair Employment Practices*, Case 506 (Washington, D.C.: Bureau of National Affairs), January 1970.
4. Gurmankin v. Costanza Ca. 3, 1977, *14 Fair Employment Practices* (Washington, D.C.: Bureau of National Affairs.)

5. For example, see Benson Rosen and Thomas H. Jerdee, "Coping with Affirmative Action Backlash," *Business Horizons*, August 1979, pp. 18–19.
6. Terry L. Leaf, William H. Holley, Jr., and Hubert S. Feild, "Equal Employment Opportunity and Its Implications for Personnel Practices in the 1980's," *Labor Law Journal*, No. 11, November 1980, pp. 669–682.
7. "Workplace Inquiries and Illnesses up Slightly in 1978," *ASPA's Occupational Safety & Health Review*, December 1979.
8. "Why Nobody Wants to Listen to OSHA," *Business Week*, June 14, 1976, p. 64.
9. Lawrence Ettkin and J. Brad Chapman, "Is OSHA Effective in Reducing Industrial Inquiries?" *Labor Law Journal*, July 1975, pp. 236–249.
10. Murray L. Weidenbaum, "Four Questions for OSHA," *Labor Law Journal* 30, 1979, pp. 528–531.
11. For an excellent discussion of the difficulty of evaluating OSHA, see "The Impact of OSHA" in James Ledvinka, *Federal Regulation of Personnel and Human Resource Management* (Belmont, Ca.: Wadsworth Publishing, 1982), pp. 181–199.
12. *Ibid.*, p. 158.
13. *Analysis of Workers' Compensation Laws*, 1980 Edition (Washington, D.C.: Chamber of Commerce of the United States).
14. For example, see Murray L. Weidenbaum, "The Cost of Government Regulation of Business," *Hearing on the Cost of Government Regulation before the Subcommittee on Economic Growth and Stabilization of the Joint Economic Committee*, 95th Congress, 2nd Session, April 11, 1978.
15. U.S. Employment Opportunity Commission, pp. 16–17.

BIBLIOGRAPHY

Brookmire, David. "Designing and Implementing Your Company's Affirmative Action Program." *Personnel Journal* 58, April 1979, 234–237.

Brown, Robert J. "Making the Promise of OSHA a Reality." *Labor Law Journal* 29, February 1978, 68–71.

Burton, Gene E., and Dev S. Pathak. "101 Ways to Discriminate against Equal Employment Opportunity." *Personnel Administrator* 22, August 1977, 42–45, 48–49.

Crickmer, Barry. "Regulation: How Much Is Enough?" *Nation's Business* 68, March 1980, 26–33.

Dhanens, Thomas P. "Implications of the New EEOC Guidelines." *Personnel* 56, September–October 1979, 32–39.

Dyer, Frank J. "An Alternative to Validating Selection Tests." *Personnel Journal* 57, April 1978, 200–203.

Ebel, Robert L. "Comments on Some Problems of Employment Testing." *Personnel Psychology* 30, Spring 1977, 55–64.

Famularo, Joseph J., Ed. *Handbook of Modern Personnel Administration*. New York: McGraw-Hill, 1972, Part IV.

Feild, Hubert, and Susan Bayley. "Employment Test Validation for Minority and Nonminority Production Workers." *Personnel Psychology* 30, Spring 1977, 37–48.

Guion, Robert M. "Content Validity in Moderation." *Personnel Psychology* 31, Summer 1978, 205–213.

Hoyman, Michele, and Ronda Robinson. "Interpreting the New Sexual Harrassment Guidelines," *Personnel Journal* 59, December 1980, 996–1000.

Koen, Clifford. "The Pre-Employment Inquiry Guide." *Personnel Journal* 59, October 1980, 825–829.

Ledvinka, James. *Federal Regulation of Personnel and Human Resource Management.* Boston: Kent, 1982.

Pati, Gopal C., and Edward F. Hilton, Jr. "A Comprehensive Model for a Handicapped Affirmative Action Program." *Personnel Journal* 59, February 1980, 99–108.

Schliebner, Joan Johnson, and Joy Sandberg. "Record Retention and Posting Requirements of the Federal Government." *Personnel Administrator* 24, April 1979, 54–59.

Schreitmueller, Richard G. "Living with ERISA Administration." *The Personnel Administrator* 22, May 1977, 26–34.

Whiting, Basil J., Jr. "Regulatory Reform and OSHA: Fads and Realities." *Labor Law Journal*, August 1979, 514–527.

Organizational Behavior

CHAPTER OUTLINE

Formal and Informal Organization
The Formal Organization □ The Informal Organization

Emergent Behavior Subsystem

Required Behavior and Sentiments

The Individual Worker
Long-term Characteristics □ Short-term Characteristics

Work Groups and Other Worker Associations
Managerial Groups □ Professional and Technical Groups □ Unions

Implications of Worker Similarities and Differences

OBJECTIVES

1. Tell why managers must learn about human behavior in organizations
2. Classify and list inputs and outputs of the basic behavioral system
3. Describe the origins of individual behavior
4. Describe the basic needs and motivations of workers
5. Classify the higher-level behavioral systems—the groups of workers—that make up the total organizational system
6. Identify similarities and differences in classes of workers

SPOTLIGHT:
Donna McGeddy

Donna McGeddy attended Taylor Business Institute. Upon graduation, she went to work for the federal government in Fort Monmouth, New Jersey, in a clerical position related to personnel administration.

Ms. McGeddy decided that the only way to get ahead in that field was to attend college, so she attended Florida Atlantic University and received a bachelor's degree in Human Resource Management. After graduation Ms. McGeddy joined Sensormatic Electronics Corporation as a Personnel Coordinator, where she conducts orientation sessions and supports the Employment Section of the Personnel Department.

Comments by Donna McGeddy

Working in personnel has been an extremely rewarding learning experience for me. One of the things I have learned is that being able to deal effectively with a wide variety of people, both individually and in groups, is an important requirement.

This skill seems to come only with a lot of experience. Through interacting with people, we can become more aware of the reasons why people act as they do in organizational situations. We can then begin to react to the different behaviors effectively. Each situation is unique, and each person has to be dealt with in a unique way.

If you also take into account that the organization is made up of various groups of people differentiated by type of education, type of work performed, and work-life goals, you may be able to reconcile the aims of such groups with company objectives. Winning over informal groups such as these helps to reduce resistance to innovation by individuals within the groups. A company "culture" of innovation, which is so important to high-tech companies, may then be developed over a period of time.

If you seek a career in management, you will need to develop understanding of organizational behavior to build positive and effective work groups.

Personnel policies seem to be dismal failures. Employee morale is low. Incentives carefully designed to increase productivity have no effect. What is wrong in these situations?

A serious defect of the policies, practices, and systems used for managing HR in many organizations is that they have been designed without consideration of behavioral science data concerning the impact of individual motivation and the influence of groups on human behavior. Countless programs and systems have failed to achieve their intended purpose because they did not adequately take into account scientific knowledge about the *causes* of human behavior. This chapter will, therefore, survey what is known about individual and group behavior, and this data will become the foundation for all HR management practices discussed throughout the remainder of this text.

In the 1980s and 1990s, most employed people will be working in groups consisting of individuals working simultaneously on the same tasks or interacting closely with others on related tasks. A large part of HR management will therefore be concerned with behavior of people in groups. Do people behave differently when they are in groups as opposed to being alone? Intuition says yes, a fact confirmed by behavioral science.

When we first look at workers in business, we are impressed with the infinite variety of groups, tasks, and individuals that comprise these groups. How in the world can we predict how such groups will behave in certain situations? How can we influence them to work in optimum ways for organizational objectives? Managers and the HR department must be able to find some approximate answers to these questions. In fact, the HR department's main concern is exactly this—to set up systems that will result in productive groups of workers. That is, we must try to influence each individual worker to try his or her *personal* best, as well as motivate workers to do their best in work groups of varying sizes.

In this chapter, we will present a picture of the behavioral system of the work group. We will identify various types of groups, characteristics of the individual in the group, and characteristics of the group itself that affect its behavior. Finally, we will show those factors that managers may control or influence to modify the behavior of groups. Most of the following chapters of this book are directed to amplifying on these factors that influence work groups.

FORMAL AND INFORMAL ORGANIZATION

Before the Hawthorne experiments in the 1920s at Western Electric, most managers viewed people as units of labor—the formal organization structure was *the* organization. The Hawthorne studies produced the revolutionary finding that the emergent *informal* organization created by the work group itself has a profound influence on output. A second important finding was that the "norms" of the work group (i.e., their expectations or standards of behavior for each other) exert a powerful influence on the behavior of group members.[1] These studies spurred further research on the behavior of work groups. Behavioral science has become more sophisticated in its study of the workplace, and it is now believed that the dominant characteristics of group behavior can best be described in terms of the informal organization. The formal organization is now seen as just one of a number of factors that influences the informal organization.

A rough comparison of concepts associated with the formal and the informal organization is shown in Exhibit 3–1.

The Formal Organization

The formal organization is based upon authority derived from owners of the business, from legal statutes in the case of government agencies, or from self-perpetuating boards of trustees in the case of some nonprofit organizations. The primary functions of the formal organization system are to set objectives for the system as a whole and to coordinate the efforts of everyone in the system to work toward those objectives. The structure of the formal organization is continually changing, but at any moment in time it may be represented by a chart such as Exhibit 3–2.

The impact of the formal organization on the human resource system as a whole depends on such factors as:

- ☐ Number of levels of management
- ☐ Subdivision of work
- ☐ Channels of communication
- ☐ Delegation of decision making
- ☐ Power
- ☐ Control

EXHIBIT 3–1
Two sets of work-group concepts

Formal Organizational Concepts	Informal Organizational Concepts
Organization chart	Roles, status, prestige hierarchy
Managers	Informal leaders
Authority	Cliques
Position descriptions	Norms
Policies and procedures	Cohesion
Standards	Sentiments
Organizational objectives	Culture
Appraisal and reward systems	Socialization
Management information systems	Grapevine
Control systems	Sanctions

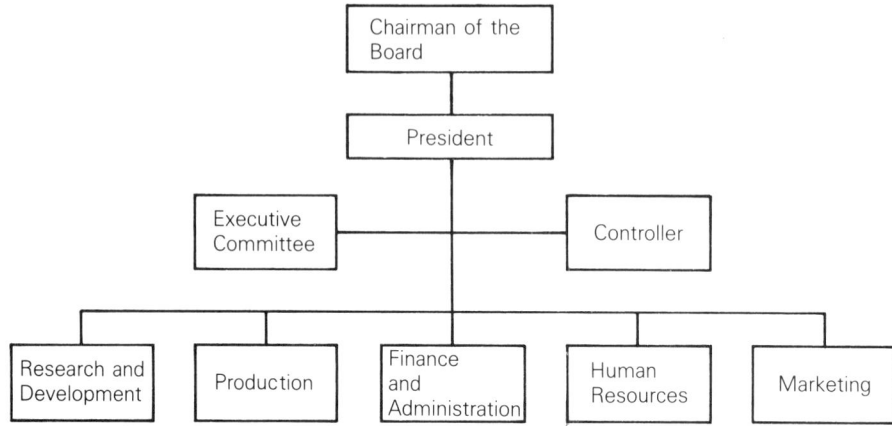

EXHIBIT 3–2
Formal organization chart

A technical system, the formal organization is, too often, designed without regard to the people who make it function. As Chris Argyris has pointed out, formal organization often places controls on mature people of such a kind that they rebel in various subtle ways. This reaction, in turn, causes the formal organization to develop increasingly greater control over the work of individuals. The result: The formal organization and the aspirations of individuals are in constant conflict.[2] Properly designed, however, the formal organization should be a positive factor in the total work environment of the individual. Increasingly, enlightened corporations are taking the perspective that "lean is better" and that flexibility and efficiency are increased as the formal organization becomes simpler.

The Informal Organization

The informal organization or social system is actually a number of subsystems ranging from small groups of workers in the same room to perhaps hundreds of workers who are united by some common interest, such as a grievance against management. The informal organization is especially important because it sets norms or standards of behavior for its members (including norms related to productivity) and represents the fastest communication system in the organization. As we saw in the previous section, the formal organization is a creation of top management, and is the system shown in the management charts. The informal organization, however, is created by the social relationships existing in the organization.

The *norms* established by the workers in a group have significant impact on all activities of the group. If the norms are not congruent with organizational objectives, management faces a serious problem. For example, most groups establish very specific norms concerning expected quality and quantity of production; these norms may often be the most influential determinant of organizational productivity. The assembly line, for example,

> **Definitions**
>
> *Norms:* Common beliefs by the group members as to how members should act or should not act
> *Group cohesion:* Attraction of the work group for its members, and degree of member support for each other within the group
> *Sentiments:* Broad category of internal states of an individual, including emotions, feelings, beliefs, aspirations, values, and attitudes
> *Culture:* Beliefs, customs, knowledge, and practices developed and stabilized over a "long" period of time within the company
> *Socialization:* Modification of behavior of a new group member to fit the norms and culture of the group
> *Grapevine:* Informal communication system among employees

may reflect more accurately the *workers'* definition of quality and quantity than the plant manager's.

Norms arise out of characteristics of the workers, the work culture, and the work environment. The strength of adherence to these norms and of resistance to change not desired by the group is a function of *group cohesion*, that is, how closely the individuals stick together.

Determining the social role the individual will play within a particular group is the individual's degree of adherence to norms. When a new member joins a work group, for example, intense efforts at *socialization* begin. This socialization consists of "teaching" the new recruit the norms of the group. The degree to which the new member is willing to adhere to these norms (or is capable of doing so) will determine whether that individual will become a regular, deviant, isolate, or leader.

One other very important factor in group behavior is the informal communication system, or *"grapevine."* Thus, the informal communications that arise may be viewed as attempts by workers to interpret their "local" environment, and may take the form of rumors, gossip, or various casual opinions that come to be regarded as fact.[3] Such communications may be heavily distorted due to the beliefs of workers and the tendency of the informal organization system to fill in gaps of information with imagination. Such misinformation may actually hamper efficiency and lower group morale.

EMERGENT BEHAVIOR SUBSYSTEM

The behavior of a work group emerges as the result of the interaction of at least six factors: environmental inputs, formal organization, characteristics of the individuals making up the work group, other associations to which workers may belong, work situations, and job design.

The model in Exhibit 3–3 illustrates the connections among these managerial, environmental, and individual causal factors, which interact to determine and create a subsystem of emergent behavior.

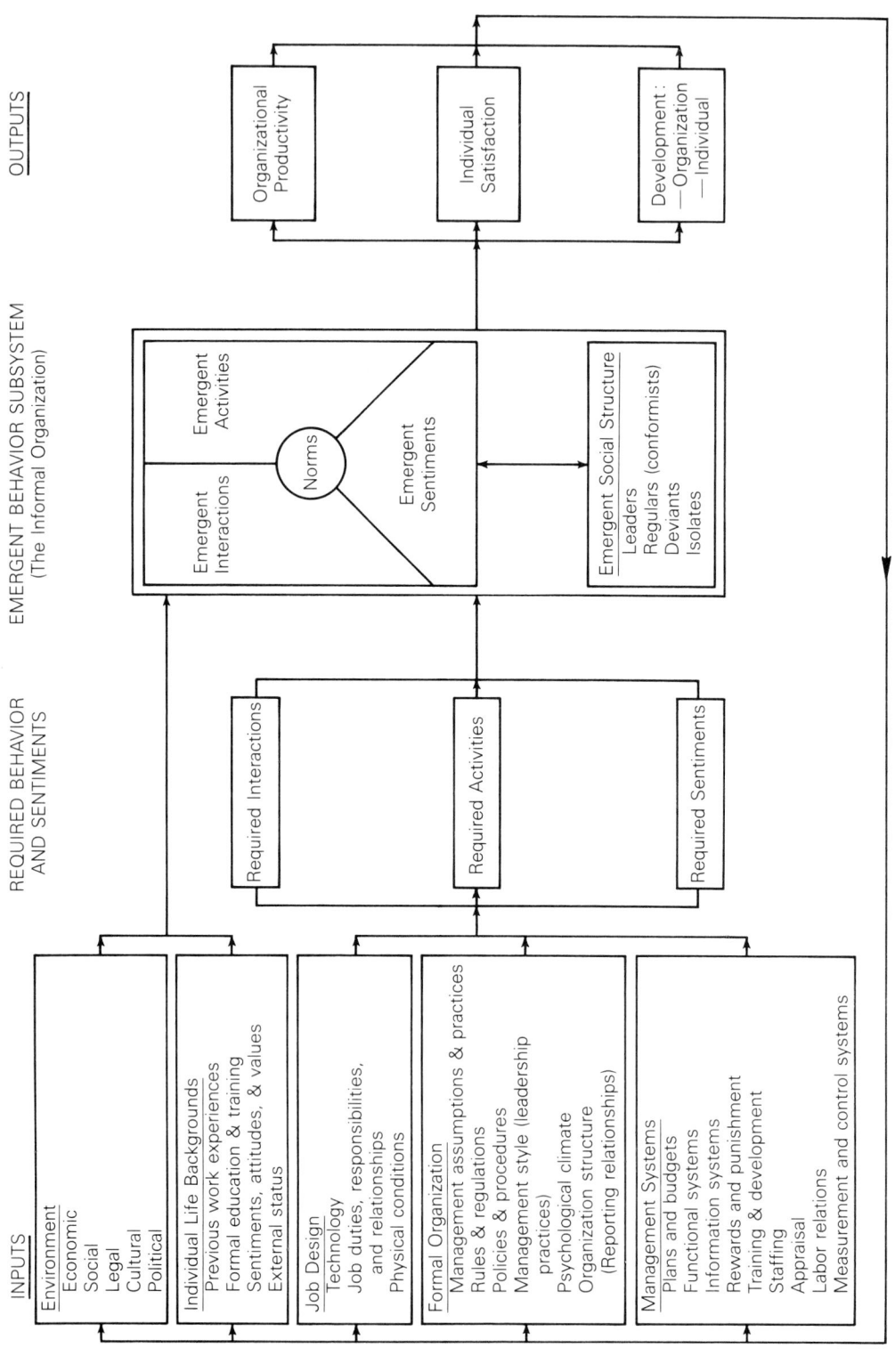

EXHIBIT 3-3
Determination of the emergent behavior subsystem (the informal organization)

Extremely important to the human resource system's total effectiveness, emergent behavior is characterized by key factors that will determine its impact:

1. Norms and goals of the emergent subsystem (are they congruent with or in conflict with the objectives of the formal organization?)
2. Communication channels within the subsystem
3. Conflict resolution within the subsystem and with other subsystems
4. Cohesiveness, or how strongly individuals are bound together in each subsystem
5. Duration of various groups (for example, groups such as taskforces may form and break up as projects are started and terminated)
6. Status and power of each emergent subsystem
7. Leadership found throughout the informal organization

Note that in the model shown in Exhibit 3-3, all behavior that "emerges" in the emergent behavior subsystem is determined or caused by the input variables in the background factors. Since many of these input variables are organizational factors routinely controlled by management (e.g., management practices, rules, job design, rewards, etc.), managers in reality have much greater influence over the kind of behavior created by the emergent subsystem than is generally recognized. This system view, in fact, makes it clear that managers should be more aware of these controllable background factors as "handles" on the informal organization. The emergence of work-group norms, sentiments, and activities congruent with organizational goals should constantly be kept in mind as an objective whenever decisions are being made regarding such background factors as job design, working conditions, selection of new employees, management practices, leadership style, rules, reward systems, information systems, and all other management systems.

REQUIRED BEHAVIOR AND SENTIMENTS

Exhibit 3-4 shows that the three immediate inputs to a work group that influence the emergent or resulting group behavior are required interactions, required activities, and required sentiments. *Required interactions* are the communications, interchange of work materials, authority roles, and cooperative relationships necessary to carry out the work directed toward organizational objectives. *Required activities* are the actual tasks that must be performed. *Required sentiments* are feelings about the job that are necessary, as a minimum, to get the job done.

These requirements are mainly established by management. Management designs the work system, the jobs, and the formal organization. It supplies the physical plant, the equipment, tools, and raw materials. It attempts to establish attitudes and values to produce required sentiments to

THE SETTING

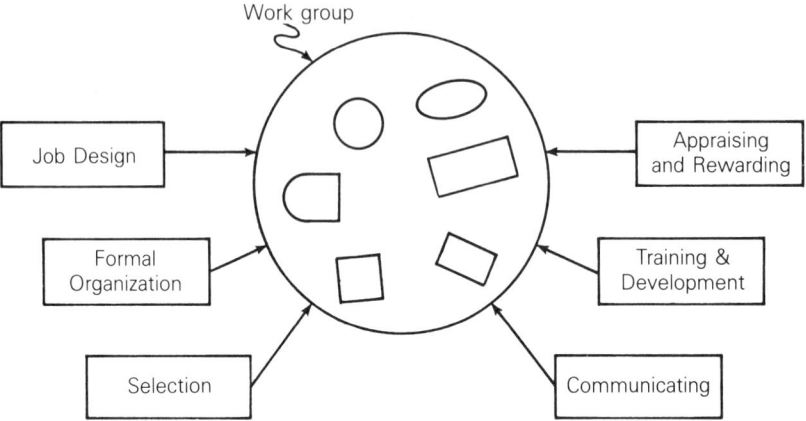

EXHIBIT 3–4
Shaping required behavior and sentiments

accomplish the work. However, every decision in the development of such requirements should be made with awareness of its impact on the behavior of individuals and of the work groups (Exhibit 3–4).

Organization Structure

Individually committed and capable people require effective organizational structures and policies to produce collective results. All too often, the structures and policies are not clearly and judiciously thought out. Competing structures and contradictory policies combine to frustrate personal energy and commitment.

The creation of consistent sets of structures and policies allows individual effort to be translated into collective results.

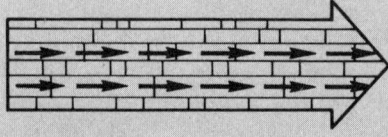

Source: Charles Kiefer and Peter Stroh, "A New Paradigm for Organization Development." Reprinted by permission of Innovation Associates, Inc., from *Training and Development Journal,* April, 1983. © Innovation Associates, Inc., 1983.

THE INDIVIDUAL WORKER

Long-term Characteristics

While the company can shape certain aspects of the work environment, it cannot modify all. Some characteristics of the individual that influence his or her behavior are long-enduring and not easily changed, so that management must either modify company goals, spend considerable effort in changing the employee's traits, or remove the worker from that particular system. Examples of long-enduring characteristics are:

1. Value systems
2. Attitudes
3. Cultural and educational background
4. Level of aspiration
5. Reference group and role models
6. Level of development in terms of perceived needs and personal "maturity"
7. "Intelligence"
8. Experience and time spent in life and work situations
9. Perceived role or self-concept
10. Life goals

Values Everyone has a unique "value system." A *value* is a concept about what is fundamentally good or desirable that the individual holds onto as a guide through life. It is analogous to a written company policy that is rarely modified. The value system is a set of concepts that truly forms a framework for the individual's preferred modes of conduct.[4] Included in this set are "prejudices," or values that other people reject as "unfair."

It is apparent that each individual probably has many such strongly held values that prescribe or limit actions. An important idea to note is that there may be conflicts or inconsistencies within the framework of values. For example, "majority rule" based on the value of democracy may infringe on individual freedom (another value).

Attitudes Attitudes are predispositions to evaluate or respond to some object or aspect of the world in a favorable or unfavorable manner. Workers may have unfavorable attitudes toward their workplace, efficiency study of their work, overtime work, or seniority as a basis for promotion. Attitudes are closely related to value systems.[5]

Culture The *culture* of the individual, the third long-enduring characteristic, includes educational background and represents the things learned and patterns of behavior acquired from the people around the individual. Language, values, likes, and dislikes are characteristics that define a society. As a result of differences in these characteristics, Eskimos, for example, view the world quite differently from Europeans. Similarly, the culture of New

Yorkers is different from that of West Virginia miners.[6] One of the most difficult cultural changes being attempted today in our country is increasing the role of women in business. Occupational and compensation stereotyping persist despite massive government efforts.

Aspiration The level of aspiration is the life-goal that an individual sets. Such a goal may change upward or downward over a period of years because of successes or failures.

Some people have clearly defined life-goals derived from their value systems. Others are unsure about "who they are." Still others have no goals or desire to have goals; they are content to drift through life enjoying the present. It is apparent that management must structure jobs, rewards, and growth opportunities differently to build effective work groups for such different individuals.

Reference Group and Role Models We all have our "reference group," or role models, people whom we desire to be like. The professor identifies with the teaching community. The shopworker identifies with co-workers, or perhaps the foreman. The construction worker identifies with other construction workers, not Wall Street brokers. We guide our behavior by the norms (that is, standards of behavior), goals, and values of our reference group.

Socioeconomic Level The level of our socioeconomic class refers to the level at which we perceive our needs and our ability to adapt to our situation. If we are uneducated, poor, work for low wages, and are in the lowest socioeconomic class, our needs are apt to be primarily economic. We tend to respond best to authoritarian leadership. At the other extreme, exemplifying a high level of socioeconomic class, are the company president or college professor. In these cases we find individuals with considerable control over their work situation. Their economic needs are apt to be relatively fulfilled, and they are more likely to respond to noneconomic factors.

Intelligence The "intelligence," or reasoning power, of a person apparently changes relatively little through life. An individual's behavior occurs within the limits of his or her intelligence.

Experience Experience is the accumulated time that a person has spent in life situations. Thus, an experienced worker would behave differently in the same position from an inexperienced worker. Experience, once attained, is a long-lasting (that is, stable) characteristic of an individual.

Self-concept The self-concept or perceived role is a very important characteristic in behavior. The military has recognized this clearly by the way it has treated recruits. A professional person or an executive drafted from civilian life enters the armed forces with a self-concept as a leader, advisor, and solid citizen to be respected. This self-concept is quickly destroyed in basic training by constant treatment of the recruit as a nobody, one among thousands. Then the rebuilding of a new self-concept is started. In the business world, self-concepts change very gradually in most cases. We tend to perceive our work role more clearly as time goes by. We behave as we believe someone in that role *should* behave. A person may hold a self-concept of being industrious, respected for integrity, and loyal to the company. To destroy this self-concept completely and suddenly would have a shattering effect upon the individual.

Short-term Characteristics

Short-term characteristics of the individual worker are more flexible and include:

1. Sentiments, opinions, or beliefs about the company, working conditions, and co-workers
2. Relationships within the informal work group (to be discussed later in the chapter when we view systems composed of two or more individuals)
3. Relationship with a formal leader or manager as established by the organizational structure
4. Mental state and physical health on any given day

More easily influenced by management than long-term characteristics, these short-term traits can be modified by identifying basic needs of people. How should the manager approach this process?

The first important point is that underlying the specific on-the-job needs of people are their life-satisfaction needs. It is important to look at this *totality* of needs because:

1. Some workers find practically all of their life-satisfactions off the job and work primarily to satisfy physical and economic needs.
2. Most workers derive at least part of their noneconomic life-satisfactions on the job.
3. The more needs a worker has an opportunity to satisfy on the job, the more likely the worker is to be highly motivated to perform the job.

Douglas McGregor's optimistic view of human nature (a view consistent with Maslow's "need hierarchy" theory discussed in Chapter 8) led to a set of beliefs—called Theory Y—about the nature of people at work.[7] Consistent with a whole new style of managing by integration and self-control, Theory Y stated that organizational objectives and individual objectives could be integrated to mutual satisfaction. Managing by integration and self-control consists of designing work situations in such a way that each individual can best achieve his or her personal goals by contributing to the goals of the organization.

One common thread running through all theories about human needs is that they assume individuals have different and widely varying needs. The strength of these needs varies from time to time within the same individual, as well as varying between individuals. Further, the behavior of workers is conditioned by their permanent characteristics and by the previous outcomes of their behavior.

One practical conclusion that seems to be shared by all the theories about human motivation is that in order to motivate people at work, managers must be able to create the conditions under which a large proportion of the work force will be able to perceive much of the time an opportunity to meet their own personal needs *best* by contributing to the achievement of organization objectives. In order for this to happen, large numbers of individuals must believe (1) that rewards which they personally value are being offered, and (2) that the receipt of these rewards will be dependent on the quality of their own performance and contribution. Seeing this connection requires (1) confidence in the resources of the organization to provide these rewards; (2) organizational ability to accurately measure performance to permit equitable distribution of rewards; and (3) organizational integrity to actively deliver what has been promised. In short, individuals must be able to perceive a *direct* causal connection between the value of their contributions and the value of the rewards received. (This concept of motivation will be discussed more fully in Chapter 8 particularly from the perspective of what the personnel department and line managers alike must do in order to create a highly motivated work force.)

WORK GROUPS AND OTHER WORKER ASSOCIATIONS

We have structured a major portion of this book around two concepts: Managing HR requires managing people as *individuals*, and also requires a system to manage *groups* within the total organization. Shown in Exhibit 3–5 are five categories of work groups: formal, informal, managerial, professional/technical, and union or trade.

The identification of groups and differentiation among them affect such processes as staffing, motivating, communicating, upgrading human resources, managing change, and resolving conflict. Groups vary in degree of permanence and degree of complexity as well as in the goals they seek.[8] The differentiation of groups must be done very carefully, however. For example, you might be tempted to lump engineers and scientists into the same group and treat them alike. Yet several studies have shown significant differences in the perceptions and needs of people in these professions.[9]

We have given considerable attention to formal and informal groups, and will now discuss the last three groups in Exhibit 3–5: managerial groups, professional and technical groups, and unions.

EXHIBIT 3–5
Work groups and associations affecting emergent behavior in the organization

Subsystem	Description	Goals
Formal organization groups	Workers grouped by organizational tasks	Organizational goals
Informal organizations	Groups who have a common interest because of similar work, close location, common outside interests, similar values and norms, and so on	Varied goals relating to both on-job and off-job interests; establishment of better communications, work norms, power, pressure on management or other groups, and so on
Managerial	Groups of managers, usually of similar levels in the hierarchy of the formal organization	Establishment of company values and objectives; higher productivity; development of people in the organization; self-advancement and personal power
Professional/Technical	Engineers, accountants, secretaries, aircraft mechanics, nurses, and other licensed or certified groups, or members of professional organizations	Development of discipline skills and remaining abreast of changes
Union or trade	Associations of workers with a common bond of skill or location	Negotiation with management over working conditions, compensation, benefits

Managerial Groups

Within the ranks of managers informal subsystems tend to form because of common goals, desire for informal communication, and desire for power. The three basic types of informal managerial groups are formed according to discipline, peer group, and the sponsor–protégé system.

The first type of managerial group is formed around a common discipline, say, manufacturing or engineering. The second is the peer group, managers at the same level who form a loose group or set of groups. At any particular level, managers from lower levels of the hierarchy are not welcomed to the group and higher-level managers don't care to join.

A third type of group, somewhat in contradiction to the concept of the peer group, is the sponsor–protégé system, which forms for a variety of reasons including mutual support. A high-level manager may provide guidance and support for a number of lower-level managers in the organization. In turn, these protégés will be a source of information and support within their peer groups. While sponsors (sometimes called mentors) and their protégés do not usually socialize (lunch, and so on) at work, the manager and a single protégé may get together for private family affairs. It is not likely that a high-level manager would meet with a group of protégés.[10]

Different groups of managers, such as line managers and staff managers, must be identified and treated differently by the members of the organization. These two groups frequently engage in power struggles that prevent optimization of the effectiveness of the total HR system. In Chapter 9, Organization Development, we give attention to changing such group behavior.

Professional and Technical Groups

While professional and technical groups provide safeguards to the organization, they also may pose severe problems. A true professional may place loyalty to discipline ahead of company goals. For example, should the company wish to sacrifice the *quality* of work in the interests of greater *quantity*, the professional may rebel against compromising quality, and feel that service is no longer professional if it is in any way dictated by the client or employer. One researcher has characterized this group as being "an especially demanding breed of people, bent on individualistic values and requiring more managerial imagination."[11] Similarly, the greater the extent of the professional's academic training, the stronger is the interest in basic, autonomous knowledge-seeking research, and the more difficult it becomes to integrate personal goals with the goals of the overall organization.

Management may find that the human resource system and company goals require safeguards—such technical professionals may be designated not as decision makers but as consultants or researchers for managers or other decision makers in the organization.

Conflict may also arise between professional ethics and job requirements. Legal restraints may prevent the professional from performing in ways management may desire. For example, the accountant may have to make reports to the S.E.C. or prepare financial statements that management might not desire. Again, an engineer will be hesitant to design a building or product in a way that endangers life because of skimping on materials or using hazardous materials.

Unions

The union—a formal organization—exists as a subsystem within the organization. The effects of unions on the human resource system vary so tremendously that a different type of formal system (leadership style) must be adopted in each situation. The union system includes such variables as:

1. Types of workers that are unionized in the company
2. Types of workers that outsiders are trying to unionize
3. Strength of unions in the company
4. History of labor–management relations
5. Number of different unions and their conflicts or cooperation with one another
6. Nature of union leadership—legalistic, power-oriented, degree of maturity, cooperativeness, strength, and so on

In the case of unions, the human resource system must adapt greatly to this second system that constitutes an environmental influence or input. Fortunately, as union–management relations have matured under economic pressure, union and business leaders have identified overriding common goals such as survival of the industry or the company. The effect of the union on the human resource system is discussed in Chapter 16, Labor–Management Relations.

IMPLICATIONS OF WORKER SIMILARITIES AND DIFFERENCES

If we were to consider a group of semiskilled workers doing office work and a group of semiskilled workers in the shop, we might notice such similarities as educational level, compensation, level of skill, and working hours. Yet differences in values, aspirations, role concept, cultural interests, and reference groups may greatly affect each work group as a system processor. Of course, it is difficult to generalize since it is possible to find a janitor who is an opera buff and a top manager who is a cultural know-nothing.

Exhibit 3–6 shows some implications of classifying workers for HR management. This is, of course, a very abbreviated table, but it does illustrate how similarities and differences of work groups may be taken into account for purposes of recruitment, selection, training and development, compensation, and bargaining.

Vital to designers of HR systems are three things: awareness of how people behave as *individuals*, as members of *emergent behavior systems*, as well as a keen appreciation of individual differences. It is important that each of the operational subsystems of HR be designed to be consistent with and to take advantage of our scientific knowledge of human behavior.

SUMMARY

Managing people both in organized groups and as individuals requires an understanding of basic concepts of behavioral systems. Managers must act as catalysts to influence change in the on-going behavioral system in order

EXHIBIT 3-6
Work groups and P/HR activities

Work Group	Recruitment	Selection	Training and Development	Compensation	Bargaining
Unskilled warehouse labor	Ad in paper; word of mouth	First come	None	Per hour	Collective bargaining
Professional accountants	Campus recruiters	Grades or exam scores; recommendation	Orientation program; external professional seminars	Weekly or monthly salary	None
First-line factory supervisors	Promotion from within	Assessment center evaluation; performance appraisals	New supervisor courses; outside seminars	Weekly or monthly salary	None
Top corporate executives	Executive recruiters; ad in paper; personal contacts	Careful evaluation of many candidates; psychological assessment	Extensive executive development	Annual salary plus bonus	Individual basis with vice president of HR management

to improve organizational outputs and adapt the organization to changing societal environments.

The principal behavioral units identified in the chapter were:

1. The individual worker
2. The formal organization
3. The informal organization
4. Managerial groups as subsystems
5. Professional and technical groups as subsystems
6. Unions as subsystems

The fact that every worker is a functioning element in two or more of these subsystems indicates the complexity of the human resource system. It also indicates that optimizing the total business system (the particular company) requires a considerable knowledge of the behavior of people both as individuals and as group members.

The worker has certain long-lasting characteristics, such as values, attitudes, and aspirations. Managers may anticipate somewhat stable responses to a particular input when these characteristics dominate in a situation. Unfortunately, the worker is also characterized by changing short-term characteristics. Much behavior depends upon changing perceived needs, according to most theorists.

Workers as individuals perform differently from groups of workers. HR management must, therefore, identify groups of workers that must be considered for management. The behavior of some of these groups, such as unions, will be treated more fully in Chapter 16. Here we have emphasized *differences* in groups to point out that groups require special attention.

KEY CONCEPTS

The formal organization	Grapevine
The informal organization	Sanctions
Norms	Emergent behavior
Group cohesion	Required sentiments
Socialization	Culture

NOTES

1. Elton Mayo, *The Human Problems of an Industrial Civilization* (New York: Macmillan, 1933).
2. Chris Argyris, *Personality and Organization* (New York: Harper & Row, 1957).

3. See Lawrence A. Klatt and David L. Kurtz, "The 'Grapevine' as a Management Tool," *Akron Business and Economic Review*, Winter 1970.
4. See, for example, Martha A. Brown, "Values—A Necessary but Neglected Ingredient of Motivation on the Job," *Academy of Management Review*, October 1976.
5. Daniel Katz, "The Functional Approach to the Study of Attitudes," *Public Opinion Quarterly*, Summer 1960. See also William C. Scott and Terence R. Mitchell, *Organization Theory*, Homewood, Ill.: Irwin, 1976, Ch. 7, "Attitudes."
6. Clyde K. Kluckholn and Henry A. Murray, *Personality in Nature, Society, and Culture*, New York: Knopf, 1953.
7. Douglas McGregor, *The Human Side of Enterprise* (New York: McGraw-Hill, 1960).
8. For a review of various perspectives and theories of groups, see Chap. 1, "What Is an Organization?" in J. Eugene Hass and Thomas E. Drabek, *Complex Organizations: A Sociological Perspective* (New York: Macmillan, 1973). See also Part 2, "Individual and Group Behavior," in William G. Scott and Terrence R. Mitchell, *Organization Theory: A Structural and Behavioral Analysis* (Homewood, Ill.: Irwin, 1976).
9. M. K. Badawy, "Organizational Designs for Scientists and Engineers: Some Research Findings and Their Implications for Managers," *IEEE Transactions in Engineering Management*, November 1975.
10. For example, see Norman H. Martin, "Thinking Ahead—Power Tactics," *Harvard Business Review*, November–December 1956.
11. Robert Chartier, "Managing the Knowledge Employee," *Personnel Journal*, August 1968, p. 559.

REVIEW AND DISCUSSION QUESTIONS

1. Explain how the individual is a "system."
2. In what ways is the behavioral system the adaptive system controlling the firm?
3. What is the relationship between job-related and nonjob-related outputs of the worker? Is one more important than the other?
4. Give specific examples of possible approaches that management may employ to control the human resource system.
5. What is a value? Show how a particular value system may influence the manager's ability to manage.
6. In what ways can a "reference group" affect the worker's behavior as a processor?
7. Why are sentiments, opinions, and beliefs about the company classified as short-term characteristics of the individual? Does this mean that they can be changed by management?
8. Of what practical value is McGregor's Theory Y?
9. Using an organization that you currently are a member of, show how you are also a member of at least two organized subsystems within that organization's human resource system. Can you think of any instance in which the goals of a subsystem may have conflicted with another subsystem in that organization?

10. In what ways does the formal organization affect the human resource system?
11. What is meant by the informal organization system? Can management influence the informal organization? Explain your answer, using specific examples.
12. Explain how each of the following subsystems have an impact on the goals of the human resource system: managerial groups, professional/technical groups, unions.
13. Write a short speech to be delivered to a group of managers on how "optimizing the total business system of a firm requires considerable knowledge of the behavior of people, both as individuals and in groups."

BIBLIOGRAPHY

Behling, Orlando, and Chester Schriesheim. *Organizational Behavior: Theory, Research and Application.* Boston: Allyn and Bacon, 1976.

Bridges, E. M., et al. "Effects of Hierarchical Differentiations on Group Productivity, Efficiency, and Risk Taking." *Administrative Science Quarterly,* January 1968.

Brown, Martha A. "Values—A Necessary but Neglected Ingredient of Motivation on the Job." *Academy of Management Review,* October 1976.

Connor, Patrick E., and Boris W. Becker. "Values and the Organization: Suggestions for Research." *Acadamy of Management Journal,* September 1975.

Gibson, James I., John M. Ivancevich, and James Donnelly, Jr. *Organizations: Structure, Processes, Behavior.* Dallas: Business Publications, 1975.

Hertzberg, Frederick. *Work and the Nature of Man.* New York: World Publishing, 1966.

Homans, G. C. *The Human Group.* New York: Harcourt, Brace, 1950.

Maslow, A. H. "A Theory of Human Motivation," *Psychological Review,* 1943. Reprinted in Robert A. Sutermeister (ed.), *People and Productivity,* 2nd ed. New York: McGraw-Hill, 1969.

McGregor, Douglas. *The Human Side of Enterprise.* New York: McGraw-Hill, 1960.

Sathe, Vijay. "Implications for Corporate Culture: A Manager's Guide to Action," *Organizational Dynamics,* Autumn, 1983.

Schoderbek, Peter P., Asterios G. Kefalas, and Charles G. Schoderbek. *Management Systems: Conceptual Considerations.* Dallas: Business Publications, 1975.

Steers, Richard M., and Lyman W. Porter. *Motivation and Work Behavior.* New York: McGraw-Hill, 1975.

PART I CASE STUDIES

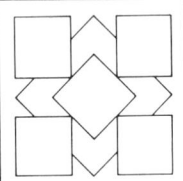

CASE STUDY:
Little Things Mean a Lot
Edward R. Toth, Jr.

For years the RMI Company had unused land adjacent to its main plant in Niles, Ohio. Not long ago the company decided to make this land available to its employees and their families to grow their own private flower and vegetable garden. Any employee may sign up for a 3,000-square-foot garden. RMI does the plowing.

It is this sort of consideration for employees by management, we believe, that has enabled us to become a leader in our industry, recognized for our exemplary personnel management. We are not great believers in managing people "scientifically." We believe in a fair, sensitive, consistent and open-ended management, with a sympathetic understanding of human feelings and desires. Simple acts that may seem inconsequential make all the difference. We learned this the hard way, and for us it has meant nothing less than company survival.

RMI employs nearly 2,000 people in six plants, four of which are unionized. Its primary product is titanium, a metal with many aerospace, defense, and commercial applications.

Five years ago, RMI was in difficult straits. In 12 of the previous 16 years, the company had operated in the red. We were stifled by labor problems, including two major strikes at our main plant. Productivity was abysmal. Product rejection rates were sky rocketing. Employee morale was low. There was little identification between the company and its employees or between the company and the community.

Communications were poor, not only between management and labor but between departments. Our market penetration was weak.

Within four years, however, all this changed. Productivity has increased by 77 percent. Product rejection rates have declined sharply. Sales have risen by more than 600 percent. The morale and pride of our workers are widely recognized by all who know us.

There is no great secret behind RMI's turnaround. We have not introduced sophisticated, costly new programs. On the contrary. We depend on a simple, straightforward relationship with our employees, based on five principles:

- ☐ We aim to instill in every employee the idea that he or she is part of a team working toward a common goal. We emphasize the merits of teamwork and the importance of each employee as a team member.

- ☐ Every employee is persuaded to realize that the best way to guarantee job security is to help ensure that the company is profitable.

- ☐ Every employee is made to understand that the company expects excellence. We believe that organizations that expect high performance will get high performance and those that accept mediocrity will get mediocrity. We set our goals high but within reach.

- Employees are encouraged to feel that they are members of the RMI family before they are members of a union or management, production or sales, or whatever.
- We encourage employee participation in community affairs because we believe such activity helps to enhance self-esteem and allows individuals to identify more closely with their community. It also improves the community's perception of the company.

Two words guide us in everything we do: communications and simplicity.

Dinner meetings are held regularly to bring together front-line supervisors, middle managers, and top managers; we use these occasions to convey our company philosophy and goals and to give a "state of the union" message. These affairs are also a means of establishing a closer relationship between all levels of management and between departments.

Informal dinner meetings held for top management and union officials have helped establish an atmosphere of mutual trust and a closer and better working relationship. Managers and union officials are seated side by side to demonstrate equality and encourage conversation. There is no head table.

In addition, union officials are frequently invited to management meetings to discuss specific items or problems, such as changes in administrative procedures, expansion plans, and new products.

Customers are also invited to make presentations to our employees at bi-monthly dinner meetings. The meetings, which are strictly voluntary, are well-attended and have helped to reinforce the importance of quality and prompt customer deliveries.

We have established an open-door policy under which every employee has the right to arrange a meeting to speak with the chief executive officer or any other executive on any serious issue. Middle managers who fear a break in the established chain of command are uncomfortable with this practice. But we believe it makes employees feel that they are respected as individuals and a part of the larger team. It has also contributed to improved union/management relations.

The ultimate success of our open-door policy depends on follow-up communications with middle managers, however. The employee's manager is informed of the meeting and the nature of the discussions. We take great pains to ensure that no confidences are breached.

As part of our communications efforts, top managers make frequent and random visits to work areas. These visits help create a feeling of togetherness and demonstrate top management's interest and concern for employees, even though they may be limited to a friendly "hello" or a quick comment on how the business is going.

Periodically and without notice, top managers greet employees near the punch-clock at the start of shifts. If an employee is late, he is reminded in a pleasant way that tardiness hinders fellow workers in their work and thus hurts the company. Punctuality has improved, and we have gained greater visibility of top management.

Accepting the premise that no one knows more about what is wrong and what is needed most than the workers themselves, RMI launched an "Action Request" program about two and one-half years ago. To date, more than 500 suggestions have been implemented, far exceeding our original expectations. In many cases, suggestions have improved service and quality, reduced costs and idle time, and improved productivity.

RMI also tries hard to interest employees' families in what occurs at work; we believe this reinforces individual workers' importance at work and makes any discussions at home about work more positive. We mail our bimonthly company newsletter, a result of an employee's suggestion incidentally, to our employees' homes. We also hold Open Houses at our plants for employees' families, with exhibits explaining how titanium is used. Tours are conducted by both shopfloor and salaried personnel.

We also endeavor to keep the physical working conditions of our employees in top condition. Some improvements have involved nothing more than a paint-up and spruce up. But this constant care has helped to raise employee morale and productivity.

We provide stickers with company symbols for employees to apply to their hardhats, luggage, and car bumpers. Banners and signs placed throughout the plants bear company messages and promote its philosophy and goals. "When you meet a man without a smile, give him one of yours," reads one. It may be corny, but it works.

In fact, all of our efforts, however small, directly or indirectly, have given the organization, from top to bottom, a new dynamism and vitality. People visiting our plants invariably comment on this. But nothing moved management more and confirmed that what we are doing is right more than the inscription on a silver cup recently presented to RMI President James L. Daniell by two local unions:

". . . in appreciation of his tireless efforts in improving plant morale, working conditions and employee relations."

Edward R. Toth, Jr., is Vice President of Operations for the RMI Company, headquartered in Niles, Ohio. *Source:* Reprinted by permission of the publisher, from *Management Review* (AMA Forum), November 1981, © 1981 by AMACOM, a division of American Management Associations, New York. All rights reserved.

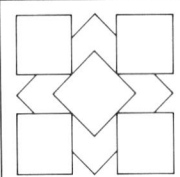

CASE STUDY:
Action and Reaction

When young Tom Babcock was put in charge of a division of a large manufacturing company and told to "turn it around," he spent the first few weeks studying it from afar. He decided that the division was in disastrous shape and that he would need to take many large steps quickly to save it. To be able to do that, he realized that he needed to develop considerable power fast over most of the division's management and staff. He did the following:

1. He gave the division's management two hours' notice of his arrival.
2. He arrived in a limousine with six assistants.
3. He immediately called a meeting of the 40 top managers.
4. He outlined briefly his assessment of the situation, his commitment to turn things around, and the basic direction he wanted things to move in.
5. He fired the four top managers in the room and told them that they had to be out of the building in two hours.
6. He then said that he would personally dedicate himself to sabotaging the career of anyone who tried to block his efforts to save the division.
7. He ended the 60-minute meeting by announcing that his assistants would set up appointments for him with

each of the remaining 36 top managers, starting at 7 A.M. the next morning.

Throughout the critical six-month period that followed, the top managers who remained at the division generally cooperated energetically with Mr. Babcock.

Source: Reprinted by permission of the Harvard Business Review. Excerpt from "Power, Dependence, and Effective Management" by John P. Kotter (July–August 1977). Copyright © 1977 by the President and Fellows of Harvard College; all rights reserved.

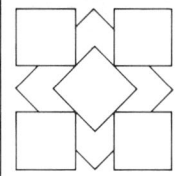

CASE STUDY:
Order Processing

It had been six months since Mr. Spear, the newly hired manager of management information systems, had arrived on the scene. Ms. Dawn Adams recalled his first visit to her office. She had shown him the work flow of her order processing organization.

Six clerks received purchase orders and sales orders by mail and orders from salespersons over the telephone. Two other clerks checked records and divided these orders into "new customer" and "old customer" groups to be logged in a record journal and then checked for credit. Six more clerks edited the orders to see whether they were complete in terms of customer information and correct in terms of stock numbers and product descriptions. Finally, three typists transferred the order information onto a standard company form for transmission to product planning and control.

Most of Ms. Adams' employees were men and women in their 40s and 50s who had worked for the company for an average of 11 years. When they were interviewed by the MIS staff analysts, they had appeared quite agitated.

Ms. Adams had just met with Mr. Spear to go over his recommended change in her order processing operation. The changes included both system changes and computerization of most of the operation. This meant that a number of personnel would have to be trained in such computer-related skills as card punching and output checking. About eight people would have to be transferred to other sections of the company.

Ms. Adams considered calling her entire group together and informing the group as a whole of the new proposal, which was logical, economical, and certain to be implemented by management. On the other hand, she envisioned weeping men and women. Should she meet with each of her subordinates individually to provide reassurance and point out the advantages of the change to the subordinate? She was aware that after one or two people had been in her office, all of the others would get the news informally without the personal reassurances.

What were *all* the causes of resistance to this change going to be, and how could Ms. Adams overcome them?

II
Planning and Staffing

Planning for Human Resources

CHAPTER OUTLINE

Advantages of Human Resource Planning

Integrated Business and Human Resource Planning

The Human Resource Planning Process

Corporate-Level Planning ☐ Intermediate-Level Planning ☐ Operations Planning ☐ Short-Term Activities Planning

The Planning Approach to Determining Manpower Requirements

Corporate Objectives and Strategy ☐ Organization Structure ☐ Sales, Work Breakdown Structure, and Current Manpower Requirements ☐ Current Manpower Inventory ☐ Future Manpower Requirements ☐ Net Change to Satisfy Future Manpower Requirements

Forecasting Manpower Requirements

Trend Projection ☐ Regression Methods ☐ Composite Department Demand ☐ Fractional Flow Models ☐ Contingency Model ☐ Decision Models with Fluctuating Product Demand

Forecasting Manpower Supply

External Supply ☐ Internal Supply ☐ Matching Demand and Supply

OBJECTIVES

1. Identify and describe the advantages of integrated business and human resource planning
2. Distinguish between the planning and the forecasting approach to determine future resource needs
3. Describe the planning approach to determining manpower needs
4. Describe various methods for forecasting future manpower requirements
5. Describe the use of models for forecasting manpower needs
6. Describe a method for estimating manpower supply

SPOTLIGHT:
Kenneth L. Otto

Kenneth L. Otto joined Tenneco in 1977, and serves as the corporation's senior employee relations executive. He was employed previously by United Technologies as Corporate Vice President–Organization and Personnel Resources. He was also Corporate Vice President, Personnel and Organization Development, for the Bendix Corporation and held a variety of management posts in organization and personnel work at the Ford Motor Company. Mr. Otto has a Bachelor of Science degree in Industrial Management from the State University of Iowa.

Comments by Kenneth L. Otto

To paraphrase Mark Twain, "everybody is talking about human resource planning, but no one is doing very much about it" (or they're not doing it very well). Perhaps having "everyone talk about human resource planning" is a step in the right direction but it does not assure a quality effort. Everyone talking about it is a relatively new phenomenon. Fifteen to twenty years ago, not much was being written about human resource planning and when it was commented upon, it was called "manpower planning." The change in title reflects an appropriate recognition of changing times and increased social awareness, but I am not sure how much else has really changed in large organizations that are doing human resource planning.

The problem with human resource planning is not that the planners don't know how to use numbers to plan, but rather they often use numbers that are irrelevant to what the plan is supposed to accomplish. There are many reasons for this, but in my experience there do seem to be some root causes.

One cause is that planning in many organizations is carried out by a group of central staff experts who assume that the human resource input can be effectively developed without fully considering the many variables that impact on the human resource equation. Our human capital investment just doesn't act and react the same way as do dollars, plant and equipment, land, technology, and other factors impacting on the plan. This suggests that there must be more active communication and cooperation between the planning experts and the human resource experts. In my opinion, enlightened organizations have only begun to stimulate this sort of interaction.

An even more basic problem that partially results from this lack of coordination and communication is human resource planning without relation to the business plan of the organization. Human resource planning that is not tied into the overall business plan is a good intellectual exercise at best and meaningless at worst. There are, unfortunately, many visible examples of this lack of coordination in the various jobs and job-training programs sponsored by the government during the last fifteen to twenty years. The overall objective of most of these government programs is to put people to work. The staff is recruited, training programs are established, and people are recruited and paid to participate in the training. Upon completing the training, they are understandably frustrated when they again return to the ranks of the unemployed. What has happened in all too many cases is that the jobs for which they were trained were not the ones that business and industry needed in their geographic area. This is a perfect example of the human resource plan (the job/jobs-training program) not being tied into the business plan (the numbers and types of jobs that are needed by the receiving organizations). While not as visible in the business community, there are many similar examples. Grandiose business plans are prepared that are models of planning efficiency that cannot be achieved because the human resource planning portion of the plan was inaccurate or nonexistent.

A human resource plan that is related to the overall business plan of the organization will consider:

☐ Possibilities of growth or retraction of human resources.
☐ Changes in the status quo.
☐ Changes in mission of the organization.
☐ Shifts in emphasis in the products or services offered.
☐ An "environmental scan" to assist in determining outside impacts on the organization's human resources.

The chapter that follows provides an overview of human resource planning techniques that were not available when I was in business school. However, the following summary may provide you with information useful in the "real world of human resource planning." The human resource plan must be an integral part of the overall business planning process, and should incorporate eight elements:

☐ It should be formulated in writing.
☐ The basic organization structure has been developed for 4–5 years hence.
☐ The number and type of executives needed for the next 4 to 5 years have been estimated.
☐ Replacements for key positions have been identified and development plans prepared.
☐ Strengths and weaknesses of executive resources have been profiled.
☐ Plans for advancing women and minority employees are available.
☐ A system for identifying high-potential performers early in their careers is in place.
☐ Recruitment programs, including college recruitment, are operational.

In a small company of 10 employees, if two leave during the year, 20 percent of the human resources must be replaced.

Exxon, a large company, hired 4199 people in the United States despite a reduction of work force.

These examples represent two extremes of human resource planning situations. What would happen if there were no planning for such changes? Are there really advantages to anticipating changes in human resources? How would such planning be carried out? Who does it? These are all questions of vital interest to the P/HR manager as well as top management.

ADVANTAGES OF HUMAN RESOURCE PLANNING

Human resource planning describes the intended actions of the organization to ensure that the organization has the right number and right mix of people at the right time and place to achieve efficiently present and future organizational goals. *The entire range of activities of the P/HR department is devoted to this concept.* In this chapter we will focus on the broad planning for human resource employment. In the following chapters, methods for planning and implementing the various subactivities of staffing, development and compensation are covered in detail.

As you will see, there are eight advantages to human resource planning:

1. Human resources are able to be deployed in support of basic strategic objectives of the company.
2. Management gains an improved understanding of the influence of business strategy on human resources and of human resource activities on business strategy.
3. People may be planned for, and used, more effectively and efficiently, in year-to-year and day-to-day operations.
4. Human resources may be continuously upgraded by the implementation of planning for recruitment, termination, training, development, career management, and rewarding for performance.
5. Employees will be more satisfied with the quality of worklife. This will facilitate the management of change, good community relations, and the recruiting of good people.
6. Easier diagnosis and solution of problems involving human resources will be possible because planning essentially provides a model of the human resource system. This implies that improved analysis of costs can be made.
7. Equal employment opportunity and affirmative action requirements may be achieved because objectives and actions are spelled out in plans.
8. Shortages of key technical and managerial skills may be reduced or prevented.

INTEGRATED BUSINESS AND HUMAN RESOURCE PLANNING

Human resource planning, just as product planning, financial planning, and equipment planning, should be an integral part of the total business. Communication of needs is central to accuracy. The manager or vice president of P/HR provides inputs such as key HR issues, HR environmental constraints, and internal HR capability constraints to the business planners. At the same time, these business managers must communicate their needs and constraints to the P/HR organization. The final corporate and business plans thus incorporate both H/R and functional plans.

Companies may prepare plans to fit four time spans:

1. Strategic plans that establish major long-range objectives, which state the principal milestones and policies to achieve them; the time span for strategic plans is usually considered to be five or more years.
2. Intermediate-range plans covering about a three-year period. These are more specific plans in support of the near-term portion of the strategic plan.
3. Operating plans cover one year, month-by-month in sufficient detail for profit, budget, and cost control.
4. Activity plans are the day-by-day and week-by-week plans; examples are the route plan for a salesperson, the production plan for the week, or the short-term work assignment of a compensation specialist. Frequently, such plans are not even documented by the supervisor.

Let us now look at the links between business planning and human resource planning. First, from Exhibit 4–1, we see that issues analysis is the connecting link between strategic business planning and strategic HR planning. HR issues are major problems that must be addressed. They arise as part of strategic business planning or strategic HR planning. For example, the company may intend to grow by the acquisition of other companies. A strategic issue may be what to do if some companies in the corporation are unionized and acquired companies are not. The P/HR department may also raise issues such as moving to guaranteed annual wages, hiring foreign labor, introducing innovative new organizational structures, and noting the effect of robotics and computers on productivity.

From Exhibit 4–1, we note that at the intermediate-range level, HR planning is linked to the business plan by the development of HR programs required for major business programs. One business program might be the development of a new personal computer product line. The HR plan would include recruiting of skilled engineers, compensation structure, training, career-planning assistance, leadership development for managers in the new organization, and creation of a work climate to motivate workers.

EXHIBIT 4-1
Linking business planning and HR planning.

Planning Level and Horizon	Business Planning Process	←Link→	Human Resource Planning Process
Strategic planning (5 or more years)	Corporate philosophy, value system, and policies Goals and objectives Key success factors Product market scope, competitive edge, allocation of resources	Issues analysis	Analysis of issues raised by external factors Employment demand projection Manpower supply analysis and projection
Intermediate-range planning (3–5 years)	Organization evoluation Programs required to implement strategy Deployment of resources Acquisitions, divestments, and internal development of product lines	Programming requirements	Forecasting total staffing level Forecasting number of managers and key personnel Forecasting net changes in managers and key personnel, year by year Planning P/HR support programs
Operational planning (12 months)	Detailing of programs to specify actions, responsibilities, cost–time schedule, and organizational profitability	Integrated control requirements	Detailing of P/HR activities that are incorporated in the one-year business plan
Activities planning (daily and weekly)	Day-to-day and week-to-week plans and work schedules decentralized throughout the company	Implementation actions	P/HR day-to-day and week-to-week assignments in support of the objectives and plans of the P/HR department

Operational planning for human resources is linked to business planning by means of the annual budget. From the smallest organizational unit up to the largest in the firm, a budget summarizes the annual plan for the organizations. That is, the tasks to be performed by each organization are listed with labor, materials, and overhead costs. From this budget, total annual labor costs for major classes of workers may be determined. Further, the budget for the P/HR department itself must be integrated into the total organizational budget. All good operational budgets and plans show a month-by-month breakdown of the total figures.

The daily HR and P/HR plans are linked to daily business planning by the joint efforts required to carry out business plans. For example, paychecks require line supervisor verification of time worked (unless the process is computerized) and verification of worker's pay rate by P/HR. Replacement of a worker who terminates, disciplinary action, promotion of an employee, and entering an employee in a training course all require business-oriented activities that involve P/HR activities and HR planning.

It is apparent by now that P/HR planning is an integral part of business planning, and you can see why P/HR planning is not done in a vacuum. Every aspect of it must be pointed toward total organizational objectives.

THE HUMAN RESOURCE PLANNING PROCESS

In Exhibit 4–1, we have shown the principal features of business planning and human resource planning. We have also shown the basic concept for linking these at each level of planning:

Level	Link
Strategic	Issues analysis
Intermediate	Programming requirements
Operational	Integrated control requirements
Activity	Implementation actions

We will now develop the HR planning process to amplify on the ideas in Exhibit 4–1. Exhibit 4–2 shows the process for conducting integrated planning at the four levels of large companies.

Corporate-Level Planning

Top management sets the tone for the development of strategy formulation by making explicit the corporate philosophy and value system through poli-

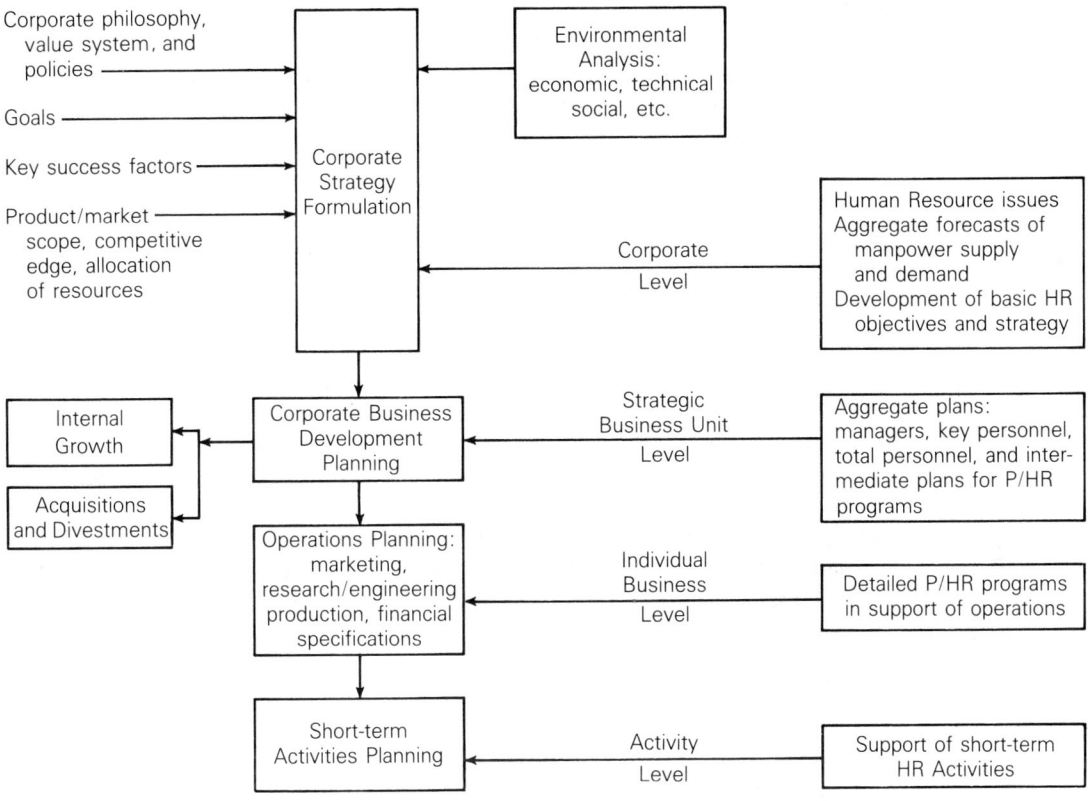

EXHIBIT 4-2
Human resource planning in the business system.

cies, public statements, and its actions. The P/HR department's role, in turn, will be to raise issues relative to the treatment of employees (as covered by the following chapters of this book). Examples of such issues are:

1. Guaranteed annual wages
2. Hiring of foreign labor
3. Subcontracting of labor-intensive operations
4. Robotics and computer effects on productivity
5. Introduction of innovative organizational structures and work design
6. Legal constraints on hiring and on closing plants

In addition, top management sets broad goals and objectives for the company, and identifies key success factors, which, if not attained, will jeopardize the existence of the firm. Top management then makes its *corporate strategy* explicit in terms of product–market matches it will pursue, its desired competitive edge, and the allocation of resources to be made. This allocation depends heavily, of course, on aggregate estimates of manpower requirements under the alternative assumptions provided by the HR departments. In parallel, the P/HR department will prepare objectives consistent with company strategy and a strategy of its own to support the firm's strategy.

Intermediate-Level Planning

Many modern corporations have grown so large that they must group subsidiaries or "businesses" into "divisions," "groups," or "sectors." For strategic purposes, special groupings of operations and businesses into a single product–market group called a Strategic Business Unit (SBU) is used. For purposes of simplification, let us just assume that there is an intermediate level of planning within the company that deals with the entrepreneurial growth and change in the firm in terms of products and markets. The P/HR department must prepare fairly specific three-year plans for all its activities to support the major changes in the firm's development. It must also prepare more specific plans for acquiring future managers, key personnel, and total number of employees in support of company requirements over the next three years.

In addition, if a new company is to be acquired, plans for integrating the "culture" of the new company, the policies (and labor contracts), training, compensation, benefits, etc., must be prepared. If a company is to be divested, or sold, by the firm, the P/HR department must have plans for separation, transfer, or retention of key people.

Operations Planning

At the lowest business profit-center levels, the one-year operating plans are the blueprints for the year ahead. Detailed monthly forecasts of sales, revenue, expenses, as well as planned accomplishments and utilization of human and material resources are documented. P/HR planning at this level includes detailed plans for all HR activities covered in the subsequent chapters of this book. These plans are designed to support the manpower requirements of other managers throughout the company. They include such diverse activities as recruiting certain skilled engineers, developing a compensation structure, assisting a manager with the design of a new job, developing leadership in managers, and creating concepts to improve work climate.

Short-Term Activities Planning

P/HR faces many varied short-term (one day to one month) problems. For example, replacement of unskilled workers who leave the company, the handling of employee benefits, the review of accident reports, and the processing of union grievances are required to support short-term company activities.

THE PLANNING APPROACH TO DETERMINING MANPOWER REQUIREMENTS

All P/HR activities, it may be recalled, are directed toward supplying and maintaining a productive workforce within cost–benefit constraints. This requires planning to obtain the right mix of the right number of workers at the right time. The basic premises for such planning are the company's strategy and the sales forecast. Plans that determine the manpower requirements are, in a sense, the central focus for all other HR planning and subsequent action.

In a very small firm, the owner can easily plan for staffing of the firm. The nature of the work will likely remain stable, and the owner knows the few employees personally and keeps informed about their plans. It is easy to anticipate retirement of an employee and prepare for replacement. But what of firms with 100 employees or several hundred thousand employees? Organization structure and jobs are continually changing. New skills are continually being demanded. The number and variety of employees' career goals complicate planning.

In order to discuss manpower planning fully, we will follow the detailed system of Exhibit 4–3. The role of the P/HR department is to achieve the objective—the net change required—by supplying the support activities on the rights, which are derived from manpower needs. We will touch briefly on inputs from line managers and the cooperating roles of P/HR and line managers.

Corporate Objectives and Strategy

The responsibility for establishing strategy is that of top management. The P/HR department provides information about human resources to top management in the conduct of strategic planning. For example, what should upper management know about the implications of doubling the size of the company in the next five years? What costs are involved in finding and hiring people with rare skills? What are the long-range implications of government labor laws and public policy? What will labor costs be five years hence for alternative strategies?

At the same time, top management must convey answers to P/HR to questions such as: Will we employ our own sales force or use manufacturers' representatives? Will we subcontract all production except finished as-

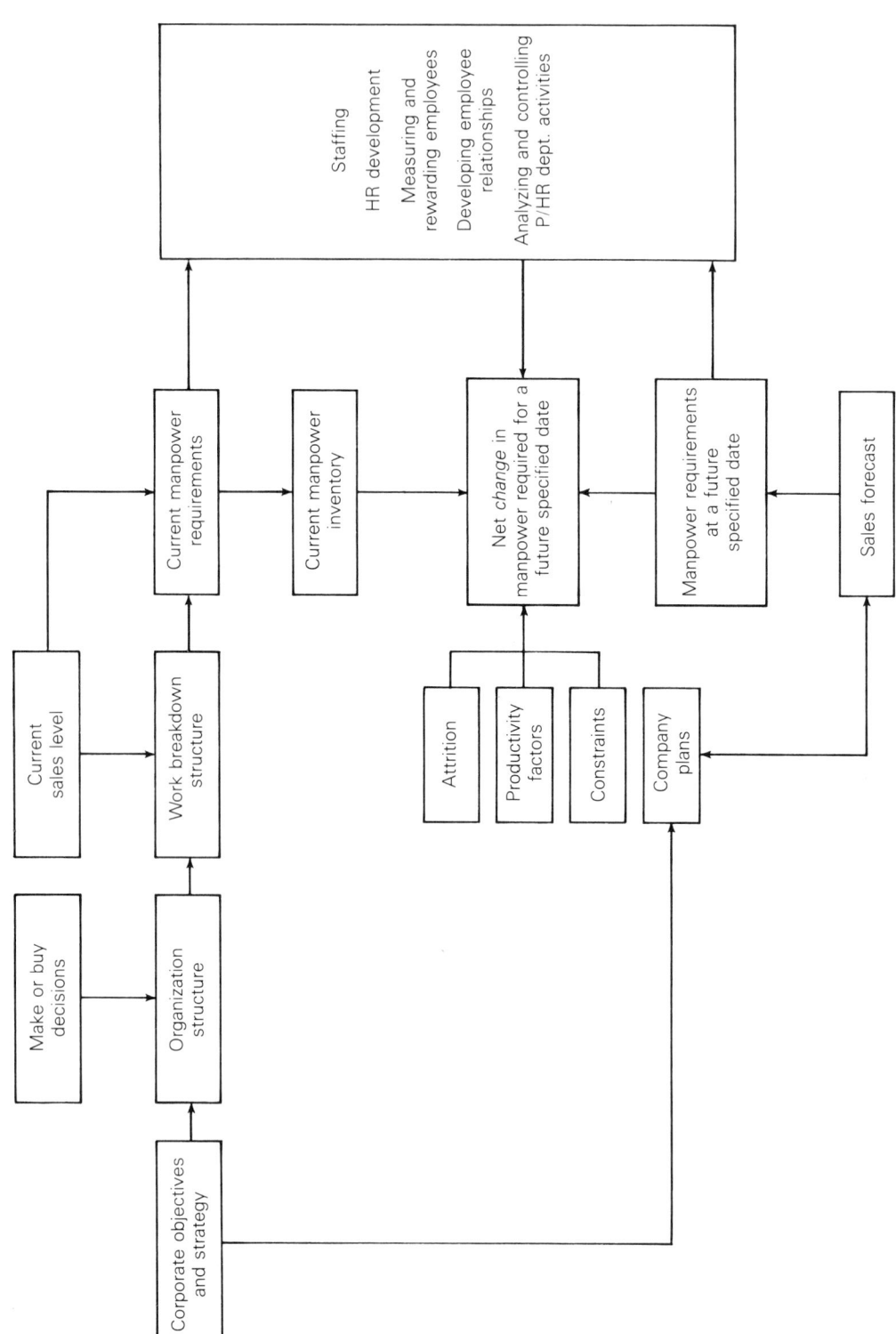

EXHIBIT 4–3
Manpower-planning model.

sembly? Will we use computer service bureaus or establish our own computer facilities? Answers to such questions provide the starting point for manpower planning.

Organization Structure

"Structure follows strategy" is a generally accepted proposition. As the strategy of a company evolves from a single-product firm through various stages to a large diversified organization, *organization structure* keeps changing. The question of whether to run a lean company or a highly staffed company also influences the structural decision. If we compare two large companies, Fuqua and Parker Hannifin, for example, we note that Fuqua has a staff of about 70 at its headquarters in Atlanta, while Parker Hannifin has 1,500 at its headquarters in Cleveland.

In addition, the company's "make or buy" decisions will modify its structure and staffing requirements. Will the company make component parts or buy them for assembly? If providing a service, will parts of the service be subcontracted or not?

Sales, Work Breakdown Structure, and Current Manpower Requirements

The type of products, number of units of products, and the breakdown of the work into tasks lead to the immediate estimate of manpower requirements. Based on the planning process results in Exhibit 4–3, we may develop a practical method for listing current manpower requirements as shown in Exhibit 4–4.

EXHIBIT 4–4
Plan relating work breakdown structure and sales to current manpower requirements.

Organization Structure
↓
Structure of Tasks (Work Breakdown Structure)
↓
Current Positions
↓

Sales Volume → Sales Mix →

Product	No. of Units	Engineers Required	Sales people Required	...	...	Drill Press Operator
A	4,000	1	1			0
B	3,000	0	1½			1
C	15,000	3	2			0
D	20,000	10	2			2
E	14,000	2	2			1
F	5,000	1	1			0
G	2,000	0	½			0

From Exhibit 4–4, we note that the type of tasks to be performed to achieve organizational objectives leads to the defining of positions. A position may or may not be filled, depending on the requirements to produce types and numbers of products at a particular time. Thus, sales volume and sales mix establishes current requirements for people to fill established positions.

Current Manpower Inventory

It would be nice and efficient if the number and types of people with specific skills on hand match current requirements. Sometimes a company may have too many people with a particular skill and have too few with another desired skill. Companies, therefore, maintain a master file of employees and their skills to compare with their needs—a *manpower inventory*. A report may, therefore, be prepared to list every position filled, the name of the incumbent, and the level of the skills possessed by the incumbent.

Future Manpower Requirements

In the planning approach, we determine the current manpower inventory, prepare, for example, a five-year business plan, plan for the manpower requirements over each of the years, and then find the net change year by year. As indicated in Exhibit 4–3, this net change is achieved by hiring employees, attrition, productivity factors, and constraints. Sometimes companies plan to hire key people in excess of their needs in anticipation of business expansion and large contracts. Even small companies may plan to hire slightly in advance of their needs to make sure that they are available when needed. These practices increase the net change between "required" inventories at present and some time in the future.

Plans for future demand are usually prepared in the form of various tables. Exhibit 4–5, for example, shows demand by type of position and year over a three-year period. Planning for the first year is more detailed, that is, month by month.

The estimate of human resources by class of worker is also useful in planning for:

1. Training, benefits, etc.
2. Payroll costs
3. Equipment required
4. Factory and office floor space

Exhibit 4–6 could be used as the basis of age distribution of employees so that there is a mixture of young, mature, and highly experienced workers. On the basis of these curves, a manpower planning table may be drawn up for various types of workers.

In Chapter 2, The Legal Environment for Human Resource Management, and in Chapters 6 and 7, Recruitment and Selection, we discuss the

EXHIBIT 4–5
Plan showing demand by type of position over a three-year period.

Job Class	19X1 J F M A M J J A S O N D	Beginning of 19X2	19X3
President and Vice Presidents			
Managers and Supervisors			
Scientists			
Engineers			
Marketing professionals			
Production professionals			
Accounting professionals			
Finance professionals			
Technicians			
Clerical			
Craftspeople			
Unskilled			

nature of EEO and affirmative action in staffing. The planning, which precedes recruitment and selection, involves preparing profiles of the work force of the future in terms of EEO classifications. In other words, we find that the future work force must be described in terms of:

1. Number of workers
2. Types of workers (skills)
3. Age distribution of workers
4. EEO classes of workers (minority workers) and their numbers

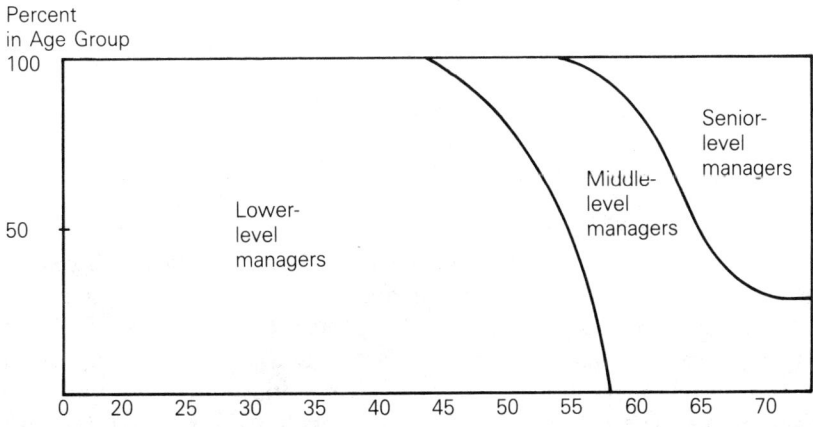

EXHIBIT 4–6
Age-distribution plan.

Exhibit 4–7 shows a form for this last purpose. Notice that it specifically refers to progression lines, the optimal lines of promotion through the organization for a given position.

Net Change to Satisfy Future Manpower Requirements

Future manpower requirements are derived basically from business plans and the sales forecast as indicated in Exhibits 4–2 and 4–3. The net *change* in requirements from the present to a specified future date, however, is affected by attrition, productivity factors, and certain constraints.

Attrition The final HR plan shows not only the people employed at various dates but the flow into and out of the company. When people leave the company, for whatever reason, this is called *attrition*. Plans usually, but not always, are made to replace them. People leave the company because they (1) quit for professional opportunities or personal reasons, (2) are terminated by the company, (3) are laid off indefinitely, (4) become disabled or too ill to work, (5) are drafted into military service, (6) retire, or (7) die.

Although it is not usually considered attrition, a rise in absenteeism that is chronic has the same effect as if employees left the company.

For a particular division within a company, attrition also appears due to promotion or transfer to some other division within the company. Somewhat analogous is the "loan" of an executive to a government agency for one to several years or leaves of absence for extended periods of time (say, for educational purposes).

Productivity Factors Fewer workers may be needed to close the gap between present inventory and future greater demand if the company can find ways to increase the *productivity*, or output per hour, of its workers. Three ways that this may be accomplished are:

1. Better management work planning, learning-curve benefits, automation, and increased investment in equipment for workers
2. Improved leadership and motivation
3. Productivity programs

The first method is primarily the responsibility of line management. The function of the P/HR manager is to estimate reduction in work force needs because of such improved management actions. In particular, the P/HR manager will likely provide the expertise on learning-curve impact. *Learning curves*, also known in manufacturing as *manufacturing progress functions* and in marketing as *experience curves*, have a major impact on HR requirements. "Learning" is the cause of reduced manhours or total costs to produce a product. Such learning actually includes improved management,

EXHIBIT 4-7
Example of a form showing profiles of the work force by EEO classification.

EEO WORK FORCE ANALYSIS
By Job Title Within Department

Department _____

Page _____ of _____
As of _____ 19___
     (Date)

Job Group No.	Job Title	EEO-1 Category	Salary Code	All Employees			Minority Employees										Progression Lines
							Male				Female					
				Total	Male	Female	Blk.	Asian	Hisp.	N. Amer.	Blk.	Asian	Hisp.	N. Amer.	Total	

TOTAL—THIS PAGE

GRAND TOTAL—LAST PAGE

BLK.—BLACK HISP.—HISPANIC N. AMER.—NATIVE AMERICAN

FOR PROGRESSION LINES INDICATE 1, 2, 3, 4, ETC.

115

EXHIBIT 4–8
A learning curve showing reduced labor hours per unit due to learning.

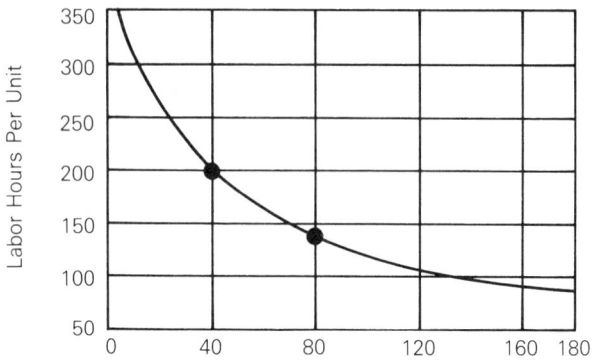

Cumulative Number of Units Produced

improved processes and procedures, and improved application of mental and manual skills to produce a product.

The model that seems to fit such a learning situation well is one that shows a fixed reduction of time or cost every time production is doubled. For example, in Exhibit 4–8, if we go from cumulative production of 40 units to production of 80 units, our cumulative production has doubled. The learning reduces the cost or time to 70 percent (140 hours down from 200) for the 80th unit compared to the 40th unit. In the aircraft industry, a reduction to 80 percent of the previous value of time or cost for each doubling of production is typical.

The introduction of the computer may or may not increase productivity, but increased capital investment per worker in the form of robots will likely produce tremendous gains in the near future.

The P/HR manager is responsible for developing leadership training programs and advising line management on methods for achieving increased motivation. In Chapter 8, Motivation and Leadership for Productivity, we will discuss in detail how the extension of improved leadership to productivity programs can lead to dramatic gains. For example, compare a Japanese auto production line to its American counterpart. The Japanese system is characterized by (1) worker involvement in ways to avoid rework and (2) increased investment per worker. Look at the results (based on Harbour & Associates data).

	Japan	U.S.
Parts stamped/hour	550	325
Manpower per press line	1	7 to 13
Time needed to build a small car	31 hours	51 hours

Constraints Not only do productivity factors reduce the net change in manpower numbers and mix, but certain constraints may reduce or change the characteristics of the net difference. These constraints are:

1. EEO and affirmative action requirements
2. Overtime policies and legal limits on overtime
3. Machine and facility constraints
4. Cash flow constraints

The EEO and affirmative action requirements, in theory, should not affect the number of people required. It is possible, however, that in order to fulfill minority hiring requirements, an employer may have to hire an individual who is qualified for a job but perhaps does not have the experience or training of an alternative non-minority candidate. This represents a constraint that influences productivity.

Another constraint that affects flexibility of operations and number of people hired is state law on overtime. Some state laws may impose limitations on the hours per week or per pay day that an employee may work. When the overtime limit is reached on an extended basis, the company will have to hire additional workers (or delay deliveries of products).

Equipment and facilities are required for production workers as well as office workers. If equipment is not on hand or the company cannot obtain it or afford to buy it within a certain time period, it would not make sense to plan for the people who would operate such equipment. Delays in building a new plant fall in the same category as lack of equipment. These situations impose constraints upon the planned human resource requirements.

Cash flow must also be considered in establishing the net change in manpower. The company must have working capital and cash available to employ additional people. If internally generated funds or external sources of funds are not sufficient, the company must reduce its expansion plans.

FORECASTING MANPOWER REQUIREMENTS

Planning represents a series of actions established in advance to achieve a desired result. Forecasting represents an estimate of the future. Thus, in the *manpower forecast*, we do not follow a logical chain of company actions but rather use some model or technique that jumps from past data to the future. Forecasting methods range from simple projections to sophisticated models. Because forecasting methods are usually mechanical (statistical or modelling) methods, the computer is a very effective tool.

Forecasting manpower requirements is a quicker, simpler, and usually less accurate approach than deriving future requirements from business and organizational planning. Forecasting is most useful for making aggregate estimates of manpower to answer "what if . . . ?" questions posed by planners. Following are some brief descriptions of forecasting techniques and models, including regression methods and composite department demand. More sophisticated are total planning system models, such as fractional flow and contingency models.

Trend Projection

The number of people in the company may be plotted against time, and a straight line or sketched curve may be drawn as a projection into the future. This may be accurate enough because such a *trend projection* may be revised annually to give good short-term estimates and rough long-term estimates.

For mathematical elegance, time series analysis and exponential smoothing methods may be used, but there is little assurance they will produce more accurate long-term forecasts.

Regression Methods

There is obviously a causal relationship between number of employees and sales. Based on past data, a *regression* curve may be fitted (see Exhibit 4–9). If sales can be forecast reasonably well, total employee requirements may then be forecast from the regression line. Suppose sales for the third year in the future are forecasted as 350,000 units. Then, from Exhibit 4–9, the number of employees would be forecast as 3,000.

Composite Department Demand

Each department may be asked to estimate the number of employees it will require on a specified future date. These estimates may then be combined into a *composite demand* figure for the forecast of total requirements.

Fractional Flow Models

Based on a *fractional flow model,* a table may be established showing the fraction of the people in one type of occupation and state (time period) that

EXHIBIT 4–9
Regression line for forecasting manpower demand.

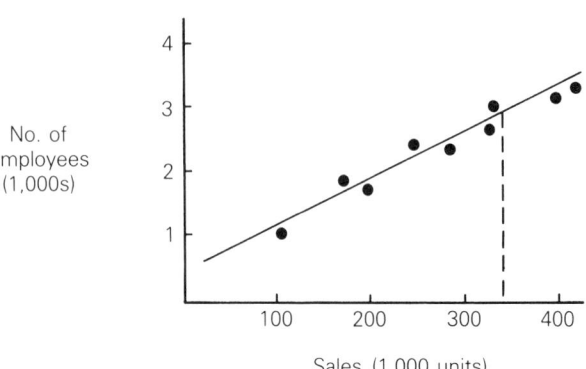

move to another occupation in the next time period. A portion of such a table would appear as follows:

To From	Retire/Leave	Salesperson	Sales Mgr.	Budget Analyst	...
Salesperson	.01	.90	.02	.01	
Budget clerk	.05	.10	0	.25	
⋮					

In this example, the first line shows that one percent of salespeople quit or retire; 90 percent remain salespeople; 2 percent become managers; and one percent become budget analysts during the next time period (usually one year). It is apparent that a very large table may be required to show the flow from positions to other positions.

Contingency Model

A forecast of manpower requirements may depend on factors outside the control of the company. In such cases, a *contingency forecasting model* may be used to produce what is shown in Exhibit 4–10, which shows three scenarios: (1) A contract to supply a large customer such as the U. S. government will mean hiring a large number of people. If the contract is not obtained, (2) normal growth will be expected. If, however, (3) a product line must be dropped later, the forecast of manpower is quite different.

Decision Models with Fluctuating Product Demand

In order to develop solutions to aggregate planning problems, mathematical models have been structured to minimize product costs by determining the

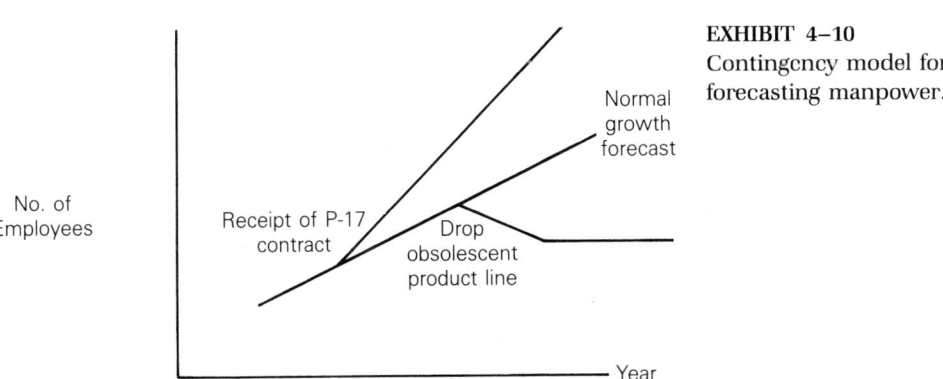

EXHIBIT 4–10
Contingency model for forecasting manpower.

work force size and production rate for future periods.[1] Four of these methods are:

1. The Linear Decision Rule (LDR) consists of two linear equations, one for the production in a specified time period and one for work force size for the same period. These are derived by minimizing a quadratic cost function.[2]
2. The Search Decision Rule (SDR) is a computerized method that starts with a trial set of work force sizes and production rates for 10 periods. Small changes are made to see if the cost is reduced. If not, the search goes back to the starting point, and changes in a different direction are tried.
3. Parametric Production Planning employs a heuristic search procedure to develop the coefficients for two decision rules for production rate and work force size. Like LDR, it assumes a quadratic cost function for work force, overtime, production rate, and inventory.[3]
4. The Management Coefficients model employs statistical analysis of management's past decisions to determine coefficients for the decision rule.[4]

FORECASTING MANPOWER SUPPLY

We have looked at various models to help the P/HR department determine future *needs*. Now we turn to the question of *supply*. Forecasting of *manpower supply* is useful because it provides (1) input to the recruiting program, (2) input to future labor cost estimates, (3) input to training needs, (4) input to capital investment plans (for equipment such as robots), and (5) input to production capacity forecasts. Forecasts of supply cover *external* supply and *internal* supply.

External Supply

The forecasting of future labor supply may be approached by starting with current supply data and then estimating the impact of various factors in the future. The principal factors to be considered are:

1. Economic conditions and unemployment rate
2. Anticipated wages and salaries
3. Participation rate of the labor force, with attention to minority groups, homemakers, retired people, and their respective leisure-vs.-income preferences
4. Part-time workers and moonlighting workers
5. Alien workers, legal and illegal
6. Local labor market
7. Mobility characteristics of various types of workers (to broaden a firm's labor market)

8. Manipulation of supply by labor unions through control of apprentice programs, etc.
9. Government policies such as funding of training programs, student financial aid, etc.

The forecast of the total available labor force and *labor force participation* by occupational group may provide a company with some indication of tight labor markets to come. The *Monthly Labor Review* contains articles from time to time dealing with such aspects of supply on a national basis. Econometric models are used to break out the total labor force into occupations and then into areas of the country.

"Participation" models may be used to show the percentage of workers of various types and classes that will be employed in the future. These projections depend on forecasts of technology and wages.

Robots Join the Working Force

New technology is making it possible to replace increasingly skilled workers. The latest computer-controlled robots are considerably more versatile than their simple-minded predecessors of just two years ago. And a new generation of robots that "see" and "feel" and even "think" is emerging from the laboratories. Some automation experts say that such smart robots could displace 65% to 75% or more of today's factory work force.

Source: *Business Week*, June 9, 1980, p. 62–63.

Internal Supply

The internal supply at a future date may be separated from the number hired up to that point for purposes of forecasting (see Exhibit 4–11). We start with our present inventory (numbers of workers by type) and trace through time the movement of workers (1) out of the organization, and (2) up (or down) the organization or to different types of jobs because of promotion (demotion) or training. Generally, the number of unskilled and low-skilled workers remaining may be projected from historical data. For managers and key personnel, individuals should be projected in their positions from year to year over the planning horizon. Such projection, once again, takes into consideration the career objectives of these employees as well as their potential.

The P/HR department plays a very important role in presenting data so that managers may easily plan for position backups, for promotion and lateral moves, for timing of such moves, and hiring of key people at all levels over the planning horizon. An example of a personnel replacement chart that might be prepared by P/HR on the basis of data from line managers is shown in Exhibit 4–12.

PLANNING AND STAFFING

EXHIBIT 4–11
Planning requirements and sources.

Estimated Supply and Requirements (Calendar year, beginning January 1)		Positions		
		P1	P2	P3
19X0	(Present) Distribution	320	50	496
19X1	Requirements	331	52	501
	Internal supply	290	40	420
	Recruits needed	41	12	81
19X2	Requirements	340	53	529
	Internal supply	301	42	426
	Recruits needed	39	11	103
19X3	Requirements	360	55	550
	Internal supply	310	42	440
	Recruits needed	50	13	110

Other information shown on some management replacement charts may be: name of incumbent as well as position for which backups are listed, salaries of individuals listed, length of time of each individual in the job, and total company service time for each individual. The backup information for the management chart is contained in the skills inventory data base. With modern computers, such information is available on a video display screen in a matter of seconds.

Matching Demand and Supply

The future internal supply may be controlled to some extent by management policies. Training policy is one way to change the mix and level of skill. One way to control attrition is by hoarding skilled employees such as engineers in anticipation of a future shortage, a technique used by large companies engaged in defense work. Compensation and retirement policies can also slow attrition. Overtime work may also be used to increase supply to some degree. The decision to retain or terminate lower-quality employees also affects the internal supply.

SUMMARY

The modern systems approach to managing human resources requires the establishment of goals and objectives followed by careful planning. We have listed the advantages of such an approach to manpower planning, which

PLANNING FOR HUMAN RESOURCES **123**

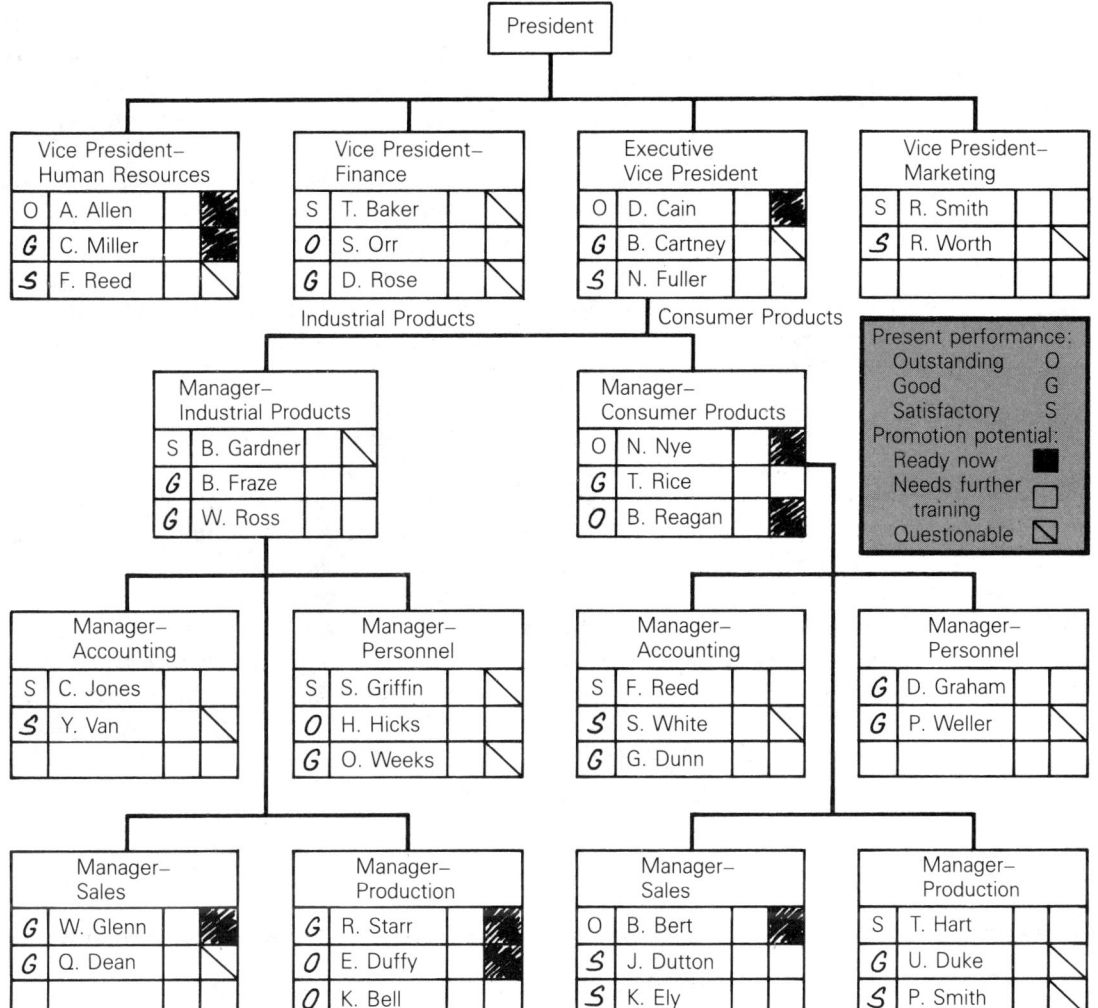

EXHIBIT 4–12
Management personnel replacement chart.

should start from overall company plans at the strategic, intermediate, and operational levels.

The P/HR manager has the responsibility for having the right number of the right kind of people at all times. Employment policy planning and implementation yields (1) effective and efficient use of human resources, (2) more developed and satisfied employees, and (3) better implementation of company business plans.

The human resource planning process is a joint responsibility of the P/HR department and line management, with each performing specified functions in the process. The P/HR manager should be consulted during all business planning. In particular, at the start, the P/HR department should provide expert advice on organization structure and position design. Organizational structure establishes the framework for the subsequent steps in manpower planning.

Once the current and future manpower requirements have been established, the dynamics of the manpower planning model take over. The factors bridging the time span are the sales forecast, attrition, productivity factors, and internal and external constraints. Future manpower requirements should be estimated by total number of employees, by types (skills) of employees, and by age distribution of managers and key workers. In addition, future requirements should be estimated by EEO classifications.

Future manpower demand may be forecasted or it may be planned for as part of the business planning in a model of causal events and company policies. Forecasting is the simpler process. Forecasting methods commonly used are regression methods relating manpower needs to sales and composite department demand. Total planning system models or simpler fractional flow models, and contingency models are sometimes used.

Manpower supply, consisting of the number and characteristics of available workers, should be estimated so that the company can plan for shortages in the future. The supply of workers comes from internal and external sources. Appropriate and timely policies and actions by the company will yield an increased supply. In particular, management replacement should be carefully planned by using such tools as replacement charts and useful personnel inventory records.

KEY CONCEPTS

Human resource planning	Trend projection
Corporate strategy	Regression
Organization structure	Composite demand
Manpower inventory	Fractional flow model
Attrition	Contingency forecasting model
Productivity	Manpower supply
Robot	Labor force participation
Manpower forecast	

NOTES

1. This section is based on Robert G. Murdick, *Product/Operations Management for Small Businesses* (Worthington, OH.: Publishing Horizons, undated).
2. E. H. Bowman, "Consistency and Optimality in Managerial Decision Making," *Management Science*, January 1963.
3. C. C. Holt, F. Modigliani, J. F. Muth, and H. A. Simon. *Planning Production, Inventories, and Work Force* (Englewood Cliffs, N. J.: Prentice-Hall, 1960).
4. W. B. Lee, and B. M. Khumawala, "Simulation Testing of Aggregate Production Planning Models in an Implementation Methodology," *Management Science*, February 1974.

REVIEW AND DISCUSSION QUESTIONS

1. Give a specific actual or hypothetical example for each advantage of human resource planning. (For example, "By means of human resource planning, IBM was able to shift smoothly more personnel to its Boca Raton, Florida, facilities in time for the rapid expansion of the personal computer market.)
2. Discuss how human resource planning fits in with corporate planning as shown in Exhibit 4–1.
3. What is the time span, approximately, for (a) strategic plans, (b) intermediate-range plans, (c) operating plans, and (d) activity plans?
4. Define (a) issues analysis, (b) programming requirements, (c) integrated control requirements, (d) implementation.
5. Distinguish between the concepts of planning for manpower demand and forecasting manpower demand.
6. Explain with a simple example a simulation to obtain a forecast of manpower demand.
7. Discuss the impact of career planning on the planning for manpower requirements.
8. Discuss the relationship between organization structure and manpower planning. Consider such factors as staff services, number of levels of management, type of departmentation, and job enrichment.
9. Sketch a learning curve where the time required to produce a unit declines 80 percent every time production is doubled.
10. Select a company listed in *Moody's Industrials* and find the number of employees for the past 10 years. (Annual reports may also provide such information.) Plot these points on a graph and draw a trend line. How many employees do you forecast on this basis five years from now?
11. Prepare a list of major contingencies that could affect a contingency forecast of manpower requirements.
12. For each of the nine factors affecting external supply of manpower, indicate what condition (increase or decrease) of the factor will produce an increase in supply.

13. Develop a different, more elaborate, manager replacement chart than that given in the text.
14. Discuss the long-range impact of computers on manpower requirements of U.S. companies.
15. Discuss the long-range impact of robots on manpower requirements of U.S. companies.
16. Discuss the impact of the changing age-profile of the U.S. population on manpower supply 10 years hence.

BIBLIOGRAPHY

Atwater, Donald M., et al. "An Application of Human Resource Planning Supply–Demand Models." *Human Resource Management*, Vol. 5, No. 1, 1982.

Baytos, Lawrence M. "Nine Strategies for Productivity Improvement." *Personnel Journal*, July 1979.

Behling, Orlando, and Chester Schriesheim. *Organizational Behavior: Theory, Research, and Application*. Boston: Allyn and Bacon, 1976.

Bogart, Dodd H. "Changing Views of Organization." *Technological Forecasting and Social Change*, 1973.

Bryant, Donald T., and Richard J. Niehaus, Eds. *Manpower Planning and Organization Design*. New York: Plenum Press, 1978.

Cohen, Stanford. *Labor in the United States*, 5th ed. Columbus, OH.: Merrill, 1979.

Cummings, Larry, and Chris J. Berger. "Organization Structure: How Does It Influence Attitudes and Performance?" *Organization Dynamics*, Autumn 1976.

Drucker, Peter F. *Management: Tasks, Responsibilities, Practice*. New York: Harper & Row, 1973.

Galbraith, William F. *Organization Design*. Reading, Mass.: Addison-Wesley, 1977.

Gehrman, Douglas B. "Objective Based Human Resources Planning." *Personnel Journal*, December 1981.

Goggin, William C. "How the Multidimensional Structure Works at Dow Corning." *Harvard Business Review*, January–February 1974.

Grinold, Richard C., and Kneale T. Marshall. *Manpower Planning Models*. New York: Elsevier North-Holland, 1977.

Kelleher, Edward J., and Kay Lillig Cotter. "An Integrative Model for Human Resource Planning and Strategic Planning." *Human Resource Planning*, Vol. 5, No. 1, 1982.

Koenig, Richard, Jr., and David Pierson. "Human Resource Planning: Three Configurations." *Human Resource Planning*, Vol. 5, No. 4, 1982.

MacCrimmon, Kenneth R. "Improving Decision Making With Manpower Management Systems." *The Business Quarterly*, Autumn 1971.

Mintzberg, Henry. *The Structuring of Organizations: A Synthesis of Research*. Englewood Cliffs, N. J.: Prentice-Hall, 1979.

Murdick, Robert G. *Production/Operations Management for Small Businesses*. Worthington, OH.: Publishing Horizons, undated.

Patten, Thomas H., Jr. *Manpower Planning and the Development of Human Resources*. New York: Wiley, 1971.

Ray, Keith. "Managerial Manpower Planning—A Systematic Approach." *Long-Range Planning,* April 1977.
Reynierse, James H. "A Goal Model of Human Resource Planning." *Human Resource Planning,* Vol. 5, No. 1, 1982.
"Robots Join the Labor Force." *Business Week,* June 9, 1980.
Scott, Bruce R. "The Industrial State: Old Myths and New Realities." *Harvard Business Review,* March–April 1973.
Shetty, Y. K., and Howard M. Carlisle. "A Contingency Model of Organization Design." *California Management Review,* Fall 1972.
Skibbons, Gerald J. *Organizational Evolution.* New York: AMACOM, 1974.
Stieglitz, Harold. "On Concepts of Corporate Structure," *Conference Board Record,* February 1974.
Walker, James W. *Human Resource Planning.* New York: McGraw-Hill, 1980.
Weisblat, D. I., and J. C. Stucki. "Goal-Oriented Organization at Upjohn." *Research Management,* January 1974.

Work Design and Job Analysis

CHAPTER OUTLINE

Work Design and Organizational Output
Productivity □ Affective Responses □ Relation of Work Design to other HR Functions □ HR Management View of Work Design

Hierarchy of Work
General Approach to Job Design
Classical Design of Jobs
Expectancy Model of Job Design
Job Characteristics Model of Job Design
Major Job Design Factors from Research
Job Design and Class of Work
Documentation of Job Design
Job Analysis Overview
Major Steps in Job Analysis
Job Analysis Techniques
Task (or Job) Inventory Concept □ Interview Guidelines □ Functional Job Analysis □ Position Analysis Questionnaire (PAQ) □ Work Performance Survey System (WPSS) □ Management Work Analysis

Job Redesign

OBJECTIVES

1. Differentiate between work design and job analysis
2. Explain the purposes and uses of job descriptions and job specifications
3. Identify the uses of job analyses for P/HR management
4. Identify the core job dimensions for job enrichment in the job characteristics model of job design
5. List the major steps in job analysis
6. Describe four general methods for collecting job analysis information
7. Describe the general features of FJA, PAQ, WPSS, and MPDQ

SPOTLIGHT:
Sidney Gael

Sidney Gael is an industrial psychologist at the Central Services Organization, Incorporated. Prior to the divestiture of the Bell System telephone companies, Dr. Gael was employed by AT&T, where, for 16 years, he conducted research on a broad spectrum of personnel issues. He received his B.S. Degree in Psychology from Hunter College (1957), his M.S. Degree from Pennsylvania State University (1959), and his Ph.D. Degree in Industrial Psychology from Ohio State University (1966).

Dr. Gael's research, method development, and writing have spanned many topics in industrial organizational psychology. He has developed a job inventory questionnaire approach to job analysis, the Work Performance Survey System (WPSS). Having conducted research on job analysis, methods, and procedures, Dr. Gael is also the author of the recently published *Job Analysis*. He has directed a series of nationwide test-validation projects that served as the basis for setting employment test standards for many Bell System jobs, and he has served as expert witness before the Federal Court in equal employment opportunity litigation. Other current interests include job performance evaluation and appraisal, and development of a Task Oriented Rating approach to performance evaluation.

Comments by Sidney Gael

Job analysis is a process whereby a job is broken down into its component parts, and the parts (elements, tasks, functions, duties, modules) are studied to determine the nature of the work. The term *job analysis* implies that there is an approach to analyzing jobs and that, of course, is not the case. There are many approaches to analyzing jobs—observation, interviews, diaries, questionnaires, etc.—and several disciplines utilize some form of job analysis as a means to accomplishing a variety of objectives; for example, industrial engineers study elemental motions to develop efficient work methods and achieve economy objectives.

When job design or redesign is the objective, job analysis is indispensable. Fortunately, job designers hardly ever have to start from scratch because few functions are entirely new. Much of job design, therefore, consists of redistributing activities and reconfiguring existing jobs. Even under circumstances where jobs are entirely new, imaginative job designers have been able to describe future activities accurately. In fact, after the analytic techniques were developed, future activities were forecast rather routinely by the United States Air Force and the National Aeronautics and Space Administration for space missions long before any space flights became a reality.

Most job analysis techniques can be applied only in situations where jobs exist. With tasks as a starting point, a bottom-up approach can be used for job (and organization) design or redesign when jobs are in place. Tasks performed by job incumbents can be determined and grouped into larger, somewhat homogeneous work activities, such as functions. When jobs do not yet exist, a panel of experts can use an organization's objectives as a starting point, a top-down approach, and identify the outputs that must be produced to attain the objectives and the functions that must be performed to produce the outputs. Functions can then be broken down into tasks. With the top-down approach, it is not necessary to refer to jobs at all to analyze tasks and functions. The panel of experts, in this case, provides the details about function and task attributes, such as task importance, whereas in a bottom-up approach, task attribute information can be provided by job incumbents and supervisors.

At AT&T we became interested in developing a job inventory questionnaire approach to job analysis. A job inventory questionnaire is composed of a comprehensive list of tasks that are performed to accomplish a job or set of jobs. Respondents are asked questions about each task, such as how important is the task to your job, and how much time do you devote to task performance. The questionnaire is structured so that job incumbents, supervisors, and other job experts can be surveyed about tasks incumbents perform. The primary reasons for adopting the job inventory approach to job analysis was because detailed information can be obtained about job activities actually performed by job incumbents directly from the incumbents themselves even though they might be working at geographically dispersed sites, and results obtained with a single survey can be used to support several personnel programs. Further, a job analysis approach was desired that managers and their staffs could apply with only a modicum of training and consulting.

The job inventory approach that evolved was named the Work Performance Survey System (WPSS). Given the kind and volume of data collected with WPSS questionnaires, it was necessary to develop special computer programs to analyze survey responses. Again, the aim was to prepare computer programs that managers and their staffs could easily apply to analyze WPSS data.

To many people, going to work every day is a great joy. They seem to be always working on interesting problems along with interesting people. There is a sense of freedom because of the way organizational goals are set. Why is it, then, that other people dread going to work, suffer daily stress, and can hardly wait to get home again? Are these two situations simply inherent in organized work so that there must be the fortunates and the unfortunates? Or can all jobs be designed to inspire the workers and be matched to their needs? How does work design and the analysis of work actually performed relate to the whole system of human resource management? These questions are as vital to the person starting on his or her career as to the management of a company.

Work design is a broad term meaning the process of defining tasks and jobs to achieve both organizational and employee goals. It must, therefore, take into account the nature of the business (organizational interest), the organizational structure, the information flow and decision processes, the differences among employees, and the reward system. Within the broad scope of work design is the design of individual jobs, that is, *job design. Job analysis* is the process of obtaining information about jobs. *Job redesign* makes use of job analysis to redefine a job in terms of tasks, behaviors, education, skills, relationships, and responsibilities required.

With the rapid changes in technology, more new types of companies are starting up than in the past, and old companies require new types of organizations and jobs. As a result, job design has achieved a greater importance today. Also, as job analysis techniques have improved, the opportunities for greatly improving the redesign of jobs have increased. Thus, although the major focus of P/HR activities in the past has been on job analysis, the forward-looking P/HR manager will try to assist managers more by providing his or her expertise on the design of jobs.

In Exhibit 5–1, the sequence of job development is shown as work design, job design, job analysis, and job redesign. The design of work to achieve organizational objectives is obviously the responsibility of managers. Organization structure is one aspect of organizing work. Some control must be maintained over organization structure at the middle and lower levels to adhere to company policies, to maintain balance in levels in the hierarchy, and to prevent weird improvisations. Therefore, it is advisable to have the P/HR department review organization structures and "sign off" on them before they are implemented. In a positive way, P/HR may work with managers in developing the organization structures.

If jobs are carefully designed, much time may be saved on later job analyses and redesign. Good job design requires close coordination between the manager and the P/HR department. The practical obstacle is that managers usually operate under severe time restrictions, and want to put people to work immediately.

For the many jobs that are already established and have incumbents, the P/HR department has major responsibilities for description and analysis. Therefore, the major part of this chapter deals with these topics. Finally,

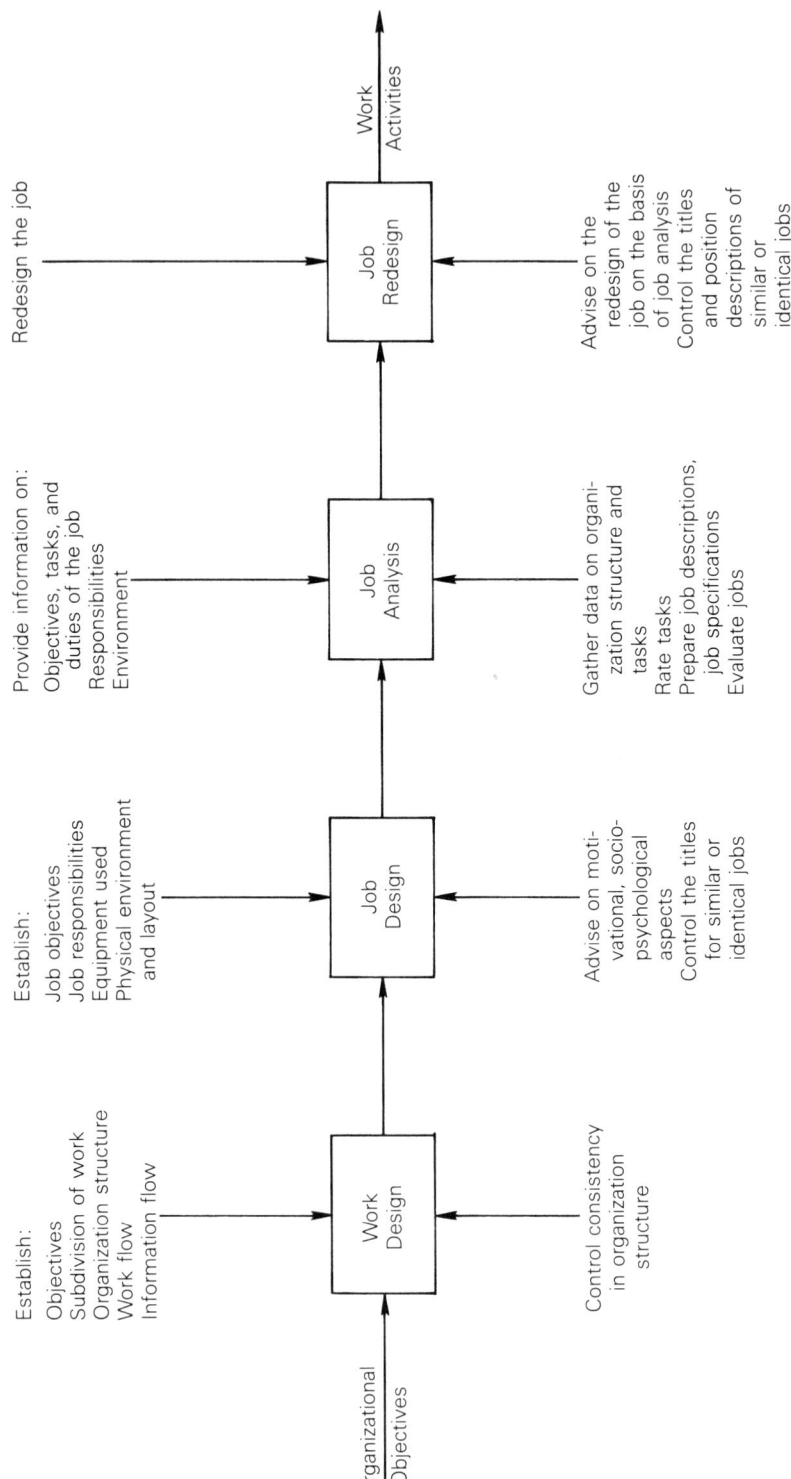

EXHIBIT 5–1
Responsibilities of managers and the P/HR department in the development of jobs.

in redesign of jobs, the P/HR department can bring to bear expertise in behavioral science, compensation, legal requirements and constraints, and productivity concepts to aid managers and provide adherence to company policies.

WORK DESIGN AND ORGANIZATIONAL OUTPUT

Work is the process by which productive systems convert inputs to outputs. Everybody in a business system does "work." The management of human resources must be concerned with the design of work to achieve organizational objectives.

Work design starts with the decisions about organizational structure. The division of the organization along product-based structures, geographical-based structures, functional structures, matrix structures, or adaptive project structures establishes the first approximation to work design. That is, organization structure specifies the types of job and job relationships. The further identification and specification of jobs is the detailed design of work.

Productivity

Work design describes the activities of a person on the job, the equipment and materials used, and the physical conditions of the job. The design process should also consider psychological, social, and physiological characteristics of the worker as well as technical capabilities of equipment and tools. In an assembly line situation, for example, the relation to the preceding job and to the subsequent job in the work process, along with information flow, are also factors in design of a particular job. Office jobs would, obviously, also share in the interdependence of job functions. It should now be apparent that the design of work and design of jobs for individuals is very complex. The ultimate goal is organizational productivity.

Affective Responses

Good work design will lead to good affective responses to the job by the worker. That is, the worker will feel that the "quality of work life (QWL)" is high and will experience satisfaction with work life. This is a desirable social benefit for businesses, which are so often criticized for lack of social responsibility.

Good work design will usually also increase motivation. Motivation relates back both to QWL and particularly to productivity. In the late 1970s, basic industries in the United States finally recognized that ignoring the behavioral aspects of work design in favor of an engineered rational approach often reduces motivation to an extremely low level.

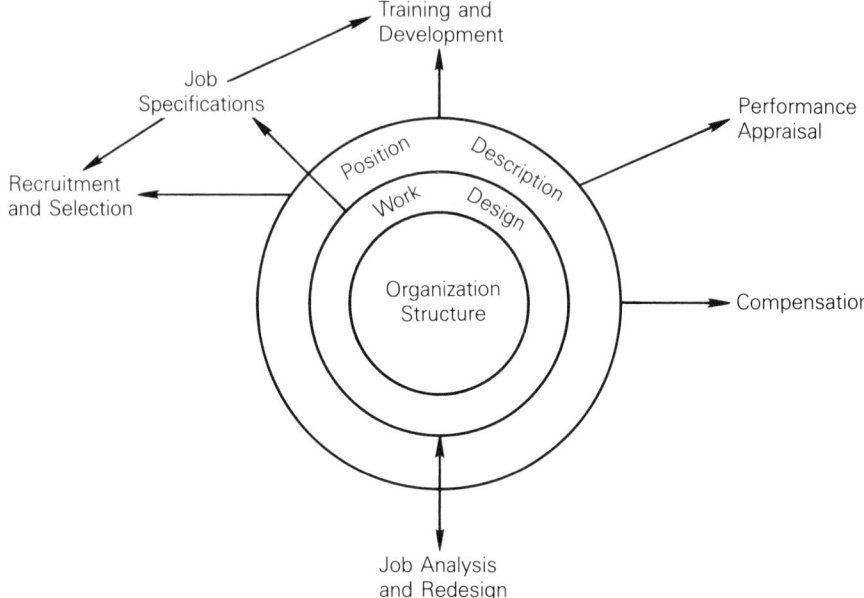

EXHIBIT 5–2
Work design as the basis for other HR functions.

Relation of Work Design to Other HR Functions

Work design is the basis for many of the other HR activities, shown in Exhibit 5–2. Specific chapters in this book will amplify on the following relationships. Work design is the basis for position descriptions and hence an amplification of the organization structure. Job analysis and redesign may lead to increased motivation and productivity (Chapter 8), and an improved description of the organization (Chapter 9). Job specifications—the description of required skills to perform a job—are derived from work design and job analysis. These specifications, along with position descriptions, are necessary for effective recruiting and selection (Chapters 6 and 7). Performance appraisals (Chapter 13) should be based on the objectives of a job as described in the position description. Therefore, training and development for an individual (Chapter 11) should follow from the position description and appraisal. Finally, compensation (Chapter 14) should be structured for the organization as a whole based on comparisons of the worth of jobs. "Worth" is determined from comparisons of tasks, responsibilities, and relationships specified in the jobs.

HR Management View of Work Design

One area of HR management that distinguishes the changing role of the P/HR manager is that of work design and job analysis. As employee value systems have changed, management has recognized the need to design jobs to be more personally fulfilling. The accelerated increase in research in organizational behavior has pointed the way to increased motivation and productivity. Proper job design offers workers opportunities to achieve social, psychological, and economic goals by achieving company goals. (The expectancy theory of motivation and path–goal theory of leadership, which deal with these concepts, will be explained more fully in Chapter 8.)

The ability of the modern P/HR manager to apply such theory to the design of work for improved productivity has greatly enhanced his influence. The P/HR department now can take the initiative in a proactive role to improve company profits directly. Work design and job analysis are ongoing activities that shape both the effectiveness and efficiency of the organization.

HIERARCHY OF WORK

It helps us understand what we are talking about if we define our terms. Such terms as work, task, jobs, and positions have been defined or not defined according to whether they are discussed by industrial engineers, job and wage analysts, project managers, or behavioral researchers. We will present a consistent set of definitions for terms as commonly used in the P/HR field.

- *Work* Work is the performance of physical and/or mental activities directed to the achievement of some economic or societal goal. In contrast, play consists of activities for self-amusement or diversion. When two or more people, as in an organization, are involved, then the design of work becomes a problem to be solved. How shall the total work be fragmented, and who shall do what parts? Equally important, how can jobs be enriched and workers motivated?
- *Element* An element of a job is the smallest step into which it is practical to subdivide any work activity without analyzing the separate motions, movements, and mental processes involved. An example would be the editing of an employee's change of status—the entering of the change in status in a computer. The *elements of a job* should not be confused with *elemental motions* such as specific separate motions of the fingers, hands, arms, and so on, involved in positioning work or operating equipment. These elemental motions are studied by industrial engineers to establish standard procedures and times.
- *Task* A task is a discrete work activity performed by an individual with a specific purpose and a clear-cut beginning and end. It may consist of several elements and is described by a statement that starts with an action verb and includes the object of that verb. Here is an example: "Estimate the costs for painting a building."
- *Duty* A duty is a large segment of the work performed by an individual and typically consists of several tasks. A secretary will likely have

many duties, such as handling the mail. This duty consists of opening the mail daily, answering some letters herself, discarding some types of mail, and classifying other types of mail for the manager by priority of urgency.
☐ *Position* A position consists of the tasks and duties that represent the work of a full-time individual. A position exists if it is defined and authorized whether or not it is filled at any moment in time.
☐ *Job* A job is a group of positions that are identical or very similar with respect to their major tasks and are sufficiently alike in total to justify their being covered by a single analysis.[1]
☐ *Occupation* An occupation is a general class of jobs corresponding to a discipline or specialty. Machinist, salesperson, accountant, and computer operator are examples.

GENERAL APPROACH TO JOB DESIGN

There are three approaches to job design used in practice. These are (1) top down; (2) bottom up; and (3) redesign whatever is in existence.

The top-down approach is related to Management by Objective (MBO) and organizational effectiveness. The overall grand objective of the organization is first established and the scope of the required work is defined. Next, the organization and organizational tasks are simultaneously subdivided *down* to the lowest level of management. At this point, managers hire people to accomplish the objectives for their units.

The bottom-up approach begins with the work at the lowest level of the organization. Job tasks are identified and combined in positions. Supervisors are employed as judged necessary by the number of positions. In practice, a top-down organization design meets the bottom-up organization structure fairly close to the first line supervisory level. That is, the bottom-up approach does not continue to combine positions and to form higher-level organizational units.

Most companies start small and expand. As a result, positions come into existence without much thought for scientific design. When a company becomes large enough to hire a trained P/HR manager, it becomes apparent that information is needed about the many jobs. At this point, the jobs may be analyzed and redesigned. Such analysis and redesign usually occur only at the level of shop workers and clerical personnel. With a proactive and knowledgeable P/HR manager, however, a review of the organizational structure and a top-down approach could be combined with job analysis.

The design of work and of jobs is a very complex activity. Consideration must be given to dynamic organizational objectives, basic policy variables in work design, the efficiency achieved by scientific methods, the workers' responses to their jobs, individual worker and work groups, a long list of factors affecting job design, and job design for classes of workers from operators to executives.

We will start first by presenting some useful models that can guide the manager. We will then expand on some of the topics just mentioned above. Throughout all of this, you should remember that jobs are continually changing, *with or without design*, as workers do whatever is necessary to meet changing objectives. Organization charts and job analysis are, therefore, often obsolete the day they are published.

CLASSICAL DESIGN OF JOBS

More pernicious and enduring than fractionation of work in organization and job structures is the effect of technological determinism which enters through the design of technical systems and their accompanying artifacts—machines, tools, computers, programs, etc. The dominant view of the 1960s which still is prevalent today, of the relationship of technology, organization and job structure, carefully nurtured for the past 150 years, is the dangerously simplistic perspective of technological determinism. This holds that technology evolves according to its own inherent logic and needs, regardless of social environment and culture. Further, it holds that to use technology effectively, and thus to gain its benefits for society, technological development and application must be uninhibited by any considerations other than those thought relevant by its developers—that is, engineers or technologists.[2]

This historical development of job design suggests a sequential process for job design. The initial approach to job design was technical task and job rationalization. The concepts of division of labor and specialization have appeared throughout history. The scientific study of work methods received its greatest impetus from Frederick W. Taylor and Frank Gilbreth and Lillian Gilbreth in the early 1900s.

In the classical model, the design of jobs is carried out by:

1. Determining the objectives of the work and the sequence of operations
2. Dividing the work into small job-tasks
3. Determining exactly how the job-tasks should be performed by applying the principles of motion economy (these principles are outlined in Exhibit 5–3); this involves the preparation of operations flow charts
4. Determining the time required for job-tasks and operations and establishing standard times; either stop-watches or predetermined time standard tables are used for this purpose
5. Developing a compensation method based on standard times

The classical model is directed toward shop or clerical workers who perform repetitive tasks. It has relatively little value to the design of work for executives, professionals, or others whose work is varied and mental. The concessions to mental characteristics of workers appear in the timing of

EXHIBIT 5-3
Outline of principles of motion economy.

Use of the Body	Arrangement of the Work Place	Design of Tools and Equipment
Hands should begin and complete motion at the same time.	There should be a definite and fixed place for tools close to the point of use and in sequence of motions.	The hands should be relieved of all work that can be done better by a jig, fixture, or foot-operated device.
Use hands rather than arms, arms rather than trunk whenever possible.		
Use smooth continuous motions in opposite and symmetrical directions.	Use proper illumination and protection from noise.	Tools and materials should be pre-positioned when possible.
Eye fixations should be as few and as close together as possible.	The seating height and work equipment should be adjusted to the individual worker.	Tools and equipment should be designed to provide the greatest possible mechanical advantage for hand and body movements.

work. An allowance is made for fatigue in setting a standard. In addition, if stop-watch timing is employed, a rating factor is introduced to find the time required for the "average" worker to perform a task.

A 1955 study ranked seven considerations for breaking work flow into tasks to achieve highest quality at lowest cost.[3] This was during a period of general prosperity and apparent satisfaction with the "good life." Ranked high on the list by engineers and data-processing managers was "making jobs as simple to perform as possible." Exhibit 5-4, which shows the rankings, also indicates that providing more job satisfaction was next to the bottom of factors considered in job design. The decline in productivity gains since that period of time suggests that the nature of the work force has changed. It now appears that gains in productivity may be achieved by making jobs more *complex* and interesting, rather than simple, and by involving workers in decisions on the other factors. In today's job design, we have to start somewhere and then modify the design because so many factors are involved. The classical approach can still provide this first rough conception of a job.

EXPECTANCY MODEL OF JOB DESIGN

The expectancy model of job design focuses on matching goals of individuals to the goals of the organization. The job must be designed so that the

EXHIBIT 5-4
Importance of seven considerations in breaking work flow into tasks to provide greatest product quality at lowest cost.

	Rank Order	
	Engineers	Systems Analysts
Maximizing throughout per unit of time	1	1
Efficient use of machine resources	2	2
Making jobs as simple to perform as possible	3	4
Reducing manpower	4	5
Providing management with better information	5	3
Providing more job satisfaction	6	6
Minimizing floor-space requirements	7	7

Source: James C. Taylor, "Job Design Criteria Twenty Years Later," in Louis E. Davis and James C. Taylor, Design of Jobs, 2nd ed. (Santa Monica, Ca.: Goodyear, 1979), p. 57.

individual sees a high probability that his or her goals will be achieved if a strong effort is made. Expectancy theory is discussed further in Chapter 8 because of its focus on motivation and leadership.

JOB CHARACTERISTICS MODEL OF JOB DESIGN

J. R. Hackman, G. R. Oldham, and others have developed, over a number of years, a model relating task characteristics to performance.[4] The model, shown in Exhibit 5-5, consists of Job Dimensions as inputs, Personal and Work Outcomes as outputs, and an intermediate stage of Psychological States. Consistent with the expectancy theory of motivation, the job characteristics model attempts to relate intrinsic worker satisfaction to an individual's need for growth.

From the model, it can be seen that meaningfulness of the work is dependent upon five important job dimensions.

1. Skill variety: the variety of skills required and the levels of these skills required; designing skill variety into a job is carried out by combining tasks and defining relationships between worker and person for whom the task output is prepared
2. Task identity: the degree to which tasks and the job result in production of a complete item or part
3. Task significance: the impact that the tasks and job have on other people
4. Autonomy: the degree to which the workers can plan and control their work through their own discretion, scheduling, and control
5. Feedback: the degree to which the worker receives direct, clear, and timely information about the effectiveness of his or her performance

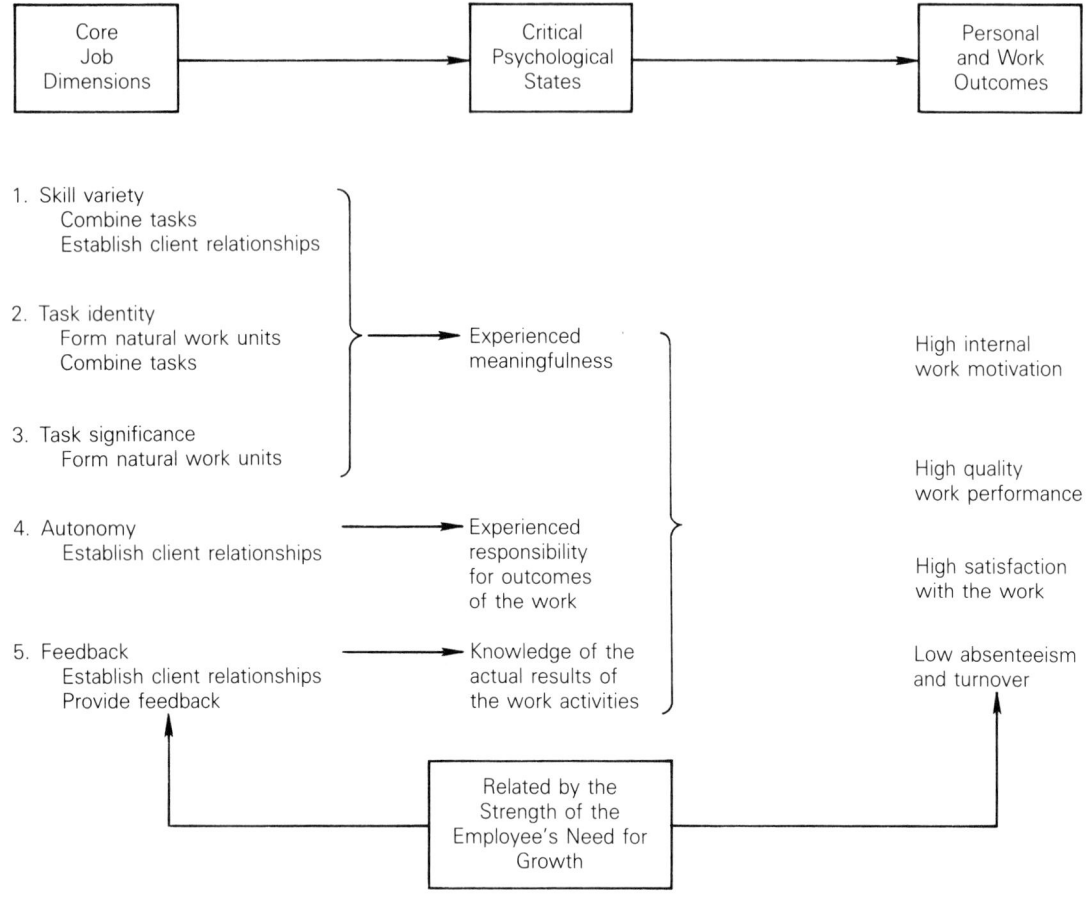

EXHIBIT 5-5
Job characteristics model of job design.
Source: Adapted from J. R. Hackman and G. R. Oldham, "Motivation Through the Design of Work: Test of a Theory," *Organizational Behavior and Human Performance* 16, 1976, 250–279.

For designing and redesigning a job and evaluating the effect of design changes on a worker, either prior estimates or work situation measurements may be used in a formula developed as part of a model. The Job Diagnostic Survey (JDS), developed by Hackman and Oldham, measures each of the five core dimensions. The summary score, which measures overall motivating potential of a job, is shown in Exhibit 5-6.

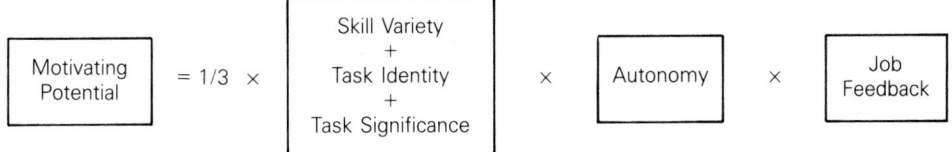

EXHIBIT 5-6
Computing the motivating potential score with the job diagnostic survey inputs.

MAJOR JOB DESIGN FACTORS FROM RESEARCH

Much research has now been done to identify factors in the job that influence work output and worker motivation and satisfaction. A lot of this research, however, has not been related to any of the systems models such as scientific management, the expectancy model, or job characteristics model. In the model of job design, Exhibit 5-7, we have extended the core job dimensions to the many underlying variables to be considered by the P/HR manager. Exhibit 5-7 shows the variables that underlie the core job dimensions of Exhibit 5-5. In addition, research has been conducted on some major job design variables included in the job design model and cross-related. The following discussion will be helpful to the practitioner, and will consider both individual and group tasks.

Contextual Factors The nature of work and a particular position or job is, plausibly, dependent on contextual factors and structural factors. Contextual factors consist of situational variables. The role of organization structure in work design has been discussed briefly at the outset. A. H. Van de Ven and Diane L. Ferry, in attempting to develop measures of organizational effectiveness, offer a model that serves well to describe the context and structure of the situation influencing work design.[5] An extension of this model, with the list of variables affecting job dimensions, is shown in Exhibit 5-7.

Physical Factors The nature of the work area and the physical effort required are physical factors in job design. Exposure to dirt and air pollutants, high-risk noise, lighting, and odors (tannery or sewer maintenance) are illustrations of unfavorable physical factors. Physical effort may vary from strenuous manual effort to motor tasks to practically none. Also, consideration must be given as to whether the physical effort is continuous, periodic, or occasional. The physiology of humans must be considered in the design of work in terms of capacity, stress, and fatigue.

Psychosocial Factors Workers on the job have varying needs for psychological satisfactions. The subdivision of work into small repetitive tasks ignores

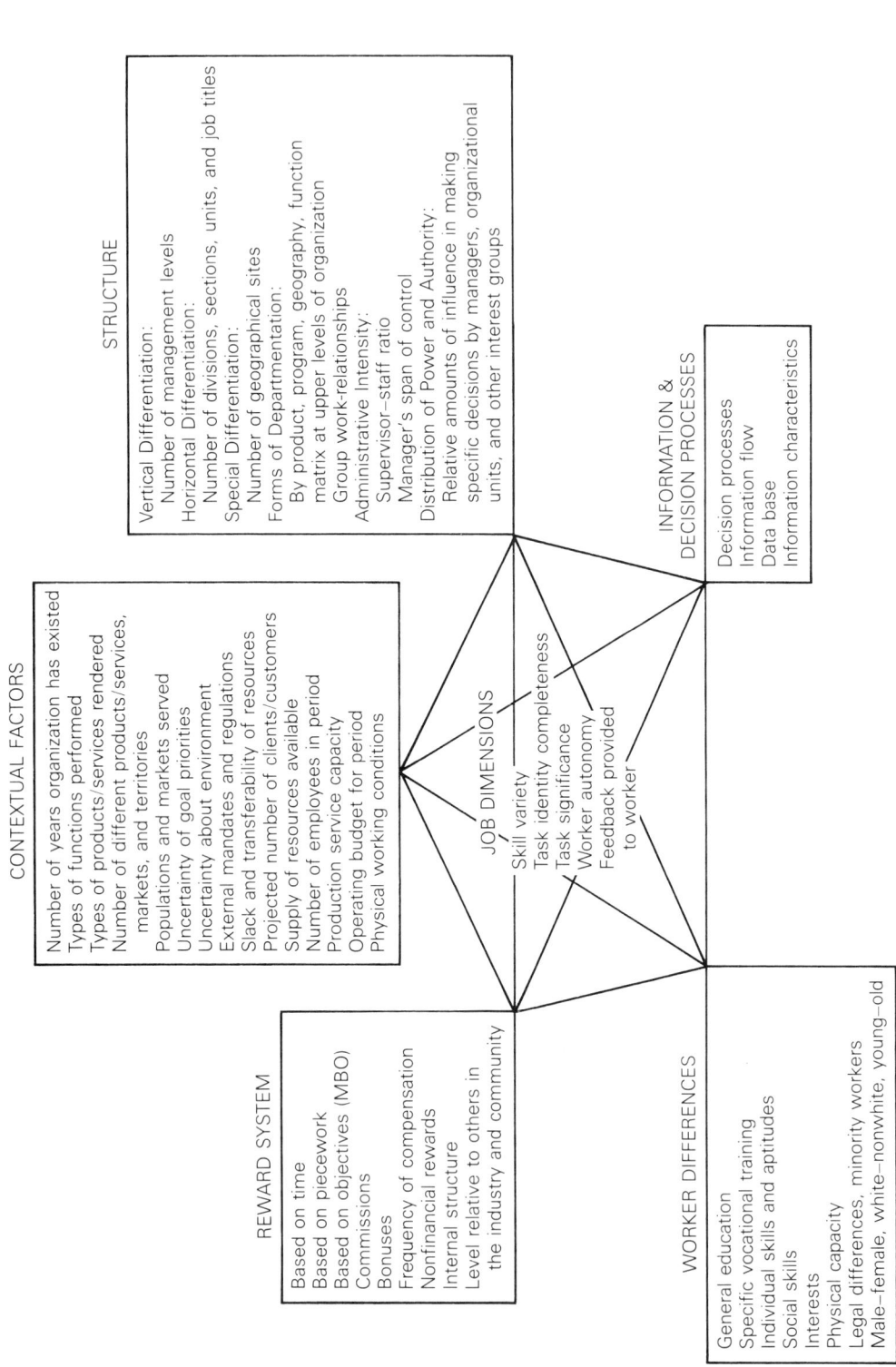

EXHIBIT 5–7
Job Design.
Source: Based on work by J R. Hackman and G. R. Oldham, and A. H. Van de Ven and D. L. Ferry.

these psychological needs, however. At the same time, workers have social and psychosocial needs that may be filled simply by being part of a work group. The implication for the job designer is that a purely rational-technical approach to job design is not the most effective.[6] Worker differences and the reward system are important inputs to job design. For HR management, recombining tasks to reduce monotony, and job rotation on a periodic basis may be used in job design.

Sociotechnical Factors: Organization Structure and Information/Decision Processes The sociotechnical approach to job design focuses on the introduction of the work group and technology. Studies in the 1950s in India and England showed that work groups could handle production problems better than management if they were permitted to make their own decisions on scheduling and work allocation. Later experiments and the quality circles have confirmed that employee involvement in work design produces good results. Task interdependence fosters autonomy and experience responsibility.[7]

Allocation of Work between Humans and Machines Some analysts have approached the allocation of work between humans and machines by listing the things that humans do best and the things that machines do best. Others view the work of humans and machines as complementary rather than comparable so that "allocation of work between men and machines" becomes meaningless. While there may be no adequate systematic methodology for distributing the machines, it is apparent that they have taken over more and more jobs performed by humans—automation and "robotization" of automobile assembly lines are good examples. Presumably, automation performs the repetitive and boring tasks so that workers are freed to perform more complex design, monitoring, and maintenance tasks.

The spread of computers to the office is also reorganizing the kinds of work that people perform. Routine tasks and repetitive decisions are programmed so that workers decide only on inputs, and then the utilization of outputs. Shoshana Zuboff points out that with "computer-mediated work, employees receive feedback only as symbols instead of as personal contact."[8] In Decision Support Systems (DSS), managers interact with the computer by requesting information and posing questions. Decision making at the lower levels often means processing information with a computer program rather than using human judgment. Work becomes more abstract as professionals and managers lose direct contact with information processing at lower and middle levels of problem solving and decision making. Social interaction may be reduced as the computer becomes one's source of information and as one's output is returned to the computer's data base. Such technology-induced changes in work design require care to prevent worker stress.

> "I'm suffering from it now," hollered Nancy Lee into the telephone. "The microcomputer is in another part of the room and I haven't got time to hop up and down to communicate with my clients. I need one at my desk."
>
> Lee, a vice president of Research & Planning Inc.—an office-technology consulting group based in Cambridge, Mass.—already had thrown a self-described "fit" earlier that day over computers in her office. It is just one example of how the new technology that is revolutionizing offices can put the people in them under siege.
>
> High-tech anxiety. Electronic stress. Cyberphobia, or fear of computers. "It all exists because so much change is happening so rapidly," said Lee, who counsels companies and workers. "It affects everybody, whether support staff or senior management."

Source: Judy Linscott, reprinted in "Technology Brings Stress to Office Life," *Boca Raton News,* June 23, 1983, p. C1.

Task-Oriented vs. Job-Oriented At the shop and clerical level, job design in the past has been task-oriented. That is, the rational-technical approach has been used, and it has been assumed that the worker will fit the job. At professional and managerial levels, however, the positions are usually modified to utilize the talents and experience of the individual. At the top-management level and for "research consultant" or "fellowship" positions in large companies, the person designs his or her own position within general constraints of company strategy and policy.

Job Rotation and Cross-Training Besides job enlargement and job enrichment, some companies have attempted to increase worker satisfaction and productivity by means of planned job rotation (on the assembly line, at management levels, or for professionals in project organizations). Cross-training to increase and broaden worker skills has also been used to reduce job monotony.

Work Modules A work module has been defined as a time-task unit of approximately two hours of work at a given task.[9] To relieve the monotony of repetitive, short time-tasks, the work module approach proposes four modules per day for a worker. Desirable and undesirable work may be alternated among workers as well.

Time Scheduling Time of work is an important factor in job design. All workers on a shift may be required to work the same hours. Now some companies have tried Alternative Work Patterns (AWP) whereby variations of this requirement are scheduled. For example, flexible work hours (flexitime) may be permitted so that workers exercise some choice over the hours they work. Some may come in early and leave early; some take long lunch breaks and make up the time; some arrive late and leave late. Usually, there is a "core" time when all employees must be present.

Job sharing is another innovation that is attractive to married couples whose family responsibilities make full-time work undesirable. In this case, two people share a single job and arrange with each other which one of them will be at work.

Common in retailing, part-time jobs include job sharing and jobs designed for individual part-time workers. An example of this type of time scheduling in a service organization is Keyboard Communications, Long Island, where 85 percent of the employees work part time.[10] The trend of part-time workers is increasing, with about 18.2 million workers working part-time in 1982.

Compressed workweeks in which the standard 40-hour week is compressed into fewer than five days such as a four-day, 10-hour-per-day week, have also been tried. In a survey of 214 organizations in the United States known to use some alternatives to the standard workweek, flexitime was most frequently mentioned among the responding firms (Exhibit 5–8).

Industrial Democracy, Quality Circles, and Task Groups The structuring of work with responsibility assigned to task groups appears to be increasing to achieve greater productivity and worker satisfaction. The opportunity for industrial democracy and quality circles to provide a means for releasing the creativity of workers has some impressive results in a few instances. A greater feeling of autonomy and self-esteem is one result.

Inputs to Job Design from Government Regulation The Occupational Safety and Health Act (OSHA) has influenced the design of the physical conditions of jobs in both trivial and significant ways. The Equal Employment Opportunity Act has affected job design by focusing on job requirements and requiring clearly stated job specifications. The impact of OSHA and of EEO regulations is determined greatly by the policy of the administration in power, however.

Type of Application	Number	Percent
Flexitime	62	48
Compressed workweek	23	18
Job sharing	13	10
Permanent part-time	31	24
	129*	100

EXHIBIT 5–8
Total number of alternative work pattern applications reported.

*Some respondents indicated more than one type of AWP in effect. *Source:* Ben Burdetsky and Marvin S. Katzman, "Alternative Work Pattern Applications," *Journal of Systems Management,* December 1981.

JOB DESIGN AND CLASS OF WORK

Job design is naturally greatly influenced by the degree to which work is manual or mental and the level of effort required. We may distinguish briefly here among six general classes of work: (1) unskilled, (2) craft, (3) clerical and office, (4) technical nonprofessional, (5) professional, and (6) managerial.

The design of manual production jobs usually requires very specific description because many positions fall within a job category. In addition, the jobs are usually limited in scope and the output must be fitted as part of a larger product. The job design requires considerable attention to physical characteristics of the workplace and the worker.

The design of jobs for clerical workers also usually results in a standardized description for work of limited scope. As with production work, the level of skills involved may vary from unskilled to highly skilled.

For both craft and professional workers, the design of jobs focuses on technical objectives to be achieved and responsibilities rather than specific procedures to be carried out. The level of complexity and interrelationships with other positions may cover a broad range.

The design of a managerial position also focuses on responsibilities. However, the managers at a given organizational level within the structure may have responsibilities assigned based on their power, preferences, skills, and experience. Thus, a manager who holds the same title over a period of a few years may have his or her job redesigned several times because of these factors.

DOCUMENTATION OF JOB DESIGN

When a job has been designed, it is usually documented, that is, described in writing in the form of a *job description.* The job description specifies the tasks, duties, and behaviors required in a given job. A *position description*, or position guide (see Exhibit 5–9), is prepared from a job description. For every employee there is a position description that describes responsibilities and relationships for the individual at a given time. For production and clerical workers, a job description may be only a single paragraph or one page. For a professional or manager, however, the position guide may extend to two or three pages. The position guide is very important for job evaluation, appraisal, and compensation.

That aspect of the job which focuses on the requirements of the worker is called the *job specification* (see Exhibit 5–10). The job specification and descriptions are important tools for recruiting (see Chapter 6).

EXHIBIT 5-9
Position guide for a manager.

POSITION GUIDE
INDUSTRIAL PRODUCTS BUSINESS DIVISION

POSITION CODE: _____

POSITION TITLE: __MANAGER-INFORMATION SYSTEMS_____

OPERATION/DEPARTMENT: __FINANCE__   SECTION: INFORMATION SYSTEMS_____

A. *Broad Function*

The Manager–Information Systems has the responsibility for identifying opportunities and needs, planning, developing, implementing, reviewing and modifying integrated information systems for the IP Business (all functions) and, in addition, for those systems required to support the entire IP Business Division. Included is the responsibility to determine the need for, obtain, schedule and operate a data processing capability to meet the needs of the Division, and be aware of current and expected information requirements through the establishment of appropriate relations both within and outside the Division.

B. *Responsibilities*

1. Collaborate with his manager in setting realistic and challenging operational goals. Contribute to their accomplishment. Periodically prepare and implement supporting projects and plans which are considered supplementary to this Guide.

    Accountability: Timeliness, completeness and degree to which such goals and plans assist in achieving effective use and integration of available resources.

2. Assure implementation of Company Policy and IP Business Division Instruction 0.1 regarding equal employment opportunity within the organization.

    Accountability: Implementation and adherence to the policy, achievement of established goals and the development of a positive climate of employee support and understanding within his organization.

3. Develop and maintain an updated, long-range information systems plan for the Division Headquarters organization, including remote plants, Distribution Service and other field operations remote to headquarters, consistent with the overall Information Systems and Business plans and objectives.

    Accountability: Feasibility of the long-range plan and degree of opportunity identified to provide assistance to the Business.

4. Develop both master and detailed plans and schedules for Division (including Headquarters, plants, field distribution, field service and field sales), Information Systems development activities (both manual and automated), defining benefits, goals and completion dates for training, systems specifications, systems design, programming, implementation, maintenance and measurements.

    Accountability: The feasibility of the plans and schedules, and the contribution to overall development and implementation of information systems projects.

5. Support and maintain existing information systems and related computer programs, assuring an adequate master and detailed data processing schedule and their successful execution as necessary to meet the needs of the Business.

    Accountability: Adequacy, cost, dependability, completeness and timeliness of systems support, maintenance and execution of required data processing.

6. Coordinate with Corporate Regional Computer Center and/or other pooled computer centers to assure adequate and economic computing capacity and to obtain necessary technical assistance to assure effective, dependable and economical use of applicable computer resources. Also, coordinate with CCPO to assure complete plans that provide an economically balanced use of Division Corporate Regional Computer Center and other pooled computer centers.

    Accountability: Adequacy, cost, dependability, completeness and timeliness of programming techniques assistance and data processing capability required.

EXHIBIT 5-9, *continued.*

7. Make significant recommendations as the result of systems, procedural forms and work simplification analyses, and provide for the development and implementation of information systems which will result in the timely generation, processing and transmission of information required to effectively and economically support the Business.

    Accountability: Quality, timeliness and overall dollar contribution of the information systems developed for the Business.

8. Provide the necessary programming to translate the information systems requirements into data processing logic and languages, and establish appropriate checking procedures to assure adequacy, dependability and timeliness of the capability.

    Accountability: Adequacy, cost, dependability, completeness and timeliness of programming capability required.

9. Maintain sound organization and manpower development and training programs required to meet high standards of performance to effectively fulfill assigned responsibilities.

    Accountability: Quality of leadership and effectiveness of overall recruitment and training program resulting in minimum manpower required to achieve objectives, and results planned in a timely manner.

10. Maintain an effective, integrated relationship with functional personnel (including Headquarters, plant, field distribution, field service and field sales) to assure adequate and timely input to information systems development, adequate information systems interfaces and ease of implementation.

    Accountability: Completeness and timeliness of functional inputs, adequacy of interfaces and ease of implementation.

11. Develop and utilize a series of feedback and measurement criteria for reporting; planning and scheduling effectiveness; manpower utilization; and improved information systems effectiveness, value, protection and security.

    Accountability: Ability and willingness to measure and the contribution of measurements made.

12. Keep Manager–Finance informed concerning matters for which he is accountable which require his advice or coordination, or which involve variations from established policies.

    Accountability: Degree to which Manager–Finance is kept informed and surprises are eliminated.

EXHIBIT 5-10
Job specification.

Secretary IV

Minimum Training and Experience

Graduation from a standard high school and three years of secretarial and/or clerical experience.
Successfully completed studies beyond the high school level may be substituted for the required experience at a rate of 720 classroom hours or 30 semester hours per year.
Possession of Certified Professional Secretary Certificate may be substituted for the required experience.
An equivalency diploma issued by a state department of education or by the U.S. Armed Forces Institute, or a qualifying score on the Division of Personnel Educational Attainment Comparison Test may be substituted for high school graduation.

Necessary Special Requirements

Ability to type at a rate of 35 correct words a minute.
Ability to take and transcribe dictation at the rate of 80 words a minute is required for designated position allocated to this class.

JOB ANALYSIS OVERVIEW

Work design is a *planning* activity; job analysis is the *analysis, measurement, control,* and *redesign* of a set of activities. Obviously, job analysis cannot be conducted until the job has been designed and there is already someone performing the job. That is, job analysis is performed upon *ongoing jobs.* A warning that is rarely mentioned should be repeated here. Like organization charts, jobs are always in the process of change. Therefore a job analysis may be obsolete shortly after it is completed.

The objectives of job analysis are to study processes, simplify methods, measure work for establishing job and time standards, provide information for compensation and incentive plans, and improve the safety, recruiting, selecting, training, appraising, and compensating of employees. These objectives of job analysis can be grouped under three headings:

1. Work simplification (job redesign)
2. Establishment of work standards
3. Support of other personnel activities

Exhibit 5–11 shows how job analysis fits into the HR management system. The combination of organization structure and job analysis provides a complete detailed picture of the performance of tasks by the company. Job analysis provides information.

Job Evaluation Job analysis leads to job descriptions and to job factors used to compare and evaluate the relative worth of jobs in the company.

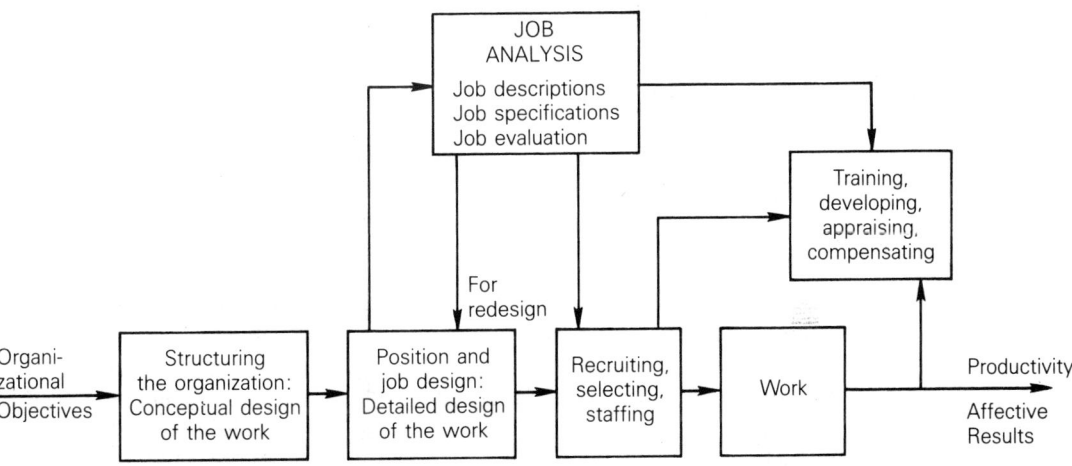

EXHIBIT 5–11
The role of job analysis in HR management.

Recruitment Job analysis supports recruitment by providing both position descriptions and job specifications. Job specifications describe the traits and skills required for the job.

Selection and Placement Job analysis and the resulting position descriptions and job specs make possible good matching of individuals to jobs and good career planning.[11]

Performance Evaluation People should be evaluated on the basis of well-defined behavior and output. Job analysis is used to determine an acceptable level of performance.

Training and Development Comparison of job descriptions shows the requirements of the current job and of desired jobs. This provides a basis for training for both present and future jobs.

Career Planning Job analysis and job descriptions provide a clear description of proposed steps in a career.

Compensation The compensation plan system should be based on job evaluation and relative worth of jobs.

Job Classification Job analysis permits grouping of jobs on some specified basis such as the nature of the work performed. This reduces the number of job titles and simplifies compensation planning.

> According to Marvin T. Runyon, President of Nissan, U.S.A., there are only four classes of technicians at Nissan Motor Manufacturing in Smyrna, Tennessee. In traditional American auto plants there are literally hundreds of narrow, stratified job classifications for hourly workers.

Source: Based on "Nissan's Way," *Miami Herald,* June 26, 1983.

MAJOR STEPS IN JOB ANALYSIS

In some firms, job analysis is a continuing activity. As jobs change or new ones are added, they become subject to analysis. Often, in continuing programs, job analysts in the wage and salary administration section of the P/HR department conduct the analyses. Their results are then reviewed by their own manager and by the managers of the workers whose jobs are analyzed.

In some cases where a new job analysis program is being initiated, a job analysis committee is created to oversee and review the analyses. The committee makes difficult decisions concerning the various job factors such as responsibility and scope of the jobs.

There are eight major steps in a job analysis program:

1. Organize and plan for the program. The company must determine who will be in charge of the program (or committee or the Manager–P/HR) and must assign responsibilities. A schedule should be established and a budget estimated.
2. Obtain current job design information. The job analyst should next obtain organization charts, current position descriptions and job specifications, procedure manuals, and systems flowcharts to the degree that these are available.
3. Conduct "needs research." The P/HR job analyst should investigate to determine which organizations, managers, or staff people require job analyses or output from job analyses. The analyst should also determine for what purpose and to what extent jobs must be analyzed and how the information will be used.
4. Establish priorities in the jobs to be analyzed. The P/HR department, working with managers of the various organizational units, identify the jobs to be analyzed and the priority of each job analysis.
5. Collect job data. Collect data about the selected jobs *as they are currently being performed* using established systematic techniques.
6. Evaluate and redesign the jobs if appropriate.
7. Prepare a job description and job classifications.
8. Prepare job specifications.

JOB ANALYSIS TECHNIQUES

The analysis of jobs requires gathering data about the jobs from (1) company *records*, (2) *interviews* with workers performing the jobs, their supervisors, and workers doing work that impinges on the jobs being studied, (3) *observations* of workers on the job, and (4) *self-reporting* by the workers through such means as diaries, logs, questionnaires, and (5) recordings (film, tape).

There are three types of job analyses: job-oriented, worker-oriented, and combined. Analysis of jobs based on describing the *tasks* required for successful performance is called job-oriented. Analysis based on *worker behavior*—what the worker does—is called worker-oriented analysis. Usually a combination of each type of analysis is used.

The job analysis techniques used for manual workers may differ considerably from those used for knowledge workers such as managers. For example, observation of the behavior of a manual worker tells us a lot about the job. On the other hand, observation of a "mental" worker may tell us nothing. A number of systemic techniques have been developed to gather

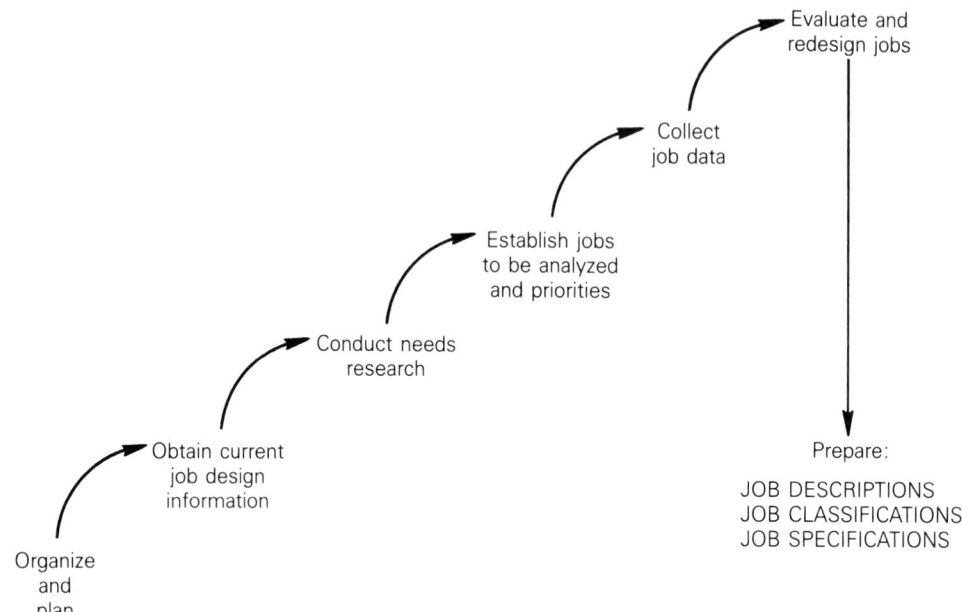

EXHIBIT 5-12
Major steps in job analysis.

and analyze data on jobs. The more advanced techniques use computers to provide a variety of analyses. We will give a brief description of several of these techniques.

Task (or Job) Inventory Concept

In recent years the development and use of *task inventories* have advanced the field of job analysis significantly. A task inventory consists of a listing of tasks and some type of response scale for each task. The list of tasks usually consists of all the tasks that can be performed by incumbents in a particular occupation.

Two types of rating scales are associated with the task inventories for the incumbent or other respondent to check. One type is concerned with the degree, if any, that the incumbent is involved with a particular task and deals with:

1. Performance (does the incumbent perform the task?)
2. Frequency of performance
3. Time spent on the task when it is performed
4. Relative time spent
5. Importance of the task to the job

The second class of scales covers a range of factors that help describe the job, such as:

1. Complexity of the task
2. Criticalness of the task
3. Difficulty of learning the task
4. Method of learning the task (on-the-job, etc.)
5. Experience needed for performing the task
6. Supervision required in task performance
7. Time required to learn the task

Three advantages of the task inventory concept are:

1. Task inventory questionnaires may be distributed to individuals at distant locations throughout the company or administered to the incumbents as a group.
2. Task inventories are continually being developed for more occupations.
3. The analyses, because scaling is used, can be made with a computer.

Interview Guidelines

The personal interview of incumbents is an important part of some commonly used job analysis systems. For unstructured questionnaires or job analysis worksheets, the analyst tries to draw out a description of the job as the incumbent sees it. For job analysis based on the task inventory concept, some methods require personal interviews to develop the task lists. It should be recognized that job analysis interviewing, just as marketing research interviewing, requires considerable knowledge and skill. The fundamental objective is to obtain complete unbiased information from the respondent. Thus, both the type of questions asked and the interviewer's manner are important to achieving this objective.

Three types of interviews are desirable. An initial interview provides most of the job information. A verification interview is made after the results from the first interview have been checked with other sources and prepared in task form. A follow-up interview with a group of incumbents and supervisors may be used to polish up the final draft for language, clarity, and correctness of terms.

Preparation for the Interview All interviewees should be notified in advance of the purpose of the study. The questionnaire, the task inventory, or other materials such as drafts of task lists should be given to the interviewee in advance. A time for the interview should be established that allows for an adequate period of questioning. Late Friday afternoons and times shortly before the lunch hour are obviously not the best. The interviewer should secure permission from the worker's supervisor to conduct the interview.

Opening the Interview Workers who participate in job analysis frequently have fears that the results will be used to lower their salaries, demean their jobs, or increase their tasks. Until rapport is established, the analyst should try to put the worker at ease with some casual talk and explanation of the service he or she is providing.

Guiding the Interview The worker should be encouraged to talk by the analyst's courteous listening and nonevaluative attitude. The worker should be asked to talk about a typical day starting from when he or she arrives. To keep the discussion from wandering, the interviewer may summarize the conversation to this point and ask, "What do you do next?"

Leading questions should be avoided. Questions should be phrased so that more than "yes" or "no" will be required. Jargon should be avoided.

Notes should be taken as unobtrusively as possible throughout the interview.

Closing the Interview The analyst should close the interview by summarizing the information obtained and discussing a convenient time for the next interview if one is required.

Functional Job Analysis

Functional Job Analysis (FJA) is a standardized procedure for developing a definition of a job and its requirements. It was developed by the Department of Labor to create the government's *Dictionary of Occupational Titles*. FJA attempts to identify what the worker *does* on the job and *what gets done*. What the worker does is defined according to four categories of information:

1. Worker function: what the worker does in relation to data, people, and things (see Exhibit 5–13)
2. Work fields: techniques and methods used
3. Equipment: machines and tools
4. Materials, products, and services: subject matter of the work

In addition, a fifth category of information, worker traits including working conditions, is also part of the data sought.

One way of organizing a task statement for FJA may be illustrated for an engineer as follows:

Performs what action (action verb):	Performs stress analyses
On what or to whom:	On mechanical products
To achieve what:	Adequate design strength for components
With what input information:	Performance specifications and reliability specs
Using what equipment and tools:	Computer and engineering materials handbooks
Work functions:	Data 60%/2, People 10%/1, Things 30%/4 (See Exhibit 5–13 for the numerical key to these activities)

EXHIBIT 5–13
Work functions.

Data	People	Things
0 Synthesizing	0 Mentoring	0 Setting Up
1 Coordinating	1 Negotiating	1 Precision Working
2 Analyzing	2 Instructing	2 Operating–Controlling
3 Compiling	3 Supervising	3 Driving–Operating
4 Computing	4 Diverting	4 Manipulating
5 Copying	5 Persuading	5 Tending
6 Comparing	6 Speaking–Signaling	6 Feeding–Offbearing
	7 Serving	7 Handling
	8 Taking Instructions–Helping	

Source: U.S. Department of Labor, *Dictionary of Occupational Titles,* 4th ed. (Washington, D.C.: U.S. Government Printing Office, 1977).

The U.S. Training and Employment Service (U.S.T.E.S.) of the Department of Labor is more involved in job analysis than any other organization. A job analysis schedule, including a completed job description, used by the U.S.T.E.S. is shown in Exhibit 5–14. The specific directions for conducting a job analysis and for preparing the job analysis schedule is given in the *U.S.T.E.S. Handbook for Analyzing Jobs.*

Functional Job Analysis (FJA) is apt to be costly because of the hiring expenses for highly skilled job analysts. These analysts must determine how the jobs relate to company goals. Also, FJA is not generally suitable for managerial, professional, and technical jobs. On the other hand, FJA is tied into the *Dictionary of Occupational Titles* so that often much time may be saved. In addition, the system is organized so that much information is coded and, therefore, can be easily manipulated by a computer. For example, six classes of physical demands, seven classes of working conditions, and nine classes of specific vocational preparation are identified.

Position Analysis Questionnaire (PAQ)

The Position Analysis Questionnaire, developed at Purdue University, is a method for analyzing jobs in quantitative form. The PAQ covers 195 job elements grouped into six sections:

1. Information input: Where and how do workers get information to do their jobs? 35 elements
2. Mental processes: What reasoning, planning, organizing, and decision making is done? 14 elements
3. Work output: What physical activities, tools, and machines are used? 49 elements
4. Relationships: What contact with other people, both in the company and outside of it, is maintained or developed? 36 elements

EXHIBIT 5–14
Job Analysis Schedule.

U.S. Department of Labor

Estab. & Sched. No.   071-3120-423

JOB ANALYSIS SCHEDULE

1. Estab. Job Title   INFORMATION DESK CLERK, receptionist-clerk
2. Ind. Assign.   ret. tr.
3. SIC Code(s) and Title(s)   5311 Department Stores

Code 237.568
WTA Group Information Gathering
Dispensing, Verifying and Related Work p. 258

4. JOB SUMMARY:

Answers inquiries and gives directions to customers, authorizes cashing of customers' checks, records and returns lost charge cards, sorts and reviews new credit applications, and requisitions supplies, working at Information Desk in department store Credit Office.

5. WORK PERFORMED RATINGS:

Worker Functions	(D) Data	(P) People	(T) Things
	5	6	7

Work Field   282-Information Giving   231 Recording
M.P.S.M.S.   890-Business Service

6. WORKER TRAITS RATING:

GED   1 2 (3) 4 5 6
SVP   1 2 (3) 4 5 6 7 8 9
Aptitudes   G 3 V 3 N 3 S 4 P 4 Q 3 K 4 F 3 M 4 E 5 C 5
Temperaments D F I J (M) (P) R S T (V)
Interests   1a (1b) (2a) 2b 3a 3b 4a 4b 5a 5b
Phys. Demands (S) L M H V 2 3 (4) (5) 6
Environ. Cond. (1) 0 B 2 3 4 5 6 7

DOT Title
Ind. Desig.

13. Machines, Tools, Equipment, and Work Aids
    Impressing Device—Small Hand-operated device, of similar construction to stapler with a nonmoving base and a moveable upper arm containing rollers which inked Impressing-Device (con) are moved by a lever in the upper arm. Charge card is placed in a groove in the base, stand-up print facing up, and paper or bill positioned over card, then the upper arm is brought down and lever depressed to bring inked rollers over paper to make impress of card's print.

14. Materials and Products
    none

EXHIBIT 5-14, continued.

```
15. Description of Tasks:
    1. Answers inquiries and gives direction to customers: Greets customers at Information
       Desk and ascertains reason for visit to Credit Office. Sends customer to Credit Inter-
       viewer to open credit account, to Cashier to pay bills, to Adjustment Department to ob-
       tain correction of error in billing. Directs customer to other store departments on re-
       quest, referring to store directory. (50%)
    2. Authorizes cashing of checks: Authorizes cashing of personal or payroll checks (up to a
       specified amount) by customers desiring to make payment on credit account. Requests
       identification, such as driver's license or charge card, from customers, and examines
       check to verify date, amount, signature, and endorsement. Initials check, and sends cus-
       tomer to Cashier. Refers customer presenting Stale Date Check to bank. (5%)

18. Analyst  A. Yessarian   Date  7/25/85   Editor  M. Major   Date  7/26/85
    Reviewed By  John Milton              Title, Org.  Credit Manager
    National Office Reviewer  W. Irving
```

Source: U.S. Training and Employment Service, Department of Labor.

    5. Job context: What is the physical and social context in which the job is performed?   19 elements
    6. Other job characteristics: What other activities, conditions, or characteristics not covered by the other categories are relevant?   41 elements

Exhibit 5–15 shows a completed page from the first section of the PAQ.

A major problem with PAQ is the time it takes for a job analyst to fill out the ratings. However, PAQ has been widely researched and tested and appears to be both reliable (among different raters) and valid (correlates with job pay).

Work Performance Survey System (WPSS)

The Work Performance Survey System (WPSS) is a highly developed and tested system for structuring task statements, preparing a survey questionnaire, and analyzing the resulting data with available WPSS computer programs. The system was developed for AT&T, but the computer programs are available to the public from AT&T Licensing in Greensboro, N.C. One big advantage of the WPSS is that it can be structured to analyze managerial and other knowledge worker jobs.

The WPSS is presented as a five-step process by Sidney Gael:[12]

1. Plan
2. Develop task statements
3. Verify accuracy and completeness of task statements
4. Prepare, try out, finalize, distribute and collect questionnaires; computerize collected data
5. Analyze the data; develop and report results

EXHIBIT 5–15
Portions of a completed page from the Position Analysis Questionnaire (PAQ).

INFORMATION INPUT

1 INFORMATION INPUT

1.1 Sources of Job Information

Rate each of the following items in terms of the extent to which it is used by the worker as a source of information in performing the job.

Code	Extent of Use (U)
N	Does not apply
1	Nominal/very infrequent
2	Occasional
3	Moderate
4	Considerable
5	Very substantial

1.1.1 Visual Sources of Job Information

1. **4** Written materials (books, reports, office notes, articles, job instructions, signs, etc.)

2. **3** Quantitative materials (materials which deal with quantities or amounts, such as graphs, accounts, specifications, tables of numbers, etc.)

3. **1** Pictorial materials (pictures or picturelike materials used as *sources* of information, for example, drawings, blueprints, diagrams, maps, tracings, photographic films, x-ray films, TV pictures, etc.)

4. **1** Patterns/related devices (templates, stencils, patterns, etc., used as *sources* of information when *observed* during use; do *not* include here materials described in item 3 above)

5. **1** Visual displays (dials, gauges, signal lights, radarscopes, speedometers, clocks, etc.)

6. **N** Measuring devices (rules, calipers, tire pressure gauges, scales, thickness gauges, pipettes, thermometers, protractors, etc., used to obtain visual information about physical measurements; do *not* include here devices described in item 5 above)

7. **2** Mechanical devices (tools, equipment, machinery, and other mechanical devices which are *sources* of information when *observed* during use or operation)

8. **4** Materials in process (parts, materials, objects, etc., which are *sources* of information when being modified, worked on, or otherwise processed, such as bread dough being mixed, workpiece being turned in a lathe, fabric being cut, shoe being resoled, etc.)

9. **2** Materials *not* in process (parts, materials, objects, etc., not in the process of being changed or modified, which are *sources* of information when being inspected, handled, packaged, distributed, or selected, etc., such as items or materials in inventory, storage, or distribution channels, items being inspected, etc.)

10. **N** Features of nature (landscapes, fields, geological samples, vegetation, cloud formations, and other features of nature which are observed or inspected to provide information)

11. **N** "Man-made" features of environment (structures, buildings, dams, highways, bridges, docks, railroads, and other "man-made" or altered aspects of the indoor or outdoor environment which are *observed* or *inspected* to provide job information; do not consider equipment, machines, etc., that individuals use in their work, as covered by item 7)

Source: Copyright by Purdue Research Foundation. By permission.

The components of a task statement are Action, Object, Qualifier. For example, the structure of one clerk's task might appear as follows:

What Is Done	To What	How, Why, Where, When, How much
(Action) Send	(Object) Purchase Order	(Qualifier as appropriate) To Customer

Scales are used for the incumbent to answer task attribute questions. These scales cover:

- ☐ How important or significant is each task to your job?
- ☐ How much time do you spend on each task?
- ☐ How frequently do you perform each task?
- ☐ How difficult is it to perform each task?

The application of the first scale is described in Exhibit 5–16, which gives the directions to the respondent for a WPSS questionnaire.

Management Work Analysis

Work analysis of managers differs considerably from that for manual or functional workers. Managers in similar jobs may give very different answers to questions about their jobs. Also, answers may reflect the manager's perception of what is the culturally "right answer" rather than actual behavior.

Rosemary Stewart has developed a model based on a series of studies to aid in understanding managerial jobs.[13] The model, shown in Exhibit 5–17, consists of an inner core of demands, an outer boundary of constraints, and an in-between area of choices. This model could be used to develop task statements by the WPSS method.

Another tool for analysis of managerial jobs is the Management Position Description Questionnaire (MPDQ). This provides a structure for constructing an inventory of activities for a manager. It currently consists of 208 items classified into ten parts:

1. General information
2. Decision making
3. Planning and organizing
4. Supervising and controlling
5. Consulting and innovating
6. Contacts
7. Monitoring business indicators
8. Overall ratings
9. Know-how
10. Organization chart

EXHIBIT 5-16
Directions for responding to a question about task significance.

Read each task statement carefully and decide whether or not the task is part of your present job. You are not expected to perform all the tasks listed, nor are all the tasks performed in every Business Service Center. It is important that you think only of your present job, not previous jobs.

Some tasks you perform are more significant for your job than others. Consider the following factors in judging the significance of a task to your job.:

   a. IMPORTANCE—the contribution of the task to effective operations in your office.
   b. FREQUENCY—how often you perform the task.
   c. DIFFICULTY—how hard the task is to do or to learn to do effectively.

Combine these factors in your mind to determine the significance of a task, and choose an appropriate rating according to the following:

0 = Definitely not a part of my job; I never do it.
1 = Under unusual or certain circumstances may be of a minor significance to my job.
2
3
4 = Of substantial significance to my job.
5
6
7 = Of most significance to my job.

Here is an example of how this is done:

TASK	SIGNIFICANCE	TIME SPENT
001 Review a completed order.	0 1 2 3 4 5 6 7	_____
002 Distribute incoming mail.	0 1 2 3 4 5 6 7	_____

For Task 001 in the example, a "5" was circled indicating that reviewing completed orders is somewhat more than of substantial significance to the job.

For Task 002, a "0" was circled, indicating that distributing incoming mail is not part of the job.

Even if you have the responsibility to see that a task is performed, but you do not perform the task, the "0" should be circled. The number you select should be your best estimate of the significance of the task to your job.

Source: Sidney Gael, *Job Analysis,* San Francisco: Jossey-Bass, 1983, p. 100.

It is apparent that job analysis for many manual operators doing similar work is highly developed and subject to thorough analysis by the computer. The challenge that remains is to develop a greater understanding of managerial work for both design and analysis.

EXHIBIT 5–17
Summary of different kinds of demands, constraints, and choices in managerial jobs.

Demands

Overall meeting minimum criteria of performance
Doing certain kinds of work. Such work is determined by:
   The extent to which personal involvement is required in the unit's work
   Who must be contacted and the difficulty of the work relationship
   Contact's power to enforce their expectations
   Bureaucratic procedures that cannot be ignored or delegated
   Meetings that must be attended

Constraints

Resource limitations
Legal and trade union constraints
Technological limitations
Physical location
Organizational constraints, especially extent to which the work of manager's unit is defined
Attitudes of other people to:
   Changes in systems, procedures, organization, pay, and conditions
   Changes in the goods or services produced
   Work outside the unit

Choices

In *how* work is done
In *what* work is done
   Choices within a defined area:
      to emphasize certain aspects of the job
      to select some tasks and to ignore or delegate others
   Choices in boundary management
   Choices to change the area of work:
      to change the unit's domain
      to develop a personal domain
      to become an expert
To share work, especially with colleagues
To take part in organizational and public activities

Source: Rosemary Stewart, "A Model for Understanding Managerial Jobs and Behavior," *Academy of Management Review,* January 1982; p. 11.

JOB REDESIGN

From the view of the P/HR department, job redesign may simply be a restatement of the job, its tasks and responsibilities, based upon job analysis. That is, in its simplest form, job redesign is just updating a job.

Job redesign may also be based on a combination of the original job design plus the job analysis. In other words, the job may be changed to something that has evolved past the original job description and the job as it actually exists. This requires retraining or counseling of the incumbents.

The chain of events that occurs begins, first, with a systems analysis of a functional area or organization. Then the system is changed, if possible, through work simplification methods. Work simplification means finding a better way of doing work. This may result in changing the sequence of jobs, eliminating them, and/or simplifying them. The people who engage in work simplification are called systems analysts.

The general method of studying the sequence of jobs, the recombining of jobs, or the elimination of jobs starts with the preparation of a flow process chart for the entire sequence of jobs. The operations are then reviewed for bottlenecks, delays, too much material movement, too much chasing around by people, or possible interchange of people and equipment.

Next, a particular job is selected. A subject would then be followed: a person, a part or article, or a paper form. The starting point and ending point are next identified. Then a brief description of every step is written down on a detailed process flow chart. The job is then challenged by asking (1) why is the job done at all? (2) why is each step performed? and (3) is every step a MUST?

Some of the tools for studying manual work for simplification are man–machine activity charts, left- and right-hand charts, and micromotion photography.

For office workers, some tools used are work sampling (to determine proportion of time spent on various tasks), observation of the job, interviews with the incumbent and the supervisor, questionnaire completed by the incumbent and supervisor, and incumbent's log or diary of work time.

Once a job has been studied and simplified, the analysis can be extended to establish work standards. In the shop, or for manual clerical work, a *standard time* may be established for tasks and jobs. This standard time is determined by timing the job with a stopwatch or by applying predetermined time standards from standard data tables. Adjustments are included for variability among workers and for fatigue and personal needs. Job analysis to develop improved methods and time standards is performed by methods engineers, time-and-motion analysts, and industrial engineers.

SUMMARY

Work design is the process of defining tasks and jobs to achieve both organizational and employee goals. The P/HR department acts as an advisor to line management in the design of jobs. Thus work design is concerned with productivity, affective responses of workers to their jobs, and the relationship of work design to other human resource management activities.

Work is the performance of physical and/or mental activities directed to the achievement of some economic or societal goal. It can be broken down into (1) a hierarchy of activities, job, job-task, operation, and work element or, (2) a hierarchy of organizational tasks and subtasks. Job design may, therefore, start with a bottom-up approach, a top-down approach, or a combination to redesign whatever is in existence.

The classical approach to job design was a rational-analytic, technological method that lacked any consideration for the motivation of workers or the satisfaction of their needs. This ignoring of many workers' needs for satisfaction and growth on the job no longer works. Task characteristics that consider workers' personal goals, as identified by Hackman and Oldham, are (1) skill variety, (2) task identity, (3) task significance, (4) autonomy, and (5) feedback.

A number of practical characteristics of jobs have been researched to find ways of increasing productivity and worker satisfaction. Some of these are (1) contextual and structural factors, (2) physical factors, (3) psychosocial factors, (4) sociotechnical factors, (5) allocation of work between worker and machine, (6) task or job orientation of the work, (7) job rotation and cross-training, (8) division of work into two-hour modules, (9) time-scheduling, and quality circles.

Job design is also greatly influenced by the degree to which the work is mental or physical. Five classes of work along such a spectrum are (1) manual, (2) clerical, (3) technical knowledge work, (4) professional, and (5) managerial.

Documentation of job design usually appears as job descriptions, job classifications, position descriptions, and job specifications.

Job analysis is the study of jobs for the purposes of simplifying work, setting job and time standards, and supplying vital information for other P/HR activities. The major steps in job analysis are (1) organizing for, and planning the program, (2) obtaining current work design information, (3) conducting needs research, (4) identifying jobs to be analyzed and establishing priorities, (5) collecting job data, (6) evaluating and redesigning the jobs, and (7) preparing job descriptions, job classifications, and job specifications.

Various methods have been developed to organize data for collection, to write task statements, and to manipulate and analyze the job data collected. Some of these are:

1. Functional Job Analysis (FJA)
2. Position Analysis Questionnaire (PAQ)
3. Work Performance Survey System (WPSS)
4. Management Position Description Questionnaire (MPDQ)

While work design and job analysis underlie all areas of human resource management, they have great importance for two particular HR activities. As part of this section on planning and staffing, we will explore this relationship in the next two chapters, Recruitment and Selection.

KEY CONCEPTS

Work design	FJA
Job design	PAQ
Job analysis	WPSS
Job redesign	MPDQ
Job description	Job characteristics model
Position description	Job-task
Job specification	

NOTES

1. *The Dictionary of Occupational Titles*, published by the U.S. Department of Labor, is the standard reference book on occupations.
2. Louis E. Davis, "Job Design: Historical Overview," in Louis E. Davis and James C. Taylor, *Design of Jobs*, 2nd ed. (Santa Monica, Ca.: Goodyear, 1979), p. 33.
3. L. E. Davis, R. R. Canter, and J. Hoffman, "Current Job Design Criteria," *The Journal of Industrial Engineering*, 1955, Vol. 16, pp. 1–7.
4. Ricky W. Griffin, Ann Welsh, and Gregory Moorhead, "Perceived Task Characteristics and Employee Performance: A Literature Review," *Academy of Management Review*, October 1981. See, in particular, J. R. Hackman and G. R. Oldham, *Work Redesign* (Reading, Ma.: Addison-Wesley, 1980).
5. Andrew H. Van de Ven and Diane L. Ferry, *Measuring and Assessing Organizations* (New York: Wiley, 1980).
6. See Davis and Taylor, *Design of Jobs*, pp. 104–108.
7. Moses N. Kiggundu, "Task Interdependence and the Theory of Job Design," *Academy of Management Review*, July 1981.
8. Shoshana Zuboff, "New Worlds of Computer-Mediated Work," *Harvard Business Review*, September–October 1982.
9. Robert L. Kahn, "The Work Module," *Psychology Today*, February 1973.
10. "Job Sharing: For Many a Perfect Answer," *U.S. News & World Report*, August 23, 1982, p. 66.
11. See *Uniform Guidelines on Employee Selection Procedures* (Washington, D.C.: The Bureau of National Affairs, 1980).
12. Sidney Gael, *Job Analysis* (San Francisco: Jossey-Bass, 1983), p. 35.
13. Rosemary Stewart, "A Model for Understanding Managerial Jobs and Behavior," *Academy of Management Review*, January 1982.

REVIEW AND DISCUSSION QUESTIONS

1. How could the P/HR department work with line managers to design the organization and new jobs in an organization? Explain the contribution that the P/HR department could make.

2. Select a job and give an example of a work element, operation, and job task.
3. Discuss how organizational objectives and organizational tasks are related in a hierarchy and how they are related to job design.
4. Should jobs be designed first from a rational-technical view or should work be first designed according to the individual's abilities and interest? Explain your answers.
5. Select a job and explain in terms of this job the meaning of skill variety, task identity, task significance, autonomy, and feedback.
6. Explain how each category of factors, structure, contextual factors, reward system, worker differences, and information/decision processes relate to the job dimensions in Exhibit 5–7.
7. Discuss possible trends in allocation of work between workers and machines for (a) engineers, (b) factory workers, and (c) managers. Give a scenario for the year 2000.
8. Develop a format (headings for items) for a position description for managers.
9. Distinguish between work design and job analysis.
10. Discuss how job analysis may be used for carrying out (a) placement, and (b) training and development.
11. Discuss how each of the four methods of data gathering could be used, or why each would not be appropriate, for analyzing a clerical job and a managerial job.
12. How would you present plans for a job analysis program to employees?
13. To what classes of jobs—manual, clerical, or managerial—would the following methods of job analysis be best suited: FJA, PAQ, WPSS, MPDQ?
14. Rank in order of your opinion as to the usefulness of the computer with FJA, PAQ, WPSS, MPDQ.
15. Write three task statements for each of the following: a. a retail clothing salesperson; b. an order-processing clerk; and c. a wage and salary administration specialist.
16. Prepare a short questionnaire to be used as an unstructured job analysis interview guide; develop 10 to 15 questions.
17. List some reports that could be prepared conveniently by a computer from a quantitative job analysis study.

BIBLIOGRAPHY

Barnes, Ralph M. *Motion and Time Study*, 7th ed. New York: Wiley, 1980.
Brousseau, Kenneth R. "Toward a Dynamic Model of Job–Person Relationships: Findings, Research Questions, and Implications for Work System Design." *Academy of Management Review*, January 1983.

Burdetsky, Ben, and Marvin S. Katzman. "Alternative Work Pattern Applications." *Journal of Systems Management*, December 1981.

Cascio, Wayne F., and Elias M. Awad. *Human Resources Management*. Reston, Va.: Reston Publishing, 1981.

Chase, Richard B., and Nicholas J. Aquilano. *Production and Operations Management*, 3rd ed. Homewood, Ill.: Irwin, 1981, Ch. 11.

Cohen, A. R., and H. Gadon. *Alternative Work Schedules: Integrating Individual and Organizational Needs*. Reading, Mass.: Addison-Wesley, 1978.

Davis, Louis E., and James C. Taylor, Eds. *Design of Jobs*, 2nd ed. Santa Monica, Ca.: Goodyear Publishing, 1979.

Dunham, Randall B., and Jon L. Pierce. "The Design and Evaluation of Alternative Work Schedules." *Personnel Administrator*, April 1983.

Gael, Sidney. *Job Analysis*. San Francisco: Jossey-Bass, 1983.

Galbraith, Jay R. *Organization Design*. Reading, Mass.: Addison-Wesley, 1977, Chapters 20 and 21.

Geinen, J. Stephen, and Eugene Jacobson. "A Model of Task Group Development in Complex Organizations and a Strategy of Implementation." *Academy of Management Review*, October 1976.

Griffin, Ricky W. "Task Design Determinants of Effective Leader Behavior." *Academy of Management Review*, April 1979.

Griffin, Ricky W., Ann Welsh, and Gregory Moorhead. "Perceived Task Characteristics and Employee Performance: A Literature Review." *Academy of Management Review*, October 1981.

Hackman, J. R. "Work Design." In J. R. Hackman and J. L. Suttle, Eds. *Improving Life at Work*. Santa Monica, Ca.: Goodyear Publishing, 1977.

Hackman, J. R., and G. R. Oldham. "Development of the Job Diagnostic Survey." *Journal of Applied Psychology* 60, 1975, 139–170.

Hackman, J. R., and G. R. Oldham. *Work Redesign*. Reading, Mass.: Addison-Wesley, 1980.

"Job Sharing: For Many a Perfect Answer." *U.S. News & World Report*, August 23, 1982.

Kiggundu, Moses N. "Task Interdependence and the Theory of Job Design." *Academy of Management Review*, July 1981.

Klinger, Donald E. "When the Traditional Job Description Is Not Enough." *Personnel Journal*, April 1979.

Melcher, Arlyn J. *Structure and Process of Organizations: A Systems Approach*. Englewood Cliffs, N.J.: Prentice-Hall, 1976.

Miller, Stanley S. "Make Your Plant Manager's Job Manageable." *Harvard Business Review*, January–February 1983.

Niebel, Benjamin W. *Motion and Time Study*, 5th ed. Englewood Cliffs, N.J.: Prentice-Hall, 1978.

Pierce, J. L., and R. B. Dunham. "Task Design: A Literature Review." *Academy of Management Review*, October 1976.

Rotchford, Nancy L., and Karlene H. Roberts. "Part-Time Workers As Missing Persons in Organizational Research." *Academy of Management Review*, April 1982.

Schmenner, Roger W. *Production/Operations Management*. Palo Alto, Ca.: Science Research Associates, 1981, Chapter 9.

Stewart, Rosemary. "A Model for Understanding Managerial Jobs and Behavior." *Academy of Management Review*, January 1982.

U.S. Department of Labor. *Dictionary of Occupational Titles*, 4th ed. Washington, D. C.: U.S. Government Printing Office, 1977.

Van de Ven, Andrew H., and Diane L. Ferry. *Measuring and Assessing Organizations.* New York: Wiley, 1980.

Zuboff, Shoshana. "New Worlds of Computer-Mediated Work." *Harvard Business Review*, September–October, 1982.

Recruitment

CHAPTER OUTLINE

The Recruitment Process
Responsibility for Recruiting □ Initiating the Process

Constraints on Recruitment
Labor Markets □ Unions □ Organizational Policies □ Public Policy

Internal Recruitment
Advantages and Disadvantages □ Internal Recruiting Practices □ Publicizing Vacancies

External Recruitment

Alternatives to Recruiting

Evaluation of Recruitment Programs
Realistic Job Previews □ Cost Effectiveness

OBJECTIVES

1. Describe the recruiting process in terms of who does it, how it is done, and how it fits into the total staffing process.
2. Discuss how certain factors, such as the labor markets and unions, affect recruiting policies.
3. Discuss internal sources for filling job vacancies.
4. Identify sources and methods for attracting new employees from outside the firm.
5. List possible alternatives to recruiting new employees.

SPOTLIGHT:
Debbie Watson

Debbie Watson graduated from Florida Atlantic University in December, 1982, with a major in Human Resource Management. As a student, she was active in a number of campus organizations and worked parttime as a student assistant in the College of Business.

After graduation, Ms. Watson was employed by the *Ft. Lauderdale News* as a personnel assistant. Within a few months, she was promoted to an employment representative and is now involved in several areas of personnel/human resource work such as recruiting and selecting new employees. Thus within a short span of time, she has had the opportunity to view recruitment from two perspectives: as a recent college graduate seeking a job and as a recruiter interviewing job applicants.

Comments by Debbie Watson

What to do!

After attending all those classes, studying to get those grades, changing careers, or just jobs, what do I do to ultimately find my place in the job market? This question becomes a reality at some time in every person's career.

There are many job-search techniques available to the person in the job market, and all possible methods should be considered. The more exposure one gets to potential employers, the greater are the opportunities to get a job. The key to successful job hunting is to choose the most effective combination of available search methods.

One easily accessible source of available jobs is the classified section of the newspaper. Other sources include trade journals, directories from which listings of companies can be obtained to send resumes, career fairs, employment agencies, and on-campus career centers, where college recruiting takes place. One of the latest innovations in recruitment has been a computer information bank that has in its memory a listing of potential candidates, their skills, interests, and other information that interested recruiters can view from terminal centers around the country. While there are advantages and disadvantages associated with each of these, the disadvantage of one source can be offset by the advantage of another, making an effective combination very important.

While the job seeker is looking for a job that will meet his or her needs, the recruiter's responsibility is twofold. First, there is the recruiter's commitment to the organization to find the best-qualified candidate for the position. Second, as a recruiter, I feel that I also have a responsibility to the applicant in matching that person's needs to a job where expectations can be met. To be efficient and effective, the recruiter must know what qualifications the applicant should possess to meet both personal and organizational needs.

This means that prior to actual recruiting, an organization must thoroughly determine the requirements of a job. To get qualified applicants, job specifications must be clearly defined. Once a need is defined, the company has several alternative sources of labor such as present employees (referrals), advertising, agencies, and educational institutions. The recruiter is concerned with making the most economical use of available sources for the type of employee sought. For example, the newspaper industry, in which I work, is unique in one sense because of the low cost for its advertising. The cost incurred for the paper is the opportunity cost of outside advertising. Another advantage is that it is a medium that reaches a large amount of people daily.

Whatever side of the recruiting function one is on, you must understand and accept the needs and expectations of the other side for there to be a successful match.

RECRUITMENT   **171**

The effectiveness of an organization at any level depends upon the skills of employees who are striving for a common purpose. The objective of the staffing process is to locate, select, acquire, and place the human resources necessary to fulfill organizational and human resource plans. The staffing process, then, may be viewed as a flow of activities that results in the placement of qualified workers in organizational positions at all levels. In some industries a particularly difficult part of this job is the smooth and timely staffing of new and radically different jobs as they are created.

We have seen in previous chapters that in order to carry out this process, management must design the work, perform job analyses, and do human resource planning in order to determine the skills that will be necessary to meet the organizational goals. As seen in Exhibit 6–1, recruitment, selection, placement, and development programs result from these human resource plans. In a broader sense, the total *staffing process* encompasses the flow of human resources into, within, and out of the enterprise. In this chapter and the next, we shall see how this process takes place in an organization. It should be noted, therefore, that organization planning and human resource planning, along with work design and job analysis are interrelated and provide the input for the staffing process.

In this chapter we will examine recruitment, an important part of the staffing process. The selection of qualified individuals from among those recruited will be discussed in the following chapter.

THE RECRUITMENT PROCESS

The *recruitment process* involves identifying and attracting candidates for current and future jobs; it is a process of developing and maintaining adequate sources for filling human resource needs. The greater the number and variety of sources of personnel, the greater the chance of finding the right individual for the job. Recruitment may be relatively simple, as when

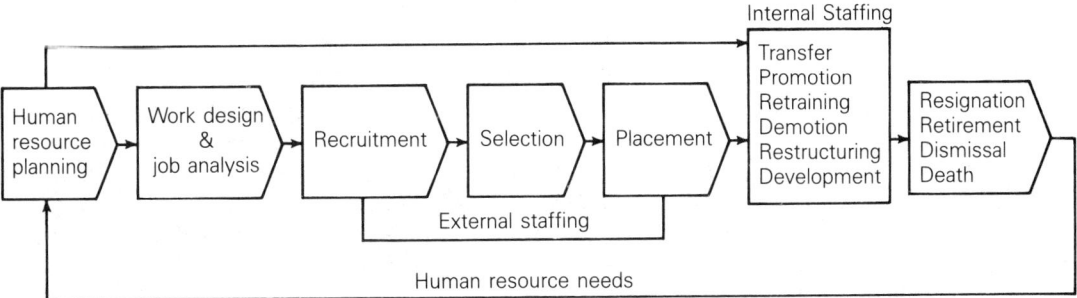

EXHIBIT 6–1
The staffing process.

the small retail store finds someone to "help out" during the busy season. In a large firm, on the other hand, recruitment may be a complex and expensive activity involving promotions from within as well as advertising, placing orders with employment offices, visiting schools and colleges, attending professional meetings, and conducting research to evaluate these sources and activities.

Responsibility for Recruiting

In a small organization, recruiting is usually done rather informally by the owner or manager. In larger organizations, the human resource department is usually responsible for developing sources of applicants. Within the human resource department there is likely to be an employment office staffed by recruiters and interviewers who do the recruiting and even initial selection of candidates for a job. Very large organizations, and firms employing large numbers of professional and managerial employees, may have a separate department engaged entirely in college recruiting.

At the same time, individual managers and employees throughout the organization may be referring promising applicants to the appropriate group in the human resource department. Similarly, the human resource department may be requesting recruitment assistance from individual managers, as may be the case when recruitment will take place at the alma mater of one of the line managers. Still other firms prefer to put together recruiting teams consisting of human resource specialists and operating personnel. For example, one or more engineers may accompany the college recruiter when recruiting for engineering personnel at technical schools and colleges.

Regardless of who does the recruiting, it is important for one department to coordinate the recruiting function in order to develop adequate sources, avoid duplication, and ensure that human resource needs for the overall organization are met.

Initiating the Process

Recruiting may be an on-going process whereby the firm attempts to develop a pool of qualified applicants for future human resource needs even though specific vacancies do not currently exist. This practice is also necessary to maintain contacts with recruiting sources.

In most cases, recruiting starts when a manager initiates an employee requisition for a specific vacancy (or anticipated vacancy). The requisition should contain the basic information describing the position to be filled, the duties to be performed, and the experience and qualifications required of the candidate for the job. The requisition in Exhibit 6–2 is typical of the format used in many firms.

Since the candidates for a given job can only come by movement within the organization or by recruitment from outside, every firm faces

EXHIBIT 6–2
Personnel requisition.

PERSONNEL REQUISITION	ASSIGNED TO	BY	DATE

DATE REQUIRED	PAYROLL CLASSIFICATION	CODE	PAY GRADE	LOCATION OF WORK

COST CENTER	JOB OR SUB. NO.	EMPLOYEE WILL REPORT TO:	DIVISION/DEPARTMENT	SECTION	SUPERVISOR	EXT

NAME OF PERSON HIRED	EFFECTIVE DATE	SOCIAL SECURITY NO	U.S. CITIZEN ☐YES ☐NO	EEO CODE

CONTACT FOR INTERVIEWS	EXT	TRAVEL REQUIRED ☐YES ☐NO IF YES EXPLAIN BELOW	REFERRED BY

DESCRIPTION OF DUTIES:

EXPERIENCE AND QUALIFICATIONS REQUIRED—INDICATE SPECIAL REQUIREMENTS, e.g., SECURITY CLEARANCE, CITIZENSHIP, ETC.

☐REPLACEMENT FOR ☐TRANSFERRED ☐QUIT ☐DISCHARGED ☐LAYOFF ☐________

☐NEW POSITION GIVE BRIEF EXPLANATION

SUGGESTED APPLICANTS		
	NAME	HOW TO CONTACT
	NAME	HOW TO CONTACT
	NAME	HOW TO CONTACT

REQUESTED BY	DATE	APPROVED BY	DATE

these questions: When, and to what extent, do we fill our vacancies from within? When do we go outside? Answers to these and other questions regarding recruitment can only be made after careful consideration of several constraints that exist within, and outside, of the individual firm.

CONSTRAINTS ON RECRUITMENT

There are many factors that limit or affect the recruiting policies of any organization. Among the most important are: the labor market, organizational policies, public policies, and unions.

Labor Markets

Changes in the *labor market* can very dramatically affect recruiting policies and practices. The unemployment rate, shortages or excessive supply in specific skills, recruiting activities of other firms, and going wage rates will all influence the effectiveness of recruitment programs.

However, defining a labor market is not an easy task. Technically, a labor market is a geographical area within which the people looking for work interact with the demand for labor and thereby determine the price for labor. Thus, if the supply of labor is low relative to the demand, the price will be high and recruiting activities may have to be broadened into another geographic area to attract qualified candidates.

In reality, the boundaries of a labor market are seldom clear-cut and vary depending on the particular skill needed. For example, the labor market for clerical employees for an individual firm may consist of the city-limits in which the firm is located. At the same time, the labor market for scientists and accountants might include all of North America. Thorough understanding of the labor markets for the individual firm is essential for a sound recruitment program.

Unions

In several industries, unions play an active role in employment practices. In the building and maritime industries, the union hiring hall is a way of life whereby the employer is required to contact the union for new employees. This practice results in the union becoming the primary recruiters of labor.

Through the collective bargaining process, many human resource policies are jointly determined and serve as constraints on recruiting activities. Rules with regard to layoffs, transfers, discharges, and demotions may limit the firm's *internal* recruitment policies. Seniority rules and rights may specify who will be promoted into a vacant position. For example, if the labor contract specifies that the most senior employee will be promoted, providing that he or she is qualified to perform the job, management is constrained from recruiting outside the firm or selecting a less senior employee (who may be more qualified) if the employee with the most seniority meets the minimum requirements for the job.

As we shall see in a later section, many labor contracts provide for some sort of job posting and bidding process for favored work assignments and job vacancies. One of the drawbacks to this process is the possible delay in filling a vacant position.

Organizational Policies

Various policies and practices of a firm outside of the human resource system will have an impact on recruiting effectiveness. For example, a firm with a favorable public image resulting from a sound product, positive business practices, and an effective marketing and public relations program, is likely to have an easier time in recruiting qualified candidates. On the other hand, an organization receiving bad publicity due to shoddy products, shady business practices, or pollution, will be at a disadvantage when competing for good applicants in the labor market.[1]

In a sense, the general policies of a firm set the overall tone and provide direction for the recruitment policies and practices. Often these general policies need to be interpreted to provide detailed recruitment policies. For example, an organization dedicated to the *spirit* as well as the letter of relevant public policy, may establish recruitment programs that aggressively seek out trainees from among the handicapped, hard-core unemployed, and ex-convicts.

Similarly, all human resource policies influence recruiting policies. Thus, a company with very rigid compensation policies may have to pass up the very qualified engineer who is already earning more than the maximum allowed by the existing salary structure. A policy of paying "as little as possible" may then make it impossible to attract top-notch applicants.

Policies of promoting from within may result in recruiting only for the entry-level or less desirable jobs. An existing affirmative action plan may specify the need to recruit more women and minorities for managerial and professional jobs. Since about one out of five job applicants obtained employment by asking friends or relatives about jobs at which they worked, sound human resource practices will play an important role in the number of job applicants.[2] That is, some firms, enjoying a reputation as a "nice place to work," have very limited recruitment programs since most jobs are filled by word-of-mouth.

Public Policy

Federal and state policies regulate the entire staffing process, including recruiting activities. We have already seen this in Chapter 2, The Legal Environment for Human Resource Management. In this section, we shall briefly survey some of the important implications for the recruiting function. We shall see essentially that equal employment opportunity and affirmative action policies have an overriding role in determining the overall approach to recruiting, the sources of recruits, and even who is responsible for recruiting.

Title VII of the Civil Rights Act of 1964 (amended in 1972) makes it illegal to discriminate against any individual in *any* employment procedure because of the individual's race, color, religion, sex, or national origin. Subsequent interpretations, executive orders, and additional legislation have created a nightmare of paper work for the human resource personnel attempting to comply with the law. For example, the Office of Federal Contract Compliance (OFCC) was set up to see that federal contractors and subcontractors do not discriminate in employment. In a standard OFCC review the following items, which have a direct impact on recruiting, would be required:

1. A list of *all* recruiting sources (e.g., colleges, schools, and so on) showing job categories for which each is used, as well as sample copies of job requisitions
2. Statistics showing the total number of applicants during the last three months, breaking down by male and female the applicants for white-collar and blue-collar positions; in addition, the number of minority-group persons in each category must be indicated
3. Copies of recruitment advertising, including recruitment brochures

Similarly, the *Equal Employment Opportunity Commission* (EEOC), which was set up to administer Title VII of the Civil Rights Act, can require companies to develop and preserve any records necessary to determine whether illegal employment practices have been in use. An EEOC review will in most cases also involve a close examination of recruiting policies and practices.

Lesser known, but equally important laws that protect other groups and constrain recruiting policies include the Amended Military Selective Service Act of 1967, the Age Discrimination in Employment Act, and the Vocational Rehabilitation Act.

The Amended Military Selective Service Act of 1967, which requires an employer to grant to a returning service man or woman a previously held job or one comparable to it.

The Age Discrimination in Employment Act as amended, which is designed to protect individuals between forty years of age and seventy. Thus, a firm, for example, cannot advertise for a secretary under 30. An exception to age criteria can be made if age is a bona fide occupational qualification as in the case where an actor is required to play a youthful role.

The Vocational Rehabilitation Act (Section 503), which requires employers with federal contracts over $2,500 to take affirmative action for the employment of handicapped persons. The Labor Department's regulations on the handicapped emphasize recruitment and communication of the employer's policy on hiring the handicapped.

As can be seen from the above brief discussion of public policies, there is an important need for someone in the human resource department to become thoroughly familiar with all the state, local, and federal regulations that affect the recruitment process. (More will be said about some of the laws that pertain to other aspects of the staffing process (e.g., testing and interviewing in the next chapter). While it is impossible to list all the "do's and don't's" for the recruiting process, any firm should as a minimum consider seven points:

1. Someone in the firm should be responsible for monitoring the recruitment program to see that it is free of unlawful discrimination. Discrimination may show up not just in formal recruiting practices

but in long-established informal practices—for example, in employee referral. To illustrate, if a firm relied entirely on referrals from employees for job applicants, the results may be the perpetuation of the present composition of an organization's membership where minorities and females are not well represented at all levels. The courts have ruled that reliance on this practice is discriminatory.
2. Record keeping is very important. For example, it would be useful to develop an "applicant flow" data system. Accordingly, the data for each applicant would show personal and job-related information whether or not a job offer was extended; if not, the reason(s) should be given. This information will enable the human resource department to analyze the recruitment practices related to minority and female applicants and to take corrective action if needed. One person should be responsible for all the record keeping.
3. An analysis of the organization's human resource inventory can suggest if an affirmative action plan is necessary. For example, if women or minorities are significantly underrepresented in the organization in overall numbers in specific job positions, an affirmative action plan might be established with the support of top management. (See Exhibit 6–3 for an excerpt of the recruitment section of an actual affirmative action plan.)
4. All recruitment advertising must conform to the requirements for nondiscrimination. For example, help-wanted advertisements cannot indicate a preference for males or females—unless gender can be shown to be a bona fide occupational qualification such as being female to work as an attendant in a women's locker room.
5. Recruiting only college graduates or only high school graduates for a given position must be justified on the basis either of job relatedness as shown in the job description or of statistical data showing significant predictive power for such requirements.
6. Recruiting efforts may need to be expanded to new sources from which minority and women applicants are more likely to be reached. For example, most firms included in a survey of recruiting policies and practices found local community agencies to be the most effective source of locating minority and handicapped workers. (See Exhibit 6–4).
7. All interviews and application-blank data must be "validated" the same as any selection tool used in the staffing process. Validation of selection tools will be discussed in the following chapter.

INTERNAL RECRUITMENT

Even if an organization wanted to fill every vacant job with an employee hired from outside, it must rely, through *internal recruitment*, upon inside sources for filling a number of its jobs. Although many jobs are similar from

EXHIBIT 6–3
Excerpt from an affirmative action directive to department heads in a state university.

Recruitment efforts will be directed at securing applications from qualified minority and female applicants. Appointments will not be made to instructional or professional positions until a good-faith effort has been made to secure the services of a woman or a person of minority identification, and until such effort can be adequately demonstrated. Public announcements and advertisements of position vacancies will be placed in local, regional, or national media, journals or professional publications, or communications to professional societies. . . .

H. AFFIRMATIVE ACTION INDICATIONS

Recruiting

1. Utilize minority group persons in:
   a. Your Administrative or Personnel Office, as staff and as interviewers.
   b. Your recruiting visits to high schools, colleges, job fairs, and similar agencies.
2. Establish contacts in the minority and women's communities. The key to good contacts is credibility—credibility between your department and the contact, credibility between the contact and the minority and women's communities, and credibility among women's groups and organizations.
   a. Contact the nationally known minority groups or women's organizations.
   b. Contact community organizations—school committees, churches, local centers. In some places, these lesser-known groups have closer contact with the people than the organizations with national reputation.
   c. If experience shows no group is an adequate contact, seek out individuals and leaders who are well known—ministers, doctors, barbers, beauticians.
   d. If these sources fail, seek out the leaders of community demonstrations. Do not be deterred by radical rhetoric; some of these leaders may have more credibility than better-known groups.
   e. Invite minority and women leaders to visit, tour, and/or lecture to your department.
   f. Make an effort to bring minority-group members and women into your vacancy information system and equalize their opportunities.

When you have a job opening,

a. Advertise it in minority and women's community media (newspapers, magazines, radio and TV stations). Utilize these media as regularly as you use other forms of advertising. Always use the phrase, "An Equal Opportunity Employer." Also, indicate that "we welcome applications from minorities and women."
b. Notify employment agencies with a large clientele of minority-group persons.
c. Make clear to non-specialized agencies that applicants will be rated on merit only, and encourage them to send minority-group and women applicants.
d. Encourage minority and women employees to refer their friends.

DO NOT:

1. Rely predominantly or exclusively on word-of-mouth referral.
2. Rely predominantly on walk-ins, especially if you are located in an all-white area.
3. Rely on qualifications which are not job-related and tend to "screen out" applicants rather than "screen in" qualified minority-group persons and women.
4. Continue restricting positions by sex, unless there is a bona fide occupational qualification involved.

Applications

Accept applications from minorities and women whether or not you have an opening. Keep the applications on file; consult them when openings develop. Minority group persons and women must be built into the system of employment. While white males may hear of future openings by word-of-mouth from present employees, minority-group persons and women most often do not.

Interview

When you interview applicants, be certain that
   a. Interviewers understand and carry out your equal employment policies.

EXHIBIT 6-3, *continued.*

    b. Interviewers are not biased by dress and grooming styles which are unique to certain ethnic or age groups.
    c. Interviewing staff is appropriately representative of group being sought in affirmative action efforts.

Employment Standards

Qualifications should reflect what the applicant needs to get the job done. Do not lose potentially good workers because you have artificially high standards.

    a. Eliminate requirements for diplomas and degrees where neither is needed for proper position or job function.
    b. Eliminate or be flexible about experience requirements when the job can be quickly learned, and reduce experience requirements which are excessive.
    c. Review a person on the basis of his or her previous success record and promise, as well as academic achievement.
    d. Assume that women do not permit marital status to affect their acceptance of employment.
    e. Assume that minorities are willing to live and work in a predominantly white community.
    f. Assume that wives of current employees are qualifiable according to standards set forth in the State Personnel Policies.
    g. Apply all of the same considerations and equalizations for minorities and women to employment of minority and women students.

one organization to another, some jobs require specialized knowledge that can be obtained only within a particular firm. For example, a firm's secret chemical process or solid-state technology may require the use of certain employees who are experienced in that process or technology. Therefore, the realities of the staffing process may require firms to select from within.

Promoting from within is a widely accepted and long-established policy in most organizations.[3] In some companies, such a policy is set forth in the collective bargaining agreement negotiated with a labor union.

EXHIBIT 6-4
Most effective recruiting sources for special groups.

	Groups		
Source	Minority Workers[*]	Women[*]	Handicapped[**]
Local community agencies	33	18	60
Advertising	19	39	8
Walk-ins	9	10	3
Employee referrals	30	27	11
College recruiting	11	17	6
Employment agencies	20	21	5

Note: Figures are percentages of all companies.
[*] Figures add to more than 100 percent because of multiple responses.
[**] Figures add to less than 100 percent because of nonresponses.
Source: *Recruiting Policies & Practices,* Personnel Policies Forum, Survey No. 126 (Washington, D.C.: Bureau of National Affairs, Inc., July 1979), p. 9.

Advantages and Disadvantages

While several reasons have been given for filling a job from within whenever possible, the justifications for an internal recruitment policy include:

1. Better-qualified employees. We are in a better position to assess the skills of an employee who has been performing satisfactorily over a period of years, than those of a person who is brought in from the outside.
2. Lower costs. It is usually less costly to transfer or promote an employee (even one who needs additional training) than to lure away an outsider from his or her present employer. In addition, the recruitment and selection process is simplified if there are only a few entry jobs and if the education and skill requirements for these are lower.
3. Motivating role. The employee who feels that he or she can get ahead by working harder is more likely to strive to succeed.

We should keep in mind, however, that an exclusive promotion-from-within policy can create "inbreeding" and prevent the infusion of new ideas and knowledge. A policy of recruiting from within also assumes, perhaps mistakenly, that the persons in the firm have the aptitudes, interest, and potential for moving ahead. In addition, as noted in our previous discussion, it may be necessary for a firm to go "outside" to correct past discriminatory hiring practices or as part of an affirmative action plan trying to attract special groups of workers.

Internal Recruiting Practices

There are three basic methods of filling job vacancies internally: *transferring* an employee from a similar job somewhere else in the company; *promoting* an employee from a lower-level job; and *upgrading* the employee now holding the job. The last method is accomplished by increasing the educational or skill level of the employee.

One approach to identifying the individuals for the transfer, promotion, or upgrading is to utilize *skills inventories* that were part of the human resource planning (see Chapter 4, Planning for Human Resources). The firm searches the files for potential candidates for the current or anticipated vacancies. The candidates are then notified and asked to apply for the position if they are interested. Today, most firms utilize their computer information system to search for qualified candidates among the existing workforce.

Publicizing Vacancies

As seen in Exhibit 6–5, *job posting* is the most commonly used method of publicizing job vacancies within the firm. In fact, 82 percent of the firms surveyed posted their blue-collar jobs on bulletin boards. Many collective bargaining agreements require that the organization post job openings for a

EXHIBIT 6-5
Publicizing internal vacancies.

	Type of Job		
Method	Blue-Collar	Office/Clerical	Professional/Technical
Posted on bulletin boards	82%	64%	48%
Circulated in memos to supervisors	12	12	20
Reported in employee publications	8	10	10
Publicized by other methods	10	15	12
Not publicized	8	20	30

Source: *Employee Promotion and Transfer Policies,* Personnel Policies Forum, Survey No. 120. (Washington, D.C.: Bureau of National Affairs, Inc., January 1978), p. 2.

minimum period of time before "going outside" the firm to recruit. Aside from unionized organizations, job posting has become more common in financial, life insurance, and governmental organizations. One reason for its popularity is the openness of the system, which allows all employees including the various minority groups to apply for positions that they consider themselves qualified for.[4] In the event that an employee is not qualified or interested, he or she may refer a friend or associate from outside the firm.

It is important that someone in the organization be responsible for providing positive feedback as soon as possible to those employees who do not receive the job they applied for. Most progressive organizations will have the immediate supervisor or someone from the human resource department meet with the "rejected" employee to do some career planning. This is an opportune time to discuss with the employee—in a positive manner—why he or she did not get the job posted, what jobs the employee might apply for in the future, what strengths need to be developed (through more training), and so on.

EXTERNAL RECRUITMENT

If necessary talents cannot be found within the firm, P/HR must go outside through *external recruitment.* Some firms look for "new blood" outside their own organization in order to keep the human resource system from growing stagnant. Other firms have found it cheaper and quicker to hire highly-trained specialists and professionals rather than to train and develop their own employees.

The particular sources and means by which workers are recruited vary widely, depending upon the types of jobs involved, the local labor market, and economic conditions. For example, during a business boom, when labor is scarce, more aggressive recruiting techniques may be required than those used during periods of high unemployment when "walk-in" applicants are likely to satisfy the bulk of a firm's human resource needs.

Effective hiring requires having a large enough number of applicants from among which to select the most suitable recruits. Depending on the job, the number of applicants might range from 3 to 5 for routine clerical and production jobs to 15 or more for management positions. Where then do organizations go to obtain the large number of applicants to fill job needs? Exhibit 6–6 shows the sources used for recruitment by the 188 firms responding in the Bureau of National Affairs study. We can see that employee referrals, walk-ins, newspaper advertising, and local trade and high schools are commonly used recruitment sources. However, it should also be noted that the importance of the source varies considerably depending on the type of job. For example, the United States Employment Service (U.S.E.S.) is utilized by nearly three-fourths of the firms to recruit plant employees, and by almost two thirds of the firms to recruit office employees. On the other hand, only 27 percent of the companies use this source for recruiting management personnel, for which newspaper advertising and private employment agencies become more important.

Let us now examine these various sources for external recruitment.

Employee Referrals Whenever possible, present employees should hear about vacancies first. If they are good workers, their recommendations may provide excellent applicants. This is probably the most fruitful source of job applicants for the smaller firm. Former employees are often acceptable if they left for good reason and under good circumstances. They may also be able to refer the manager to qualified friends.

"Walk-in" Applicants In a loose labor market there may be a substantial number of qualified applicants in this category. This is a most common source of applicants for plant and office personnel. This is a very inexpensive source of applicants, especially for the firm that enjoys a favorable image in the community and thus has people stopping by to fill out a job application for employment.

Advertising As seen in Exhibit 6–7, newspaper advertising overall seems to be the most effective recruiting source used by the firms responding to the Bureau of National Affairs study. As we have already noted, it is also one of the most frequently used sources.

A number of factors will influence the response rate to advertisements for job applicants. Four important considerations are the image or reputation of the organization, labor market conditions, media selected, and the wording of the advertisement.

For example, a large, well-known firm with a favorable public image is likely to receive a good response rate to its job ads. However, this same firm will likely receive fewer responses for the identical ad run in the same newspaper in a tight labor market than when unemployment is high. Similarly,

EXHIBIT 6–6
Sources used for recruitment, by employee group.

Source	Office/Clerical (N = 184)	Plant/Service (N = 155)	Sales (N = 96)	Professional/Technical (N = 182)	Management (N = 181)
Employee referrals	92	94	74	68	65
Walk-ins	87	92	46	46	40
Newspaper advertising	68	88	75	89	82
Local high schools or trade schools	66	61	6	27	7
U.S. Employment Service (U.S.E.S.)	63	72	34	41	27
Community agencies	55	57	22	34	28
Private employment agencies	44	11	63	71	75
(company pays fee)	(31)	(5)	(49)	(48)	(65)
Career conferences/job fairs	19	16	19	37	17
Colleges/universities	17	9	48	74	50
Advertising in special publications	12	6	43	75	57
Professional societies	5	19	17	52	36
Radio–TV advertising	5	8	2	7	4
Search firms	1	2	2	31	54
Unions	1	12	0	3	0

Note: Figures are percentages of companies providing data for each employee group as indicated by the numbers in parentheses for each group.

Source: Recruiting Policies & Practices, Personnel Policies Forum, Survey No. 126 (Washington, D.C.: Bureau of National Affairs, Inc., July 1979), p. 2.

EXHIBIT 6-7
Most effective recruiting sources by employee group.

Source	Office/Clerical	Plant/Service	Sales	Professional/Technical	Managerial
Newspaper advertising	39	30	30	38	35
Walk-ins	24	37	5	7	2
Employee referrals	20	5	17	7	7
Private employment agencies	10	2	23	25	27
U.S. Employment Service (U.S.E.S.)	5	6	0	1	1
Local high schools or trade schools	2	2	0	0	0
Colleges/universities	1	1	8	15	2
Community agencies	1	3	0	1	2
Unions	0	2	0	0	0
Career conferences/job fairs	0	1	2	2	1
Professional societies	0	1	1	0	2
Search firms	0	0	2	5	17
Radio–TV advertising	0	1	0	0	1
Advertising in special publications	0	0	3	5	8

Note: Figures are percentages of companies providing data for each employee group as indicated in Exhibit 6–6. Columns may add to more than 100 percent because of multiple responses or less than 100 percent because of nonresponses.

Source: Recruiting Policies & Practices, Personnel Policies Forum, Survey No. 126 (Washington, D.C.: Bureau of National Affairs, Inc., July 1979), p. 5.

certain publications will be more effective for recruiting certain types of applicants. For example, trade magazines or national newspapers such as the *Wall Street Journal* are generally used for managerial and professional personnel. The classified ad section of the local newspaper, on the other hand, may be more effective for recruiting production or clerical personnel. An effective ad should also avoid generalities and furnish adequate information about the job, the organization, and possibilities for advancement.[5] A "shotgun" approach to advertising such as might appear to be suggested in Exhibit 6–8 will probably result in wasting the recruiter's time as hundreds of college graduates may apply for the job.

Since effective advertising for recruitment is a complex and difficult task, the human resource department should consult the organization's advertising or public relations department (if one exists) or contract with an outside advertising agency. An advertising specialist will analyze the recruitment goals and develop an effective advertising program.

Schools Local high schools and trade schools often have a placement service for their students and alumni. Even if the school lacks such a service, teachers are often interested in helping their graduating students get good jobs.

The successful recruiter maintains personal contact with local schools through company participation in programs such as Junior Achievement, Career Day, or cooperative science projects. Personal contacts with counselors and teachers can aid in getting the better students referred to the company.

Employment Agencies There are three different types of employment agencies: public, private, and search consultants. Let us consider each one separately.

Of *public agencies*, the United States Employment Service (U.S.E.S.) is the largest employment agency in the United States. Through 2,400 offices

---

MANAGEMENT TRAINEES

We are looking for good people to grow with our company. If you are a college graduate with ambition, drive, and a willingness to learn, please call Mr. Mopair at 393–3656 for an appointment.

KUB INDUSTRIES, INC.

120 Fleming Dr.   Deerfield, Fl.

An Equal Opportunity Employer

EXHIBIT 6–8
Recruiting Ad.

located in all states it processes more than 8 million job openings per year. The agencies are staffed by state employees, but operating guidelines and funds come from the federal government. Without charge to applicants or employer, these agencies attempt to place applicants on the basis of education, experience, and testing. Unknown to many employers, the U.S.E.S. will, upon request, do job analyses, as well as testing and screening of job applicants.

Since an unemployed worker is required to register with the state employment office in order to receive unemployment compensation, these agencies have an image of dealing only with the unemployed and especially low-level applicants. In recent years, however, a growing number of employed persons at all occupational levels who are interested in a job change have been utilizing the state employment office. A number of firms use the U.S.E.S. as their sole recruiting source.

The U.S.E.S. has also established an automated system called the Job Bank, which exists in over 50 major cities throughout the United States. Accordingly, job openings in the metropolitan area are programmed into a computer. Each day a new listing is printed out including the pertinent information for each job such as number of openings, educational and physical requirements, and pay rates. This program shows considerable promise as an efficient and quick way of distributing job information.

Reliable *private agencies* can be quite useful in locating applicants. Most private agencies specialize in certain types of applicants, such as clerical, sales, health-care, part-time, and so on. In recent years, some firms have even specialized in counseling black women in higher-level positions.[6]

Private agencies charge a fee for their service that commonly would amount to 50 to 100 percent of one month's salary. Some agencies charge the employer; others the applicant. When dealing with private agencies, as well as public agencies, it is important for the employer to supply details about the job opening since the agency will do initial screening of applicants.

Search consultants, in a sense, may be considered to be another type of private employment agency. However, they merit separate discussion for several reasons. To begin with, they are highly specialized agencies that locate candidates for executive positions. Many grew out of the practice of many management consultants who were requested by clients to recommend applicants for top-level positions.

Often called "headhunters," the search consultant may work on a retainer fee basis and be paid a commission as high as 30 percent of the executive's first-year salary if the candidate is hired. The search consultant may have to be highly aggressive and tactful in canvassing and seeking out promising candidates in an attempt to "pirate" them away from their existing firms. An advantage of the search firm is that it can contact and screen a promising candidate who is currently employed while maintaining the anonymity of the organization seeking the individual.

EXHIBIT 6-9
The three components of a successful recruiting program.

Programs	Objectives	Success Measured By
On-campus visit	Increase student awareness of company, promote a company image, inform students about jobs available.	Number of students signed up
Company visit	Determine if the candidate visiting is suitable for any of the jobs available. Give the student a positive impression of the company, regardless of outcome.	Offer/visit ratio
Mentoring	Answer lingering questions. Make the student feel part of the corporate family.	Offer/hire ratio

Source: "The Successful Components of College Recruitment," by Bonnie Nunke, copyright November 1981. Reprinted with the permission of *Personnel Journal,* Costa Mesa, California; all rights reserved.

Colleges and Universities For most organizations, colleges and universities are the main source for higher-level personnel. Thus, college recruiting is a large-scale operation at many companies. In fact, college recruiting provides employers in this country with about two-thirds of new hires for college-level jobs. Competition among firms is especially keen for the students to fill positions in engineering, accounting, computer systems, and fast-track management training.[7]

Effective college recruiting means much more than visiting college campuses. Exhibit 6–9 shows three components necessary for a successful recruiting program, which includes the on-campus visit, the company visit, and mentoring. We can see that each component has a specified objective and measure for success. The component of mentoring is often missing from recruiting programs. According to mentoring, usually the hiring supervisor will tailor a plan to enhance the student's knowledge of the company and keep communications open after a job offer has been extended. This is accomplished by such techniques as sending additional information, calling to discuss what was sent, and so forth.[8] Exhibit 6–10 illustrates a situation in which an employment offer was extended during the second week in February with a decision to be made by the applicant by the last week in April.

Smaller organizations tend to recruit at local campuses in order to reduce travel and other recruiting cost. There is also the general belief that the candidate from the local school is likely to know the firm and is also more likely to favor working in the area.

Among medium- and large-size organizations, the selection of a college may be based on several factors, including:

1. Reputation of the school
2. Proximity to location of job openings

EXHIBIT 6–10
Sample timetable.

When	What Action Taken	Who Acts
Feb., week 3	Call: Was offer letter received? Any questions?	Hiring supervisor
March, week 1	Mail additional benefit information	Personnel
March, week 2	Call: Was benefit information received? Highlight items of importance to particular candidate.	Personnel
March, week 4	Mail house organ or technical journal	Personnel
April, week 1	Call: Explain that you are trying to give the applicant a feel for the company. See how decision process is going.	Hiring supervisor
April, week 2	Send local newspaper or regional magazine	Personnel
April, week 3	Call: Explain that you are trying to give the applicant a feel for the community.	Personnel or hiring supervisor

Source: "The Successful Components of College Recruitment," by Bonnie Nunke, copyright November 1981. Reprinted with the permission of Personnel Journal, Costa Mesa, California; all rights reserved.

3. Type of majors and degrees offered
4. Size of school
5. Personal preference of management[9]

Summer Internships and Cooperative Programs A growing recent practice of larger corporations and public agencies has been to hire college students during the summer as interns. This allows such organizations to get some work done during the summer while exposing their full-time staff to potential employees. Many of the interns serve as ambassadors back on campus who "spread the word" about career opportunities with the organization. Equally important, the organizations can carefully evaluate the capabilities of the interns as future permanent employees on the basis of actual performance, thus improving their selection judgement.

The same benefits are found with cooperative programs whereby a promising student may work either full- or part-time with the firm while attending classes. In some programs the student will receive academic credit for the time spent working with the firm.

Trade and Professional Associations Many trade and professional associations maintain placement services for the benefit of their members. Professional associations include such varied occupations as personnel managers, physicians, engineers, and legal secretaries. Trade organizations, which may consist of thousands of firms in an industry such as printing, farm equipment manufacturing, or retail hardware also tend to provide some recruiting services for managerial and higher-level technical personnel for their members.

Typically these trade and professional associations publish a journal or magazine that lists job openings and/or job applicants. They might also publish annual or semiannual rosters of job vacancies that are mailed to members. Most professional associations provide a placement facility at national and regional meetings to enable job applicants to be interviewed by member organizations.

With the labor force becoming more and more specialized and professionalized, individuals with similar training and work experience tend to get to know each other through attendance at meetings, conventions, and day-to-day business dealings. As a result, much recruiting takes place through these informal networks that tend to develop. For example, if a firm needs an engineer with some highly specialized skills, the human resource manager may be able to locate several candidates by calling a few other human resource managers in the local area who will recommend a qualified individual "looking" for a job. Similarly, if a company needs a qualified sales manager, a call to the local sales-executive association might be beneficial.

Other Sources Various other alternatives exist for recruiting on the outside. Customers and suppliers are in a position to recommend specialized personnel. In some industries, such as the building trades, the hiring hall of the local union has the responsibility to supply the employer with personnel. If properly matched to jobs, the handicapped, ex-convicts, and older workers are capable of reliable and superior performance. The state vocational rehabilitation office can provide information on the hiring of handicapped workers, while the National Alliance of Business has an ex-offender job-placement program.

Firms involved in affirmative action recruiting should develop contacts with local community organizations. Some of the more productive groups include the Urban League, NAACP, local Hispanic-American organizations, and the local Veteran's Administration.

Some firms have taken more creative approaches to filling their human resource needs. For example, Atlantic Richfield Company (ARCO) has a program designed for the older worker. As part of the program, ARCO uses part-time scheduling as well as giving the individual some latitude regarding work hours (flexitime). Other companies reassign older workers to different duties, to use their experience for problem solving but freeing them from day-to-day responsibility. Control Data Corporation has a program for former employees who are "homebound." With the use of computer terminals in their homes, the employees are trained as business application programmers.[10]

ALTERNATIVES TO RECRUITING

We have seen that human resource planning translates the goals of an organization into the number and type of people needed. However, rather than recruit to fill existing or future needs, management has several other alternatives, including:

Subcontracting work Forced with a forecasted increase in demand for the firm's goods or services, management may simply decide to subcontract the additional work to another firm. This alternative is especially appealing if the demand is viewed as short-term. If the firm is unionized, however, the union contract may have strong provisions that restrain management from subcontracting work.

Overtime Generally, because of the savings in recruiting and selection costs, overtime is another important option to filling human resource needs. Most employees welcome a limited amount of overtime work because of the obvious higher pay. However, if overtime becomes excessive or continues for a prolonged period of time, fatigue may set in and productivity may decrease. A related problem occurs when workers force themselves to ensure that overtime will be available. Again, if the firm is unionized, the union typically will want to influence the procedure to be followed for assigning overtime.

Temporary Help About nine out of 10 companies in this country have used temporary help agencies to meet their short-duration human resource needs. In fact, temporary help agencies are now a $2-billion industry.[11] Most organizations utilizing "temps" do so for clerical and lower-level hourly positions. While most temporary help firms tend to specialize in providing temporary office and blue-collar help, even scientific and technical personnel are available through such sources.

Companies that utilize such agencies mention such advantages as lower recruiting and selection costs, less record keeping, and lower benefit costs since the "temporary help" employee usually does not receive the various fringe benefits paid to full-time employees of the company. On the other hand, the "temp" employee may not have the same commitment to the organization as does the permanent employee. Again, the union contract frequently has provisions regarding the use of temporary help.

EVALUATION OF RECRUITMENT PROGRAMS

More research needs to be done on the effectiveness of recruitment programs. Studies in the area of recruitment have been relatively limited in number and scope. Most studies have focused on recruiting sources as they relate to subsequent employee turnover. For example, several studies have found that employee referrals are among the best sources of long-tenure employees and newspaper advertisement and private employment agencies are among the worst.[12] This is apparently not consistent with recruiters' perceptions of recruiting sources inasmuch as we have seen earlier in the chapter that newspaper advertising is one of the most frequently-used sources for recruiting.

Of course, how long a recently-hired employee stays with the firm says nothing about the quality of that employee. We need to know how various aspects of recruitment, such as sources and methods, relate to such things as absenteeism, performance, and job satisfaction. A recent study among research scientists suggests that recruiting sources and methods do make a difference. College recruiting and newspaper advertising tended to turn up less effective performances with higher rates of absenteeism. On the other hand, direct applications turned up the best performers. At the same time, recruiting source and method made no difference in terms of job satisfaction.[13]

Realistic Job Previews

A traditional approach to recruiting involves the recruiter attempting to "sell" the organization and/or the job to the applicant. The recruiter would praise, unrealistically, the benefits of the organization and extol the challenges and opportunities of the job being discussed. The applicant, in turn, might accept the position with impossible expectations of challenging work and rapid advancement to the top. The new employee then becomes disillusioned and feels misled by the organization.

As a result, organizations are attempting to improve the accuracy of applicants' expectations about job factors before an employment offer is made by providing a *realistic job preview*. Accordingly, applicants are provided with work samples or other information that describes the positive and negative factors they can expect to find in the job. Realistic information about such things as supervisory style, prospects for advancement, autonomy, and workplace is furnished.

Research has demonstrated that employees who were hired using realistic job previews tend to be more satisfied with their jobs and are less likely to leave than those recruited by traditional methods.[14] Thus, the use of realistic job previews is another step in the direction of attempting to match organizational needs with the needs of the job applicant—an important aspect of the recruiting process.

Cost Effectiveness

In the last analysis, each firm needs to evaluate the effectiveness of its own recruiting program. Since recruiting is expensive, the firm needs to consider the cost of various sources and methods of recruitment. Without some system of collecting recruiting cost and effectiveness data, the firm cannot make intelligent choices among recruiting alternatives. Exhibit 6–11 illus-

EXHIBIT 6–11
Examples of measures used to evaluate the recruiting process (per source and method).

Search	Screening	Offers and Hires	Results
$\dfrac{\text{Number of applicants}}{\text{Source and method}}$	$\dfrac{\text{Visits offered}}{\text{Applicants}}$	$\dfrac{\text{Offers extended}}{\text{Visits accepted}}$	Performance rating of hires
$\dfrac{\text{Number of applicants}}{\text{Source and method per unit of time}}$	$\dfrac{\text{Visits accepted}}{\text{Invitations}}$	$\dfrac{\text{Offers extended}}{\text{Total applicants}}$	Tenure of hires
			Exit interview data
Cost per applicant	$\dfrac{\text{Qualified applicants}}{\text{Unqualified applicants}}$	$\dfrac{\text{Offers extended}}{\text{Qualified applicants}}$	Costs per level of performance
$\dfrac{\text{Qualified applicants}}{\text{Total applicants}}$	$\dfrac{\text{Qualified applicants of each protected group}}{}$	$\dfrac{\text{Offers accepted}}{\text{Offers extended}}$	Time lapsed
$\dfrac{\text{Applicants of protected groups}}{\text{Total applicants}}$	Total visits offered	Time lapsed	
		Costs/hire Same indexes by each protected group	

Source: William E. Glueck, *Personnel: A Diagnostic Approach,* 3rd ed. (Plano, Tx.: Business Publications, Inc., 1982), p. 265. © 1982 Business Publications, Inc.

trates a number of indexes or measures that can be used at different stages of the recruiting process depending on what aspect of the recruitment program we want to evaluate.

Caution must be exercised in interpreting any evaluation measures. For example, in evaluating the cost effectiveness of several geographic areas as sources for recruiting, one area might be temporarily affected by an unusual labor market occurrence, such as a temporary layoff of certain types of employees by a large employer. Thus, any attempt at evaluating a recruitment program needs to be a continuous process rather than something done once every few years.

SUMMARY

The objective of the staffing process is to locate and acquire the human resources necessary to fulfill organizational and human resource plans. We have seen that staffing is a process involving a flow of activities that results in continuously meeting the firm's human resource needs.

Recruitment is a process of developing and maintaining adequate sources for filling human resource needs. It involves identifying and attracting candidates for current and future needs. Today, there are many factors that limit or affect the recruiting policies of any organizations. Among the most important constraints are labor markets, unions, organizational policies, and public policy.

Candidates to fill job needs must come either by movement within the organization or by recruitment from the outside. Every firm faces the question, "When and to what extent do we go outside?" In this chapter we have suggested some guidelines for answering that question. We have also examined internal recruitment, the major sources for external recruiting, and alternatives to recruitment. Since recruiting is an expensive but necessary activity, each firm should evaluate the effectiveness of its recruitment program. Several measures that can be used at different stages of the recruiting process have been suggested.

KEY CONCEPTS

Staffing process

Recruitment process

Labor market

Internal recruitment

Job posting

External recruitment

Realistic job previews

NOTES

1. "For Companies with an Image Problem, Hiring Top Talent Can Take Ingenuity," *Wall Street Journal*, October 17, 1980, p. 48.
2. U.S. Department of Labor, "Job Seeking Methods Used by American Workers," *Bulletin 1886*, 1975, p. 7.
3. For example, see John Curley, "More Companies Look Within for Managers," *Wall Street Journal*, October 28, 1980, p. 33.
4. James W. Walker, *Human Resource Planning* (New York: McGraw-Hill, 1980).
5. Van M. Evans, "Recruitment Advertising in the '80s," The *Personnel Administrator* 23, December 1978, p. 23.
6. "The Specialized Recruiter," *Business Week*, August 27, 1979, pp. 124–30.
7. S. J. Wilhelm, "Is Campus Recruiting On Its Way Out?" *Personnel Journal*, April 1980, p. 302.
8. Paul F. Wernimont, "Recruitment Policies and Practices," in *ASPA Handbook of Personnel and Industrial Relations*, ed. by Dale Yoder and Herbert G. Heneman, Jr. (Washington, D.C.: The Bureau of National Affairs, 1979), pp. 4–97.
9. See Joan Lindroth, "How to Beat the Coming Labor Shortage," *Personnel Journal*, April 1982, pp. 268–272.
10. Howard Rudnitsky, "A Cushion for Business," *Forbes* 123, Feb. 5, 1979, p. 78.
11. *Ibid.*

12. James A. Breaugh, "Relationship between Recruiting Sources and Employee Performance, Absenteeism, and Work Attitude," *Academy of Management Journal* 24, No. 1, 1981, pp. 142–147.
13. *Ibid.* Also see J. P. Wanous, *Organizational Entry: Recruitment, Selection, and Socialization of Newcomers* (Reading, Ma.: Addison-Wesley, 1980).
14. John G. Wanous, "Realistic Job Previews: Can a Procedure to Reduce Turnover Also Influence the Relationship between Abilities and Performance?" *Personnel Psychology* 31, 1978, pp. 249–258.

REVIEW AND DISCUSSION QUESTIONS

1. Who is responsible for recruiting in an organization?
2. Discuss several alternatives to recruiting. Under what conditions might each be used?
3. What factors influence the degree to which a firm will be involved in the recruiting process?
4. How has public policy affected the recruiting process of all organizations?
5. "Promotion from within is a good policy, but it results in a stagnant organization." Discuss.
6. For each of the following jobs, list the sources you would utilize to locate suitable candidates: (a) management trainee; (b) tool and die maker; (c) secretary; (d) manager, human resources.
7. As employment manager for the ABC Corporation, you receive a requisition for a management trainee. Assuming the firm has a policy of promoting from within, how would you proceed?
8. Discuss the necessary components for a successful college recruiting program.
9. Draw up a list of more "uncommon" external sources for recruiting hard-to-find employees. Be creative.

BIBLIOGRAPHY

Brecker, Richard L. "Ten Common Mistakes in College Recruitment—or How to Try without Really Succeeding." *Personnel* 52, March–April 1975, 19–28.

Bureau of National Affairs, Inc. *Fair Employment Practices Manual.* Washington, D.C., 1979.

Dahl, David A., and Patrick R. Pinto. "Job Posting: An Industry Survey." *Personnel Journal* 56, January 1977, 40–41.

Edson, Andrew S. "How Other Companies Assess MBA Recruitment: Some Make It Big, Others Stumble." *Management Review* 68, April 1979, 13–14.

Evans, Van M. "Recruitment Advertising in the '80s." *Personnel Administrator* 23, December 1978, 21–24.

Freund, Madalyn, and Patricia Somers. "Ethics in College Recruiting." *Personnel Administrator* 24, April 1979, 30–34.

Kosnik, Thomas J. "Aiming for the Right Company: Alternative Strategies for Recruitment." *Advanced Management* 44, Winter 1979, 52–57.

Miner, Mary G., and John B. Miner. *Employee Selection within the Law*. Washington, D.C.: Bureau of National Affairs, 1978.

Neuberger, T. S. "Sex as a Bona Fide Occupational Qualification under Title VII." *Labor Law Journal* 29, 1978, 425–29.

Schwab, Donald P. "Recruiting and Organizational Participation." In *Human Resource Management*, eds. K. Rowland and G. Ferris. Boston: Allyn & Bacon, 1982.

Sweeney, Herbert J., and Kenneth S. Teel. "A New Look at Promotion from Within." *Personnel Journal* 58, August 1979, 531–535.

Taylor, H. Nathaniel. "Job Posting Update." *Personnel Administrator* 22, January 1977, 45–46.

U.S. Department of Labor. *The Operation of the Federal and State Employment Service System*. Washington, D.C.: U.S. Government Printing Office, May 24, 1976.

Walker, James W. *Human Resource Planning*. New York: McGraw-Hill, 1980.

Wanous, John P. *Organizational Entry*. Reading, Mass.: Addison-Wesley, 1980.

Wernimont, Paul F. "Recruitment Policies and Practices." In *ASPA Handbook of Personnel and Industrial Relations*, eds. Dale Yoder and Herbert G. Heneman. Washington, D.C.: Bureau of National Affairs, 1979.

Selection

CHAPTER OUTLINE

Selecting Human Resources
Responsibility for Selection □ Factors in Selection Decisions

Determining Validity and Reliability for Selection Techniques
Validity □ Reliability

The Selection Process
Preliminary Screening □ Review of Application Blanks □ Employment Testing □ Reference Checks □ Employment Interviewing □ Physical Examinations

Assessment Centers

Legal Influences on the Staffing Process
Affirmative Action Programs □ Meeting the Challenge of Equal Employment Opportunities

Selection Strategies
Multiple Predictors □ Placement □ Cost-Benefit Analysis

Evaluation of the Selection Process

OBJECTIVES

1. Describe some of the important factors that affect selection decisions.
2. Define validity and reliability, and explain how they relate to the selection process.
3. Identify the key steps involved in the selection process.
4. Discuss how affirmative action and equal employment opportunity have influenced the staffing of an organization.
5. Specify ways to evaluate the selection process.

SPOTLIGHT:
Larry Spiller

Larry Spiller is currently a staff manager-personnel for Southern Bell Telephone and Telegraph Company. His varied staffing responsibilities include the coordination of EEO requirements, conducting internal EEO Compliance Reviews, coordinating the management evaluation plan, and coordinating the company's Quality of Work Life program.

Prior to his current position, he was Staff Manager of Training, responsible for first- and second-level management training programs. He was also Manager of the Management Assessment Program, which evaluated nonmanagement personnel for first-level management positions.

Comments by Larry Spiller

In today's highly competitive environment, more demands than ever are now being placed on corporate management to select qualified personnel. Businesses are actively seeking individuals who are able to find ways of advancing the business rather than simply projecting minor alterations, or even worse, repeating the status quo routinely year after year.

Recruiting efforts today are truly geared toward selecting those individuals who recognize the need for the effective management of the "human resources" of an organization. It is this emphasis that will play an important role in determining the success rate of an individual entering the business world.

Many of the large corporations today have established their own Assessment Centers to assist in identifying those individuals who demonstrate the potential and skills, such as oral and written communication skills, leadership, organizing and planning, decision making, etc., needed to perform effectively in a management position. The result of this assessment process, however, is only one of the factors considered in selecting an individual for a management position. An individual's job performance, the available job openings, and the EEO considerations of the company are also factors that will influence the final decision to hire or promote an individual into a management position. These same factors may also apply to many of our nonmanagement positions. All of these factors considered collectively will help to insure that the most qualified individual is selected for the position.

Individuals who are presently in the workforce, or those about to enter it, must prepare themselves today for the ever-demanding needs of the business world of tomorrow.

SELECTING HUMAN RESOURCES

Managers have always been concerned with the problem of selecting "winners" from available candidates—passing by a promising prospect or hiring someone who later does not measure up to requirements can be very costly. Further complicating the manager's job of selecting the "right" candidate are the legal and administrative constraints that have come into existence.

Every decision to select an individual for employment or promotion suggests a prediction that the candidate will succeed if placed on the job. *Selection*, therefore, may be viewed as a process of making predictions by matching differences in people to differences in job requirements. The basic objective of human resource selection is to obtain employees who are most likely to meet desirable standards of performance. This holds true regardless of whether the selection process is used to hire new employees for entry-level jobs, to transfer current employees, to assign employees to specialized training programs, to promote employees to higher level jobs, or to hire highly skilled technicians or managers.

Responsibility for Selection

Decisions on staffing policy are primarily a function of line management, as are selection and placement decisions. However, the human resource staff department has the responsibility for improving these decisions through competent professional assistance and recommendations. For example, test construction, evaluation, and interpretation are not within the expertise of line managers. Expertise in these areas requires professional training and experience, which are usually furnished by the human resource staff department (or by an outside consultant working with the staff department).

In addition, the many government regulations pertaining to hiring practices make it difficult, if not impractical, to have each manager performing all the selection activities for his or her department. A recent survey found that the vast majority of firms have centralized the screening procedures for employment.[1] While in smaller organizations even one full-time employment specialist may not be feasible, most larger firms have centralized the selection activities within a specialized group, usually called the employment office, which is part of the human resource department.

In practice, then, selection tends to be a shared responsibility. The employment office performs most of the preliminary screening of candidates; the managers make the final decision to hire within guidelines jointly determined with the human resource department. In some organizations, most lower-level positions are filled by the employment office. However, there are many variations of the selection procedure among organizations.

Factors in Selection Decisions

All organizations make selection decisions. In a smaller business, selection is likely to be done on a rather informal basis. In a large firm, selection may be a very costly, formalized procedure. Regardless of its size, an organization should consider a number of factors when making decisions regarding the selection of human resources.

The selection process is likely to vary according to the type of position to be filled. For example, technical and professional applicants will probably undergo more thorough evaluation to verify their competence than will unskilled laborers. If a firm is new, its approach to staffing is likely to be less structured than that of a well-established firm.

Social pressures also frequently play a part in selection decisions. For example, boycotts by minority groups have forced some businesses to disregard their traditional selection policies in an effort to hire more employees in these groups. In a union shop, seniority may be the basic criterion for selecting employees for some jobs, whereas in a nonunion shop, skills and abilities may be the sole criteria.

We must also keep in mind that the staffing process in general, and selection in particular, must be tailored to fit the needs of the given organization. This means that consideration must be given to such things as the level and complexity of the job, the organization costs if the selected employee fails on the job, the length of the required training period, and the cost of the "ideal" selection process. For example, some firms follow the practice of intentionally overhiring with the intent of "weeding out" poor performers during a probationary period. This practice tends to be costly for many reasons, including the expense of turnover and training. To illustrate, one large bank calculated its cost of replacing one teller as follows:

Recruiting	$105
Selection (three hours)	45
Medical examination	50
Reference check	25
Training time (one week)	200
Not fully productive for one month (one fourth of monthly salary)	220
Clerical and payroll costs	90
Indirect training costs	190
	$925

The number of applicants for a particular job will also affect selection decisions. For example, if the firm has a very effective recruiting program and there are a number of very qualified candidates, the selection process can indeed be very selective. On the other hand, if recruiting efforts have only produced a few applicants for a job requiring highly-specialized skills, whoever is available may have to be selected.

We shall also see in this chapter that some traditional selection techniques have been ruled discriminatory. A growing number of court cases have made it clear that any nonjob-related employment practice is illegal if such a practice has an adverse impact on minority group members, women, or persons aged 40 to 70. The high legal costs involved in defending company selection practices, plus lack of expertise in validating "job relatedness," have caused some companies to simply discontinue the use of certain selection tools such as tests. Before discussing specific steps, or selection techniques involved in the selection process, let us consider two important underlying concepts, validity and reliability.

DETERMINING VALIDITY AND RELIABILITY FOR SELECTION TECHNIQUES

In selecting employees for a position, we are concerned with predicting which applicants will perform satisfactorily on the job. In order to do this, we establish a selection process consisting of selection techniques or instruments. Before we use any of these techniques, such as tests or interviews, which will be discussed later in the chapter, we need to know (1) how valid the technique is in predicting success on the job, and (2) does it produce *consistent* results under varying conditions? Let us examine how we can go about answering these basic questions.

Validity

A selection technique has *validity* if it measures what it is supposed to measure. For example, if an employer is using an employment test to select someone for a job, the test is valid if it is directly measuring the applicant's ability to perform the job as evidenced by some acceptable criterion. Thus, while a yardstick may be a valid measure of length, it has no validity for measuring intelligence or ability to type.

While there are several types of validity, human resource managers are primarily interested in (1) content, (2) construct, and (3) criterion-related. It should be noted that while we shall illustrate these three types with regard to testing, they are relevant to any selection technique.

Content Validity In a content validation study the organization shows, usually through job analysis, that the content of the test, or interview, or other selection technique, is actually a representative sample of the work performed on the job. For example, a firm might test applicants for a bank-teller job on speed and accuracy with figures. On the other hand, if a job calls for more abstract (and less observable) behavior, such as leadership, content validity is not appropriate.

Construct Validity This concept of validity involves identifying the psychological trait or "construct" that underlies successful job performances. These constructs include such traits as verbal ability, leadership, and creativity, which are inferred from job behaviors and duties indicated in the job analysis. When this identification is accomplished, a selection technique is devised to measure the presence and degree of the trait. As an example, if leadership and creativity could be shown to be related to successful performance of a job, the firm might use a test that measures these two traits. It is important, however, that the test measure the trait it is *supposed* to measure, and that the trait be related to performance on the job. Construct validity thus requires showing that a relationship exists between the selection procedure (in this case, a test) and the construct.

Criterion-related Validity According to this concept, a selection procedure is justified by a statistical relationship between test scores and measures of job performance such as supervisory evaluations, absenteeism, or units produced. Two methods of established criterion-related validity are called predictive and concurrent.

The *predictive method*, which is the most preferred by the Equal Employment Opportunity Commission, is the most difficult to do. It involves using the selection device on *all* candidates but hiring them without regard to the score received on the test. After the employees are on the job long enough to identify successful and unsuccessful employees, their performance is statistically correlated with their scores on the selection device used when they were hired. This then becomes the criterion to be used as a predictor for future selection.

On the other hand, the *concurrent method* of establishing validity statistically relates a selection technique to the performance of employees currently on the job. This approach is more practical since it can immediately determine the usefulness of a selection technique.

Reliability

The *reliability* of a test selection device is the extent to which it produces consistent results. If the results of a test, for example, are not consistent, our ability to draw conclusions about its validity is also reduced. Thus, if a test is not reliable, its statistical validity will be low.

If an applicant took a test on Monday and scored well, we would expect the applicant to receive a relatively high score the following week (assuming something unusual, such as illness, did not occur on one of the test days). Thus, if we wanted to determine the reliability of a test we would correlate the scores of applicants given the same test on two different occasions.

THE SELECTION PROCESS

The selection process may vary from a ten-minute interview to a highly involved series of evaluations over an extended period of time. In a more complete program, the selection process is based upon careful job analysis, comprehensive human resource planning, and effective recruitment. The steps in the actual selection process usually include six steps:

1. Preliminary screening of applicants
2. Review of application forms
3. Employment testing
4. Reference checks
5. Employment interviews
6. Physical examinations

The sequence in which these six steps are applied may vary. You should also keep in mind that each of these steps is a tool or technique for collecting information on which to judge whether or not the applicant is qualified for a specific job (see Exhibit 7–1).

Preliminary Screening

This initial screening is intended to eliminate obvious misfits in order to reduce the time and cost of actual selection. For example, all applicants might be given a ten-minute screening interview to determine whether they have the necessary education, training, interest, and experience for the job. The interviewer might tell the applicant about the nature of the job opening and minimum requirements.

The preliminary screening is an important step in the selection process since it results in a pass–fail decision. This means that a potentially qualified applicant could get screened out at this point if the initial requirements are improper or if the interviewer is not qualified. The firm should, therefore, set specific and minimum standards for rejection that can be accurately determined in a brief interview (for example, job requires a college degree in physics).

If the requirements of the company and the qualifications and interests of the applicant appear to match in the initial screening, the individual would be given a more detailed interview. In most cases the applicant would be asked to complete an application form and then move on to another step in the selection process. It is also possible that the applicant may not qualify for one position but may have the requirements for another. Thus, even at this preliminary level it is important that the individual doing the screening be properly trained and informed of all human resource needs.

Application Blanks

Next to the interview, the application blank (or form) is the most commonly used selection tool. Typically, the application form gathers information

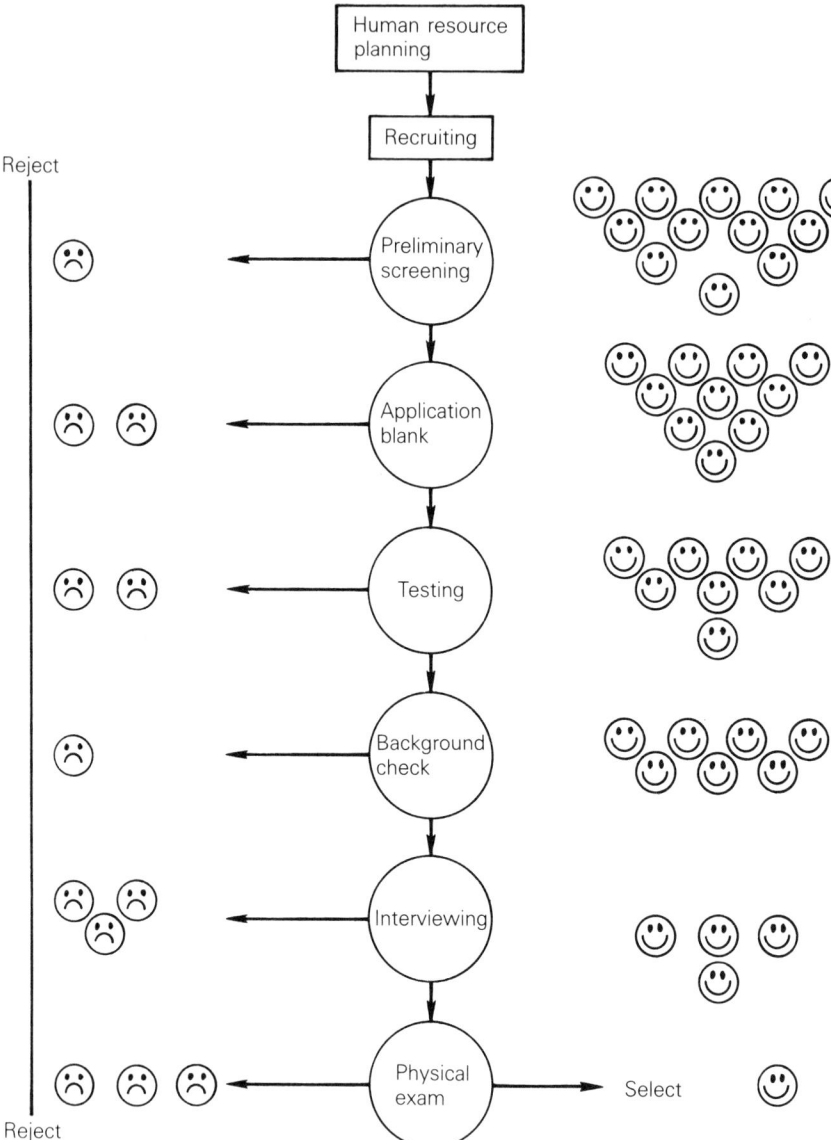

EXHIBIT 7-1
The selection process.

about the education, experience, and personal characteristics of the applicant, as illustrated in Exhibit 7-2 on page 206. Different forms may be used for different kinds of jobs. One form may be used for hourly employees, another for managerial and professional employees, and still another for sales and clerical personnel. Some firms use a short form when an applicant applies for a job with no immediate vacancy and a long form when the applicant will be considered for a current job opening.

Application forms should be tailor-made for a specific firm, and the content of the forms should vary as necessary to cover special job requirements. For low-level jobs where the applicant is likely to have little education and cultural attainment, the form should reflect this in its overall appearance, wording, and instructions. Items referring to race, religion, or national origin should not appear on the application form.[2]

Weighted Application Blank In recent years a growing number or organizations have attempted to determine the validity of their application blank by trying to correlate each item on the form with actual job success. In so doing, a firm may find that some items predict success better than others. The *weighted application blank* results and these items may then be given more weight than others in selecting employees. To illustrate, a company may find that its successful engineers ranked average in their graduating class but had been active in student organizations. These factors can then be given a definite statistical score when evaluating an application. Since it will take considerable time and effort to develop a *weighted application blank*, we would want to develop one only for those jobs that require considerable hiring.

Studies have shown weighted application forms to be useful in predicting such diverse factors as creativity and mechanical ingenuity, scientific and engineering performance, and turnover of factory workers. Attempts have been made to market "standard" weighted application forms for use in any company. Research has indicated, however, that ordinary aptitude tests can generally produce better results for less cost.

Besides the time and cost of developing such application forms, another drawback is that the form must be updated every few years to be sure that the factors identified are still valid predictors of job success. These shortcomings are probably the reasons why only 4 percent of almost 200 firms surveyed were using a weighted application form.[3]

Current Problems Recent court rulings, state laws, and administrative guidelines under federal legislature have challenged the job relatedness of many items formerly found on application forms. Questions regarding race, color, religion, national origin, age, marital status, handicaps, or arrests, are either prohibited or curtailed, unless the employer can prove their job relatedness. In addition, questions about child-care arrangements, a spouse, height and weight, pregnancy, membership in organizations, or home ownership or rental are also generally prohibited or curtailed. Such questions by themselves do not violate existing laws if the information is a necessary qualification for a particular job. However, the burden of proof is with the employer if a complaint is filed, and an adverse impact exists.

A review of applications from 151 of the largest corporations found that all but two had at least one "legally inappropriate" question on their

SEARS, ROEBUCK AND CO.

APPLICATION FOR EMPLOYMENT

PLEASE PRINT INFORMATION REQUESTED IN INK.

Date ____________

SEARS IS AN EQUAL OPPORTUNITY EMPLOYER and fully subscribes to the principles of Equal Employment Opportunity. Sears has adopted an Affirmative Action Program to ensure that all applicants and employes are considered for hire, promotion and job status, without regard to race, color, religion, sex, national origin, age or handicap.

To protect the interests of all concerned, applicants for certain job assignments must pass a physical examination before they are hired. Alternative placement of an applicant who does not meet the physical standards of the job for which he/she was originally considered is permitted.

NOTE: This application will be considered active for 90 days. If you have not been employed within this period and are still interested in employment at Sears, please contact the office where you applied and request that your application be reactivated.

Name ____________ (Last / First / Middle) Social Security Number ____________ (Please present your Social Security Card for review.)

Address ____________ (Number / Street / City / State / Zip Code)

County ____________ Current phone or nearest phone ____________

Previous Address ____________ (Number / Street / City / State / Zip Code)

If hired, can you furnish proof of: Age? ☐ Yes ☐ No U.S. Citizen? ☐ Yes ☐ No
or Alien legally entitled to work in U.S. ☐ Yes ☐ No

(Answer only if position for which you are applying requires driving.)
Licensed to drive car? ☐ YES ☐ NO
Is license valid in this state? ☐ YES ☐ NO

Have you ever been employed by Sears? ☐ YES ☐ NO If so, when and where last employed? ____________ Position ____________

Former employes of Sears and certain Subsidiaries may be entitled to service credit under the Pension Plan based on prior employment with Sears, Roebuck and Co., Homart Development Co., Sears Investment Management Co., Sears Roebuck Acceptance Corp., Sears, Roebuck de Puerto Rico, Inc., Sears Roebuck Overseas, Inc., Sears Securities Sales, Inc., Terminal Freight Handling Co., Allstate Insurance Company and their Subsidiaries, Lifetime Foam Products, Pacific Installers, and Sears, S.A. (Central America).

Have you a relative in the employ of Sears in the store or unit to which you are applying? ____________

A PHYSICAL OR MENTAL DISABILITY WILL NOT CAUSE REJECTION IF IN SEARS MEDICAL OPINION YOU ARE ABLE TO SATISFACTORILY PERFORM IN THE POSITION FOR WHICH YOU ARE BEING CONSIDERED.

Do you have any physical or mental impairment which may limit your ability to perform the job for which you are applying? ____________

Do you have any Service related disability? ☐ Yes ☐ No

EDUCATION	School Attended	No. of Years	Name of School	City/State	Graduate?	Course or College Major	Average Grades
	Grammar						
	Jr. High						
	Sr. High						
	Other						
	College					Degree	

MILITARY SERVICE	BRANCH OF SERVICE	DATE ENTERED SERVICE	DATE OF DISCHARGE	HIGHEST RANK HELD	SERVICE-RELATED SKILLS AND EXPERIENCE APPLICABLE TO CIVILIAN EMPLOYMENT

What experience or training have you had other than your work experience, military service and education? (Community activities, hobbies, etc.)

I am interested in the type of work I have checked:

Sales ____ Office ____ Mechanical ____ Warehouse ____ Other (Specify) ____________

Or the following specific Job ____________

I am seeking (check only one):
☐ Temporary / ☐ Permanent — Employment

If temporary, Indicate dates available ____________.

I am available for (check only one):
☐ Part-Time / ☐ Full-Time — Work

If part-time, indicate maximum hours per week ________, **and enter hours available in block to the right.**

HOURS AVAILABLE FOR WORK	
Sun	To
Mon	To
Tues	To
Wed	To
Thurs	To
Fri	To
Sat	To

Have you been convicted during the past seven years of a serious crime involving a person's life or property?

NO ☐ YES ☐ If yes, explain ____________

10534 Rev. 1-81 (SEE REVERSE SIDE)

EXHIBIT 7–2

Sample application form. Courtesy of Sears, Roebuck and Co.

application forms. In fact, 57 of the firms had more than 10 "inappropriate" questions.[4] Thus, it is important that an organization examine the application form used to determine if all the information sought is a necessary qualification for the job. Consulting the EEOC guidebook for employers would also prove beneficial.[5]

EXHIBIT 7-2, continued.

Employment Testing

Employment tests are usually administered after a preliminary interview has been conducted and the application blank has been examined. Tests have been developed in an effort to find more objective ways of measuring the qualifications of job applicants, as well as for use with employees being considered for transfer or promotion. A properly developed and administered testing program can provide a more objective way of judging job applicants and improve the accuracy of the selection process. Some of the more commonly used tests include performance or achievement tests, intelligence tests, aptitude tests, interest tests, personality tests, and polygraph tests.

Performance or achievement tests measure how much the job-seeker already knows about the job or how well he or she is able to do the job. For example, prospective typists may be asked to type a page, a computer operator may be asked to do some programming, or a widget machine operator may be asked questions about the equipment.

Intelligence tests attempt to measure the individual's capacity or overall ability to learn. Although such tests have been proven valid for certain high-level jobs, they have often been misused to screen applicants for jobs that should be measured with performance or aptitude tests. For example, the reasoning factor in the Wonderlic or Otis tests is not very predictive of ability to be a file clerk. Certain tests (of aptitude) of perceptual speed, however, are effective in selecting file clerks.

In general, while intelligence tests are often useful in selecting individuals who can do well in training or learning, intelligence in itself has not proven to be a valid predictor of job success. Even people who do not score high on intelligence tests may be found performing a broad spectrum of jobs with a wide range of skill levels. This is especially true for those jobs whose preparation does not involve a great deal of "academic"-type training.

Aptitude tests attempt to measure ability to learn specific jobs. These tests may be multiaptitude or specific aptitude. *Multiaptitude tests* measure a number of traits. For example, the three-hour Differential Aptitude Test is a series of eight tests covering clerical speed, verbal reasoning, abstract reasoning, mechanical reasoning, numerical ability, space relations, spelling, and sentences. *Specific aptitude* tests measure specific patterns of abilities necessary to perform certain jobs. For example, mechanical aptitude tests such as the SRA Mechanical Aptitude are useful in selecting apprentices for skilled mechanical trades.

The most widely used and extensively researched aptitude test battery is the General Aptitude Test Battery (GATB), which is the official U.S. Employment Service aptitude test. Used by state employment agencies throughout the country, the GATB is composed of 12 subtests that measure nine aptitudes found to be important for successful performance in a wide variety of occupations. These nine aptitudes are general intelligence, verbal, numerical, spatial, form perception, clerical perception, motor coordination, finger dexterity, and manual dexterity.

Interest tests (often referred to as inventories) attempt to measure the applicant's interest. Although the test results may indicate whether a person likes a particular job, the results are not necessarily related to job success. Therefore, interest tests are primarily used in job or vocational counseling. Examples of interest tests are the Kuder Preference Record and the Strong Vocational Interest Blank.

In the set of interest questions shown below, for example, the person taking the test would be asked for each set of activities, which would he or she most and least like to do:

	Most	Least
1. a) Design a chair	_____	_____
b) Build a chair	_____	_____
c) Sell a chair	_____	_____
d) Repair a broken chair	_____	_____

Personality tests (also referred to as inventories) attempt to measure different facets of the personality such as achievement orientation, dominance, and sociability. Like interest tests, personality tests have neither right nor wrong answers, but if properly administered and interpreted, can assist in predicting how someone will handle situational stress or will relate to other people.

Examples of these types of tests would be paper-and-pencil inventories such as the Minnesota Multiphasic Personality Inventory (MMPI) and projective techniques, such as the Rorschach Inkblot Test, which require trained specialists for their interpretation. Personality tests are far behind the other types of tests in terms of demonstrated usefulness for selection and placement in industry. Severe criticism of these tests strongly suggests that much more research is needed before they become useful in the selection process. At any rate they should only be administered by a competent psychologist.

Polygraph tests measure the individual's galvanic skin response (GSR), heart and pulse rate, and breathing rate. Incorrectly referred to as a "lie detector," the polygraph is used for different purposes by about one-fifth of the largest employers in the United States.[6] Organizations dealing with security and law enforcement, as well as banks and retail firms are common users of polygraphs.[7]

The person being tested with a polygraph is asked a series of neutral questions such as: "Is your name Mary Smith?" Once a series of normal responses are achieved, the individual will be asked a stressful question such as "Have you ever stolen from your former employer?"

In recent years, the use of polygraph for selection purposes has come under heavy criticism. Questions about its constitutionality and invasion of privacy have been raised. A more serious question is whether the test is valid and reliable. It must be remembered that the polygraph merely records physiological changes in response to stress—which may or may not be caused by "lying." Thus, there are some people who can lie easily and end up "beating" the polygraph. Other people who respond emotionally to certain types of questions may be labeled as liars. Since the polygraph provides only raw data, its credibility is solely based on the judgment and interpretation of the administrator.

As a result of these concerns, several bills have been introduced in Congress to regulate or ban polygraph usage for employment selection. Thus, the future usage of polygraph tests as a selection device appears to be in the hands of the courts and Congress.

Benefits of Tests The United States Employment Service (U.S.E.S.) through its 2,400 offices located in every state throughout the country, is by far the largest user of employment tests. The extent of test usage is illustrated in Exhibit 7-3. Based on their research and review of existing studies of different methods of selecting workers, the U.S.E.S. has concluded that *"occupa-*

EXHIBIT 7–3
Examples of the extent of usage of U.S. Employment Service testing programs for selecting employees.

> Nissan Motors, Inc., maker of Datsun, is opening the first Japanese auto plant in the U.S., located in Tennessee. All 2,000 workers to be hired are being recruited by the U.S. Employment Service (U.S.E.S.) and screened for selection with the use of ES tests.
>
> The Tennessee Valley Authority (TVA) hires all candidates for training in 17 different crafts based upon the exclusive use of ES tests. About 4,000 placements have been made at TVA during the past five years.
>
> It is standard practice for ES tests to be used in selection of candidates for apprenticeship jobs established under standards set by the Bureau of Apprenticeship and Training. During the year, the ES will achieve 9,000 placements for apprenticeship jobs in the electrical industry alone.
>
> In Kentucky, ES placed 3,500 test-selected workers at the Ford plant in Louisville. The company has since reported a drastic drop in turnover from 25 percent to 5 percent annually.
>
> Volkswagen of America identified ES tests as the best tools for screening applicants for their auto plant in Pennsylvania. The ES placed 2,000 test-selected employees using the aptitude test for automobile assembler.
>
> The ES in Iowa, Michigan, New York and other states has exclusive agreements to provide recruitment and testing services as a means of making thousands of placements in various city and state merit system jobs.
>
> Numerous large firms have agreements with local offices of the ES to test all applicants referred for jobs at some of their local plants. Examples of such firms include: General Electric, Bethlehem Steel, Phillip Morris, Texas-Gulf, R.R. Donnelley, Carolina Telephone and Telegraph, Continental Can, Safeway, the major auto companies, Borg-Warner, Bendix, Wang Labs, Parker Bros., Dayton Power & Light, Rockwell, GMAC, and ITT.

Source: Based on "Occupational Testing Services Contribute to ES Productivity," position paper by U.S. Employment Service Office of Program Operations, Division of Counseling and Test Development, July 6, 1982.

tional tests are by far the most accurate method of selecting the most productive workers."[8]

The benefits of using properly selected and administered tests as part of the selection process can be substantial. For example, in a recent study of two groups of production workers—one group tested and one group not tested—the test-selected workers were more productive, had lower turnover, and cost less to train (see Exhibit 7–4).

Current Problems in Test Usage Civil rights issues have had a major impact on the use of employment tests. Conflicting rules and guidelines coming from court decisions and federal agencies have confused managers as to what is legal and proper with regard to employment testing. Consequently, a growing number of organizations have dropped their testing programs. A Bureau of National Affairs survey found that 90 percent of the respondents were using tests in 1963, whereas only 55 percent were using them in 1971.

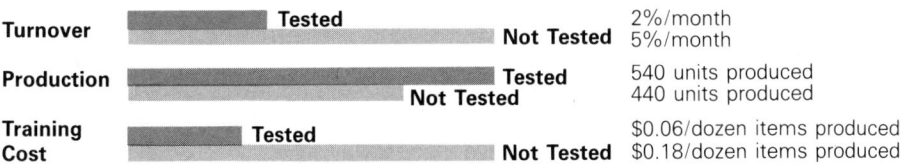

Turnover	Tested / Not Tested	2%/month / 5%/month
Production	Tested / Not Tested	540 units produced / 440 units produced
Training Cost	Tested / Not Tested	$0.06/dozen items produced / $0.18/dozen items produced

EXHIBIT 7–4
Comparison of two groups of newly hired workers: one group test-selected and one group not tested. *Source: Employer Guide to Job Service Testing Program,* Michigan Employment Security Commission (Detroit, Mich., April 1980), p. 1.

A 1976 survey reported only 42 percent of companies were using employment tests.[9] Similarly, a survey conducted by the American Society for Personnel Administration revealed that most firms were confused about their testing responsibilities according to federal guidelines. As a result, over 36 percent said that they did not test at all, and most of the others had reduced their testing in the preceding few years.

Court decisions have put the burden of proof on the company to show that its tests are predictive of job success. For example, in the case of *Myart* v. *Motorola* a black worker was denied a job because of his low score on an intelligence test. The company was told that it could use the test *if* it could show that the test predicted job success. This is difficult to do since studies have shown that certain tests may not be equally predictive of job success in white and black workers.[10]

Opponents of testing claim that tests may discriminate against minorities, are given too much weight in selection decisions, and are often unrelated to job success. On the other hand, if tests are properly developed, administered, and used in conjunction with other selection tools, they can be an important component of the selection process.[11]

Suggestions for Test Usage The use of testing as a selection tool will probably be increasing again since the publication of the *Uniform Guidelines on Employee Selection Procedures* were adopted by the EEOC, Department of Labor, and the Department of Justice. Some of the uncertainty regarding test requirements has thereby been removed. In general, the manager should follow certain guidelines on the effective use of tests, such as:

1. Do not make tests the sole tool for selecting applicants.
2. Use the right tests for the job for which you are hiring.
3. Be sure that a test measures what you want to measure.
4. Try a test on present employees before adopting it.
5. Seek the advice of competent consultants in test development or selection.
6. Have the test administered by competent professionals.

If you desire to learn more about testing, consult the reading materials on testing listed in the bibliography of this chapter.

Reference Checks

There is a good deal of variation among firms in the types of references requested, methods of verifying references, and the consistency with which references and applicant data are checked. Although little research has been done on this subject, it appears that most firms have found it useful to learn how the applicant performed on previous jobs.[12] Phoning or interviewing the applicant's past supervisors can be a helpful source of information. Probing is often required since people are very cautious about what they say regarding past employees.

In addition to verifying the accuracy of what the applicant has said in the application form or in an interview, a reference check may disclose further information about the applicant. When conducting a reference check, it is wise to be on the watch for incorrect dates of employment, claims of a higher level of responsibility than that actually held, inflated salary figures, and falsified information about experience or education. Since studies reveal that 90 percent of past employers and supervisors comment favorably when asked to rate a previous employee, there is some doubt as to how much weight should be placed on such ratings. Whenever possible, objective data should be sought, including such information as grades shown in school transcripts and data recorded on personnel records.

Some firms use outside organizations, such as commercial credit-rating companies, to provide information on an individual's work history, character, and financial condition. Such reports are now governed by the Fair Credit Reporting Act, and the applicant must be notified in writing that such information is being sought.

Since Congress passed the Privacy Act in 1974, legislation and judicial rulings have had a major effect on reference checks. According to the law, applicants have the right to examine reference checks regarding their employment unless the right is waived in writing. One way to get around the privacy law is for the applicants to sign a release form stating that they waive the right to examine the reference checks. Still, objective reference letters are becoming difficult to obtain. Many employers now will only put in writing the following information regarding former employees: job title, dates of employment, whether or not the company would rehire, and salary.[13]

It should be noted that court rulings and labor agreements are placing more restrictions on what can be retained in a personnel folder. For example, some organizations are restricted from keeping any medical records, grievances, or disciplinary correspondence after one year.

Although background information may be getting more difficult to obtain, it is probably now more important than ever as the amount of credential fraud appears to be increasing.[14] Thus, a reference check can determine if the applicant has the experience and qualifications listed on the application blank. Sometimes the discrepancy is not the result of fraud but merely a difference in job definition. For example, the "engineer" at one company may have performed the job duties similar to that of a "technician" at the investigating company. Similarly, a "manager" might be a highly paid clerk at one firm and an important decision maker at another.

Employment Interviewing

The employment interview remains the most widely used and the most important tool in the selection process. An effective interview enables the interviewer to learn more about the job applicant's background, interests, and values; it also gives the applicant an opportunity to find out more about the job and the organization.

The different techniques of conducting interviews have been classified in many ways. For example, we might consider an employment interview to be structured, unstructured, or a combination of the two. Although studies have found the structured interview to be more reliable, no single technique or approach is appropriate in all cases. The type of information desired suggests the approach to use. Let us briefly consider these different approaches or techniques.

Interviewing Techniques In a *structured*, or *patterned interview*, we determine in advance the questions and their sequence, based upon the job description and specifications. A form is generally used, whereby we go down a list of questions and record the applicant's replies. Exhibit 7–5 is an illustration of a structured interview guide.

EXHIBIT 7–5
Structured interview guide (sample questions).

Work Experience
What is your previous work experience?
What were your duties in your previous jobs?
Why did you leave your previous place of employment?
What kinds of work do you like best? Least?
Why do you want to work for this company?

Education
What is the highest level of education you achieved?
What were your best subjects? What subjects did you do less well in?
Have you considered further schooling?
Any special achievements in school?

Career Plans
What are your salary requirements?
What are you looking for in a job?
What can you contribute to this company in the way of abilities and experience?
What kind of work would you like to be doing in five years? In ten years?

In the *unstructured,* or *nondirective, interview,* we have a general topic to discuss and follow no preplanned strategy. The objective is to get the applicants to do the talking, and they have considerable leeway in determining the direction of the discussion and in emphasizing what they feel is important. An unstructured interview might include such questions as "Tell me about yourself" or "What are your career plans?"

Few employment interviewers use a purely nondirective technique. For example, the interviewer might ask the applicant some specific questions about the job duties performed on the former job. These questions might be followed by a nonstructured approach such as "Tell me about the kind of work you like to do."

Similarly, even though a structured interview is being used, it need not be rigid. The skillful interviewer using a series of patterned questions will avoid reading the questions and continuing down the list in an inflexible manner. The interviewer will probe with such questions as "That's interesting; tell me more about it" until a satisfactory understanding of the applicant's response to the patterned question has been obtained.

A special type of interview, which is much talked about but not commonly used, is the *stress interview.* It is intended to disorient the applicants to see how they will respond under anxiety and pressure. However, this technique is of questionable value since rarely is the stress created in an interview format similar to that found on the job. In addition, a negative image of the interviewer and company may develop which in turn may carry over to the job in the event that the applicant is hired.

Current Problems with the Employment Interview   While the interview is one of the more researched selection tools, it is not known to be valid. It is, in fact, a relatively weak tool for predicting the job success of an applicant. Why then is it almost universally used as a selection tool? For one thing, it may be the best, if not only, way to obtain certain information about the applicant, such as communication skills, attitudes, and clarifications of information on the application blank. It also allows the interviewer to inform the applicant more fully about the job and organization, if necessary, and to "sell" the applicant on the job.

At the same time, it is important to remember that interviewing is an art—not a science. This means that poorly trained interviewers can, and will, make errors. A common mistake is the tendency to stereotype people (for example, "Southerners are slow workers"; "farm workers are dull"; "physically handicapped people are unreliable"). Another mistake is to phrase questions in a way that results in unreliable answers (for example, "You do like sales work, don't you?"). Studies have found that, generally speaking, the more structured the interview and the more training the interviewer has, the more reliable the interview.[15]

Frequently, it is the way in which questions are asked rather than the content of the question that results in emotional barriers to communications. For example, in Exhibit 7–6 we can see some less direct ways of asking sensitive questions of the applicant.

The interview, like the employment test and an application blank, is a selection tool and, therefore, must meet the standards of job-relatedness and nondiscrimination. In one EEOC case the court ruled that by relying on questions not related to the job applied for when selecting employees, interviewers violated EEOC guidelines.[16]

As more managers and human resource specialists are trained in interviewing, we can expect that the interview as a selection tool will correspondingly increase in usefulness and reliability. Let us now consider a few suggestions that will increase the effectiveness of our own interviews.

EXHIBIT 7–6
Sensitive questions and their alternatives.

Too Direct or Sensitive	Less Direct or Sensitive
Why were you fired from your last job? or Why are you looking for another job?	What are some of your reasons for considering other employment at this time?
Did you have trouble with your boss?	How would you describe your boss?
Why did you leave school before you got your degree?	Was there any particular reason that you decided to leave school when you did?
To what do you attribute your poor employment record?	I see you have changed jobs several times. What were some of your reasons for seeking new opportunities? or Everyone has problems with some aspects of their jobs. Could you describe some of the things that posed problems for you on previous jobs?
Did you get along with your co-workers?	Could you describe your relationship with a co-worker or colleague whom you were particularly close to?
What didn't you like about your last job?	Most situations have some aspects that are not as pleasant as others. Were there any less pleasant aspects of your last job?
Are you free to move?	How would you feel about moving to another city at the present time? or If you were relocated to another area, what problems would this present for you? (Note: The relocation question usually takes more time and should not be approached so directly. The whole topic can become a separate area of nondirective inquiry. . . .)
Your sales record must have been poor last year, since you didn't get a bonus.	How would you describe your sales success during the past year? or We all realize that sales often reflect various conditions of the economy. Could you comment on some factors that might have precluded your meeting last year's quotas?
You mean to say you're unemployed? I suppose you're on unemployment, huh?	At present you're not employed, then, is that correct? Were you eligible to receive unemployment compensation after you were laid off?
Why would you think you are qualified to go into research and development, with your background?	Would you comment on how you feel you could use your background in our research and development area?

Source: Table 2.1 (pages 24–25) from *Selection Interviewing for Managers* by Thomas L. Moffatt. Copyright © 1979 by Thomas L. Moffatt. Reprinted by permission of Harper & Row, Publishers, Inc.

Suggestions for Improving the Interview Research has shown that trained interviewers using sound procedures can and do achieve good results. Managers desiring to improve their interviewing skills will want to read one or more of the many books dealing with employment interviewing. In general, you can improve the quality of your interviewing by observing eight rules:

1. Formulate the objective of the interview and the questions to be asked before seeing the applicant.
2. Conduct the interview in private, and put the applicant at ease with a few general remarks about the business and the job.
3. Encourage the applicant to talk by asking pertinent questions and listening attentively to the answers.
4. Avoid any suggestion of discrimination. That is, avoid the topics of race, religion, national origin, age, and political views.
5. Retain control of the interview. Don't be dominant, but keep the interview headed toward the objective.
6. Probe into relevant topics raised by the applicant and pursue additional topics you have planned to cover.
7. Allow plenty of time, but don't waste it.
8. Record the facts obtained in the interview while they are fresh.

Even when interviewing for the lowest-level jobs, it is a good practice, whenever possible, to have the applicant interviewed by at least two persons, preferably on different days. The applicant's prospective supervisor should definitely be one of the interviewers.

Physical Examinations

In most firms, the final step in the selection process is a physical examination. Such examinations have not been shown to be highly reliable predictors of future medical problems. However, they are valuable in screening out applicants whose physical qualifications are inadequate to meet the requirements of the job they are being considered for.

Again, it must be emphasized that physical standards for jobs need to be realistic and job-related. Otherwise, potentially qualified job candidates may be rejected by unnecessary or unrealistic medical standards.

Physical examinations are also used to record physical and health problems at the time of hiring in order to protect the firm against unwarranted workers' compensation claims. In a more positive light, progressive companies use physical examinations in an attempt to place persons who are employable but whose physical handicaps require assignment to certain jobs only. It is also relevant to note that the Department of Vocational Rehabilitation can issue a "secondary certificate" for a person with a known physical condition. This limits the employer's liability and can have a positive affect on Worker's Compensation Insurance premiums.

ASSESSMENT CENTERS

A somewhat newer method used for selecting managerial talent is the *assessment center*. AT&T has formally assessed over 75,000 employees, and numerous other firms, such as IBM, J.C. Penney, General Electric, Standard Oil of New Jersey, and Sears, have established assessment centers. Smaller firms have had some success in utilizing such centers through consultants who provide the service on a fee basis. The use of assessment centers in managerial selection has been described by many writers. Parker, for example, reports that over 2,000 companies have used the assessment center approach.[17]

Assessment centers typically process candidates in groups of 10 to 15, exposing each group to various exercises for one to four days. These exercises may include such standard selection tools as interviews and tests. However, the assessment center takes a "broad-band" approach whereby candidates are observed in many settings, including management games and in-basket and problem-solving exercises. Meanwhile, experienced managers observe and note the behavior of each candidate and the patterns of interpersonal relations that develop. Candidates are selected on the basis of the evaluations of these managers.

The assessment center also shows substantial promise for identifying management potential among women and minority group employees. For example, a study at the Michigan Bell Telephone Company found that assessment center ratings of both white and black females were very predictive of ratings made by superiors some time after the women were promoted to supervisory positions.[18]

While studies to date support the assessment center procedure as an effective and valid method of managerial selection, it is not without some disadvantages.[19] The most important limitation of the procedure is the high cost. Dunnette and Borman also caution that "the rapid growth of assessment centers may be accompanied by sloppy or improper application of assessment procedures."[20]

LEGAL INFLUENCES ON THE STAFFING PROCESS

The staffing process is subject to legal scrutiny from several directions. Major legal influences stem from federal, state, and local laws prohibiting employment discrimination because of race, sex, or age. Other legal influences result from privacy rights as protected under consumer credit laws. It should be noted at the outset that the law is more than the words stated in legislation; it also includes how the courts interpret those words, and such interpretation is constantly evolving. The decisions of lower courts, for example, have been reversed by higher courts.

A striking example of court reversal is the *Griggs* v. *Duke Power Company* case. The federal district court and the Fourth Circuit Court of Appeals both upheld the Duke Power Company's position. The U.S. Supreme Court then reversed the lower courts by a vote of 8 to 0. The implication of the Supreme Court decision in this case is that if any employment practice eliminates a higher percentage of minority applicants, or women, or any other group protected by the law, the burden of proof is on the employer to show that the practice is job-related and predicts job performance.

Affirmative Action Programs

As discussed in Chapter 2, Title VII of the Civil Rights Act is enforced by the Equal Employment Opportunity Commission (EEOC). At first the courts required strict proof of discrimination in hiring practices before ruling against an employer. It had to be shown, for example, that a qualified minority worker did, in fact, seek a job and that a less qualified white was hired instead. Now the courts are looking to results rather than to the methods by which employees are hired. If a company located in an area with a substantial minority population has a small number of minority employees, the EEOC may inquire into the company's selection process, and the results may well be that the firm will have to take remedial action to ensure the reduction of "inequality." The focus has also shifted from hiring women and minorities at lower-level jobs to increasing the proportionate representation of women and minorities at all levels, including management. Remedial action may be costly. In one case, nine steel companies and the steelworkers' union were required to give an estimated $31 million in back pay to 45,000 minority and female workers who were determined to have suffered loss of income because of company–union promotion policies that restricted them to lower-paying jobs.

The Office of Federal Contract Compliance (OFCC) is responsible for seeing that employers who receive federal government contracts file an affirmative action plan. If an employer does not have an approved plan, OFCC can institute proceedings to cancel the contract. The employer's plan must have specific steps and timetables to remedy "underutilization" of women and minorities in each job classification.

Meeting the Challenge of Equal Employment Opportunities

It is apparent from the above that recent laws, regulations, and court decisions have had a significant impact on the entire staffing process. Equal employment opportunity is now the law of the land. At the same time, as we have seen, it is not always clear when a firm is operating within the law. As a result, a growing number of firms are employing EEO specialists who have an in-depth knowledge of EEO requirements and who keep abreast of court decisions relating to the various EEO laws and regulations. Other firms turn to outside consultants for assistance in operating within the law.

Many of the lower court decisions must still be resolved by the U.S. Supreme Court. Meanwhile, it is important that the firm develop a positive approach toward an EEO program. Such a program must be viewed as an important and integral part of the firm's total human resource system and not "just another personnel department program." The types of questions management might ask regarding its selection requirements and procedures are presented below from the official handbook of the American Society for Personnel Administration.

Are all job requirements based upon a careful analysis of the job? Are the job descriptions and job requirements in writing? Are the job requirements job related? Could they be defended as such in court? Do the job requirements exceed those of a number of satisfactory incumbents in the job? If so, they can be challenged.

Are there questions on the application form which are not job related and which reject a higher percentage of minority applicants or women? Or which reject on the basis of age? Some of the questions which may be illegal in some states or challenged on a federal basis are: date of birth, age, sex, marital status, citizenship status, draft status, arrest record, number of dependent children, "own your own home," color of eyes and hair, friends or relatives working for the employer, garnishment record, height, weight, maiden name, Mr., Miss, or Mrs., spouse's name, spouse's work, widowed, divorced, or separated? If these items are needed for identification purposes they may be obtained for personnel records after the hire. If the items are not specifically forbidden by law, they may be left on the application, but if they are used in hiring and cause a differential rejection rate, then the burden will be on the employer to show that they are job related. In many cases the use of this data is based on flimsy reasoning which would not stand up in court.

Do you have clearly supportable evidence that interviewers have received training on federal and state law? Have clear instructions been issued to them on hiring? Are their final selection decisions based on clearly supportable job-related job requirements?

Are education requirements clearly supportable? Do you insist on a diploma or a degree when in fact a certain number of years of experience might suffice in lieu of the educational requirement? Are your college-degree requirements clearly job-related? Do your college-degree requirements exceed those of a number of successful incumbents? If so, they may be challenged.

Are your experience requirements reasonable? Are you inclined to favor persons with five years of experience in an area when two years would clearly suffice to make the person qualified?

Are your promotion procedures sufficiently well defined to avoid the possibility of even a semblance of discrimination? Is your procedure in writing? Is there more than one avenue through which a person may be considered? Are employees aware of the requirements for promotion? Can they get information on job openings as they occur? Is there a procedure for review of selection decisions for compliance with legal requirements?

PLANNING AND STAFFING

> Where performance is a factor in promotion, is the evaluation of performance systematized? Does the person know where he stands? Has he been apprised of the things he may need to do to prepare himself for advancement?*

SELECTION STRATEGIES

The final decision of which applicant should be selected for a specific job position should be based on a selection strategy that considers several key concepts. Let us briefly consider each of these: multiple predictors, placement measures, and cost–benefit analysis.

Multiple Predictors

When more than one predictor or selection technique is used, it is necessary to decide how we are going to combine them to make an employment decision. There are three approaches: multiple hurdle, compensatory, and combined. In *multiple hurdles*, each selection device is reviewed as a hurdle over which the applicant must pass before proceeding to the next one. Thus, the applicant, after being initially screened, must pass a review of his or her application form, then a test, followed by a background check, and so on (see Exhibit 7–1). Failing to pass any hurdle results in the applicant being rejected for the job.

In the *compensatory approach* to selection, the applicant is not automatically rejected because of failure at any one hurdle (selection device). An applicant might score low at one step in the selection process but that score might be offset by a very high mark in another area. For example, an applicant who is nervous might receive a low score on the interview but yet do very well on the performance test and reference check. Typically, firms using this approach will allow all applicants to complete the selection process, after which the applicants are compared to each other.

In the *combined approach*, the selection process starts with multiple hurdles and ends with a compensatory approach. For example, one organization has found that a minimum score on a validated aptitude test was a requirement for success in an entry-level job. Therefore, all applicants were first screened on the basis of the test. Those not meeting the minimum score were rejected; the other applicants completed the remainder of the selection process. A compensatory approach was then taken to filling the job from among the latter pool of applicants.

Placement

In a sense selection is a limited process in that we are involved in choosing or rejecting applicants for a specific position. *Placement*, on the other hand,

---

*Reprinted by permission from "Equal Employment Opportunities" by Howard C. Lockwood in ASPA Handbook of Personnel and Industrial Relations, D. Yoder and H. Heneman, Jr., eds., pages 4-278–4-279, copyright © 1979 by The Bureau of National Affairs, Inc., Washington, D.C.

is a broader process that considers an applicant for more than one position. That is, while the applicant may not qualify for one position, the applicant's abilities, interests, skills, or other characteristics may qualify him or her for other jobs.[21]

A placement strategy as opposed to a traditional select/reject approach, is especially important to consider during a tight labor market where an adequate supply of candidates is in short supply. Large organizations with diversified jobs especially find a placement strategy to be effective. Studies have also found that a placement strategy can lower recruiting and selection costs.[22]

Cost–Benefit Analysis

Essentially, there are two types of costs involved in selecting an employee. First, there is the actual cost of filling the position such as recruiting, testing, interviewing, and so on. Second, there are potential costs resulting from an incorrect selection decision. These include (1) the "false positive," in which the costs involve selecting someone who fails in the job, termination costs, the expense of selecting another employee, and low productivity; and (2) the "false negative," in which the costs are associated with rejecting an applicant who could have been successful on the job; these will include the opportunity cost of having a successful employee who could have added to the productivity of the organization.

The amount of these costs will vary according to the hiring standards set in the selection process. However, at some point total costs will generally increase as hiring standards increase. This means that the human resource department should periodically examine its selection technique and standards to see if they are cost effective. Or, to state it another way, we could spend a great deal of money to increase our prediction of an applicant's success on the job. However, at some point, the cost involved may outweigh the benefits of getting the added precision.

EVALUATION OF THE SELECTION PROCESS

There is little justification for making outlays in selecting human resources without determining how effective the selection process is. However, it is difficult to develop adequate yardsticks by which the selection process can be measured. A decision to select a candidate is based on expected performance as suggested by the various tools used in the selection process. In a sense, then, if these expectations hold true when the candidate is placed in the job, we could conclude that the selection program is valid and effective. It is difficult, however, to isolate all of the other conditions that might be influencing the job performance.

To illustrate, a company inaugurated a new testing program as part of the selection process for new salespeople. In a follow-up study it was found that all of the salespeople selected during the first year of the new program had more total sales during their first year than new salespeople had had in earlier years. It was also discovered that turnover among the newly hired salespeople was lower than that of newly hired salespeople in earlier years. The temptation was to immediately attribute these results to the new testing program. However, someone pointed out that sales for all sales personnel had been considerably higher that year. Moreover, that year the firm had recruited from different schools. In addition, the job market was considerably softer for sales people in the industry.

Despite the difficulty in providing proper yardsticks, every firm should make systematic efforts to evaluate the effectiveness of its selection process. Periodic audits, research, and other evaluation techniques are as essential for human resource programs as they are for programs in marketing, production, or any other function. Such evaluation techniques should be directed toward answering this fundamental question—is the selection process providing the type and quality of human resources specified in human resource plans?

As previously suggested, a key yardstick in our evaluation will be the job performance of newly hired employees. The important indicators will include performance appraisals and results, such as supervisory ratings, attendance records, productivity rates, and length of service. We can then compare these indicators of job success with the predictions recorded at the time of selection. Although comprehensive evaluation procedures are beyond the scope of this book, we can suggest several areas and questions that should be covered in a systematic evaluation of the selection process:

1. Have well-defined selection policies been developed? Are they consistent with public policy?
2. Why are we using the employment standards we have? How are they related to actual performance on the job?
3. Do we maintain accurate records of why each candidate was rejected? ("Not qualified" is not sufficient.) What percentage of those who apply are hired?
4. What contribution does each of the steps in the selection process (interviewing, testing, reference checks, and so on) make to the overall program?
5. How much does each of the steps and tools in the selection process cost?
6. Can we successfully defend our selection process in court?
7. Have these selection tools been properly validated?
8. What percentage of the newly hired is discharged during the probationary period?
9. Is there a correlation between degree of success on the job and the predictions made at the time of selection?
10. Is there an exit interview to help measure how well we are matching people and jobs?

SUMMARY

An effective selection program is based upon careful job analysis, comprehensive human resource planning, effective recruitment, and a proven set of evaluation techniques. The actual selection process is likely to include several steps or tools that assist us in deciding whether or not the applicant is qualified for a specific job.

The selection process includes:

1. Preliminary screening
2. Review of application blanks
3. Employment testing
4. Reference checks
5. Employment interviewing
6. Physical examinations

The basic objective of the process is to obtain employees who are most likely to meet desirable standards of performance. The assessment center is a more recent method that is receiving growing attention in managerial selection.

A decision to select a candidate is based on expected performance as suggested by the selection process. It is vital, therefore, that we periodically evaluate this process to determine whether it is providing the types and quality of human resources specified in human resource needs plans. The final decision of which applicant to select should also be based on a selection strategy that considers such concepts as multiple predictors, placement, and cost–benefit analysis. In view of recent federal antidiscrimination efforts, we must also examine our staffing program in general and our selection process in particular to see whether our efforts are consistent with public policy.

KEY CONCEPTS

Selection
Validity
Reliability
Weighted application blank

Employment tests
Structured interview
Assessment center
Placement

NOTES

1. Harriet Gorlin, *Personnel Practices I: Recruitment, Placement, Training Communication,* Information Bulletin, No. 89 (New York: The Conference Board, 1981), p. 14.

2. For a good discussion of application forms, see C. Harold Stone and Floyd L. Puch, "Selection, Interviewing, and Testing," in *Staffing Policies and Strategies* (Washington, D.C.: Bureau of National Affairs, 1974).
3. *Selection Procedures and Personnel Records*, No. 114 (Washington, D.C.: Bureau of National Affairs, 1976), p. 3.
4. Ernest C. Miller, "An EEO Examination of Employment Applications," *Personnel Administration*, March 1980, pp. 63–81.
5. Equal Employment Opportunity Commission, *Affirmative Action and Equal Employment: A Guidebook for Employers*, Vol. 1 (Washington, D.C.: U.S. Government Printing Office, 1974).
6. John A. Belt and Peter B. Holden, "Polygraph Usage among Major U.S. Corporations," *Personnel Journal* 57, February 1978, pp. 80–86.
7. "Business Buys the Lie Detector," *Business Week*, February 6, 1978, pp. 100–104.
8. "Occupational Testing Services Contribute to ES Productivity," July 6, 1982, an unpublished position paper by the Division of Counseling and Test Development, Office of Program Operations, United States Employment Office, p. 6.
9. *Selection Procedures and Personnel Records*, Bureau of National Affairs, p. 7.
10. Edward Puda and Lewis Albright, "Racial Differences on Selection Instruments Related to Subsequent Job Performance," *Personnel Psychology*, Spring 1968, pp. 31–41; see also Charles Sparks, "Validity of Psychological Tests," *Personnel Psychology*, Spring 1970, pp. 39–46.
11. See John B. Miner and Mary Green Miner, *Personnel and Industrial Relations* (New York: Macmillan, 1977), Chap. 10, "The Logic of Selection."
12. One study was conducted by Allan N. Nash and S. J. Carroll, "A Hard Look at the Reference Check," *Business Horizons*, October 1970, pp. 43–49; see also *Selection Procedures and Personnel Records*, Bureau of National Affairs, p. 4.
13. For example, see Liz Gallese, "Campus Concern: Student Job Referrals by Teachers Hit Snags Due to a Privacy Law," *The Wall Street Journal*, January 14, 1977, p. 1; and Edward L. Levine, "Legal Aspects of Reference Checking for Personnel Selection," *The Personnel Administrator*, November 1977, pp. 14–17.
14. Kenneth C. Cooper, "Those Qualified Applicants and Their Phony Credentials," *Administrative Management* 38, August 1977, p. 44.
15. David Tucker and Patricia Rome, "Relationship Between Expectancy, Causal Attributions, and Final Hiring Decisions in the Employment Interview," *Journal of Applied Psychology*, February 1979, pp. 27–31.
16. Richard D. Arvey, *Fairness in Selecting Employees* (Reading, Ma.: Addison-Wesley, 1979), p. 165.
17. Treadway C. Parker, "Assessment Centers: A Statistical Study," *Personnel Administration* 25, February 1980, pp. 65–67.
18. Ann Howard, "An Assessment of Assessment Centers," *Academy of Management Journal* 17 (March 1974), pp. 115–134; Wayne F. Cascio and Val Silbey, "Utility of the Assessment Center as a Selection Device," *Journal of Applied Psychology* 64, April 1979, p. 107.
19. James R. Huck and Douglas N. Bray, "Management Assessment Center Evaluations and Subsequent Performance of White and Black Females," *Personnel Psychology* 29, Spring 1976, p. 13.
20. M. D. Dunette and W. Borman, "Personnel Selection and Classification Systems," in *Annual Review of Psychology*, ed. M. Rosenzweig and L. Porter (1979), pp. 477–526.
21. Stone and Puch, "Selection, Interviewing, and Testing," pp. 4–122.

22. For example, see M. D. Dunette, *Personnel Selection and Placement* (Belmont, Ca.: Wadsworth, 1966), pp. 183–199; and Sidney A. Fine, "What's Wrong with the Hiring System?" *Organizational Dynamics* 4, Autumn 1975, pp. 55–67.

REVIEW AND DISCUSSION QUESTIONS

1. In what ways might the selection process vary among (a) a small retail store; (b) a research organization with 40 employees; and (c) a large multi-plant manufacturing firm?
2. Give concrete examples and situations in which it would be advisable to alter the steps in the selection process as discussed in this chapter.
3. What is an employment test? Distinguish between a performance test and an aptitude test.
4. Opponents of testing claim that tests may discriminate against minorities and, therefore, should be abolished from the selection process. Do you agree? Explain.
5. What kinds of information can be adequately obtained through the employment interview? Suggest several ways in which you could increase your effectiveness as an interviewer.
6. What is an assessment center? How important is it as a selection tool?
7. Arrange to speak with the personnel director of a large company in your city.
8. In what ways does the external environment affect the staffing process in every firm?
9. In what ways have federal and state equal employment opportunity laws caused organizations to alter their human resource policies and practices?
10. What are the relationships among human resource planning, recruitment, and selection?

BIBLIOGRAPHY

American Psychological Association. *Principles for the Validation and Use of Personnel Selection Procedures.* Washington, D.C.: APA, 1975.

American Psychological Association. "Testing: Concepts, Policy, Practice, and Research." (Special Issue) *American Psychologist* 36, October 1981, 997–1189.

American Society for Personnel Administration. "Test Justification and Title VII." *The Personnel Administrator* 21, January 1976, 46–51.

Arvey, Richard D. *Fairness in Selecting Employees.* Reading, Mass.: Addison-Wesley, 1979.

Arvey, Richard D. "Unfair Discrimination in the Employment Interview: Legal and Psychological Aspects." *Psychological Bulletin* 86, July 1979, 736–765.

Black, James M. *How to Get Results from Interviewing.* New York: McGraw-Hill, 1970.

Bureau of National Affairs, Inc. *Equal Employment Opportunity: Programs and Results.* Personnel Policies Forum Series No. 112, March 1976.

Buros, O. K. (Ed.) *The Sixth Mental Measurements Yearbook.* Highland Park, N.J.: Gryphon Press, 1965.

Cronbach, Lee J. "Five Decades of Public Controversy over Mental Testing." *American Psychologist* 30, January 1975, 1–14.

Dipboye, Robert L., Howard L. Fromkin, and Kent Wiback. "Relative Importance of Applicant Sex, Attractiveness and Scholastic Standing in Evaluation of Job Applicant Resumes." *Journal of Applied Psychology* 60, February 1975, 39–43.

Fisher, Cynthia D., Daniel R. Ilgen, and Wayne D. Hoyer. "Source Credibility, Information Favorability, and Job Offer Acceptance." *Academy of Management Journal* 22, March 1979, 94–103.

Gael, Sidney, Donald L. Grant, and Richard J. Ritchie. "Employment Test Validation for Minority and Non-minority Telephone Operators." *Journal of Applied Psychology* 60, August 1975, 411–419.

Gatewood, Robert D., and James Ledvinka. "Selection Interviewing and EEO: Mandate for Objectivity." *Personnel Administrator* 24, December 1979, 51–54.

Goleman, Daniel. "The New Competency Tests: Matching the Right People to the Right Jobs." *Psychology Today* 15, January 1981, 35–46.

Grant, Donald L., and Douglas W. Bray. "Validation of Employment Tests for Telephone Company Installation and Repair Occupations." *Journal of Applied Psychology* 54, February 1970, 7–14.

Greenlaw, Paul S., and John P. Kuhl. "Selection Interviewing and the Uniform Federal Guidelines." *Personnel Administrator* 25, August 1980, 74–80.

Howard, A. "An Assessment of Assessment Centers." *Academy of Management Journal,* March 1974, 115–134.

Howell, N. L. "Complying with the Fair Credit Reporting Act." *Personnel Administrator,* January–February 1972, 10–12.

Huck, J. R. "Assessment Centers: A Review of the External and Internal Validities." *Personnel Psychology,* Summer 1973, 191–212.

Lipsett, Lawrence. "Selecting Personnel without Tests." *Personnel Journal* 51, 1972, 648–654.

Lockwood, Howard C. "Equal Employment Opportunities." In *Staffing Policies and Strategies,* Washington, D.C.: Bureau of National Affairs, 1974.

Moffatt, Thomas L. *Selection Interviewing for Managers.* New York: Harper & Row, 1979.

McCormick, E. J., and A. S. De Nise. "An Alternative Approach to Test Validation." *Personnel Administrator,* January 1976.

Miner, John B., and Mary Green Miner. "The Logic of Selection." In *Personnel and Industrial Relations.* New York: Macmillan, 1977.

Novit, Mitchell. "Physical Examinations and Company Liability: A Legal Update." *Personnel Journal,* January 1982.

Sparks, C. Paul. "The Not So Uniform Employee Selection Guidelines." *Personnel Administrator,* February 1977.

Stone, C. Harold, and Floyd L. Puch. "Selection, Interviewing and Testing." In *Staffing Policies and Strategies.* Washington, D.C.: Bureau of National Affairs, 1974.

Yoder, Dale, and Herbert G. Heneman. (Eds.) "Staffing Policies and Strategies." In *ASPA Handbook of Personnel and Industrial Relations.* Washington, D.C.: Bureau of National Affairs, 1979.

PART II CASE STUDIES

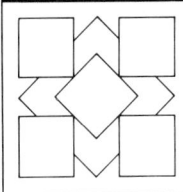

CASE STUDY:
Company Growth and Good Ole Boys (and Girls)

The Honeygood Company was born in the electronic age. As a manufacturer of modems and control computers primarily, it was on a fast growth track. It employed about 800 people and had annual sales of about $30 million in 1984. At that time, it had no organization chart and management operated very informally.

The company was highly personality-oriented. The chairman of the company, Larry Gooing, exclaimed, "Organization charts? I hate them!" He and the president of the company, Ms. Intel Lect, a graduate of MIT, had adjoining offices looking out over an office area where informality was the custom.

If an organization chart of the Honeygood Company were drawn, it would look like that shown in the accompanying illustration.

Despite the informality, the chairman and the president agreed that the company should expand in its areas of strength by adding certain computer hardware products to its line over the next five years. They estimated that sales would double and that the number of employees would increase to about 1,500.

Because of the informality, there were only two layers of management. Since the span of managers was large, coordination, control, and feedback of information about problems were slow. The manager of finance and accounting had been pressing for the development of an improved organization structure, human resource planning, and a management information and control system to prepare for the future.

Ms. Intel Lect has agreed that there may be a limit to informality when it comes to long-range planning. You have been hired as a consultant to prepare organization and human resource plans for Honeygood.

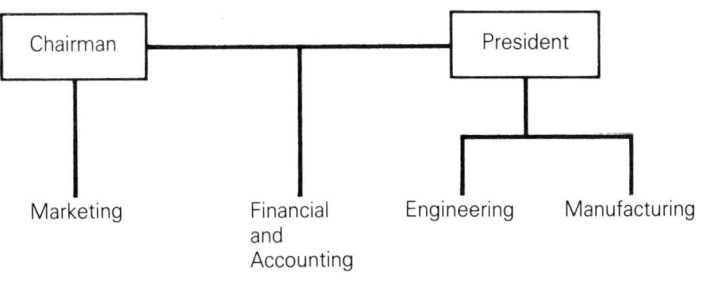

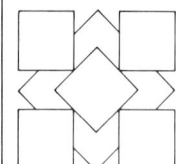

CASE STUDY:
Management Resource Planning: Keys to Success

J. B. Carlisle, CEO, was about to go into the monthly meeting of the corporate management review committee (CMRC). Carlisle chaired this committee which was made up of the top six senior executives of the company. This group also formed the central policy committee which met weekly on matters of key policy and operational significance. Management development is an important subject at this company as evidenced by the fact that this committee exists and that they recently decided to expand the amount of time dedicated to management resource planning (MRP) considerably. The purpose of the CMRC was to review the key management positions and people in the company in terms of their performance and developmental needs, and to plan the replacements for these key people/jobs.

Top management felt that MRP was an important part of their responsibility. Carlisle felt especially strong about this. In fact, he was personally responsible for setting up the extensive process used throughout the company nearly eight years ago. XYZ, a four-billion-dollar company, had nearly 70,000 employees and was organized on a divisional basis. Every effort was made to provide the divisions with maximum autonomy. The MRP process was a bottoms-up approach, not complicated but time consuming. It was corporate policy that all divisions use the same process for middle-level management positions and above. Therefore, once each year the process was reviewed and updated for all middle manager positions and above. The division had an option to do the same for lower levels of management. There were two fairly simple forms. One was completed by the employees and contained a summary of their work experience and their career goals. The second form was filled out by their managers and summarized current performance levels, long-term potential, specified the most likely next jobs for each person, identified specific developmental needs as well as appropriate developmental actions such as special assignments or training. It also specified the names of two or three people who could replace the incumbent.

The division presidents were responsible for management succession within their organization and were required to use the corporate system. Most of the division presidents had formed their own version of the CMRC with their division senior executives, performing similar functions as the corporate committee but within their division. Beyond that, in several of the divisions, such committees were common at lower levels, e.g., the manufacturing plant manager headed a committee which oversaw all management succession activities for management positions in that plant. No assignment could be made without their review and approval. This was done in order to assure that management development needs (not just the immediate needs of the business) were a primary factor in assignments. The plant manager felt that this was important because there was a natural tendency for managers to fill critical jobs with the most qualified candidate due to the pressure in meeting near-term business objectives. Naturally, these were the assignments which were also best for testing younger managers who showed exceptional potential.

The divisions have considerable autonomy in their management resource activities. However, in addition to the requirement to use the corporate process and forms, there were other corporate "demands." Once each year, the division presidents had to visit corporate headquarters specifically to review their management resources with the CMRC. It was required that they review each of the senior positions reporting to the division president. Those reviews covered the incumbent's management resource information as well as the two most likely replacements for each of those positions. It was common for these meetings to be lively since many of these people were known by the members of the CMRC, and these meetings had to end in agreement on their next moves, replacements and development for each person and position reviewed.

It was also required at these meetings, that the division presidents discuss lower level "high potential" managers who would be put through special developmental experiences to test, challenge and prepare them for senior division positions within the next ten years. Lastly, each division president was required to review people who had been identified as having the potential to fill the most senior corporate positions within the next ten to fifteen years. The CMRC took great interest in this group because they were potentially their replacements. Once they were approved by the committee, these people became "corporate resources" and all developmental plans, job assignments and compensation actions had to be approved by the CMRC.

Carlisle felt that this was necessary in order to assure the identification and long-term development and preparation of the future senior executives. It was natural for the division presidents to want to keep their best people within the division. In fact, many of them felt that they could provide these people with adequate development opportunities within their division without any corporate involvement. Carlisle strongly disagreed. He believed that future senior executives needed assignments in several businesses and functions, in at least two different divisions and preferably an international assignment, to have the thorough understanding and knowledge of all key aspects of the business and to have a broad perspective. Therefore, these corporate high potentials became part of a separate process. This process was administered by the Manager, Management Resources on the Corporate Personnel staff. He was responsible for coordinating all the management resource actions for the corporate high potentials, which involved about 200 people. More detailed long-term developmental plans were created for each of these people. These long-term plans were created by the division but required the approval of both the Manager, Management Resources and the CMRC.

In reflecting on the meeting he was about to start, Carlisle was proud of the company's program and of his own foresight in setting it up despite cries of corporate bureaucracy from the divisions, and the fact that it was established when the company was much smaller and the need less clear. Of course there were some problems, but for the most part he felt it had worked quite well as evidenced by the fact that in the last three years they only had to go outside the company twice to fill key executive positions.

However, he knew this meeting would be a difficult one. The president of the largest division was in for his annual MRP review. Carlisle knew he had some specific gripes which would be aired in the meeting. First of all, he and his senior people were upset because a new senior corporate position had recently been created to manage a new acquisition and the job had been filled from outside the company because "we didn't feel anyone inside had the appropriate understanding of the technology needed in the newly acquired company." Secondly, the division did not meet its sales and profit targets for 1982 and the division president felt it was partly because two of his most talented people in critical assignments had been moved for developmental purposes to other divisions. The performance of their organization had declined during the transition to their replacements.

Carlisle was not satisfied with the number of minority and female names on the division's management resource review last year and was looking for significant improvements. Also, during the past year, Carlisle had received an open-door letter from a middle manager in that division who "sensed there were very few opportunities for development in that division and wanted to know what top management could do about it." A similar letter was received from a manager who had been there for twenty years and who felt that the division management resource process was discriminatory because none of the division high potentials were over forty years of age.

Source: Reprinted by permission of the publisher from *Human Resource Planning,* Volume 5, Number 4, 1982. Copyright 1982 by the Human Resource Planning Society.

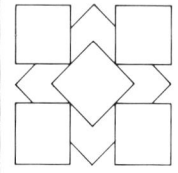

CASE STUDY:
KMS Industries

KMS Industries is a relatively small but rapidly growing firm with about 400 emloyees. It is a closely held firm [owned by usually 3 to 10 stockholders], established about eight years ago by the current president. Although the company has been very profitable, turnover among employees has been a constant problem. In fact, the third person in the past two years to hold the position of sales manager has just submitted his resignation. In the past three years, 12 managers have either quit voluntarily or been asked to resign. Turnover among nonmanagerial employees is about 80 percent higher than the industry average.

Each year the personnel director hires about ten college graduates from universities located in a tri-state area. He has full authority to hire new graduates and will occasionally hire on the spot if the applicant appears to be really outstanding.

Most managerial and technical employees are recruited via employment agencies and advertisements in newspapers and trade publications. The selection tools include an application blank, a personality test, and interviews with the personnel director and with executives responsible for the area in which the applicant will be placed. Mr. Zim, the president, indicated that if the applicant had "shifty eyes" or generated "bad vibrations" during an interview, the company would take a careful look at the applicant and run a reference and credit check.

Mr. Zim made the following additional remarks about the selection of employees. "You don't have to spend a lot of time or money selecting people if you really know what it is your looking for. I can usually tell in the first five minutes if the applicant is what KMS Industries needs. What we want are clean-cut nice-looking people who are willing to work hard and grow with the company. We don't want any longhair types, prima donnas, or people who are more concerned with our retirement benefits."

The executive vice president was calling a meeting of all top and middle managers to discuss the company's recruitment and selection process. He had just learned through the grapevine that two supervisors were planning to quit next week. He had also heard that a disgruntled female employee was bringing a sex discrimination charge against the company. She claimed that KMS Industries had hired a black male for a managerial job that she said she was qualified to do.

Mr. Murd, the personnel director, thought it might be a good idea to bring in an outside consultant to evaluate the entire KMS staffing process. He had had very little previous background in human resource management and was not entirely satisfied with the way things were going. He felt, for example, that there must be a better way of matching up the right person with the right job than the one KMS was using.

III
Development

Motivation and Leadership for Productivity

CHAPTER OUTLINE

Productivity
Meaning of Productivity ☐ Factors Determining Productivity ☐ Motivation and Leadership: P/HR Management Concerns

Motivation
Needs Theories ☐ Expectancy and Goal Achievement ☐ Operant Conditioning: The Individual As Systems Component ☐ Overview

Leadership
Leadership Concept for HR Management ☐ Theories of Leadership ☐ Application of Theory

Quality Circles: Application of Motivation/Leadership Theory

OBJECTIVES

1. Explain the meaning and nature of productivity of people.
2. Relate motivation to P/HR functions.
3. Explain several "needs" theories of motivation.
4. Explain operant conditioning as a means of getting people to work for organizational goals.
5. Relate the concept of leadership to motivation.
6. Describe generally major theories of leadership.
7. Relate leadership and motivation to quality circles.

SPOTLIGHT:
Mary Coeli Meyer

Mary Coeli Meyer is a classical eclectic, having pursued a diversity of interests both educationally and in business. Dr. Meyer received her Bachelor's Degree in Education from National College of Education. There, she focused her attention on sociology, science, and education. Prior to that she was a scholarship student in music at Kent State University. Dr. Meyer taught for several years in the public school system while pursuing doctoral studies in International and Comparative Education at Indiana State University. She served as both an educator and a curriculum consultant during these years until she shifted her attention to a career in business.

Dr. Meyer's business career is characterized by broad exposure. Beginning in operations management, she moved into advertising and public relations, and then became Director of Employee Relations for a division of one of the Fortune 500 companies. While attending Case Western Reserve University Management Institute, she had the opportunity to work on the curriculum for the evolving Organization Development department. While she was there she discovered that not only was it interesting but much of the work she was doing was closely related to this new school of thought. As a result Meyer "read every book that had been written on the subject—which wasn't that many." Discovering that the field was new and in need of good minds, she pursued her MBA at California Western University and followed that up with a Ph.D. in Business Administration from California Coast University.

For the past decade, Dr. Meyer has been on the cutting edge of sociotechnical systems design, authoring more than 49 professional articles, and contributing to three books and authoring two books. She has addressed audiences worldwide on the future of Human Resource Systems and human capability, including state departments, corporate boards, and public forums. Appearing with regularity in the media, Meyer is known for her candor and for her ability to raise questions that require insightful answers.

Dr. Meyer is President of Cheshire Ltd., an international management consulting firm, headquartered in Wheeling, Ill. The company specializes in sociotechnical system consulting, training and development, design/delivery and product lines, and personal development product lines. Meyer also lectures at Harper College, Business Division.

Comments by Mary Coeli Meyer

As we pursue the topic of motivation and leadership theory, you will begin to note that there are dozens of thoughts on the subject, with new thoughts continually emerging. It appears that we have been searching for the solitary button that, when pushed, will yield the fully productive individual who is both satisfied with the job and inspired by it. Practically speaking, the search is for a mechanical button, often times managed by the Personnel Department and garbed in MBO's, performance appraisals, and merit reviews . . . not to mention a host of other mechanical carrot-and-stick devices that we hope will inspire productivity irrespective of motivation. This interest in human productivity surfaced about the same time as Frederick Taylor and his theory of "scientific management," and has not lost its momentum or direction to this day. The only ingredient missing in most of these equations and theories is the *real* human being.

There is a certain irony in this pursuit, given that people come motivated and that we have never addressed the subject of how to manage motivated employees. Indeed, the authentic leader either intrinsically or through acquired skills knows how to do this, but it is still a rare commodity in the world of work. It is rare that managers are actually held accountable for managing the motivation of those who do the job. The emphasis is still on output, costs, and waste—items that can be measured with extreme accuracy and generated with the push of a button. It is with this in mind that operant conditioning in the form of human engineering has come into play. The hope is that motivation can be encapsulated into measurable segments and generated through a modified button-pushing mechanism. The irony is that motivation is not the function of a button over the long term—it is the function of human expression exercised by choice.

Let us look at the idea that all people come motivated to the work environment. Let us also consider that if motivation is not directed toward a mutually satisfying end result, it will seek its own satisfaction, particularly because it is essentially human. Hence, Theory X is, to a large degree, a misinterpretation of what human motivation is all about. If it appears that an individual does not want to work, is the individual "not" motivated, or is it true that his or her motivation is not channeled in our direction? Oddly enough, *we continue to define motivation as if it belonged to us rather than belonging to the individual*. In the absence of giving it to us, we categorically say that the individual is not motivated. Such is not the case. The truth of the matter is that the individual is motivated—however, the goals are not those which the particular department, supervisor, or company desire.

Well, then, how does a leader discover what motivates a person? Certainly not through observation or assumption. For example, suppose a particular employee is observed working late. Is this person's motivation "brownie points," avoidance of a spouse, the need to finish up, being seen by the late-working, attractive co-worker, boredom with life away from the work environment? The observation of seeing a person working late tells us nothing of his or her motivation, only that this person is staying late. It does not even tell us about output.

Second, motives are part and parcel of our personal development, particularly our development in childhood. Indeed, the priorities or expressions of a particular motive might change but seldom does the underlying need, desire, or expectation (i.e., motive) change. Hence, to assume that as a leader, we can influence an individual's motive, is an exercise in futility. As a leader we can only influence the expression of a motive, providing we have taken the time to determine what the motive is. Making this determination requires dialogue, an investment in the person that you are trying to lead. This is somewhat like reading the instruction manual to a particular machine—not all machines of the same type but a *particular* machine. The machine doesn't work properly until you know where to find the "on" button and its unique properties. In the case of the individual, the only manual that is accurately available is the individual himself or herself. It is the individual that is or is not productive.

Adhering the motivation of the individual to that of the department requires the development of a psychological contract. Discussion and dialogue yield this important ingredient to productivity. The dialogue takes place between the leader and the motivated "potential" follower. Through this discussion the "potential" follower determines whether he or she is going to commit personal motivation to the leader or whether the energy of motivation is going to be directed toward its own satisfaction (i.e., perhaps totally unrelated to company goals). The psychological contract is fundamentally a statement that says, "I believe . . ." Its power lies in its potential to integrate the individual with the organization.

Regardless of whether the discussion takes place during the job interview or task assignment, the key to channeling and directing motivation lies in the completeness and truthfulness of the discussion. After all, having one's motivation channeled and directed is largely a matter of free choice on the part of the owner of the motive. During the conversation, each party formulates expectations that yield either a positive or negative "I believe" statement of significant potency. Assuming that the statement was positive, the person who leaves the conversation and then relates it to an important other, in essence, re-tells it by saying, "I believe that this will be the end result." A part of this commitment is that the individual wants to believe and then those beliefs are either reinforced and made stronger or negated. Hence, his or her motivation will either be aligned with the organization or with himself.

Given that the psychological contract

is clearly defined to both parties, its life span is dependent upon continuous clarification. Thus, if changes take place in a particular department in the company, the psychological contract must purposefully be renegotiated or renewed as pertinent to the situation. Failure to do this allows for the erosion of the contract and the dispersal of the motivation toward its own fulfillment exclusive of department or company goals.

Today, the manager of the human resource has a challenge equivalent to the challenge presented by the development of the assembly line. Workers are not only more highly educated and more sophisticated, but they are also more concerned with "whole life" management rather than compartmentalization. There is a societal move towards decompartmentalization of work, self-fulfillment, leisure, learning, loving, and a search for a unified life-style. The true leader, not necessarily a manager/supervisor, recognizes this transition and is responsive to it.

Every day headlines proclaim statistics like the following: "Japan has 23 percent of the American car market, 90% of motorcycles, 50% of recording equipment, 50% of radios, 30% of cameras, and 25% of televisions."[1] Foreign nations such as Japan and Germany have given us shock after shock by producing better goods at lower prices with better service. Why is this so? Do foreign workers work harder? Are they more motivated? Are they more "productive"? Why has productivity in the United States increased over the years at a much lower rate than in many other industrialized countries? (See Exhibit 8–1.)

In this chapter we will examine the two principal behavioral aspects of workers and managers that relate to organizational performance—motivation and leadership, which underlie all HR management processes as discussed in the HR management process chapters that follow. For example, training and development activities are designed to develop leadership and channel motivation. The selection and staffing process should be based on selection of workers whose goals and leadership skills are congruent with company objectives. Compensation programs must be related to motivation and rewards for good leadership. While Chapter 3 provided descriptive background for understanding behavioral aspects in the rest of the book, this chapter prescribes actual measures that the HR specialist can take to improve productivity. First, however, we will discuss an area critical to today's organization—and its survival in the world marketplace. Let us look at productivity.

PRODUCTIVITY

Meaning of Productivity

Traditionally, measures of productivity have placed a heavy emphasis on countable items and their counting. For example, *productivity* may be measured by dividing the number of units of product produced by a company by the total cost of operations. Another calculation—total output of units of product per month divided by the number of employees—will give a measure of output per employee. But what if many of the units are defective? Shouldn't quality also be considered along with quantity? Is playing the "Minute Waltz" in 45 seconds an appropriate measure of productivity?

The issue of measuring productivity is extremely complex and an extended discussion is beyond the scope of this book. There are three measures of productivity, however, that should be considered in managing human resources:

1. *Strategic objectives:* Are our organizational objectives correct, as nearly as we can determine?
2. *Effectiveness:* To what degree are we achieving our objectives in terms of quality and quantity?

DEVELOPMENT

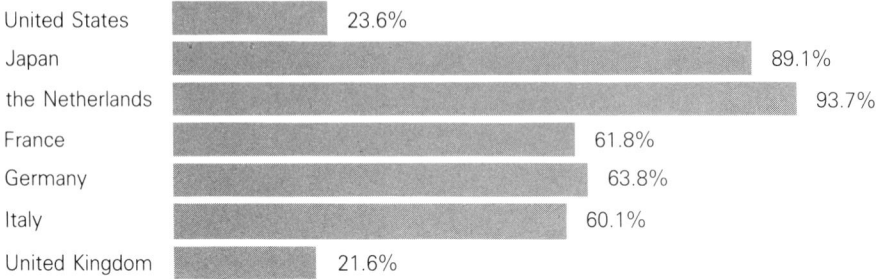

EXHIBIT 8-1
Productivity growth in some major industrialized nations.
Source: Based on data from the Bureau of Labor Statistics, United States Department of Labor, December 1979. (Courtesy of Westinghouse).

3. *Efficiency:* What is the $\frac{\text{output}}{\text{input}}$ ratio where the output measure includes both quantity and quality?

For example, the P/HR manager may set as a *strategic objective* the upgrading of all middle-level managers so that there will never be a problem of filling higher-management openings. The *effectiveness* of this upgrading activity may be measured by such counts as percentage of managers trained, degree of readiness for promotion as reflected in appraisals, and historical results of promotions in terms of individual managerial success. The *efficiency* would be the dollar value of in-house training relative to the cost of the program.

Factors Determining Productivity

Certain factors may facilitate the increase in productivity, while others may constrain productivity. We can use Exhibit 8-2 to summarize these factors.

The three internal forces with special impact on productivity are managerial processes, managerial leadership, and motivation. Managerial processes are the planning, organizing, integrating, and controlling of activities. They provide the systems and methods for accomplishing tasks. If the systems are poorly structured, productivity may be low regardless of the effort of the individual workers. Managerial leadership is concerned with both looking ahead to set new organizational goals and providing conditions that cause workers to try to do their best. Motivation is the sustained desire of workers to achieve goals, including, from the HR management view, organizational goals.

The three external forces with special impact on productivity are government regulation, unions, and innovation. Government regulation, while

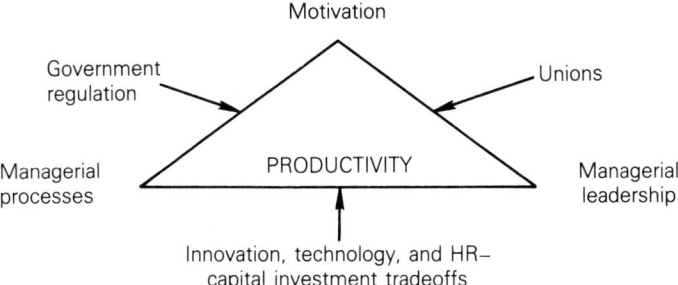

EXHIBIT 8-2
Factors affecting productivity.

usually reducing productivity, may in some instances bring about improved quality. Unions, like government, generally affect productivity negatively because they restrict managerial process and innovation. Innovation may be either managerial or technological, and breakthroughs have occurred in both with considerable impact on productivity.

It is clear from our above discussion that productivity is not just a matter of each worker working harder. The largest gains in productivity can come from management's working *smarter*. Management works smarter by making the job easier and simpler for the worker. Although often big gains may be achieved from technological advances, there are some pitfalls. The cost of new superequipment may actually reduce productivity as measured by cost per unit of output.[2]

Motivation and Leadership: P/HR Management Concerns

The manager of P/HR makes his or her greatest contributions to company productivity by developing means for increasing motivation and improving leadership for this purpose. This is no easy task.

From a behavioral point of view, leadership and employee motivation are opposite sides of the same organizational coin, and interact to affect the efforts of workers. They are, therefore, very important concerns of the P/HR manager and his or her staff in carrying out their responsibilities. From a practical viewpoint, the P/HR manager must know how people are motivated and what leadership characteristics and behavior can lead to higher levels of motivation. While we do not have any precise mathematical models to answer such questions, we do have cumulative research that expresses various perspectives and provides some general guidelines.

In particular, the manager of P/HR applies motivation theory to practically every aspect of HR management as shown by the examples in Exhibit 8-3.

EXHIBIT 8–3
Examples of application of motivation theory to HR management functions.

Area of Application	Examples
Organization and design of work	Worker relationships and tasks are designed to consider goals of workers.
Selection of new employees	Historical work patterns and psychological tests may indicate degree of motivation so that the most productive workers may be hired and very low-motivated workers may be screened out.
Training and development	T & D may be used as a means for bringing about increased motivation for workers desiring promotion or increased skills. T & D may also change attitudes and thus increase motivation.
Rewarding employees	The development of reward systems should be based on an understanding and application of motivation theory. Incentive programs in particular should be based on sound motivation theory. The assignment of rewards should also be made in the light of the effects on all employees.
Appraising	Managers should be coached or trained by the P/HR department to conduct appraisals so that employees do not have negative feelings after appraisal interviews, but are motivated to improve performance.
Industrial relations	Motivation is a consideration for determining why the union presses for specific demands. Company objectives in negotiation should take into account the impact of agreements on motivation.
Controlling	Control systems must be based on motivation theory. Too tight control may have a very negative effect on motivation, while formal, self-imposed control expressed by the worker may increase motivation.

MOTIVATION

What is it that makes people do the things they do? Or, as many a manager has said after hearing about some action of a subordinate, "Now why in the world would he do a thing like that?" The fantasy of P/HR managers is to find the secret of how to get all employees to be deeply committed to organizational goals and objectives and then pass this secret on to line managers.

Motivation is an *internal* driving force that results in the direction, intensity, and persistence of behavior. It is obviously a result of the combination of a particular individual's characteristics and the situation in which the individual is placed. There are many theories of motivation. Most of these appear very plausible on the surface, but many have little basis in testing by research. Managers use unsubstantiated theories and may not even have heard of the more complex but somewhat more validated theories. Is practice a better measure than research, or is it simply a case of things working out in real life by muddling through?

Regardless of whether all the theories of motivation discussed here are research-tested, they all contribute insights to motivation. They present different perspectives that help us get a feeling for the concept and for its application to actions. In addition, apparently all of the theories lead to a common set of guidelines for managers.

Needs Theories

The dynamic force that activates the individual is called motivation. According to the needs theories, *motivation is simply the drive to reduce a tension caused by an unsatisfied need*. Exhibit 8–4 gives an illustration of this statement. If managers were able to *satisfy* all of an individual's needs, the individual would not be motivated to act. Fortunately, new goals and learned needs keep arising. The individual keeps developing higher-level and more complex needs as present needs become satisfied.

Underlying the specific on-the-job needs of people are their life-satisfaction needs. It is important to look at the totality of needs because:

1. Some workers find practically all of their life satisfactions off the job and work primarily to satisfy physical and economic needs.
2. Most workers derive part of their noneconomic life satisfactions on the job.
3. The more needs a worker has an opportunity to satisfy on the job, the more likely the worker is to be highly motivated to perform the job.

Maslow's Need Hierarchy Theory Abraham Maslow developed a theory explaining the individual's hierarchy of basic life needs that we may relate

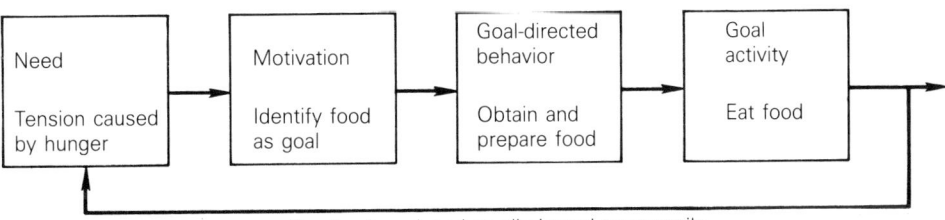

EXHIBIT 8–4
Motivation, according to need theory.

to satisfactions on the job and off the job. According to this hierarchy, individuals generally try to satisfy the lower-level needs in the hierarchy first. A particular higher-level need does not become potent as a motivator until lower-level needs have been satisfied reasonably well.

Starting at the lowest-level, first-to-be-satisfied needs, the hierarchy is:

- *Physiological:* basic physical needs (air, food, water, sex)
- *Safety:* need for physical and psychological security
- *Social:* need for satisfying social relationships with others
- *Ego:* need for self-respect and the esteem of others
- *Self-actualization:* the desire to be all that one can be, to fully utilize one's talents[3]

In Exhibit 8–5, we have indicated examples of needs for each level of Maslow's hierarchy.

A review of the literature shows little support for Maslow's theory because the needs are ambiguous and overlap, rather than being distinct and independent. In some studies, the lower-order needs formed a cluster and the higher order needs formed a cluster. As J. A. Lee writes:

> Science seems to have no quarrel with Maslow's physiological need level. This seems to be the most personally plausible of the five levels, because, although everyone does not know if he self-actualizes, he knows that he eats, wants sex and goes to the bathroom. Maslow's highest need level—self-actualization—seems to be not much of a problem, either, but mainly because most people are somewhat unsure of what it means. In between these, his model appears sufficiently ambiguous and therefore difficult to refute or support. . ."[4]

Nevertheless, Maslow's theory is easy to understand and plausible to the practitioner. It keeps the manager aware of higher-level human needs when the manager makes personnel decisions.

Herzberg's Two-factor Theory   Herzberg's theory of motivation parallels Maslow's in stating that in modern industrialized societies workers have satisfied their lower-order needs so that higher-order needs are the sources of their motivation. The lower-order needs are maintenance or "hygiene" needs (also called "dissatisfiers") that, if *not* present, produce dissatisfaction. Their presence, however, does not necessarily motivate employees; they *are* needed, however, to provide at least a feeling of "no dissatisfaction." Along this first continuum, the opposite of dissatisfaction is no dissatisfaction.[5]

Motivational factors or "satisfiers" are, however, intrinsically different from hygiene factors, in that, if present, they do increase satisfaction. Here, along this second continuum, the opposite of satisfaction is no satisfaction.

From structured interviews with 200 engineers and accountants in nine companies, Herzberg and his associates developed 6 motivators (satisfiers) and 10 hygiene factors (dissatisfiers) as shown in Exhibit 8–6. Herz-

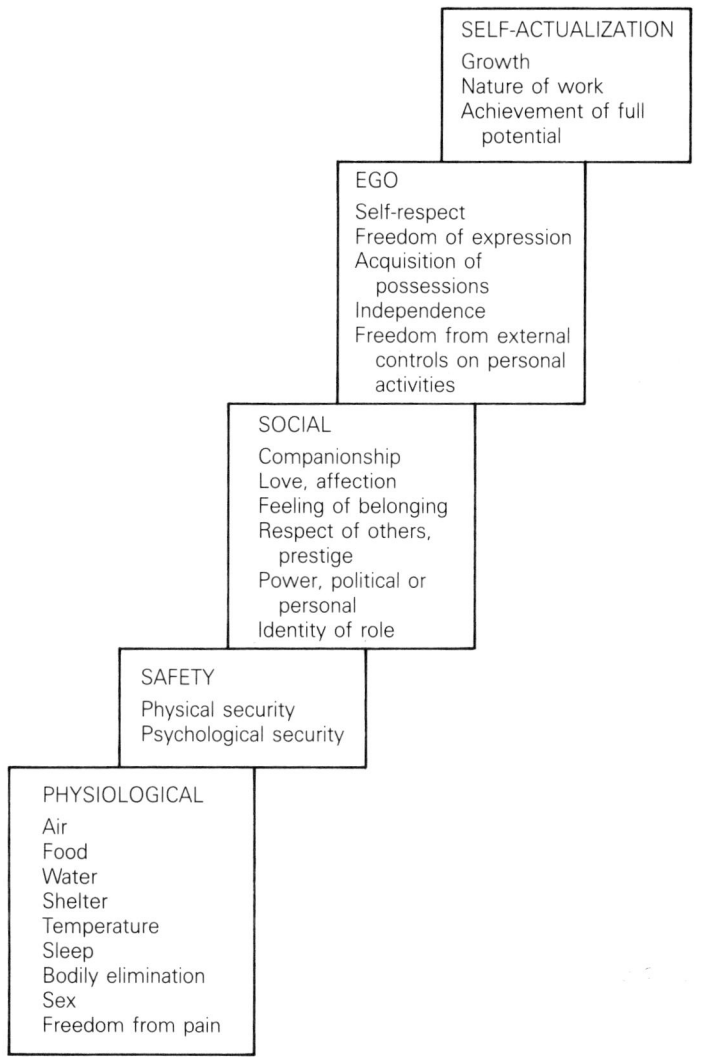

EXHIBIT 8-5
The hierarchy of needs.

berg's studies stimulated a great amount of research into motivation of people at work. In addition, he focused attention on work-goal achievement as a source of satisfaction.

Herzberg's work has led to the concept and application of job enrichment as a means of inducing motivation by restructuring factors relating to the job and responsibility for one's own performance. In addition, the jobs are designed so that the worker will increase his or her skills with time.

Herzberg's theory has been criticized on the basis of methods used. Other researchers have questioned whether his factors are mutually exclu-

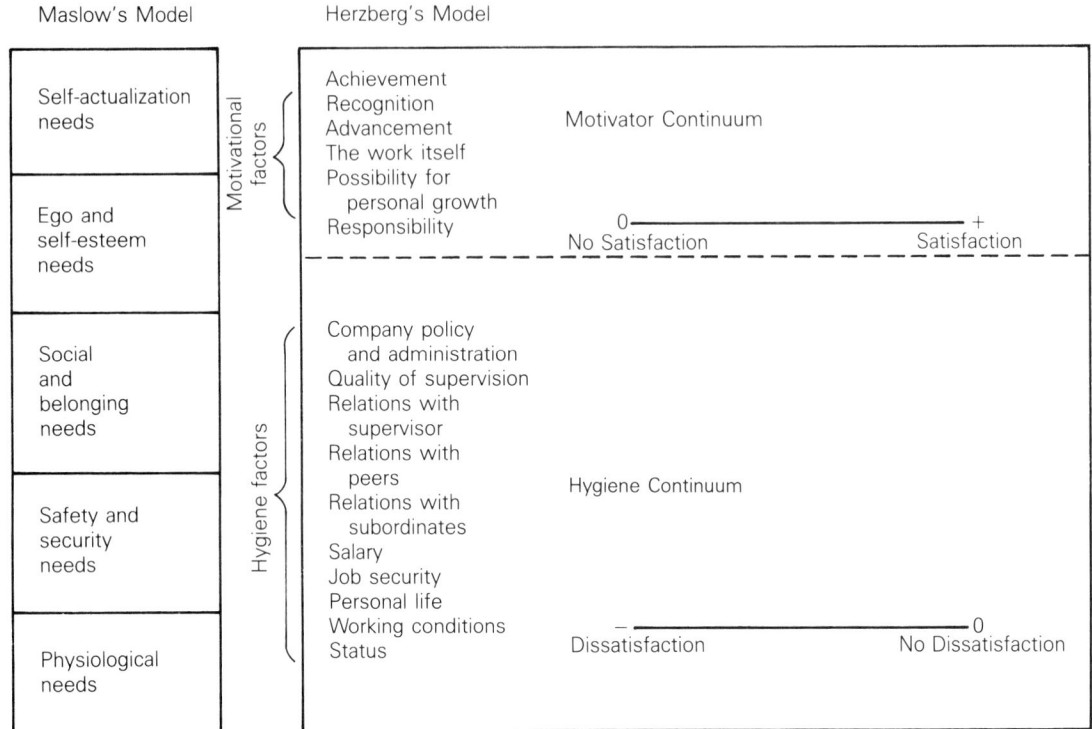

EXHIBIT 8-6
A comparison of Herzberg's model to Maslow's model.

sive. For example, salary is a hygiene factor in Exhibit 8-6, yet the salary of very highly paid executives may be primarily a form of recognition they strive for. Others have criticized the theory as being too simple. J. Lee states that "The evidence to date clearly eliminates Herzberg's theory as a general or universal theory of work motivation."[6] Steers and Porter take a more positive view by saying, "It appears that a fruitful approach to this 'controversial' theory would be to learn from it that which can help us to develop more improved models, rather than to accept or reject the model totally."[7]

Probably the great significance of Herzberg's theory is (1) it is easy for managers to understand; (2) it has the plausibility of Maslow's theory; (3) it has received wide publicity in management circles; (4) it has been developed and applied widely in business; and (5) it has stimulated research on improved models.

Need for Achievement in Motivation David C. McClelland and his associates set out (1) to prove high achievement motivation was a prerequisite for economic development of a country and (2) to develop successful programs for increasing the need to achieve.[8] McClelland and J. W. Atkinson continued the study of motivation in a laboratory setting. The need for achieve-

	Symbol	Definition
Achievement	n Ach	The need to set high attainable goals and be measured against them
Affiliation	n Aff	The need for warm, friendly, interpersonal relationships
Power	n Pow	The mastery need to control and manipulate the environment

EXHIBIT 8–7
McClelland-Atkinson need outline.

ment is indicated by persons who consistently set high but attainable goals for themselves and who select tasks over which they have control and which provide clear feedback on performance. Included in the model are achievement, affiliation, and power (see Exhibit 8–7).

McClelland found that achievement needs were relatively stable and developed over a person's childhood. This stresses the importance of identifying long-enduring characteristics of workers entering the company as discussed earlier in the behavioral systems section. Also, the implication for P/HR managers is that training and development may improve skills but it has little impact for motivation. For this reason, the selection process in staffing should focus heavily on identifying people with high achievement needs.

More recently, McClelland has attempted to increase achievement needs through training programs. In one case, three different groups of small-business workers were given 70 hours of achievement training and assistance. The findings were impressive. For example, for one group, median profits increased from $280/month to $670/month.[9]

Expectancy and Goal Achievement

Victor H. Vroom and the coauthors Lyman Porter and Edward Lawler, have developed separate "expectancy" models of motivation.[10,11] Basically, the *expectancy model* treats motivation as dependent upon the strength of an individual's desire for a set of goals and the likelihood that a specific type of behavior will lead to the achievement of the individual's goal. These models are consistent with need satisfaction, but *start* with the end needs and work backward to a choice of action by the individual to fulfill them. The expectancy theories essentially state that motivation is induced because the individual *believes* that certain performance will lead to satisfactions. Former theories stating that providing satisfactions will motivate performance have been abandoned.

Three terms used in expectancy theory are:

☐ *Effort:* how hard and how persistently an individual works
☐ *Performance:* behavior that directly promotes organizational goals; when a supervisor asks an employee to perform a work-related task, the doing of the task is "performance"
☐ *Outcomes:* individual's feelings derived directly from the person's work, organizational rewards such as pay, and the social and physical environment in which the work is performed; other terms used for job satisfaction are "satisfactions" and "rewards"

In a simplified depiction of expectancy theory (Exhibit 8–8), the worker is motivated because he or she has a goal of higher pay, promotion, or what-not, and believes that if he or she performs well (organizational tasks are accomplished), rewards will be obtained.

There are some uncertainties that slip into the picture when we deal with the future and the behavior of other people, however. We deal with these uncertainties as probabilities, or "expectancies." Our own characteristics also enhance or impede our ability to perform. With these additional concepts, the general model appears as in Exhibit 8–9.

There are two other considerations that are included in Vroom's expectancy model of motivation:

☐ *Valence:* the strength of an individual's desire for a particular outcome
☐ *Instrumentality:* the individual's perception that a first-level outcome will lead to a particular second-level outcome

Porter and Lawler have advanced a variation that includes perception of equity of rewards and role perceptions as well as abilities and traits.[12]

There has been general support from research on expectancy models. However, there have also been some problems with the models. The assumptions that people survey all goals, valences, estimate expectancies, and that calculations can be made to predict behavior do not hold up. On the other hand, the models do provide some guidance for managers. A manager, for example, should attempt to identify goals of individuals in his or

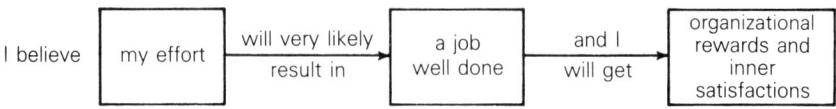

EXHIBIT 8–8
Simple model of expectancy theory.

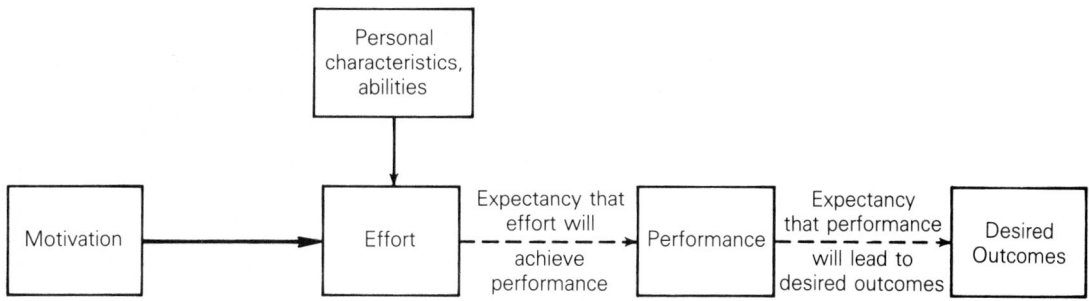

EXHIBIT 8-9
Expanded expectancy model.

her group that have high valences for the individuals. The manager should then set rewards that relate to these goals. The manager should also communicate clearly the measure of performance and define the links between effort, performance, and reward so that expectancies will be high and realistic.

Operant Conditioning: The Individual As Systems Component

B. F. Skinner is the outstanding proponent of *operant conditioning*, which views the human as a system. On the basis of his research, he has attempted to discredit the idea of autonomous human beings. Skinner rejects explanations that humans autonomously initiate behavior, and states that the human is a passive processor of inputs. Behavior is determined by its consequences, and management may, therefore, control the behavior of workers by prompt positive reinforcement of desirable behavior.[13] The concept of needs as an explanation and a predictor of behavior is superfluous.

Four basic types of conditioning consequences have been identified: positive reinforcement, neutral or nonresponse, punishment, and escape (negative reinforcement, or removal of a noxious stimulus). Continuous positive reinforcement is the most effective way of operant (behavior) conditioning. The manager would carry out a procedure as follows:

1. Specify objectives and desired standard of performance
2. Provide immediate feedback to the worker on his performance
3. Provide positive reinforcement when performance meets standards by praise, incentive payments, and so forth; provide encouragement when performance does not meet standards but the worker has tried hard
4. Do nothing when the worker has loafed or gone off in the wrong direction

The concept of operant conditioning has been criticized because it ignores social processes, neglects conflicting stimuli, manipulates the individual, and is a technology rather than a theory. Its success under other names has been impressive, however. Wage incentive systems, commission plans, and Management by Objectives (MBO) are examples. Also, an examination of other theories of motivation indicate that, in practice, operant conditioning is applied in some manner.

Overview

Each model discussed provides some insights into motivation of workers. Despite their apparent differences, they all suggest a similar management technology. (1) Managers induce motivation by (2) identifying goals (needs) of workers, (3) designing work systems so that (4) workers can achieve their goals (5) through satisfactory organizational performance, and (6) communicating this process to the workers. Workers' goals may be intrinsic (personal satisfaction) or extrinsic; they may be noneconomic or economic. Management must create the environment to reinforce desired behavior through goal achievement.

LEADERSHIP

The manager may induce motivation toward organizational goals by either creating the environment and reward system or by his or her personal behavior and influence. The latter method is referred to as *leadership*. Leadership is not an end in itself; its purpose is to increase motivation for productivity and increase worker satisfaction.

The P/HR department has a strong supporting role in the development of leaders within the company. First, by means of recruiting and selecting entry-level personnel for hiring by managers, the P/HR manager makes sure there is a steady inflow of leaders as well as specialists. The recruitment and selection of middle managers as well as promotions to middle management often depends upon criteria established by the P/HR department and input evaluations from the P/HR department. Other examples of the application of leadership theory to achieve P/HR objectives are shown in Exhibit 8–10.

Leader development is a continuing development carried out by line managers and training programs developed by the P/HR department. There is a large amount of evidence about success in training leaders.

Leadership Concept for HR Management

Bernard Bass states that there are many definitions of leadership, depending on the person defining it. Many of these definitions present different facets of leadership and together enrich the concept. Some of the definitional approaches discussed by Bass are depicted in Exhibit 8–11.[14] Effective leadership in the context of human resource management may be defined as influencing individual and group behavior toward optimal obtainment of the firm's goals. If a manager can initiate action, induce oth-

EXHIBIT 8-10
Applications of leadership theory to achieve P/HR objectives.

P/HR Activity	Examples of P/HR Department's Applications of Leadership Theory
Organization and design of work	Design of organization and job tasks to give the manager flexibility in assigning responsibilities directed toward individual's goals
Selection of new employees	Development of application forms, interview patterns, and assessment methods to select future leaders
Training and development	Design and implementation of leadership programs and courses to develop leaders at various stages of their careers
Appraising employees	Design and implementation of appraisal methods to reward leaders on the basis of productivity of their groups and worker satisfactions
Rewarding employees	System to reward leaders adequately for innovation, risk taking, and improvements in group productivity
Controlling	Advice to management on control system design so that leadership and motivation will not be repressed

ers to engage in it, and direct the action toward goals, he or she is performing the primary functions of leadership.

We shall extend our definition of the leader, however, as suggested by Katz and Kahn, to mean a person who exerts a significant amount of influence over and above that required to obtain routine compliance with the routine directives of an organization.[15] This is in sharp contrast to the bureaucrat who is concerned with doing routine activities efficiently. Accordingly, an effective leader is one who is able to go beyond expected role

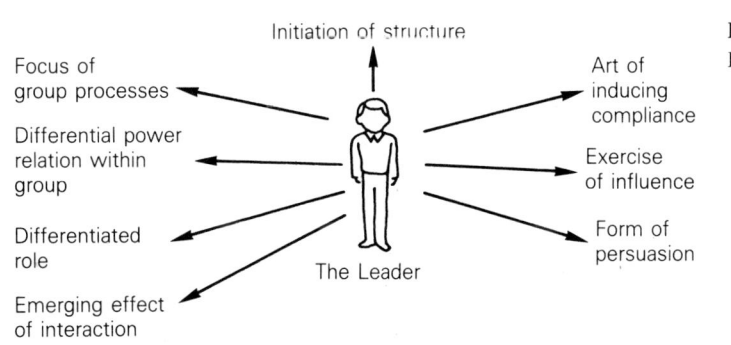

EXHIBIT 8-11
Leadership definitions.

performance to realize more fully the potential of his or her position of influence. This chapter will also point out that effective leadership is a complex matter, involving the consideration of a wide variety of factors.

The term *influence* is frequently used in connection with two other related terms—*power* and *authority*. Sometimes these terms are used interchangeably; at other times they are regarded as mutually exclusive concepts. Our approach will be to view influence as the all-inclusive concept that covers any means by which behavioral change is induced in individuals or groups. Because power and authority usually are important factors in leadership in business organizations, we will discuss these first.

Power Power is the capacity to do or affect something, such as depriving an employee of some reward or inflicting some cost on an employee for nonperformance. There are two important characteristics of power: (1) It consists of an individual's capacity to influence another to do something that otherwise would not be done; (2) it is not an attribute of a given person.

Authority Authority may be defined as the "legitimate" right to direct or influence the performance of others. Early writers on the subject of management perceived authority as the *right* and *power* to get performance from other persons. This view of authority held that the source of authority was at the top and flowed downward through the hierarchy. In more recent times, most behavioral scientists have held that authority stems from a willingness of followers to accept orders from others. For example, if an employee disagrees with an order given by the manager, the employee can circumvent that order in a number of ways without actually refusing to carry it out. Slowdowns, absenteeism, and sloppy work are just a few examples. This suggests that to be effective authority requires the consent of the employee.

Authority, therefore, comes both from the top down and from the bottom up. Agreement must exist between leaders and followers. In a given situation, the authority and the power may reside with management, in which case the employee may be compelled to do as ordered. That is, the consequence of nonacceptance is so distasteful that the employee accepts the authority. In other situations, the employee may be in a position to exercise considerable influence over the way orders from above are followed and even over whether the orders are followed at all. Such might be the case where a powerful labor union exists.

Chester Barnard's "acceptance theory of authority" has helped to explain the limits placed on authority by the response of subordinates. According to this theory, there are orders "which are clearly unacceptable, that is, which certainly will not be obeyed; there is another group somewhat more or less on the neutral line . . . and a third group unquestionably acceptable."[16] In addition, there are many degrees of compliance to an order, ranging from enthusiasm to reluctant resignation.

In summary, authority is a basis for influencing behavior in the human resource system. At the same time, it is not enough to ensure the desired response from subordinates. When greater reliance must be put on different means of influencing behavior, leadership becomes the important factor.

Theories of Leadership

For as long as there have been leaders, people have been intrigued with the phenomenon of leadership. For centuries, writers and the general public believed that true leaders were "great," that such leaders were "born" and not "made" in terms of education and training.

An investigation of the numerous books dealing with leadership reveals that leadership has been heavily examined from the perspective of experience. Rather than scientific research, much of the literature is based on *how* or *why* a particular person was successful in "leading," with the writer suggesting that the solution is to adopt that person's style of leadership.

Trait Theories A great deal of early research was aimed at identifying traits and characteristics that differentiated successful leaders from unsuccessful ones. Characteristics such as height, weight, physique, energy, appearance, and fluency of speech were studied to determine if they differentiated leaders. Traits such as intelligence, scholarship, knowledge, judgment, originality, extroversion, dominance, integrity, self-confidence, social skills, and so on were likewise studied.

Bernard Bass, after an extensive review of research findings, concludes that factors associated with leadership could be grouped as follows:

1. *Capacity:* intelligence, alertness, verbal facility, originality, judgment
2. *Achievement:* scholarship, knowledge, athletic accomplishments
3. *Responsibility:* dependability, initiative, persistence, aggressiveness, self-confidence, desire to excel
4. *Participation:* activity, sociability, cooperation, adaptability, humor
5. *Status:* socioeconomic position, popularity

Generally, it may be concluded that leaders exceed the *average* of their groups in intelligence, scholarship, dependability, social participation, and socioeconomic status. Traits that correlate highest with leadership are originality, popularity, sociability, judgment, aggressiveness, desire to excel, humor, cooperativeness, liveliness, and athletic ability.[17]

The reader may recognize some other limitations to the approach of trait theories: (1) the theories overlook subordinates, who certainly must have an impact on the performance of the leader. (2) We do not know the relative importance of the desirable traits. (3) There may be no universal set of traits of a leader because different situations require leaders with different sets of traits. (4) The construct of "leader" has been based on prevailing ideas of leadership; that is, Machiavellian traits were not investigated.

(5) Most important, although we can see that successful leaders have certain traits, it is not clear whether the traits make the leader or whether the accomplishments of the leader make *the traits* noticeable.

The trait theories have been more or less abandoned by researchers since the 1960s. From a HR management view, it would be convenient if trait theory could be used for the selection process. In addition, much leadership training is probably based on trait theory and development of traits. The manager of P/HR should keep line managers aware of the unreliability of the trait approach during selection and promotion of employees.

Leadership Styles: The Behavioral Approach Another approach to understanding leadership concentrates on what the leader does and on how the leader behaves in conducting his or her leadership function. Trait theories explain leadership according to what the leader *is;* behavioral theories explain leadership according to what the leader *does.* Many behavioral theories advocate the effectiveness of one style of leadership over that of others. In this section we shall analyze several basic types of leadership behavior. We shall also see that individuals in leadership positions may follow contrasting approaches to leading people (see Exhibit 8–12).

EXHIBIT 8–12
Contrasting approaches to leading.

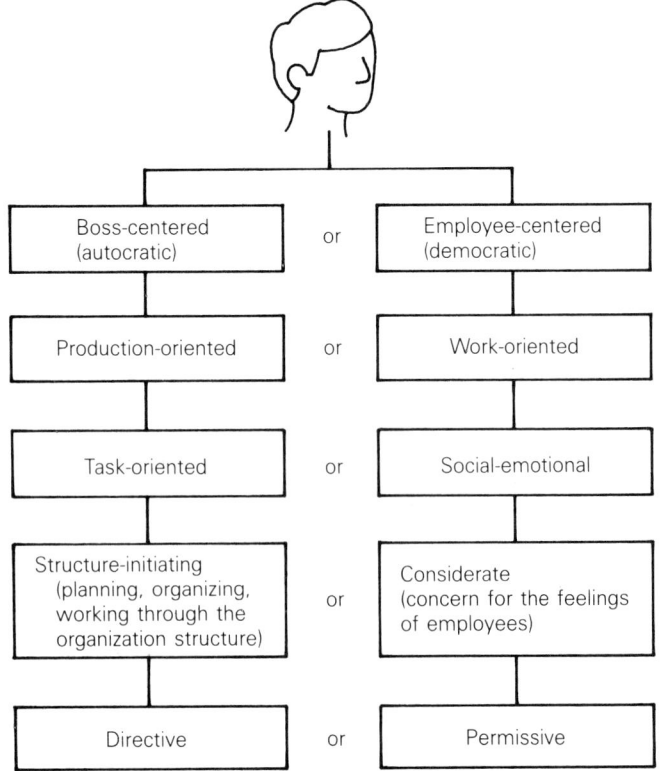

Boss-centered or employee-centered leadership. Over the years, researchers examined two divergent styles of leading people, known as the boss-centered or autocratic style, and the employee-centered or democratic style. The difference between the two styles lies in the degree of authority used by the manager and in the amount of freedom available to the subordinate in making decisions. The leader actions characterize the manager who delegates decision-making authority.

The continuum also suggests that a number of leadership styles may be employed. According to this approach, effective leaders are those who can adapt their style to different kinds of situations. That is, they would delegate authority according to their own capabilities, employees' abilities, and the goals to be accomplished.

The two-dimensional theory of leadership. As a result of extensive investigations undertaken by researchers at Ohio State University, two dimensions of leadership behavior have been identified.[18] The two dimensions, initiating structure and consideration, were used to describe leader behavior in different types of organization settings.

Initiating structure, which is task-oriented, emphasizes the needs of the organization. Consideration, which is more relationship-oriented, stresses the needs of individual employees. Managers with high scores on the "initiating structure" dimension were those who structured their own role and those of their employees toward reaching preestablished goals. They were also active in planning work activities, scheduling work, and communicating pertinent information. High scores in "consideration" went to managers who developed a work atmosphere of mutual trust, respect for subordinates' ideas, and consideration of employees.

These two dimensions of leader behavior have been tested in several different studies with somewhat conflicting results. For example, foremen who were rated as most effective by their bosses scored high on "initiating structure" and low on "consideration," whereas among managers in staff departments, this relationship was reversed. In general, it has been found that grievances, accidents, absenteeism, and turnover are likely to be higher among the employees of managers who are rated as high in "structure" and low in "consideration."

Situational Theories As more research on leadership traits and styles have been conducted, it has become apparent that the traits or style required by an effective leader depends on the particular situation. Many of the situational theories suggest that the effective leader is one who is capable of adapting his or her style to deal with the situation at hand and the personality of the subordinates. Leadership is a function of the leader's personality, the group's personality, and the situation. This means that a successful leader in one situation, say, the dean of a business college, may not be as effective in another situation, for example, as the manager of a large industrial plant.

> In a year when most retailers are taking their lumps, J. C. Penney Co. shines....
>
> For years, Penney followed personnel policies usually associated with the Japanese. The company adheres strongly to employment security and to nonadversarial relations with customers and employees. Now, with those practices firmly ensconced, Penney seems to be successful in adopting another quintessentially Japanese business concept: consensus management.
>
> To develop leaders comfortable with Penney's aggressive new merchandising thrust and its entry into new fields such as insurance, its chairman and chief executive, Donald V. Seibert, allows his managers an equal voice in almost every major decision.

Source: "Teamwork Pays Off at Penney's," *Business Week,* April 12, 1982, p. 107.

Based on many years of empirical research, Fred E. Fiedler has developed the leadership contingency model. He specifies three important leadership dimensions as influencing the effectiveness of the leader:

1. *Leader–member relations.* This is the extent to which the leader "gets along" with the subordinates and to which the subordinates maintain confidence in and loyalty to the leader.
2. *Task structure.* This refers to how routine and predictable the work group's task is. For example, well-defined jobs in which each aspect is spelled out have a high task structure.
3. *Position power.* This is the influence inherent in the position held by the leader. It includes the rewards and punishments associated with the position as well as the support the leader receives from his or her superiors and the overall organization.

We notice that "leader–member relations" is much like the "consideration" (or relationship-oriented style) concept previously discussed. Similarly, "task structure" is closely related to "initiating structure" (or task-oriented style). Fiedler, however, goes beyond these approaches by defining what characteristics of the situation are important in determining which leadership style is more effective. According to Fiedler's model, the situation variables determine the degree to which the leader is able to exert influence over his or her group.[19]

Howard M. Carlisle has pointed out several important implications of the contingency approach to leadership that are often contrary to current practices in human resource management:

> Organizations tend to restrict the criteria for selecting leaders to individuals who possess certain traits (aggressiveness, decisiveness, etc.) or who have demonstrated unusual technical expertise. However, these are only two factors that determine leadership effectiveness. This effectiveness is a function of many variables and conditions relating to the group and broader situational factors.

No one leadership style should predominate throughout an organization. This sort of inbreeding is damaging, because different elements of the organization will display characteristics that call for different types of leaders.

There is no one training approach to leadership because there is no one best style. Furthermore, attempts to change basic styles are often hazardous and always difficult. Leadership training should emphasize flexibility in behavior and skill in diagnosing situations.

Selecting and capitalizing on effective leaders involves matching the skills, attitudes, values, and personality traits of the leader with the characteristics of members, organizational climate, and other variables. If a mismatch exists or changes are desired, rather than concentrating on changing the leader, more success will usually be achieved by modifying factors in the situation such as tasks, position power, organization structure, and other such variables.[20]

We wish to emphasize the last point by suggesting that, although leadership skills can be learned, it is difficult, if not nearly impossible to change an individual's personality. As many human resource departments have found out, you cannot expect, for example, to change an autocratic, production-oriented foreman into a participative, employee-oriented department manager. It may be much more effective to adjust the situation than to attempt to change the style of leader. Accordingly, the autocratic, production-oriented foreman would be assigned to highly structured departments. The participative, employee-oriented manager would be assigned to a group whose work is less structured and more challenging. If possible, employees may be transferred to areas in which they would be more compatible with the leader.

Vroom-Yetton Model Victor Vroom believes that the behavioral sciences should attempt to go beyond descriptive theory and provide useful guides to solving real-world problems. He feels that the central problem of managers is choosing a leadership style for deciding among problem solutions so that the solution will be effectively implemented by the work group. The Vroom-Yetton model provides a clear-cut operational procedure for doing this.[21]

Vroom developed a set of management decision styles as shown in Exhibit 8–13. The model specifies the appropriate choice(s) of decision styles based on empirical research. The conceptual basis of the model requires us to distinguish three attributes of the outcomes:

1. The quality or rationality of the decision
2. The acceptance or commitment of the individuals in the group to implement the decision effectively
3. The time required to make the decision

Some problems are so trivial or so familiar to the manager and the organization that group acceptance is insured. It is more effective for the

EXHIBIT 8-13
Examples of management decision styles, according to the Vroom-Yetton model.

AI	Manager solves the problem and decides on the solution alone.
AII	Manager asks his or her group of subordinates for information but makes the decision alone. Group members may or may not be told what the problem is.
CI	Manager shares the problem with individuals in the group, but not as a group, and asks for ideas and information. The manager makes the decision.
CII	Manager shares the problem with the collective group for group discussion. The manager makes the decision.
GII	Manager and subordinates meet as a group to discuss the problem, and the group as a whole makes the decision.

Note: A = Alone   C = Consultation   G = Group

manager to make a decision alone in such a case. At the other extreme, complex problems that affect all subordinates might be better solved as a group. Such a decision style has to weigh tradeoffs of cost, effectiveness of the solution, and worker commitment (motivation) to implementation. In order to provide a procedure, seven diagnostic questions requiring only a "yes" or "no" answer have been developed. By following through the branches of this decision tree, we find acceptable solutions for 14 problem types.

Path–Goal Theory The close link between motivation and leadership is demonstrated by the *path–goal theory* of leadership.[22] This theory is essentially based on the expectancy theory of motivation. Leadership is viewed in terms of both its motivating impact and need satisfaction impact on workers. The effective leader will help to define the *paths* of workers toward their goals and will influence the perceptions of the goals themselves (Exhibit 8–14).

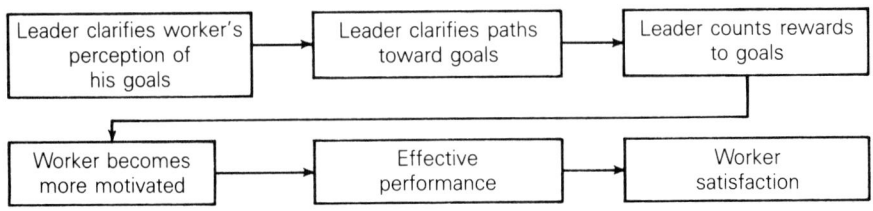

EXHIBIT 8-14
Path-goal leadership process.

Application of Theory

The P/HR specialist is responsible for initiating programs to develop the leadership of company managers. These programs fall within the area of "Management Development" as part of the total company training and development activity. The various theories discussed can be taught by a combination of techniques:

1. Role playing, for awareness of situations and subordinates
2. Case method, for decision making, awareness of situations, subordinate and peer interactions, and complexity
3. In-basket methods, for diagnosis
4. Kepner-Tregoe (decision-making technique that combines elements of case method and role playing), for problem identification and solution

Finally, the Vroom-Yetton model provides a prescriptive approach to leadership development that can be taught by combinations of the above techniques.

QUALITY CIRCLES: APPLICATION OF MOTIVATION/LEADERSHIP THEORY

It is no longer news that American industry has lost a strategic advantage to the Japanese, that of quality in products. It has taken some years for U.S. management to recognize that one of the causes of poor quality is poor

---

Employe "Circles" Help Management Solve Problems and Establish Policy

Robert Dodge, *Miami Herald* Bureau Writer

A group of about 10 maintenance workers at Eastern Airlines solved an inventory control problem and saved the company thousands of dollars. They did it through quality-circle management—an employe-participation management technique once used only in Japan.

Employes participating in quality circles—there are usually three to 15 in a group—meet on a regular basis to identify, analyze and propose solutions to problems in their work areas. Participation is voluntary and the groups receive special training.

The Eastern group found that some of the less expensive parts removed from jet engines during overhaul were unnecessarily discarded. As a result of that finding, an airline official said, the carrier was able to cancel a spare-parts order for $54,000. (Undated mimeo.)

management. Management has not established the system, the work environment, the leadership, or the reward system that will produce the quality of goods that the consumer desires.

Many companies are now developing organizational approaches based upon the Japanese development of quality circles (QC). A *quality circle* consists of from three to 15 members doing related work and who meet regularly to identify, analyze, and solve product-quality and production problems and improve operations. Participants are trained in problem-solving methods and statistical techniques for quality control. QCs provide opportunities for workers to participate in activities that, in the United States, were reserved for management. The chance to grow on the job, to satisfy the need for pride in doing good work, and the related recognition and rewards lead to increased motivation. Management's role is to establish such a system and treat it as important. Exhibit 8–15 shows how QCs are organized. Exhibit 8–16 shows how the QC system operates to provide opportunities for recognition at higher levels.

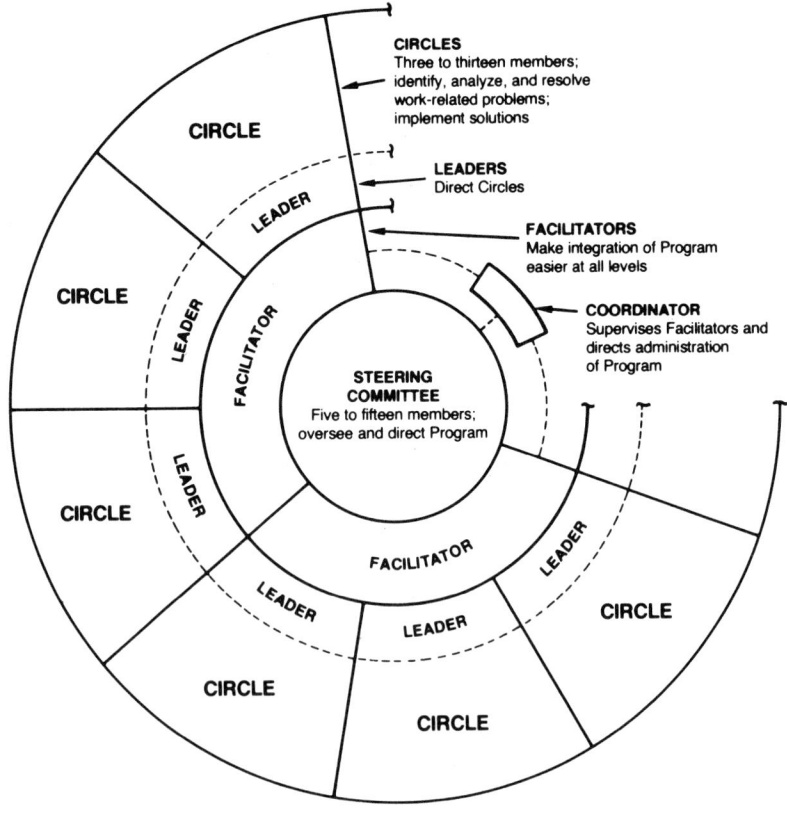

EXHIBIT 8–15

Quality circles organization. *Source:* Joseph Hanley, "Our Experience with Quality Circles," *Quality Progress,* February 1980, p. 24.

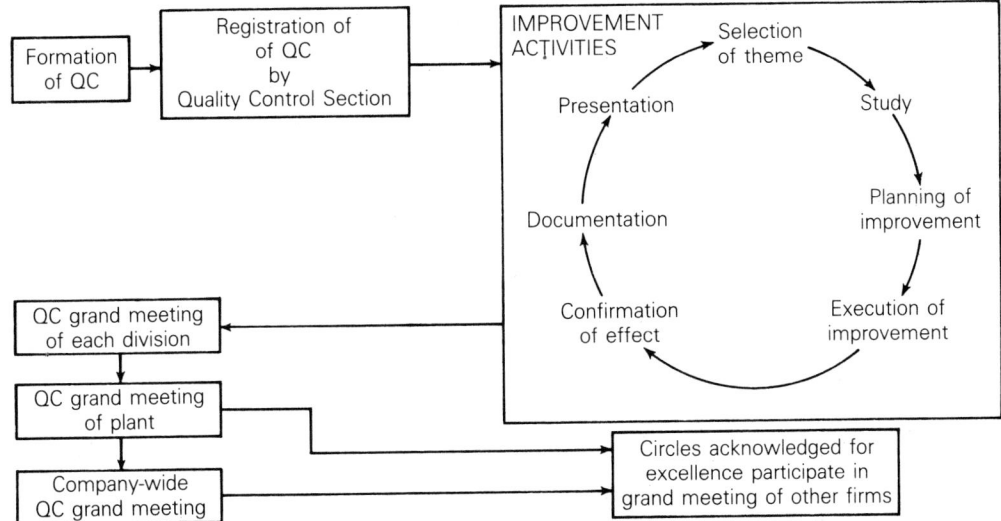

EXHIBIT 8-16
How the QC system operates.

Quality circles represent the application of the various theories of motivation and leadership as follows:

Theory	Application
Maslow	QCs satisfy needs for self-fulfillment and affiliation.
Herzberg	QCs satisfy needs for achievement, satisfaction with the work itself, and desire for responsibility, and provide job enrichment in general. They also provide hygiene factors such as improved relations and working conditions.
McClelland	QCs provide workers with a feeling of achievement because they will feel their work and products are important.
Expectancy theory	Workers will anticipate improvement in work efficiency, and quality of products will lead to greater company profitability and, therefore, greater rewards for themselves.
Operant conditioning	Not clearly applicable when bonus system is used.
Path–goal theory	In QCs, the leader's behavior is an immediate source of satisfaction. The leader shares authority, supports the QC group, and seeks rewards for the group based on performance.
Behavioral theories	In QCs, both "initiating structure" and "consideration" activities by the leader are increased.
Situational contingency theories	In QCs, the leader must get along well with members of the group or be replaced. Task structure is high, but means for achieving tasks allow for

	worker creativity. Leader "power" is deemphasized so that workers feel they have more control over their jobs. The leader is primarily supportive. These factors produce an environment that promotes achievement, personal growth, and recognition to motivate workers.
Vroom-Yetton model	Helps distinguish between decisions to be made by leader and those to be made by the QC group on the basis of the situation and type of problem.

SUMMARY

We have introduced the basic organizational goal of productivity. All P/HR activities should be directed first toward this goal. Productivity has three components: strategic objectives, effectiveness, and efficiency. Leadership and motivation must be combined positively to strive for these objectives.

Motivation is the internal force that produces behavior on the part of the individual. Maslow proposed a hierarchy of needs as a basis for motivation. From lowest (primary) to highest, these needs are: physiological needs, safety needs, social needs, ego needs, and self-actualization needs. Despite their plausibility, these needs are apparently not independent, and the model of motivation is untestable.

Herzberg proposed a dual-factor theory paralleling Maslow's theory. He stated that hygiene needs, if not present, act as dissatisfiers. Such needs include company administration, quality of supervision, relations with others, salary, job security, personal life, working conditions, and status. Herzberg identified the motivators (satisfiers) to be achievement, recognition, advancement, the work itself, personal growth, and responsibility. Herzberg's theory has had wide impact on managers because it is easy to understand and appears to be plausible. Research on the model has been controversial.

Consistent with Herzberg and Maslow, McClelland and Atkinson emphasized the need for achievement as a drive. They also included the needs for affiliation and power.

Modern cognitive motivation models are tending toward expectancy and goal models. The individual estimates the likelihood that his or her effort will result in attaining organizational goals and the probability that such performance will result in desired rewards. The probabilities in this chain are called expectancies, and the strength of desire for a goal is called its valence. This theory permits management to structure tasks, rewards, and communications processes to produce higher motivation.

A theory of motivation proposed by B. F. Skinner is operant conditioning. When a worker is presented with a stimulus such as a goal, he or she may select various behaviors. Management rewards (reinforces) desired behavior and essentially ignores undesirable behavior (unless it becomes a serious problem).

In essence, the technology for all the motivational models is the same. Management determines the goals of the workers and then creates an environment of task structure and rewards to permit the worker to achieve his individual goals.

Leadership is essential for the effective management of human resources. A manager, however, is not necessarily a leader. The essence of leadership is found in the extent to which a manager can influence the behavior of peers or in the extent to which he or she can influence the action of employees. If the manager can initiate action, induce others to engage in it, and direct it toward goals, he or she is a leader.

To begin with, we have seen earlier in this chapter that the influence system provides the broad setting within which leadership occurs. Power and/or authority underlie the entire spectrum of ways to influence behavior. It takes leadership, however, to obtain results that are "above the call of duty." The leadership system involves three basic elements—the leader, the follower, and the situation. In addition, leadership is affected by such important variables as the external environment, the task, and the organization.

Certain personality traits are helpful for effective managerial leadership, but are neither required nor sufficient. Above-average intelligence, initiative, and supervising ability are most important among traits identified. Effective leaders tend to be good listeners and to encourage meaningful two-way communication. They also typically exhibit a flexible personality as well as flexible leadership styles. That is, they are able to adjust to a particular individual or group in a particular situation and at a particular time. They recognize that effective leadership is a function of a complex combination of factors that are part of the broader human resource system. They know that effective leadership requires the integration of individual and organizational goals. This means that they have a high concern both for the objectives of the firm and for the goals of their followers. They believe that their followers' goals can be best attained through making contributions to the achievement of organizational objectives.

The personality of the leader will, of course, dictate a preference for a particular style of leadership. An aggressive, authoritarian manager would tend to be a more directive type of leader. On the other hand, a very democratic manager with a strong commitment to human values will probably use a more free-rein or participative leadership style. However, this does not mean that one style will always be more effective. For example, when subordinates prefer self-control and autonomy, the participative approach would be more effective. However, if the employees are dependent, avoid responsibility, and have a low commitment to group goals, a more directive style would be advisable.

We have seen that an appropriate leader is one who resembles the group in such things as values, attitudes, and personality. Although this does not mean that the characteristics of the leader must be the same as the characteristics of the group, it does suggest that a certain type of leader might not harmonize with a given group.

For example, if previous leaders of a group have been very directive and task oriented, this would have a major influence on that group's expectations regarding the type of leadership style for a new leader. A similar variable is the degree of homogeneity of the group. If the group is highly diverse and lacks common characteristics, a more directive leadership style might be more effective.

Exhibit 8–17 illustrates several group characteristics that influence the leader–follower relationship. Accordingly, situations with the characteristics identified on the left-hand side call for a more autocratic or directive leadership style, whereas situations with the characteristics identified on the right-hand side call for a participative or free-rein style.

The tasks to be performed are an important determinant of effective leadership. Each job or position has specialized assignments and requirements associated with it. The fact that an individual has been an effective leader in one position does not mean that he or she will necessarily be effective in leading a group of workers performing different tasks. For example, the captain of the company's softball team may be very ineffective as sales manager. Similarly, we know that simple, repetitive tasks that provide few intrinsic rewards require a more directive leadership approach. On the other hand, a more supportive leader would be effective if the tasks to be accomplished were complex and intrinsically rewarding.

The characteristics of the organization are an equally important determinant of leadership effectiveness. Organizations may be private or public, large or small, highly structured or loosely organized, task centered or relationship oriented, economic oriented or social oriented. Too large a discrepancy between the personality of the leader and certain characteristics of the organization may result in ineffective leadership. A retired army general, for example, may be ineffective as a hospital administrator. The vice president of a large state university may be ineffective as the president of a small liberal arts college.

EXHIBIT 8–17
Situational variables in leadership (leader and follower characteristics excluded).

	Group Characteristics	
Quantity of interaction	Little	Extensive
Group unity	Conflict	Cooperation
Trust	Low	High
Membership	Heterogeneous	Homogeneous
Existing leadership roles	Directive	Free rein
Existing member roles	Obedient	Independent

Source: Adapted from Howard M. Carlisle, *Management: Concepts and Situations* (Chicago: Science Research Associates, 1976), pp. 505–506.

The characteristics of the environment external to the organization are another important determinant of leadership effectiveness. For example, a relatively authoritarian or directive leadership style may be effective in a business firm in financial crisis due to a severe business recession. Similarly, leadership must conform to the broader societal culture to be effective. This means, to take an extreme example, that a successful, democratic-oriented manager in the United States may be ineffective if he or she is transferred to a foreign country with a more authoritarian culture.

KEY CONCEPTS

Productivity

Motivation

Expectancy model

Operant conditioning

Leadership

Path–goal theory

Quality circles

NOTES

1. "Anti-Japanese Sentiment Is Rising on the West Coast," *Miami Herald*, June 4, 1982, p. 3D.
2. *The Unpredictability of "Modern" Technology and What To Do About It*, PIMSLETTER, No. 2, The Strategic Planning Institute, Cambridge, Mass., 1977.
3. Abraham H. Maslow, "A Theory of Human Motivation," *Psychological Review*, July 1943. Reprinted in Robert A. Sutermeister (Ed.), *People and Productivity*, 3rd ed. (New York: McGraw-Hill, 1976).
4. James A. Lee, *The Gold and the Garbage in Management Theories and Prescriptions*, Athens, Ohio: Ohio University Press, 1980, p. 72.
5. Frederick Herzberg, B. Mausner, and D. B. Snyderman, *The Motivation to Work* (New York: Wiley, 1959).
6. James A. Lee, *The Gold and the Garbage in Management Theories and Prescriptions*, Athens, Ohio: Ohio University Press, 1980, p. 101.
7. Richard M. Steers and Lyman W. Porter, *Motivation and Work Behavior*, 2nd ed. (New York: McGraw-Hill, 1979), p. 395.
8. David C. McClelland, *The Achieving Society* (Princeton, N.J.: Van Nostrand, 1961).
9. D. Miron and D. C. McClelland, "The Impact of Achievement Motivation Training on Small Business," *California Management Review*, Summer 1979.
10. Victor H. Vroom, *Work and Motivation* (New York: Wiley, 1964).
11. Lyman W. Porter and Edward Lawler III, *Managerial Attitudes and Performance* (Homewood, Ill.: Irwin, 1968).
12. Porter and Lawler, *Managerial Attitudes*, p. 165.
13. B. F. Skinner, *Beyond Freedom and Dignity*, New York: Knopf, 1971. See also David K. Hart and William G. Scott, "The Optimal Image of Man for Systems Theory," *Academy of Management Journal*, December 1972.
14. Bernard M. Bass, *Stogdill's Handbook of Leadership*, rev. ed. (New York: The Free Press, 1981).

15. Daniel Katz and Robert L. Kahn, *The Social Psychology of Organizations* (New York: Wiley, 1966), pp. 300–302.
16. Chester I. Barnard, *The Function of the Executive* (Cambridge, Mass.: Harvard University Press, 1960), pp. 168–169.
17. Bass, *Stogdill's Handbook*, p. 66.
18. R. M. Stogdill and A. E. Coons (Eds.), *Leader Behavior: Its Description and Measurement* (Columbus Bureau of Business Research, Ohio State University, 1957).
19. Fred E. Fiedler, *A Theory of Leadership Effectiveness* (New York: McGraw-Hill, 1967).
20. Howard M. Carlisle, *Management: Concepts and Situations* (Chicago: Science Research Associates, 1976), pp. 514–515.
21. See Victor H. Vroom, "A New Look at Managerial Decision-making," *Organizational Dynamics*, Spring 1973, and Victor H. Vroom and Phillip W. Yetton, *Leadership and Decision Making* (Pittsburgh: University of Pittsburgh Press, 1973).
22. Robert J. House and Terence R. Mitchell, "Path–Goal Theory of Leadership," *Journal of Contemporary Business*, Vol. 5 (1974), pp. 81–97.

REVIEW AND DISCUSSION QUESTIONS

1. Discuss why it appears that the Japanese workers are more productive than the American workers.
2. Discuss the meaning of productivity.
3. What are the three internal company forces that influence productivity and how are they related?
4. In what general ways can the P/HR organization contribute to improving leadership and motivation?
5. What is the general nature of the "needs" theories of motivation?
6. Distinguish between the expectancy theory of motivation and Herzberg's model.
7. Why would Skinner's operant conditioning theory of behavior likely be rejected out of hand by psychologists? Discuss.
8. What common result is obtained from all theories of motivation and behavior covered in the text?
9. Develop a definition of "leadership" as a process within a system.
10. Distinguish among the following concepts: (a) influence, (b) power, (c) authority, (d) leadership.
11. What plausible explanation can you give for highest leadership effectiveness occurring when the situation is unfavorable but the leader's style is task oriented?
12. Explain what quality circles are, and why you think they are called quality circles instead of productivity circles.
13. What is the role of the P/HR department in promoting increased motivation?
14. Why is the development of leadership an important objective of the P/HR department? Discuss the contribution of various P/HR functions to leadership development and measurement.

15. Identify and describe two contingency (situational) theories of leadership. Why do Vroom-Yetton criticize such theories?

BIBLIOGRAPHY

Bass, Bernard. *Stogdill's Handbook of Leadership* (rev.). New York: The Free Press, 1982.
Bowers, David C., and Stanley Seashore. "Predicting Organizational Effectiveness with a Four-Factor Theory of Leadership." *Administrative Science Quarterly,* April–June 1966.
Byars, Lloyd L. "Solutions to Productivity Problems." *Journal of Systems Management,* January 1982.
Gilmore, Harold L. "Quality of Employee Performance." *Quality Program,* May 1980.
Green, Stephen G., et al. "Personality and Situational Effects on Leader Behavior." *Academy of Management Journal,* June 1976.
Gregerman, Ira B. *Knowledge Worker Productivity.* New York: AMACOM, 1981.
Hersey, Paul, and Kenneth H. Blanchard. *Management of Organizational Behavior,* 2nd ed. Englewood Cliffs, N.J.: Prentice-Hall, 1972.
Hinricks, John R. *Practical Management for Productivity.* New York: Van Nostrand Reinhold, 1978.
Hunt, James G. "Breakthrough in Leadership Research." *Personnel Administration,* September–October 1967.
Hunt, James G., and Lars L. Larson (Eds.). *Contingency Approaches to Leadership.* Symposium held at Southern Illinois U., May 17–18, 1973.
Jago, Arthur G. "Leadership: Perspectives in Theory and Research." *Management Science,* March 1982.
Latham, Gary P., Larry L. Cummings, and Terence R. Mitchell. "Behavioral Statistics to Improve Productivity." *Organizational Dynamics,* Winter 1981.
Levinson, Harry. "Executive Development: What You Need to Know," *Training and Development Journal,* September 1981.
Macarov, David. *Worker Productivity: Myths and Reality.* Beverly Hills, Ca.: Sage Publications, 1982.
Moore, Brian E., and Timothy L. Ross. *The Scanlon Way to Improved Productivity: A Practical Guide.* New York: Wiley, 1978.
Owens, James. "A Reappraisal of Leadership Theory and Training." *Personnel Administrator,* November 1981.
Reddin, William J. "The 3-D Management Style Theory." *Training and Development Journal,* April 1967.
Rubin, Irwin M., and Max Goldman. "An Open System Model of Leadership Performance." *Organizational Behavior and Human Performance,* May 1968.
Stogdill, R. M., and A. E. Coons (Eds.). *Leader Behavior: Its Description and Measurement.* Columbus Bureau of Business Research, Ohio State University, 1957.
Tannenbaum, Robert, and Warren H. Schmidt. "How to Choose a Leadership Pattern." *Harvard Business Review,* March–April 1958.
Vroom, Victor, and Philip Yetton. *Leadership and Decision Making.* Pittsburgh: University of Pittsburgh Press, 1973.
White, Harold C. "Personnel Administration and Organizational Productivity: An Employee View." *Personnel Administrator,* August 1981.

Organization Development

CHAPTER OUTLINE

What Is Organization Development (OD)?
Objectives □ Underlying Themes

Three Main Approaches to OD

Conducting An Effective OD Program
Steps for Action Research □ Intervention Techniques

The Impact of OD

OBJECTIVES

1. Describe the origins and objectives of organization development.
2. Define and show the importance of organizational climate.
3. Explain the difference between behavioral and nonbehavioral interventions.
4. Show the relationship between human resource management, OD, and training.
5. Discuss in detail two or more models of organization change.
6. Describe each of the basic steps in action research.
7. Define laboratory training and discuss its objectives.
8. Differentiate the concepts of team building, managerial grid, and MBO.
9. Discuss the future of organization development.

SPOTLIGHT:
H. Gregory Calvert

Vice President and Director of Human Resources for Landmark Banking Corporation, H. Gregory Calvert is employed in this Florida-based bank holding company headquartered in Fort Lauderdale, Florida, with assets of 1.6 billion dollars. Prior to joining Landmark, Mr. Calvert was the Compensation Manager for Maryland National Bank in Baltimore, Maryland.

Mr. Calvert currently serves on the Florida Banker's Association Human Resources Committee and is a director and faculty member of the Association's Supervisors Academy. He is an Accredited Personnel Manager with the American Society of Personnel Administrators and is a member of the American Compensation Association and American Society of Training and Development.

Mr. Calvert's educational background includes a Bachelor of Science degree in Personnel and Labor Relations from the University of Baltimore.

Comments by H. Gregory Calvert

In the next decade Organization Development will be the two most talked about but least understood buzz words in the human resource vocabulary.

I share with you my thoughts and beliefs about what it means to me:

- ☐ The feelings employees have toward their jobs are based more on the job environment and how they are treated than the inner feeling of their personalities; therefore, any effort to change feelings about the job or the company should be geared more toward how the person is treated, than toward getting the person to change.
- ☐ An organizational philosophy and/or climate that meets the needs of its human resources as well as the requirements of the organization, tends to excel in quality and quantity of production.

- Motivation comes from within. Today's employee seeks challenging work and the responsibility and accountability for accomplishing organizational objectives they are a part of and committed to.
- The superstructure of any organization is groups (teams) of people; the units of change, therefore, are groups not individuals. Additionally, the growth of the groups will flourish when the participants are open and honest, trusting and supportive, and willing to accept change.
- Organization development must come from within. I believe people are committed to what they help create or participate in. The effectiveness of change will be in direct proportion to the degree of ownership of the participants involved.
- The effectiveness of any organization is a direct result of the people who make it move. The more openness, trust, and participation that exist, the more effective the organization will be.

These are my thoughts and beliefs, I have no scientific data nor research to support these statements. I simply say they are true. . . .

In his classic book, *The Human Side of Enterprise*, Douglas McGregor says that "the limits on human collaboration in the organizational setting are not limits of human nature but of management's ingenuity in discovering how to realize the potential represented by its human resources."[1] This statement aptly summarizes the underlying rationale for the process of organization development. Organization development (or OD as it is often called) is a process for responding to McGregor's challenge to "realize the potential represented by human resources."

Organization development has been defined by Richard Beckhard as "an effort that is planned, organization-wide, and managed from the top to increase organizational effectiveness and health through planned interventions into the organization's process, using behavioral science knowledge."[2] The term organization development (OD) thus stands for both a general approach and a variety of techniques directed toward achieving McGregor's Theory-Y type of organization. In such an organization, mutual trust and individual responsibility permit each worker to reach for self-fulfillment in the work climate.

The goals of OD include company-wide change as well as change on the individual level. One aim of OD is to help each employee achieve at his or her full potential. Another aim is to improve working relationships among individuals and groups. From a systems view, then, OD is a means for improving the functioning of the total system for managing human resources, and is thus closely related to all of the other functions of human resource management. It does this by modifying the climate of the organization, its policies, regulations and procedures, and the behavior of individuals.

Organization development represents a specific application of the systems view of human resources, since the major thrust of OD is the improved functioning of the total system.

WHAT IS ORGANIZATION DEVELOPMENT (OD)?

Organization development (OD) is a varied set of techniques directed toward improving organizational performance. The approach consists of modifying the organizational climate to instill such new behavioral values as openness and trust. Once an overall OD strategy has been determined, it may be decided that a part of this strategy should include the training and development of individuals. Thus, OD is very much a "macro" approach to development as contrasted with individual training and development, which is essentially a "micro" approach.

Exhibit 9-1 shows the relationship of the OD process to human resource management and training and development (this important latter subject is discussed more fully in Chapter 11, Individual Training and Development). The principal difference in emphasis between OD and training

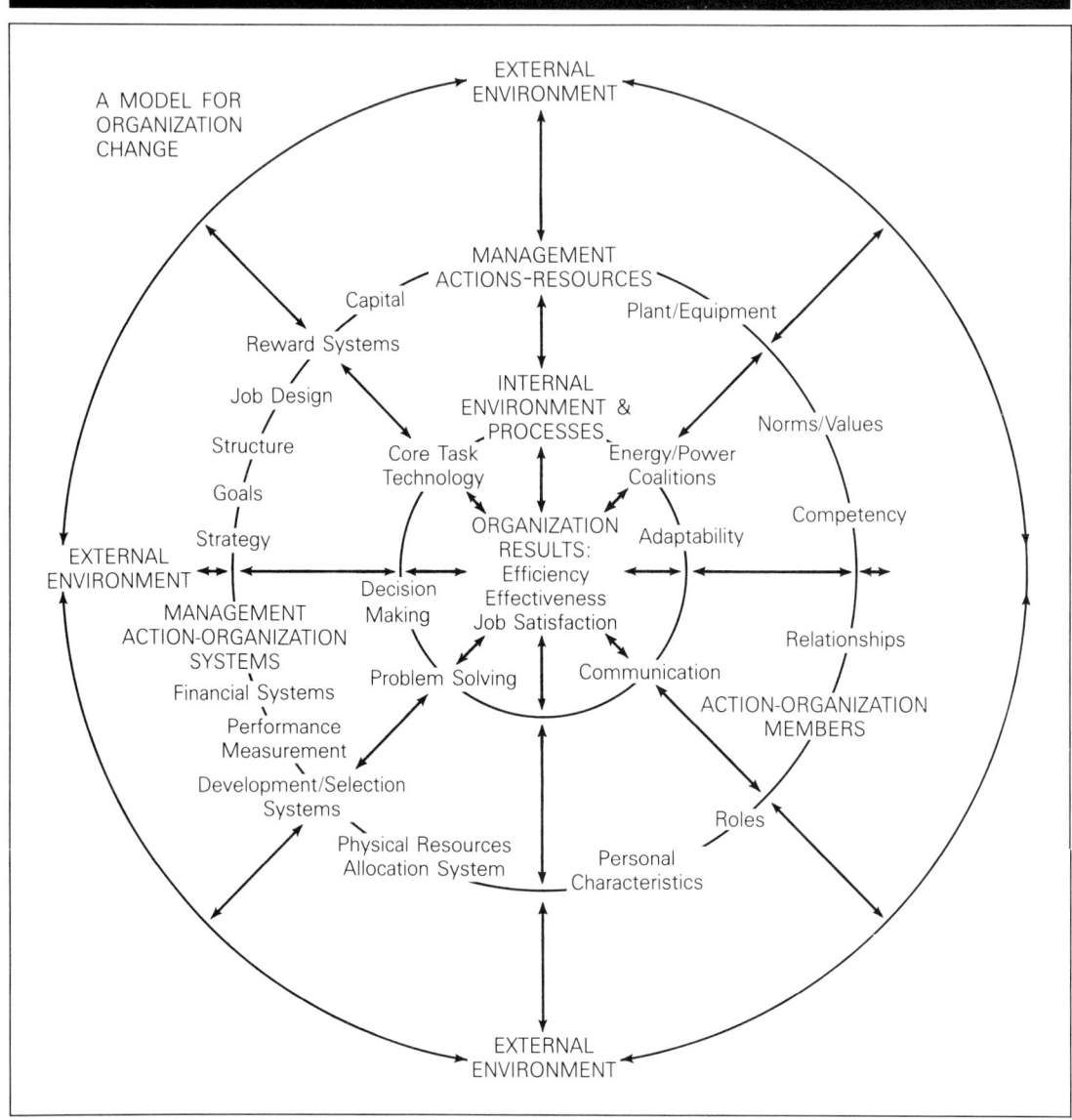

Source: Noble McKay and Serge Lashutka, "The Basics of Organization Change: An Eclectic Model," *Training and Development Journal*, April 1983, p. 68. © 1982 Noble McKay and Serge Lashutka.

and development is that OD focuses on the working climate whereas training and development focuses on the individual. The specific differences are summarized in Exhibit 9–2. Further, if we explain the meaning of "working climate" more specifically, we will gain a better understanding of the focus of OD.

ORGANIZATION DEVELOPMENT 273

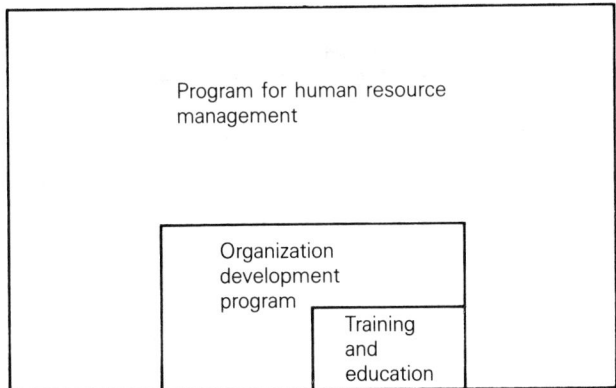

EXHIBIT 9-1
The partitioning of human resources management.

Just as we live in a climate of weather, we work in a "climate" of other people's behavior and organizational forces. A climate may provide stimulation and motivation to encourage the performance of human resources. It may also contain constraints, blockages, and frustrations that inhibit this performance. The organization climate is as intangible as the wind in our physical climate. It is felt but cannot be seen. It affects every member's performance. The organization climate is a composite of many factors, some of which are the managerial style of individual managers and the dominant management style of the organization; the values held by individual managers and reflected in the organization as a whole; and the formal organization (rules, policies, organization structure, the reward system), the informal organization (norms of behavior, beliefs, values, and attitudes of the emergent behavioral system), the communications system, and all other managerial systems.

Objectives

Organizations embark on organization development programs in order to achieve a wide variety of specific objectives. However, most of these objectives can be classified into three types:

1. Improved organizational performance as measured by such indexes as profitability, turnover, innovation, and share of market
2. Improvement of the organization's adaptation to its environment, including the willingness of members to face up to organizational problems and their effectiveness in consistently reaching creative solutions to those problems
3. Improvement in internal behavior patterns, including such things as interpersonal and intergroup cooperation, the level of trust and support, owning up to feelings and emotions, openness and completeness of communication, and widespread participation in the planning of organization strategy

EXHIBIT 9–2
Comparison of traditional training and the organization change process.

Dimension	Traditional Training	Organization Change Process
Unit of focus	The individual	Interpersonal relationships—teams, work units, intergroup relations, superior–subordinate relations
Content of training	Technical and administrative skills	Interpersonal and group membership skills—communication, problem solving, conflict management, helping
Target subjects	Primarily first-line employees and supervisors; managers trained outside organization	All levels; usually initial intervention with upper management in-house
Conception of learning process	Cognitive and rational	Cognitive, rational, emotional-motivational
Teaching style	Subject matter and teacher centered	Participant, immediate experience, problem solving, and subject matter centered
Learning goals	Rationality and efficiency	Awareness, adaptation, and change
View of organization	Discrete functional skill units	Social system

Source: William B. Eddy, "From Training to Organization Change," *Personnel Administration,* January–February 1971, pp. 37–43. Reprinted by permission of the International Personnel Management Association, 1313 East 60th Street, Chicago, Illinois 60637.

Underlying Themes

Although organization development has the appearance of being quite new, its roots (and some of its techniques) go back to the Hawthorne experiments of the 1920s and 1930s.[3] These research studies conducted at the Hawthorne plant of the Western Electric Company were among the earliest systematic studies applying the experimental method to the analysis of behavior in organizations. They provided the basis for such concepts of organizational behavior as informal work groups, "emergent behavior," group norms, values and sentiments, and the significance of participation in decision making—concepts that remain central to the various techniques of organization development.

There are thus two underlying themes that you should keep in mind throughout our discussion of organization development. One of these is the systems approach to developing organizations. The other is commitment to a value system that emphasizes openness, trust, mutual confidence, confrontation, participation, and motivation of the individual through involvement in the decision-making process.

THREE MAIN APPROACHES TO OD

Although there are numerous OD approaches or models, we will discuss the three that have received the most attention in management literature. One of these is the three-step model of Kurt Lewin, consisting of "unfreezing," "changing," and "refreezing."[4] In Lewin's model, unfreezing involves readying the organization for change when an apparent challenge or problem makes it clear that change will be required. Changing means going from old behaviors to experimentation with new behaviors to solve the organizational problem. Refreezing consists of reinforcement activities for the new behaviors that will strengthen them and make them a part of the new behavior system of the organization. The most commonly utilized intervention technique, laboratory training, was a direct outgrowth, an application, of Lewin's model.

A more recent model by Larry Greiner also looks at change from the standpoint of sequential stages or steps in the process. A diagram illustrating Greiner's model is shown as Exhibit 9–3.[5] An important finding of Greiner's research was that for the organization change process to be effective, it appeared to be vital that each of the steps or phases occur in the particular sequence indicated in the model. Thus it appeared to be critical that the change process be initiated by *outside pressure* or stimulus on the top management of the organization, followed by a decision of the top management to take action. The succeeding phases of intervention by a change agent, diagnosis of problem areas, invention of new solutions, experimentation with these solutions, and reinforcement from positive results appeared to be crucial for the effectiveness of change processes.

Harold J. Leavitt has suggested a somewhat different approach to an organization change model.[6] Unlike Lewin's or Greiner's models that emphasize sequential steps or phases of organization change, Leavitt's model considers the different parts of a system on which change efforts might focus and the interactive nature of those parts. Leavitt views an organization as a system of four interacting variables—task, structure, technology, and people. Exhibit 9–4 gives an idea of Leavitt's approach.

There are two important features of Leavitt's model from the practical perspective of a manager. The first is that task, structure, technology, and people are interactive—that is, changing any one of these variables automatically produces change (some of which may be uncontrolled and unwanted) in the other variables. Thus, in planning and implementing change, it is important that the manager focus not only on the specific intended change but also on the effects which that change will have on the other

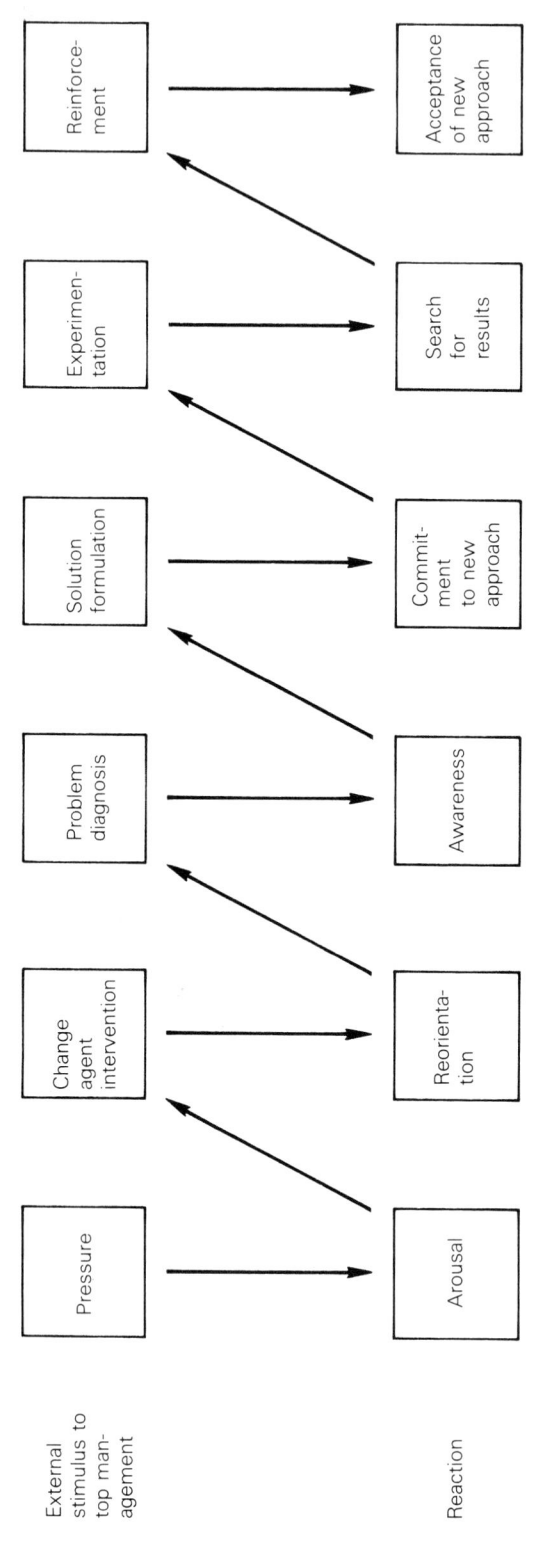

EXHIBIT 9-3
Greiner's model of the dynamics of successful organization change. *Source:* Based on Larry E. Greiner, "Patterns of Organization Change," in Gene W. Dalton, Paul R. Lawrence, and Larry E. Greiner (eds.), *Organizational Change and Development* (Homewood, Ill.: Richard D. Irwin, 1970), p. 222.

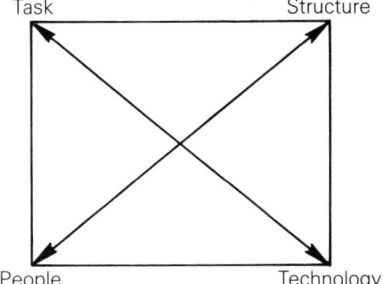

EXHIBIT 9-4
The four interacting variables of an organization. *Source:* Based on Harold J. Leavitt, *New Perspectives in Organization Research* (New York: Wiley, 1964).

variables. The second important feature is that change can effectively begin with any one of the four variables. Depending on the manager's diagnosis of the total situation, he or she might elect to start up an organization development effort with interpersonal behavior training of some sort, or to make a purely technological or structural intervention, or to simply modify the tasks.

CONDUCTING AN EFFECTIVE OD PROGRAM

Although many specific strategies have been designed to achieve organization development, the *action research model* is the heart of the OD process. Most OD practitioners (despite their many differences regarding specific strategies and interventions) agree that in a genuine OD strategy each of the five basic steps of the action research model must take place. These steps are intervention, data gathering, organizational diagnosis, data feedback and discussion, and action intervention (Exhibit 9-5). Thus, the considerable disagreement that exists among various OD practitioners centers primarily on the many techniques that can be utilized for each of the steps in the basic OD process.

This is particularly true of the action intervention stage, as hundreds of specific intervention techniques have been experimented with by OD practitioners. Many of these intervention strategies have been published, even though in some cases the strategy may have been utilized by only one practitioner or only one organization. Because OD is still in its infancy, there has not been much rigorous validation of the various intervention techniques, although research on OD is growing. At this stage, OD is very much an art rather than a science.

Steps for Action Research

It will be obvious from the above that a detailed discussion of the various techniques utilized for each of the stages in the OD process is beyond the scope of this book. We will, however, attempt to summarize the important aspects of each of the stages and to discuss briefly some of the most commonly used techniques.

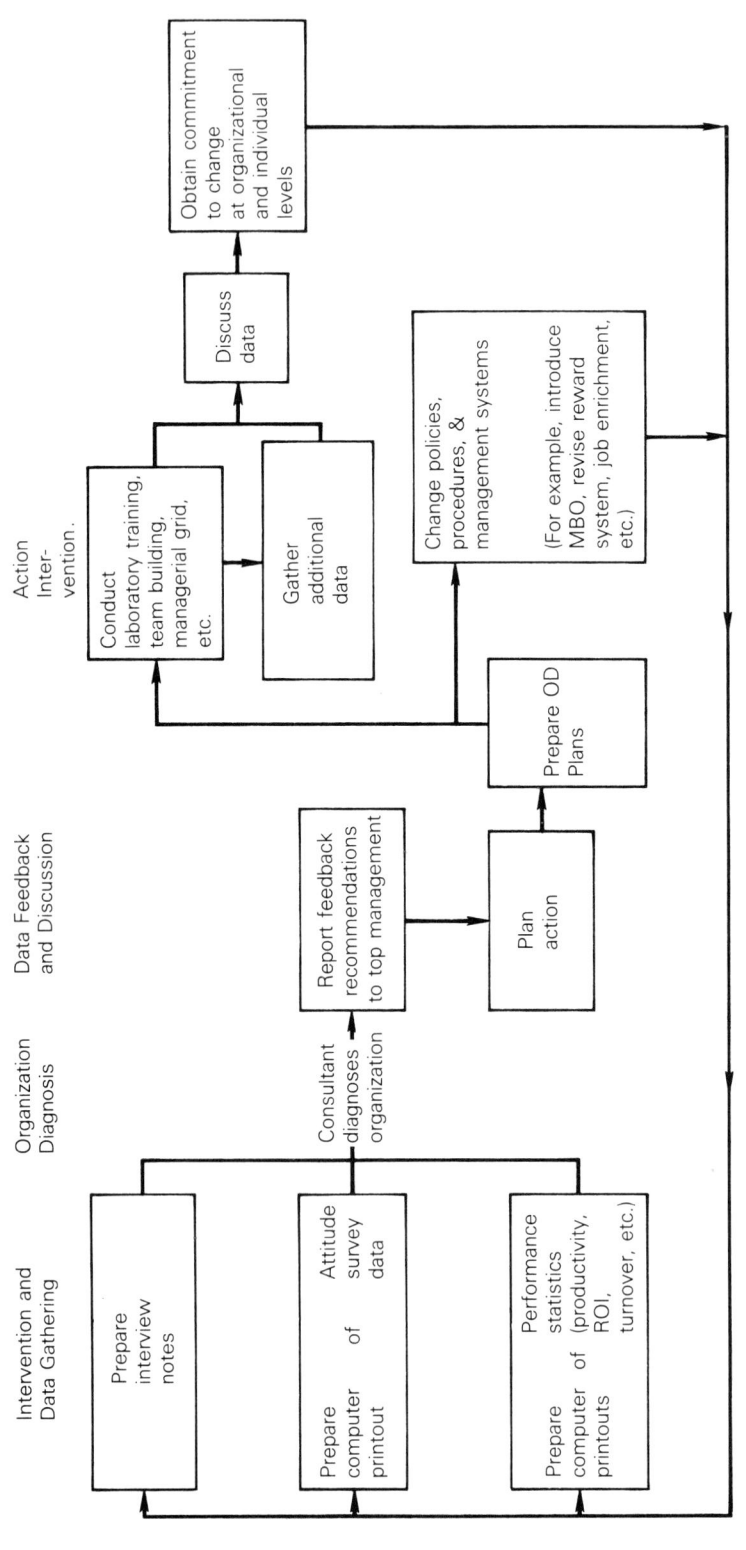

EXHIBIT 9-5
Action research model of organization development.

1. *Intervention.* OD begins with the intervention of a change agent from inside or outside the organization. Usually entering at the invitation of top management, this person is brought in in response to some perceived organizational problem (or, less frequently, a perceived opportunity) related to the ability of organization members to work cooperatively and effectively. Frequently this *change agent* is a consultant who has no permanent tie to the organization. The advantage of using such a consultant is that the change agent has both objectivity and relative independence from the power structure of the organization. There is a growing trend for larger organizations to have their own internal change agents, who are relatively independent staff members at the corporate level working in the same manner as external change agents with the various line organizations and divisions of the corporation. While internal change agents may lack, or appear to lack, the objectivity of external change agents their offsetting advantage is often better knowledge of the organization and insights into the causes and ramifications of the important issues that surface within the OD process.

2. *Data gathering.* The first major task of the change agent is to gather data for diagnosis of the organization's ability to function effectively and for the determination of specific problems. There are two primary methods of data gathering, the interview method and the survey questionnaire. It is not uncommon for OD practitioners to combine these two methods; however, some practitioners use one method exclusively. (It should be noted, incidentally, that the data-gathering process itself constitutes an action intervention because it disrupts the status quo.)

In the interview method, the top executives of the organization are interviewed individually by the consultant. In virtually all cases this would include at least the chief executive and each of his or her immediate subordinates. Depending on the size of the organization and the time allocated for this step, a sample of the next level of executives might be interviewed. Usually, if the first set of interviews uncovers potential problem areas, reporting executives will receive additional interview attention.

Although practice varies widely, the typical interview consists of a one-to-three-hour informal discussion session in which the consultant begins with some very open-ended questions, such as these: "How do you assess the overall effectiveness of this organization?" "Are there any specific obstacles that you believe are holding back the performance of the total organization or some part of the organization or your own performance?" "What frustrations do you experience in this organization, and what things would you like to see changed?" This interviewing is always done with the understanding that the replies of any single individual will be treated in complete confidence. It is also understood that the problems identified (particularly those identified by several executives) will be reported back to others in the organization.

In the second method for gathering data, a written questionnaire is given to a group of executives, either alone or in combination with individual interviews. Usually, a larger number of executives participate in a survey questionnaire than would be involved in the use of the interview technique. One advantage of the survey questionnaire technique is that it permits data to be gathered from a much larger range of executives with relatively less expenditure of consultant time. Some experts maintain that the survey questionnaire is more objective and "scientific" than the interview in that each executive respondent is asked exactly the same questions in exactly the same way, while simultaneously guaranteeing anonymity. Other experts argue that this is, in fact, the major *disadvantage* of the survey questionnaire—it does not permit individual follow-up by the consultant to probe for the deeper meaning of superficially expressed opinions.

A balanced view recognizes that both the interview technique and the survey questionnaire have unique advantages. The most effective data gathering should probably include both of these techniques. An example of a typical survey questionnaire instrument is shown in Exhibit 9–6.

It could be said that the whole purpose of organization development is to increase both the kinds of data available on the functioning of the organization and the application of these data in the organization. Data gathering attempts to supplement the usual kinds of information about the performance of an organization with information on the climate of the organization, the norms and values of work groups, and people's sentiments and attitudes about such things as management practices, status and power in the organization, communication, and information sharing. Thus, OD focuses both on generating new data about such issues and on encouraging the consideration of such issues as legitimate executive activity.

3. *Organizational diagnosis.* The next stage in the OD process is the preliminary diagnosis of the organizational situation by the consultant in conjunction with the top executive(s). This stage would usually include the informal or formal feedback of some of the data gathered to the top executive(s) along with the consultant's interpretation and/or questions. The primary purpose of the *preliminary diagnosis* is to enable the consultant to propose the next steps to be taken in the OD process and to obtain the agreement of the organization's leaders for these further steps.

A growing issue in the field of organization development is the recognition of the need for some procedures to assist in the diagnosis of organizational difficulties. It is increasingly being recognized that there would be great benefit from using a standard diagnostic procedure to assist in the initial identification of organizational difficulties. One such approach that has proven quite versatile and helpful is the differentiation and integration model of Lawrence and Lorsch.[7] Another diagnostic model, previously used to illustrate inputs into the work group that influence group behavior, is illustrated in Exhibit 3–4.

4. *Data feedback and discussion.* The data-feedback stage may overlap with the previously discussed stage of preliminary diagnosis. However, it is helpful to separate data feedback for purposes of description. In the data-feedback stage, the data obtained from the members of the organization through the combination of interviews and survey research are reported

Human Resources Index

The objective of this survey is to determine how members of this organization feel about the effectiveness with which the organization's human resources are managed. The survey provides you an opportunity to express your opinions in a way that is constructive. Your views will be valuable in assisting the organization to evaluate and improve its performance.

The survey is to be done anonymously. Please **do not put your name** on the response sheet or identify your response in any way. Responses can in no way be traced to any individual. The frank and free expression of your own opinions will be most helpful to the organization.

Listed below are a series of statements. After you have read each statement, please decide the extent to which the statement describes your own situation and your own feelings, using the following scale:

A) almost never
B) not often
C) sometimes (i.e., about half the time)
D) often
E) almost always

Then, using a No. 2 pencil darken the appropriate box on the response sheet. For example, if you believe that the statement is true "sometimes" darken block C on the answer sheet next to the number corresponding to the indicated statement.

Questions 65 and 66 should be answered in **pencil** on the back of the **response sheet.**

When you have completed the survey, please return the response sheet and this survey form in accordance with the directions in the cover letter.

IN THIS ORGANIZATION:

1. There is sufficient communication and sharing of information between groups.

2. The skills and abilities of employees are fully and effectively utilized.

3. Objectives of the total organization and my work unit are valid and challenging.

4. The activities of my job are satisfying and rewarding.

5. I have received the amount and kind of training which I need and desire to do my job well.

6. Leadership in this organization is achieved through ability.

7. Rewards are fairly and equitably distributed.

----

*Copyright ©, 1977, Fred E. Schuster, Professor of Management, Florida Atlantic University, Boca Raton, Florida.

EXHIBIT 9-6
A typical survey questionnaire instrument. Copyright ©, 1977, Fred E. Schuster, Professor of Management, Florida Atlantic University, Boca Raton, Florida.

back to groups of executives for their information, discussion, and reaction. Frequently, this data report is in a fairly formal form in which the consultant attempts to summarize the most significant aspects of the data obtained. The consultant may or may not provide interpretation of these data and may or may not raise specific questions for the executives. In any case, at this stage the organization's executives discuss the data leading to the identification of the concerns and issues to be dealt with. The executives are also asked to confront the needs for organization development. They consider various alternative strategies that might be utilized. The primary purposes of the data-feedback stage are to ready the organization for further development activities and to plan the specific intervention techniques that will be utilized in the continuing OD effort. Exhibits 9–7 and 9–8 illustrate two typical samples of feedback data used by executives at this stage of the process. You may refer to Exhibit 9–6 to see part of a questionnaire survey used to obtain the results shown in Exhibits 9–7 and 9–8.

5. *Action intervention.* The action intervention stage is the last phase in an effective OD program that may take several forms, ranging from behavioral to nonbehavioral interventions, or a mixture of the two. The next section deals with this last phase, which attempts to integrate information obtained to create positive change.

Intervention Techniques

Most action interventions in OD have traditionally been *behavioral interventions*, that is, designed to affect the behavior of individuals and groups. It is, however, perfectly consistent with the theory of organization development to consider *nonbehavioral interventions*, which are much more structured and include changes in the organization structure, work design, technology, or compensation system. These are also a legitimate part of intervention strategy in an overall OD effort. A number of other intervention techniques, including climate surveys for data feedback and discussion, job enrichment, quality circles, and productivity committees, are discussed elsewhere in this book. Let us now examine some of the most commonly used intervention techniques.

1. Laboratory training. The most commonly utilized OD intervention technique is *laboratory training*. Laboratory training is so named because it is conducted by creating an experimental "laboratory" situation in which people are brought together in groups to interact in an unstructured environment. The group is then challenged with a "dilemma" for which normal behavior patterns appear to be inadequate, and it is encouraged to experiment with new individual behaviors and new group interactions in order to resolve the dilemma. Thus, the objective is to create an experimental laboratory atmosphere in which both individual and group behavioral learning and development may occur. Laboratory training originated in the late 1940s and has taken on a variety of specific formats. A principal offshoot of laboratory training is T-group training or sensitivity training, a specific set of laboratory training techniques originated by the National Training Laboratory.

The duration of laboratory training may vary from a few hours ("microlabs") to two weeks or more. The most common length of laboratory

```
FACTOR 1.  REWARD SYSTEM
           INCLUDES STATEMENTS: 7 22 26 33
                                        N =  696       % OF N      % OF TOTAL

     1. ALMOST NEVER                            84        .12         .12
     2. NOT OFTEN                              155        .22         .22
     3. SOMETIMES (I.E. ABOUT HALF THE TIME)   248        .36         .35
     4. OFTEN                                  137        .20         .19
     5. ALMOST ALWAYS                           72        .10         .10
        BLANK                                    8                    .01

     MEAN = 2.94   10TH PERCENTILE = 1.83   MEDIAN = 2.44   90TH PERCENTILE = 4.03


FACTOR 2.  COMMUNICATION
           INCLUDES STATEMENTS: 1 9 13 18 24 27 30 34 41 60 64
                                        N = 1908       % OF N      % OF TOTAL

     1. ALMOST NEVER                           101        .05         .05
     2. NOT OFTEN                              260        .14         .13
     3. SOMETIMES (I.E. ABOUT HALF THE TIME)   604        .32         .31
     4. OFTEN                                  522        .27         .27
     5. ALMOST ALWAYS                          421        .22         .22
        BLANK                                   28                    .01

     MEAN = 3.47   10TH PERCENTILE = 1.35   MEDIAN = 2.98   90TH PERCENTILE = 4.55


FACTOR 3.  ORGANIZATIONAL EFFECTIVENESS
           INCLUDES STATEMENTS: 2 6 8 36 39 47 57 61 62 64
                                        N = 1740       % OF N      % OF TOTAL

     1. ALMOST NEVER                            38        .02         .02
     2. NOT OFTEN                              142        .08         .08
     3. SOMETIMES (I.E. ABOUT HALF THE TIME)   559        .32         .32
     4. OFTEN                                  572        .33         .32
     5. ALMOST ALWAYS                          429        .25         .24
        BLANK                                   20                    .01

     MEAN = 3.70   10TH PERCENTILE = 1.96   MEDIAN = 3.23   90TH PERCENTILE = 4.59
```

EXHIBIT 9–7
Sample feedback data in computer-printout form.

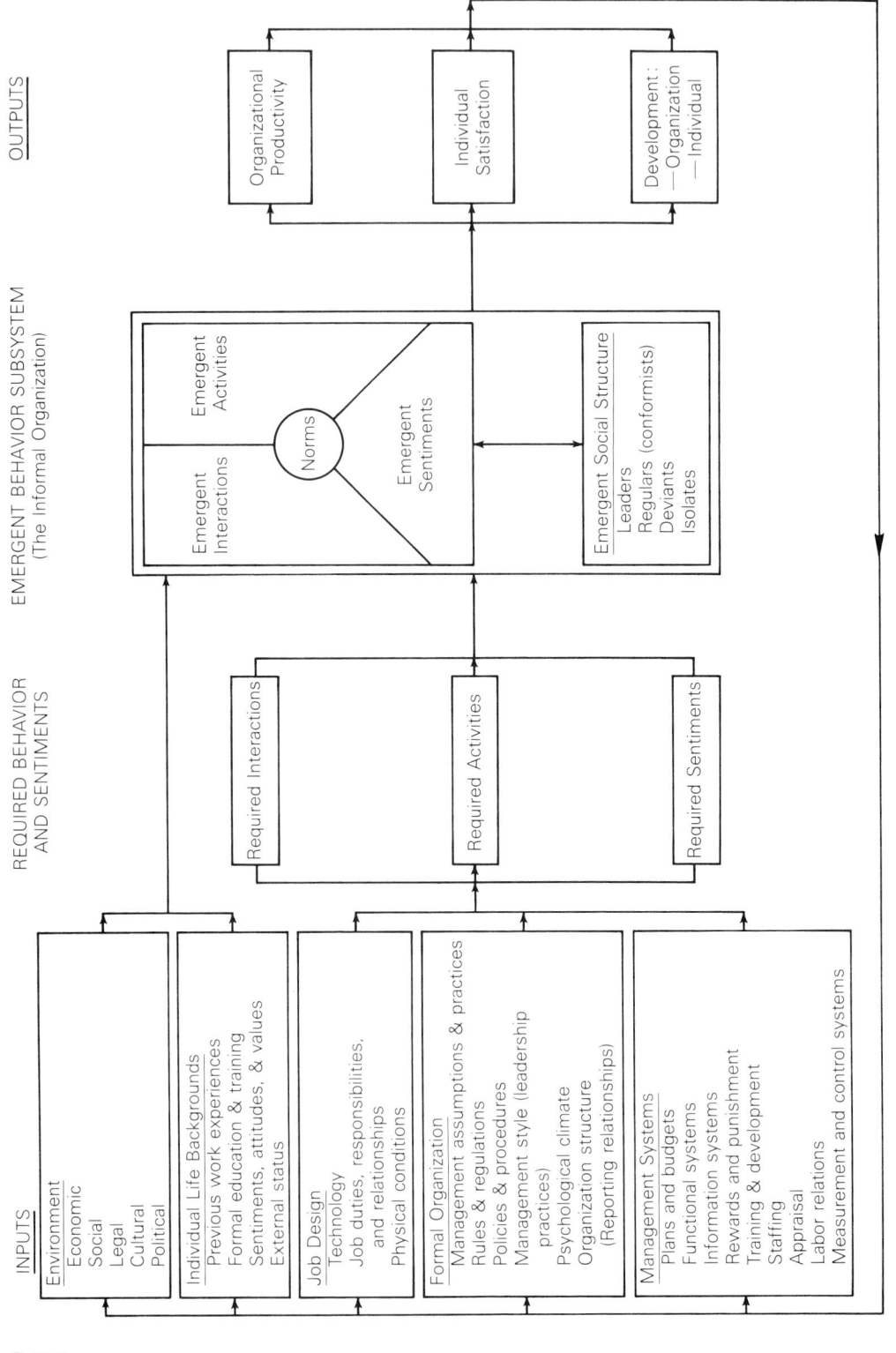

EXHIBIT 9–8
Sample feedback data in graph form pertaining to Exhibit 9–7.

programs is probably three to five days of intensive work. The content of the sessions may also vary widely. Commonly the leader or trainer announces at the beginning of the sessions that he or she will take a relatively passive role in the training process—that is, the leader will attempt to assist the group in learning, but the group will have control of the agenda and the leader will not direct the group's processes.

Usually the trainer's introductory remarks will focus the attention of each member of the group on perceiving his or her own behavior and the behavior of others. The trainer will attempt to create a nonpunishing environment in which each person's feelings and reactions to others can be openly expressed to the group as data for consideration. Although the trainer invariably indicates that there is no specific agenda, the group members are encouraged to learn about their own behavior from their experiences in the group. After these introductory remarks the trainer usually remains silent.

The silence and apparent lack of direction are perceived as an uncomfortable situation by most group members. This leads to the development of further group behavior which, with the assistance of the trainer, becomes the focus for discussion and learning. The role played by the trainer may vary widely, depending on the trainer, the type of laboratory, the type of group or organization in which the laboratory exists, and the behavior of the participants. Usually, however, the trainer will encourage participants to think about, and then to verbalize, their feelings about the activities of the group.

The major distinction between laboratory training and T-group training is that T-groups focus almost exclusively on the kinds of behavioral interactions just discussed. Laboratory training usually places a heavy emphasis on such activity, but in addition it may include role playing, management games, discussions of theory, and even lectures.

One of the problems of laboratory training is the question of the most effective basis for organizing groups. For example, if "stranger labs" are used, there is the difficulty of translating the learning to interactions with another group of people who have not gone through the same experience. It is clear that much laboratory training has been ineffective for this reason. Thus, the logic goes, it is much better to train a cross-section of the organization, and, best of all, to train an actual work group so that the skills learned in the training can be applied more readily on the job.

Although "family groups" seem to provide the greatest potential for the learning and application of new behaviors, such groups—for essentially the same reason—also pose the greatest danger to the individuals involved. It is one thing to expose our innermost feelings to those with whom we do not work (and whom we will never see again) and quite another thing to expose those feelings to members of the work group with which we associate every day. Without doubt, people have been harmed, both psychologically and in terms of their careers, by participation in "family groups." And

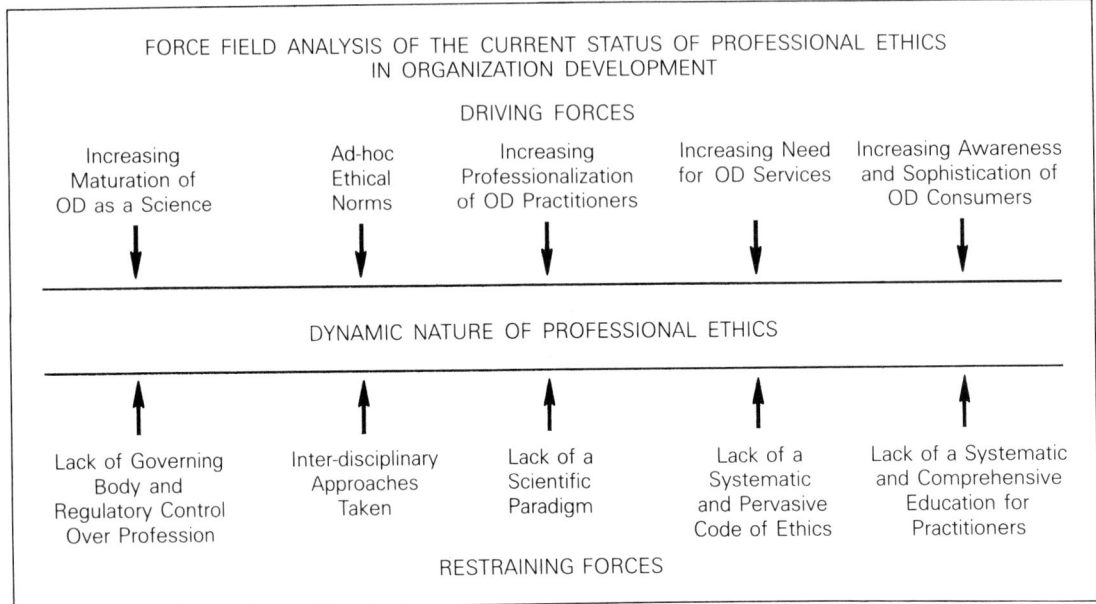

Source: Kevin C. Wooten and Louis P. White, "Ethical Problems in the Practice of O.D.," *Training and Development Journal*, April 1983, p. 18.

yet, equally without doubt, in such groups lies the greatest potential of laboratory training.

Unfortunately for the practice of laboratory training, there are no clear-cut research findings regarding the effectiveness of such training. Although considerable research has been conducted, its interpretation is still controversial. Proponents of laboratory training point to some demonstrable successes and conclude that it is the most valuable organization development technique yet devised. Opponents point to some undeniable failures and to some serious health problems, including mental breakdowns, attributable to laboratory training.

Two very careful research studies to evaluate such training have been performed by John P. Campbell and Marvin D. Dunnette and by Robert J. House.[8] Significantly, both studies regard the evidence as inconclusive. Campbell and Dunnette state that laboratory training can produce changes in behavior, but they point out emphatically that it has not yet been demonstrated that a tie exists between such changes and job performance. As managers, we might, therefore, hesitate to invest our company's money in laboratory training programs. A more recent study by Nichols[9] (1982) has demonstrated a significant correlation between OD intervention and hard criteria of performance such as productivity and profitability.

2. Team building. The idea of team building arose from the belief that the most effective laboratory training would take place among people who actually worked together as a team. *Team building* is nothing more than the application of the general technique of laboratory training to actual working groups, usually comprising a group of peers and a superior.

The techniques used in team building may run the full gamut of those already discussed in connection with laboratory training—all the way from T-group or sensitivity training through managerial games, exercises, and role playing. One team-building technique increasingly being utilized is data feedback and discussion using attitude survey data (such as the Human Resources Index shown in Exhibit 9–6) as the basis for team-building exercises. Regardless of the techniques employed, team building dwells on improving the ability of the members of the team to work effectively with one another to accomplish the common purpose of the team on the job.

Although the most common application of team building is to a natural work group consisting of a manager and immediate subordinates, team-building techniques are also being applied to short-term task teams. This is a very useful application of behavioral science technique, since one of the common problems of a short-term task team is the necessity of developing rather quickly effective norms to guide the group.

Efforts to improve intergroup relations and effectiveness are a further outgrowth of team building. Such efforts bring together the members of two or more different teams in laboratory training directed toward improving the ability of the teams to work together.

3. The Managerial Grid. A specific methodology for team building that has received widespread attention and application in American industry is the *managerial grid* of Blake and Mouton.[10] Sometimes referred to as "instrumented laboratory training," managerial grid training is a structured version of laboratory training. It consists of a series of carefully planned individual and group exercises designed to develop awareness of individual managerial style, interpersonal competence, and group effectiveness; grid training is thus directly related to the issue of leadership discussed in Chapter 8, Motivation and Leadership for Productivity. The "grid" refers to the chart used to record the individual's relative positioning on the issues of "concern for people" and "concern for production" (see Exhibit 9–9).

The managerial grid is in part an attempt to achieve the benefits of sensitivity training or T-group training at reduced risks in terms of individual and/or organizational dysfunction. Thus, instead of focusing on individual perceptions of the behavior of others and giving critical feedback on that behavior, the managerial grid focuses on the observation of behavior in exercises specifically related to work. The feedback given does not refer to the individual's personality but to his or her performance in group exercises. Blake and Mouton feel (and most practitioners agree) that this is a much safer type of laboratory for a family group or a work team.

Using interpersonal and intergroup exercises as the basis of behavioral observation, participants in grid training are encouraged and helped to evaluate their own managerial style. The individual's style of managerial behavior is graphed on a chart according to the two dimensions of concern for people and concern for production. This style can then be discussed in the group and related to the style of other group members as well as to the style of the group as a whole.

There is certainly no denying the fact that many of America's leading corporations made a major investment in managerial grid training during the 1960s and 1970s. At present in the 1980s, the managerial grid remains one of the most widely utilized laboratory training techniques.

4. Management by objectives (MBO). Another change strategy or technique that may be used quite effectively with an overall OD effort is *management*

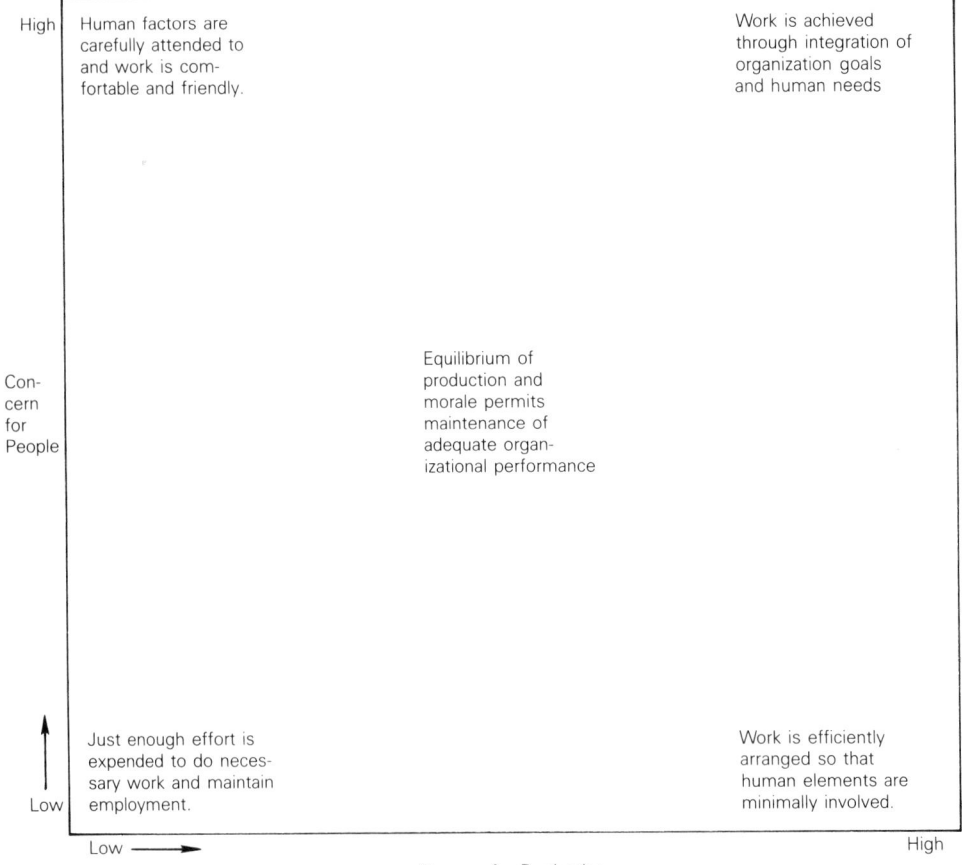

EXHIBIT 9-9
Simplified Managerial Grid.
Source: Based on R. R. Blake, Jane S. Mouton, L. B. Barnes, and L. E. Greiner, "Breakthrough in Organizational Development," *Harvard Business Review,* November–December 1964, pp. 37–59.

by objectives (MBO). As was pointed out earlier, many OD practitioners are concerned about a loose use of terminology in which any MBO program may be referred to as "organization development." Nevertheless, there seems to be agreement that management by objectives may legitimately be considered a specific change strategy to be introduced in the action intervention stage of an OD effort.

There is a growing belief among OD practitioners that MBO can be particularly effective. It ties together the underlying Theory-Y philosophy of OD, the behavioral learning of the laboratory training that should precede the implementation of MBO, and a very practical management planning and control technique. This managerial planning and control technique appears work related and realistic to even the most traditional manager.

To illustrate the relationship that he sees between MBO and OD, Thomas H. Patten uses the diagram in Exhibit 9–10, an adaptation of the "organizational iceberg" concept of Stanley Herman.[11] Note that in this figure Patten points out the distinction between the older, limited concept of

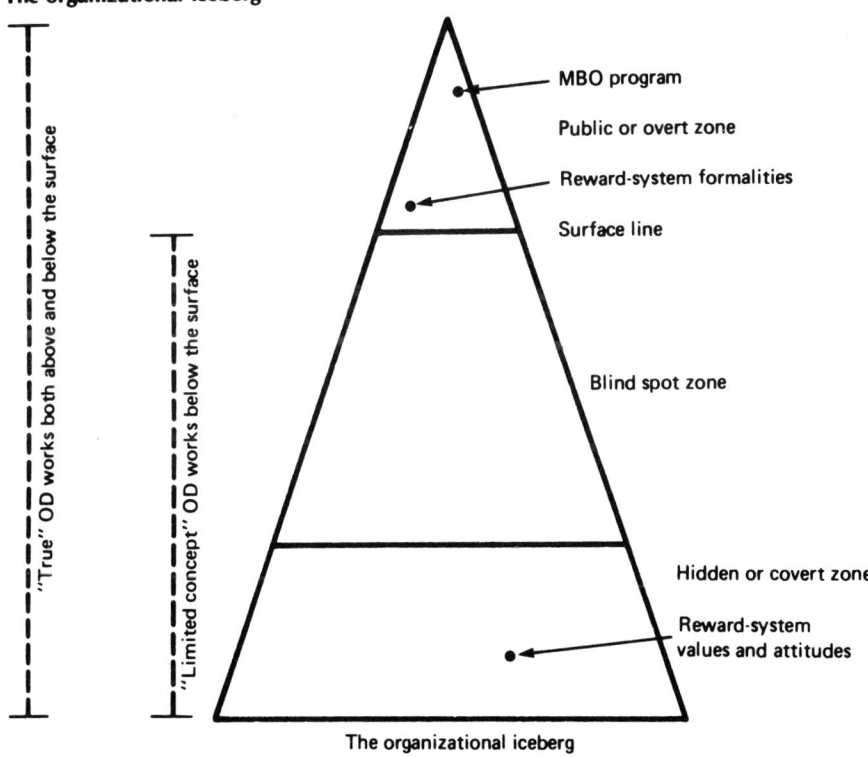

EXHIBIT 9–10
The organizational iceberg.

Source: Thomas H. Patten, Jr., "O.D.—MBO and the Reward System." Reproduced by special permission from *O.D.—Emerging Dimensions and Concepts.* Copyright 1973 by the American Society for Training and Development, Inc.

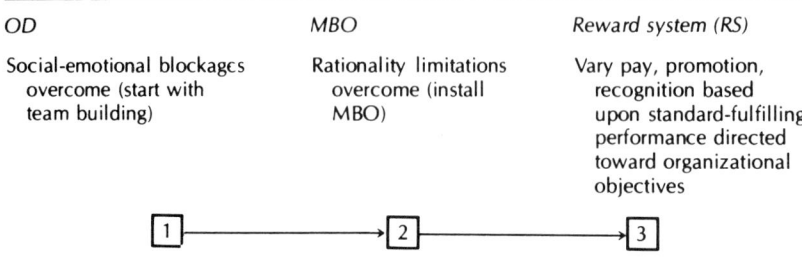

EXHIBIT 9-11
Optimal sequence of organizational development.
Source: Thomas H. Patten, Jr., "O.D.—M.B.O. and the Reward System." Reproduced by special permission from *O.D.—Emerging Dimensions and Concepts.* Copyright 1973 by the American Society for Training and Development, Inc.

OD, which sees OD as working only at unconscious levels of behavior, and the newer, more inclusive view of OD. This newer view sees organization development as an overall effort to improve organizational performance by involving not only changing perceptions, values, attitudes, and behaviors but also, optionally, changes in the structure or practices of the formal organization, including such things as MBO and the reward system.

Patten develops the theme that not only are OD, MBO, and the reward system significantly related, but that there is also an optimal sequence in which attention should be given to these specific managerial activities as part of an overall OD effort. The optimal sequence suggested by Patten is OD–MBO–reward system, as illustrated in Exhibit 9–11.

THE IMPACT OF OD

Scientific evidence regarding the effectiveness of OD technology is very hard to obtain. In view of the attention focused on OD and its widely heralded potential, it is surprising that so little rigorous research has been done. One paper presented at the 1976 meeting of the Academy of Management observed, "Although organization development (OD) as a change strategy has been widely used, the number of reported attempts to conduct systematic research on the impact or effectiveness of OD has been appallingly slim. Despite repeated calls for systematic research (Bennis, 1969; Raia, 1972; Huse, 1975; Kimberly and Nielsen, 1975), personal testimonies and anecdotal data have continued to dominate the field."[12]

After surveying 37 recently reported studies of OD methods and techniques in order to "bring together previously scattered information and provide future researchers with direction relative to researchable gaps in the field," Tate, Nielsen, and Bacon conclude that "more systematic, longitudinal research on OD is needed."[13]

The plain fact is that very few attempts to objectively evaluate OD technology have yet been made, and even the most rigorous of these studies do not involve satisfactory experimental control. This lack of research is probably due in part to what Newton Margulies calls the "myth of nonresearchable variables"—namely, the belief that OD programs are impossible to measure scientifically and that research would interfere with the OD process.[14] The lack of research is also due in part to the relatively long time dimension of OD work—at least five years from initial intervention until measurable results can be expected. This time dimension hinders researchers' ability to isolate the effects of experimental variables from those of uncontrolled variables that intervene in any real situation. The lack of research may also result from practitioners' reluctance to step back from intervention activity long enough to observe it objectively, and perhaps even from their unconscious fear that OD might not be able to withstand rigorous scientific evaluation.

Nevertheless, the literature is full of comments, generally positive, by executives and consultants regarding their subjective evaluation of specific OD efforts in a particular organization. Moreover, there are at least a few studies that represent attempts at objective evaluation.

One such study is Blake, Mouton, Barnes, and Greiner's grid OD effort in a major corporation, called Sigma in the study.[15] The researchers concluded that OD appeared to have had a powerful positive impact on the organization. It also quoted several executives who perceived a strong tie between the OD effort and improved organizational performance.

A second widely quoted study by Paul, Robertson, and Herzberg of a series of job enrichment interventions did utilize control groups and also reported positive results.[16] The authors state:

> During the trial period the experimental group increased its sales by almost 19 percent over the same period of the previous year, a gain of over $300,000 in sales value. The control group's sales in the meantime declined by 5 percent. The equivalent change for both groups the previous year had been a decline of 3 percent. The difference in performance between the two groups is statistically significant at the 0.01 level of confidence.[17]

Although control groups were utilized, these studies should be interpreted as indicative of OD effectiveness rather than as conclusive evidence of its effectiveness. This is because it is unclear whether the activity measured constituted a full-blown OD effort as OD has been defined here and elsewhere, or whether the activity measured merely constituted a specific organizational intervention.

On the other side of the debate, Frank and Hackman have recently reported a carefully controlled and measured OD program that admittedly failed to achieve its objectives.[18] It seems safest to conclude at this point that the evidence regarding the effectiveness of OD is still inconclusive and that much research work remains to be done.

In a study of the Fortune 500 largest industrial organizations, Schuster found in 1982 that 36.8 percent of the Fortune 500 companies utilize OD processes. Of these companies, 91 percent feel that the OD work is either moderately successful or highly successful in achieving its objectives. This is obviously a subjective evaluation, but it is interesting that such a high percentage of these companies express satisfaction with the results of OD. Furthermore, 35 percent of these firms claim that their positive evaluation of OD is based on a "systematic attempt to directly measure the success of the OD process." Of the companies attempting to measure the impact of OD on objective criteria, 33 percent report measurable improvements in productivity, 63 percent report improvement in teamwork and cooperation, and 41 percent report a reduction in conflict and destructive competition.

SUMMARY

Organization development embodies the systems view of the organization's human resources because the major thrust of OD is the improved functioning of the total system. The two underlying themes of this chapter have been:

1. The systems focus on developing the functioning of a total organization (system) as opposed to developing individuals
2. The commitment to a value system that emphasizes openness, trust, mutual confidence, confrontation, participation, and the motivation of the individual through involvement in the decision-making process

Although the roots of OD go back to the Hawthorne experiments of the 1920s and to the T-groups of the 1940s and 1950s, most of the processes and techniques now called organization development have evolved over the last 15 years. Organization development has been defined as "an effort that is planned, organization-wide, and managed from the top to increase organizational effectiveness and health through planned interventions into the organization's processes, using behavioral science knowledge."[19] Although behavioral intervention techniques have been emphasized in this chapter, the authors believe that it is highly useful to keep in mind that both behavioral and nonbehavioral interventions may legitimately play a part in a concerted OD effort.

Although the specific objectives of organizations may vary, the overall objectives of most OD efforts are improvements in the organization's performance, adaptation to its environment, and internal behavior patterns.

Several models describing the OD process were discussed, and the action research model was highlighted as the basic intervention model that runs through all organization development. Action research consists of five steps: (1) intervention, (2) data gathering from the organization, (3) preliminary diagnosis, (4) data feedback and discussion, and (5) implementation of action strategies. The decisions to be made and the actions typically taken by the change agent at each of these stages in the OD process were also discussed.

Among the action interventions discussed were several behavioral and nonbehavioral interventions: (1) laboratory training, (2) sensitivity training or T-groups, (3) team building, (4) the Managerial Grid, and (5) management by objectives.

KEY CONCEPTS

Organization Development (OD)
Change agent
Action research model
Behavioral interventions
Nonbehavioral interventions

Laboratory training
Team building
Managerial grid
MBO

REVIEW AND DISCUSSION QUESTIONS

1. Discuss the relationship between Theory Y and organization development.
2. Describe the role and function of organization development as a part of the overall human resource management process.
3. Trace the historical development of OD and show its relationship to behavioral science research.
4. Outline a complete OD process for a well-established consumer goods manufacturing company of 5,000 employees that has recently developed serious problems of deteriorating profits, shrinking markets, rising costs, and internal communication difficulties.
5. Differentiate between: (a) Behavioral and nonbehavioral interventions; (b) Team building and intergroup training; (c) Laboratory training and managerial grid training; and (d) Individual training and organization development.
6. Describe each of the basic steps in the action research model.
7. Visit the personnel director of a major firm in your area. Discuss with him or her that firm's approach to organization development and report your findings back to the class.
8. Describe and contrast two models of organization change.
9. What training, experience, and other preparation would you recommend for the director of organization development in a major diversified corporation?

NOTES

1. Douglas McGregor, *The Human Side of Enterprise* (New York: McGraw-Hill, 1960), p. 196.
2. Richard Beckhard, *Organizational Development—Strategies and Models* (Reading, Mass.: Addison-Wesley, 1969).
3. F. Roethlisberger and W. J. Dickson, *Management and the Worker* (Cambridge, Mass.: Harvard University Press, 1939).
4. Kurt Lewin, *Field Theory in Social Science* (New York: Harper & Row, 1951).
5. Larry E. Greiner, "Patterns of Organization Change," in Gene W. Dalton, Paul R. Lawrence, and Larry E. Greiner (Eds.), *Organizational Change and Development* (Homewood, Ill.: Richard D. Irwin, 1970), p. 222.
6. Harold J. Leavitt, *New Perspectives in Organization Research* (New York: Wiley, 1964).
7. Paul Lawrence and Jay W. Lorsch, *Organization and Environment: Managing Differentiation and Integration* (Boston: Division of Research, Harvard Business School, 1967).
8. John P. Campbell and Marvin D. Dunnette, "Effectiveness of T-Group Experiences in Managerial Training and Development," *Psychological Bulletin*, August 1968; and Robert J. House, "T-Group Education and Leadership Effectiveness: A Review of the Empiric Literature and a Critical Evaluation," *Personnel Psychology*, Spring 1967.
9. John M. Nichols, "The Comparative Impact of Organizational Development Interventions on Hard Critieria Measures," *Academy of Management Review* 4 (53), 1982, p. 42.
10. Robert R. Blake and Jane S. Mouton, *The Managerial Grid* (Houston: Gulf, 1964).
11. Thomas H. Patten, Jr., "OD–MBO and the Reward System," in *OD—Emerging Dimensions and Concepts* (American Society for Training and Development, 1973); and Stanley Herman, "The Shadow of Organization Development," paper presented at the Conference on New Technology in Organization Development, New Orleans, February 1974.
12. Larry E. Tate, Warren R. Nielsen, and Paula C. Bacon, "Advances in Research on Organization Development: Toward a Beginning," *Proceedings of the 36th Annual Meeting of the Academy of Management*, August 11–14, 1976, p. 389.
13. *Ibid.*
14. Newton Margulies and Anthony P. Raia, *Organizational Development: Values, Process, and Technology* (New York: McGraw-Hill, 1972).
15. R. R. Blake, Jane S. Mouton, L. B. Barnes, and L. E. Greiner, "Breakthrough in Organizational Development," *Harvard Business Review*, November–December 1964, pp. 37–59.
16. William J. Paul, Keith Robertson, and Frederick Herzberg, "Job Enrichment Pays Off," *Harvard Business Review*, March–April 1969.
17. *Ibid.*
18. L. L. Frank and J. R. Hackman, "A Failure of Job Enrichment: The Case of the Change That Wasn't," *Journal of Applied Behavioral Science*, October–December 1975.
19. Beckhard, *Organizational Development, ibid.*

BIBLIOGRAPHY

Allen, Robert F., and Frank J. Dyer. "A Tool for Tapping the Organizational Unconscious." *Personnel Journal*, March 1980, 192–198.

Baker, H. Kent. "The Hows and Whys of Team Building." *Personnel Journal*, June 1979, 367–370.

Beer, M., and S. W. Kleisath. "The Effects of Managerial Grid Labs on Organizational and Leadership Dimensions." In E. F. Huse *et al.*, *Readings on Behavior in Organizations*. Reading, Mass.: Addison-Wesley, 1975.

Bell, Cecil H., and Wendell L. French. *OD Behavior Science Interventions for Organization Improvement*. Englewood Cliffs, N.J.: Prentice-Hall, 1978.

Bennis, W. G. "Unresolved Problems Facing Organizational Development." *Business Quarterly*, October–December 1969.

Berger, Lance A. "The Staffing Grid: An Integrated Approach to Organizational Development." *Personnel Journal*, August 1979, 544–546.

Blake, Robert R., and Jane Srygley Mouton. "Why the OD Movement is 'Stuck' and How to Break It Loose." *Training and Development Journal*, September 1979, 12–19.

Blake, Robert R., and Jane Srygley Mouton. "Principles of Behavior for Sound Management." *Training and Development Journal*, October 1979, 26–28.

Blake, Robert R., and Jane Srygley Mouton. "OD Technology for the Future." *Training and Development Journal*, November 1979, 54–64.

Blake, R. R., J. S. Mouton, L. B. Barnes, and L. E. Greiner. "Breakthrough in Organizational Development." *Harvard Business Review*, November 1964.

Bowers, D. G. "OD Techniques and Their Results in 23 Organizations: The Michigan ICL Study." *Journal of Applied Behavioral Science*, January–February 1973.

Buchanan, Paul C. "An OD Strategy at the IRS." *Personnel*, March–April 1979, 42–52.

Connor, P. E. "Values and Assumptions in OD: Some Critical Observations." In *Proceedings of the 35th Annual Meeting of the Academy of Management*, August 1975.

Cuba, Richard, and Gene Milbourn. "OD Techniques and the Bottom Line." *Personnel* 58, May–June 1981, 34–42.

Digman, Lester A. "Let's Keep the OD People Honest." *Personnel*, January–February 1979, 22–29.

Dyer, William G. "Selecting an Intervention for Organization Change." *Training and Development Journal* 35, April 1981, 62–68.

Ends, Earl J., and Curtis W. Page. *Organizational Team Building*. Cambridge, Mass.: Winthrop Publishers, 1977.

Fitz-Enz, Jacques. "Measuring Human Resources Effectiveness." *Personnel Administrator*, July 1980, 33–37.

Frank, L. L., and J. R. Hackman. "A Failure of Job Enrichment: The Case of the Change That Wasn't." *Journal of Applied Behavioral Science*, October–December 1975.

French, Wendell. "Organization Development: Objectives, Assumptions, and Strategies." *California Management Review*, Winter 1969.

Goad, Tom. "Needed: A New OD Model." *Training and Development Journal*, September 1979, 46–48.

Golembiewski, R. T., and R. Munzenrider. "Persistence and Change: A Note on the Long-Term Effects of an Organization Development Program." *Academy of Management Journal*, December 1973.

Greiner, Larry E. "Red Flags in Organization Development." *Business Horizons*, June 1972.

Hackman, J. R., G. R. Oldham, R. Janson, and K. Purdy. "A New Strategy for Job Enrichment." *California Management Review*, Summer 1975.

Hand, H. H., B. D. Estafen, and H. P. Sims, Jr. "How Effective Is Data Survey and Feedback as a Technique of Organization Development? An Experiment." *Journal of Applied Behavioral Science*, July–September 1975.

Harrison, R. and J. Kouzes. "The Power Potential of Organization Development." *Training and Development Journal*, April 1980, 44–47.

Hautaluoma, J. E., and J. F. Gavin. "Effects of Organizational Diagnosis and Intervention on Blue-Collar 'Blues.'" *Journal of Applied Behavioral Science*, October–December 1975.

Hersey, P., and J. Keilty. "One-on-One OD Communications Skills." *Training and Development Journal*, April 1980, 56–60.

Herzog, Eric L. "Improving Productivity Via Organization Development." *Training and Development Journal*, April 1980, 36–39.

Holmes, Robert A. "What's Ahead for Personnel Professionals In The 80's." *Personnel Administrator* 25, June 1980, 33–37.

Huse, E. F. *et al. Readings on Behavior in Organizations.* Reading, Mass.: Addison-Wesley, 1975.

Jamieson, David W. "Training and OD: Crossing Disciplines." *Training and Development Journal*, April 1981.

Jones, Rob. "A Caution Signal for H.R.D." *Training and Development Journal*, April 1981.

Kegan, D. L., and A. H. Rubenstein. "Trust, Effectiveness, and Organizational Development: A Field Study in R & D." *Journal of Applied Behavioral Science*, July–August 1973.

Kimberly, J. R., and W. R. Nielsen. "Organization Development and Change in Organizational Performance." *Administrative Science Quarterly*, June 1975.

Kleiner, Brian H. "A Manager's Guide to Organizational Change." *Personnel*, March–April 1979, 31–38.

Kur, Edward C. "OD: Perspectives, Processes, and Prospects." *Training and Development Journal* 35, April 1981, 28–34.

Luke, R. A., P. Block, J. M. Davey, and V. R. Averch. "A Structural Approach to Organizational Change." *Journal of Applied Behavioral Science*, September–October 1973.

Margulies, Newton, and Anthony P. Raia. *Organizational Development: Values, Process, and Technology.* New York: McGraw-Hill, 1972.

Margulies, Newton, and John Wallace. *Organizational Change: Techniques and Applications.* Glenview, Ill.: Scott, Foresman, 1973.

Martin, Wallace. "What Management Can Expect From an Employee Attitude Survey." *Personnel Administrator* 26, July 1981, 75–79.

McGregor, Douglas. *The Human Side of Enterprise.* New York: McGraw-Hill, 1960.

McNamar, Richard T. "Building a Better Executive Team." *California Management Review*, Winter 1973.

Muczyk, J. P. "A Controlled Field Experiment Measuring the Impact of MBO on Performance Data." In *Proceedings of the 35th Annual Meeting of the Academy of Management*, August 1975.

Myers, M. Scott, and Susan S. Myers. "Toward Understanding the Changing Work Ethic." *California Management Review*, Spring 1974.

Nadler, D. A., and P. A. Pecorella. "Differential Effects of Multiple Interventions in an Organization." *Journal of Applied Behavioral Science*, July–September 1975.

Nielsen, W. R., and J. R. Kimberly. "Designing Assessment Strategies for Organization Development." *Human Resource Management*, June 1976.

Pate, L. E. "A Reference List for Change Agents." In *The 1976 Annual Handbook for Group Facilitators*, eds. J. W. Pfeiffer and J. E. Jones. La Jolla, Ca.: University Associates, 1976.

Pate, Larry E., Warren R. Neilsen, and Paula C. Bacon. "Advances in Research on Organization Development: Toward a Beginning." *Proceedings of the 35th Annual Meeting of the Academy of Management*, August 1979, 389–394.

Patten, Thomas H. "Team Building Part 1. Designing the Intervention." *Personnel*, January–February 1979, 11–21.

Patten, Thomas H. "Team Building Part 2. Conducting the Intervention." *Personnel*, March–April 1979, 63–68.

Paul, William J., Keith Robertson, and Frederick Herzberg. "Job Enrichment Pays Off." *Harvard Business Review*, March–April 1969.

Raia, A. P. "Organizational Development—Some Issues and Challenges." *California Management Review*, Summer 1972.

Randolph, W. Alan, John Ferrie, and George Brennan. "An Experiential Design for Training in OD." *Training and Development Journal*, November 1979, 76–87.

Scobel, Don. "HRD—Changing Organizational Systems in the 80's." *Training and Development Journal*, January 1980, 40–41.

Soat, Douglas M. "An OD Strategy at Parker Pen." *Personnel*, March–April 1979, 39–43.

Solomon, Robert J. "An Examination of the Relationship Between a Survey Feedback OD Technique and the Work Environment." *Personnel Psychology* 29, 1976, 583–594.

Varney, Glenn H. "Developing OD Competencies." *Training and Development Journal*, April 1980, 30–35.

Warrick, D. D., and T. Donovan. "Surveying OD Skills." *Training and Development Journal*, September 1979, 22–25.

Warrick, D. D., and John Thompson. "Still Crazy After All These Years." *Training and Development Journal*, April 1980, 16–22.

Wilson, Clark L. "Assessing Management and OD Needs," *Training and Development Journal*, April 1980, 71–76.

Woodworth, W., and R. Nelson. "Witch Doctors, Messianics, Sorcerers and OD Consultants: Parallels and Paradigms." *Organizational Dynamics*, August 1979, 16–33.

Developing Communications

CHAPTER OUTLINE

Roles of Communication in the HR System

Responsibilities of the HR Manager for Development of Communications

Line Managers and the Human Resource Department

Development of Formal Communication Systems

Development of Informal Communication Systems

Nature of Interpersonal Communication

Models of Communication

Objectives of Manager–Subordinate Communication

Guides for Improving Communication with Employees

Develop a Company-Wide Communications Program □ Build Trust □ Get the Facts in Advance □ Plan the Discussion □ Set a Mutually Agreeable Time □ Set an Appropriate Meeting Place □ Advise the Employee in Advance □ Anticipate Barriers □ Tell What and Why □ Summarize □ Terminate the Discussion Constructively □ Followup □ Listen and Understand

OBJECTIVES

1. Describe the role of communicating in the human resource system.
2. Distinguish between broadcast and interpersonal communication.
3. Discuss the major forms of formal organizational communication.
4. List objectives of manager–subordinate communication.
5. Present guidelines for improving interpersonal communication.

SPOTLIGHT:
William V. Machaver

William V. Machaver is Vice President, Industrial Relations and Personnel, at Sun Chemical Corporation, a company that has a comprehensive and innovative approach to communication as a key element of its HR management strategy. At Sun Chemical Mr. Machaver was a pioneer in developing a very innovative device for upward communication called the Labor Relations Audit. In the audit, a team of five executives conducts face-to-face, individual interviews with each employee in the company once a year in order to measure the management climate and to determine if there are any organizational problems or complaints requiring management's attention. To provide reassurance to employees that their individual comments will be kept confidential, the executives auditing a particular facility are cross-assigned from other divisions and locations. The results are reported in summary form only to the executive in charge of the facility. The data stop at this level and are not reported to higher management unless the audit team feels that insufficient action is being taken by the executive receiving the audit data.

Mr. Machaver's philosophy of communication is reflected in the following comments.

Comments by William Machaver

Modern management recognizes that a key ingredient in ensuring a high level of productivity and the profitable growth of the enterprise is understanding, developing, and coordinating large groups of people engaged in many varied activities. Effective communication plays the most vital role in the operation of an efficient organization. Communication is synonymous with human relations since most personal relationships are carried on through some form of communication.

The growth and complexity of modern industry have placed pressure upon management at all levels to develop effective means of transmitting to lower echelons information that is vital to the continuing, efficient operation of the business. The passing on of orders, policies, and plans necessary to modern industrial life is the backbone of efficient management.

There are additional gains from encouraging employees to talk freely and honestly. By revealing the degree to which ideas and directives are accepted and by stimulating individuals to participate in the operation of their departments, communication encourages them to defend the decisions and policies that they have cooperatively developed with management.

Effective communication also results in valuable ideas contributed by employees and helps to avert the potentially explosive situations that may arise daily in industry. Communication is dynamic. It must flow up as well as down if it is to stimulate mutual understanding at all levels of a company.

Sharing information with subordinates tends to diminish fears and suspicions and to afford the security and feeling of belonging so necessary for efficiency. Effective communication improves morale and helps people to understand and accept the frequent changes that are part of a modern dynamic business.

Of 27 human resource activities studied in a recent ASPA/Towers, Perrin, Forster & Crosby survey of senior management views of the human resources function, "employee communication" finished a close second to "productivity improvement" as the most important HR management function. One chief executive in a followup interview said, "I agree this [employee communication] is a top priority item and would rate it higher than productivity improvement. Improving communications increases productivity."

One of the responses to the written questionnaire said "communication was the single largest key to productivity improvement." Other reasons senior managers gave for the high ranking of "employee communication" included:

1. Vital to helping employees attain a feeling of belonging
2. Increase dedication, motivation, and feeling of belonging
3. There's not enough feedback
4. To maintain good employee relations and preserve nonunion status
5. For morale, team building, and success in reaching objectives
6. To foster involvement of personnel at all levels
7. To improve performance through understanding departmental and company objectives
8. To achieve quality and organizational results
9. To assure that we are listening to employees and reacting on a timely and responsive basis

A key part of the survey involved senior management's view of the HR function in the future. One senior manager predicted "employee communication," along with "job evaluation and internal equity" and "determining competitive benefits levels" to be the three major areas of change in the human resources function during the last five years. When asked to name the internal issue that would have the greatest impact on human resources activities over the next five years, another replied, "The adequacy and totality (up and down) of communication to ensure that everyone will know what we want to do as a company and what each must provide to ensure that we get there."[1]

The communication subsystem is perhaps the most underrated subsystem of HR management. Many P/HR textbooks give little or no attention to communication—and yet, it may well be the single most critical element of HR systems in the 80s. This is true, first of all, because effective downward and upward communication is fundamental to making all of the other subsystems of HR management operational. Secondly, in many organizations improved communication represents the single most cost-effective means of improving productivity and performance.

While the cost of a sophisticated, complete communication program can be relatively modest, the value of the results can potentially be substantial. This is a reality long ago discovered by the Japanese, but only recently has it become widely recognized in American industry. Attention to communication is the single most distinctive characteristic of the Japanese management style. In fact, emphasis on communication is the thread of consistency that ties together the seemingly disparate Japanese practices of decision making through consensus, de-emphasis of status differences or status symbols, quality circles, open office landscaping, and extensive off-the-job socialization of all levels of employees. The Japanese simply practice the belief that effective organized activity stems from full sharing of all information about the organization (both upward and downward) through constantly open channels of communication.

Although such attention to communication is admittedly time-consuming, the Japanese believe this is a necessary investment in order to produce commitment, motivation, and maximum contribution from each individual. Some major American corporations, among them Motorola and General Motors, have recently begun to adopt this point of view as a part of their extensive efforts to become more competitive with their Japanese counterparts.

ROLES OF COMMUNICATION IN THE HR SYSTEM

Communication in organizations has four basic purposes: (1) coordination, (2) problem solving and innovating, (3) leading, and (4) appraising and regulating.

1. Coordination When two or more people are working together to achieve common objectives, their efforts must be related in action and timing. Interpersonal communication is required. For larger numbers of people, managers are required as "communication centers" for coordination. They must keep the workers informed about objectives, progress, and problems.

2. Problem solving and innovating Many problems are solved day in and day out by individuals who apply specialized skills to their jobs. On the other hand, such problems as long-range planning, organization development, engineering projects, or even the "fires" and crises that break out in business are solved by group efforts. In such situations, innovative solutions are stimulated by communication among members of work groups. This communication will range from the complex and formal (systems, procedures, forms) to the informal and interpersonal.

3. Leading To inform and influence subordinates, peers, and superiors, managers must have good communication skills. They must be able to present situations in a light which motivates subordinates. Leadership has been discussed in Chapter 8 in relation to motivation, and will be discussed further in subsequent chapters.

4. Appraising and regulating Communication provides the means for carrying out the vital tasks of appraising human performance and regulating the performance of the human resource system. Here the role of communication is to feed back information to managers and workers so that they may take any corrective action required.

RESPONSIBILITIES OF THE HR MANAGER FOR DEVELOPMENT OF COMMUNICATIONS

An objective of the HR manager is to propose communication systems to line management that will increase (1) productivity of workers, (2) quality of working life, and (3) ability of the company as a whole to solve problems and react to environmental changes.

Two types of communication systems must be developed: formal and informal. *Formal communication systems* consist of established procedures, policies, information processing, and scheduled reports. The formal system may be both impersonal (written or videotaped) or interpersonal (face-to-face meetings for regular performance appraisals or committee meetings). The contribution of the HR manager to the formal system consists of advice to line management on design of broadcast systems (company publications) and establishment of policies, and the design of HR information systems (see Chapter 20, Human Resource Management Control, Problem Diagnosis, and Research).

Informal communication systems consist of nonformalized, nonplanned, written or interpersonal communication facilitated by company philosophy and operating policies. The contribution of the HR manager to the development of informal communication is through OD, job design, training and development, and advice to line management on the content of policies to encourage such informal exchange.

Exhibit 10–1 indicates the general dimensions of the communications systems in an organization. Communications may be formally structured or informal and random. In either case, they may be personal or nonpersonal. Further, communications may flow down, up, or laterally within the organization. In the exhibit, examples of communications to which the HR manager contributes are shown. For example, the HR manager may propose appraisal forms, provide training for line managers on the appraisal interview, and prepare policies relative to frequency and use of appraisals. The completed appraisal forms and the appraisal interview will then be the actual communication methods.

EXHIBIT 10-1
Examples of communication methods to which the HR manager contributes.

	Downward	Upward	Lateral
Formal communication system	Performance appraisals Permanent committees Promotion announcements Weekly top management staff meetings Policy statements Broadcast announcements Job openings Safety regulations Union negotiations and contracts	Annual review of HR plans Permanent committees Weekly top management staff meetings MIS reports Attitude surveys Suggestion systems	OD sessions Permanent committees Weekly top management staff meetings Information system reports
Informal communication system	Accidental conversations Work-dictated conversations Ad hoc group meetings Memos Occasional reports Notification of problems	Accidental conversations "Open-door" conversations Ad hoc group meetings "Open door" memo or letter Memos or reports as feedback on problems	Accidental conversations Ad hoc group meetings

LINE MANAGERS AND THE HUMAN RESOURCE DEPARTMENT

Line managers are responsible for communicating with their subordinates on work-related topics. Essentially they are responsible for keeping the human resource system operating to perform the myriad of necessary tasks properly.

The human resource department acts as adviser to line managers and as monitor of the communication system. As a crude analogy, it is like a maintenance crew that guards against breakdowns and works on repairs. It guides line managers on a personal basis and develops training programs to improve communication.

In areas where line managers do not have highly specialized expertise, the communication process is transferred to the human resource department. Examples include psychological counseling, interpreting company-sponsored physical examinations of employees, and handling questions concerning pension benefits.

A fairly recent innovation is the much greater emphasis placed on *upward communication* through the use of attitude surveys, telephone hotlines, speak-up programs, brown-bag meetings, and employee advisory groups.

DEVELOPMENT OF FORMAL COMMUNICATION SYSTEMS

Effective communication, as we have pointed out, is top down, bottom up, and lateral. The following list shows a well-rounded formal communication system, including nine top-down forms, four mixed give-and-take forms, and three bottom-up formats.

1. Orientation Programs New employee orientation should set the stage for a positive long-lasting relationship between the employee and the organization. Most companies fail to understand who the new employees are, where they come from, and what they value. The corporation should focus on the information the new employee will need immediately. On the first day, for example, the "corporate story" should be supplemented with a session devoted to an open discussion of fears, expectations, and general concerns about the new environment. This discussion will lay the foundation for trust. The orientation effort should be an on-going program, which means inviting the groups to participate in other programs. As organizations learn to meet the *needs* of the new hire they will build a stronger, more responsive, and more committed workforce.

2. Employee Handbooks The basic objectives of employee handbooks are (1) to acquaint all personnel with the key information and guidelines for company operations; (2) to communicate company philosophy, goals, policies, and procedures; (3) to promote employer–employee understanding; (4) to build awareness of company operations and responsibilities; (5) to help employees gain a sense of belonging to a company; and (6) to provide a source of ready reference and answers for common employee concerns.

3. Bulletins Special bulletins are used for urgent or emergency announcements. They should be extremely brief and to the point. Special bulletins should originate only from top management and should be used very judiciously. They also should be printed on only a brightly colored paper reserved for this use.

Weekly bulletins, on the other hand, are used to inform employees in a routine manner of upcoming events. Topics are restricted to the company and related activities and must be of a general interest. Weekly bulletins may be originated by individual employees, for example, to publicize travel packages, and upon department request. They are approved by a manager responsible for bulletins and are issued from a central source.

4. Official Reports This medium keeps employees abreast of and/or analyzes important company information in an official format and on a regular schedule. Official reports usually are classified by types, such as special, routine, single, or recurring.

5. Newsletters The primary purposes of newsletters are to introduce new ideas, suggest solutions to problems, and inform employees of company activities.

6. Bulletin Boards and Posters Bulletin boards are designed to keep employees informed of current and future plans, company activities, important safety and sanitation issues and procedures, and to cite company problems and achievements.

Posters can be more effective than bulletin boards when communicating simple, yet crucial messages. As with bulletin boards, sole responsibility for posting and removing posters should be with the personnel manager.

7. Job Posting This procedure simply posts all job vacancies so that employees may apply for promotions. In many organizations both management and staff believe that communication improves due to the public announcement of successful job candidates as well as to posting vacancies. Employees say they now have a greater voice in where their talents can be put to good use. Supervisors have learned to state their needs and standards of performance more clearly. Unsuccessful nominees have identified needed skills and gained a more realistic idea of additional training or experience required for practical career alternatives.

8. Policies and Procedures Manuals Without a sound set of operating guidelines, progress can be stifled by decision conflicts and operational chaos. Well-written policies can provide clear guidelines by giving structure and direction to the organization. The policies manual provides an effective "one shot" means of communicating the company's policies to present and new employees.

An extremely useful management tool, the policy manual answers employees' questions pertaining to benefits and helps to achieve uniformity of action. It guides the manager in matters requiring fairness and objectivity. The primary goal of the policy manual is to communicate. Therefore, the manual must be clearly written and carefully reviewed at least once a year.

9. TV Video is superior to film because of its instant feedback advantage, which allows the company to create, edit, and show a program in a few hours if necessary. British Petroleum uses video for its major stories concerning everything from new plant openings to new products. ICI uses video to explain their year-end financial situation. On this program a panel of employees quizzes the chairman. They also make a video presentation when the company changes its policies. Companies are also finding video a useful tool in motivating work forces. Hambro Life uses video to remind the sales force of the targets and policies to which they have committed themselves. Video is also used for training.

One bank uses a video program to spell out corporate objectives to its employees. This enables employees to be fully informed about new banking policies and keeps all employees working toward a common purpose. One tape deals with reasons behind new promotions, implications they will have for the bank's staff, and how expected increased workload will be absorbed. The bank feels that a well-informed staff will lead to a more profitable company. American Can Company uses a video-cassette presentation as the primary means of introducing to employees a major change in its benefits program.

10. Special-Purpose Programs A formal communications program was developed by a manufacturing company when it was noted that many work days were lost due to workplace injuries. Led by the company's top management, the program began with formal presentations using slides. Explaining management's concern about employee accidents, the program solicited questions and recommendations from the employees. A brochure was developed later to summarize key points brought out during the meeting. T-shirts, banners, and posters all displaying safety messages were distributed.

11. Open Forums Cedars-Sinai Medical Center uses an open forum for two reasons: (1) to inform middle managers about "why we do what we do," and (2) to educate top management about day-to-day problems. The open forum is a two-way, face-to-face, question-and-answer session between top and middle management. Department heads are excluded so that there will be a more open discussion of issues. Employees are brought up to date on problems that are raised and the resolutions that are now underway. The total cost of this invaluable program is a mere $400 per quarter.

12. Regular Staff and Committee Meetings In many companies, top managements have formalized regular weekly staff meetings with a fixed set of topics on the agenda. The following day, each manager attending the meeting then meets with his or her subordinates at another staff meeting. This method of communication provides downward, upward, and lateral communication. Standing committees, which may draw upon a more unrelated cross-section of employees, also provide for similar formally structured communications.

13. Communication Audits A communication audit looks at the communication needs, policies, practices, and capabilities both internal and external to the firm. The audit then provides data and recommendations on the firm's communication program. Subjects covered by the audit include the communication philosophy, objectives and goals, existing communication

> ### The Oldest (and Best) Way to Communicate with Employees
>
> In most organizations employee communication is a bastard function. Either no one is willing to acknowledge parentage and advocate the function's right to life or it is embroiled in a halfhearted (though in some cases heated) custody fight—with public relations claiming the tasks and personnel claiming the charter. Whichever way this peculiar conflict is resolved, custody battles do the function no good. Through the years it has suffered from lack of definition, inadequate budgets, limited professional staffing, and nearsighted vision.
>
> But out of necessity the tide may finally turn. Corporate management is beginning to face the fact that you can't take your people for granted, that domestic indifference soon leads to domestic trouble. Thus the longtime orphan function may get a chance to establish its place in the family.
>
> Why the sudden desire to do better? There are two major reasons: first, companies are dealing with a different kind of employee than heretofore—an employee who is looking for job satisfaction, who believes in personal options, and who wants meaningful work. But, you may protest, this has been the case for at least a decade. That's correct. Yet when this first reason is coupled with the success of the Japanese—who regard their workers highly and who are evidently having great success in human resource management (as well as in international markets)—companies face powerful indicators for self-examination.
>
> However, even when it spends considerable time trying to improve the flow of communications, management largely ignores the importance of the human transmitter. The result is overemphasis on expensive, often ineffective, equipment and one-way communication to an audience that is demanding an opportunity for dialogue.
>
> #### The threatening corridor
>
> Management consultant Scott Myers tells a story that shows how simple yet complex the communication function is. He was called in by a client to suggest ways management might communicate better with its work force. The company, always run along traditional lines, was trying to update itself and its communication practices. Before retaining Myers, management had decided to stress the traditional media methods—more articles in the company paper on corporate objectives and employee benefits, improvement of bulletin board displays, and a new monthly letter from the president.
>
> In his initial talk with the president, Myers learned that the company was about to spend almost $300,000 to install what it saw as the most effective and up-to-date way to transmit messages to employees: closed-circuit television monitors scattered throughout the premises. Myers, dismayed by this news, asked for a short delay of the order until he could size up the situation and make some recommendations. The president reluctantly agreed.
>
> In the course of examining the organization's communication efforts, Myers discovered an inter-

programs, meetings, attitudes toward existing communications, and so forth. Basically the method used is one of planning (determining audit's objectives), researching (top management and employee beliefs are gathered through interviews and questionnaires), and feedback (the results are publicly disclosed).

14. Suggestion Systems   Suggestion systems provide forms on which employees may make suggestions for any kind of constructive improvement in operations or for new product ideas. Suggestion boxes and forms are usually located throughout the plant or office. Suggestions may come from employees who wish to remain anonymous, who wish to bypass a likely veto by their manager, or who sign their names to achieve recognition and possible rewards. The suggestions go to a committee for evaluation rather than to a single manager. Suggestion systems are, therefore, a formal upward communication system.

esting practice. For some years employees had had a common coffee break during which all coffee machines were programmed to dispense the beverage free. At the same time, a cart carrying free pastries for everyone was wheeled into each area.

Watching the proceedings one morning, Myers recognized an opportunity. At his next meeting with the president, Myers suggested that he join his people out in the corridor at a coffee bar. The president smiled patiently and said that he couldn't do that. Asked why not, he replied that "it simply wasn't done." Top officers all had their coffee in their own offices dispensed from a mahogany cart. They never mingled with other employees during breaks. It would have been bad form and might even constitute an intrusion.

Myers persisted, however, and reluctantly the president agreed to try the radical idea. His first attempt was an abysmal failure. He didn't even know how to work the coffee machine. A bystander, seeing him fumble with coins, walked over and told him the coffee was free. Red-faced, he took the cup in hand and looked for someone to begin a conversation with. No one approached him; employees were clustered in little groups quietly discussing their various concerns and glancing curiously at him. He drank his coffee and walked back into his office.

To Myers he pronounced the experiment a flop—they wouldn't talk to him. Myers told him that the problem was twofold. He made his appearance too formal; instead of wearing his suit coat, he should have gone out in his shirt sleeves. Moreover, the workers weren't used to seeing him in their area. To make this a fair test, Myers urged, he must go back tomorrow. At first the president was emphatic in his refusal to subject himself again to such humiliation. Eventually he agreed to try it one more time, but with his coat off.

This time he got his coffee without incident and screwed up the courage to break into the perimeter of a small gathering. After some conversation about the weather, he asked how things were going and heard some pleasantries from the group indicating that everything was fine.

The following morning, after doing some homework on a current concern of the work force (the opening of a plant in Europe), he raised the subject with a coffee-break group and explained the logic behind the decision. He was surprised to find himself in the middle of an animated discussion about the plant.

The next day and the next the president went out to the corridor for his morning coffee. In time he found himself holding forth on all kinds of company issues with employees, who now felt comfortable enough to air their concerns. The kaffee-klatsches were working so well that he asked his senior staff to begin mingling with *their* people at coffee time. He also canceled the TV equipment in favor of the simpler and more effective technique of firsthand, face-to-face communication.

Source: Copyright © 1982 by the President and Fellows of Harvard College; all rights reserved. Reprinted by permission of the Harvard Business Review. "The Oldest (and Best) Way to Communicate with Employees" by Roger D'Aprix, September–October 1982.

15. Attitude Surveys *Attitude surveys* also provide a means for formal upward communication. The purpose of the employee attitude survey is to increase motivation by soliciting their opinions and ideas. In turn, it can strengthen internal communications, initiate feedback on employee policies, pinpoint reasons for excessive turnover, identify wage or benefit concerns, and identify promotion and discipline problems. Management will benefit if it listens to problems and does something about them. Top-level management must get back to employees within a short time after the survey is administered. The results should be discussed in meetings where employees can provide additional information. An effective follow-up program should be instituted in order to ensure continuing good relations.

Over the long run the ultimate criteria for measuring the effectiveness of human resource management are such hard data as return on investment, productivity, absenteeism, turnover, grievance rate, and so on. Because changes in these data may lag behind changes in the condition of the organization's human resources by many months, however, it is highly useful for management planning and control to supplement these measures with interim measures of the attitudes, motivation, and satisfaction level of the organization's human resources.

Use of an information system to evaluate the quality and commitment of the human organization is one of the newest developments in the field of human resource management. It is undoubtedly an aspect that will receive greatly increased attention during the 1980s because it represents a major opportunity for increasing productivity.

A number of leading firms including IBM, Texas Instruments, Xerox, and American Can are pioneers in the development of survey feedback systems to measure the attitudes of the organization's human resources. One such system for upward communication and control, called the "Human Resources Index" or HRI, has been designed to be applicable in a wide range of organizations who wish to (1) have the advantage of comparing employee responses in their organization with norms determined by the responses of individuals in a broad cross-section of other organizations, and (2) to obtain the advantages of the climate survey process without the heavy investment of time and money to develop internally their own survey instrument.

To give an idea of what confronts an employee when he or she is asked to participate in a survey, turn back to Exhibit 9–6 on p. 281, the Human Resources Index. The HRI, as well as being a device for improving organizational development, is necessarily an instrument of communication. It contains a total of 64 items, all positive statements about the organization, regarding which the employee is asked to indicate his or her level of agreement. The last two items provide an open-ended opportunity for the respondent to indicate things that are "most liked" about the organization and things that he or she would "most like to change."

Because survey results tend to indicate both strengths and weaknesses in any organization, it is often helpful for an organization to compare results against a standard of norms established for a cross-section of other organizations. This is one of the real advantages of using a standardized survey. For example, the HRI provides a means for comparing results against norms established by data from other organizations as well as against internal norms established in other departments.

Pioneering work in cross-organizational exchange of data has been done by the Mayflower Group, a group of more than 30 companies including Xerox, GE, and Prudential Insurance. The Mayflower Group, which formed in the mid 1970s, was so named because its initial organization meeting was held at the Mayflower Hotel in Washington, D.C.

As reported in *Business Week*, "Last year more than 100,000 employees—ranging from production workers to senior managers—minced no words in telling their bosses exactly what they thought of them, the company they work for, and their fellow workers. But instead of being fired, they were encouraged to sound off. Their companies were using a management tool called climate surveys, which not only get employee opinions out in the open but force managers to face up to—and correct—often unpleasant situations."[2]

One company discovered that a unit of welders was extremely dissatisfied with pay levels, even though the company paid competitively. In a survey feedback session, the workers said they had been reading want ads for welders offering pay of "up to $7.84 per hour." When it was pointed out to the welders that no company hires at the maximum wage, the grumbling stopped. Such feedback sessions are the key to making climate surveys work. As we saw in Chapter 9, Organization Development, climate surveys can be used both to take the pulse of the organization and to effect change.

16. Grievance Procedures Companies that fail to effectively communicate with their employees and who seem uninterested in employees' problems are those that easily fall prey to unionization action. Grievance procedures let employees voice complaints and get relief from hasty or unfair company actions. To make a grievance procedure work, the idea must be sold to employees. (Grievance procedures are more fully discussed in Chapter 16, Labor–Management Relations.)

The Human Resources Index

In Chapter 9 Exhibit 9–6 shows a segment of the Human Resources Index. This is a questionnaire that has proved effective in a number of organizations to:

- Measure attitudes, level of satisfaction and commitment to organizational goals
- Pinpoint specific trouble spots and issues of concern requiring concentrated attention
- Provide a work-related and, therefore, meaningful basis for opening up real two-way communication and initiating a process of organizational development

The 64 items on the HRI are scored and reported individually; more importantly, however, they are also used to determine a composite score on each of the following 15 factors.

1. Reward system
2. Communication
3. Organization effectiveness
4. Concern for people
5. Organizational objectives
6. Cooperation
7. Intrinsic satisfaction
8. Structure
9. Relationships
10. Climate
11. Participation
12. Work group
13. Intergroup competence
14. First level supervision
15. Quality of management

The scores on the 15 factors become the initial focus in analyzing and comparing results from one organization with another or in comparing changes over time within a single organization. Once critical factors are identified, the scores on individual items become very important in pinpointing the cause of a particular attitude and in understanding its significance for the organization.

DEVELOPMENT OF INFORMAL COMMUNICATION SYSTEMS

Communication occurs at various system levels within the organization. The communication system that links all the workers in the organization to the ideas and concepts of management is a general *broadcast system.* Most of this system is usually nonpersonal, and the same messages must reach many people. The media for broadcast methods are company policies and procedures, the company newspaper, the bulletin board, newsletters, and public announcements. The broadcast system is designed to present objectives and the unifying purpose of the company.

EXHIBIT 10-2
Formal and informal information systems.

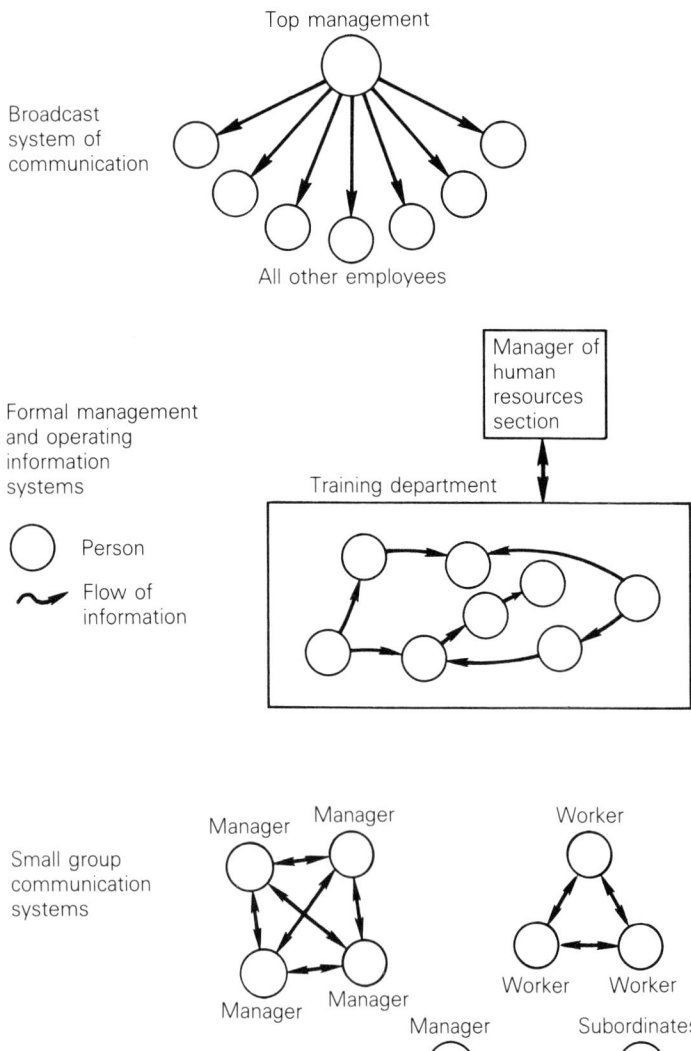

Also at the macro level are the formal information systems. These systems provide for communication among all workers who need specific information in order to do their daily jobs (see Exhibit 10–2).

Both of the above systems are supplemented by small group and interpersonal communications to provide clarification, amplification, and feedback. The lowest system level of communication is the typical two-person manager–subordinate interchange. Such interchanges may be written (memos), telephonic, or face-to-face (see Exhibit 10–2).

Let us now look at a single individual in terms of face-to-face discussion. At the intrapersonal level, we would study the communication system within the individual. This deals with physiological and psychological systems of sensing, interpreting, encoding, and decoding messages; channel capacity; speed of response; and transmitting and receiving meaning.[3]

At the interpersonal level, we see the manager dealing with one or more subordinates or others involved in problem solving. Studies have been made of communication patterns in three-, four-, and five-person task-solving groups. Exhibit 10–3 shows that the manager may establish different systems of communication with different characteristics. In addition, if the manager meets with subordinates as a group, interaction between the manager and any single subordinate is greatly influenced by the presence of the others.

Systems of communication			
Speed	Slow	Fast	Fast
Accuracy	Poor	Good	Good
Organization	No stable form	Slowly emerging but stable	Almost immediate and stable
Morale	Very good	Poor	Very poor

EXHIBIT 10–3
Task-solving patterns.

EXHIBIT 10-4
The development of interpersonal communication.

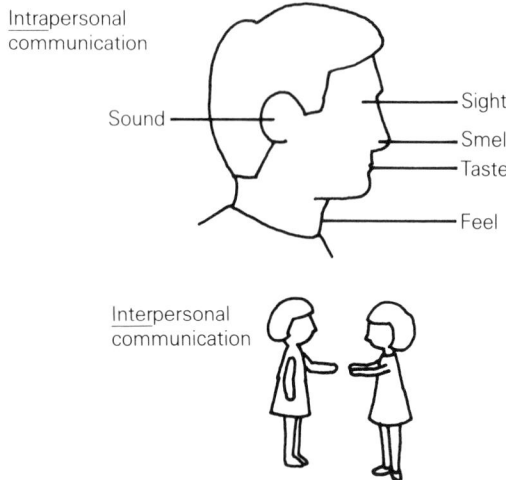

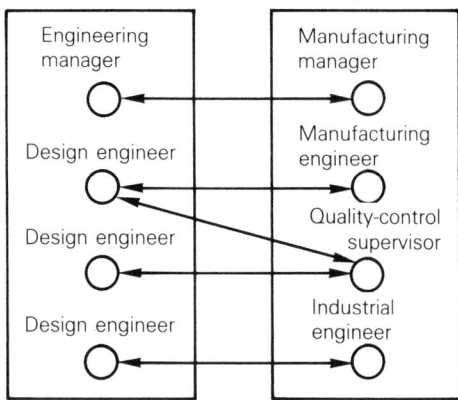

Also at the interpersonal level, an entire organization unit may communicate with another organization unit through many individual contacts. For example, engineering may communicate with manufacturing in this way, or accounting with finance. In Exhibit 10-4 you may see the development of interpersonal communication from the starting point of the individual's intrapersonal communication to intergroup contacts.

Nature of Interpersonal Communication

We have been discussing communication as if we all know exactly what it is. It is now proper to check our mutual understandings. For instance, is communication a one-way process or a two-way process between two or more people? What are the possible channels of communication? What is the process of communication? What is communicated? Does communication occur between people and machines? Between machines and machines?

What are the basic purposes of interpersonal communication? Although we may not answer all of these questions here, we do want you to think about the many aspects of the communication process that are important to human resources management.

What Is Communication? *Interpersonal communication* is the process by which one person transmits ideas, concepts, images, or sentiments to another. Not only is information exchanged, but the feelings and attitudes of the people involved are affected. Communication between people takes place when those involved attach significance to each other's behavior.

Basic Objectives of Communication The basic objectives of interpersonal communication are to: (1) inform, (2) appraise, (3) persuade, and (4) solicit information (feedback).

In work situations, the manager frequently informs a worker of new developments—techniques unknown to the worker—or both informs the worker and solicits the worker for information. All people in organizations constantly transmit appraisals of other people and work situations. Managers use communication to persuade subordinates to carry out certain tasks wholeheartedly. Subordinates use communication to persuade managers to accept proposals for programs. Much of daily communication is concerned with persuasion. Finally, problem-solving and conflict situations require one person to elicit information from another. From the first person's point of view, this is, in a sense, the opposite of informing.

What Is "Information"? If you send a memo to a person in your company who doesn't read it, are the contents information? If your computer files are loaded with data, do those files contain information? If your mind is wandering so that you blocked out the words of the person talking to you, do those words constitute information?

For our purposes we will refer to such content as *data*. We *transmit* data. By information, we will mean data that affect our behavior, beliefs, or attitudes. We *communicate* information. A computer can only receive data, but it may *communicate information* to a manager, who uses its output to make a decision. Two people who are talking and listening to each other are communicating. Exhibit 10–5 shows the distinction between communicating information and transmitting data.

Quality of Information One of the biggest problems for managers and people in general is determining the quality of information. What you think you see and what you hear may be incomplete and distorted. The many ways that communication may be disrupted are covered later in the discussion of barriers to communication. Basically, however, the quality of information is affected by:

1. Reliability or trustworthiness
2. Precision, or the range of the possible error

EXHIBIT 10-5
Communicating information versus transmitting data.

Communicating information = Affecting behavior, opinions, attitudes

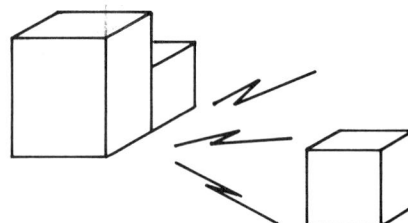

Transmitting data = Exchanging signs that are having no impact on behavior

3. Accuracy, or the difference between what is communicated and the truth
4. Bias, or consistent difference from the actual facts
5. Validity, or the degree to which a statement represents what it is said to represent; for example, does a personnel selection test actually measure what it is claimed to measure?
6. Currency, or up-to-dateness of information
7. Redundancy, or unnecessary repetition of information
8. Freedom from "noise," either extraneous data in the message or in the communication process

What's in a "Message"? People communicate ideas as a "message," or a spurt of information. For clear communication, particularly in writing and in more formal speaking, you should plan these messages. That is, you should consider:

1. *The number of ideas in the message.* If you wish to communicate only one idea, you are apt to have a high degree of success. If you attempt to communicate many, the receiver of your message may forget or confuse some of the ideas.

2. *The rate of information flow.* If you speak too rapidly, your listener may be unable to grasp what you are saying. Poor managers often try to keep up with every detail so that reports (messages) pile up and overload them. As a manager, therefore, you must be selective about the kind of information you get so that you can absorb it in the time available.

3. *The relative importance of your ideas.* The organization of messages should make clear which ideas are most important. A sort of "priority for action" can thus be established.

4. *The coverage of each idea.* The coverage or detail given to each idea in a message must be considered. More important or complex ideas usually require greater amplification than do less important or simpler ideas.

5. *The relationship of ideas.* Related ideas are usually grouped together. Alternatively, ideas may be presented in the sequence of the required action. Consider a manager discussing with a sales employee the tasks to be completed over the next three months. The manager could organize the discussion around products, customers, administrative reports, and pricing. Or, using the sequential approach, the manager could discuss plans for the areas and the customers to be covered, travel plans, the time to be spent with each customer, the products to emphasize with each customer, and daily reports.

Exhibit 10–6 portrays the planning of a message.

Psychological Aspects of Interpersonal Communication Without realizing what they are, all human beings are bound by psychological constraints. We also follow many cues in interpersonal communications without consciously thinking of them.

Personal filters and selective perception. Each of you is unique in the way that you construct the world outside yourself. Your perceptions and your expectations about the world are based upon your past experiences and your conception of self. You selectively perceive or filter information. People tend to avoid information about occurrences that appear to be inconsistent with beliefs about themselves or the world. People also tend to forget such information or to discount it. Such filtering of information obviously distorts communication.

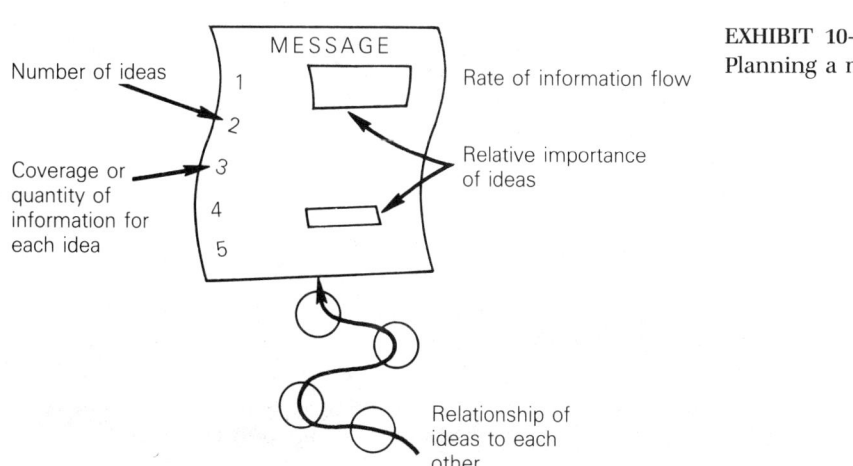

EXHIBIT 10–6
Planning a message.

Verbal and nonverbal communication. What we say is usually not the whole message, and, in fact, may be the opposite of what we mean. Sarcasm is an illustration. How then do we fully communicate in interpersonal discussions?

We must view interpersonal communication as consisting of four parts: verbal + vocal + body movements + use of space. In face-to-face discussions we note the gestures, the arm and leg movements, and the total body movements of the individuals. Examples include the use of gestures to communicate on a noisy shop floor, and the unconscious mirroring of others' body language, an action signifying agreement.

Each culture has its own distinctive set of movements and meanings.[4] One of the most significant and complex body movements is mutual eye contact. Centering; the duration of eye contact; movement up, down, or sideways when eye contact is broken—all have important meanings. The Arab businessman, for example, will expect eye contact at close range, whereas the Japanese executive will be offended by it, preferring to have his tie-knot focused on in conversation.

Source credibility. Communicating with another person means leaving the security of one's own concepts and entering the experiential field of another. The degree to which this occurs depends upon the credibility of the other person. Former president Lyndon Johnson experienced a "credibility gap" in his explanations of the Vietnam War. Credibility depends upon trust, situation, and time.

Credibility is an extremely important concept in managing people. Too often, managers are unable or unwilling to deal with unpleasant topics in face-to-face discussions with employees. In such instances, the employee later learns the facts indirectly through the grapevine. Often a form of double-talk is employed in dealing with employees. A classic example of double-talk in the political arena may be drawn from Governor Nelson Rockefeller's statement of his position on Vietnam at a 1968 press conference:

> Surely, my position on Vietnam is very simple. And I feel this way. I haven't spoken on it before because I haven't felt there was any major contribution that I had to make at the time. I think our concepts as a nation, and that our actions have not kept pace with the changing conditions, and therefore our actions are not completely relevant today to the realities of the magnitude of the complexity of the problems that we face in this conflict.

Power. Power in communication is the potential of one person to influence another. The power of the corporation president or the capacity of a manager to exert strong sanctions will affect what the other person in a discussion says and how he or she listens. Power means the ability to determine the location, the time, and the length of a discussion. Both power and trust are bases for credibility. When both discussants strive for power, conflict arises.[5] It should be the purpose of communication to prevent or curb conflict.

Listening. If one person is talking and the other is hearing but not listening, little communication is taking place. In manager–subordinate interchanges, the subordinate is likely to listen carefully because of the power relationship. In fact, the subordinate is often oversensitive to each aspect of the manager's message.

On the other hand, managers are often so intent on expressing their own ideas that they fail to listen to their subordinates. Listening is an active process. It consists of giving attention, of receiving stimuli from the sender, and, finally, of perception, which is the assignment of meaning to whatever stimuli are received.

Physical Aspects of Interpersonal Communication North Americans demand more space about them than do the people of most countries. This is evident in the dispersion of residences, the size of offices, and, finally, in the space maintained between two people engaging in conversation. Space is also maintained by using such barriers as furniture and by suppressing odors with deodorants and mouthwashes. We resent people, consciously or unconsciously, who press against us or intrude on our sphere of privacy in conversation.

Another physical aspect of interpersonal communication is the orientation of the participants. Steinzor and later Bass and Klubeck showed that two people sitting opposite each other tend to interact more than do two people seated side by side.[6]

Time Aspects of Interpersonal Communication Usually the manager or supervisor is under a time constraint that does not permit topics to be covered leisurely. In such circumstances, people often neglect courtesies and fail to listen to the messages that the other person is sending. This suggests that you should schedule discussions when you have adequate time or else limit the topics covered.

The time of day or the time of week selected for discussion affects the information received, as does the mood of the participants and the apparent importance of the meeting. For example, a manager who calls a meeting a few minutes before normal quitting time on Friday afternoon cannot expect full attention from participants.

Semantic Aspects of Interpersonal Communication Semantics is concerned with the relations among thought, language, and behavior. For semantics the meanings of words lie not in the words themselves but in our reactions to them. The same word may mean different things to different people. Thus such words as *scab*, *rate-buster*, and *management tool* arouse intense emotions among hourly union workers while producing little effect on professional workers.

Barriers to Communication The discussion above has introduced factors that affect communication, an understanding of which will guide you to-

EXHIBIT 10-7
Barriers to communication.

1. Differences in perceptions of events in the world
2. Misinterpretation of messages received
3. Heightened emotions
4. Laziness in trying to understand or transmit messages
5. Resistance to change
6. Failure to "listen" actively, letting the mind wander, or thinking about what *you* want to say
7. Uncritically and mistakenly assuming that you understand what the speaker means
8. Failure of the speaker or writer to recognize the situation and frame of reference of the listener or reader
9. Cultural and social differences that affect the language, viewpoints, and values of the people who are attempting to communicate
10. Confusing "facts" with inferences and sentiments
11. Failure to appraise motives or to ask what the other person is really trying to accomplish
12. Failure to obtain related information before interpreting the other person's meaning
13. Overgeneralization or projection of the other person's meaning by listening to that person's first ideas and then jumping to conclusions
14. Assuming that everything is either black or white or failing to see that many characteristics may assume a whole range of values
15. Lack of feedback between people who are trying to communicate. Do you attempt to phrase the other person's ideas in your own words for checking?
16. Overcommunication so that you cannot identify the main ideas of the message
17. Confusing words with concrete phenomena. The word *John* and the person John are not the same.
18. Inability of language and symbols to give some shadings of the meanings desired
19. Use of "gobbledygook," *the ostentatious application of hypertechnical terms and ororverbalization as an instrumentality of nugatory communication*
20. Lack of organization and failure to emphasize ideas
21. Conflict between verbal communication and behavioral signs. The receiver of the message may incorrectly interpret one or the other.
22. Interruptions to the communications process
23. Outside "noise" or interference
24. Distance between the sender and the receiver, which may reduce such aids to communication as the observation of behavior or the tone of voice
25. Inappropriate channel of communication
26. Time between origin of message and receipt of message
27. Structure of the formal and informal organizations
28. Status and other social barriers
29. Number of people involved in the communication process

ward improved communication techniques. We may amplify further by identifying some specific ways in which barriers to communication may arise because of lack of such understanding. These barriers, listed in Exhibit 10-7, are generally self-explanatory. Since we have not grouped them according to the factors we have discussed, you may wish to test your understanding of the barriers by so grouping them.

MODELS OF COMMUNICATION

Models (diagrams and descriptions) help to unify knowledge and improve understanding of a subject. A number of models have been developed that attempt to show relationships among the factors affecting interpersonal communication and/or to present the basic process.

An early model of the communication process treated information from a statistical standpoint, without regard to semantic content.[7] Although this model dealt with electrical signals, it was extended to interpersonal communication. The basic model in Exhibit 10–8A presents the communication process and the "noise" that interferes with the process. Exhibit 10–8B expands the model to indicate that whoever generates a concept or receives a communication shapes it according to his or her background and emotional state. "Encoding" means converting an idea into a language. "Decoding" is, of course, the reverse process. Interfering noises throughout the

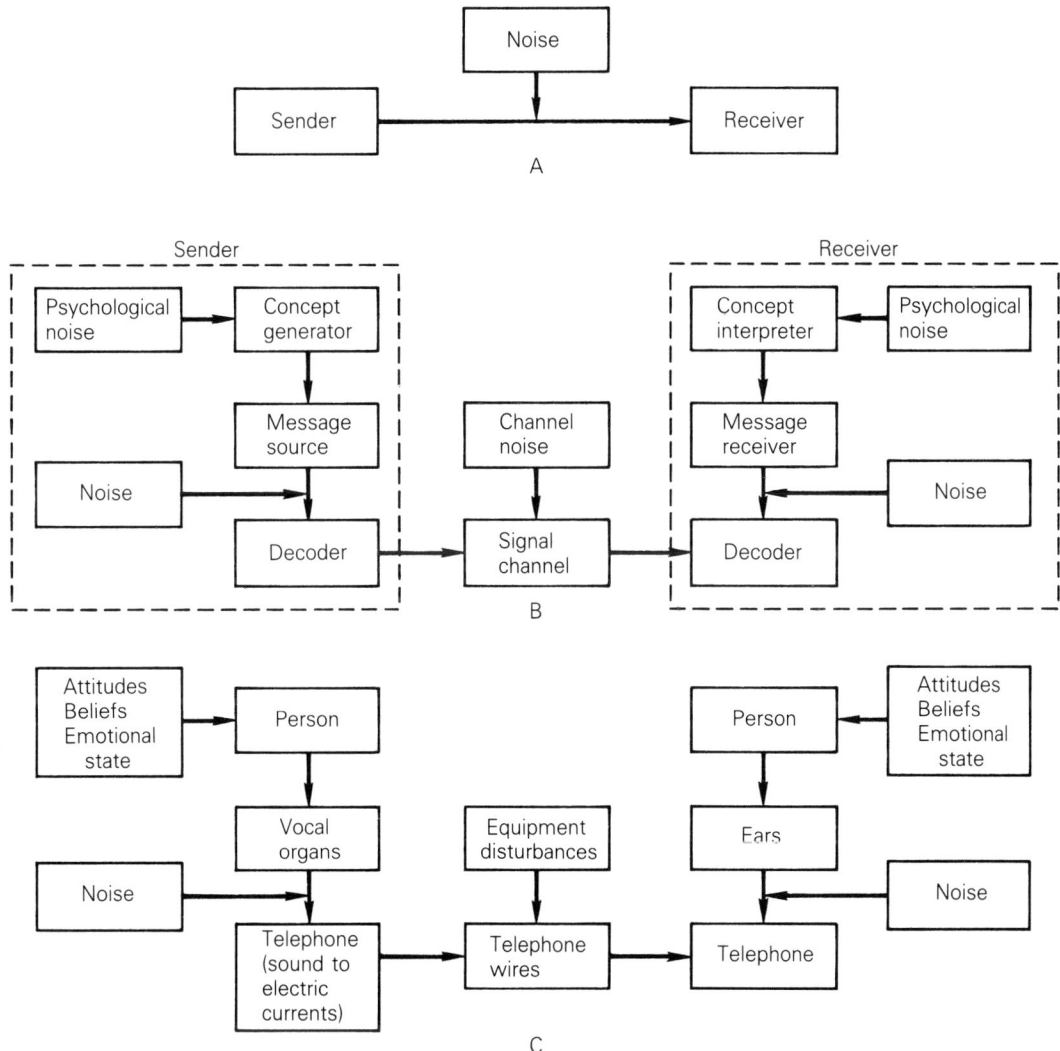

EXHIBIT 10–8
(A) Basic model of a communication system; (B) expanded model showing encoding and decoding; and (C) model showing source of interference.

EXHIBIT 10-9
A simplified Johari Window model of interpersonal communication
Source: Adapted from Joseph Luft, *Of Human Interaction* (Palo Alto, Ca.: National Press Books, 1969).

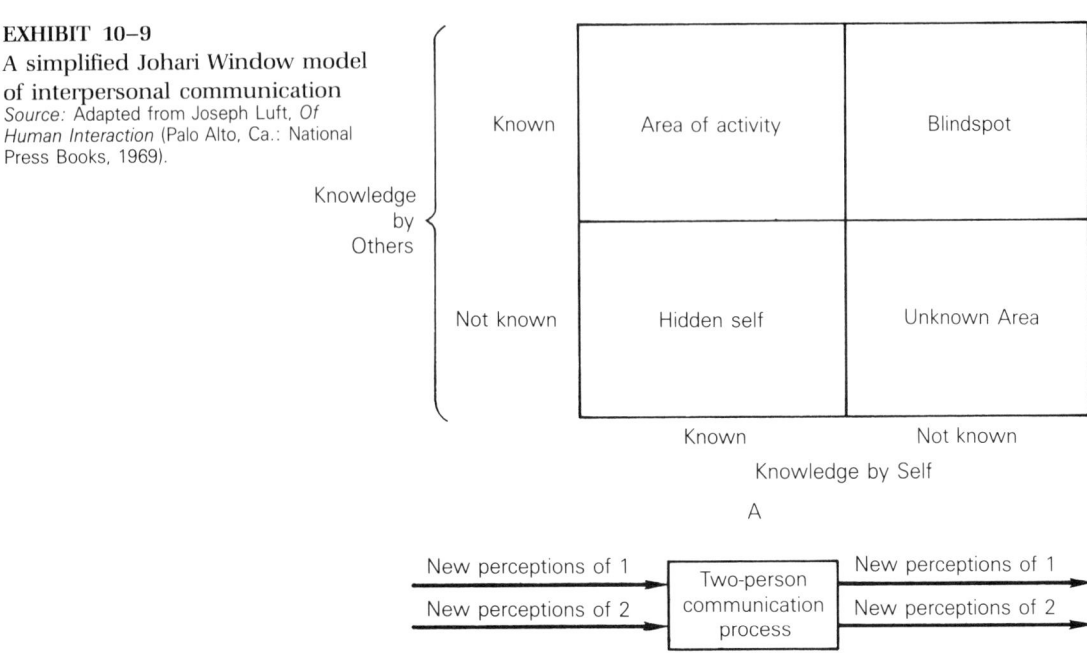

system may distort communication. Exhibit 10–8C illustrates an application of this model.

Joseph Luft has proposed a model that he calls the Johari Window model for interpersonal communication.[8] This suggests the model in Exhibit 10–9A, which shows four possible states of awareness between two people. When both persons have an awareness or knowledge of a subject, this is the arena of the discussion. When one person knows something that the other does not know, the latter has a blind spot in the discussion. When either of the participants enters the discussion with incorrect facts or perceptions, this may well lead to conflict. Finally, if neither party is aware of certain information, there will be an "unknown" area excluded from communication.

From the systems view, then, Exhibit 10–9B represents the two-person discussion process as acting upon inputs (the knowledge and perceptions of each person) and yielding revised knowledge and perceptions.

OBJECTIVES OF MANAGER–SUBORDINATE COMMUNICATION

The first step in designing a system is to set its objectives. After doing this, you may develop plans and make sure that all parts of the communication system are operating effectively. In the following discussion, we take up eight typical objectives or purposes of the person-to-person communication involved in managing human resources.

Communicating Organizational Objectives and the Individual's Responsibilities When a new employee is first hired, he or she is usually given a brief orientation to the objectives and policies of the company. Someone from the human resources department may meet with a group of new employees or with a single new employee. Orientation literature is usually provided. Sometimes a series of company managers or staff people will make brief presentations.

The manager to whom the new employee is assigned will also seek to communicate information about the work group. Another objective will be to discuss the work to be performed by the new employee and the other members of the group.

Communicating Policies, Procedures, and Practices In order to ensure consistency in action and a unified sense of direction, the manager needs to communicate the company's policies, procedures, and practices. Although this information is usually available in manuals, it requires explanation and interpretation for most employees.

Providing Employees with Feedback and Evaluation To keep the human resource system going in the established direction, managers at every level must let their group members know how they are doing. If information on a person's performance versus plans is supplied, the person can usually correct his or her performance when things start to go wrong. For example, if a training director receives cost reports, attitude measurements of students and managers, and student examination results, the director may be able to revise programs to make them more efficient and effective. Chapter 13, Appraising Performance, deals with communicating during the appraisal process.

Providing Employees with a Sense of Direction The good manager will communicate to those in the work group a sense of mission, a feeling that the organization's objectives are important, and that each individual should give his or her all. In sports, we sometimes see this esprit de corps when a theoretically weaker team beats a much stronger team. The toughest thing for a manager to do is to maintain this sense of mission in each employee over a long period of time.

Disciplining and Other Unpleasant Topics Communication between manager and subordinate has many positive objectives. Unfortunately, some objectives of communication in managing are "last resort" processes. Disciplining, demoting, or terminating an employee (for whatever reason) produces discomfort for both.

Counseling Employees A more pleasant objective of communication in managing is that of counseling an individual. Here the objective is to help a person improve on the job or find solutions to career or personal problems. The manager or a specialist from the human resources department may perform the counseling function according to the employee's situation.

Hearing and Resolving Employee Desires and Grievances Most workers desire control over their work and modification of their work situation. Such desires may be presented as proposals for which the employee simply seeks his or her manager's approval. In other cases, the employee may voice the desire as a complaint about a present situation and may or may not propose a solution. The source of the employee's grievance may be his or her manager or a third party. In all such cases, the manager and the employee should communicate fully to uncover the real problem and possible solutions.

Exit Interviews A major purpose of the exit interview, which is conducted when someone leaves the firm, is to uncover the attitudes and feelings of the interviewee toward the company and to diagnose organizational problems. This usually requires the nondirective interviewing technique which is discussed later in this chapter. It is also desirable that the employee who quits or is fired feels that he or she has been treated as fairly as possible. Such people may harm or enhance the reputation of the company through contact with other people.

GUIDES FOR IMPROVING COMMUNICATION WITH EMPLOYEES

Since communication is a big subject, we can only give some guides to improving communication within the company.

Develop a Company-wide Communications Program

In a large company, an individual within the human resources department should be appointed to develop and maintain a communication program. The small company should probably use the services of a specialist in communication from a management consulting company to develop the program. Then an employee could be assigned part-time to maintain it. The development of a communication program would consist of:

1. Reviewing organizational goals
2. Auditing the present communication activities
3. Establishing communication objectives
4. Establishing communication policies
5. Establishing communication activities

6. Establishing communication modes
7. Evaluating goal-related behavior

The above company-wide broadcast program provides the backup system for face-to-face manager–subordinate discussions. The following are guides for holding effective discussions.

Build Trust

Trust is not an instant gift. It is true that social standing, role, and power favor the development of trust. Generally, however, the manager must build a reputation for credibility over a period of time. Then, on the basis of trust, the subordinate will accept persuasion better and will also share his or her own ideas and feelings more honestly and freely.

On your side, *understand,* like, and trust your subordinate. Review, in your mind at least, all that you know about the person with whom you will be communicating. What is his or her education, work experience, background, and personality? How has he or she responded in similar conferences in the past? Since you depend on this person, you should review his or her strong points, those that caused you to hire the person. Prepare yourself to enter the discussion with an attitude of liking and trust.

Get the Facts in Advance

Each participant in a discussion should obtain as much information as is appropriate before the meeting. This prevents blind spots and areas of conflict.

Plan the Discussion

As manager, you should jot down a plan of points to be covered and objectives to be reached in the discussion. If the discussion is to involve joint work on a technical problem, it may be worthwhile to send an agenda to the other person.

Note specifically what you hope to accomplish. Note the minimum satisfactory outcome.

Example: One of your subordinates has fallen behind in a project that she has taken. Your objectives are (1) to determine what her problems are, (2) to help her lay out a course of action that will overcome the problems, and (3) to arrange for such support or expertise as she will need for the next two weeks.

In planning discussions, such as interviews, plan *how* you will structure the interchange. Should your approach be "directive" or "nondirective"? In the directive approach, the manager (or interviewer) guides the interchange, seeks answers to specific questions, and gives advice. This approach is useful in covering routine matters, matters of fact, and reports of progress.

In the nondirective approach, the manager (or interviewer) seeks to uncover feelings or beliefs that the other party is reluctant to expose. In fact, a nondirective discussion may be used to help either party evolve or clarify thoughts that he or she was unaware of. If the manager has a specific objective in mind for the discussion, then the manager must stimulate the other person's thinking and responses by:

1. Asking questions and then listening without interruption or criticism until the other person has finished and remains silent for a time
2. Making reflective comments, such as "Could you explain a little more?" "I see." "You feel that . . . ?" "Uh huh."
3. Observing the other person's facial expressions, body movements, tone of voice and inflections, and change of rate in speaking in order to determine points for probing questions
4. Withholding criticism, judgments, and arguments

Set a Mutually Agreeable Time

If the matter at hand deals with a current work problem, you may call the employee into your office or visit his or her office immediately for a brief informal discussion. On the other hand, if a matter of importance affecting the employee's performance or career is at issue, the time and place should be chosen with care. Often layoffs, terminations, or other bad news is discussed late Friday afternoon so that the employee can adjust to the shock over the weekend. On the other hand, promotions may be discussed at any time unless there are serious side issues, such as transfers to another location.

In dealing with bad news, the manager should present and discuss possible alternative courses of action for the employee. The supervisor should reassure the employee by helping the employee to find a constructive solution to the problem. Adequate time must be allowed.

The lunch hour, after work hours, and Saturday mornings should be evaluated as possible times for meetings in different situations.

Set an Appropriate Meeting Place

The place of the meeting and the physical setting have an important impact upon the way an interpersonal discussion will go. Casual topics should be discussed in convenient places—at the individual's work station, in the cafeteria, or even at the coffee machine.

More formal and serious subjects are usually taken up in the manager's office or a conference room. Correction interviews and evaluation interviews should be carried out in private and without interruption. Such topics as the promotion or transfer of an executive may be discussed at a restaurant or country club, or a business convention in a vacation spot.

Advise the Employee in Advance

Let the employee know the subject of the discussion far enough in advance so that he or she may prepare technically or psychologically. If the discussion is to be on an unpleasant topic, however, it is sometimes better to just call the employee in and develop the discussion of the problem together.

Anticipate Barriers

Check the possible barriers to communication. Which are most likely to hamper your communication at the forthcoming meeting? How can you reduce these barriers?

Tell What and Why

Good communication requires risk and the exposure of feelings. Tell the employee the problem as you see it, the alternatives that appear possible, and why you are recommending a particular course of action.

If you and the employee have developed mutual trust, encourage and help the employee. What feedback has the employee received previously?[9]

Correctional and disciplinary interviews deserve special attention as adjustments to the malfunctioning of the human resource system. As much as possible, the worker should be given responsibility for corrective action. The first such interview, therefore, should be conducted to determine whether the employee is aware of the objectives, duties, or rules involved. If so, the discussion should center on the future action planned by the employee. The employee is not criticized. Rather, forward-looking action is discussed.[10]

If the employee does not take corrective action within a specified time, a second interview will be necessary. Has the employee been taking the corrective action previously agreed upon? Are other employees failing to cooperate or to provide required inputs, so that corrective action is not possible? Is the employee simply not competent or not trying? If following rules is the issue, did the employee again accidentally (forgetfully) or deliberately violate the rule? At this point, possible changes in the employee's position or possible disciplinary action may be identified. If the employee has deliberately or carelessly broken a rule for a second time, disciplinary action is called for. Such action should be objective, related to the particular individual, and consistent with the union contract if one exists. A record should always be kept of disciplinary interviews, and a contract expert from the human resources department should be present if it appears that disciplinary action will be required. Resist distractions. Give the other person a chance to marshal his or her ideas and to present them completely. Don't argue.

Don't evaluate what the other person says until there has been a full exchange of views. Judge the content and not the delivery. Be flexible; an idea that appears off-target may be great with some modification.

Probe, question, and summarize in your own words what the other has said and ask whether he or she agrees that this was the idea presented. Use mirror questions, or signs indicating that you understand, that the speaker should continue.

Remember that nonverbal communication (body language) has a great influence on the other person. Make sure that your signs and expressions don't convey the opposite of active listening.

Summarize

At the end of the discussion, summarize the points of agreement and the action to be taken. Check to see whether the other person agrees with your summary. In some cases, notes should be prepared on the spot and initialed by both parties.

Terminate the Discussion Constructively

Complete the meeting courteously. Make constructive comments about the future or about possible future meetings. Even if there is substantial disagreement, offer to keep communications open by meeting again if this seems feasible.

Follow up

Whatever agreement, objectives, or action are agreed upon, put a note in your tickler file to follow up. This may call for another meeting and a person-to-person review. Without such a follow-up, the benefits of the meeting may slip away.

Listen and Understand

Communication is a two-way process. As a manager, cultivate the skill of *listening*. Look at the other person, not out the window.

In their article "Communication: An Alternative to Job Enrichment," Hak C. Lee and John J. Grix describe a creative attempt at General Motors' Lordstown plant to use the communication process as a basis for achieving a better relationship between management and the workers, and as a basis for solving some serious problems of worker resentment and alienation.[11] The article illustrates the importance of effective formal communications and reflects the potential contribution that such a communication system can make to the achievement of improved productivity.

Lee and Grix conclude that it is difficult to single out accurately the effects of a communication program from a multitude of factors affecting the organization. But, based on some formal measures of organizational effectiveness and informal feedback from the workers as well as supervisory personnel, the communication program has played a major role in improving both organizational climate and worker–management relations.

While the results so far measured and reported are short-run effects, longer-run effects are yet to be measured. However, the attempts undertaken by the Lordstown management represent a new structural approach to communication in countering workers' job alienation and improving the worker–management relations in the situation where management alternatives are severely limited by overwhelming technological considerations and competitive marketplace pressures. The attempts also represent a new direction in dealing with worker problems in an industry where human problems have typically been met by "hygiene" solutions such as pay, fringe benefits, and so on, through collective bargaining.

The experience in the Lordstown plant demonstrates the importance of communication as a possible substitute for job enrichment or OD programs—especially in the situation where management has limited flexibility to design such programs due to highly structured, integrated, and unalterable technology.

SUMMARY

This chapter has emphasized the importance of communication as a broad and fundamental aspect in the 1980s of any systematic approach to managing human resources. Communication has been described as perhaps the most underrated subsystem of HR management because the cost of a sophisticated communication program can be relatively modest, and yet for many organizations improved communication may represent the single most cost-effective means of improving productivity and performance.

The importance of upward as well as downward communication and the role of both formal and informal means of communication have been discussed.

This chapter has discussed 16 important types of formal communication programs and has shown the complementary responsibilities of human resource staff specialists and of line managers for the design and implementation of the communication subsystem. Specific methods for improving interpersonal communications within an organization have also been discussed.

KEY CONCEPTS

Formal communication systems	Attitude surveys
Informal communication systems	Interpersonal communication
Broadcast system	Feedback
Upward communication	Information

NOTES

1. Roy G. Foltz, "Communication Concerns," *The Personnel Administrator*, September 1982, p. 31.
2. *Business Week*, October 16, 1978, p. 168.
3. See, for example, C. David Mortensen, *Communication: The Study of Human Interaction* (New York: McGraw-Hill, 1972), Part 2, "The Intrapersonal System."
4. For a technical discussion, see Merwyn A. Hayes, "Nonverbal Communication: Expression without Words," in Richard C. Huseman, Cal M. Logue, and Dwight I. Freshley (Eds.), *Readings in Interpersonal and Organizational Communication*, 2d ed. (Boston: Holbrook Press, 1973).
5. L. R. Pondy proposed five stages of conflict: latent, perceived, felt, manifest, and aftermath. See L. R. Pondy, "Organizational Conflict: Concepts and Models," in John M. Thomas and Warren G. Bennis (Eds.), *Management of Change and Conflict* (Middlesex, England: Penguin Books, 1972).
6. B. Steinzor, "The Spatial Factor in Face-to-Face Discussion Groups," *Journal of Abnormal and Social Psychology* 45, pp. 552–555; and B. M. Bass and S. Klubeck, "Effects of Seating Arrangements in Leaderless Group Discussions," *Journal of Abnormal and Social Psychology* 47, pp. 724–727.
7. Claude E. Shannon and Warren Weaver, *The Mathematical Theory of Communication* (Urbana, Ill.: University of Illinois Press, 1949); and Robert G. Murdick and Joel E. Ross, *Information Systems for Modern Management*, 2d ed. (Englewood Cliffs, N.J.: Prentice-Hall, 1975), especially pp. 447 and 453–456.
8. Joseph Luft, *Of Human Interaction* (Palo Alto, Ca.: National Press Books, 1969); and Jay Hall, "Communication Revisited," *California Management Review* XV, Spring 1973, pp. 56–67.
9. For a taxonomy of feedback events, see David M. Herold and Martin M. Greller, "Feedback: The Definition of a Construct," *Academy of Management Journal*, March 1977.
10. For a good concise discussion of disciplinary interviews, see O. Jeff Harris, Jr., *Managing People at Work* (Santa Barbara, Ca.: Wiley/Hamilton, 1976), Chap. 14, "When Disciplinary Action Becomes Necessary."
11. Hak C. Lee and John J. Grix, "Communication: An Alternative to Job Enrichment," *Personnel Administrator*, October 1975.

REVIEW AND DISCUSSION QUESTIONS

1. List some company-wide or organization-wide programs that seek to improve communication among employees.
2. Discuss the use of communication in coordinating a specific project or task that you know of.
3. Discuss the role of communication for two people working on a project or problem versus its role for 1,000 people working on a project or problem.
4. Discuss the process of appraising the performance of the individual who receives reports directly versus the process of appraising the per-

formance of the individual who receives all reports through his or her manager. Which communication system do you think would be more effective, and why?

5. Develop a diagram to show the flow of information upon the hiring of a new employee.
6. List all the ways that two people communicate with each other in business (written, face-to-face, and so on).
7. Distinguish between the *intra*personal and *inter*personal communication systems.
8. Give examples drawn from business situations of each of the four basic objectives of communication.
9. Take an example of business information, such as the sales forecast, and discuss the likely quality of the information in terms of the eight characteristics of information covered in this chapter.
10. Give the substance of a recent conversation that you had in which the filters and perceptions of each party made communication difficult.
11. List the body gestures or positions that you have noticed people using when they talk, and give your interpretation of these gestures or positions.
12. Discuss the meanings and connotations of the terms *boss, manager,* and *leader.*
13. Prepare a plan for discussing an employee's breach of a no-smoking rule and possible disciplinary action. Have another student play the role of the employee, and act out the meeting.
14. Play the role of manager in a discussion, with another student playing the role of a subordinate whose grievance is that members of the work group keep hiding his tools.

BIBLIOGRAPHY

Aveleira, Enrique. "Hurdling the Barriers to Effective Communication." *The Internal Auditor,* August 1980, 81–83.
Beam, Henry H. "Good Writing: An Underrated Executive Skill." *Human Resource Management* 20, Spring 1981, 2–8.
Benford, Robert J. "Found: The Key to Performance." *Personnel,* May–June 1981, 68–77.
Bensahel, J. G. "Mixing the Formal with the Informal." *International Management* 36, January 1981, 37–39.
Blake, Robert R., and Jane S. Mouton. "Increasing Productivity through Behavioral Sciences." *Personnel,* May–June 1981, 59–67.
Brush, Douglas P. "The New Technology." *Public Relations Journal* 37, February 1981, 10–14.
Coyle, Lee. "RSVP: The Ohio Bell Approach." *Public Relations Journal* 37, February 1981, 24–27.

Davidson, Jeffrey P. "Communicating Company Objectives." *Personnel Journal*, April 1981, 292–293.

Dickey, John D. "Managing Dissatisfaction." *Personnel*, May–June 1981, 12–21.

Driver, Russell W. "Opening the Channels of Upward Communication." *Supervisory Management*, February 1980, 24–29.

Foltz, Roy G. "Internal Communications." *Public Relations Journal*, April 1981, 28.

Foltz, Roy G. "Productivity & Communication." *Personnel Administrator*, August 1981, 12.

Foltz, Roy G. "Quality of Work Life Effects on Productivity." *Personnel Administrator*, May 1982, 20.

Foltz, Roy G. "Communication Concerns." *Personnel Administrator*, September 1982, 31–32.

Guildea, Joyce. "45,000 Employees Judge Effectiveness of Internal Communication." *Journal of Organizational Communication*, 1981–1982, 3–11.

Guildea, Joyce Asher, and Miriam Emmanuel. "Internal Communications: The Impact and Productivity." *Public Relations Journal*, February 1980, 8–12.

Hall, Jane L., and Joel K. Leidecher. "Is Japanese-Style Management Anything New? A Comparison of Japanese-Style Management with U.S. Participative Models." *Human Resource Management*, February 1981, 14–21.

Hall, Jay. "Communication Revisited." *California Management Review* XV (3), 1973, 56–67.

Hatfield, John D., Richard C. Husman, James F. Luhiff. *Interpersonal Communication in Organizations: A Perceptual Approach*. Boston: Holbrook Press, 1977.

Keeber, L. C. "Marketing Employee Benefits." *Pension World*, April 1981, 33.

Lee, Hak C., and John J. Grix. "Communication: an Alternative to Job Enrichment." *Personnel Administrator*, October 1975.

Levine, E. L. "Let's Talk: Tools for Spotting and Correcting Communication Problems." *Supervisory Management* 25, July 1980, 25–37.

Lewis, Carl B. "How To Make Communications Work." *Public Relations Journal*, February 1980, 14–17.

Matchin, John. "The Least Inter-Manager Communications: Matching up to Expectations?" *Personnel Management*, January 1981, 26–29.

McCallister, Linda. "The Interpersonal Side of Internal Communications." *Public Relations Journal*, February 1981, 20–23.

Moravec, Milan. "How Performance Appraisal Can Tie Communication to Productivity." *Personnel Administrator*, January 1981, 51–54.

Olsen, Marie. "Implementing a Successful Suggestion System." *Personnel Administrator*, May 1982, 75–80.

Otis, I. "Effective Communication in Industry." *Industrial Management* 22, September–October 1980, 11–14.

Owen, James L., L. Page, and Gordon I. Zimmerman. *Communication in Organizations*. New York: West Publishing, 1976.

Penley, L. E., and B. L. Hawkins. "Communicating for Improved Motivation and Performance." *SAM Advanced Management* 45, Spring 1980, 39–44.

Personnel in Practice (column). "What Goes with a Formal Communications Policy?" *Personnel Management*, January 1981, 26–29.

Preston, Paul. *Communication for Managers*. Englewood Cliffs, N.J.: Prentice-Hall, 1979.

Randsepp, Eugene. "Are You Getting through to Your Staff?" *Company Decisions*, May 1981, 146–148.

St. John, Walter D. "Management Principles to Make Employees Feel like Somebodys." *Personnel Journal*, January 1981, 25.

Samaras, J. T. "Two-way Communication Practices for Managers." *Personnel Journal* 59, August 1980, 648.

Tavernier, Gerard. "Using Employee Communications to Support Corporate Objectives." *Management Review*, November 1980, 8–13.

White, Tod. "Address the Right Issue." *Training and Development Journal* 35, May 1981, 12–20.

Wycoff, Edgar B. "Cannons of Communication." *Personnel Journal*, March 1981, 208–212.

Individual Training and Development

CHAPTER OUTLINE

The Systems View
Individual and System Obsolescence □ Roles of Managers and the HR Department in the T & D System

Determining T & D Needs

Long-Range T & D Objectives and Policies for HR Management

Organizing for T & D

Identifying and Selecting T & D Methods and Techniques
Framework for T & D □ Characteristics of T & D Programs □ Underlying Learning Theory □ Career Objectives and Characteristics of Trainees

Developing the T & D Programs
Characteristics of Programs □ Levels of Learning

Implementing the T & D Program
Developing the T & D Subjects, Content, and Techniques □ Selecting Types of Training Methods □ Recruiting and Training the Instructors □ The Process of Teaching–Learning □ Preparing Instructional Materials □ Arranging for Facilities and Times □ Recruiting Trainees

Conducting the Teaching Activities

Evaluating the T & D System

Modification and Maintenance

The T & D Information System

The Computerized T & D Management System

OBJECTIVES

1. Identify company problems that T & D may help solve.
2. Identify, and describe briefly, methods for identifying T & D needs.
3. Relate company objectives to T & D objectives.
4. Identify T & D methods.
5. Describe briefly the major learning theories.
6. Describe the process for development of T & D programs.
7. Describe the process for implementing T & D programs.
8. Describe evaluation of T & D in terms of what is evaluated, by whom, and by what means.

SPOTLIGHT:
John Pattan

Dr. John Pattan is Manager of Training and Development, Brown and Williamson Tobacco Corp. at Macon, Georgia. He earned a B.A., M.A., and Ph.D. in philosophy, an M.A. in history, and a graduate degree in theology and counseling at Catholic University, Washington, D.C. He received an MBA from the University of Dayton and a diploma in organization development from the U.S. Army.

Between 1969 and 1978, he did counseling and organization development work and taught philosophy in Buffalo, N.Y., and Columbus, Ohio. In 1978, he left his position as philosophy department chairman at the Josephinum College to start at the bottom of the business world as management training instructor with the Metropolitan Atlanta Rapid Transit Authority. Within 18 months he was promoted to Manager of Training and Development. In 1982 he moved to his present position with Brown and Williamson.

Comments by John Pattan

The Brown and Williamson Tobacco Corporation is the third largest manufacturer of cigarettes in this country, making Barclay, Belair, Viceroy, Raleigh, and Kool cigarettes. The company operates manufacturing plants in Petersburg, Va., Winston-Salem, N.C., and Macon, Ga., plus a leaf-processing facility in Wilson, N.C. The Macon plant is considered to be the most modern facility of its type.

The corporation is dedicated to equipping its employees with the most effective technical and supervisory skills for optimal job performance. We have a 31-member training department at Macon, which delivered about 150,000 hours of technical and management training to over 1,800 employees in 1982. New production workers receive up to 10 weeks of initial technical training. Formal cross-training courses are given as an ongoing activity after initial training. Management training programs vary in length from half a day to five days.

At the Macon plant, we offer 19 management development programs and over 90 technical courses. In addition, our employees may attend in-house management training at our corporate offices in Louisville, Ky., and external technical and professional development seminars. The corporation also offers generous educational assistance to employees who wish to further their undergraduate or graduate education.

Two of the most important issues in industrial training are: (1) what courses to develop and deliver, and (2) how to evaluate their effectiveness in terms of return and investment. The identification of training programs to be designed and conducted is called training needs assessment.

Business plans determine staffing requirements, that is, how many employees our corporation needs to attain its business objectives. Technological developments in the industry determine what kinds and levels of skills the employees should have both to prevent obsolescence and to have the improved competence. In the light of these business goals and technological forecasts, then, joint management–union training councils in each technical area propose curriculum plans. In the management development area, training needs are identified by needs assessment surveys and personal interviews. Training councils in both technical and management training areas also determine the new courses to be developed or existing courses to be revised. The line managers and hourly employees on the training councils assure that the training department develops courses in such a way that they best satisfy the job-performance needs of employees, the customers of the training staff.

The evaluation of training programs occurs in several steps. The training councils review our training materials in the light of the course objectives. They look at both what was developed and also how it was presented for easy understanding. When finishing a program, participants fill out course critiques. This gives instant feedback to instructors about their courses. Participants also complete a follow-up questionnaire three months after the course. It assesses how relevant and useful the course was for doing their work. In technical training, supervisors complete follow-up questionnaires on how well their employees have applied to the job what they had learned. Such monitoring is conducted for several weeks after the training program.

In management training, supervisors have a pre- and post-training meeting with the participants. At the pre-training meeting, they discuss the reasons and goals for taking the course. Upon their return from training, their supervisors discuss with them the behavior and performance improvements they expect of the employees in applying the course content to their jobs. The supervisors also monitor how well their employees transfer their management training to long-term performance. The training councils also monitor the effectiveness of all training programs in their respective areas.

Our training philosophy divides the responsibility for the training of employees among the training department, the supervisors, and the employees themselves. Our training activities are aimed at improved productivity and bottom-line results.

Do the following statements surprise you? If the answer is yes, you are like the majority of Americans today.

Managers are developed, not born.
The Bell System spends in excess of $500 million annually on training.
It is practically impossible to define and describe the full dimensions of training in business and industry today.[1]

Although there is a serious lack of information on training, development, and education in business in the United States, it is obvious that large, progressive companies strongly believe in developing their organizational capabilities by these processes. The U.S. is spending about $40 billion a year on job training—$30 billion by corporations and the remainder by federal, state, and local agencies.[2] In a survey of 141 personnel executives, it was found that 55 percent of the companies had formal in-house training programs and 90 percent had tuition-refund programs. From these and other data, it appears that training and development is considered vital to developing the human dimension of company productivity.[3]

THE SYSTEMS VIEW

Training and development (T & D) is a subsystem of the HR management system. The primary objective of the T & D subsystem is to change the behavior of people in the company so that performance of the company as a whole is improved. T & D is also the most commonly used organizational development method (see Chapter 9). In this chapter, we focus on upgrading the individual members of the organization by involving them in many types of planned learning experiences. The *learning experience* results in a *relatively permanent change* in the behavior of the individual and hence in the company as a system.

Organizational renewal and improvement are possible through planned teaching–learning on a continuous basis. T & D makes the company more effective and more efficient by upgrading people who must solve such problems as:

1. Filling vacancies for highly skilled workers
2. Need to improve quality
3. Need to improve productivity
4. Excessive scrap
5. Excessive absenteeism and turnover
6. Inadequate planning and cost control

As for all P/HR activities, it is important to evaluate T & D programs. Generally, the costs can be estimated, but objective measurement of benefits in many cases is difficult. A discussion of evaluation is presented later in the chapter.

Individual and System Obsolescence

When a superior product replaces an old product, the old product is said to be obsolete. The horse and buggy are obsolete for modern cross-country transportation. People may become obsolete, too, if they do not update themselves with new work methods, skills, and knowledge about the environment. An entire organization may become obsolete if it lacks a systematic means for continually developing organizational capabilities. It has been estimated that an engineer's knowledge of his or her field is cut in half every 10 years because of the advancement of the field—unless he or she continues to study. The 10-year period in this case is called the half-life of the occupation and is a measure of the rate of obsolescence (Exhibit 11–1).

The rapid development of the computerized work station, automation, technology, and legal constraints, in particular, require continual retraining.

Roles of Managers and the HR Department in the T & D System

Top management determines the general scope and types of T & D programs, usually after consultation with the HR Department manager. Within policies thus established, the T & D manager investigates the desires of the line managers and of employees. He or she often proposes courses and programs for their consideration.

The line managers are responsible for the selection of trainees, although this may often be routine approval of applications initiated by employees. The HR manager should work closely with line managers to identify T & D needs of promotable employees and career paths of all employees.

The implementation of the actual T & D is the responsibility of the T & D manager. He or she must handle the many details involved in setting times of meetings; finding classroom space; obtaining instructors and training them in teaching methods; preparing instructional material; and evaluating course content, instructors, and trainees.

Exhibit 11–2 illustrates the complex structural relationships that de-

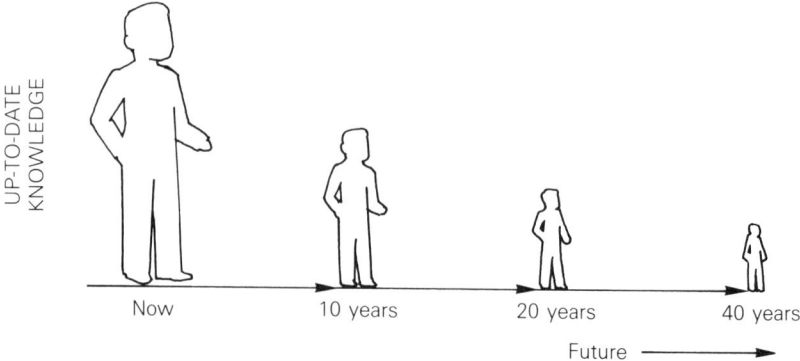

EXHIBIT 11–1
Decline of knowledge of current concepts for a half-life of 10 years.

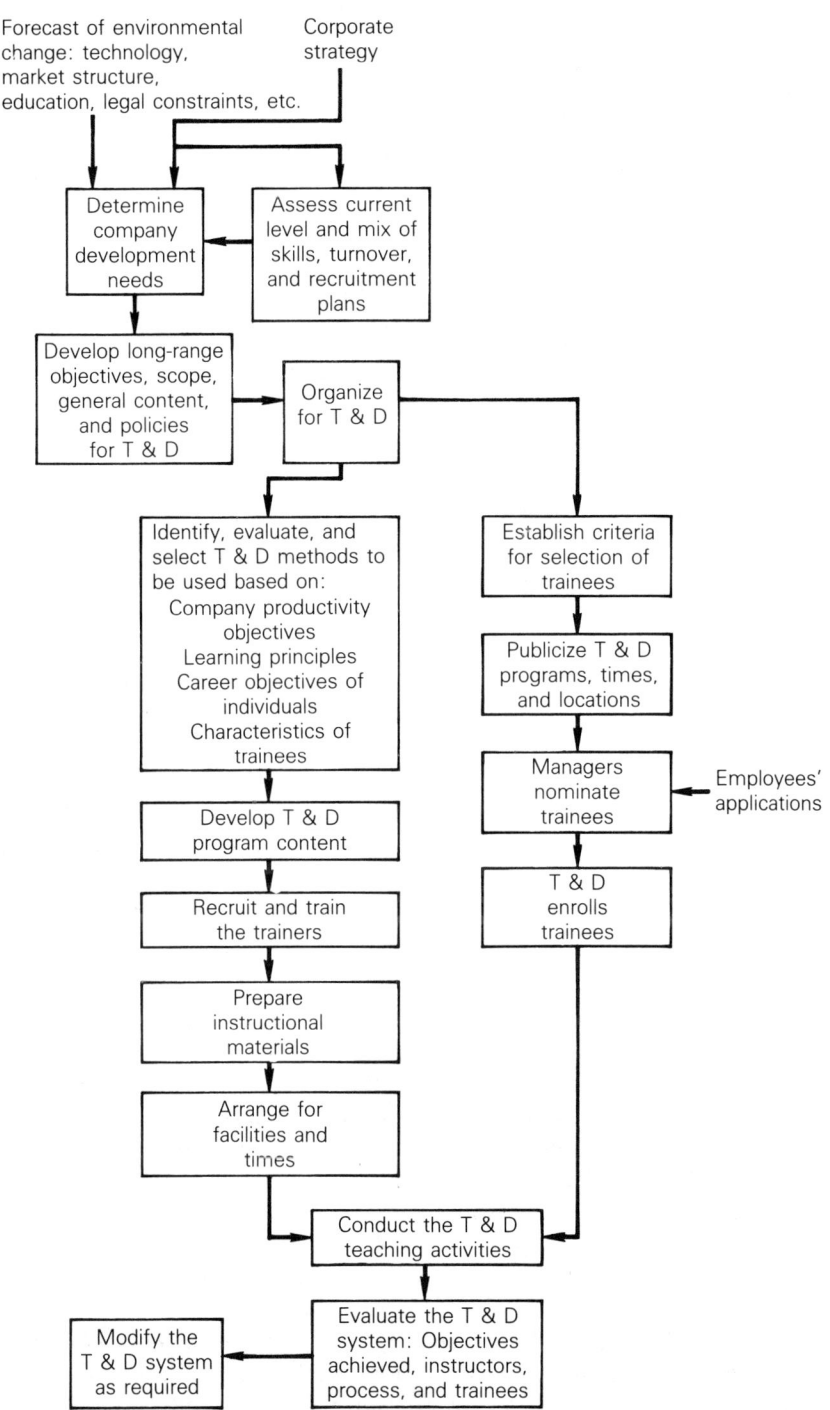

EXHIBIT 11-2
The training and development system.

EXHIBIT 11-3
Closing the performance gap.

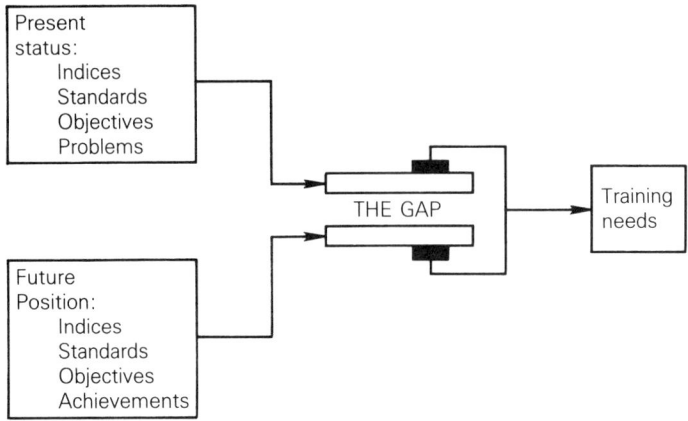

velop in making a T & D system effective. The rest of this chapter explains the nature and implementation of this system.

DETERMINING T & D NEEDS

T & D needs arise from two perspectives. From the view of the company as a system, T & D is needed to:

1. Orient new employees
2. Maintain performance of the system by preventing obsolescence
3. Build a skilled work force for the future
4. Assist in meeting legal obligations such as EEO and affirmative action
5. Motivate employees by offering opportunities for growth

From the viewpoint of company employees, T & D is needed to (1) avoid obsolescence, (2) prepare for a better or different and more rewarding job, and (3) follow a planned career path.

Exhibit 11-3 shows the general approach to determining T & D needs. Basically, the company must determine its present position, decide what its desired future will be like, and then determine how to close the gap through its development of human resources.

Training needs may be suggested by the following 10 techniques and then evaluated in terms of closing the performance gap:

1. Interview with Potential Participants The manager or company career counselor may interview a worker to identify training that would improve job performance or prepare the worker for future jobs. Either the worker or the manager could initiate such an interview. Part of the annual performance appraisal discussion should be devoted to possible T & D.

2. Questionnaire Survey Questionnaires may be sent to employees and managers to identify training needs that may not be available currently. Questionnaires may be used to compare employees' desires for specific T & D courses with managment's beliefs as to what is needed. Information about length of courses, times given, and type (company, university, outside seminars) may also be solicited.

3. Analysis of Personnel Inventory Files If personnel inventory files are available from a computer, a printout of each worker's career objectives and his or her progression through T & D courses may be obtained by the training director. The employee's manager may then attempt to match the employee's need for T & D with company needs in the future. The manager then makes recommendations to the training director for specific courses and programs.

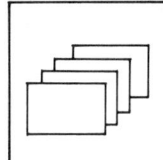

4. Management Requests Managers may request the training director to admit certain people to specific courses, request that specific courses be given, or request the development of a new T & D program.

5. Observation of on-the-Job Behavior Observation of workers' behavior, communications, work flow, and relationships on the job may suggest needs for technical training, training in communications, and organizational development.

6. Job Analysis and Job Competencies Job analysis, as discussed in Chapter 5, leads to the development of job specifications. If a worker does not meet the job specs set for the job, training may likely be the answer.

7. Tests Many companies give tests such as typing or stenographic tests to determine promotability. The Federal Civil Service System bases promotions and transfers on tests of job-skills education. In addition, tests offered by state and private agencies such as the Certified Public Accountant exams and so on lead to company T & D programs for preparation.

8. Outside Consultant In some cases, an outside consultant may be called in by the P/HR department to review the T & D program and make recommendations. For small companies without a training director, this may be especially beneficial. Outside consultants provide a fresh view, greater breadth of experience, and help to support the training director's final proposals to management.

9. Group Problem Analysis Although group problem analysis to develop T & D needs is probably rarely used, it has some strong advantages. All managers concerned with problems of a specific business system meet to identify the problems and causes. Often, training of employees is a major part of any solution.

10. Assessment Centers Assessment centers are widely used for evaluating employees for promotion, placement, and further T & D (see Chapter 13). AT&T had 60 assessment centers at which about 15,000 people a year were assessed for a variety of jobs.[4]

According to a study of 47 large corporations by L. A. Digman, T & D needs are specified for managers and for individuals according to Exhibit 11–4.

One of the worst errors in T & D is to establish mandated training. This leads to apathy and dislike on the part of the trainees. There is usually no carryover to the job. This is a case of trying to fit *needs* to conceptualized goals instead of determining true needs.[5]

LONG-RANGE T & D OBJECTIVES AND POLICIES FOR HR MANAGEMENT

Line managers are responsible for the company's short- and long-range development plans. In making such plans, each manager projects the number of people and skills required over the planning period. The human resources department then compiles the totals for all managers, evaluates the feasibility of hiring the needed people, and plans the training programs required to supplement the hiring by increasing the present capabilities of the organization.

EXHIBIT 11–4
Methods for identifying training needs.

Needs for Manager Development		Needs for Individual Employees	
Method	% Using	Method	% Using
Projection of management personnel requirements	83	Individual performance	93
Analysis of problem areas	83	Planned promotion or reassignment	80
Part of on-going regular program	74	Existence of problem situation	76
As needs appear	74	Prescribed or periodic development	63
Periodic survey	11	Accomplished promotion or reassignment	59
Other	2	Unit performances	33
		Other	15

Source: Adapted from L. A. Digman, "How Companies Assess Development Needs," in Richard C. Huseman (Ed.), *Proceedings of the 40th Annual Meeting of the Academy of Management,* Detroit, Mich.: August 9–13, 1980.

The long-range T & D objectives should parallel the company's strategy. A brief example is given in Exhibit 11–5.

Although it would appear that we should survey the needs of employees in terms of the needs for developing organizational capabilities, the "deployment of resources" limits us. With anticipated sales and cash flow, we must allocate funds among plant, equipment, human resources, and dividends to stockholders. If we increase the number of dollars going to one of these, we must decrease the number of dollars going to another. Therefore, the systems approach tells us that a good *balance* in distributing our funds will probably ensure good growth for the firm. What this leads to is, "Here are *X* dollars for training and development, Mr. Human Resource Manager. Please set up a long-range program to meet our organizational needs as best you can."

D. H. Bullock recommends that the T & D department prepare a Training Mission Statement (TMS) to guide the development of policies. The TMS would follow the following outline:

1. Nature of the T & D function: relationship to the corporate mission and resources
2. Services and products: desired outputs of the T & D functions
3. Primary clients and users: specification of the organizational users

EXHIBIT 11–5
Long-range T & D objectives and company strategy.

Company objectives	T & D objectives
Scope: Lubricating oil products in Eastern U.S. markets	Sales, production, and technical personnel
	Train all groups
Risk: Medium risk in investment of funds	Hire slowly so as to have too few rather than too many.
	Develop enough managers so that expansion may be carried out rapidly if needed.
Competitive edge: Technical quality of product	Specialized programs in technology
	Tuition-refund programs at the graduate level
Specifications (T & D only): 2,250 employees five years hence—1,000 production, 150 marketing, 80 managerial, 20 human resources, 600 technical, 400 supporting services	Provide training and development for 50 percent of employees at the average rate of $1,000/year
Deployment of resources (T & D only): Emphasis on technical and managerial training and development	Same
	Concentrate on employees under 50 years of age and minority groups

who benefit and the relation of the benefits to the corporate mission
4. Secondary clients who may benefit
5. Desired results: primary indicators or measures of efficiency and effectiveness of T & D relative to corporate mission
6. Operations/Processes: very generally, the work/information flows for T & D[6]

The human resources department may recommend one of several basic policies to follow with regard to developing the capabilities of the organization's members to meet new challenges. The choice will depend on the value system of the company, on industry practices, and to a great extent on the size of the company. Alternative policies are:

1. Laissez-faire
2. Encouragement
3. Joint company–individual commitment
4. Aggressive company development
5. Replacement instead of development

In the first case, the company does nothing about developing its human resources. It assumes that people will prepare themselves and that the good ones will rise to the top. With the proper work climate and a suitable incentive system, this policy may be successful in a stable industry where innovations are rare.

The second policy is one of benevolent paternalism. The company may give some courses for employees. It may encourage employees to attend local colleges and record the results in the employees' personnel files. It may send a limited number of people to professional meetings each year. This policy is obviously an unstructured approach to long-range T & D.

The joint company–individual development policy is a planned system. The company first establishes development objectives and plans and means for implementing the plans, then matches employee needs to courses or programs offered. A wide range of techniques for development is likely to be used.

Aggressive company development programs are usually found in the large multinational companies. In one such company, the only route to becoming a financial manager was to complete a two-to-three year company program of courses given after working hours. In some high-technology companies, engineers must either take company or university courses every year or risk being released.

Finally, we come to a less common policy. A company may decide to upgrade through a hiring process rather than a development process. One firm let it be known unofficially that at the end of each year the poorest 10 percent of the professional people would be told to start looking for another job.

Well-managed companies clarify their educational and development system by means of written policies, program catalogs, and forms.

ORGANIZING FOR T & D

A single employee, a training specialist, may be made responsible for T & D activities. At the other extreme, there may be a training specialist just for production and clerical workers, a specialist for professional workers, a specialist for supervisory training, and a management development specialist. The expertise required in each of these areas is different enough to justify such positions in large companies.

In some companies, the T & D organization may also include some of the trainers. This is the case when the same courses are to be given repeatedly. Very large companies with separate product divisions conduct both corporation-wide programs and local product division T & D. Each product division has its own T & D director as does corporate headquarters. The somewhat complex relationships are depicted in Exhibit 11–6.

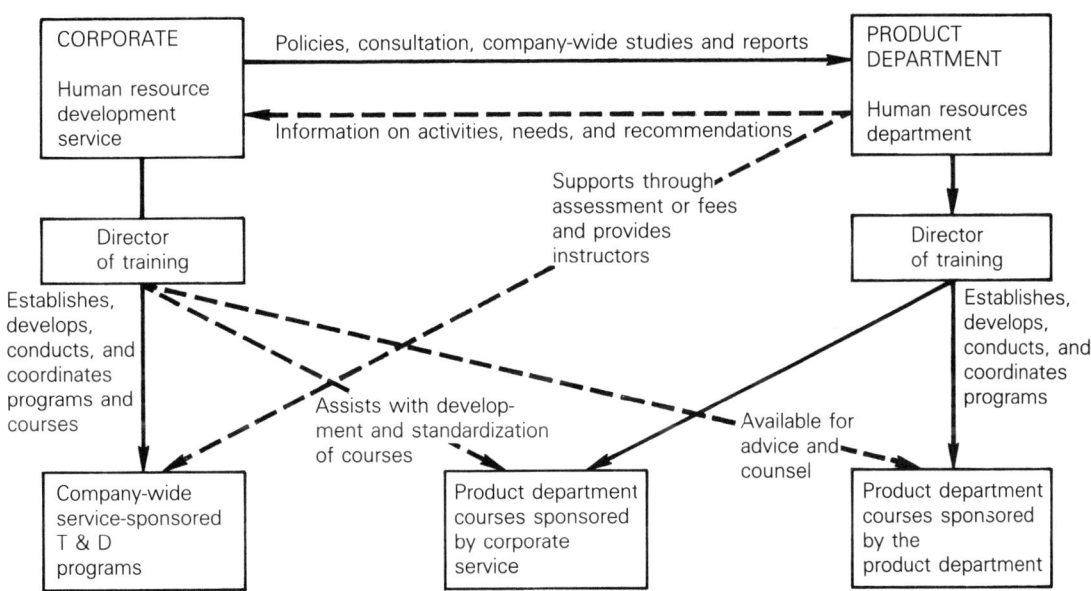

EXHIBIT 11–6
Relationships between corporate services and product departments for human resource development programs and courses.

IDENTIFYING AND SELECTING T & D METHODS AND TECHNIQUES

Once the T & D needs have been established, policy decisions must be made to establish general training methods to be used. The choice of a general method depends on the number of employees of a particular type to be trained, the company facilities and teaching skills available, the financial resources of the company, and the comparative cost–benefit ratios for each general method for that particular company.

Framework for T & D

From the practitioner's perspective, T & D is viewed in a framework of four major objectives: training, development, education, and rehabilitation. The definitions of these objectives follow.

1. *Training* is a systematic way of altering behavior to prepare an employee for a job or to improve the employee's performance on the present job. For example, a stenographer may receive training to increase the rate of dictation that he or she can take. A manager may be trained in public speaking so that the speeches he or she gives for the company will be better. Training is used to develop mental or manual skills, to increase knowledge, and to change attitudes. Training is a *job-related* experience.

2. *Development* is *person-oriented.* It is preparing an employee for a broader role in the company. Development focuses on improving the conceptual, decision-making, and interpersonal skills in complex, unstructured situations.

3. *Education* is also individual-related learning experience. The focus here, however, is on improving *breadth* of knowledge—the understanding and thinking processes of the individual to *broaden* the range of responses. As John Dewey said, "It is that reconstruction or reorganization of experience which adds to the meaning of experience, and which increases ability to direct the course of subsequent experience."[7]

4. *Rehabilitation* is experience-oriented toward the special skills and attitudes required by some people in order to remain or become useful to society. Some companies, for example, make a special effort to employ and retain physically handicapped people. Many companies have unpublicized programs for employees who have become alcoholics.

Characteristics of T & D Programs

T & D methods may vary from programmed learning at home to paid leaves of absence to obtain a Ph.D. degree. The T & D program is usually differentiated to develop five groups of employees:

1. Managers
2. Professional personnel
3. Semiprofessional employees (technicians)
4. Office and clerical help
5. Factory and other production personnel

Managers may receive training to update them in their functional fields, to develop them for future promotion, or to make their responses to society, the public, and their customers more sophisticated and less provincial. The development of managerial capabilities is a never-ending process that parallels managerial experience. The use of seminars for the interchange of ideas, case-study techniques, and workshops are highly favored for management development. Some companies offer top-level managers educational renewal programs at universities both in the United States and abroad. Companies such as Xerox and General Electric have built their own management schools away from the demands of the plant and headquarters.

Professional and semiprofessional development courses may range from one-day seminars to two- or three-year accounting, engineering, or manufacturing programs. Although some courses may be given on company time and at the plant, many are given after hours. Tuition-refund programs and seminars away from the company plant are common, but the use of company instructors is popular because in this way courses can be focused on company problems. The advantage of sending students outside the company and away from their work is that this gives them fresh outlooks.

Office and clerical help are requiring a tremendous amount of retraining because of the introduction of microcomputers, computerized data storage and retrieval systems, and newly designed work stations. Generally, workshops and short seminar courses are most useful for such training in information systems.

Factory and other production workers are also strongly influenced by computerized information systems as well as automation. Again, the same techniques that fit clerical workers are applicable here.

Underlying Learning Theory

The attainment of the objectives defined above and the basis of the T & D programs rest upon various theories of learning developed by psychologists over the years. Definitions of learning have varied according to particular theories of the learning process.

> Learning involves change. It is concerned with the acquisition of habits, knowledge, and attitudes. It enables the individual to make both personal and social adjustments. Since the concept of change is inherent in the concept of learning, any change in behavior implies that learning is taking place or has taken place. Learning that occurs during the process of change can be referred to as the *learning process*.

Source: L. D. Crow and A. Crow (Eds.), *Readings in Human Learning* (New York: McKay, 1963), p. 1.

Learning theories have generally been classified into two groups: behaviorist and cognitive theories. The behaviorist theories are also known as stimulus–response, or reductionist theories because they reduce apparently complex behavior to simple explanations involving stimuli and responses. Some researchers who contributed to conditioning theories are E. L. Thorndike, Ivan Pavlov, J. B. Watson, C. L. Hull, and B. F. Skinner.

The models of this behavioral learning theory are viewed as mechanistic or behaviorist because only observable behavior is considered to represent learning. In *classical conditioning*, Thorndike's Law of Effect states that a strong stimulus–response bond depends on the reinforcer (reward or punishment following a behavior). Thus, behavior depends upon its consequences. This leads to the concepts of acquisition of new behavior and extinction of old behavior. On-the-job training may be viewed as an application of these concepts when immediate reinforcement is frequent. In Skinner's *operant conditioning* theory of behavioral learning, only positive rewards for "emitted" behavior are employed, and undesired behavior is believed to be extinguished when it is repeated without any reinforcement (i.e., ignored).[8] One of Skinner's most notable contributions is the development of programmed learning techniques.

The second major group of learning theories is characterized by the cognitive approach. *Cognitive learning theory* includes E. C. Tolman's sign learning, Gestalt, and field theory. Generally, the cognitive model views the individual as interacting with a life-space of many forces. Tolman's ideas formed the basis for modern expectancy theory (discussed in Chapters 3 and 8). He believed that people could recognize the relationships between signs in the environment and their desired goals. The individual learns meanings of signs and a route to a goal, not a pattern of behavior. Adults in business usually have goals that, through expectancies, provide the basis for motivation during T & D experiences.

The greatest influence on modern cognitive learning has been Jean Piaget. He describes distinct, identifiable stages of development of the intellect through childhood to maturity and the conditions that facilitate each stage of transition. Robert M. Gagné believes that classical and operant conditioning also help in understanding learning in childhood. In a classification that retains ideas from many major theories, Gagné proposed eight types of learning:[9]

1. Signal learning (classical conditioning)
2. Stimulus–response learning (operant conditioning)
3. Chaining of behavior learning
4. Verbal association learning
5. Multiple discrimination learning
6. Concept learning
7. Principle and role learning
8. Problem solving

Another important concept in the application of learning theory is that adult learning situations should be constructed differently from those for children. In the past, most research has dealt with *pedagogy*, the teaching of children. It is only in recent years as many older adults returned to college that attention became focused on *andragogy*, the teaching of adults.

This is despite the fact that business has been training adults for many years.

E. C. Lindeman identified several basic concepts about adult learners that have been supported by more recent research:

1. Adults are motivated to learn by their needs and interests. Therefore, adult learning should be organized around these.
2. Adults' outlooks are *life*-centered; therefore, life situations rather than narrow subject matter should be the basis for organizing the learning process.
3. Adults have wide experience so that the teaching methodology should be based on the analysis of experience.
4. Individual differences among people increase with age so that style, time, and pace of learning must be adapted to each individual or group.[10]

Exhibit 11–7 distinguishes between the characteristics of pedagogy, which is reactive, and andragogy, which is proactive. That is, pedagogy tends to be reactive because the student does not initiate ideas for discussion or criticize ideas and material. Andragogy, however, involves proactive participation by the adults in the teaching–learning process.

From Exhibit 11–7, we note that the reactive approach is typical of teaching in the lower grades in child education. The child is willing to be dependent and is committed to learning in order to progress through grades. Usually a competitive atmosphere is fostered by examinations and awards.

In contrast, adults bring a broad experience, curiosity, and skepticism to the classroom or conference. They measure progress more in terms of their feeling of improved performance at work and in the world. Competition, therefore, is replaced to a great extent by mutual assistance and group projects. Adults also desire to have greater impact on the direction and content of the learning experience.

It is apparent from the above that T & D in a business organization requires an entirely different approach than the "teacher-knows-all-and-is-always-right" approach as practiced in elementary schools and even in some college courses. In T & D in many company programs, participants do not take examinations to be checked out on the "right answers." Rather, attendance, participation in projects, and application of course concepts on the job are used as loose measures of the learning taking place.

Career Objectives and Characteristics of Trainees

Career objectives may vary from (1) becoming a general manager to (2) becoming a skilled professional engineer, to (3) becoming a skilled tool designer or craftsman. Decisions as to use of in-house apprenticeship programs or college tuition-refund programs, for example, will be based upon

EXHIBIT 11-7
Pedagogy as a reactive learning situation vs. proactive andragogy.

Resources for Learning	Required Conditions	Required Skills
Reactive Teacher in traditional course	Willingness to be dependent. Respect for authority. Commitment to learning as means to an end (e.g., degree). Competitive relationship with fellow students. (The way most of us were taught to learn—not recommended)	Ability to listen uncritically. Ability to retain information. Ability to take notes. Ability to predict exam questions.
Proactive Printed materials (and experts)	Intellectual curiosity. Spirit of inquiry. Knowledge of resources available. Healthy skepticism toward authority. Criteria for testing reliability and validity. Commitment to learning as a developmental process.	Ability to formulate questions answerable by data. Ability to identify data available in printed materials (e.g., by Table of Contents, Index, etc.). Ability to scan quickly. Ability to test data against criteria of reliability and validity. Ability to analyze data to produce answers to questions.
Resource people (supervisors, experts)	Institutional commitment to individual growth as capital investment. Definition of role of supervisor as including "resource for learning." Time availability by both supervisor and employee for conferences. Inclusion of both supervisor's and employee's learning accomplishments in reward system. Spirit of mutual assistance in growth and development.	*By Supervisor:* Ability to convey respect, caring, and support. Ability to provide data (and feedback) objectively and nonthreateningly. Ability to ask probing questions while keeping locus of responsibility in employee. Ability to use employees as resource for own learning. Ability to listen emphatically. *By Employee:* Ability to formulate goals. Ability to assess present level of performance. Ability to collect and analyze data about performance nondefensively. Ability to relate to supervisor as a resource for learning. Ability to be open and honest with supervisor.

EXHIBIT 11-7, continued

Resources for Learning	Required Conditions	Required Skills
On-the-job and life experiences	Collaborative relationships with colleagues. Commitment to learning as a developmental process. Institutional support for learning from mistakes. High valuation of self-direction.	Ability to collect data through: (1) own observation, (2) feedback from supervisors, peers, and subordinates, (3) analysis of records. Ability to use data for self-diagnosis of needs for self-improvement. Ability to accept responsibility for own learning. Ability to experiment with new behavior.

Source: From the *Journal of Continuing Education and Training,* Baywood Publishing Co., Inc, Farmingdale, N.Y.

anticipated career objectives, education, and experience of potential trainees—*and* anticipated company expenditures for T & D.

Recent research by Georgoff and Murdick covered several hundred large corporations and a review of the psychological learning literature.[11] Georgoff and Murdick developed a training and development grid that relates basic individual objectives to organizational objectives. This T & D Grid ©, shown in Exhibit 11-8, may be used as a practical tool to identify the priority of individuals' needs. Rank numbers indicate one individual's priorities that are being worked out by counseling. The grid also lists under cognitive, affective (emotional), and psychomotor objectives. When all activities have been listed appropriately on the grid, overlapping, overemphasis, underemphasis, and voids will be revealed.

DEVELOPING THE T & D PROGRAMS

The T & D program is specified in terms of "courses," on-the-job plans, and other experiences. The learning experiences should be presented in a "catalog" available to all employees. An example of pages from such a catalog issued by Westinghouse Electric Corp. are shown in Exhibit 11-9.

Characteristics of Programs

As indicated by Exhibit 11-9, companies may have a combination of various programs such as:

1. Courses directed toward immediate preparation for a new job
2. Courses directed toward improvement on the job

EXHIBIT 11-8
T&D grid©.

	Purposes			
	A Improvement of the individual's performance in his or her present position	B Improvement of the individual's ability to perform in an upgraded position	C Improvement of the general performance level of the organization	D Improvement of the individual independent of his or her job
Cognitive				
To understand and recall discrete and factual information	1			
To comprehend the meaning of concepts and abstract terminology				
To develop understanding of relationships among combinations of facts, terminology, and concepts				
To improve analytic and problem-solving skills		4		
To improve planning ability—that is, the ability to arrange and work out the details of a plan or idea		3		
To improve imaginative and creative thinking				
Affective				
To change prevailing attitudes, beliefs, and/or sentiments			2	
To improve the individual's behavior in interactions with others				
Psychomotor				
To improve motor, manual, and physical skills				

EXHIBIT 11-9
Catalog description of a typical course offering. *Source:* 1984 Education and Development Course Catalog. Courtesy of Westinghouse Electric Corporation.

803

Women in Business Management Seminar

Objectives:
This course prepares women to:

assume increased responsibility in managerial, professional, and other roles in Westinghouse

understand the principles of career planning and career development

grow in their ability to understand and apply management techniques

communicate effectively

handle interpersonal and intergroup relationships

participate equally with men in the management of the corporation

Description:
The opportunities available to women in business are expanding rapidly. This course addresses the many vital subjects to which women have had little exposure. Its primary objective is to help women further develop their business acumen and gain self-confidence in their ability to use it effectively in business careers. Women participating in this three day course will get an overview of management techniques, motivation, communication, career development, and interpersonal relationships. A major by-product of the course is the communications network that is established by the women attending this course.

Candidate Selection:
Ideal for newly appointed women managers or those about to be promoted, and for women in professional positions. Higher levels of clerical positions will also benefit greatly.

Length:
Three days, with evening sessions.

Management:
W. F. Morrison
Manager
Functional and Support Training

---

3. A hierarchy of courses within a field such as accounting or marketing
4. Corporate-wide integrated programs that lead to a high level of competence in management, accounting, engineering, etc.

Later in this chapter we will discuss courses according to their training methods. This T & D grouping includes apprentice programs, vestibule training, on-the-job training, off-the-job training, and on-and-off-the-job training.

Other characteristics of T & D programs that must be considered in developing policies for company T & D are:

1. Types of employees to be trained
2. Number of courses
3. Number of sessions per course
4. Length of meetings

5. Time of meetings: on company time, on personal time, or on part of each
6. Number of students per course and per class
7. Share of costs borne by employees, if any
8. Reward or promotion, if any, upon completion

Levels of Learning

A complete statement of instructional objectives should also include the level of achievement that the student will be asked to attain. It is helpful to illustrate the levels of learning by means of a simplified example. Suppose we wish to teach the student about leadership. At the lowest level of teaching, we would say that leadership is inducing someone to work toward a predetermined objective. We would explain "induce" and the total idea, and then require the student to be able to *recall* the meaning of leadership upon request. This level is the lowest step in Exhibit 11–10, which shows a five-step model for levels of learning.

The next level of learning is the *application* level. We would tell the student what things he or she must do to lead. In other words, the student applies principles.

Analysis, the next stage of advancement, means that the student can break up material into parts for greater understanding. We would examine the elements of leadership behavior, why such behavior induces people to act, and what research about leadership behavior appears to mean. A student who has a thorough understanding of leadership could then pass to *evaluation* of the behavior of specific individuals to say which of their actions promoted leadership and which did not.

EXHIBIT 11–10
Levels of learning.

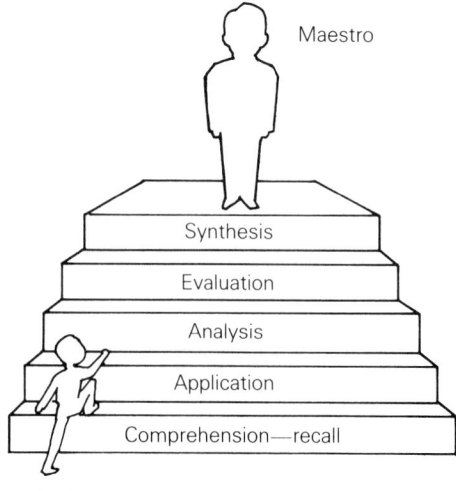

Finally, the most difficult level of teaching–learning is the level of *synthesis*. Synthesis is the creation of new ideas and patterns of thought. The instructor cannot give a formula or rule for synthesis; he or she can only *stimulate* the student to think independently. Thus, a student might arrive at a new description of leadership behavior or originate a new experiment that shows an unsuspected characteristic of leaders.

IMPLEMENTING THE T & D PROGRAM

Once the T & D program has been developed and the general direction and T & D organization have been established by long-range plans, the program must be implemented. Two major sets of activities must be carried out: (1) conducting instructional activities, and (2) recruiting, selecting, and enrolling the trainees.

The operations involved in carrying out the instructional activities are usually performed in parallel, and interact with the recruiting, selecting, and enrolling of trainees. We will, however, for convenience, discuss these two activities serially.

Developing the T & D Subjects, Content, and Techniques

Recently, much attention has been focused on training for job competencies. With this approach, a job is analyzed to determine exactly what skills are required to perform the job. Next, a particular training course is developed for subjects and content to train directly for these skills. Then appropriate techniques for teaching these skills are selected. The range of such techniques is indicated in Exhibit 11–11, which provides a guide to optimal matching.

Course material to be selected must be considered in terms of type of work as well as specific job. That is, should we train operative employees, professional employees, and management employees? How should we allocate funds to each of these groups? The answers are usually derived from judgments by top management based on recommendations from the P/HR manager.

Selecting Types of Training Methods

Once the subjects, the course contents, and the techniques to be used have been established, the types of training methods may be selected. (In many companies, the type of training program is established first and then the subject, contents, and techniques are chosen.) There are four basic training methods:

Apprenticeship and Cooperative T & D *Apprentice training* may be mainly off-job or entirely on-job training. The apprentice may attend a vocational

EXHIBIT 11-11
Teaching techniques.

Technique	Description	Suitability	Check points
Lecture	A talk to explain material, with little or no participation by the class in the form of discussion or questions.	For large groups. For orientation or easy-to-understand material.	Unless the preparation is very good, the audience may get lost at some point and miss all of the following ideas. Short lectures and brief applications or quizzes help.
Case study	A business problem situation is described in detail, with both relevant and irrelevant information given. The student is required to identify problems, develop alternative solutions, evaluate.	For small groups. Requires discussion and participation by all participants. The case-study method is used to develop skills at analyzing and solving complex unstructured problems and to provide broad simulated experience. It may also be used to develop group decision-making skills.	Students may get frustrated because the data are pretty much limited to the case material. Even in real life, however, similar limits are set by time and cost. Some students fail to participate unless called upon, and others may dominate the discussion unless controlled. Arguments may evolve around opinions rather than analysis of the "facts" of the case.
In-basket technique	Trainees are given a description of a company in some detail. Memos are then given to the trainees posing problems or asking for decisions.	For small groups. For developing analytical and decision-making skills. Outside data may be introduced by the trainees.	A good case and good questions are required. Considerable time may be required for discussion of students' replies.
Conferences and seminars	A speaker may lecture, or there may be no speaker, only a conference leader. Knowledge, ideas, and opinions are freely interchanged among all participants.	For broadening knowledge, stimulating new ideas, and changing attitudes. "Workshop seminars" may be used to develop skills.	Participants may stray from the subject. Hardening of attitudes and conflict may occur. Seminars away from the company tend to keep politics out of the viewpoints expressed.
Programmed instruction and computer-assisted learning (learner-controlled instruction)	Programmed instruction and, usually, computer-assisted learning are rigid self-learning devices. The student is given material and tested on it immediately before proceeding to	For either large or small groups where cost is critical. Permits people to study at their own convenience.	Appropriate programs must be available. Students may drop out by stretching out their work.

EXHIBIT 11-11, continued

Technique	Description	Suitability	Check points
Simulation and gaming	A business situation or an entire industry is modeled so that the student may take actions and have the results reported back. Usually the model is stored in a computer.	For group projects. For developing decision-making skills requiring the integration of many factors.	The model should not be too simple, and the required learning of input formats should not be too complex. The students may just guess at their input decisions instead of making a good preanalysis. Computer reports of results should be returned to students well in advance of subsequent decisions.
Video and audio self-development programs	Lectures and rote learning material may be given on video equipment or tape cassettes.	For individual study at student's own pace. For learning facts. For developing skills when responses to the equipment are clear. For inspirational purposes, such as in sales training.	If the material is not clear, the student will become frustrated and drop out. The student's motivation must be strong to carry out a self-development program where reinforcement of motivation may be absent.
Remote TV live teaching	Instructor lectures to groups of students at remote classrooms. Usually, two-way voice communication is provided.	For a highly skilled lecturer working with groups of students located at widely separated company plants, this is an economical method. For courses that require relatively few questions to clarify points.	Instructors may outpace students if students do not take the initiative to slow them down. Associated written assignments have to be corrected and returned in the period between lectures to be effective.
Laboratory training	A change agent (consultant) devises means for groups of people in an organization to clarify their values, attitudes, and problems to improve understanding, motivation, and the working climate in general.	For groups of almost any size. For changing an organization's attitudes. For increasing organizational problem-solving capabilities.	Top management must understand its role and give strong backing to the change agent. Considerable time will be required before the impact of laboratory training becomes evident. High-level executives may have to devote a good deal of time to such programs.

357

EXHIBIT 11-11, continued

Technique	Description	Suitability	Check points
Managerial grid sessions	Six-phase program lasting from three to five years. Starts with upgrading managers' skills, continues to group improvement, improves intergroup relations, goes into corporate planning, develops implementation methods, and ends with an evaluation phase.	For rapidly growing and large companies where the considerable investment has time to pay off.	Check on progress in achieving objectives. Check on turnover of the managers involved.
T-group sessions, sensitivity training, group dynamics sessions	Participants are put in situations in which the views, behavior, and personality of each are subjected to examination and critique by the others.	For developing better understanding and better perceptions of co-workers.	Participants may not be able to stand the stress involved in learning about themselves. They may withdraw from the group or suffer psychological damage. Problems arising within the group must be resolved before the group breaks up.
Correspondence courses	Correspondence courses require students to read material on their own or to actually work on equipment that is supplied. Students mail their answers to the company or university that offers the course. In some cases exams must be proctored by local professional teachers.	For development of technical/manual skills. For training in specialized business subjects, such as accounting. For managerial development and broadening (for example, the Alexander Hamilton program).	Students must be highly motivated to study on their own. In some cases, students may have friends do the homework. Proctored exams will help reduce this problem.

school and work part time for a company or a skilled tradesman. In the United States the government regulates apprentice training under the Apprenticeship Act of 1937 and subsidizes many such programs. An apprentice program may run from two to 10 years.

Cooperative programs are also part on-job and part off-job programs. They are for people seeking professional and subprofessional careers. People in these programs are college students who either take reduced loads or who alternate between college and a selected company that cooperates with the college on the program. Such students get practical experience and some income while the cooperating company gets an opportunity to evaluate them as potential employees in the future. Such programs are usually initiated and controlled by the college.

Vestibule Training In *vestibule training* the employee works in a simulated environment to achieve the skills required on the job. For example, a machine shop with an instructor may be established at a plant to train shop workers. Vestibule learning makes it easy to transfer skills to the job. The advantage of vestibule training is that the machine and work conditions simulate the actual shopwork conditions, and a trainer works closely with the trainees. It is used for training workers thoroughly and quickly where the high cost is justified. A constant flow of trainees utilizing this duplicate machinery will help keep costs per trainee down.

On-the-Job Training *On-the-job training* consists of both formal training (supervision) and informal training. Formal training may be in the form of internships, job rotation, task-force or committee assignments, and the "buddy" system for new employees. Essentially, the trainee works closely with skilled people, perhaps under the sponsorship of a single person, and learns by watching, doing, and listening to instructions and evaluations of his or her work. It is applicable to almost all employees and occupations. On-the-job training should be a part of all jobs. In some cases, however, specific learning objectives may be established and a schedule set. "Grooming" an executive to take over as president of a company or training a clerk to become a production planning and control specialist are examples.

Off-the-Job Training *Off-the-job training* includes going to college, vocational school, high school, or special seminars and conventions. It may include correspondence courses and tuition-refund programs. For high-level company executives, it may be working for the federal government for one or two years on a leave of absence. It is generally more expensive than other types of training for large numbers of employees. It is advantageous when only one or two people require training in a specific skill or when no expertise is available within the company. It is advantageous because it brings in fresh ideas to the company.

Recruiting and Training the Instructors

When traditional courses are given, that is, those that require instructors, coaches, or seminar leaders, these people must be identified and recruited. Often the new instructors are very competent technically but need some coaching in teaching. In other cases, when a number of instructors for different sections of the same course are required, the instructors must be trained in the course material itself.

> A 2,000-employee division of a large company wished to introduce a course in reading improvement. A psychologist in the Personnel Department developed the course and materials. He conducted the course several times and recruited instructors from the graduates. The course could then be offered several nights a week to different small groups of professional and managerial personnel. The psychologist gathered evaluation data and coached the instructors from time to time.

Special training must be provided for instructors guiding *Learner-Controlled Instruction (LCI)*. LCI is effective for adults because it is adapted to the particular experience, level of knowledge, and time availability of a variety of trainees. In essence, the learner manages his or her own learning under a "contract" to achieve specified objectives (Exhibit 11–12). Video, computer-assisted, and programmed learning manuals are commonly associated with LCI. There are many instances when more freeform approaches such as independent research or creative expression are more appropriate.

The Process of Teaching–Learning

The training director wants to make sure that all instructors thoroughly understand the teaching–learning process. Learning is not accomplished

EXHIBIT 11–12
Learner-controlled instruction (LCI).

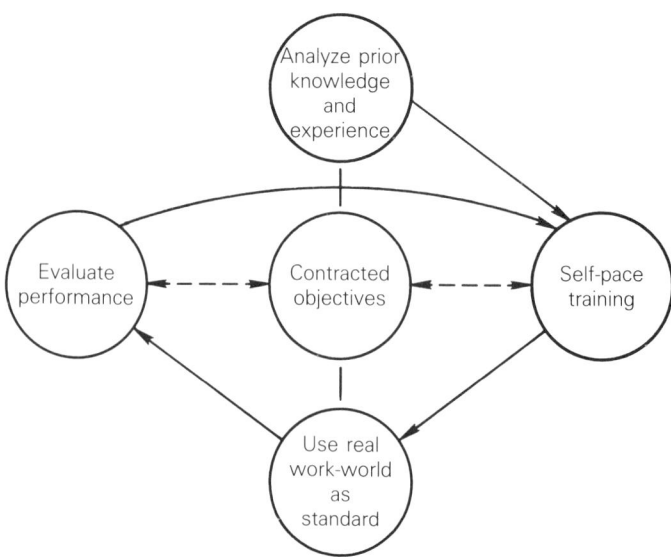

by mere notetaking; ideas must be actively interchanged between instructor and student.

There are eight steps in the teaching–learning process. (1) The would-be learner must be receptive and motivated to learn. If the organizational climate has not led to this motivation, the burden on the instructor is a heavy one. All instructors should try to reinforce the student's interest in learning, regardless of initial readiness.

The training director (2) prepares objectives for the course. In general, is the course supposed to train, develop, educate, or rehabilitate? Then, more specifically, what will the instructional goals be? Robert F. Mager, an authority on instructional objectives, states that such objectives should give:

1. A statement of the desired behavior of the student at the end of the course
2. The conditions under which the student can perform the desired behavior
3. The level of achievement he or she will be asked to attain[12]

The instructor (3) must analyze the student's present level of performance—his or her initial behavior. (4) The teaching–learning tasks may now be identified. In other words, what does the student need to know or do in order to perform the behavioral objectives?

The instructor (5) prepares the course by developing stimuli that will lead to the next step. (6) The student responds. For example, the student might be asked to read through these steps in the teaching–learning process and then to draw a diagram such as Exhibit 11–11. If the response is a good one, the next step follows. (7) Reinforcement is given in the form of a passing grade. The major reinforcement is passing the entire course. Each time the student passes one portion of the course, he or she will feel one step closer to achieving the goal of getting credit for the whole course.

Finally, in many learning situations, (8) the learner must be able to *generalize* his or her behavior. For example, if students are being taught how to interview a particular job-seeker, could they apply the principles learned whenever required to interview another candidate?

Preparing Instructional Materials

The preparation or selection of good instructional materials is sometimes taken for granted despite its importance. Good notes prepared and distributed in professional binders can contribute to the trainees' perceptions of the importance of the course. Good audiovisual material can make the learning process easier. In some courses, machinery, lab equipment, or special equipment (such as devices to pace speed-readers) are a necessity.

The preparation of instructional materials is frequently a joint operation of the instructor, who has the technical expertise, and the training director, who has experience with teaching processes. The training director is also concerned with keeping such expenses within budget.

The training director also must make sure that the materials are available on time. The two major factors to be considered are time to prepare the notes, and the time to edit the notes, do the artwork, and reproduce the notes. If the reproduction is to be done by a vendor, the training director must determine the lead time, get the material to the vendor sufficiently early, and then follow up on progress.

Arranging for Facilities and Times

The matching of facilities, times of classes, courses, and instructors for large T & D programs requires careful planning. One table or chart can show this match (Exhibit 11–13).

The experienced training director will probably have a checklist whenever facilities are being arranged for. A few matters (among many) that may be overlooked include:

1. Are the facilities and courses being held after work with too little time for dinner or too much time between the end of work and beginning of class?
2. Are there alternate plant sites so that a class may be located near the trainees?
3. Is the class ending late at night in a high-crime area?
4. Is the classroom large enough to accommodate the enrolled trainees comfortably?
5. Have arrangements been made with plant engineering to have air conditioning or heat as necessary?

TRAINING COURSE SCHEDULE FALL 1985

DAY	CLASS MEETS	COURSE TITLE	INSTRUCTOR	CONF. ROOM #	NO. ENROLLED	COURSE CHG. NO.
MONDAY	5-7	PRINC. OF MATH	MR. BROWN	B6	28	70-350
	10-11:45	R16.58	DR. KING	B1	15	60-405
TUESDAY	5-6:30	FILM TECH	DR. SHERMAN	A2	25	60-358
	5-7	REPORT W'NG	DR. WOOD	G2	12	60-360
WEDNESDAY	10-11:45	R16.58	DR. KING	B1	15	70-405
	5-7	TRANSISTORS	MR. WONG	D2	18	60-407
THURSDAY	5-7	VIBRATIONS	DR. LASKY	D2	18	60-356
	5-7	HEAT TRANSFER	DR. PION	A6	16	60-410
FRIDAY	2-3:15	NUM. METHODS	MR. HOUGH	B1	22	70-412

EXHIBIT 11–13
T & D planning board.

6. Has the assignment of the classroom been scheduled in advance and confirmed recently by a formal process?

Recruiting Trainees

The process of recruiting and selecting trainees depends on four considerations:

1. Desired career paths and personal career goals of individuals
2. Managers' selection of employees for reasons such as preparing employees for promotion or raising performance in problem areas
3. Fulfillment of affirmative action and EEO requirements for protected classes of workers
4. Aid to workers of particular government and social interest, such as hardcore unemployed, older workers, handicapped workers, ex-convicts, or rehabilitated drug/alcohol abusers

Selection of trainees implies that these people are being prepared for higher-paid work or promotion. Completion or grades on courses have been used as *criteria* for future assignments or *predictors* of future career advancement. This brings the selection process fully within EEO and affirmative action imperatives.

Basic policies may restrict some T & D programs to certain classes of workers, for example, managers only or sales employees only. Educational requirements for certain technical courses such as a college degree in engineering may be justified. General courses such as speed-reading, introduction to computers in business, business writing, interpersonal skills, and so forth may attract more candidates than can be handled at one time. The managers must then establish priorities in terms of company criteria and goals, the career status of the individual, and EEO considerations.

Once criteria have been established for selection of trainees, the forthcoming courses or other T & D offerings should be publicized in a memo or brochure giving criteria, times, and locations. Employees then apply for T & D based upon past management appraisals or their own special desires. Managers nominate employees for the programs on the basis of these applications or their own initiatives. The T & D director notifies managers if the classes are oversubscribed so that the manager can drop low-priority candidates.

CONDUCTING THE TEACHING ACTIVITIES

The T & D director should monitor the actual teaching to make sure that classes are being held as scheduled, that instructors are receiving support in terms of preparation of teaching materials and availability of supplies, and that trainees are attending sessions.

Certificates must be prepared to award graduates, and grades or completion notifications must be entered in the HR information system.

EVALUATING THE T & D SYSTEM

The cost and difficulty of measuring the impact of T & D upon the individual trainees and upon the productivity of the company usually discourage companies from the attempt. "We know it pays off, but not how much" is the usual feeling of top management. The decision that an evaluation should be carried out is, therefore, the starting point of the process.

All *T & D evaluation* is done by applying judgement to data. An evaluation should be valid, that is, based on evidence that is reasonably complete and accurate, represents what it is intended to represent, and identifies cause and effect. The evaluation should be reliable in that reasonably consistent conclusions would be reached by qualified evaluators who use the same data.

The subjects or phases of T & D and their evaluation will now be discussed.

Purposes The purposes of the evaluation should be defined in terms of the users and their purposes. The evaluation that top management desires and the evaluation that an instructor desires, for example, are quite different. Top management, for example, will be interested in the "bottom line," that is, the cost–benefit relation, while the instructor will evaluate the results according to whether the course is achieving specified learning objectives. The format may be a brief summary for managers and lengthy and technical for lower-level P/HR staff people.

What Will Be Measured and Against What Standards? The purposes, scope, and objectives of the overall T & D program should be measured. Are the purposes defined? Is the scope adequate for the purposes? Are T & D objectives applicable to jobs? Are measurable objectives defined? Will the program meet future needs?

The organization and administration of the training should be measured. Exhibit 11–14 suggests a possible assessment format.

The training itself should be measured in terms of what is learned. Course learning objectives can be established as standards and evaluation may be made by the instructor, by the trainees themselves, or by auditors. The teaching methods and performance of the instructors may be measured with consideration for course content and trainee capabilities.

Finally, the results of the T & D may be measured. Some criteria could be:

1. Impact of the total program on the productivity of the company
2. Applicability of T & D objectives to careers and impact on careers
3. Impact of T & D on individual job performance

Scope and Comprehensiveness Evaluations cost money and therefore cost–benefit considerations apply here also. Evaluations may be one-shot

EXHIBIT 11-14
Evaluation of organization and administration of training.

Item to be evaluated (add others appropriate to specific situation)	Excellent	Satisfactory	Weak	Inapplicable	Kind of data used as basis for judgment in evaluating	Remarks and observations
1. Is there a clear statement of training policy?						
2. Have resources necessary to implement it been provided?						
3. Is line responsibility for training recognized?						
4. Is enough staff assistance on training provided?						
5. Is delineation of line and staff responsibilities understood and accepted?						
6. How effectively are line and staff training efforts coordinated?						
7. What is the level of competence of the training staff?						
8. What is the level of training competence of the line?						
9. What is the general attitude of management (all levels) toward training?						
10. What is the general attitude of employees toward it?						
11. How well are orientation and induction accomplished in actual practice?						
12. How effectively are such resources as staff conferences, job rotation, guided experience used in meeting training needs?						

EXHIBIT 11-14, continued

Item to be evaluated (add others appropriate to specific situation)	Excellent	Satisfactory	Weak	Inapplicable	Kind of data used as basis for judgment in evaluating	Remarks and observations
13. How adequately does the plan for determining training needs operate?						
14. How clear are the goals of the training that is given?						
15. How carefully are plans for training made?						
16. etc.						

Source: U.S. Civil Service Commission

affairs for one-shot courses or may extend over years for continuing courses or the entire T & D program. In many cases, it may be found that T & D solves a problem in the workplace so that no further evaluation is worthwhile. Simple tools, such as questionnaires, may be used, or complex, statistically designed experiments may be applied. Exhibit 11–15 shows the application of such experiments in five organizations.

Authority and Responsibility If evaluations are to be made, assignment of authority and responsibility for the evaluations must be clearly assigned by management. Adequate funds and trained personnel must be provided. The evaluator should have credibility for competence and objectivity.

Sources of Data The evaluations require that methodology be carefully planned to gather valid data. Sources of data are:

1. General impressions of people concerned with the T & D program and its results
2. Reports by managers or staff people
3. Supervisors' ratings of trainees who have completed the programs vs. nontrainees
4. Observed behavior of trainees
5. Scores on tests
6. Interviews with trainees
7. Questionnaires completed by trainees
8. Before and after measurements of trainees and measurements of successive groups of trainees over time
9. Costs vs. estimated benefits[13]

EXHIBIT 11–15
Research summary measuring T & D effectiveness in five organizations.

Organization	Study Type: What Measured	Summary of Methodology	Results
Hospital	Measuring on-the-job behavior change as rated by subordinates and managers.	Measurement of change from before training to post-training, and comparing experimental and control groups. Ratings by subordinates and boss.	Statistically significant behavior change ranging from .0001 to .001 level of confidence.
Electronic	Measuring on-the-job behavior change as rated by subordinates and managers.	Measurement of change from before training to post-training, and comparing experimental and control groups. Ratings by subordinates and boss.	Statistically significant behavior change ranging from .01 to .03 level of confidence.
Food warehousing and distribution	Measuring on-the-job behavior change as rated by subordinates and managers.	Measurement of change from before training to post-training, and comparing experimental and control groups. Ratings by subordinates and boss.	Statistically significant behavior change ranging from .01 to .03 level of confidence.
Pharmaceutical	Measuring on-the-job behavior change as rated by subordinates and managers; measure of knowledge improvement.	Measurement of change from before training to post-training, and comparing experimental and control groups. Ratings by subordinates and boss. Pre- and post-test of knowledge of supervisory skills.	Statistically significant behavior change ranging from .0001 to .001 level of confidence; knowledge improvement of 64%.
Hospital	Measuring on-the-job behavior change as rated by subordinates and managers; measure of knowledge improvement.	Pre- and post-test of knowledge of supervisory skills. Ratings by subordinates and supervisor's managers on behavior change.	Statistically significant behavior change at or beyond .05 level of confidence; knowledge improvement of 90%.

NOTE: Statistical significance of .01 indicates that a change of difference as large as the one observed would occur only one time in one hundred; .001 that a change that large would occur once in a thousand times by chance. The accepted standard of significance in the social sciences is the .05 level, or that a change of that magnitude would occur only five times in one hundred by chance.

Source: John H. Zenger and Kenneth Hargis, "Assessing Training Results: It's Time to Take the Plunge," *Training and Development Journal,* January 1982, p. 15. Copyright 1982, *Training and Development Journal,* American Society for Training and Development. Reprinted with permission. All rights reserved.

DEVELOPMENT

Exhibit 11–16 shows some evaluation methods used to collect data and who makes the evaluation.

Reporting Unless the evaluations are reported to decision makers, they will be wasted. Short summary or exception reports and cost–benefit reports

EXHIBIT 11–16
Evaluation strategies.

Focus	Evaluation Methods	Who evaluates?
Employee-students		
Mental skills	Achievement tests, before and after	Instructor
	Reports	Instructor
	Work performance appraisal	Manager
Attitudes	Attitude measurement questionnaires	Training director
	Course evaluation	Training director
	Behavioral measures, such as attendance records	Instructor, manager
Manual skills	Work performance appraisals	Manager
	Job performance tests	Foreman or supervisor
	Observation by others	Key employees
	Rating scales	Supervisor
Instructors		
Teaching–learning skills	Questionnaires	Student, training director
	Auditing of class sessions	Training director
Effectiveness	Measure of improvement in student or degree of achievement of behavioral objectives	Manager, training director
Training director		
Administration of the training program	Measures of organizational performance, before and after	Manager of human resources and line managers
	Observation of preparatory and support activities	Manager of human resources
Value of the program	Cost–benefit analysis	Manager of human resources

should go to top management, and technical analysis to the T & D department.

MODIFICATION AND MAINTENANCE

We can always improve any man-made system, and the T & D system fits this category. Improvements may be made based on evaluations or analysis of the total system in a redesign effort. In addition, changes in organization of the company, changes in the company's environment, and changes in the characteristics of the work force may require *maintenance* changes in the T & D system.

Specifically, maintenance are those changes not requiring system-wide redesign. For the computerized HR management system, maintenance is required for increasing the scope of the data base, generating new T & D files and output reports, modifying or adding computer application programs, and correcting errors in data entered in the data base. Additions or transfers of output or input terminals for instructional purposes would also be considered maintenance.

Introduction of new department policies (e.g., eligibility for refund), new course application forms, or the development of a new process for enrolling course applicants are other examples of system maintenance.

THE T & D INFORMATION SYSTEM

In companies that use a manual *T & D information system*, the following documents are utilized:

- □ *Inputs*
  Company plans
  HR management plans
  T & D resource allocations
  Personnel profile records
  Records of potential instructors
  Company T & D policies
  Policies and EEO guidelines
  Employee T & D application forms
- □ *Outputs*
  Course offerings and course outlines
  Schedule of course times and locations
  Approved application forms
  Evaluation reports
  Budget proposals
  Reports to managers on course completion by their subordinates
  Updated personnel inventory records
  EEO-required information reports

THE COMPUTERIZED T & D MANAGEMENT SYSTEM

A computerized HR management system greatly facilitates the management of T & D. Described briefly, several features of such a system permit greater efficiency:

1. The career plan, the educational background, and the planned courses for each individual may be called out on a video terminal. The manager, in conference with the individual, may review, revise, and recommend training for the next term. (Chapter 12, Career Management, discusses career planning and expands on the relationship between T & D and careers.)
2. A catalog of courses, course descriptions, and instructors may be stored in the computer and easily updated; this catalog may be searched at a terminal or printed for distribution.
3. Records of each course completed by an employee may be easily retained and included in personnel inventory printouts. Also, for a given course, a list of all people who completed it, or the number who have enrolled for it in the past may be called out at a terminal.
4. A file of instructors may be maintained by course, by quality of teaching based on past evaluations, and by time availability.
5. The computer can match facilities and instructors to times of availability of each.
6. Student enrollments in terms of applications, approved applications, and dropouts at any point of time may be made available to plan courses and required instructional materials.
7. Computers may be used in the instructional process, even permitting students to take the course at home.
8. Student evaluation of facilities, instructional methods and materials, and instructors may be entered directly on a terminal and the results analyzed by computer.
9. T & D expenses may be analyzed and compared with estimated benefits. Summary reports to managers may be readily prepared.

SUMMARY

The development of individual capabilities of members of an organization is a process performed by a subsystem of the human resource management system. This we have called the T & D subsystem. The system is composed of line managers, the manager of human resources, and the training or development director and staff. The inputs processed are the employees of the company.

Companies adopt a particular basic policy with respect to T & D. It may be laissez-faire or it may consist of a major, integrated systems effort.

In order to understand and apply principles for T & D, you must study some basic concepts. These concepts deal with:

1. The long-range objectives of the T & D process
2. The processes of teaching and learning
3. The levels of learning
4. Teaching–learning techniques
5. The characteristics of programs for manual workers, professional employees, and managers
6. Organizing for T & D
7. Developing program content
8. Identifying and selecting trainees
9. Administering the instruction
10. Evaluating the system
11. Modifying and maintaining the system

Once you have these background concepts in mind, you are ready to lay out a plan for T & D and to execute the plan. In essence, the plan must start with macro objectives—the total organizational needs for development over a two-to-five-year period, let us say.

Next you need to establish the amount of money to invest in this T & D program.

Within the scope of macro objectives and allocated funds, you may then establish basic policies for the T & D system. You would determine policies for matching the employees to be developed to the funds that are available.

The stage is now set for the detailed development of courses and execution of the program. You would plan specific courses for the year ahead, obtain instructors, classrooms, equipment. You would schedule class times, in line with predetermined policies. Publicize the courses and obtain definite enrollments approved by employees' managers. You would then conduct and monitor the courses.

Every operation or process in business should be measured to determine how well the system involved is working. You may measure the T & D system as a whole, and you may measure "components" in the system. You are interested in system effectiveness, that is, in the degree to which the T & D system is achieving system objectives. You are also interested in the relationship between the benefits and the cost of the system.

The structure and process of the T & D system are tied together by the flow of information. The typical hardcopy forms and reports for such an information system are listed as inputs or outputs of the system. When the T & D management system is computerized as part of a computerized HR management system, tremendous improvements in planning, implementing, and controlling T & D are possible. One of the most important gains is the rapid preparation of all kinds of reports useful to trainees, their managers, top management, the training director, and the P/HR manager.

KEY CONCEPTS

T & D needs

Training

Employee development

Education

Rehabilitation

Behavioral learning theory

Cognitive learning theory

Pedagogy

Andragogy

Apprentice training

Vestibule training

On-the-job training

Off-the-job training

Learner-Controlled Instruction (LCI)

T & D evaluation

T & D information system

NOTES

1. William R. Tracey, *Managing Training and Development Systems* (New York: AMACOM, 1974), p. 4.
2. Jeremy Main, "Work Won't Be the Same Again," *Fortune*, June 28, 1982, p. 60.
3. *Training Programs & Tuition Aid Plans*, PPF Survey No. 123, Washington, D.C.: The Bureau of National Affairs, October 1978.
4. Lester A. Digman, "How Well-Managed Organizations Develop Their Executives," *Organizational Dynamics*, Autumn 1978.
5. Judy Cureton and Bob Cureton, "Is Training an Ivory Tower?" *Training and Development Journal*, February 1983.
6. D. H. Bullock and T. F. Gilbert, *Human Competence* (New York: McGraw-Hill, 1978), and Brian P. Murphy, "Policy, Procedure, and Practice in Technical Training," *Training and Development Journal*, March 1983.
7. John Dewey, *Democracy and Education* (New York: Macmillan, 1916), pp. 89–90.
8. See for example, Robert M. W. Travers, *Essentials of Learning*, 4th ed. (New York: Macmillan, 1977), Part II, "The Reductionist Position."
9. See Nelson F. DuBois, George F. Alverson, and Richard K. Staley, *Educational Psychology and Instructional Decisions* (Homewood, Ill.: Irwin, 1979), and Travers, *Essentials of Learning*, ibid.
10. Eduard C. Lindeman, *The Meaning of Adult Education* (New York: New Republic, 1926).
11. David M. Georgoff and Robert G. Murdick, "A Matrix Model for Planning the Training and Development for Employee Groups," *IEEE Transactions on Engineering Management*, May 1980, p. 43.
12. Robert F. Mager, *Preparing Instructional Objectives* (Palo Alto, Ca.: Fearnon Publishers, 1962).
13. See, for example, Stephen B. Sloan, "How Milliken Measures Training Program Effectiveness," *Management Accounting*, July 1981.

REVIEW AND DISCUSSION QUESTIONS

1. Distinguish among training, development, rehabilitation, and education.
2. How would you diagnose T & D needs in terms of company objectives and employee objectives?
3. What techniques are used to gather data for diagnosing T & D needs?
4. (a) Obtain several annual reports of companies. From statements of company objectives, give several possible T & D objectives for the companies: (b) Develop a T & D mission statement for one of the companies.
5. Distinguish between the behaviorist and cognitive theories of learning. Discuss how each theory could be applied in corporate T & D.
6. What is the role of reinforcement in learning new concepts or extinguishing old ones? Give an example of each in a business setting.
7. In what ways should the teaching of adults be different from the teaching of children?
8. For each technique listed in Exhibit 11–11, give a hypothetical problem in a business where the technique could be applied appropriately in T & D to solve the problem.
9. Describe and discuss each level of learning, giving a specific example of each.
10. What are the two major activities for implementing a T & D program? List the implementation steps.
11. (a) Consider the decision as to whether classes should be held on company time, on the employees' time, or on part of each. Give the advantages and disadvantages for each. (b) Consider the decision as to whether (1) a course should be given by the company at its plant, or (2) the employees should be sent to a noncompany-sponsored seminar or university course. Give the advantages and disadvantages of each.
12. A company wishes to give a course in reading improvement (speed and comprehension) to about 20 executives with an average salary of $35,000. Prepare a list of estimated costs and benefits stating your assumptions. Convert all benefits into dollars (estimated).
13. Discuss the potential uses and roles of the computer in corporate T & D 10 years hence.

BIBLIOGRAPHY

Bartlett, C. J. "Equal Employment Opportunity Issues in Training." *Human Factors* 20, 1978.

Bass, Bernard, and James A. Vaughan. *The Psychology of Learning for Managers.* American Foundation for Management Research, 1965.

Bass, Bernard M., and James A. Vaughan. *Training in Industry: The Management of Learning.* Belmont, Ca.: Wadsworth, 1966.

Bower, Gordon H., and Ernest R. Hilgard. *Theories of Learning*, 5th ed. Englewood Cliffs, N.J.: Prentice-Hall, 1981.

Carnevale, Anthony, and Harold Goldstein. *Employee Training: Its Changing Role and an Analysis of New Data*. Washington, D.C.: American Society of Training Directors, 1983.

Cone, William F. "Guidelines for Training Specialists." *Training and Development Journal*, January 1974.

Cox, John H. "A New Look at Learner–Controlled Instruction." *Training and Development Journal*, March 1982.

Craig, Robert L., Ed. *Training and Development Handbook: A Guide to Human Resource Development*. New York: McGraw-Hill, 1976.

Craig, Robert L., and Christine J. Evers. "Employers As Educators: The Shadow Education System." In *Business and Higher Education: Towards New Alliances*, ed. Gerald G. Gold. San Francisco: Jossey-Bass, 1981.

Deming, Basil. *Evaluating Job-Related Training*. Englewood Cliffs, N.J.: Prentice-Hall, 1983.

Digman, L. A. "How Companies Assess Development Needs." In *Proceedings of the 40th Annual Meeting of the Academy of Management*, ed. Richard C. Huseman. Detroit, Michigan, August 9–13, 1980.

Feeney, Edward J. "Beat the High Cost of Training Through LCI." *Training and Development Journal*, September 1981.

Galagan, Patricia. "The Numbers Game: Putting Value on Human Resource Development." *Training and Development Journal*, August 1983.

Georgoff, David M., and Robert G. Murdick. "A Matrix Model for Planning the Training and Development Programs for Employee Groups." *IEEE Transactions on Engineering Management*, May 1980.

Glueck, William F. *Personnel: A Diagnostic Approach*, 3rd ed., revised by George T. Milkovich. Dallas: Business Publications, 1982.

Harel, Gedaliahu H., and Loretta K. Conen. "Expectancy Theory Applied to the Process of Professional Obsolescence," *Public Personnel Management Journal*, Spring 1982.

Kirkpatrick, Donald L. "Determining Supervisory Training Needs and Setting Objectives." *Training and Development Journal*, May 1978.

Knowles, Malcolm. *The Adult Learner: A Neglected Species*, 2nd ed. Houston, Tex.: Gulf, 1978.

Langdon, Danny G. "The Individual Development Program." *Training and Development Journal*, March 1982.

Levinson, Harry. "Executive Development: What You Need to Know," *Training and Development Journal*, September 1981.

Lindeman, Eduard C. *The Meaning of Adult Education*. New York: New Republic, 1926.

Lusterman, Seymour. "Education for Work." *Conference Board Record*, May 1976.

Mager, Robert F. *Preparing Instructional Objectives*. Palo Alto, Ca.: Fearon Publishers, 1962.

McGehee, William. "Training and Development Theory, Policies and Practices." In *ASPA Handbook of Personnel and Industrial Relations*. Washington, D.C.: Bureau of National Affairs, 1979.

Moore, Michael L., and Philip Dutton. "Training Needs Analysis: Review and Critique." *Academy of Management Review*, July 1978.

Owen, Steven, H. Parker Blount, and Henry Moscow. *Educational Psychology.* Boston: Little, Brown, 1978.

Reeser, Clayton. "Managerial Obsolescence—An Organizational Dilemma." *Personnel Journal*, January 1977.

Smith, E. Paul. "Measuring Professional Obsolescence: A Half-Life Model for the Physician." *Academy of Management Review*, October 1978.

This, Leslie E., and Gordon L. Lippitt. "Learning Theories and Training." *Training and Development Journal*, June 1979.

Tracey, William R. *Managing Training and Development Systems.* New York: AMACOM, 1974.

United States Civil Service Commission. *Assessing and Reporting Training Needs and Programs.* Washington, D.C.: U.S. Government Printing Office, December 1961.

Warren, Malcolm W. *Training for Results: A Systems Approach to the Development of Human Resources in Industry*, 2nd ed. Reading, Mass.: Addison–Wesley, 1979.

Weiss, Alan. "How to Tell if HRD is Paying Off in Your Organization." *Training HRD*, October 1978.

Wexley, Kenneth N., and Gary P. Latham. *Developing and Training Human Resources in Organizations.* Glenview, Ill.: Scott Foresman, 1981.

Wong, Martin R., and John D. Raulerson. *A Guide to Systematic Instructional Design.* Englewood Cliffs, N.J.: Prentice-Hall, 1974.

Yoder, Dale, and Herbert G. Heneman, Jr., Eds. *Training and Development.* Washington, D.C.: The Bureau of National Affairs, 1977.

Zenger, John H., and Kenneth Hargis, Eds. "Assessing Training Results: It's Time to Take the Plunge." *Training and Development Handbook: A Guide to Human Resource Development.* New York: McGraw-Hill, 1976.

Career Management

CHAPTER OUTLINE

Reasons for Interest in Career Management

What Is a Career?

Career Management

Relationship to other HR Management Activities □ Responsibility for Career Management

Career Planning

Organizational Career Planning □ Individual Career Planning

Career Development

Job Assignments □ Training and Other Learning Experiences □ Evaluation and Feedback

Summary

Key Concepts

Notes

Review and Discussion Questions

Bibliography

OBJECTIVES

1. Define what is meant by a career.
2. Explain organizational career planning and describe how it is done in a firm.
3. Describe how career paths can be used within an organization.
4. Develop a career-planning process for an individual.
5. Explain how career management, career planning, and career development are interrelated and, in turn, related to other HR management activities.

SPOTLIGHT:
Louis P. Benson

Louis P. Benson, Ph.D., is both an educator and businessman. He has served on the faculties of Kent State University in Kent, Ohio, and the City University of New York. Presently he is an adjunct professor in the College of Business of Nova University.

Following a full-time career in academe, Lou Benson entered the world of business as a consultant, designing personnel and management programs. His company, Benson and Associates, established in 1979, is currently one of the largest and most diversified personnel recruiting firms in South Florida.

Comments by Lou Benson

Progressive organizations are beginning to recognize that career management is an important component of effective human resource management. Unfortunately, many career programs are ill-conceived or fail to recognize that any career planning must consider individual needs as well as organizational needs. This is vividly illustrated by the following true-life situation:

"Hello, John, I'm Bill Rogers. I'm a recruiter for an executive search firm and I've been following your progress—or lack of it—with your bank. Do you have a few minutes to talk?"

Without hesitation, John replied, "Let me shut the door."

During the ensuing conversation, John detailed his career at the bank. He had been hired by the bank over 10 years ago after a two-year stint with a smaller bank. His current employer had been good to him, and he was relatively happy. The bank had paid for John's MBA program and had even given him a paid leave so he could go to school full-time one summer. He was promoted quickly at first from Assistant Branch Manager to Commercial Loan Officer. It had been over three years since his last promotion to Senior Vice-President.

The recruiter sensed some dissatisfaction and probed deeper into John's career with the bank.

"I feel like I've been sent to every seminar offered by the American Banking Association and the American Management Association. They keep moving me from branch to branch, department to department. They say it's cross-training. I say it's busy work. The bank president introduced me to the chairman of the board once. He shook my hand and said he's heard of me and great things were in store. That was a year ago and nothing has changed."

The recruiter suggested John see his client company, an aggressive bank looking for a new president. John did not ask about salary. He just wanted to show his boss how the bank had underutilized him. John went on the interview and was hired.

John's boss, the bank president, was angry when he heard of John's resignation. He immediately called the director of human resources into his office and demanded an explanation. The director of human resources had pushed hard to have a career planning program implemented. The president fought for board approval and John was to be their showcase. John was being "groomed" to take over as president of the bank's newly acquired branches in the adjoining three-county area. The president and director of human resources knew they would face the ire of the chairman if they lost John to another bank.

The president then called John into his office and presented him with a counteroffer of the regional presidency. John felt the offer was too little, too late. He felt that if they had really wanted him and had been grooming him for a top management position, they would have communicated the opportunities *before* his resignation. Therefore, John stuck by his resignation and joined the competition.

In this case, the president and human resource director know the advantages of career planning. However, with their *organization-centered* approach, the bank developed a career plan to be implemented by the personnel department with careful attention given to the *organization*'s future growth but minimal consideration given to the employee's needs. The company made it a practice to promote from within, and each new employee was hired with a view to his or her future in the company. Employees like John were selected early in their careers to receive special attention as "fast trackers" with high management potential.

The career planning program allowed for employees to train for future assignments, and training included tuition payment for college courses and financial assistance to attend relevant seminars.

Unfortunately, John felt like a pawn in a bank chess game. Transfers and promotions were given without advance consultation. John recalled the case of a "fast track" accountant who was "promoted" to assistant branch manager, but resigned within a few months to return to his accounting career. The human resources department could not understand why he left such a good opportunity.

The moral of the story? Career planning must involve the individual in the planning process. In this case, organizational goals were not communicated to the employees whose careers were being planned. John appreciated the training and support, but with no clear purpose attached to the training, he wondered, "What was it all about?"

Had the bank involved John in the career planning, he would have realized all of the training and job rotation was to give him the breadth of experience to function as a regional bank president. Increased communication, involvement, and goal-setting between the bank and John would have prevented the resignation. John would never have shut the door.

We live in a society of highly mobile workers and ever-changing values, a society where the meaning of work and what constitutes a "successful" career are constantly being questioned and reevaluated. As a result, in recent years organizations as well as academicians have been displaying increasing interest in "careers," especially the management of careers.

A person's career is a major part of his or her life. Each individual should be aware of the need to manage work on the job, to manage career, and to manage life—in the sense that life represents an ongoing striving toward each individual's goals. The employer should recognize that human resources can appreciate with time if the employer actively aids each worker to develop his or her career. The HR manager plays a major role in conducting such efforts.

REASONS FOR INTEREST IN CAREER MANAGEMENT

Several factors account for the growing interest in career management:

1. Technological change and obsolescence have resulted in layoffs and underemployment, causing both individuals and organizations to recognize the need for planning a career and for developing multiple skills.
2. Increased education has created rising expectations about what constitutes a happy and fulfilling life. Workers of all ages, especially younger ones, are demanding greater personal and career autonomy and are less concerned with the demands of the organization.
3. Continuing pressure from affirmative action programs ensures not only that firms hire more females and members of protected groups, but also that they plan for the development and steady movement of these individuals through the organization structure.
4. Organizations typically lose as many as 30 to 50 percent of their "younger" employees during the first two years on the job. Similarly, there is a growing trend toward job changes in midcareer as members seek greater career satisfaction and a higher quality of life. Also, organizations are seeking ways to reduce the expensive turnover as more workers ask, "Am I in the right job?" "Would I be happier doing something else?" This type of question is being asked by all kinds of employees, from blue-collar to professional to top management.
5. Shortage of capable managers and certain skilled, professional, and technical workers has resulted in organizations looking for ways to develop such personnel from within through career planning and development.

As a result, human resource specialists are performing an ever-increasing role in designing and implementing programs to help employees focus on career goals in line with both company needs and personal goals. Let us now consider what a career is and clarify some important related terms.

What Is a Career?

A "career" means different things to different people. One person may think of a career as a series of jobs, as in "her career has encompassed four different jobs with three separate companies." Another individual may view a career as analogous to an occupation (i.e., "his career is in electronics"). All in all, the many different uses of the term *career* seem to have five distinct meanings:

1. Career = advancement. This views a career as mobility, usually upward, in an organization or professional hierarchy.
2. Career = profession. According to this viewpoint certain occupations constitute a career (such as managers, professionals, and military personnel), while other occupations are thought of as "jobs," such as waiters, laborers, or clerk-typists.
3. Career = lifelong sequence of jobs. Here we view a career as a rather objective summation of an individual's job history.
4. Career = lifelong series of role-related experiences. This is a subjective approach that focuses on the way one experiences work history, including such things as self-conceptions, aspirations, and failure.

The fifth meaning of "career" is the definition that most meets our purposes in this book: As proposed by Douglas T. Hall, a career is an individually perceived sequence of attitudes and behaviors associated with work-related experiences and activities over the span of the person's life.[1] This definition includes both objective aspects (item 3 above) and subjective aspects (item 4 above) over an entire lifetime. At the same time, it makes no judgments as to what represents advancement (item 1) for a particular individual. That is, the degree of "success" of a person's career is based on one's own assessment rather than someone else's.

A few other concepts are basic to understanding this chapter and need to be defined. They are career planning, career development, career paths, and career management. *Career planning* is the process of choosing occupations, organizations, and routes one's career will follow. *Career development* comprises those programs and activities undertaken to achieve a personal career plan. A *career path* is the sequential pattern of jobs that form one's career. *Career management* is the process of designing and implementing goals, plans, and strategies to enable the organization to satisfy human resource needs while allowing individuals to achieve their career goals. Thus, career management involves the integration of career planning and career development. We will consider these concepts in some length in this chapter and will begin by examining what is involved in career management and how it relates to other HR management activities.

CAREER MANAGEMENT

We have defined career management as a process of designing and implementing goals, plans, and strategies to enable the organization to satisfy human resource needs while allowing individuals to achieve their career goals. Thus, it is a highly inclusive process in which managers, human resource specialists, parties external to the organization, and individuals themselves all share in the responsibility.

As illustrated in Exhibit 12–1, career management integrates the three distinct but highly interrelated functions of individual career planning, or-

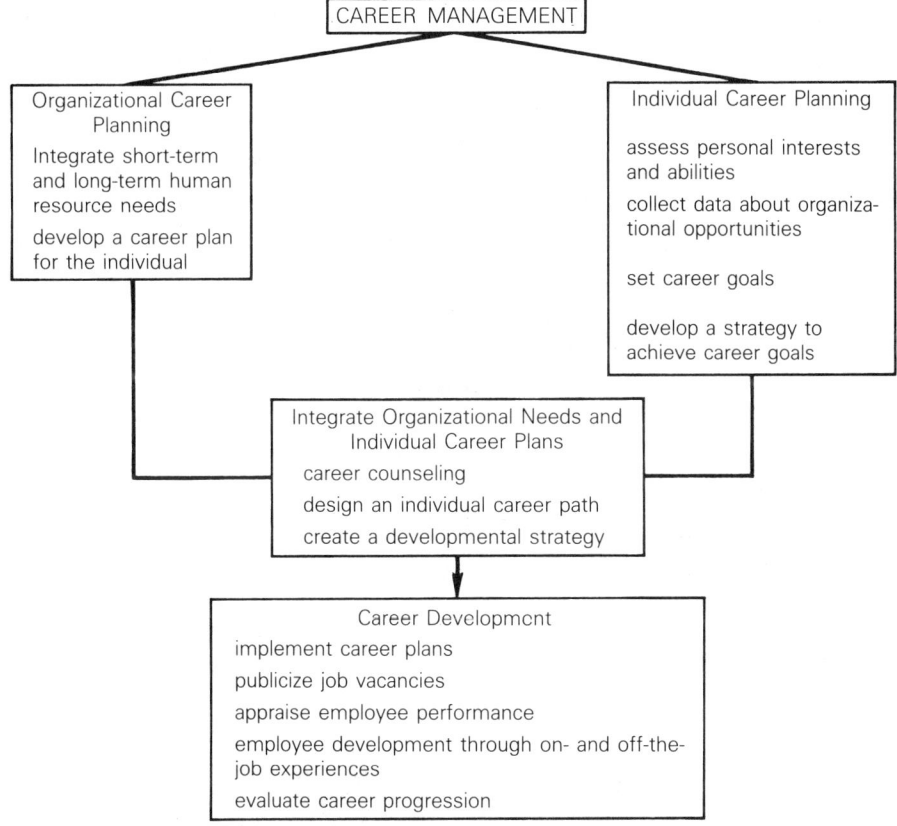

EXHIBIT 12–1
The career management model.
Source: Michael R. Carrell and Frank E. Kuzmits, *Personnel: Management of Human Resources,* Columbus, Oh.: Merrill, 1982, p. 408. Copyright © 1982 by Charles E. Merrill Publishing Co. Reprinted by permission.

ganizational career planning, and career development. Since career management is an integrating function, let us consider two important questions: How does it relate to other human resource activities? Who is responsible for it?

Relationship to Other HR Management Activities

Career management is related to all human resource development activities such as recruiting, selection, training and development, compensation, and promotion. For example, one's choice of an organization is influenced by recruiting policies and practices; job choice and job assignments are affected by selection and internal staffing policies; career progression is influenced by job design and performance standards; even transfers and retirement are influenced by benefits and compensation programs.

At the same time, career management must be an integral part of human resource planning if it is to succeed. (See Exhibit 12–2.) Unless the

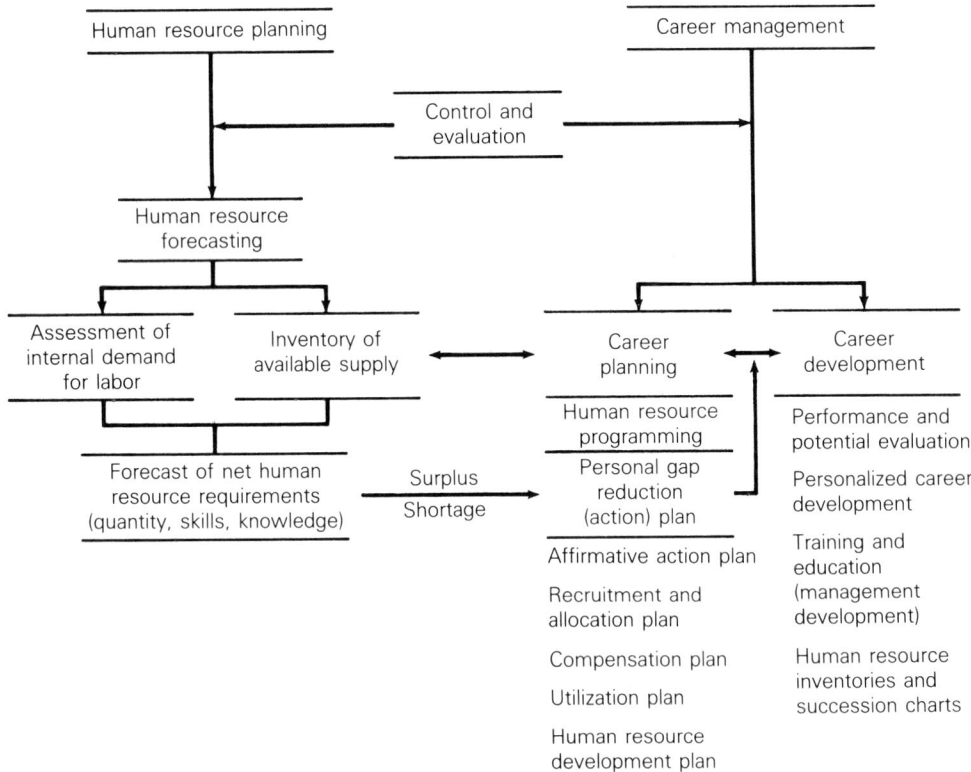

EXHIBIT 12–2
Interface between career management and human resource planning.

Source: Adapted from Thomas Gutteridge, "A Comparison of Perspectives," in Lee Dyer, Ed., *Careers in Organizations: Individual Planning and Organizational Development* (Ithaca, N.Y.: New York State School of Industrial and Labor Relations, Cornell University, 1976). Used by permission.

organization knows what positions will be open and when, career management cannot be practiced. Similarly, the individual will find it difficult to do career planning unless the organization has done its planning and is able to present the individual with a realistic career plan and development program. Exhibit 12–3 summarizes many of the human resource activities involved in career management and shows how they relate to other human resource activities.

Responsibility for Career Management

For career management to be effective, it must be a shared responsibility. In a sense, the ultimate responsibility for career planning and development rests with the individual employee. Company policy cannot dictate to the employee in these matters. The employee cannot be forced into planning a career convenient to the firm, or developing abilities to correspond to career goals.

At the same time, the responsibility for the administration, maintenance, and effective utilization of a career management program rests with the organization. For example, management is responsible for identifying and tracking candidates, notifying employees of opportunities and paths for advancement, designing appropriate training and development programs, and providing the necessary evaluation and feedback.

Most importantly, if career management is to be effective, it must be a recognized, formal program. Commitment on the part of top management is vital in order to gain the support of all managers. Without top management support, line managers are likely to give minimal attention to career management activities. In most organizations the personnel/human resource department is given the responsibility for coordinating the career management program. Thus, the personnel/human resource department and line managers who share the responsibility for carrying out the program, must work closely to be sure that line and staff activities are coordinated and program objectives are met.

CAREER PLANNING

Career planning is the responsibility of both the organization and the individual. In the past, most organizations kept track only of the rising stars and the managers. If employees were not identified early in their careers as exceptional, they were left to shift for themselves. The stars, on the other hand, were given special training and assistance. They were scheduled for upward promotions from job to job to follow the "fast track."

Most individuals, on the other hand, hoped that if they performed well and were politically astute, they would be rewarded with a promotion. There seldom existed any formal mechanism by which the individual became part of the career planning process. While this situation still exists in

EXHIBIT 12-3
Career management and HR management activities.

Career Management Aspects	Human Resource Planning Issues
Recruitment	
Attracting a flow of applicants	Knowing/influencing the supply of talent available
Defining hiring requirements	Use of agencies or search firms
Selection	Defining staffing needs
Induction and orientation	Defining bona fide job requirements
	Providing realistic information to recruits
	Validation of selection process
	Shortening of the learning curve
	Minimization of early turnover
Placement	
Defining job requirements and career paths	How to define professional and managerial job requirements and job families/career paths
Inventories and placement systems	What to put into an inventory and how to put it to use
Job posting and bidding	How much employee involvement is desired/appropriate
Selection procedures	Validation of internal selection procedures and practices
Fast-track programs	
Management succession programs	Managing accelerated career progress for high-potential employees
Relocations	Minimizing disruptive effects of relocations, controlling relocations
Training and development	
Individual career planning	Equipping employees with tools to do their own effective career planning
Training needs analysis	Managing raised expectations
Program design and development	Defining training and development needs objectively
Research and evaluation	Weighing alternative approaches for meeting these needs
	Evaluating the costs, benefits, and quality of programs
Decruitment and alternatives	
Terminations	Policies and philosophy regarding reverse or lateral career steps
Retirements	Policies governing terminations and ensuring legal compliance
Demotions and transfers	Effecting flexible retirement policies and practices

Source: J. W. Walker, *Human Resource Planning,* New York: McGraw-Hill, 1980, p. 250. Copyright © 1980 by McGraw-Hill, Inc. Reprinted with permission.

a number of firms, more and more organizations are establishing formal career management programs and are including the individual in career planning. To be effective, career planning must find a workable balance between the organization's human resource needs and the individual's career goals. Exhibit 12–4 illustrates the integration of individual and organization needs in the career planning process.

We should emphasize that career planning and development carried out by the organization is not a cost to be borne in the name of social responsibility. Proactive career planning provides such company benefits as:

1. An upgrading of the work force for increased productivity
2. Lower absenteeism
3. Lower turnover and hence savings in recruiting costs
4. Increased goodwill and better business contacts as the company helps executives move to other companies (since room at the top is limited)

The two sides of career planning—the organizational level and the individual level—are shown in Exhibit 12–5. This table shows what both the company and the individual should be doing in their common interest. We will treat both sides of career planning in this chapter.

Organizational Career Planning

The basis for career planning is the human resource planning discussed in Chapter 4. The HR requirements represent bench marks in time at which

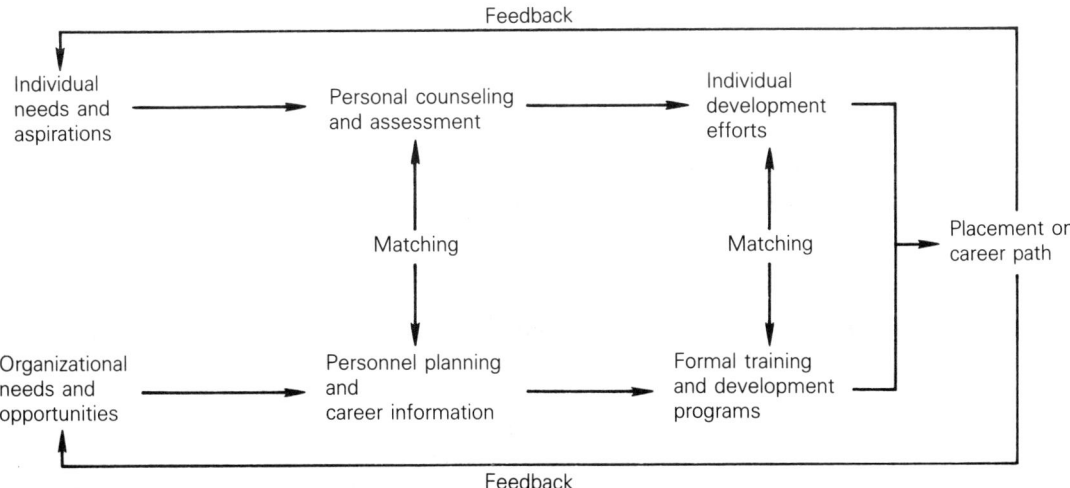

EXHIBIT 12–4

A career planning process. *Source:* Reprinted, by permission of the publisher, from "Career Development: An Integration of Individual and Organizational Needs" by John C. Alpin and Darlene K. Gerster, *Personnel,* March–April 1978, p. 25. © 1978 by AMACOM, a division of American Management Associations, New York. All rights reserved.

EXHIBIT 12-5
The two sides of career planning.

Organizational Career Planning	Individual Career Planning
Human resource needs development	Identifying your interests, skills, and potential
Upgrading of human resources for increased productivity	Identifying your life-goals and career goals
Career paths definition	Developing a written plan (including schedule) to achieve your goals
Assessment of individual potential	Seeking and obtaining the best first job
Matching of organizational needs and career needs	Communicating to management your career plan
Career counseling for quality of work life	Seeking counsel from your manager and from the HR organization on career plans and progress
Audit and control of the career planning and development system	Evaluating internal and external (other company) opportunities
	Seeking aid from sponsors
	Making known (publicizing) yourself and your accomplishments

points career stages must be matched. While conceptually this is helpful, it is not very practical because of changes in the work force. As we saw in Recruitment (Chapter 6) and Selection (Chapter 7), the dynamic nature of staffing adds to the career planning problem and thus requires proper planning. We now propose four steps for organizational career planning.

Identify Employees in the Program Ideally all employees should be in the career planning program. Some employees will just not want to participate, however. These may be employees (1) who have "disengaged" from the company early, as they have "plateaued" or leveled out, or neared retirement, (2) whose interests lie mainly outside of their work, or (3) who are hostile to the company or regard it as an adversary.

Companies tend to identify only managers, professionals, and some clerical-secretarial groups in their career planning systems. This obviously leads to a tremendous loss in appreciation of human resource assets. There are many operators and shop workers who have potential to grow into larger or different jobs, but lack education or training. The stock clerk may be a potential purchasing agent. The machinist may be a potential tool designer or inventor. The mail clerk may have potential to be (and some have become) president. The company should identify workers in all types of work who are willing to increase their awareness of opportunities, accept training, and seek greater, high-level job responsibilities.

A recent survey by The Conference Board found that approximately two-thirds of the companies provided job counseling and career planning assistance for office, clerical, and lower-level management personnel. While 45 percent had such programs for production and operations employees,[2] the scope of these programs varied considerably. Some merely provided job opportunity information; others involved career planning workshops. It is equally important for the concerned clerical worker or production worker to know where he or she stands in the company and what options are open. More will be said about career counseling in the section on career development.

Establish Career Paths Organization career planning involves establishing career paths that show logical progression of people between jobs. In a sense, these paths are "ladders" or routes that a worker can follow to advance in certain organizational units. For example, one might enter the personnel/human resource department as an interviewer, then work on testing and evaluation, be promoted to employment manager, serve as regional personnel director, and then be appointed vice-president personnel/human resources.

Career paths need not be described in writing in order to exist. However, for purposes of career management they are useful only when they are formally defined and documented. Developing realistic career paths should involve four steps:

1. Determine through job analysis (Chapter 5) the skills, knowledge, and other qualifications required to perform the various jobs in the organization
2. Identify similarities among jobs based on their content and skills/knowledge requirements
3. Group similar jobs into job families
4. Identify logical possible progression lines among these job families, which then represent career paths (see Exhibit 12–6).

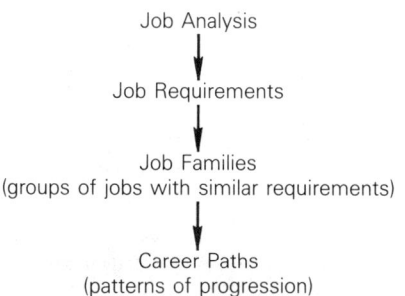

EXHIBIT 12–6
Developing career paths.

388 DEVELOPMENT

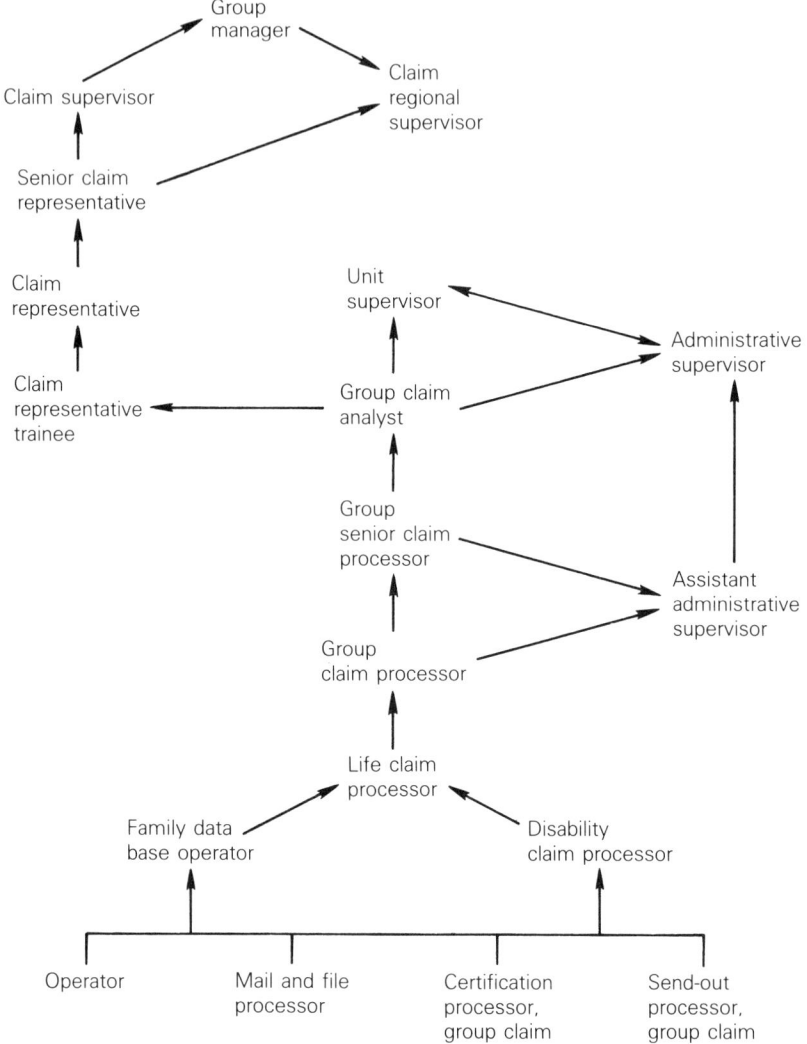

EXHIBIT 12–7
Group manager career path.
Source: Manuel London and Stephen A. Stumpf, *Managing Careers* © 1982 Addison-Wesley, Reading, Massachusetts. Pg. 140, Fig. 5.5. Reprinted with permission.

A somewhat complex career path to becoming a group manager is illustrated in Exhibit 12–7. You can see that it involves a number of steps and alternatives, and provides two career possibilities for individuals not desiring to reach the top once they have progressed along the group manager path.

Establish Program Responsibilities By means of top management directives, policies, and procedures, responsibility for the career planning and development program should be established. These responsibilities must be divided into two sets, one assigned to line management and one to the HR department career specialists. Line managers plan for the work to allow the individual to grow, guide the individual on the job, and appraise the work. With this background, the employee's manager may advise on careers in his or her functional field. Few line managers possess expertise on the *breadth* of career counseling, however. Such counseling should be the responsibility of the HR department. A career specialist will have the facts about job opportunities and an unbiased view toward the employee. (In some cases, in fact, the employee and the supervisor have such a poor relationship that the career counselor may be the only avenue left for the employee to find a more suitable job.)

Develop Individual Plans As we have seen, changing values have resulted in employees becoming more resistant to having their careers planned for them. As a result, more and more career planning is providing for increased freedom of career selection in the organization. This is accomplished by establishing open types of systems whereby employees might bid on different jobs and/or select the type of training programs they will attend in order to prepare for upward or lateral moves in the organization. In order to develop these individual plans, the organization must:

1. *Manage information.* Career planning must be based on objective information. Extensive and frequently updated records must be kept on each individual's skills. Computers have enabled management to establish data bases on skills inventories, and have the capacity to retain complete personal profiles for each employee. These computer profiles can be revised as employees acquire additional education, skills, and work experiences.

    Similarly, the employee needs to know about career opportunities, career paths, and related requirements. The employee also needs feedback about his or her performance and potential. Assessment centers (discussed in Chapter 7) and performance appraisal are useful tools to assist in preparing the career plan.

2. *Broaden the range of options.* It is useful to "open up" career paths and put more emphasis on the behavioral aspects of various jobs. That is, we often can find striking similarities in jobs even when the functions performed or technical specialties are different. For example, an individual with the necessary skills and training can be a sales representative regardless of the product, industry, or territory differences.

    An open career system also allows individual workers, through career development, to change their particular job or even occupation. Thus, a secretarial position, often viewed as a dead-end job, might lead to management in a career plan that includes employee development through completing an associate of arts degree at the local community college.

3. *Establish sponsors (mentors).* Why should only the fortunate few, fast-track stars be the only ones to have a sponsor–protege relationship? Why shouldn't everyone in the company have a higher-level sponsor to go to for career advice and counsel? While such a program may not be practical in all organizations, an implemented "godparent" relationship can lead to enormous gains in worker satisfaction and productivity.

Individual Career Planning

While organizational career planning focuses on jobs and the long- and short-run needs of the organization, individual career planning focuses on goals and skills of the employee. Therefore, an important consideration on individual planning might be movement to another organization. For example, an outstanding employee, through a process of self-assessment and goal-setting, might leave a company if a career goal can better be reached with another firm.

Since career management attempts to carefully match organizational needs with personal career goals, it is important to understand what is involved in individual career planning. To begin with, let us see what factors affect career choice.

Influencing Factors A number of studies suggest that four factors influence our choice of careers:

1. *Self-identity:* A career reflects our self-image and at the same time molds it.
2. *Interests:* We tend to follow careers that we perceive as matching our interests.
3. *Personality:* Our personal orientation as well as our needs such as affiliation, achievement, power, and so on, affect our choice.
4. *Social background:* Included here are a number of considerations such as the education, occupational level, and socioeconomic status of the parents.[3]

Certainly other considerations play a role in our choice of careers. Many of them are related to our environment, for example, the state of the economy and existing opportunities. One employee at his retirement party told how, after receiving his master's degree in accounting during the height of the Great Depression, he took a "temporary job" as a sales agent with a life insurance company because it was the only job he could get. Forty-five years later he retired, still selling insurance for the same company.

Besides our values and expectations, job counseling received (or not received) influences our career choice. Studies have found that people typically are passive and react to the work environment when it comes to career planning. As suggested by the title of one book, "If you don't know where you're going, you'll probably end up somewhere else."[4]

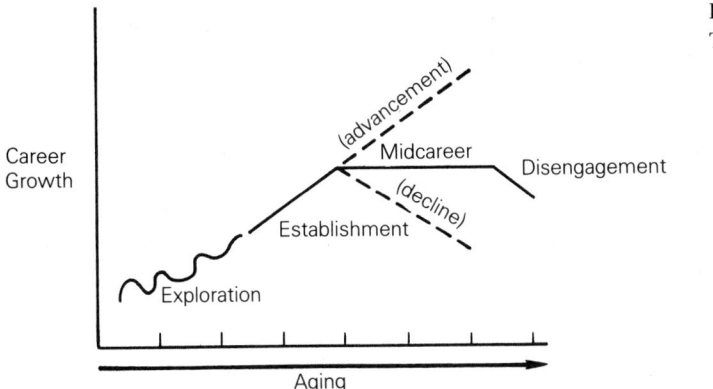

EXHIBIT 12-8
The four career stages.

Career Stages A useful way to understand careers and career planning is to consider the current *career stage* of the individual.

As seen in Exhibit 12-8, most of us go through four distinct stages regardless of the work we do. Since the issues to be resolved differ at each stage, the career planning will by necessity differ.

Stage 1: Exploration. During the exploration period employees are trying to "find themselves" and "fit into" the working role. Jobs may be tried and rejected; but throughout this period, the young worker is gaining skills and knowledge, and developing a self-image.

For the college graduate, this period may include the process of searching for, and being recruited by prospective employers. This may be followed by being placed in a first assignment. Transfers and promotions may take place during this period. If the individual decides to leave the organization, the process of exploration and trial may start over again. For most employees, this stage will end during their mid-twenties.

Stage 2: Establishment. In the establishment stage, the employee becomes involved in new work experiences such as special assignments, additional transfers, and/or promotions. Individuals who are seen as having high potential are given experiences that allow them to compete for higher-level positions. Feedback and goal-setting are critical as the individual develops a feeling of success or failure. Just as stage 1 was a period of "binding" oneself, this also is a period where one is likely to make mistakes. Learning from these mistakes may lead to increased responsibilities.

Both the employee and the organization must learn the capabilities of the other during this stage. Opportunities to demonstrate them must be provided by both sides. Establishing a mentor or sponsor relationship with a higher-level individual may be essential at this stage.

Stage 3: Midcareer. By the midcareer stage, one is expected to have gone beyond apprenticeship to journeyman status, from learner to doer. Work assignments are of a more vital nature, and mistakes carry penalties. Those who are successful receive greater rewards and responsibilities. Those who fail face a time for reassessment, adjustment of career plans, or job changes.

Most people do not face their first career crisis until the midcareer stage. This may be brought about by events external to the organization or job, such as divorce, illness, or alcohol or drug abuse. It is a time when many individuals first recognize their own mortality and limits, causing a reassessment of accomplishments and a change in goals and even life-style. Developing interests outside of work or planning a second career may take place during this period. Some employees may return to the exploration stage and make major changes in their careers. Some careers may continue on a smooth progression, with new experiences, higher status, and greater responsibility.

Stage 4: Disengagement. After a midcareer of rapid or slow growth, many individuals will settle for a slower growth or a plateau. It is a mistaken impression that they must face a decline, however. Disengagement may take many forms. Employees may "disengage" from the fast pace and instead provide advice, counsel, and invaluable judgment. They may engage in new and broader activities—the high performer may relinquish the limelight and become more of a teacher and mentor. Because this is a period of adjustment to change in life and work-style, disengagement counseling should help the individual make the transition in a way that also benefits the company. In some cases, companies loan top managers to government service. In other situations, retired executives are retrained by their company to become consultants. On the other hand, many people wish to retire with a clean break to start another career, travel, or pursue avocations.

Every career stage contains different issues and problems. Understanding these stages will (1) enable the organization to do a more effective job of career development, and (2) encourage the individual to take a more active role in his or her career planning. We now examine this career planning process in more detail.

Career-Planning Process We have seen that the trend is for effective career management to consider the individual's career plans. But how does the individual go about planning a career? The last decade has seen a proliferation of self-help books, workshops, seminars, and career kits designed to assist people in planning their careers. Most of these aids suggest that the individual engage in considerable self-assessment, whose benefits include (1) the identification of strengths and weaknesses, which helps the individual set realistic career goals; (2) a resulting list of compatible and incompatible jobs; and (3) an information base from which to draw for preparing a job application, applying for a promotion, or answering questions in a job interview.

Most experts suggest a three-step decision format:

1. Gather information on your individual interests, skills, and values
2. Convert this information into general career fields and specific goals
3. Test your choice against reality[5]

Interview With Daniel J. Levinson, Psychologist

Q: What are the stages of personal development that lead up to midlife crisis?

A: A midlife crisis may occur in various periods in adult development. The nature of this crisis depends on the period involved.

Let's start with the beginnings of adulthood. After adolescence, from about age 17 to 22, comes a period that I call the Early Adult Transition. During this time, we're beginning to separate ourselves from our parents and think about what we want to become as adults.

The next period, called the Entry Life Structure, starts at around 22 and ends at around 28. During this time, we are beginning to work, to form an occupation. We marry or get involved in relationships that lead to marriage. We move out of the parental home and form a new home base of our own. Or, if we live at home part of this time, we're trying to become more independent.

Then, at around 28, people go into the Age 30 Transition, which lasts to about 33. In this period they question the life that they have built and try to find ways to make it better. For instance, a woman who has been working during her 20s but does not have a family is likely to be asking: "Is it enough for me to have this career? Where do I go from here? Do I want to have a child?"

A man who married young and has a couple of kids or has been working along a certain path for six or eight years will often begin at 28 or 30 to question those earlier decisions. He may find that he and his wife are growing apart. And he has to ask whether they can get together or—if things are very difficult—what he wants to do about that troubled relationship.

The fourth period is the Culminating Life Structure, which lasts roughly from age 33 to 40. By around 33 or 34, a person comes up with some of the answers to the questions raised in the Age 30 Transition and begins to build a new life—a life that will, he hopes, fulfill the dreams and goals of youth.

Source: "Midlife Crisis—Is It Unavoidable?" *U.S. News and World Report,* Oct. 25, 1982, p. 73. Reprinted by permission.

Gather information. An essential aspect of career planning is the exchange among employees, family, and friends of experiences, likes, dislikes, and plans. This will give you insights and information on jobs, occupations, and organizations. Books and periodicals on careers are helpful, such as *The Occupational Outlook Handbook,* published annually by the U.S. Department of Labor, or the *Encyclopedia of Careers and Vocational Guidance,* which describes over 600 occupations.

Career counseling centers operate in every major city in the country and at most high schools and colleges. Most centers will provide testing, counseling, and guidance. Tests such as the *Strong Vocational Interests Blanks* can help determine your interests and with proper counseling relate these interests to your career choices. Exhibit 12–9 is a useful form to help you determine your "carreer expectation gap," the difference between what you are and what you desire to be. When you have done this, you can see the differences and similarities in each of six areas related to job rewards.

Continue your self-assessment by listing every job you have held, and what you liked and disliked about each. List what skills or experiences you gained from each job or extracurricular activity.

Establish career goals. Based on the information you have gathered in step 1, you should be able to identify general occupational fields you would like to pursue. At first, you may find many options. However, after you talk to people in these fields or do further research on these general occupations, you will begin to realistically focus on a limited number of occupations. As you look at such things as educational requirements, social status, earning potential, and so on, it will become apparent that few occupations will match your interests, skills, and values.

After selecting your job or occupation, you should set your career goal based on this initial choice. Many experts even suggest establishing timetables and necessary plans for this goal.

Test against reality. This is the implementation stage of your career planning process. Here you undertake the necessary training, or seek the desired job, or join the appropriate organization. Reality may substantiate that you made a correct assessment and correctly matched a job. On the other hand, for any one of a multitude of reasons (the job is boring, the training is tough, the mobility too slow, and so on), you may need to revise your career goal.

As we pass through the career stages discussed above, we change and organizations change. Thus the process of individual career planning may take place several times during one's working career. Exhibit 12–10 is a model used by an organization to help their employees with their individual career planning. Accordingly, we can see that through understanding both self and environmental factors, and job and educational options, the individual can integrate this knowledge into necessary decisions for goal development. How well the self and environment are integrated is influenced by certain factors such as midlife transitions, marriage, and health.

CAREER DEVELOPMENT

Career development is a long-term process covering an employee's entire working career. We have previously defined career development as those programs and activities undertaken to achieve a personal career plan. Before discussing some of the more important specific development programs and activities, let us consider what a career development framework might look like.

Exhibit 12–11 illustrates the relationship between career planning and

EXHIBIT 12-9
Job rewards expectation gap worksheet.

Job Rewards	What I Am Today	What I Want to Be
Field of Work		
Job Satisfactions 1. _____ 2. _____ 3. _____		
Personal Growth 1. _____ 2. _____ 3. _____		
Job Growth Opportunities		
Work Environment Characteristics 1. _____ 2. _____ 3. _____		
Economic Rewards Salary: $ _____ 1. _____ 2. _____ 3. _____		

Source: William E. Perry, *Orchestrating Your Career* (Boston, Mass.: CBI, 1981), p. 55. Copyright © 1981 by CBI Publishing Company, Inc.

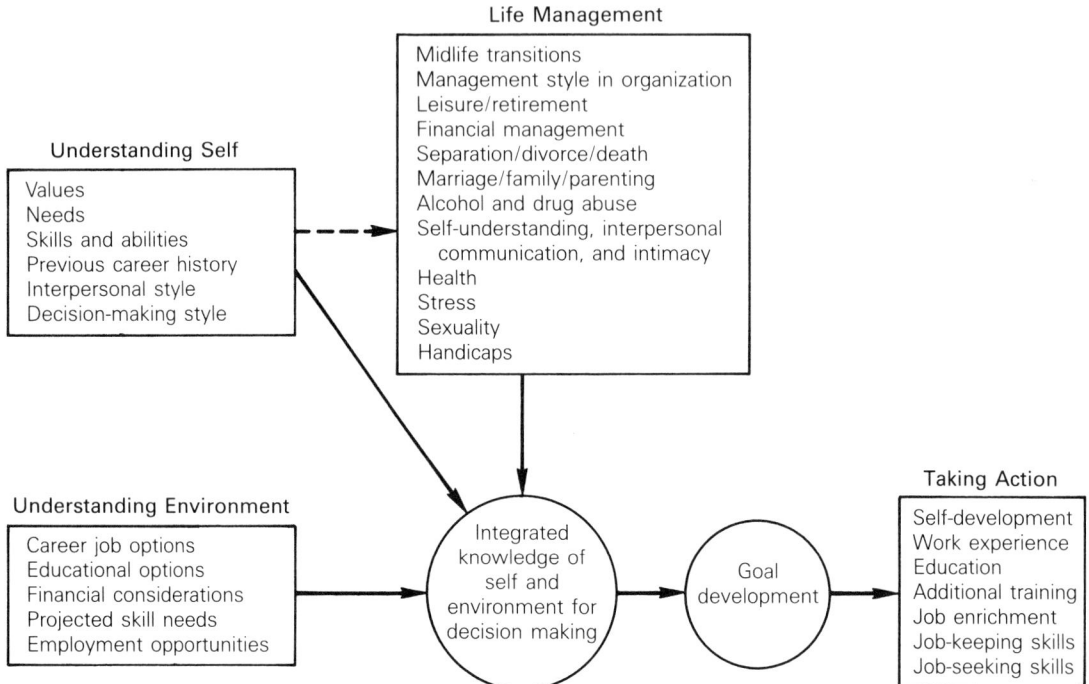

EXHIBIT 12-10
Model used to help employees with career planning.

Source: I. Marlene Thorn, Francis X. Fee, and Jane O'Hara Carter, "Career Development: A Collaborative Approach," *Management Review,* September 1982 (New York: AMA Membership Publications Division, American Management Associations, 1982), p. 39.

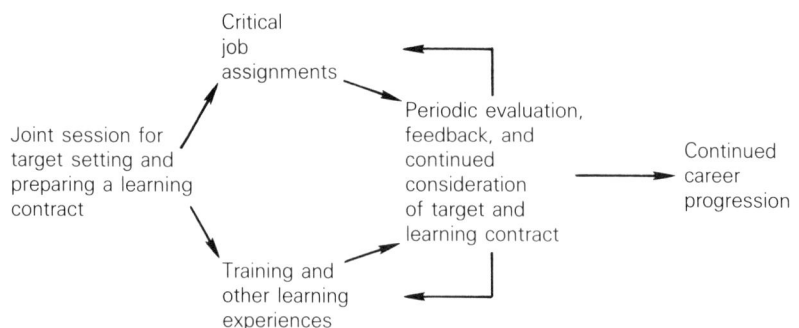

EXHIBIT 12-11
A career development framework.

Source: Manuel London and Stephen A. Stumpf, *Managing Careers,* © 1982, Addison-Wesley, Reading, Massachusetts. Pg. 164, Fig. 6.1. Reprinted with permission.

career development. Thus, we can see that after initial target setting through career planning, development consists of a series of practical job assignments and training experiences building toward a career target or goal. Periodic evaluation, feedback, and reconsideration of the target will then take place. Let us consider briefly two important components of career development: job assignments and training experiences.

Job Assignments

Based on the individual career plan, a development program should include a variety of job assignments. The number and length of the assignments will depend on the individual and the career goal. Job assignments can take the form of lateral transfers, vertical promotions, or assignments organized around new tasks, such as being made part of a special projects task force.

New and different assignments present new experiences to the employee. If successfully handled, these opportunities can provide feedback that will suggest new responsibilities and challenges. Some organizations have planned rotation programs that utilize replacement charts to coordinate organizationally who is to be moved, and where and when. Systematic rotation (1) helps develop generalists out of specialists; (2) provides employee visibility and gives a manager opportunity to compare several candidates for promotion; (3) provides variety, challenge, and fresh ideas; and (4) presents "the big picture" instead of one department's view. At the same time, management must balance the advantages of job rotation in each situation against several disadvantages: (1) A large part of the time is spent learning a new job or finding one's way around a new department; (2) job rotation encourages the employee to emphasize short-run successes or "payoffs" since he or she will soon be in another job; and (3) too much movement (especially geographic relocation) may be disruptive to one's family and cause considerable stress.

Training and Other Learning Experiences

Various types of training and other learning experiences have already been discussed in the previous chapter on individual training and development and will not be repeated here. However, we should note a couple of aspects of training that are unique to career development. To begin with, the training should follow a planned sequence of activities. The worker might even write jointly with his supervisor a "learning contract" during a career planning session.

The worker's individual development needs should be identified and agreed upon during the career planning process. Based on targeted career goals, the worker, in conjunction with the supervisor or designated career development specialist, can set up the action plans that will move him or her toward these goals. These action plans, in addition to job assignments discussed above, will identify the training and other learning experiences needed and determine where they are located, both inside and outside the organization.

Specific training programs fall into three classifications:

1. *Orientation:* indoctrination for a newcomer or sessions designed to acquaint a newly promoted worker to a new process, new procedure, or new peers and supervisors
2. *Technical skills:* designed to focus on new skills, new technologies, or recent advances; may be "in-house" by company experts or long-term and off-site such as a university. Might even include a *sabbatical* whereby the individual is given time off from work to pursue the added skills on a full-time basis.
3. *Managerial skills:* intended to increase those skills required by all managers; may be short workshops or seminars on company prem-

---

Career Development Sessions

The purpose of career development discussions is to allow both the supervisor and the individual to explore future areas of growth to satisfy their respective needs.

The content of the session should be as employee-centered as possible, with the supervisor providing structure and feedback. The range of areas that can be covered is practically limitless, but here are some suggested topics:

- Discover what the individual truly wants. Is this different from your own original estimate of the goal that he should strive for? If so, why are these two objectives different?
- Examine the individual's "self-selling" technique and offer suggestions for improving it.
- Is the individual being relatively objective in the assessment of his own strengths and weaknesses?
- Is the individual limited in his scope? Is he aware of the wide range of alternatives available to him?
- Is the individual neglecting consideration of some positions because of the personalities of the persons currently in those positions? Is he overrating other positions for similar reasons?
- Can the employee verbalize both the pros and cons of a position, or does he focus solely on the positive?
- Is the individual motivated more by the salary and/or status of a job than by the duties themselves?
- Is the individual sincere, or is he just saying what he thinks you, the supervisor, want to hear?
- Is the employee sufficiently motivated to undergo the training required for a new position?
- Has the individual incorporated previous supervisory feedback into his thinking?
- Is the individual focusing only on long-range goals, or has he developed smaller, more immediate steps?
- To pursue the individual's overall goal, can be expect to achieve it within the organization, or should he be looking elsewhere for satisfaction?

Source: Lee R. Ginsburg, "Career Planning: Help Your Organization Grow," *Supervisory Management,* June 1977, pp. 14–15.

ises or executive development courses at universities lasting from a few days to one year to an MBA degree requiring two or more years. Most training experiences for lower levels of management are intended to develop specific skills such as communication, resolving conflicts, or managing time. Training for those more advanced in their career is likely to emphasize planning or productivity improvement.

Evaluation and Feedback

As we have seen in the career development model (Exhibit 12–11), the career development process should include periodic evaluation and feedback to the participant. In most organizations with formal career development programs, the employee's progress toward career goals is measured annually or biannually, often during an annual performance appraisal session.

During the evaluation, the employee's career progress is discussed with a supervisor or a designated career specialist such as someone from the personnel/human resource department. Some organizations have a management committee that meets periodically with management trainees to review their career progress. The use of a mentor or sponsor appears to hold promise as an evaluation and feedback device as he or she periodically meets with the individual to discuss career progression and comments from others in the organization.

Emphasis at this stage is on success in meeting career goals and timetables. Failure to have met goals may result in reassessing original goals or in remedial programs in the form of additional job assignments or training experiences. Finally, completion of goals will reinforce performance and continue the individual along his or her career path.

SUMMARY

Technological changes, obsolescence, increased education, rising expectations, affirmative action programs, turnovers, and shortages of capable managers have all led to increased emphasis on careers and career management in particular. Career management is the process of designing and implementing goals, plans, and strategies that enable the organization to satisfy human resource needs while allowing individuals to achieve their career goals.

Career planning and career development are the two important components of career management. Career planning may be offered from either the individual or the organizational point of view. While organizational career planning focuses on jobs and the needs of the organization, individual career planning looks at goals and skills from the individual's frame of reference. Career paths and career stages were discussed to obtain a better understanding of the career planning process.

Career development is a long-term process involving an employee's entire working career. It involves those programs and activities undertaken to achieve a personal career plan. We have seen that career management is related to all HR management activities and is an integral part of human resource planning. Effective career management is a shared responsibility that needs the commitment of top management.

KEY CONCEPTS

Career	Career path
Career planning	Career stages
Career development	Career management

NOTES

1. Most of the definitions in this section are adapted from Douglas T. Hall, *Careers in Organizations* (Pacific Palisades, Ca.: Goodyear, 1976), pp. 3–5.
2. Harriet Gorlin, "Personnel Practices I: Recruitment, Placement, Training, Communication," *Information Bulletin*, No. 89 (New York: The Conference Board, 1981), p. 25.
3. For example, see Hall, *Careers in Organizations*, pp. 11–13.
4. Daniel Campbell, *If You Don't Know Where You're Going, You'll Probably End Up Somewhere Else* (Niles, Ill.: Argus Communications, 1974).
5. For example, see Irving R. Schwartz, "Self-Assessment and Career Planning: Matching Individuals and Organizational Goals," *Personnel*, January–February 1979, p. 48.

REVIEW AND DISCUSSION QUESTIONS

1. What is meant by a "career"?
2. How is career management related to other HR management activities?
3. Who is responsible for career management?
4. How does organizational career planning differ from individual career planning?
5. Differentiate between career planning, career development, and career management.
6. Describe the interrelationship among the employer, the employee's supervisor, and the human resource specialist in career development.
7. "Your age and career stage evolve together." Discuss.

8. What are the advantages of self-assessment in career planning?
9. Describe the steps involved in the career planning process.
10. Explain the relationship between career planning and career development.

BIBLIOGRAPHY

Aplin, J. C., and D. K. Gerster. "Career Development: An Integration of Individual and Organizational Needs." *Personnel*, March–April 1978, 23–29.

Benson, P. G., and G. C. Thornton III. "A Model Career Planning Program." *Personnel*, March–April 1978, 30–39.

Hall, Douglas T. *Careers in Organizations*. Pacific Palisades, Ca.: Goodyear, 1976.

London, Manuel, and Stephen A. Stumpf. *Managing Careers*. Reading, Mass.: Addison-Wesley, 1982.

Mikal, William L., Patricia A. Sorce, and Thomas E. Comte. "A Process Model of Individual Career Decision Making." *Academy of Management Review*, January 1984, 95–103.

Morgan, D. C. "Career Development Programs." *Personnel*, September–October 1977, 23–27.

Morgan, Marilyn A. *Managing Career Development*. New York: Van Nostrand, 1980.

Perry, William E. *Orchestrating Your Career*. Boston, Mass.: CBI Publishing, 1981.

Schein, E. H. *Career Dynamics: Matching Individual and Organizational Needs*. Reading, Mass.: Addison-Wesley, 1978.

Stair, Lila B. *Careers in Business: Selecting and Planning Your Career Path*. Homewood, Ill.: Irwin, 1980.

Van Maanen, J., E. H. Schein, and L. Bailyn. "The Shape of Things to Come: A New Look at Organizational Careers." In *Perspectives on Behavior in Organizations*, eds. J. R. Hackman, E. E. Lawler, and L. W. Porter. New York: McGraw-Hill, 1977, 153–162.

Walker, J. W. "Does Career Planning Rock the Boat?" *Human Resource Management*, Spring 1978, 2–7.

Walker, J. W., and Thomas G. Gutteridge. *Career Planning Practices*. New York: American Management Association, 1979.

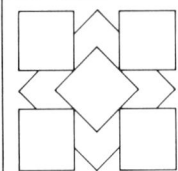

CASE STUDY:
NTEL, Inc.

NTEL, Inc., is an international firm that employed 13,000 people worldwide in 1984. It consisted of an Industrial Division, a Building Division, a Services and Leisure Division, and a Consumer Products Division. With plants all over the world and continuing rapid expansion, NTEL was having communication problems. As a result, the achievement of profit targets was beginning to slip badly in the various divisions for reasons that had not been precisely identified.

Although top management, headquartered in New York, tried to visit major plants at least once a year, these visits apparently did little to alleviate the problems. Language barriers created further complications, particularly with regard to the efforts of corporate staff executives to develop and obtain adherence to companywide policies.

Managers (both in the United States and abroad) felt that corporate headquarters management did not understand local problems. Local managements often lamented that "high-level staff lives in an ivory tower."

Further, there was considerable friction over responsibility for local plant decisions. For example, corporate management would often express exasperation with the failure of local management to make a specific decision. At the same time, plant managers and their staffs might complain bitterly about delays in getting the staff approvals from headquarters needed to finalize local decisions.

In order to break through some of these difficulties, the president of NTEL, William Sabastian, had scheduled a meeting of 178 executives, including the top management of the company, to be held in June 1984 in Paris. While preparing his plans for the meeting, he had a long conversation with an old friend, Larry Jones, who headed his own OD consulting firm. As a result, Sabastian asked Jones to help identify NTEL's organizational problems and perhaps suggest some solutions.

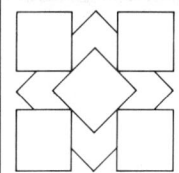

CASE STUDY:
Transforming the Transformer Company

Dr. Al Sklar, president of Transformer International Company, swiveled in his chair at 10:00 P.M. to look out of the window from his 30th-floor office. As he surveyed the expanse of the city skyline glowing with hundreds of thousands of lights, he mused about the role of transformers in supplying the lighting.

Sklar, an outsider, had taken over the helm of the company six months earlier. He had found it to be a conservative, sound engineering company living off its past reputation. Transformer International was a follower rather than a leader. Before any of its employees took a step, they wanted to be sure that the same step had been taken before by somebody else and had worked. For example, the general approach to design used by the engineers was to study all the available designs and then to try to incorporate the best features of each. There was no attempt to develop advanced, innovative designs.

Sklar was well aware that technological developments were occurring at a mind-boggling rate in the world around him. He had tried unsuccessfully to persuade his staff that product leadership was essential in the transformer business. As he sat there, he wondered whether Laura Lusk, the new manager of human resources, could help him.

The next day he met with Ms. Lusk to discuss the problem. Together they developed a list of items that needed to be explored just to identify the problem fully:

1. Definition of change variables
2. The human resource system at TI
3. The objectives of a change program
4. Methods of change
5. Changing individuals and their relationships
6. Changing group and intergroup relationships
7. Changing the physical environment
8. OD
9. MBO
10. Management information systems

At the end of the conference, Sklar asked Ms. Lusk to prepare a practical, cost-effective program that would encourage creativity and innovation in all of the company's activities.

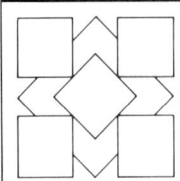

CASE STUDY:
A Question of Training

First Banktrust of Florida was organized as a multibank holding company in 1972. It has grown to 15 banks located from Miami to Orlando. The rapid growth has made it difficult to find good management. Further, on-the-job training of nonmanagement personnel has not been working well because many positions in banks today require considerable technical knowledge and skills.

The organization of the home office bank is shown in Figure A. Management is considering installing a training section in the Operations Department, as shown in Figure B.

You have just been hired as head of training and asked to present a proposal for a companywide training program within the next 60 days.

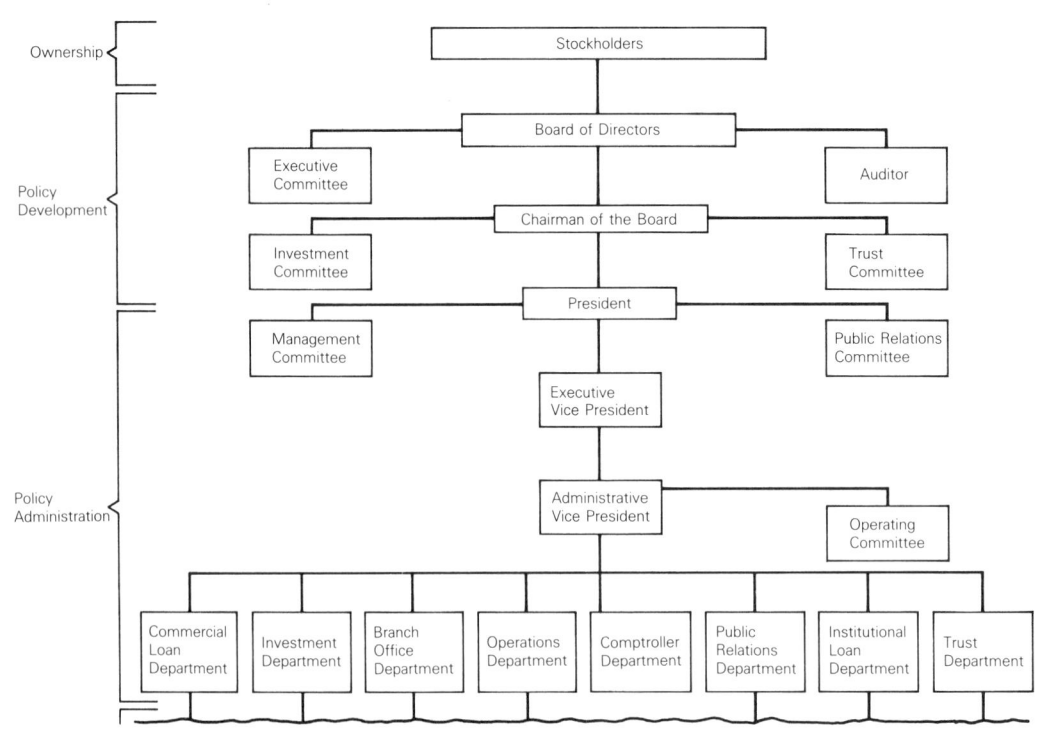

FIGURE A
Bank functional chart

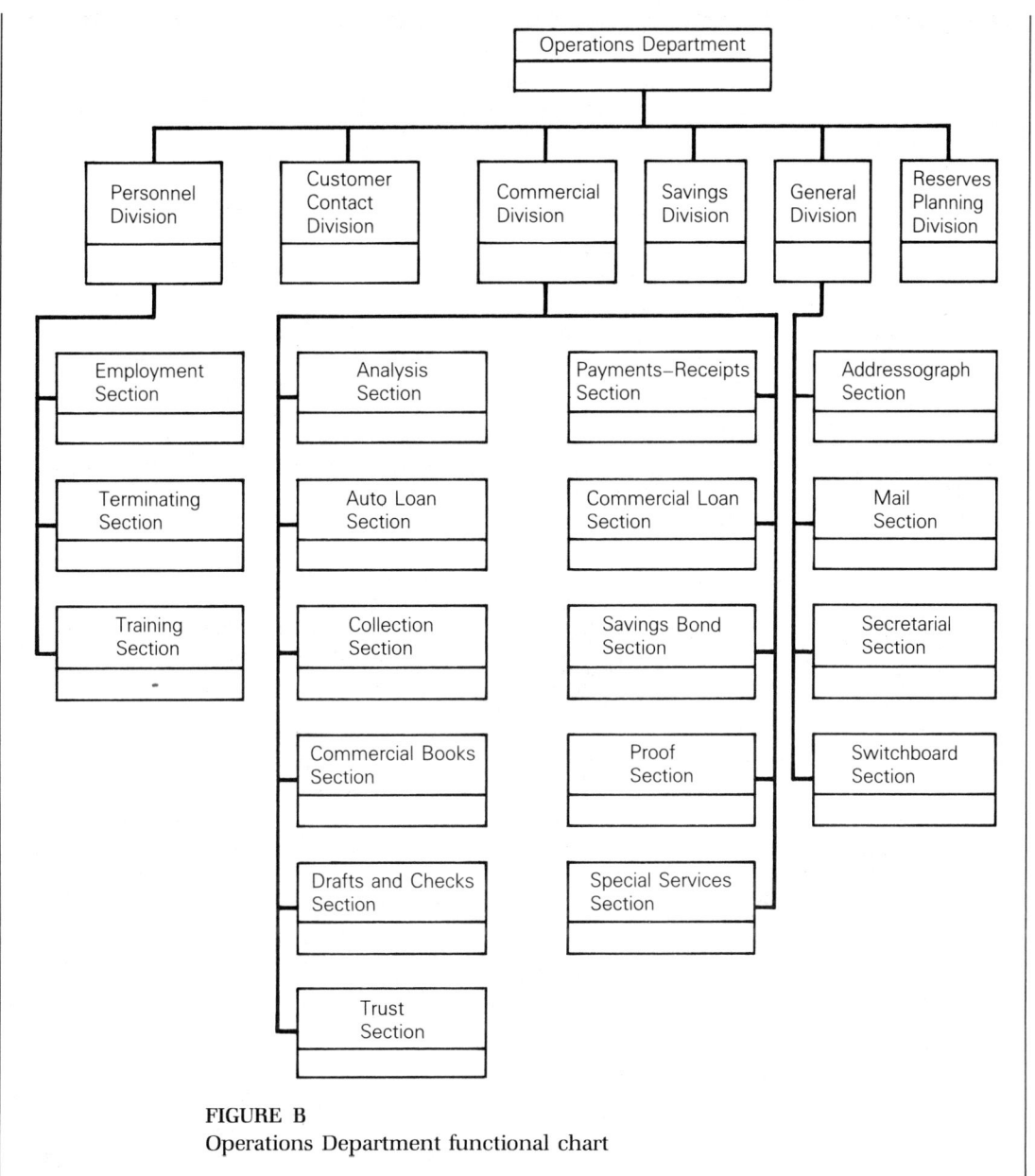

FIGURE B
Operations Department functional chart

405

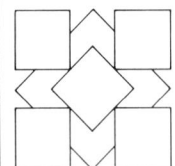

CASE STUDY:
The Case of Anne Greblad

Anne Greblad is the reference librarian of the City Public Library. In the last seven years she acquired considerable experience in developing library displays and in providing library service to the two local hospitals. She was considered to be one of the most capable workers at the library—until this year.

For several months Greblad has been creating serious difficulties for Joan Kay, the associate director, because of her arbitrary, sullen disposition and her frequent critical "popping off" in the presence of other librarians. Kay has felt that something had to be done because Greblad's attitude has been damaging the morale of the other librarians. Friction has also been increasing between the two, and Greblad's job efficiency has been adversely affected. Kay has been unable to get at the problem herself, so she has told the library director that something has been bothering Greblad but that she has been unable to find out what it was.

Kay and the library director called Greblad in for a conference after working hours on Saturday. They told her that they were concerned about her performance and were anxious to help.

At first, Greblad belligerently blamed her co-librarians for their lack of cooperation. The director and associate director continued to listen. Finally, the following conversation took place:

Director: Anne, you used to be one of our most capable workers and did an outstanding job in providing library service to our hospitals.

Greblad: I enjoyed the work when there was time to provide proper services, but that hasn't been possible since we went on this management by objectives kick. I was discussing this situation only last night with Tom in Acquisitions.

Kay: I explained to you earlier this year, Anne, that the purpose of the City Public Library has been expanded to provide books and information not only for the people in the city but for all residents of Howard County who wish to use its resources. Furthermore, we want to make information and material available to everyone within two days of the request.

Greblad: The percentage of requests filled within this time limit will be low.

Director: Progress comes from establishing goals that exceed the routine requirements of your job.

Greblad: I still think that a high priority should be given to providing library service to hospitals.

Director: I agree with you, Anne, but we do have to satisfy the overall objectives of the library.

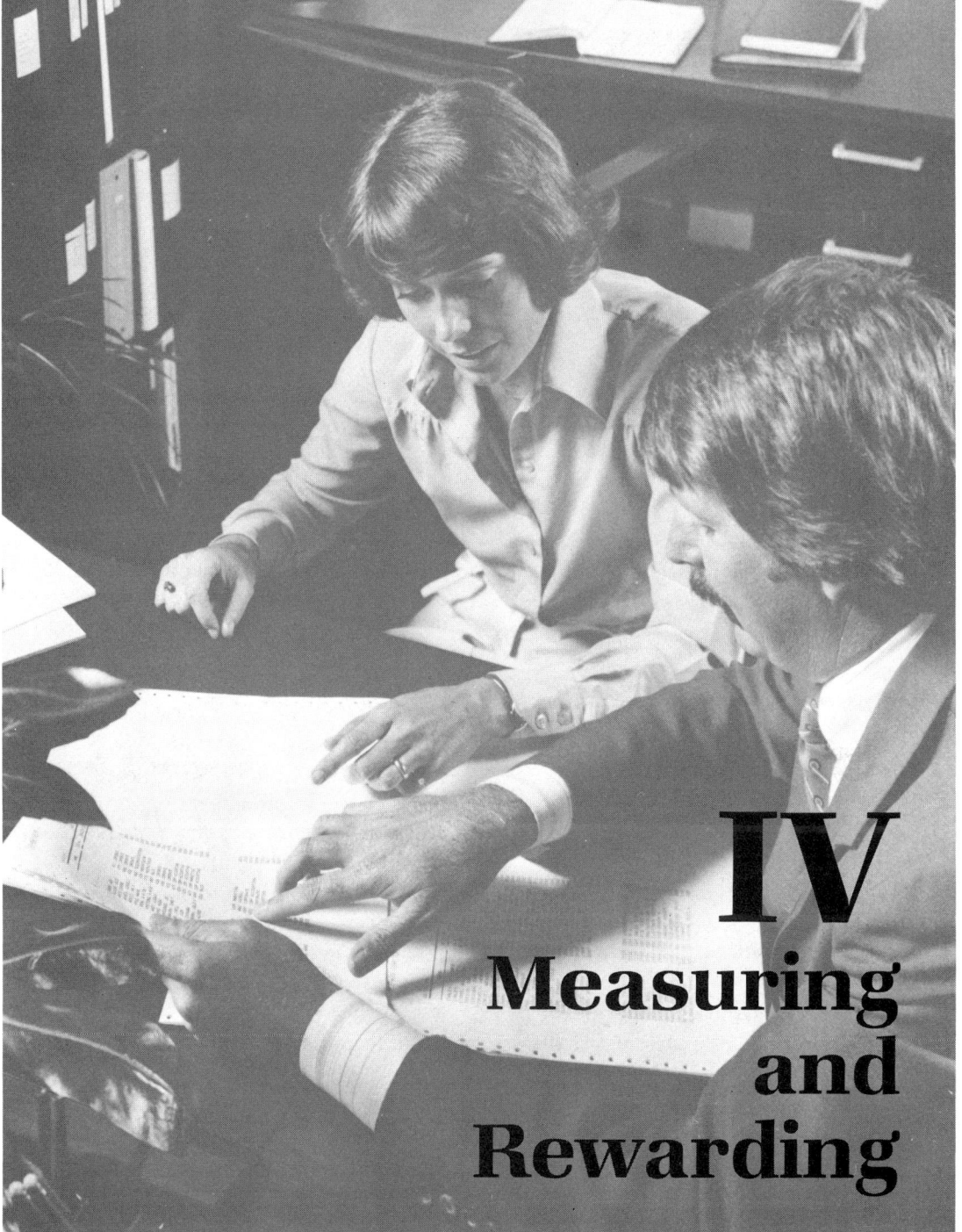

IV
Measuring and Rewarding

Appraising Performance

CHAPTER OUTLINE

Role of Performance Appraisal

Approaches to Appraisal

Current Practice in Performance Appraisal

Formalized Appraisal Programs ☐ Types of Plans ☐ Purposes and Uses of Appraisals ☐ What Is Evaluated? ☐ Who Is Involved in the Appraisal Process? ☐ Rater Training ☐ Dynamic Nature of Appraisal Systems

Current Status of the Appraisal Process

Conclusions and Recommendations

Legal Considerations in Performance Appraisal

Relating Performance Appraisal to Rewarding

Step-by-Step Implementation Procedure for a Performance Appraisal System

Conducting the Performance Appraisal Interview ☐ Comparing Performance with Accepted Standards ☐ Setting Nonfinancial Rewards ☐ Relating Performance to Compensation Budgets ☐ Taking Other Managerial Action ☐ Communicating the Final Appraisal and the Action to Be Taken

OBJECTIVES

1. Describe several approaches to performance appraisal and indicate their advantages and disadvantages.

2. Custom-design a contingency-based approach to appraisal that best fits the needs and expectations of your own work group and organization.

3. Distinguish between hierarchical and participative approaches to appraisal and know when each is appropriate.

4. Identify the theoretical and research basis for the MBO approach to performance appraisal.

5. Describe the desired relationship among performance, rewards, equity, and motivation.

6. Recognize the key motivational role of appraising and rewarding for performance.

7. Implement a six-step process for appraising and rewarding your subordinates.

SPOTLIGHT:
Robert L. Berra

Robert L. Berra is Senior Vice President, Administration, for Monsanto Company. Born in St. Louis in 1924, Berra was graduated from St. Louis University in 1947 with a B.S. degree in Commerce and Finance. Subsequently, he received his MBA degree from the Harvard Graduate School of Business. He has also done graduate work in psychology at Washington University, St. Louis.

Following four years as a member of the Business School Faculty at St. Louis University, Mr. Berra joined Monsanto Company in 1951 as assistant training manager at the former Plastics Division, Springfield, Massachusetts, plant and subsequently served there as employee relations manager, director of sales training, and director of sales administration. In 1959 he was appointed director of personnel for the Plastics Division. Becoming director of administration for the Plastics Products and Resins Division in February, 1966, Mr. Berra became assistant director of the Corporate Personnel Department in June, 1967.

From October, 1970, until June, 1974, Mr. Berra was employed by Foremost-McKesson, Inc., as Corporate Vice President of Personnel and Public Relations. He rejoined Monsanto Company as Vice President, Personnel, in June of 1974. In April, 1980, he was made Senior Vice President, Administration. In December, 1981, he was appointed an Advisory Director to the Monsanto Board of Directors.

Berra is the author of several articles in the area of management and motivation and a past president and member of the Executive Committee of the American Society for Personnel Administration.

Comments by Robert Berra

We all know that compensation is not the only thing that motivates managers. But if we do a poor job here, the manager's tolerance level erodes. Too often this translates to a drop-off in morale and productivity, and occasionally loss of a valuable person to another organization.

Although compensation problems normally exist throughout the organizational hierarchy, I've found the greatest challenge at the middle-management level. Most who reach top management have their ego needs satisfied in a number of ways, are used to dealing with less well-defined responsibility areas and are generally involved in critical decisions. Except in unusual situations they tend to know instinctively where they stand—be it good or bad. Visibility is high. Sustained tenure in the limbo of mediocrity is seldom possible.

For middle managers, it's different. Unless the individual is on a fast track, time in grade can be discouragingly long. Expectations outpace career progress. Without patient, honest counsel, the inevitable result is frustration. The individual becomes introspective. Concerns narrow, and tangible rewards are overemphasized.

Too many supervisors find it difficult to face up to candid performance appraisal. Thus, a disproportionate number of middle managers are rated too high. Given budget limitations, they cannot all be paid in accordance with their bloated evaluations—thus destroying the credibility of the compensation system.

Honest evaluation and sensitive counseling are inextricably bound to the reward system. Experience shows that individuals will respond positively to objective review of their performance, particularly if they see the process as helping them move toward the fulfillment of their potential.

Getting managers to accept and practice these fundamentals is not an easy task. But the potential rewards to the individual and the organization resulting from unleashing in middle management the latent leverage, or ability to influence behavior change, make it a worthy goal.

How does one "evaluate" another human being on the job? This is a ticklish issue, and numerous procedures have been developed to replace older measures traditionally criticized for their subjectivity and one-sidedness. The appraisal and reward systems are now designed to measure the effectiveness of job performance, gauge its value, and provide appropriate rewards (or punishment) as payment.

It is this reward for performance that reinforces the behavior and provides the motivation for future behavior. Thus, it is crucial that the appraisal system measure performance *accurately* and that the rewarding system reward it *equitably*. These two systems directly affect the probability that human resources will be motivated to achieve organizational objectives in the future. The quality of the appraisal subsystem thus determines the productivity of human resources in the future.

For the above reasons, appraisal and rewarding have been the subject of considerable scientific research over the last fifty years—and a challenge for the 1980s. "Appraisal" means to measure and evaluate against a standard of performance. "Rewarding" means to repay equitably for a service, in appropriate relationship to the quality of the service performed.

Because of the key roles of performance appraisal and rewarding, it is not surprising that these systems are receiving a great amount of attention in the 1980s not only for their previously mentioned role in determining productivity but also for their interest to the equal employment opportunity movement. Since the appraisal subsystem so directly affects the pay that individuals receive, it is, along with employee selection procedures, receiving great emphasis by the proponents of equal employment opportunity.

ROLE OF PERFORMANCE APPRAISAL

Appraising the performance of individuals and organizations is an inherent aspect of managing. Simply stated, it is impossible to make intelligent managerial decisions about individuals without measuring their performance in some manner. Hence, formal performance appraisal is as old as the concept of management, and informal performance appraisal is as old as human history. Attempts at formal appraisal go back many centuries, and in this century rigorous scientific studies of appraisal techniques and methods have a history of well over 50 years.

The primary responsibility for performance appraisal belongs to line management. Top management must make the final policy decisions on the methods to be utilized, and managers at all levels must implement appraisal and rewarding procedures. Nevertheless, there is often an important role for expert human resource staff advisers both in keeping line management informed of new research findings and technology and in proposing alternative appraisal plans for the consideration of top management.

Historically, appraisal has generally been used for administrative purposes, such as promotions and salary increases, as well as for individual

> ## Common Rater Errors
>
> Much of the research and experimentation over the past 50 years concerning performance appraisal has focused on attempts to eliminate, or at least minimize, the sources of error made by the individual appraising the performance of another. There are four common sources of rater error:
>
> *Leniency error* occurs when an evaluator consistently evaluates *all* subordinates at the high end of the rating scale (positive leniency error) or at the low end of the rating scale (negative leniency error). The real difficulty arises when it is necessary to compare the appraisals of individuals rated by different supervisors, since differences in the appraisals may be caused by differences in rater standards rather than by actual differences in performance.
>
> *Halo error* occurs when the evaluator allows his or her assessment on one trait or characteristic to influence the assessment of the same person on other traits or characteristics.
>
> *Central tendency* is the error of rating all individuals at about the center (average) point on the scale either because of failure to look at enough detailed performance data to differentiate or simply because it is "easier" to rate everyone at the middle of the scale instead of having to explain and defend any extreme evaluations.
>
> *Similarity error* is bias in favor of those individuals who the rater perceives to have personal characteristics similar to his or her own, or bias against those the rater perceives to be "different."

development and motivation. Other frequent uses of appraisal information have been employee selection and placement, feedback to guide and reinforce training, personnel planning, and organization planning. The relative emphasis on these uses of appraisal information has tended to shift over time, from early application in this country solely to compensation and placement decisions, to its current role in both administration and motivation. This shift has been a basic cause of the considerable controversy over

EXHIBIT 13–1

Uses of appraisals or ratings in 316 leading industrial corporations.

Uses of Appraisals	Responses	
	Number	Percent
Merit increases or bonuses	238	75.3
Counseling the ratee	278	88.0
Planning training or development for the ratee	270	85.4
Considering the ratee for promotion	266	84.2
Considering the retention or discharge of the ratee	184	58.2
Motivating the ratee to achieve higher levels of performance	269	85.1
Improving company planning	178	56.3
Other	28	8.9
Total companies reporting	316	

the last 20 years concerning the most effective approaches and techniques for appraisal.

A study by Schuster and Kindall described the performance appraisal practices of *Fortune*'s 500 largest industrial corporations. Of the 403 companies responding to the survey, 316 (or 78 percent) reported the use of some type of formal performance appraisal plan. When asked about the uses to which appraisals were put, these 316 companies replied as shown in Exhibit 13–1. Their responses indicate that the vast majority of companies today attempt to use performance appraisals for both administrative and developmental-motivational purposes.[1]

APPROACHES TO APPRAISAL

Until recently, almost all appraisal practices have been based on the implicit assumption that the superior is the person in the best position to judge the performance of his or her subordinates. Appraisals have thus emphasized the hierarchical relationship of superior and subordinate, and have placed the superior in the position of "playing God" by passing judgment on the subordinate.

In this emphasis on passing judgment from above, the vast majority of the earlier appraisal approaches employed some form of trait rating. Basically, the trait-rating approach requires the superior to evaluate, in some numerical or descriptive fashion, the subordinate's possession of certain personality and behavior traits. Two types of forms typically used for trait appraisal are shown in Exhibits 13–2 and 13–3.

As you can see, trait appraisals often bear a striking resemblance to segments of grammar-school report cards. In the 1960s, social science research revealed that this reliance on judgments from above may actually *reduce* the effectiveness of the appraisal process in achieving its motivational and developmental goals. For example, the work of Rensis Likert and others at the Social Science Research Center has shown that hierarchical control may lead to lower motivation and may restrict rather than encourage individual development. In contrast, these researchers assert that participative, supportive management tends to foster higher motivation and to encourage the development and personal growth of the employee.

Research findings indicate that over the past several years a trend away from traditional trait-oriented performance appraisal and toward a more positive motivation-oriented approach has been developing in the field of human resource management. The origin of this new approach lies in the writings of commentators such as Peter Drucker and Douglas McGregor, who have suggested that a participative, motivation-oriented approach to appraisal should lead to higher performance levels than does the traditional trait-oriented approach.

The question of whether there might be such a conflict between hierarchical appraisal and motivation, however, was raised early in the history

EXHIBIT 13–2
Employee performance review worksheet.

Employee name	Department	Rated by	Date

Instructions:

1. Check the block beside each factor that contains the closest description of employee with regard to that factor only.
2. Enter rating points (0, 1, 2, 3) for each factor in the far right column.
3. Add the points in each section and divide the results by the figure shown. Round fractions as follows: 0.5–1.4 = 1; 1.5–2.4 = 2; 2.5–3 = 3. Should you not rate a job on a particular factor, divide by the number of factors rated rather than by the figure shown.
4. Enter the "rating" on the rating card.

Quality

Factors	Poor—0	Fair—1	Good—2	Excellent—3	Rating points
Appearance of work	Work is generally sloppy and incomplete. Employee has little or no regard for appearance. Work must be redone often.	Some work is sloppy and incomplete. Employee tries to do acceptable work, but rework is required often enough to cause repeated reminders.	Work is generally neat and complete. Employee has pride in work. Rework seldom required.	Work is exceptionally neat, well organized, and complete. Employee has exceptional pride in work. Rework rarely required.	
Accuracy of work	Continuously makes errors. Makes no effort to check own work. Work must be checked 100 percent by others.	Frequently makes errors. Checks own work fairly often. Work must be checked 50 percent of the time by others.	Occasionally makes errors. Almost always checks own work for accuracy. Only spot checking required by others.	Rarely makes errors. Always checks own work. Little or no checking required by others.	
Supervision required	Constant direction required with little effect.	High degree of direction required to maintain level of quality.	Needs occasional direction to maintain a high level of quality.	Rarely requires direction to maintain outstanding level of quality.	
				Total points	
				Divided by	
				Rating	

Recommendations for improvement:

____ Has improved
____ Little or no change
____ Has regressed

EXHIBIT 13-2, *continued*

		Quantity			
Factors	Poor—0	Fair—1	Good—2	Excellent—3	Rating points
Volume	Volume of work is below acceptable level. ___	Volume of work meets minimal acceptable level. ___	Volume of work meets that of average worker. ___	Volume is exceptional, exceeding average requirements. ___	
Utilization of time	Frequently wastes time between assignments. ___	Occasionally wastes working time. ___	Wastes very little of available working time. ___	Utilizes working time to the fullest. ___	
Work pace	Work not organized; rarely meets deadlines. ___	Work is partially organized; frequently misses deadlines. ___	Work is well organized; occasionally misses deadlines. ___	Work is exceptionally well organized; rarely misses deadlines. ___	
Supervision required	Constant direction required to obtain quantity produced. ___	Frequent direction required to obtain quantity produced. ___	Occasional direction required to obtain quantity produced. ___	Rarely requires direction to obtain quantity produced. ___	
	Recommendations for improvement:			Total points ___	
___ Has improved				Divided by ___	
___ Little or no change				Rating ___	
___ Has regressed					

Other Comments

EXHIBIT 13-3
Trait appraisal form.

Rate the employee in the following traits, using this scale: 3—Excellent
                                                              2—Acceptable
                                                              1—Needs development
                                                              0—Not observed

Appearance	_____	Ability to learn	_____
Self-confidence	_____	Accuracy	_____
Ability to express self	_____	Meets deadlines	_____
Alertness	_____	Health	_____
Ambition	_____	Enthusiasm	_____
Initiative	_____	Attitude and acceptance of responsibility	_____
Energy	_____	Use of time	_____
Knowledge of department	_____	Organizes work to get a job done	_____
Contacts with superiors	_____	Independence	_____
peers	_____	Adaptability	_____
customers	_____	Maturity	_____

Overall Evaluation

All factors considered, my overall evaluation of this employee is (circle one):

1. Outstanding
2. A good employee who should do well
3. A sound employee
4. An adequate but limited employee
5. Only just satisfactory

If reviewed, employee's reaction or comments:

Reviewed with employee by: _____ Date: _____

---

of performance appraisal. In 1926, Arthur Kornhauser presented the classical arguments in favor of conventional, numerical rating scales but also set forth a program for testing the usefulness of rating scales. To an amazing degree, he anticipated the later criticism of Likert, McGregor, and others. Kornhauser pointed out that the arguments in favor of rating scales were based on opinion and that scientific research would be required to determine whether psychological factors existed that would limit the usefulness of such ratings.[2] The effect of research by Likert, by Kay, Meyer, and French, and by Meyer and Walker has been to show that such psychological limiting factors do indeed exist.[3]

Changes in the work environment have also stimulated shifts in emphasis in performance appraisal. According to Whisler and Harper, the following changes have had a significant impact:

1. Shifts in the occupational structure toward higher skills
2. Development of automation
3. Increasing size of organizations

4. Unionization
5. Increase of staff activities
6. Greater specialization in the roles of organization members, combined with increasing technical education
7. Changes in the philosophy of management from scientific management to human relations, and then to quantitative decision techniques and overall corporate planning[4]

In addition to the above, the movement toward greater decentralization and the creation of profit centers have had a major influence on performance appraisal practices.

The impact of these changes has been to reorient the emphasis of performance appraisal away from hierarchical judgment directed only toward controlling wages and salaries. The emphasis has recently shifted toward participation to stimulate motivation and development as well. The following list of appraisal techniques reflects this evolution.

Essays and Checklists Some of the earliest formal appraisal plans used in this country employed open-ended essay appraisals or some form of adjective checklist (see Exhibit 13–4). Because these approaches lacked objectivity and precision, the attention paid to psychometrics in the early 1920s led to the development of graphic rating scales.

Rating Scales Rating scales employed a list of traits, but in addition the rater was required to indicate his or her judgment of the amount of each trait possessed by the ratee by marking a point on a graphic scale, or continuum (see Exhibit 13–5). The major technical flaw of this approach was that because of the halo effect, most ratings tended to cluster at either the high end or the low end of the scale.

Forced-Distribution Since the failure to obtain a distribution of ratings was seen as the primary flaw of appraisals, attention shifted toward the development of methods to force a normal distribution of appraisals around the average or mean performance of all members of the work group. This led to the development of the forced-distribution technique (see Exhibit 13–6). Although the forced-distribution technique solved the technical distribution problems, it foundered on the logical objection of raters that many work groups did not reflect a normal distribution of individual performance.

Further Refinements Further technical refinements led to such approaches as ranking (rating the members of a work group from best to worst in the order of their relative performance), paired-comparison (a refinement of the ranking method that involves the systematic comparison of each member of a group with each of his or her peers in the group to produce the overall ranking), forced-choice (a series of choices between equally positive

EXHIBIT 13-4
Essay appraisal form.

Name _____   Position _____
Date of employment _____   Years in present position _____
Office _____   Previous position _____
Reports to _____

Performance, results, and methods—give production figures (be specific).

1. What has this person accomplished since the last appraisal? (Consider quantity and quality of work.)

2. How does this person go about getting his/her work done?

3. How well does this person work with people?

4. List outstanding personal qualifications or characteristics that help or hinder this person.

5. Recommended action to improve performance in present position.

The performance and personal qualification sections of this appraisal have been discussed with the employee by:

Name _____   Position _____   Date _____
Approved _____

---

and equally negative descriptive phrases), and critical-incident (the systematic recording, as they occur, of actual instances of significantly good or significantly poor performance) techniques. Exhibits 13-7, 13-8, and 13-9 represent three of these methods.

Although these later approaches have been relatively successful in overcoming some of the technical obstacles to appraisal, none of them has been widely adopted, primarily because of various practical difficulties. For example, the critical-incident technique has been shown to be relatively objective and reliable, but it is also prohibitively expensive for many appraisal situations.

Profit Performance Measurement Largely in reaction to the many difficulties encountered with such rating programs, in the 1950s researchers and management experts began to devise a number of novel approaches as alternatives to conventional ratings. One of the important alternatives suggested was profit performance measurement. Under this approach, which was designed to evaluate the performance of profit center managers, a man-

EXHIBIT 13-5
Graphic rating scale.

Name _____

Division/Department _____ Present position _____

Instructions: Read carefully each of the factor descriptions. Judge the employee on the basis of the work now being done. Consider each factor separately; do not let your rating of one factor influence your rating of another factor. Rate each factor by placing an x mark at the appropriate point along the line.

Ability to learn: Consider how quickly employee learns (ability to retain instruction and information).

Outstanding _____ Poor

Initiative: Consider ingenuity (self-reliance and resourcefulness; ability to know what needs to be done).

Outstanding _____ Poor

Job attitude: Consider the interest and enthusiasm shown.

Outstanding _____ Poor

Knowledge of job: Consider the knowledge of job and related work.

Outstanding _____ Poor

Industry: Consider responsibility to duties (ability to apply time and energy).

Outstanding _____ Poor

Quality of work: Consider accuracy of work regardless of volume (ability to perform work efficiently).

Outstanding _____ Poor

Cooperation: Consider ability and willingness to work in harmony with and for others.

Outstanding _____ Poor

Personality: Consider ability to get along with co-workers (personal conduct, courtesy, tact, friendliness).

Outstanding _____ Poor

Appearance: Consider neatness, personal dress, and personal habits.

Outstanding _____ Poor

---

ager was to be judged almost solely on the basis of the profitability of the organization for which he or she was responsible. Further refinement of the logic and application of this approach led to management by objectives.

Management by Objectives Peter Drucker proposed a new approach to performance appraisal, which he called "Management by Objectives and Self-Control." Drucker explains the concept as follows:

> Some of the most effective managers I know . . . have each of their subordinates write a "manager's letter" twice a year. In this letter to the superior, each manager first defines the objectives of his superior's job and

EXHIBIT 13-6
Forced distribution.

Key:
1. Outstanding, exceptionally high level (top 5 percent)
2. Superior, exceeds the expected level (next 10 percent)
3. At the expected level (middle 70 percent)
4. Below the expected level (next 10 percent)
5. At a marginal level (bottom 5 percent)

I. Accountabilities (as listed in approved job description) — *Performance*

II. Work traits — *Performance*

Attitude:	Willingness to adjust to changes
	Degree of interest and enthusiasm
Communication:	Ability to convey ideas and plans
	Written
	Oral
Cooperation:	Ability to work with and through others, including:
	Supervisor
	Peers
	Subordinates
	Government officials, educators, bankers, etc.
Delegation:	Ability to effectively assign work to others
Development:	Ability to develop attitudes, knowledge, and skills in:
	Self
	Subordinates
Organization:	Ability to effectively organize time and effort on work assignments
Forward planning:	Ability to plan ahead in order to meet changing needs
Judgment:	Ability to arrive consistently at sound decisions
Volume of work:	Ability to produce expected results in a given time

III. Current overall performance

Having rated each accountability and work trait, please indicate what the employee's overall performance is in his or her present position.

1. _____ Performs at an outstanding level (5 percent could be here)
2. _____ Performs at a superior level (10 percent could be here)
3. _____ Performs at the expected level (70 percent should be here)
4. _____ Performs at below the expected level (10 percent could be here)
5. _____ Performs at a marginal level (5 percent could be here)

EXHIBIT 13–7
Ranking scale.

Consider all of your employees in terms of their total performance. Then select the one you would regard as having the best total performance. Put his or her name in Column I, below, on the first line, numbered 1. Next pick out the person having the worst total performance. Put his or her name at the bottom of Column II, on the line numbered 20. Now, from the *remaining* names, select the one having the best total performance. Put his or her name in the first column on line 2. Keep up this process until all names have been placed in the scale.

Column I (Best)	Column II (Worst)
1. _____	11. _____
2. _____	12. _____
3. _____	13. _____
4. _____	14. _____
5. _____	15. _____
6. _____	16. _____
7. _____	17. _____
8. _____	18. _____
9. _____	19. _____
10. _____	20. _____

EXHIBIT 13–8
Forced-choice method.

Out of each set of five statements, check the one that best describes the employee and the one that least describes the employee.

	Best	Least
1. Would be very difficult to replace	____	____
Very valuable in a new operation	____	____
Alert to new opportunities for the company	____	____
Good for routine supervisory job	____	____
Tends to delegate things that will not reflect credit on him/her	____	____
2. Not willing to make decisions unless he/she has very complete information	____	____
Lets difficulties get him/her down	____	____
Makes snap judgments about people	____	____
Tries to run things his/her own way	____	____
Has not demonstrated up to now that he/she has the ability to progress further	____	____

EXHIBIT 13-9
Typical samples of critical incidents.

Negative Incidents			Positive Incidents		
Date	Item	Incident	Date	Item	Incident
2/14	M	Customer complaint on rudeness	4/3	B	Covering duties of ill co-worker

Item M refers to Public Relations responsibility. Customer complained that employee was rude and abusive when customer criticized his handling of transaction.

Item B refers to Cooperation. Employee voluntarily took over critical duties of an ill co-worker for period of three days in addition to performing his regular duties. As a result, department was able to maintain its performance standards.

of his own job as he sees them. He then sets down the performance standards which he believes are being applied to him. Next, he lists the things he must do himself to attain these goals—and the things within his own unit he considers the major obstacles. He lists the things his superior and the company do to help him and the things that hamper him. Finally, he outlines what he proposes to do during the next year to reach his goals. If his superior accepts this statement, the "manager's letter" becomes the charter under which the manager operates. The greatest advantage of Management by Objectives is perhaps that it makes it possible for a manager to control his own performance. Self-control means stronger motivation: a desire to do the best rather than just enough to get by. It means higher performance goals and broader vision. Even if Management by Objectives were not necessary to give the enterprise the unity of direction and effort of a management team, it would be necessary to make possible management by self-control.[5]

Another major contributor to the development of contemporary performance appraisal practice was Douglas McGregor.[6] McGregor was concerned with the fact that most appraisal systems involved ratings of traits and personal qualities that he felt were highly unreliable. Besides, the use of such trait ratings produced two main difficulties: (1) The manager was uncomfortable about using them and resisted making appraisals, and (2) it had a damaging effect on the motivation and development of the subordinate.

McGregor's criticism of trait rating was solidly supported by previous research in the social sciences. For example, Ronald Taft, a psychologist, had concluded from a survey of the extensive literature of research into human judgment that few individuals are qualified to judge the traits and aptitudes of others. Taft had found that ability to judge is a personality trait and that individuals vary widely in their ability to judge the traits and aptitudes of others.[7]

McGregor felt that Peter Drucker's concept of management by objectives offered an unusually promising framework within which to seek a solution to this problem, and he proposed a new approach to performance appraisal based upon Drucker's concept.

Building upon the logic of both Drucker and McGregor, Kindall and Gatza proposed a detailed plan for implementing a five-step performance appraisal program:

1. The individual discusses his job description with his superior, and they agree on the content of his job and relative importance of his major duties—the things he is paid to do and is accountable for.
2. The individual establishes performance targets for each of his responsibilities for the forthcoming period.
3. The individual meets with the superior to discuss the individual's target program.
4. Checkpoints are established for the evaluation of his progress; ways of measuring progress are selected.
5. The superior and subordinate meet at the end of the period to discuss the results of the subordinate's effort to meet the targets he had previously established.[8]

A typical set of forms used for the *management by objectives approach* to appraisal is shown in Exhibit 13–10. The forms used by different companies for this approach vary considerably, and some companies prefer to use only a blank sheet of paper. It will also be noted that the forms in Exhibit 13–10 emphasize an explicit relationship between the appraisal of performance against objectives and the determination of incentive bonuses. This direct tie between compensation and the accomplishment of objectives is not uncommon; however, some companies make the tie less explicit and prefer to use appraisal data only as an input to a separate compensation decision process.

A series of articles by Meyer, Kay, and French in the mid-1960s reported on General Electric's "Work Planning and Review" program, which was a major effort to apply the ideas of Drucker and McGregor. The program included controlled research to compare the results of conventional appraisal with those of a management by objectives approach. The latter approach proved to be clearly superior for motivating and developing subordinates.[9]

Meyer, Kay, and French also concluded that the developmental and compensation uses of appraisal need to be clearly separated in time. More recently, Cummings and Schwab have emphasized the importance of clearly separating the evaluative and developmental purposes of appraisal.[10] They suggest that three types of appraisal systems be distinguished: (1) those designed to enhance development and growth; (2) those designed to maintain performance at acceptable levels; and (3) those designed to improve unacceptable performance. They conclude that all three systems are likely to be operating simultaneously in a particular organization and that a single individual will be appraised by more than one system in the course of his or her career.

By the seventies, performance appraisal had been formalized by most organizations, and significant changes in the legal environment had re-

EXHIBIT 13–10

Management by objectives. (A) Sample performance standards for a supervisory position.
Performance Standards for Regular Routine
Responsibilities for Period January 1, _____ to December 31, _____

JOB: M&E Superintendent

Regular, Routine Responsibilities	Review Periods	Standards of Performance			Actual Performance
		Poor	Average	Excellent	
1. Maintenance Management indicators	Quarterly				
a) Performance		70	75	80	
b) Effectiveness		70	80	90	
c) Emergencies		20	15	10	
2. Cost Control					
a) Regular Repairs	Quarterly	$125,000/mo	$115,000/mo	$100,000/mo	
b) Overtime	Monthly	12% of total manhours	10% of total manhours	8% of total manhours	
3. Inventory Control	Quarterly	$75,000	$70,000	$65,000	
4. Completion of C&R Jobs	Upon completion of job				
a) Time		Within one month of completion date	Within one week of completion date	Completed one month early	
b) Cost		10% above budget	Budget	10% below budget	
c) Were desired objectives obtained on C&R Projects		90% of projects	95% of projects	99% of projects	
5. Downtime	Monthly				
a) Direct–paper machines		25 hrs/mo	15 hrs/mo	10 hrs/mo	
b) Indirect–equipment in others causing machine downtime		10 hrs/mo	5 hrs/mo	0 hrs/mo	
6. Industrial Relations	Annually				
a) Number of grievances		12	8	4	
b) Number of grievances reversed		3	2	1	

EXHIBIT 13-10, continued

JOB: M&E Superintendent

Regular, Routine Responsibilities	Review Periods	Standards of Performance			Actual Performance
		Poor	Average	Excellent	
7. Safety–frequency	Quarterly	5.25	4.35	3.00	
8. Development of Staff (percent promotable)	Annually	40%	50%	60%	
9. Housekeeping	Daily	Required cleanup causes overtime	Required cleanup without overtime	Stays clean as regular practice	

(B) Summary of objectives for review by both manager and employee.

1. The following items represent significant accomplishments (discuss as appropriate):

_____

2. The following major items were not accomplished as planned (give reasons):

_____

3. The following problems have been identified:

_____

4. Additional comments:

_____

Review by _____ **Date** _____
Employee _____

Progress Review of Objectives

Date _____

Objectives	Progress to Date	Problems	Suggested Action to Be Taken

(check one) Manager's copy _____
Employee's copy _____

425

EXHIBIT 13–10, *continued*

(C) Bonus percents by grade and performance.

Summary Appraisal	Salary Grade							
	10	11	12	13	14	15	16	17
Unusually high level of accomplishment on all targets. ☐ →	20–22.5%	33–37.5%	46–52.5%	65–75%	65–75%	78–90%	91–105%	104–120%
More than reasonable. Results against all targets were slightly better than normal expectations. ☐ →	17–19%	28–32%	39–45%	55–64%	55–64%	66–77%	77–90%	88–103%
Reasonable, normal achievement for managerial personnel. Did well on all the more important targets. ☐ →	14–16%	23–27%	32–38%	45–54%	45–54%	54–65%	63–76%	72–87%
Adequate performance against targets. However, achievement on the most important target could have been better. ☐ →	11–13%	18–22%	25–31%	35–44%	35–44%	42–53%	49–62%	56–71%
Results against several important targets could have been better. ☐ →	7.5–10%	12.5–17%	17.5–24%	25–34%	25–34%	30–41%	35–48%	40–55%
Failed to achieve minimum acceptable level of performance on all important targets. ☐ →	0	0	0	0	0	0	0	0

Bonus percent recommended: _____

sulted in litigation regarding merit pay and promotion decisions. With this litigation came renewed concern about the subjective nature of the appraisal process and the need to make it more valid and reliable. Such pressure intensified the effort to move away from trait-oriented appraisal toward job-related measurements, and toward techniques that recognize the "multidimensional" nature of performance. One result is the development of behaviorally anchored rating scales (BARS). The experience with BARS was carefully studied to determine its effectiveness in reducing measurement errors and in providing a basis for identifying training and development needs.

Behaviorally Anchored Rating Scales Behaviorally anchored rating scales (BARS) are designed to identify the critical areas of performance for a job, and to describe the more effective and less effective job behaviors for getting results. Performance is evaluated by asking the rater to record specific, observable job behaviors of an employee and to then compare these observations with a "behaviorally anchored rating scale." (Exhibit 13–11 provides an example of such a scale that has been designed to evaluate a department manager's ability to meet day-to-day deadlines.) As a result, the supervisor is in a position to compare the employee's actual behavior with behavior that has been previously determined to be more or less effective. Proponents of BARS claim many advantages for this approach. They argue that such a system differentiates among behavior, performance, and results, and consequently is able to provide a basis for setting developmental goals for the employee. Because it is job-specific and identifies observable and measurable behavior, it is a more reliable and valid method for performance appraisal.

Empirical studies of behaviorally anchored rating scales (BARS) have provided a fertile ground for study by both theorists and practitioners. The BARS experience has helped to clarify three major controversies of the appraisal process. One was the previously discussed issue of rating content (trait vs. job related). A second controversy involved the multidimensional nature of performance. The administrative uses of appraisal had encouraged rating systems to produce an overall ("global") measure of performance, which tended to mask differences in performance in the key result areas ("performance dimensions") critical to job results. The third controversy involved the issue of the most effective way to anchor the rating scales (numerical or behavioral). By anchoring the scales behaviorally, the BARS approach was expected to produce more valid and reliable results by reducing measurement errors (leniency, halo effect, central tendency, and similarity).

EXHIBIT 13–11
Behaviorally Anchored Rating Scale (BARS).

NAME _____

In the job of department manager, how well does this person do in meeting deadlines? Consider only day-to-day or typical job behavior.

Write *typical* on the scale opposite the action that seems to fit most closely when doing a usual or typical job in meeting deadlines.

	_____ Could be expected never to be late in meeting deadlines no matter how unusual the circumstances.
Could be expected to meet deadlines comfortably by delegating an unusually high number of assignments to two highly rated associates.	
	_____ Could be expected always to get his or her associates' work schedules made out on time.
Could be expected to meet seasonal deadlines within reasonable length of time. _____	
	_____ Could be expected to offer to do the assigments at home after failing to get them out on the deadline day.
Could be expected to fail to schedule additional help to complete assignments on time.	Could be expected to be late all the time on weekly assignments for his or her department. _____
Could be expected to disregard due dates for assignments in his or her department.	
	_____ Could be expected to leave assignments in a desk drawer for several weeks even when they had been given by a superior and called to his or her attention after due dates.

In their review of the BARS literature, Schwab, Heneman, and DeCotis conclude that "findings from research have not been very encouraging." Evidence regarding the effect of behavioral anchors on measurement errors, they reported, was inconclusive. They hypothesized that the "major advantage of BARS may stem from the dimensions generated rather than from any particular superiority provided by behavioral versus numerical anchors."[11]

CURRENT PRACTICE IN PERFORMANCE APPRAISAL

The previous sections provide a historical perspective on the evolution of appraisal techniques, and suggest theoretical guidelines for the development and implementation of performance appraisal systems. The purpose of this section is to describe current practice in performance appraisal. What appraisal techniques are being used at the present time by major American companies? Which employees have their performance appraised? What are the primary uses of appraisals? And, most importantly, what effect do the answers to the latter two questions have on the type of appraisal techniques used in a particular company?

Formalized Appraisal Programs

A study by Locher and Teel indicated that 89 percent of their respondents have formal performance appraisal programs.[12] This is consistent with a BNA study that reported that 84 percent have "regular procedures for evaluating office employees." Only 54 percent of the companies in the BNA study have formal programs for evaluating production workers, however. The BNA study further reports that "for 81 percent of the office groups and 76 percent of the production employees, a standard rating form is used in making performance evaluation."[13]

Types of Plans

Exhibit 13–12 shows the types of formal appraisal plans used by 304 leading industrial corporations surveyed by Schuster and Kindall. Somewhat surprisingly, 106 companies, or 34.9 percent, indicated they used only a management by objectives plan, and 75 companies, or 24.7 percent, indicated they used a management by objectives type plan (for a part of the work force or a part of the organization) in combination with another type of appraisal plan. Thus, 181 companies, or 59.6 percent, said that management by objectives served as the basis of performance appraisal for at least part of their work force. A total of 29 percent of the companies used some sort of trait

EXHIBIT 13–12
Appraisal plans used in 304 leading industrial corporations.*

Type of Plan Used	Responses	
	Number	Percent
Number or descriptive rating of only one general item, "How well does the ratee perform his job?"	16	5.3
Numerical or graphic trait ratings	27	8.9
Trait checklist	61	20.1
Forced-choice system of rating	11	3.6
Management by objectives	106	34.9
Other	8	2.6
Combination of management by objectives and another plan	75	24.7
Total	304	100.0%

*Twelve of the 316 respondents did not specify type of plan used.

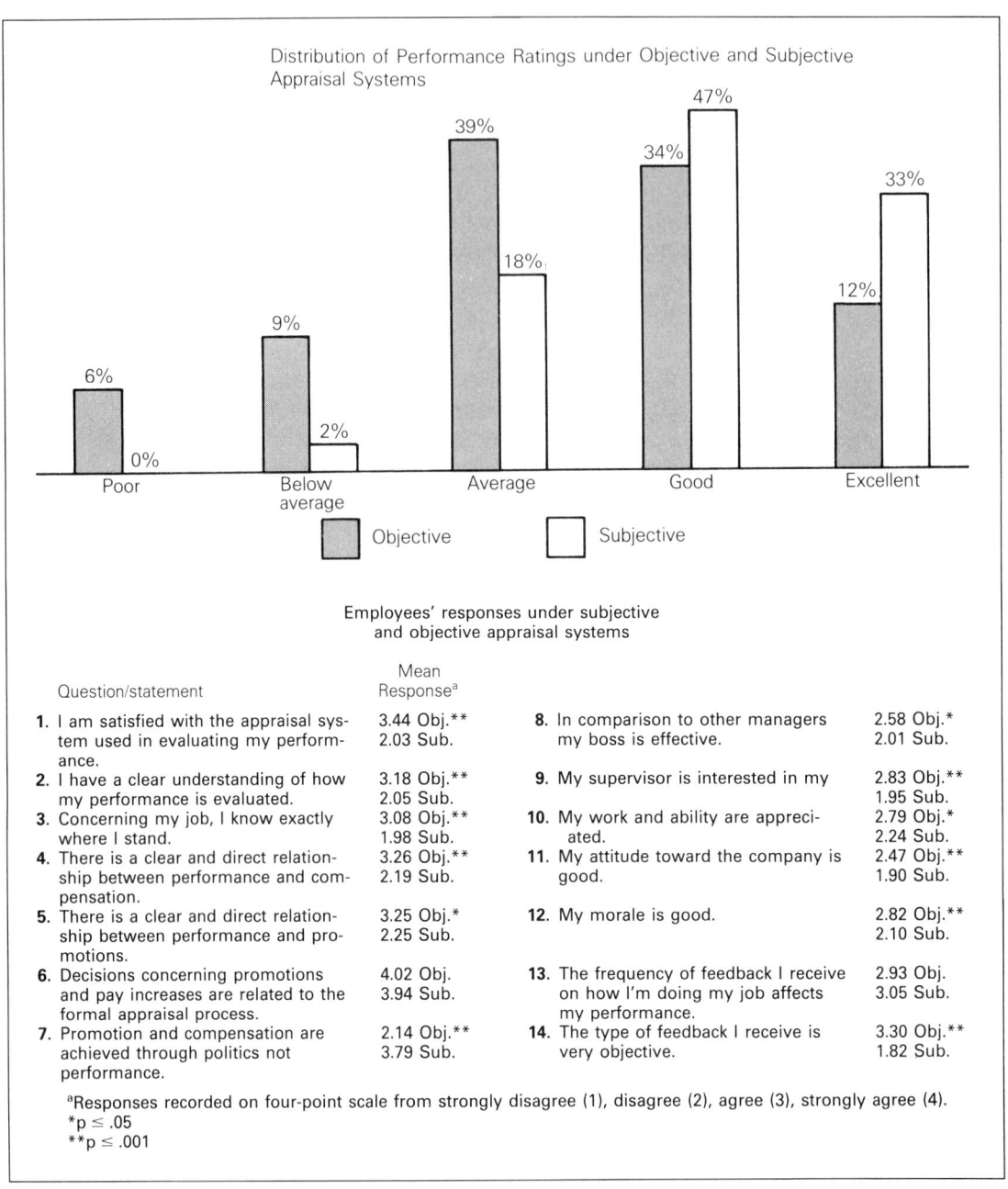

rating, and this was the only alternative besides management by objectives chosen by a significant number of companies.[14] Each remaining alternative was chosen by less than 6 percent of the companies; all together, the remaining alternatives were chosen by 11.5 percent. It thus seems clear that in the late sixties, management by objectives was by far the most common basis for performance appraisal in the largest industrial companies.

More recent studies provide conflicting evidence regarding the employment of management by objectives as an appraisal tool. The Downs and Moscinski study found MBO in use by 71.4 percent of the companies they studied, with more than half of the companies using a combination of MBO and essays.[15] Locher and Teel, however, found that only 12.7 percent of their respondents used MBO as their "primary" appraisal technique, and concluded, "Perhaps the most surprising finding of the survey was the limited use of MBO as an appraisal technique."[16] Even the Downs and Moscinski study, which supported the Schuster and Kindall study, found discrepancies in responses to their questionnaire.

It is more than likely that MBO is still the most widely used technique for appraising managerial personnel, and Odiorne is probably correct in stating that MBO is the "dominant form" of management in the United States.[17] Nonetheless, there is strong evidence that MBO, as currently practiced, is failing to fulfill the high expectations often held for it. Kondrasuk reached the following conclusion after reviewing 185 studies of MBO:

> We have found some evidence, but not conclusive proof, for the effectiveness of MBO. It appears we are headed toward a contingency approach to MBO. We still need to determine what aspects of MBO are most effective in which situation.[18]

For nonmanagerial workers, however, it is clear from all of the studies that the rating scale in combination with some form of narrative comment is the dominant technique currently in use. Teel in 1980 noted a trend toward multiple appraisal techniques and an increasing use of the narrative comment.[19] Other methods such as critical incidents, paired-comparison, and forced-choice are apparently used infrequently. A comparison of results-oriented and trait-based performance appraisals is shown on p. 430.

Purposes and Uses of Appraisals

For lower- and middle-management personnel, a recent Conference Board study ranked the following uses of appraisal in their order of importance: (1) management development, (2) performance measurement, (3) performance improvement, and (4) compensation administration. This was also true for top management except for a reversal of the top two purposes. For top executives, performance measurement was ranked number one.[20]

For office and production personnel, the BNA study indicated that performance appraisal is primarily used for "determining wage increases," "promotion decisions," and "determining training needs." "Determining wage increases" was number one for office workers, whereas "promotion decisions" ranked first for production employees.[21] Locher and Teel also concluded that appraisals are most widely used for compensation decisions and individual performance improvement programs, and "are being used today for essentially the same purposes that they have served for many years in the past."[22]

It is important to note that there appears to be a clear difference in viewpoint regarding the primary goal of performance appraisal between those companies using MBO alone and those companies using it in combination with other approaches. This can be seen in Exhibit 13–13 where the modal response (31.1 percent) of companies having an MBO approach to appraisal was that the principal purpose of the plan is the motivation of employees. Another 20.8 percent of these companies said the principal purpose of the MBO program was the planning of training and development of employees.

Significantly, management by objectives is the only appraisal approach for which the modal primary use is motivation. Only 20 percent of the companies having a combination of MBO and some other appraisal approach said that motivation was the primary goal of their appraisal program; and the modal response (22.7 percent) of this group was that the program was used primarily to determine merit increases or bonuses.

What Is Evaluated?

Surprisingly, in spite of the growing recognition of the subjectivity and bias built into systems that rate personal characteristics, most rating scales are "trait-oriented" rather than "job-oriented." Even the Conference Board study of management appraisal systems reported widespread use of such personality characteristics as attitude, drive, stability, and integrity. The following comment about terms commonly appearing on rating forms appears in it:

> Many of these terms seem to refer to personality traits rather than to specific behaviors. It is possible, however, that these terms have more specific meanings in the firms that use them. At least, when asked directly to rank the importance of the performance areas they appraise, the firms in this study put "performance results–goal achievement" at the head of the list and "personal characteristics" at the end.[23]

From this and other studies, nonetheless, it appears that in many instances the stated preference for job-related factors is more "lip-service" than reality.

Who Is Involved in the Appraisal Process?

Locher and Teel observed that appraisals are primarily made by the superior of the employee being appraised, and without any direct employee input. In a later study, Teel noted a trend toward a review by the manager

EXHIBIT 13–13
Primary use of various types of appraisal plans.

Type of Plan	Not Answered	Merit Increases or Bonuses	Counseling	Planning Training or Development	Promotion	Retention and Discharge	Motivation	Improve Company Planning	Other	Total (rounded)
Overall performance	25.0%	50.0%	0.0%	12.5%	0.0%	0.0%	6.3%	6.3%	0.0%	100%
Traits:										
Numerical	14.8	25.9	29.6	11.1	3.7	0.0	14.8	0.0	0.0	100
Descriptive	21.3	21.3	13.1	14.8	4.9	0.0	16.4	4.9	3.3	100
Forced-choice	45.5	9.1	0.0	9.1	9.1	18.2	9.1	0.0	0.0	100
MBO only	18.9	14.2	1.9	20.8	0.9	0.0	31.1	9.4	2.8	100
Other	25.0	25.0	0.0	12.5	0.0	0.0	25.0	12.5	0.0	100
MBO plus another	29.3	22.7	4.0	13.3	1.3	0.0	20.0	5.3	4.0	100
TOTAL	39.0%	17.4%	5.5%	12.2%	2.0%	0.5%	16.6%	5.0%	2.0%	100%

immediately above the one who makes the appraisal. Teel also concluded that the employee's role in the appraisal process is still a passive one.

> Most organizations follow a "tell and sell" approach, in which the manager completes the appraisal, shows it to the employee, explains the reasons for the ratings and/or narrative comments, discusses what might be done to improve performance, and asks for employee reaction. In short, the manager prepares the appraisal and tries to justify it to the employee.[24]

The BNA study described the following formal procedures for providing the employee feedback regarding the appraisal:

> In nearly all the companies with evaluation procedures the evaluation is discussed with the employee; this is true for 97 percent of office groups and 24 percent of production; in many instances the employee must sign the evaluation form indicating it has been discussed with him. The evaluation or review form becomes part of the employee's permanent personnel record in 92 percent of both office and production groups.[25]

Many writers are also reporting the increased use of both peer and subordinate appraisals. In fact, the Conference Board study provides a case study of the RCA "Talent Inventory," which provides for multiple assessment. The employee is rated by five to seven individuals within the employee's work network. Of these, two or three must be superiors, two or three must be peers, and one or two must be subordinates to the person being rated. Although many writers are recommending the use of multiple assessors, there is no evidence of its widespread use in current practice.

Rater Training

Less than half of the companies responding to the Conference Board study report the existence of formal training programs for raters. Similar findings were revealed by the Downs and Moscinski and Locher and Teel studies. Where training is provided, it primarily consists of short sessions involving two to four hours of instruction. Such programs are likely to include an explanation of the forms to be used, a discussion of measurement errors (e.g., halo effect, leniency error, central tendency and similarity), and some help in conducting the appraisal interview.

Since current performance appraisal research clearly indicates the vital nature of rater motivation and skill, there should be increased interest in the development of effective programs for training the rater in the future.

Dynamic Nature of Appraisal Systems

Both the Downs and Moscinski and the Conference Board studies conclude that two-thirds of the managers surveyed are reasonably satisfied with the appraisal systems currently in use. Yet all of the studies seemed to describe systems in the process of changing.

Although there is no evidence of any significant effort on the part of companies to formally evaluate the effectiveness of appraisal systems, the tendency for companies to frequently change their systems does indicate an awareness of problems in the appraisal process and a desire to solve them.

CURRENT STATUS OF THE APPRAISAL PROCESS

Teel summarized the problems of the appraisal process as follows:

> One is how to arrive at a single overall performance evaluation, often needed for compensation decisions, based on a series of individual ratings and/or narrative statements. A second is how to get managers to follow a strictly merit philosophy, rather than giving approximately the same percentage increases to everyone. A third is how to get greater employee involvement in the appraisal process so that it will become more of a joint problem-solving discussion and less of a "tell and sell" session. The final problem is how to reconcile the developmental and administrative requirements of an appraisal system, since an approach that satisfied one often is unsuitable for the other.[26]

In addition to the problems of inflated ratings and rater bias, Downs and Moscinski found great concern for the lack of preparation on the part of raters, the pressures of time, which made it difficult for raters to do the job properly, and the tendency for raters to view the appraisal process as an obligation rather than an opportunity.

Most companies do have formal programs for performance appraisal, and the larger ones in particular are working to make them more effective. MBO is still widely used for appraising managerial and professional personnel, and will probably continue to be the dominant form of management in the United States. Currently, the rating scale in combination with narrative statements is the technique most often used for evaluating both office and production workers. There is growing awareness of the subjective nature of the trait appraisals, and in response to pressures from the legal environment, there will be increased experimentation with "job-oriented" rating scales.

CONCLUSIONS AND RECOMMENDATIONS

In order to make the appraisal system more effective, we make four recommendations in the areas of management climate, training, evaluation, and investment.

1. Management Climate The effort to find the "right form" or the right "system" must be matched with an effort to create the right climate for appraisal. Rater motivation is critical to the evaluation process. To be effective, the type of appraisal plan adopted must be seen by all concerned as being consistent with the basic assumptions and style of management prevalent in the organization. Management by objectives as an approach to appraisal, for example, works best within a climate that emphasizes participation and a high degree of mutual trust and confidence within a framework of basic commitment to management by shared objectives and self-control.

2. Training Training programs must be developed to help the raters understand the importance of the appraisal, and to clarify both the purposes and methods of the system. In addition, the raters must be helped to develop the skills required, not only in the interview (e.g., asking questions, listening, responding to employee ideas, and handling defensive behaviors), but in the development of a performance management system (e.g., setting goals, establishing performance standards, and documenting performance.)

3. Evaluation Formal evaluation procedures should be implemented to determine the effectiveness of the appraisal system. Is it integrated with the basic strategy of the organization? Is it consistent with equal employment opportunity guidelines? Does it apply sound principles of human resource management?

4. Investment Be willing to commit the resources required to improve the system. It takes a considerable investment of time and money to do the job of communicating, motivating, and training that is required. Be prepared to undertake what often seems an overwhelming task of developing a job-oriented rating system.

LEGAL CONSIDERATIONS IN PERFORMANCE APPRAISAL

More recently, actions of the Equal Employment Opportunity Commission and subsequent court decisions have underscored the importance of accurate and objective records of employee performance in order to defend against charges of discrimination. All of this has led to increased recognition of the importance of performance appraisal and a corresponding awareness of the shortcomings of existing appraisal systems.

Several recent articles have emphasized the legal requirements and constraints that affect the design and operation of performance appraisal subsystems. Performance appraisals have been held by the courts to be a form of selection test. They must, therefore, meet stringent criteria for validity under the Uniform Guidelines on Employee Selection Procedures. Because performance appraisals are used in making decisions for promotion, layoff, merit raise, job transfer, and training placement, they must be an accurate reflection of job performance. If they are not, charges of discrimination may be brought against an employer.

In summarizing a number of landmark court decisions regarding the legal requirements for performance appraisal systems, Feild and Holley concluded:

> Successful defendants' appraisal systems tended to possess the following characteristics: the case was brought against a nonindustrial organization, individuals responsible for evaluating employees were given specific written instructions on how to complete the appraisals, appraisals were made using a system that was behavior-oriented rather than trait-oriented, job analysis was used to develop the content of the appraisal system, and the results of the appraisals were reviewed with each employee. On the other hand, defendants who lost the discrimination suits tended to have appraisal systems described as follows: the case was brought against an industrial organization, evaluators of employees were not given specific instructions on how to complete the appraisals, the appraisal system was trait-oriented rather than behavior-oriented, job analysis was not utilized in developing the content of the appraisal system, and the results of the appraisals were not reviewed with each employee.[27]

The following checklist has been suggested for auditing performance appraisal systems to assure that they are legally defensible:

POLICY CONSIDERATIONS
- ☐ Is there a written company policy covering performance appraisal?
- ☐ Are the objectives of performance appraisal clearly specified?
- ☐ Does the policy cover frequency of rating? Who is to perform the evaluation and give feedback?
- ☐ Does the policy provide for variations in frequency of rating, and so forth, under special circumstances? Are the circumstances defined?

TRAINING
- ☐ Have the evaluators been trained?
- ☐ Has the training been specific to the forms and procedures now in use?
- ☐ Can the training be documented as to who attended and what material was covered?

COMMUNICATIONS
- ☐ Do those evaluated know the policy, objectives, and procedures?
- ☐ Are those evaluated aware of the standards upon which they will be judged?
- ☐ Are those evaluated informed of the evaluation?
- ☐ Are the members of the organization informed of promotional opportunities?
- ☐ Can communications be documented?

METHODS
- ☐ Can job relatedness be demonstrated through job analyses?
- ☐ Do the methods of appraisal, such as Management by Objectives, incorporate elements of job analysis in the appraisal process?

□ Are there provisions for obtaining input from others, particularly if immediate supervisors do not have daily contact with those evaluated?
□ Are the evaluations as objective as possible?

USES OF APPRAISAL DATA

□ Are performance appraisals used as intended in policy and announced objectives?
□ Are there standardized methods and procedures for combining data from other types of evaluation in making decisions?
□ Is the weight each measure carries, with respect to the total, fixed?
□ Have safeguards for privacy been established? Are they followed?

RELATING PERFORMANCE APPRAISAL TO REWARDING

The managerial actions that may be taken to recognize and reward performance include praise (private and public), written commendation, published commendation, increased autonomy, change in job title, status symbols such as office space or furnishings, performance bonuses, salary increases, promotions in grade, increase in responsibilities, and various forms of supplementary compensation. It is most important to recognize the responsibility of the manager to match the rewards both with performance and with the perceptions and needs of the individual. Depending on the manager's analysis of the individual employee, he or she will wish to emphasize nonfinancial rewards, financial rewards, or a mixture of the two in order to reward each employee in such a way that (1) the employee will perceive the reward to relate equitably to his or her effort and accomplishment, and (2) the employee will perceive the reward to be the most attractive and motivating among the equal alternatives from which the manager selected.

Modern motivation theory (both reinforcement theory and expectancy theory) emphasizes the importance of a direct tie between performance and reward. For the reward to have the desired motivational impact, it is imperative that it be directly related to performance and that it be clearly perceived as such. In order to be effective motivationally, rewards must be perceived by the recipients to be equitable in light of their inputs and outcomes (that is, results).

No matter how accurate, the appraisal is likely to be worthless unless it is followed by appropriate rewards. Conversely, rewarding can be effective only to the extent that it is based on an accurate appraisal. This underscores again the fact that performance evaluations must be both reliable and valid if they are to serve a useful motivational purpose.

Although the responsibilities of the manager remain constant regardless of the approach to appraisal used, a considerable body of evidence indicates that, all things being equal, the management by objectives approach to appraisal is likely to result both in higher validity of the evaluation itself and in an increased perception of equity on the part of subordinates.

These would appear to be powerful arguments indeed in favor of adopting an MBO approach to appraisal whenever the situation makes it feasible.

A research study by W. H. Mobley lends additional support to the conclusion that a direct relationship between the management by objectives process and the financial rewards system is desirable. The results are summarized by Mobley:

> Due to the wide divergence of opinion on the value of linking MBO and merit compensation activities, 625 middle to top level managers were asked to indicate their perceptions of the relationship. The results of the study tend to reinforce the position that the arguments favoring linkage outweigh those against it.
>
> To the extent that pay is a valued reward, linking it, along with other desirable rewards to performance, should enhance motivation and performance.[28]

One argument for establishing a link between the MBO process and merit compensation, Mobley points out, is that "it permits establishment of the performance–reward contingency suggested by reinforcement and expectancy–instrumentality theories of motivation and performance."[29] See Exhibit 13–14 for one example of how this can be done.

STEP-BY-STEP IMPLEMENTATION PROCEDURE FOR A PERFORMANCE APPRAISAL SYSTEM

The preceding part of this chapter has been conceptual in nature. We have described in principle an approach to appraising and rewarding for performance that is consistent with both (1) the systems approach for managing human resources taken throughout this book, and (2) what is known about human motivation. Athough a "cookbook" recipe is inappropriate for a contingency-based approach to managing, there is practical utility in providing some step-by-step guidelines for the manager. We are, therefore, detailing a six-step process through which each manager may discharge responsibilities for appraising and rewarding performance. The steps in this process are:

1. The performance appraisal interview
2. Comparison of performance
3. Setting nonfinancial rewards
4. Relating performance to compensation budgets
5. Taking other managerial actions
6. Communicating the final appraisal and the action to be taken

Conducting the Performance Appraisal Interview

As indicated previously, a number of very different approaches to the appraisal process may be taken. Regardless of the specific format used

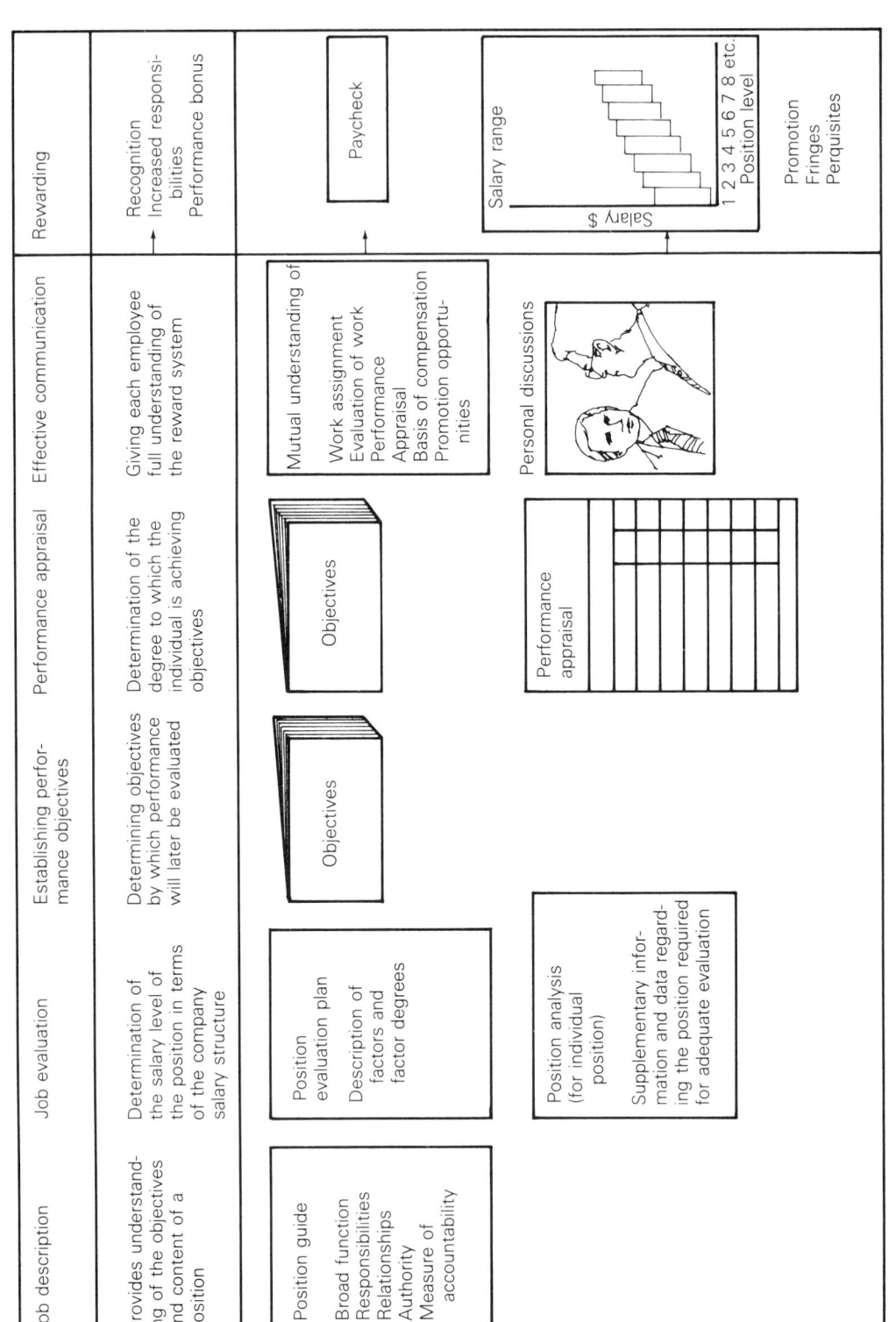

EXHIBIT 13–14
Tying rewards to performance.

(whether trait-rating, critical-incident, MBO, or something in between), however, and regardless of whether the basic approach is hierarchical or participative, two elements are essential to an effective appraisal interview.

The *first* element is that some of the data for the appraisal must come from the subordinate. Clearly, this will be especially true for MBO-based appraisals, in which a great deal of the data will come from subordinates. Even in the most hierarchical type of appraisal, however, it is important that the subordinate be given an opportunity to provide data on his or her performance. This is so because the subordinate may often be aware of performance elements not known to the superior. A minimal perception of equity by the subordinate requires that the superior take all relevant data into account in arriving at the appraisal.

The *second* essential element of the appraisal is a face-to-face conference at which the subordinate has an opportunity to present personal perceptions of his or her performance, to comment on the superior's preliminary appraisal, and to supply additional data which he or she feels have been omitted in the superior's appraisal. Again, the purpose of the face-to-face meeting is both to increase the validity of the appraisal and to increase the employee's perception of equity.

If an MBO process is being used and is operating well, drafting the performance appraisal is a very simple and straightforward step. Since specific and measurable objectives were set at the beginning of the period, and since performance data are available on accomplishments, all that is required is to match up the accomplishments with the objectives. The performance appraisal merely reports the facts, along with a brief explanation of the reasons for the results.

Although simple to describe (and, in fact, simple to do), this step nevertheless involves two things that are often not present in an organization until the implementation of management by objectives.

First, this match-up step requires that factual data measuring and evaluating the accomplishment of objectives be available. Frequently such data (in sufficient detail to permit the easy evaluation of objective accomplishment) are not available prior to MBO. This means that in order to make MBO operational, new control data and reports must be generated.

Each objective requirement should have matching control data to evaluate its accomplishment. Where such data are not already available in the organization, or where they are not available in the appropriate form, they must be created or modified.

Second, this match-up step requires that the necessary data be in the hands of the individual employee. This often means providing data to individuals who have not previously received them.

Providing feedback data on performance during the performance period so that the individual performer may adjust his or her performance in time to achieve objectives by the end of the period is not really a new concept. In fact, it is wholly consistent with the most traditional forms of scientific management. What *is* new is that this concept must be operational if MBO is to be effective.

Aside from its necessity for MBO, the provision of feedback data to enable the individual to adjust his or her performance is a highly valuable procedure in its own right. After the fact it does little good to tell a person that he or she has failed. What is helpful is to let the person know that he or she is in trouble before the opportunity to improve the performance and to achieve the desired results has been lost.

At the end of this step, the individual will have drafted a document that says, in effect, "I accomplished the following objectives, and here is how, and I failed to accomplish the following objectives, and here is why."

The next step in the appraisal interview process involves the discussion of the draft appraisal by the manager and the subordinate. Frequently, the manager will have little to do at this step except agree with the appraisal, perhaps add some content, and question a few minor details. Nevertheless, at this step, too, the boss may have to be a boss.

If the manager feels that the self-appraisal has been slipshod or that it glosses over failures, it is his or her responsibility to say so and to demand a more complete evaluation from the subordinate. Finally, if a complete appraisal is not forthcoming from the subordinate, it is the boss's job to provide one.

Again, experience shows that this degree of direction is rarely required. This is particularly true because of the factual nature of the MBO process. It should be remembered that we are dealing with specific and measurable objectives, and with factual data reporting the extent to which they have been accomplished. Since "facts are facts," there is little room for opinion or disagreement. Objectives have either been achieved or they have not been achieved, and there is usually little room for debate. This fact alone makes MBO highly desirable to a manager.

Comparing Performance with Accepted Standards

The next step in the appraising and rewarding process is for the manager to compare the individual subordinate's performance with accepted standards of performance. If an MBO process is being used, this step involves comparing achievement with objectives. If other procedures are being used, it involves comparing the individual's performance with the job description. How does the individual's performance compare with the performance expected of a typical employee at this individual's position in grade? If the particular individual is currently at the midpoint in his or her salary grade, is the performance about what would be expected at that stage, is it far in excess of what would be expected, or is it about what one would expect from a beginner rather than a seasoned employee?

Finally, the manager will want to compare on a person-to-person basis individuals who are in the same or very similar jobs and/or individuals who are at approximately the same salary grade and position within grade even though their specific duties may vary. This step will be absolutely essential in situations where the rewards available to the manager are inadequate. Even in the rare circumstances in which ample rewards are available, the manager will want to make appropriate person-to-person comparisons in order to ensure that all individuals are being rewarded equitably in relation to their relative performance (that is, inputs and contribution).

Setting Nonfinancial Rewards

Having completed the preliminary appraisal, the fact-finding conference with the subordinate, and the comparison of the subordinate's performance to the subordinate's position description, position in grade, and performance of other employees, the manager must decide on the appropriate reward mix for each subordinate.

The manager's first step in making that decision is to consider what nonfinancial rewards will be equitable in terms of each individual's performance, motivating in terms of each individual's needs, and feasible given the traditions and managerial practices of the particular organization. The many different types of nonfinancial rewards available to the manager include such things as recognition, increased responsibility, greater freedom and autonomy, and praise.

We recommend that nonfinancial rewards be considered first simply in order to ensure that these rewards (which are often neglected) be given proper consideration. Also, nonfinancial rewards often prove to be less expensive options.

Relating Performance to Compensation Budgets

In ideal circumstances the manager will have sufficient resources to award each subordinate whatever increase in compensation appears to be appropriate in order to equitably reward the subordinate for performance in light of the subordinate's job description, position, and salary grade, and of the performance of other individuals. In such situations the manager has a relatively simple job. The manager merely determines the appropriate increase in compensation (and/or the appropriate performance bonus) for each individual. These increases and bonuses are then added together to determine the total compensation increases and bonus expenditures for the year.

Of course, the organization may have policy guidelines and limitations that determine the maximum amounts that may be awarded. The organization may set an absolute limit (such as 20 percent) as the largest salary increase that may be awarded, regardless of circumstances. Or, there may be guidelines saying that individuals may receive increases of up to 20 percent if they are below the midpoint of a salary grade but that increases for individuals above the midpoint of the salary grade are limited to 10 percent. Whatever the policy constraints are, the manager will naturally have to abide by them. In our example, however, there are no budget limits on the total amount that the manager may spend on salary increases and/or bonuses for all subordinates.

Although ideal in theory, this degree of freedom and flexibility rarely occurs in practice. It is far more likely that in specific situations managers will be constrained not only by policy limits but also by a compensation budget that sets absolute limits on the total amount that they may award to all subordinates. Often this amount will be less (sometimes far less) than their appraisal and comparison has led them to believe would be appropriate if "equitable" salary action were taken for each individual subordinate. In this fairly common set of circumstances, managers are then called upon to take the additional step of determining how to allocate an inadequate compensation budget to reward the performance of their subordinates.

Although seldom emphasized in texts on appraisal and compensation, this step is perhaps the most difficult one for the manager. The previous steps in this process, though technically demanding, can lead to what the manager perceives as the "right" solution. Unfortunately, at this step of relating performance to the budget for financial rewards the manager for the first time is required to aim for something less than an optimum solution. Now, the manager must recognize that all subordinates cannot receive the treatment that he or she has determined to be equitable; instead, *the manager must aim at minimizing inequity.*

There are no magic formulas for handling this dilemma, although, clearly, person-to-person comparisons are now called for in earnest. In addition to making even more searching person-to-person comparisons than may have been necessary before, the manager will also want to rethink the opportunities for nonfinancial rewards. After this has been done, a variety of techniques may be considered, including the following:

1. Treating everyone equally by reducing all "equitable" compensation actions by the same percentage
2. Giving preference to the individuals whose performance is most outstanding and reducing the increases of the individuals whose performances are marginally satisfactory
3. Awarding all subordinates some minimum percentage increase, then allocating increases above that minimum on a person-to-person comparison basis
4. Some combination of these approaches

Although it has not been possible to suggest any perfect solutions to this dilemma, it should be pointed out that performing this step with extreme care and precision is critical if employees are to perceive their compensation to be equitable. It is bad enough that due to extraneous constraints beyond the employees' control they will not receive the rewards that their manager determined to be appropriate in relation to their performance. If employees also feel that they are receiving an inequitable share of inadequate rewards, motivationally this would be the last straw.

Taking Other Managerial Action

After deciding on an allocation of both nonfinancial and financial rewards, managers should turn their attention to such other actions as promotion, demotion, transfer, and training. While discussed elsewhere in this book, these activities should flow directly from and be directly related to the results of performance appraisal. Moreover, they are a part of the total rewarding process, and as such they should be a part of what is reported to the individual employee as being the compensation for his or her contributions.

Communicating the Final Appraisal and the Action to Be Taken

The final step in the appraising process is communication of the final appraisal and action taken by the manager to each individual subordinate. It is not sufficient for the manager to casually comment to the subordinate that, following the fact-finding conference, adjustments were made in the preliminary appraisal. And it is clearly not sufficient that the subordinate find out about the compensation action taken when he or she receives the next paycheck or a bonus check.

Whether the news is good or bad, it is absolutely essential from the standpoint of the subordinate's perception of equity and motivation that the manager communicate clearly in a private, quiet conference and in detail the action taken and the specific reasons for it. The whole complex and demanding process of appraising for performance comes to fruition at this step. Depending on how well the communication job is done, the opportunity to create a sense of equity and to strengthen motivation is either realized or is lost. It is not too strong to say that all of the other steps in the appraising and rewarding process lead up to this.

At this step more than at any other, the manager has the opportunity to emphasize the direct tie between individual performance and the rewards received. Here (and only here) can the payoff to the manager and the organization occur in terms of motivation and perception of equity.

For all of these reasons, managers should consider this conference with each individual subordinate to be one of their most important responsibilities. This mental set will lead managers to provide the appropriate amount of time, to make sure that the subordinate is in a receptive mood, to prepare themselves very carefully for the conference, and to listen carefully and respond alertly to what is said.

SUMMARY

This chapter has emphasized a contingency-based approach to appraisal that recognizes the usefulness of a broad spectrum of appraisal techniques, ranging from hierarchical trait appraisals to highly participative management by objectives approaches. Which approach is best will depend on the particular situation, including the subordinates (their experiences, expectations, and abilities), the manager and his or her capabilities, and the traditions, climate, style, and policies of the organization. Each of the different forms of appraisal has unique advantages and drawbacks.

Although no one approach to appraisal is clearly best for all situations, an impressive accumulation of research evidence indicates that, for purposes of perceived equity and motivation, the management by objectives approach has a great deal of potential. This is because the MBO approach emphasizes a direct tie between performance and reward.

The critical importance of appraising and rewarding for performance as the final step in the human resource management process was emphasized throughout the chapter. From the standpoint of motivating future organizational performance, the whole process of managing human resources effectively comes to fruition at the step of appraising and rewarding performance. If this step is performed badly, all the preceding steps in the process lose their value.

Finally, a six-step implementation process provides specific guidelines to enable individual managers to discharge their responsibilities in appraising and rewarding performance: (1) conducting the performance appraisal interview, (2) comparing performance with accepted standards, (3) setting nonfinancial rewards, (4) relating performance to compensation budgets, (5) taking other managerial action, and (6) communicating the final appraisal and the action to be taken.

The following chapter discusses the design of a flexible reward system that will allow the organization to compensate its employees equitably in relation to both their appraised performance and individual needs.

KEY CONCEPTS

Appraisal	Central tendency error
Rewarding	Similarity error
Leniency error	Management by Objectives
Halo error	Appraisal interview

NOTES

1. Fred Schuster and Alva F. Kindall, "Management by Objectives—Where We Stand," *Human Resource Management*, Spring 1974.
2. Arthur Kornhauser, "What Are Rating Scales Good For?" *Journal of Personnel Research*, September 1926.

3. Rensis Likert, *New Patterns of Management* (New York: McGraw-Hill, 1961); E. Kay, H. H. Meyer, and J. R. P. French, "Effects of Threat in a Performance Appraisal Interview," *Journal of Applied Psychology*, October 1965; Herbert Meyer and W. B. Walker, "A Study of Factors Relating to the Effectiveness of a Performance Appraisal Program," *Personnel Psychology*, Autumn 1961; H. K. Downey, D. Hellriegel, and J. W. Slocum, Jr., "Congruence between Individual Needs, Organizational Climate, Job Satisfaction, and Performance," *Academy of Management Journal*, March 1975; and Marvin D. Dunnette (ed.), *Handbook of Industrial and Organizational Psychology* (Chicago: Rand McNally, 1976).
4. Thomas Whisler and S. F. Harper, *Performance Appraisal Research and Practice* (New York: Holt, Rinehart and Winston, 1962).
5. Peter F. Drucker, *Management: Its Tasks, Responsibilities, Challenges* (New York: Harper & Row, 1974), pp. 438–439.
6. Douglas McGregor, "An Uneasy Look at Performance Appraisal," *Harvard Business Review*, May–June 1957.
7. Ronald Taft, "The Ability to Judge People," *Psychological Bulletin*, January 1955; and Robert W. Hollmann, "Supportive Organizational Climate and Managerial Assessment of MBO Effectiveness," *Academy of Management Journal*, December 1976.
8. Alva F. Kindall and J. Gatza, "Positive Program for Performance Appraisal," *Harvard Business Review*, November–December 1963.
9. H. H. Meyer, E. Kay, and J. R. P. French, "Split Roles in Performance Appraisal," *Harvard Business Review*, January–February 1965.
10. Larry L. Cummings and Donald P. Schwab, *Performance in Organizations: Determinants and Appraisal* (Glenview, Ill.: Scott, Foresman, 1973).
11. D. P. Schwab, H. G. Heneman, and T. A. DeCotis, "Behaviorally Anchored Rating Scales: A Review of the Literature," *Personnel Psychology* 28, 1975.
12. A. H. Locher and K. S. Teel, "Performance Appraisal—A Survey of Current Practices," *Personnel Journal*, May 1977.
13. BNA, *Employee Performance: Evaluation & Control*, PPF Survey No. 108, February 1975. (Report is based on responses from 150 employers who are members of BNA's Personnel Policies Forum.)
14. Schuster and Kindall, "Management by Objectives," *op. cit.*
15. C. W. Downs and Paula Moscinski, "A Survey of Appraisal Processes and Training in Large Corporations." Paper delivered to Annual Meeting of Academy of Management, Detroit, 1980, p. 3. (The study was based on a sample of companies obtained by cross-referencing the Fortune 500 companies with lists of members in the American Society for Training Directors. Questionnaires were mailed to 200 of the top 250 of the Fortune 500. Sixty-seven questionnaires were returned.)
16. Locher and Teel, *op. cit.*, p. 246.
17. G. S. Odiorne, *M. B. O. II*, (Belmont, Ca.: Fearon, 1979).
18. J. N. Kondrasuk, "Studies in MBO Effectiveness," *Academy of Management Review* 6 (no. 3) 1981, pp. 419–430.
19. K. S. Teel, "Performance Appraisal: Current Trends, Persistent Progress," *Personnel Journal*, April 1980, p. 297.
20. R. T. Lazer and W. S. Wikstrom, *Appraising Managerial Performance: Current Practices and Future Directions* (New York: The Conference Board, 1977), p. 22.
21. BNA, *Employee Performance, op. cit.*
22. Locher and Teel, *op. cit.*
23. Lazer and Wikstrom, *Appraising Managerial Performance, op. cit.*, p. 20.

24. Teel, "Performance Appraisal," *op. cit.*, p. 301.
25. BNA, *Employee Performance, op. cit.*, p. 6.
26. Teel, "Performance Appraisal," *op. cit.*, p. 316.
27. Hubert S. Feild and William H. Holley, "The Relationship of Performance Appraisal System Characteristics to Verdicts in Selected Employment Discrimination Cases," *Academy of Management Journal*, June 1982, p. 398.
28. W. H. Mobley, "The Link between MBO and Merit Compensation," *Personnel Journal*, June 1974.
29. Idem.

REVIEW AND DISCUSSION QUESTIONS

1. "Employees should be concerned only with their own compensation. What others are paid is none of their business." Discuss.
2. Describe and distinguish among the following approaches to appraisal: (a) adjective checklist; (b) rating scale; (c) forced-distribution; (d) forced-choice; (e) critical-incident; and (f) MBO.
3. Discuss the advantages and disadvantages of each of the above approaches. Describe situations in which each approach might be particularly appropriate.
4. Outline a performance appraisal plan for a small public accounting firm consisting of 3 supervising partners, 15 staff accountants, and 6 clerical workers.
5. What is meant by the term *equity* within the context of performance appraisal and compensation?
6. What is the relationship among rewards, equity and motivation?
7. Discuss the role that appraising and rewarding performance plays within the overall process of managing human resources.
8. Discuss the six-step implementation process for appraising and rewarding. Comment meaningfully on the efficacy of each step and the hoped-for result.
9. "MBO is the best theoretical management program ever conceived." Do you agree or disagree? Why?
10. Imagine that you are the personnel director of a major department store chain consisting of 20 stores of varying sizes. Draft performance objectives for your own job for the next six-month period.
11. Contact a number of large companies and organizations in your area to find out whether they use MBO. Present a summary of the experiences with and the results obtained from MBO programs by those organizations using them.

BIBLIOGRAPHY

Alpander, Guvenc G. "Training First-Line Supervisors to Criticize Constructively." *Personnel Journal* 59 (3), March 1980, pp. 216–221.

Baker, H. Kent, and Steven R. Holmberg. "Stepping Up to Supervision: Conducting Performance Reviews." *Supervisory Management* 27, April 1982, pp. 20–27.

Beatty, Richard W., and Craig Eric Schneier. "Developing Behaviorally Anchored Rating Scales." *Personnel Administrator*, Augutst 1979.

Beatty, Richard W., and Craig Eric Schneier. "Combining BARS and MBO: Using an Appraisal System to Diagnose Problems." *Personnel Administrator*, September 1979.

Beaulieu, R. "An Easier Look at Performance Appraisal." *Training and Development Journal*, October 1980.

Beer, Michael. "Performance Appraisal: Dilemmas and Possibilities." *Organization Dynamics* 9, Winter 1981, 24–36.

Birch, William J. "Performance Appraisal: One Company Experience." *Personnel Journal*, June 1981.

Brett, Randal, and Alan J. Fredian. "Performance Appraisal: The System Is Not the Solution." *Personnel Administrator*, December 1981, 61–68.

Brinkerhoff, Derick W., and Rosabeth M. Kanter. "Appraising the Performance of Performance Appraisal." *Sloan Management Review* 21, Spring 1980, 3–14.

Brinks, James T. "Is There Merit in Merit Increases?" *Personnel Administrator* 25 (5), May 1980, 59–64.

Cederblom, Douglas. "The Performance Appraisal Interview: A Review, Implications and Suggestions." *Academy of Management Review* 7, 1982, 219–227.

Danzig, Selig. "What We Need to Know about Performance Appraisals." *Management Review*, February 1980.

Delamonfagre, R. P., and J. B. Weitzul. "Performance Alignment: The Fine Art of the Perfect Fit." *Personnel Journal*, February 1980.

DeNisi, Angelo S., and George E. Stevens. "Profiles of Performance Evaluations and Personnel Decisions." *Academy of Management Journal* 24, September 1981, 592–602.

Dhanens, Thomas P. "Implications of the New EEOC Guidelines." *Personnel*, September 1979.

Drakey, George. "How to Help People Be Productive." *Management Focus*, New York, Peat Marwick & Mitchell, August 1981.

Ellig, Bruce. "The Mysteries of Employee Pricing Solved." *Supervisory Management*, January 1981, 16–22.

Giglioni, Giovanni B., Joyce B. Giglioni, and James A. Bryant. "Performance Appraisal: Here Comes the Judge." *California Management Review* 24, Winter 1981, 14–23.

Grant, Philip C. "A Model for Employee Motivation & Satisfaction." *Personnel*, September 1979.

Hawkins, Andrea. "Designing and Using Effective Performance Appraisal Forms." *Training*, February 1981, 36.

"The Hidden Traps in Performance Appraisals." *EEO Review*, April 1979.

Hills, Frederick S. "Job Relatedness vs. Adverse Impact in Personnel Decision Making." *Personnel Journal*, March 1980, 211–215.

Hobson, Charles J., Raymond M. Mendel, and Frederick W. Gibson. "Clarifying Performance Appraisal Criteria." *Organizational Behavior and Human Performance* 28, October 1981, 164–188.

Holley, William H., and Hubert S. Feild. "Performance Appraisal and the Law." *Labor Law Journal*, July 1975.

Holley, William H., and Hubert S. Feild. "Will Your Performance Appraisal System Hold Up in Court?" *Personnel* 59, January–February 1982, 59–64.

Hunter, R. W., and B. R. S. Silverman. "Merit Pay in the Federal Government." *Personnel Journal*, December 1980.

Hurt, E. H. "Performance Evaluation: The Key to Employee Effectiveness." *Management World* 9, November 1980, 32–33.

Johnson, S. L., and W. W. Ronon. "Exploratory Study of Bias in Job Performance Evaluation." *Public Personnel Management*, September 1979.

Kahalas, Harvey. "The Environmental Context of Performance Evaluation and Its Effect on Current Practices." *Human Resource Management*, Fall 1980, 32–39.

Kaye, Beverly L., and Shelley Krantz. "Preparing Employees: The Missing Link in Performance Appraisal Training." *Personnel* 59, May–June 1982, 23–29.

Kearney, William J. "Behaviorally Anchored Rating Scales—MBO's Missing Ingredient." *Personnel Journal*, January 1979.

Kearney, William J. "Pay for Performance? Not Always." *MSU Business Topics*, Spring 1979.

Klasson, C. R., D. E. Thompson, and G. L. Lubben. "How Defensible Is Your Performance Appraisal System?" *Personnel Administrator*, December 1980.

Klinger, D. E., "Does Your MBO Program Include Clear Performance Contracts?" *Personnel Administrator*, May 1979.

Lazer, Robert I. "Performance Appraisal: What Does the Future Hold?" *Personnel Administrator*, July 1980, 69–73.

Linenberger, Patricia, and Timothy J. Keaveny. "Performance Appraisal Standards Used By The Courts." *Personnel Administrator*, May 1981.

Lubben, Gary L., Duane E. Thompson, and Charles R. Klasson. "Performance Appraisal: The Legal Implications of Title VII." *Personnel*, May–June 1980, 11–21.

McAfee, R. Bruce. "Performance Appraisal: Whose Function?" *Personnel Journal*, April 1981, 298–299.

McFillen, J. M., and P. G. Secker. "Building Meaning Into Appraisal." *Personnel Administrator*, June 1978.

McGuire, P. J. "Why Performance Appraisals Fail." *Personnel Journal*, September 1980.

McMaster, John B. "Designing an Appraisal System that is Fair and Accurate." *Personnel Journal*, January 1979.

McMillan, John D., and Hoyt W. Doyel. "Performance Appraisal: Match the Tool to the Task." *Personnel* 57, July–August 1980, 12–20.

Michaeltree, P. K. "Subjectivity in Appraisal—the Supervisor's Role." *Training and Development Journal*, February 1979.

Miller, Ernest C. "Concensus: Pay for Performance." *Personnel*, July 1979.

Mode, V. A. "Making Money the Motivator." *Supervisory Management*, August 1979.

Morano, Richard. "The Rx for Performance Appraisals." *Personnel Journal*, May 1979.

Moravec, M. "How Performance Appraisal Can Tie Communication to Productivity." *Personnel Administrator*, January 1981.

Morrison, Ann M. "The Shape of Performance Appraisal in the Coming Decade." *Personnel* 58, July–August 1981, 12–22.

Munson, L. S. "Performance Standards: Do Training Directors Practice What They Teach?" *Personnel Journal*, May 1980.

Nemeroff, Wayne F., and Joseph Cosutino. "Utilizing Feedback and Goal Setting to Measure Performance Appraisal Skills." *Academy of Management Journal*, September 1979.

Percy, I. D. "Performance Appraisals: An Investment in People." *California Management Review*, February 1979.

Pitts, R. E., and K. Thompson. "Supervisor's Survival Guide: Using Job Behavior to Measure Employee Performance." *Supervisory Management*, January 1979.

"Poor Design of Employee Appraisal Hampers Results." *Savings & Loan News*, December 1980.

Pringle, Charles D., and Justin Longenecker. "The Ethics of MBO." *Academy of Management Review* 7, April 1982, 305–312.

Rendero, T. "Performance Appraisal Practices Survey." *Personnel* 57, November–December 1980, 4–12.

Rendon, Gloria J., and Laurence L. Epperson. "Customizing Performance Appraisal for the '80's." *Training and Development Journal* 35, May 1981, 147–149.

Rosinger, George, Louis B. Myers, Gerard W. Levy, Michael Loar, Susan A. Mohrman, and John R. Stock. "Development of a Behaviorally Based Performance Appraisal System." *Personnel Psychology* 35, Spring 1982, 75–78.

Sackett, R. R., and M. D. Hake. "Temporal Stability and Individual Differences in Using Assessment Information to Form Overall Ratings." *Organizational Behavior and Human Performance*, February 1979.

Salloway, Roberta A., and Alan Dayton. "Personal Scorecards." *Management Focus*, New York, Peat Marwick & Mitchell, August 1981.

Sauser, William J. "Evaluating Employee Performance: Needs, Problems and Possible Solutions." *Public Personnel Management*, January–February 1980.

Scanlon, Sally. "Inspiration at the Right Price—Sales and Management Survey." *Sales and Management*, April 1981.

Schaffer, Robert H. "Want Better Performance? Insist on It." *Administrative Management*, December 1979.

Shick, M. "The 'Refined' Performance Evaluation Monitoring System: Best of Both Worlds," *Personnel Journal*, January 1980.

Sikula, A. F., and J. P. Sikula. "Rethinking Present Appraisal Systems." *Supervisory Management*, March 1979.

Smith, Charles A. "Lump Sum Increases—A Creditable Change Strategy." *Personnel* 56 (4), July–August 1979, 59–63.

Smith, M. "Documenting Employee Performance." *Supervisory Management*, September 1979.

Spencer, George. "Keeping Salary Scales in Tune with Merit." *Personnel Management* 12 (3), March 1980, 40–42.

Steele, James W. "In Praise of Appraisal." *Advanced Management Journal* 46, Summer 1981, 12–18.

Teel, Kenneth S. "Performance Appraisal: Current Trends, Persistent Progress." *Personnel Journal*, April 1980, 296–316.

Tosti, Donald T. "Performance Measures for Job Certification and System Validation." *Training and Development Journal*, February 1979, 20–22.

White, Robert N. "Documenting Employee Problems." *Supervisory Management* 27, August 1982, 38–42.

Williamson, D. "Primer on Performance Appraisals." *Supervisory Management*, September 1979.

Winstanley, N. B. "Comment on Patterns 'Pay for Performance or Placation'." *Personnel Administrator*, May 1978.

Winstanley, N. B. "How Accurate Are Performance Appraisals?" *Personnel Administrator*, August 1980.

Winstanley, N. B. "Legal and Ethical Issues in Performance Appraisal." *Harvard Business Review*, November–December 1980.

Yager, Ed. "A Critique of Performance Appraisal Systems." *Personnel Journal*, February 1981, 129–133.

Zippo, M. "Dealing With the Poor Performer." *Personnel* 58, January–February 1981, 44–45.

Compensation and Benefits

CHAPTER OUTLINE

Role of the Reward System
Balancing Financial and Nonfinancial Rewards □ Dividing Rewards Fairly □ Applying the Contingency Approach: Flexible Compensation □ Flexible Reward Systems □ Employee Participation in Pay Decisions □ Other Considerations

The Extrinsic Reward System
Money As the Universal Reward □ Nonfinancial Extrinsic Rewards

The Intrinsic Reward System
Models of the Person □ Interaction of Intrinsic and Extrinsic Rewards

Requirements of an Effective Reward System
Operant Conditioning Theory □ Expectancy and Path–Goal Theories □ Equity Theory □ The Pay Secrecy Issue

Forms of Compensation
Salary □ Hourly Wages or Measured Daywork □ Sales Commissions or Bonuses □ Piece Rates □ Productivity Bonuses □ Plantwide Productivity Plans □ Performance Bonuses □ Profit-sharing Plans □ Stock-related Supplemental Compensation Plans

Noncash Benefits
Statutory Benefits □ Privately Funded Benefits

Recent Trends in Compensation and Benefits

OBJECTIVES

1. Describe how rewards are related to the overall human resource management system.
2. Differentiate among extrinsic rewards, intrinsic rewards, financial rewards, and nonfinancial rewards.
3. Discuss equity and equity theory.
4. Show how different aspects of the reward system satisfy different levels of needs.
5. Show the advantages and disadvantages of emphasizing money as the sole element of the reward system.
6. Understand how performance and reward must be linked if the reward system is to be a motivator.
7. Show why the contingency model provides the best basis for a reward system.
8. Describe the various forms of compensation.
9. Describe the many kinds of statutory and privately funded benefits.

SPOTLIGHT:
Sal J. Giudice

Sal J. Giudice, Executive Vice President and Special Assistant to the Chairman, is responsible for the American Can Company Foundation. Mr. Giudice has 33 years of business experience at American Can in sales, marketing, general management, and human resources. In his role as the head of human resources, he was instrumental in planning and organizing the flexible benefits program for the corporation—a much heralded and widely discussed concept offering greater choice for employees and improved financial controls.

He was appointed to his current position in July, 1983. From 1981 until 1983 he was Executive Vice President, Corporate Relations, for American Can Company, with responsibility for the public affairs, human resources, and legal functions of the company, and the American Can Company Foundation. He was Senior Vice President, Human Resources and Administration, from 1975 until 1981. He joined the company in 1950, and held various sales and marketing positions in Chicago and New Orleans. He transferred to the corporate headquarters in 1960 with the Beverage Marketing Group and was made a vice president in 1966. He was promoted to Vice President, Marketing, for all of American Can's packaging operations in 1969 and served as general manager of several major business units.

Mr. Giudice was born in New York City in 1923. After service with the armed forces, he graduated from Bowling Green State University with a Bachelor's Degree in marketing and economics. He later attended the Advanced Management Program at the Harvard Business School.

Comments by Sal Giudice

Since the end of World War II, the United States has experienced social and economic changes that have been unparalleled in history with regard to their speed and far-reaching impact.

One such socioeconomic change has been the overwhelming growth in the scope and cost of employee benefits. Employee benefits have grown from a relatively small part of overall compensation to where they are today—representing more than 40 percent of industry's total payroll costs.

Moreover, competitive pressures, union demands, and direct employee input have resulted in a wide range of new benefits being initiated, ranging from dental coverage to day care.

As employee benefit programs began to approach close to one half of business' annual payroll costs and to constitute a significant—and for the most part, tax-free—portion of every employee's income, getting the most from benefit programs is a vital concern to both employer and employee alike.

Despite the large sums of money being spent on benefits, most companies nevertheless fail to get the most value from their benefit programs by persisting in:

- Providing a single, uniform "benefit package" to all their employees—regardless of the actual needs of their employees; and
- Viewing benefits as separate and distinct from other forms of pay, rather than as an integral part of a comprehensive compensation package provided to each employee.

The results of these policies are both unfortunate and avoidable. First, most companies completely surrender control of their benefit costs to forces outside their influence, such as inflation. In addition, many employees see little ongoing value in their benefits until a particular need or emergency arises.

The time has passed when the human resource function can play a passive or reactive role. We must truly optimize benefit, compensation, and other related programs. That is, we must design and execute programs to effectively meet the changing needs of our employees in a cost-efficient manner; contribute to the bottom line by improving productivity and morale; and attract and retain the best qualified employees at all levels of the corporation. In other words, we must become and remain *innovators*.

While there was little question as to the appeal of a flexible benefits program, critics were quick to point out the pitfalls. And, a company considering the implementation of such a program did face some real problems:

- The tax laws affecting such programs were complex and not entirely clear;
- Adverse selection by employees could drive costs up;
- Computer programs capable of dealing with the complexities of a flexible program had to be developed; and
- A major effort in employee communications had to be undertaken.

Now, from the perspective of more than five years experience, it's clear to us at American Can that flexible benefits *are* successful, but not the *final* answer. We now see flexible benefits as only the first step in the evolution of a completely flexible compensation program that will permit employees to trade off between benefits and pay. This program eventually will include other areas, such as hours worked, career options, and ultimately, every aspect of the employee work environment.

At American Can, we regularly measure the results of the program. A recent comprehensive survey showed that American Can's Flexible Benefits Program is extremely popular among our employees:

- 89 percent of our employees like being able to select new benefits each year;

- 74 percent rate the Flex Program very good to excellent;
- 65 percent favor a choice between Flex credits and cash as far as increases in future compensation are concerned.

The survey also underscored the importance of employee communication, a key element of our effort. The study showed that the better an employee understands our program, the more he or she likes it.

Perhaps most significant in these inflationary times, flexible benefits permit a company to respond to unique needs of employees in a *cost-effective* fashion. In addition to traditional benefits, companies are able to incorporate demographic information in a flexible program. Coverage can be offered for such needed services as: child care, adoption assistance, legal counseling, financial/tax counseling, automobile/home insurance, dependent tuition assistance/student loans. American Can now offers all of the above programs with the exception of legal services. Each new plan option was identified through surveys and adopted within the flexible program in relatively short order.

For the future, to truly optimize our investment in our people, we are planning a "final phase" to the program, a phase that we call our "Totally Flexible Human Resources System."

As we envision this system, it will consist of three basic elements:

- *Benefits and compensation:* covering base pay, incentive/bonus plans; capital accumulation/thrift plans; benefit plans, and perquisites
- *Work environment:* covering flexible hours; special summer hours; reduced work weeks; job sharing; work at home; and phased retirement
- *Career development:* providing access to:

    Dual career paths that allow integration of both managerial and technical skills; interdisciplinary changes permitting and even encouraging employees to make career shifts from one field to another; management development programs that are clearly communicated and consistently applied to employees; and second career development programs that allow employees, and even their spouses, to develop and expand areas of interest, especially as part of a preretirement program.

> A union official approached a worker who had been showing up with some regularity only four days a week.
> "How come you're working four days a week?" the union representative asked the worker.
> "Because I can't make enough money in three," was the reply.
>
> John Lowell[1]

ROLE OF THE REWARD SYSTEM

This chapter and the next deal with a key subsystem of human resource management—the reward system. Like organizational climate, the reward system is a crucial element of the work environment. In many ways the reward system is closely related to the organizational climate, since both constitute major elements of the internal environment of the firm. As such, both the organizational climate and the reward system communicate much to each employee about the organization in which he or she is working. Moreover, the reward system determines the basis on which individuals in an organization will be able to satisfy their personal needs.

Since the opportunity to satisfy personal needs is the only basis for the individual's association with the organization, the reward system is a critical element in determining each individual's relationship to the organization. In turn, the organization's overriding purpose for the reward system is, first, to induce individuals to offer their services to the organization and, second, to secure their motivation and commitment to achieving the goals of the organization.

Important differences exist, for example, between Japanese and American assumptions concerning the proper relationship of pay and productivity. The economic implications of the differences in approach are clear, and suggest the direction in which compensation in America must move if our economy is to again prosper.

Balancing Financial and Nonfinancial Rewards

Traditionally, personnel textbooks placed primary emphasis on a compensation and benefits system, with a passing reference (at most) to the fact that nonfinancial rewards are also important. A more recent development has been the overemphasis of intrinsic factors—achievement, recognition, and growth—leaving the implication that money is relatively unimportant. Both of these emphases represent oversimplifications. This chapter will consider both nonfinancial and financial aspects of a *total reward system*.

Research in the behavioral sciences has demonstrated that most people are not motivated solely by financial rewards. Other needs are important to most people, and for at least a few people, these other needs can be more important than pay. Nevertheless, "good pay" remains very important to most employees. A point emphasized throughout this chapter and the next is that it is a nonsense question to ask, "Which are more important, financial rewards or nonfinancial rewards?" It would make just as much sense to ask, "Which is more important, the front wheel of a motorcycle or the back wheel?" An effective reward system requires both financial and nonfinancial rewards. Although both are needed, the emphasis should vary, contingent on both situational and individual differences.

Dividing Rewards Fairly

As has been pointed out by J. Stacy Adams and other researchers, the equity or fairness of pay is just as important to people as its amount.[2] Thus an effective reward system requires not only that the absolute level of compensation paid by an organization compare favorably with that of other organizations; it also requires that the compensation be divided up among the organization's employees in a way that they perceive as equitable.

Applying the Contingency Approach: Flexible Compensation

Another idea that should be emphasized is the importance of applying a contingency approach to the reward system. Traditional approaches to compensation and benefits have started from the assumption that most employees in an organization are essentially alike in their needs, their motivations, and their responses to different types of rewards. A contingency approach assumes, on the other hand, that employees are quite variable—that some respond primarily to *extrinsic rewards* (pay), that others respond primarily to *intrinsic rewards* (achievement, etc.), and that still others respond best to a combination of extrinsic and intrinsic rewards (see Exhibit 14–1). A number of research studies have indicated that both individuals and groups differ in terms of the perceived importance of pay and the effectiveness of money as a motivator.[3] Furthermore, a contingency approach recognizes that although all employees probably seek "equity,"

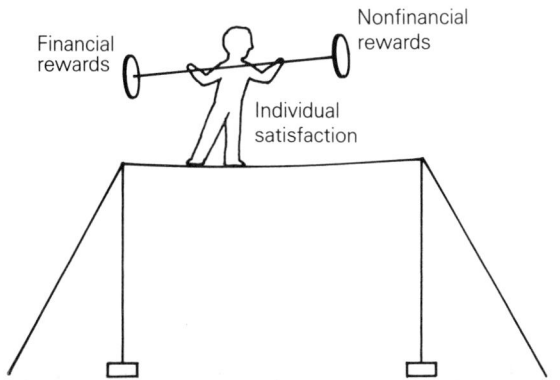

EXHIBIT 14–1
The contingency approach to flexible compensation.

there may be many conflicting definitions of "equity," so that what will appear equitable to one employee may not necessarily appear equitable to another.

Cafeteria compensation An excellent means to facilitate a contingency-based reward system is *flexible compensation* or, as it is sometimes called, "cafeteria compensation." Flexible compensation gives each individual a number of options as to the form and timing of his or her total compensation package, instead of informing the individual of the company's unilateral decision regarding the portion of total compensation that will be given in the form of cash, a retirement plan, life insurance, health insurance, vacation time, and so on. The employee is told how many compensation cost units have been granted to him, and perhaps also the required minima in such areas as cash compensation, retirement, and health insurance. The employee is then allowed to use the remaining compensation units to "shop" from among the options offered, much as one would select a meal in a cafeteria.

Advantages of the cafeteria approach This approach appears to have a number of practical advantages. First of all, the organization can supply an array of equal-cost alternative rewards and allow each individual (within limits) to select his or her own. This will, of course, maximize each individual's opportunity to choose rewards that meet personal need structure, attitudes, and preferences. Moreover, although the cost to the company remains the same regardless of the combinations chosen, the psychological value of the reward for each person should be higher since the employee is getting 100 percent of the rewards that are of greatest personal value and none of the rewards that might represent a cost to the company but be of no personal value. Psychologically, this is like giving the employee a raise at no cost to the company. Another value of this approach is that it allows employees to participate in a vital decision that relates to their jobs. This opportunity to play a decision-making role rather than a passive role in a job-related area of vital concern is itself a satisfier of higher-level needs, and thus should have its own motivational impact.

The cafeteria approach also makes obvious to each employee the economic value of each fringe benefit that is chosen. In many organizations this is no small matter. A number of research studies have shown that employees often grossly underestimate the cost, and therefore the economic value, of the fringe benefits supplied by their employers. Since they underestimate the cost, they underestimate the total compensation they receive from the company. The flexible compensation approach makes this unfortunate result virtually impossible.

Limitations of the cafeteria approach None of the practical constraints and problems that need to be solved in implementing flexible compensation appear to be insurmountable. However, the matter of tax treatment for optional benefits will require careful attention. IRS tax treatment of many types of compensation and benefits has been designed on the assumption that all or a large percentage of the employees in an organization participate on a nondiscriminatory basis in each of the benefits offered. In order to maximize the tax advantages of benefits, therefore, it will be necessary to plan carefully and perhaps to work directly with the IRS in arranging options that will meet the IRS tests for favorable tax treatment.

A particular example is the retirement plan. One IRS requirement for retirement plans that receive favorable tax treatment is nondiscrimination in participation as to both salary and organizational level. Since the IRS applies this test, not to the *opportunity* to participate, but rather to *de facto participation*, care will have to be exercised to prevent the voluntary formation of "discriminatory groups" of participants.

Another area of difficulty is the adverse selection of certain insurance coverages. It will be necessary to provide either minimum levels of coverage for all employees and/or limitations or medical qualifications for coverage to avoid the problem that under voluntary participation only employees anticipating heavy medical expenses would elect the highest levels of medical insurance coverage, and only older employees would elect the highest life insurance coverage. One possible solution to adverse selection of medical insurance would be to require a medical examination for supplementary levels of coverage (though not for the base level). A possible solution to adverse selection of life insurance would be to charge differential rates based on attained age rather than a standard rate for all employees.

Thus, the practical problems that must be worked out to make flexible compensation operational appear to be solvable. Although little has been reported on this subject, American Can Co., TRW Systems, Cummins Engine, and Educational Testing Service are among the pioneering firms that have flexible compensation plans in operation. Many other companies are rapidly implementing such plans, and it now appears that the widespread adoption of flexible compensation will be one of the major HR management trends during the 80s.

Employee Participation in Pay Decisions

One of the real advantages of flexible compensation is that it involves the individual with important decisions concerning his or her pay. Flexible compensation represents an expression by management of confidence and trust in the individual employee. At the same time, it allows an employee to custom tailor a pay and benefits package that maximizes the value of the reward package to the individual employee. Flexible compensation thus has both economic and psychological value to the employee as a step away from paternalism and toward participation/independence.

Research by Ed Lawler points out another advantage of a pay system in which the employee has some control over the form of pay. Lawler states that one of the advantages of such an approach is that "employees are more likely to trust a pay system of their own design because they have more control over it."[4] Experiences from his consulting practice indicate that employee participation in the determination of compensation and benefits can be a practical and effective procedure. He discusses one particular situation in which a plan the workers created was carefully thought out, conservative, and effective.

Other desirable aspects of employee participation in pay decisions include worker membership on job-evaluation committees and employee participation on productivity-improvement review committees that are a part of Scanlon plans and other productivity-gain-sharing plans. (Scanlon plans will be explained later in this chapter in more detail.)

Other Considerations

Larry Cummings has succinctly stated that "three fundamental dimensions . . . underlie the successful designing of a human performance environment:

1. Valued rewards are offered,
2. these rewards are based on productivity, and
3. employees can directly influence performance and productivity through their efforts."[5]

Other important considerations that play a role in the design of the reward system are methods of wage payments (by time or by output), incentive compensation, the role of government in such matters as the minimum wage and social security, the role of unions, and finally, the appropriate mix of supplementary employee benefits to be provided in addition to cash salary.

The independent considerations mentioned above, which together determine the resulting reward system, are sometimes complementary, but unfortunately they often have a conflicting impact on the reward system. Realistically, then, it is far more accurate to view the reward system at any point in time as the resultant of many often conflicting forces rather than as a scientifically determined system, although the latter is obviously the objective toward which the designers of reward systems should always struggle.

THE EXTRINSIC REWARD SYSTEM

The *extrinsic reward system* refers to all rewards external to the job itself. The extrinsic reward system can also be thought of as that part of the reward system that must be supplied to an individual by a representative of the organization, typically his or her manager. The extrinsic reward system thus consists of both financial and nonfinancial rewards meted out to the individual by some representative of the organization, presumably in response to the quality and quantity of his or her performance.

Money as the Universal Reward

Faced with what has already been described as the highly complex task of designing an effective reward system that consists of many elements, some modern-day managers long for the simpler age of the 20s and 30s when the "reward system" consisted simply of base wages. In that simpler age, about the only decision management had to make about its "reward system" was how much money would have to be paid to hire and retain the workers needed. Some managers may be heard to ask today (and probably many more have thought), "Why can't we simply pay people enough money to satisfy them and forget about all of these other nonfinancial and intrinsic rewards?" It is probably possible to do just that if an organization really wishes to. This is so because of the unique status of money as the universal reward. Money can be exchanged for goods and services to satisfy basic physiological needs. As an economic good it also satisfies security needs. Money, however, has another facet sometimes overlooked by behavioral scientists: It is a symbol of achievement. In our American culture we tend to evaluate individuals by the salaries they make and the money they possess. Therefore, compensation is a very powerful symbolic recognition of achievement, success, growth, and (for that matter) personal worth. In this sense, money can serve very nicely as a satisfier of higher-level needs.

Thus, it is quite accurate to say, as a few managers have, "All people really need to motivate them is money." To observe that money can satisfy both lower-level and higher-level needs, however, is by no means to conclude that making money the sole reward is the most cost-effective approach from the organization's standpoint.

There is ample evidence that this would be an enormously expensive solution. As a matter of fact, a number of organizations have unconsciously been pursuing just such a policy. Skyrocketing wage demands that appear to have no end in sight may well result from a situation in which the only possibility for satisfying needs is seen to be higher and higher wages.

Although money can theoretically be used to satisfy all levels of employees' needs, a much less costly strategy involves the effective use of nonfinancial rewards to reduce the total cost of the reward system. There is no doubt that a basic level of financial rewards is a necessary component of the reward system; however, it is equally clear that a second layer of the reward system dealing with the satisfaction of higher-level needs can emphasize either financial or nonfinancial rewards.

Nonfinancial Extrinsic Rewards

Nonfinancial extrinsic rewards comprise the nonmonetary means of recognizing the contributions of individual employees and classes of employees. These means include status symbols, physical working conditions, titles and promotions, control over time at work, public recognition, and informal oral praise.

THE INTRINSIC REWARD SYSTEM

By contrast, the *intrinsic reward system* consists of those rewards that come from the work itself. An intrinsic reward results from a transaction between an individual and his or her task without the intervention of any third party. The reward comes from the individual's own responses to the performance of the task—a sense of responsibility, a sense of challenge, a sense of mastery or control, a sense of participation, and so on.

Thus, extrinsic rewards are determined and delivered by a third party representing the organization, whereas intrinsic rewards are determined by the individual in interaction with the task. We should not lose sight of the fact, however, that both intrinsic and extrinsic rewards are products of the human resource management system. It is not possible for management to stand by and hand out intrinsic rewards. It *is* a responsibility of management to design jobs in such a way that intrinsic rewards are possible for those members of the organization who seek them. This may mean using such techniques as job enrichment to encourage a sense of responsibility in jobs that historically failed to do this; or a sense of challenge in place of routine; or an opportunity for mastery and control where only a sense of activity has been possible; or participation where only response to directives has been asked for in the past. It seems safe to conclude that virtually all employees seek some intrinsic rewards all of the time and that some employees seek intrinsic rewards to an even greater extent than they seek extrinsic rewards. Thus, it is a primary responsibility of management to identify individuals or groups that might be motivated by intrinsic rewards and then to design jobs in such a way as to give these individuals and groups the maximum opportunity for achieving the intrinsic satisfactions they desire.

Although intrinsic rewards seem to flow from satisfaction of only the highest levels of need, ego need, and self-fulfillment need, the extrinsic reward system is related to all levels of need. (See Chapter 8 for a discussion of Maslow's hierarchy of needs theory.) Exhibit 14–2 shows the relationship between human needs and the reward system. A better understanding of the basis for intrinsic rewards can be obtained by examining the development of "models of the person."

Models of the Person

Behavioral science research has pointed increasingly to the inadequacy of our simplistic models of the person, including the economic model, the social-system model, and the self-actualizing model. A more sophisticated model is required. A contingency model thus seems to be the model of the person around which an effective reward system for the 1980s should be built.

This model hypothesizes that human behavior is not fixed but rather dependent on each situation. Thus, the contingency model assumes that

EXHIBIT 14-2
Rewards and Human Needs—A Contingent Relation.

	Extrinsic Rewards		Intrinsic Rewards
	Financial	*Nonfinancial*	
Lower level needs			
Physiological	Pay (economic value)		
Safety–security	Benefits (security)	Rules and regulations Supervision	
Social		Status	Participation, interaction, status
Higher level needs			
Ego, self-fulfillment	Pay (symbolic value)	Recognition Praise Promotion in *title* New responsibilities New assignment Participation in decisions Challenge Control	Achievement Exploration Mastery Growth Participation Responsibility Autonomy

there is no one right solution to any management problem. Rather, the uniquely right solution for each problem is determined by a number of factors, such as the organization (its climate, history, environment, structure, rules and regulations, managerial style, and so on), the nature of the task itself (including the degree to which intrinsic rewards are available), the measurability of performance, and the individual (his or her needs, attitudes, abilities, and preferences with regard to intrinsic versus extrinsic versus mixed rewards).

Specifically, a contingency approach requires that we design, not a static reward system, but rather a flexible system that can vary for different parts of the organization, different tasks, and particularly for different individuals or subsets of individuals within the organization. The process of designing and implementing such a flexible system will be discussed in the next chapter, Administering the Compensation Program.

Interaction of Intrinsic and Extrinsic Rewards

Finally, it is important to recognize that intrinsic and extrinsic, financial and nonfinancial rewards all interact—as part of a single reward system, they are not independent. For example, workers who find little opportunity for intrinsic satisfaction in their jobs (i.e., limited opportunity for a sense of achievement, mastery, growth, etc.), and who are also frustrated in their attempts to obtain extrinsic nonfinancial rewards (recognition, esteem, status, etc.) may focus their attention exclusively on demanding greater and greater financial rewards simply because money is the only form of reward they have had any success in achieving in the past.

REQUIREMENTS OF AN EFFECTIVE REWARD SYSTEM

Now that we have discussed both the intrinsic reward system and the extrinsic reward system in principle, let us examine the critical connection between performance and reward. A considerable body of research shows that for rewards to be effective it is important that the employee perceive a direct relationship between performance and the attainment of the desired reward. This means that the mere establishment of an adequate reward system does not provide the basis for employee motivation. It is equally important that the system be communicated in such a way that each employee perceives that the attainment of desired rewards flows directly from successful performance.

Operant Conditioning Theory

One of the important lines of research leading to this conclusion is operant conditioning theory, developed by B. F. Skinner.[6] Operant conditioning theory observes that among both animals and human beings behavior that is rewarded tends to be repeated and behavior that is not rewarded tends not to be repeated (to be "extinguished"). Operant conditioning theory does not require that there be a cognitive connection between the behavior ("operant") and the reward, only that it be a sequential relationship. The theory simply observes that if a particular behavior is exhibited in the presence of certain stimuli and followed by the receipt of a reward, that behavior will tend to be repeated in the future in the presence of similar stimuli.

Expectancy and Path–Goal Theories

A separate, though complementary, line of research leading to the same conclusion is the *expectancy theory* of Vroom and the path–goal theory of Porter and Lawler.[7] Their research has demonstrated that a number of things are required for any reward system to be effective in eliciting desired behavior from employees:

1. The employee must perceive both the existence of the reward and that it is attractive to him or her.
2. The employee must perceive accurately what specific behavior will lead to the desired reward.

3. The employee must perceive that he or she is capable of that behavior, and be, in fact, capable.
4. There must be a direct tie between the behavior and the receipt of the reward, and the employee must perceive that tie.
5. If the employee's performance is to be evaluated by others and the receipt of rewards is to be dependent on such evaluation, he or she must perceive that the evaluation will be accurately and equitably performed.

Thus, the operant conditioning, expectancy, and path–goal theories all seem to lead to the conclusion that effective reward systems require:

1. An array of intrinsic and extrinsic rewards that are available to individuals on a self-selection basis
2. A clear statement of the direct relationship between behaviors and anticipated rewards
3. An accurate performance appraisal system and an effective merit increase plan that assure performance will be accurately measured and rewards received will be directly commensurate with objectively measured performance
4. An effective communication system that makes the existence of items 1, 2, and 3 widely known and understood throughout the organization

These findings may help to explain the apparently contradictory results of various research studies designed to determine the motivational impact of money. Some studies (notably those of Herzberg et al., covered in Chapter 8) have seemed to indicate that money has little value as a motivator and that it can act primarily as a source of dissatisfaction. On the other hand, over the years a number of research studies have concluded that money can sometimes act as a very powerful motivator.

Perhaps the explanation of these apparently inconsistent findings lies in the notion that the motivational value of money depends upon the individual's perception of the total situation. Where pay is closely tied to achievement and is seen by others in the organization as a form of recognition, it may operate as a very potent motivator indeed. On the other hand, in organizations where there is little perceived relationship between performance and compensation, where pay is not used as an incentive, money may very well have no effect whatsoever as a motivator and may serve only as a potential source of dissatisfaction.

Equity Theory

Furthermore, *equity theory* research by J. Stacy Adams has shown that for a reward system to be effective in motivating behavior, it is necessary that employees perceive the system to operate equitably.[8] For this perception to exist, "inputs" (which include such factors as age, education, skill, seniority, social status, and effort expended) should relate to "outcomes" (rewards) in the same way for the individual as he or she perceives them to relate for others. Adams' research has shown that people do, in fact, adjust their input to the perceived equity of their input–output relation as compared to the input–output relation of others.

The Pay Secrecy Issue

Because a perception of equity and a perception of direct relationship between performance and reward are neccessary for effective motivation, it becomes important that people in an organization be familiar with how the reward system operates and that they have detailed and accurate information on the rewards received by others. A research study by Lawler has shown that the traditional secrecy of pay practices in most organizations is likely to be highly dysfunctional.[9] Specifically, Lawler found that people in an organization who are not told the salaries of other people tend to misperceive reality, not on a random basis, but in a consistent pattern. Because people consistently underestimate the pay of their superiors and overestimate the pay of their subordinates, misperception of pay in an organization tends to severely reduce the motivational effect of the pay system. Thus, another requirement for an effective reward system would seem to be publication of at least ranges of pay for each pay grade and each individual's grade, if not indeed the publication of individual salaries.

In another research study, Charles Futrell in 1978 examined the effects of decreasing pay secrecy at a large organization. Three of the firm's nine sales units lessened their total ban on employee awareness about peers' salaries; they released information about the sizes of raises and the identity of recipients. Employee satisfaction increased markedly in these units. A research study conducted at DuPont appears to lend support to the notion of disclosing data on pay ranges and grades only rather than actually publishing individual salaries. In this study, only 18 percent of the employees voted for a completely "open system."[10] Because of the importance and universal use of financial rewards, we will focus next on different forms of compensation and fringe benefits.

FORMS OF COMPENSATION

Although the flexible compensation approach makes cash compensation and "fringe benefits" largely interchangeable, traditionally, various forms of pay have been described as compensation and various forms of other benefits as fringe benefits. The balance between cash compensation and fringe benefits may be expected to evolve through the 1980s to a considerably different benefits ratio in the next century.

Although there are hundreds of variations, the major nine categories of cash compensation include salary, hourly wages or measured daywork, sales commissions or bonuses, piece rates, productivity bonuses, plant-wide productivity plans, performance bonuses, profit-sharing plans, and stock-related plans.

Salary

Salaried workers are paid a set wage by the week or the month and are expected to work a standard set of hours each week (36–40 hours per week is the most common schedule). Usually salaried workers are not subject to pay loss for absences due to illness (normally up to an annual limit) or even for modest absences for "personal business." For this reason, salaried workers are not usually asked to punch a time clock, although some salaried workers fill out time cards reporting their attendance to the minute.

One implicit assumption of salaried compensation is that the work is of a qualitative nature under the control of the individual so that attention and careful work are of more importance than mere attendance. Another implicit assumption is that salaried individuals can be trusted to deliver a full day's work for a full day's pay without the necessity of close monitoring. There is perhaps even an implicit assumption that most salaried employees are motivated in part by higher-level needs.

Normally relatively little variation is anticipated in the work required from persons in salaried jobs so that the company can afford to, in effect, guarantee 40 hours or 36 hours of work each week. Alternatively, it may be felt that the volume of work demanded will vary slightly but that the increased motivation due to salaried status will more than offset the possible savings of paying for a variable number of hours per week in response to demand.

Hourly Wages or Measured Daywork

Hourly wages are a set wage paid for each hour the employee is actually at work or actually works. Sometimes standards of the amount of work expected in a typical hour are established, and this is referred to as measured daywork. Usually hourly workers are required to punch a time clock or to fill out a time record of some sort. Pay at the end of each week or month is computed on the basis of the number of hours worked. Usually no allowance is made for time off for personal business, but often there is allowance for time off due to illness or other specified causes. The primary objective of hourly pay is to provide flexibility for the employer in scheduling hours of work per week.

Over the last 20 years unions have made a number of inroads on this advantage through such devices as supplementary unemployment benefits and the guaranteed annual wage (really a guarantee of a minimum number of hours of work per year). Consequently the flexibility provided by hourly pay has become relatively less advantageous for some employers. There has been a decline in the popularity of hourly wage rates, although this is still the most common method of compensating production workers.

Traditionally, hourly wages have been associated primarily with blue-collar work, in contrast to the association of salaried status with white-collar, professional, and managerial work. One disadvantage of hourly pay from the employer's standpoint is its potential for conferring second-class status on hourly workers and thus making them feel less a part of the organization or less committed to the organization. On the other hand, the flexibility of scheduling hourly workers and paying only for hours worked is still an overriding economic advantage for many firms.

Gillette Safety Razor, IBM, and Texas Instruments have already changed the status of their large hourly work forces to that of salaried employees. These prominent companies follow the philosophy of salaries for all employees as a means of both demonstrating the organization's commitment to providing full employment for everyone and as a means of breaking down barriers between blue collar and white collar employees. These firms obviously feel that the gain in motivation, cooperation, commitment, and loyalty more than offsets any cost. There appears to be at the present time a slight but perceptible trend for an increasing number of companies to adopt this philosophy. On the other hand, it is important for any organization to carefully assess the impact on costs and other elements of organizational strategy before adopting such a policy.

It is undoubtedly true that there are other organizations whose situations make them ready for a move to salaried status for all employees. Nevertheless, the contingency approach to reward system design would rule out the automatic application of one compensation method to all employees. Rather, the contingency approach requires a detailed analysis of the specific situation to determine the best arrangement for the particular organization, jobs, and individuals.

Sales Commissions or Bonuses

The mechanics and the underlying theory of sales commissions or bonuses are virtually identical with those of piece rates. However, piece rates are most commonly associated with production work, whereas sales commissions or bonuses are paid exclusively to salespeople. As with piece rates, sales commissions or bonuses can be paid on every unit sold or only on units beyond a certain minimum. Furthermore, like piece rates, sales commissions can be paid on a level basis per unit, regardless of the number of units sold, or on an increasing rate per unit. It is somewhat more common with sales commissions than with piece rates to make the unit commission the total basis for compensation. This is particularly true in real estate sales.

The objective of sales commissions or bonuses is to maximize sales, and its advantage is similar to that of piece rates in providing pay in direct proportion to the performance of useful work. This relationship may be very significant motivationally, particularly for people who are motivated primarily by extrinsic rewards, because it provides immediate positive feedback each time a sale is completed.

Piece Rates

Piece rates are one of the many so-called incentive compensation plans. Piece rates provide an incremental payment for each unit of production completed. Usually, piece rates are paid as a bonus on top of an hourly or weekly wage. Piece rates can be paid on the basis of either individual production or group output.

Group piece rates are usually paid when several employees work together on a single product or in situations where considerable cooperation among a group of employees is required for effective performance. It is most common for piece-rate plans to provide either a constant or an increasing piece rate after a certain "standard" level of production has been attained, but not to pay a piece rate for units produced up to this standard number. The primary objective of piece rates is to lower unit cost of production for the employer by motivating the employee to maximize output in relation to machine time utilization, overhead costs, and the base wage.

Piece rates for each item of production are usually set by company time-study engineers. Since it is vital that piece rates be accurate and up-to-date, the monitoring of piece rates can be a relatively expensive administrative procedure. Furthermore, piece rates may be the subject of frequent and heated debate or negotiation with the union.

Historically, piece rates have been a source of considerable friction between workers and managers, and they appear to have been a common basis for the alienation of workers who, rightly or wrongly, believed that they were being exploited by unfair piece rates.

A considerable amount of research evidence indicates that the effectiveness of various incentive systems can vary greatly, depending on such factors as the preferences of workers, the norms of the work group relative to the restriction of output, whether the task is liked or disliked, and whether the task is simple or complex.[11]

The research also tends to show that the reaction to incentive plans is dependent on personality differences among individuals, including their level of achievement motivation and the reference groups with which they identify.[12] Specifically, individuals high in achievement motivation seem to be less influenced by financial incentives (because they are already motivated), whereas individuals low in achievement motivation respond relatively more strongly to financial incentives; employees from metropolitan areas who have working-class backgrounds and identification tend to be unresponsive to financial incentives, whereas employees with middle-class values and norms and employees who identify strongly with higher occupational groups are relatively more influenced by financial incentives.

Productivity Bonuses

Productivity bonus plans provide wage payments based on units of production that exceed the standard rate or on the completion of tasks in less than the standard time. *Productivity bonuses* may be paid on either an individual or a group basis. Such bonuses are not nearly as common as piece rates.

Plantwide Productivity Plans

Although somewhat related to productivity bonuses, plantwide productivity plans such as the Scanlon plan are far more ambitious in their objectives and more complex in their administration. The Scanlon plan provides incentive compensation based on plant performance. Its primary emphasis is to stimulate management–union or management–worker cooperation.

It does this by setting up a series of joint committees consisting of representatives selected by management and by workers at each level in the organization or in each department. These committees review suggestions for the improvement of productivity. Suggestions adopted by the committees are implemented in the organization.

When increases in productive efficiency are realized—that is, when unit labor costs decrease—the employees and the company share the dollar value of the savings according to a predetermined ratio, with a larger amount usually going to the workers. The major objectives of the Scanlon plan are to stimulate worker ideas for improving efficiency, to gain the commitment of workers to the objective of efficiency, to improve worker–management relations, and to provide an equitable basis for sharing increases in efficiency. The Donnelly Mirror Corporation, for example, has a total reward system consisting of substantial nonfinancial rewards in addition to an unusual financial reward system that includes a plantwide productivity plan (Scanlon plan).

Early in the 1970s the U.S. General Accounting Office initiated a project to create the Federal Productivity Measurement Program. In March 1981 it published a broadscale study of plantwide productivity-sharing plans such as the Scanlon plan. The GAO concluded:

> These plans offer a viable method of enhancing productivity. This is especially important now when the United States is faced with a serious decline in national productivity growth and high inflation rate, both of which affect the competitive position of many firms as well as the standard of living of every citizen.
>
> While productivity sharing plans are not a panacea for every firm or the solution to the Nation's economic problems, they warrant serious consideration by firms as a means of stimulating productivity performance, enhancing their competitive advantage, increasing the monetary benefits to their employees, and reducing inflationary pressures.
>
> Many of the firms included in the study achieved significant savings from their productivity sharing plans and also enjoyed many nonmonetary benefits. Firms that provided financial information on the results of their plans averaged savings of almost 17 percent in work force cost. Other benefits attributed to the plan included improved labor–management relations, reduced absenteeism and turnover, and fewer grievances.[13]

Performance Bonuses

Performance bonuses are similar to productivity bonuses except that they are paid for total performance, including performance that goes beyond mere productivity. Any measurable item of performance can be subject to such bonuses. Thus, performance bonuses can be applied to executive, professional, technical, clerical, white-collar, and blue-collar workers.

Profit-Sharing Plans

Profit-sharing plans typically provide that a stated percentage of profits will be shared by all employees of the organization or by certain groups in the organization. Profits can be shared on a level percentage basis beginning with the first dollar of profit, but a more popular arrangement is to share an increasing percentage of the profits beyond a certain base. The timing of payment may be current, deferred, or mixed.

Stock-related Supplemental Compensation Plans

There are several variations of supplemental compensation plans related to company stock. These variations include stock purchase plans, stock option plans, phantom stock plans, and performance shares. Stock purchase plans are usually offered to virtually all employees in the company. Although it was once quite common to sell stock to employees at a discount below the market rate, the tax treatment of this practice has changed; hence it is now more common to sell stock at the market rate. Under some forms of stock savings plans a portion of the employee's contribution is partially matched by the company either in additional stock or in cash.

Stock options are granted to an executive at the current market price for the stock, with provision for exercising the option within a limited period of time. Thus, if the company is successful and the stock increases in value, the executive may exercise his option at any time within the stated limits and realize the gain in value between the option date and the exercise date. In order to obtain favorable tax treatment for the transaction, it is necessary that the shares be held for a minimum period of time before resale. Although stock options were extremely popular and considered quite glamorous in the 1960s, they are considerably less popular today and are probably still waning in popularity due to less advantageous tax treatment.

A variation of the stock option is the use of phantom stock. Under this arrangement an executive is granted a *mythical* share of stock, thus enabling the executive to avoid the problem of having to lay out the money needed to exercise stock options. At the end of the specified period the executive is simply paid in cash the value of the appreciation of the mythical unit of stock, together with the accumulated dividends.

A fairly recent innovation is the concept of performance shares. Granted to an executive as a stock option would be granted, the shares, however, are not irrevocably the executive's, but merely set aside in his or her name. These shares must be earned by achieving certain performance objectives established between the executive and a performance evaluation committee. At the end of the performance period the committee grants the executive all, some, or none of the shares that were set aside, depending on its evaluation of the executive's performance.

Performance shares have grown significantly in popularity over the last 10 years, and this trend appears to be continuing. It is consistent with the reward system ideas developed in this chapter that performance shares might be applied gradually to broader segments of the work force. Performance shares would fit very nicely within the framework of a contingency-based reward system, since it would be possible to provide such shares as an optional form of incremental compensation.

NONCASH BENEFITS

We have already discussed the advantages of considering cash compensation and noncash benefits as parts of a total reward package to facilitate a contingency-based reward system incorporating the "flexible" approach to compensation and benefits.

There is a second financial reason why this approach seems highly desirable in the 1980s. Employee benefits were originally referred to as fringe benefits or "fringes" because initially they represented a small portion of the employer's total compensation cost. Typically, early fringe plans involved pensions, life insurance, and medical insurance, with the employee paying all or a substantial portion of the total cost. Much of the value of these plans came from the actuarial, administrative, and buying power advantages of large group plans as opposed to individual purchase. In general, these advantages were more important than the employer's part in funding the cost of the "fringes."

As is well known, this situation has changed dramatically. Benefits now represent a substantial portion of many employers' total compensation cost. Nevertheless, as we have already mentioned, research studies have shown that most employees vastly underestimate the cost of employer-financed benefits. This means that the employer is getting insufficient credit for these expenditures.

A study conducted by the U.S. Chamber of Commerce "showed that in 1981 a sampling of 994 companies paid on the average $6,627 per employee each year for so-called fringe benefits."[14] This figure represented more than 37 percent of the companies' total employment costs. The same study reported that whereas wages and salaries in these firms rose 115 percent during the 10-year period 1971–1981, the cost of fringe benefits increased by 161 percent (see Exhibit 14–3).

Dollar cost and the proportion of total compensation cost represented by benefits are rising rapidly. Increases in the costs of the various fringe benefits in 1981 (as reported in the U.S. Chamber of Commerce study) were broken down as shown in Exhibit 14–4.

The primary cause of escalating fringe benefit costs has been the in-

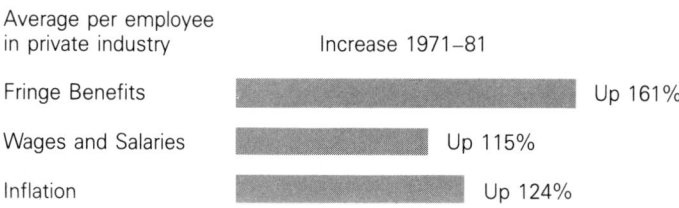

EXHIBIT 14-3
Gains in "fringes" far outpace wages and inflation.
Source: Reprinted with the permission of the Chamber of Commerce of the United States of America from *Employee Benefits 1981.*

creasing cost of such benefits as social security, pensions, vacations, and insurance. A second cause, however, has been the rapidly mounting list of fringes that have been developed over the last 20 years. A fairly common pattern has been for a new fringe benefit to spring up in only one or two

EXHIBIT 14-4
Costs by type of benefit.

Weekly Employee Benefits, Per Employee	1971	1981	Percent change
Old age, survivors, disability and health insurance (FICA taxes)	$7.15	$21.60	+202
Insurance (life, medical, etc.)	7.10	20.63	+191
Pensions (nongovernment)	7.73	17.88	+131
Paid vacation	7.69	16.96	+121
Paid holidays	4.69	11.48	+145
Paid rest periods, coffee breaks	5.38	11.46	+113
Workers' compensation	1.58	4.94	+213
Paid sick leave	1.56	4.60	+195
Unemployment compensation taxes	1.15	4.25	+170
Profit-sharing plans	1.65	3.69	+124
Dental insurance	*	1.29	*
Short-term disability	*	1.23	*
Thrift plans	0.31	1.23	+297
Christmas/suggestion bonuses	0.67	1.17	+ 75
Long-term disability	*	0.79	*
Tuition reimbursement	0.15	0.77	+413
Free meals	0.25	0.58	+132
Employee discounts	0.23	0.48	+109
Other benefits	1.63	2.41	+ 48
Total employee benefits	$48.92	$127.44	+161

*Not available

Source: Reprinted with the permission of the Chamber of Commerce of the United States of America from *Employee Benefits 1981.*

companies or in only one industry as the result of a peculiar situation or a unique union demand, to spread slowly at first to related companies or related industries, and after a few years to spread more rapidly, becoming common throughout industry.

Among the newer benefits receiving attention in the 1980s are family counseling for workers' off-the-job problems, company day-care centers, dental care, prepaid legal service, free use of employer-owned golf courses, assistance in making out income-tax returns, and free psychiatric care. Although each of these items is being discussed in the literature as a novelty, the chances are good that more than one of them will be a standard benefit within the next 10 years.

One of the principal advantages of a flexible compensation approach is that it demonstrates that benefits costs are compensation and should be considered as a part of the total reward received for performance. One result of this approach should be heightened awareness of the total value of each employee's compensation and benefits package. Another result might be decreasing pressure for new and more exotic benefits if employees realize that these are a substitute for cash or other benefits.

Statutory Benefits

There are two basic types of employee benefits—statutory benefits (those required by law and toward which the employer is legally required to make contributions) and privately funded benefits (those determined unilaterally by the company or as a result of company–union negotiation). Privately funded benefits may be paid for by the employer, by the employee, or by both the employer and the employee.

For most employees the most important statutory benefit is social security. The Social Security Act of 1935, as amended, provides for retirement income, income for survivors, and disability income. Although social security was originally envisaged as a system that would provide a minimal subsistence income, the level of coverage has steadily risen. Today, social security is thought of as the solid base around which most private retirement plans are designed. Under the most recent revision of the Social Security Act, employers and employees in 1984 each contribute 6.7 percent of the first $36,000 earned annually. Further increases in social security contributions are already scheduled in existing legislation.

Another important feature of the act is the incorporation of automatic cost-of-living escalators. Under this provision, each time there is an increase in the Bureau of Labor Statistics Consumer Price Index, the benefits paid under social security automatically increase. As can be seen, there has been a trend toward the liberalization of social security benefits, and social security is being thought of more and more as the primary basis for retirement income rather than as minimal subsistence-level income.

Another piece of legislation to come out of the Depression is the Federal Unemployment Tax Act of 1935, which requires employers of a certain minimum size to pay an unemployment insurance tax. Under the provisions of this act, employees who become unemployed through no fault of their own are eligible for 26 to 52 weeks of compensation. Through a fairly complicated arrangement, much of this act is administered by state governments, with a sizable portion of the employers' contributions going to the states.

Workers' compensation provides payments to workers or their families in the case of job-related accidents, injuries, diseases, or deaths. Although workers' compensation programs exist in all states, they are based on state law rather than federal law. Hence, standards, administrative practices, and costs vary somewhat from state to state. In all states, however, the total cost of workers' compensation is paid by the employer.

Although medical insurance plans and pension plans (other than social security) are not statutory benefits, the federal government in recent years has expressed increasing interest in these two areas. It appears to be entirely possible that either or both of these benefits will become statutory benefits.

Congress has already exerted a major influence on privately funded pension plans through the Employee Retirement Income Security Act of 1974 (ERISA). The enactment of this legislation was widely interpreted as ushering in a new era in which pension plan operation would be subject to increasing government regulation.

ERISA neither forces a company to set up a pension plan nor dictates the size of benefits, but it does set minimum standards for employee pension rights (vesting), the funding of pension obligations, and the administration and investment of pension funds. The pension plans of most large corporations embodied the standards of ERISA prior to its enactment. However, the act will undoubtedly be significant in safeguarding the rights of employees previously covered by inferior plans.

Privately Funded Benefits

An employer has wide latitude in designing the mechanics of a pension plan within the minimum requirements of ERISA, and within constraints set by the Internal Revenue Service if favorable tax treatment is to be obtained. Some pension plans are paid for by the employer, others by the employees. The largest number, however, are paid for through joint employer–employee contributions.

The most common formulas for determining retirement benefits incorporate years of service, level of income (career average or average of highest five or ten years), and age at retirement.

Another common form of privately funded benefits is medical insurance. Typically, medical insurance provides coverage for both the employee and dependents, with at least a portion of the employee's coverage paid for by the employer. Although the employee commonly pays all or part of the cost for the coverage of dependents, the funding of all medical coverage by the employer is becoming more and more common.

The most common form of medical coverage is basic hospitalization insurance of the type offered by Blue Cross–Blue Shield. Major medical insurance to provide supplementary coverage over and above the limits of basic hospitalization and doctor coverage has grown rapidly in popularity.

RECENT TRENDS IN COMPENSATION AND BENEFITS

A fairly recent development has been the growth in many areas of the country of health maintenance organizations (HMOs), which contract with individuals to directly provide full health-care services, including prevention as well as full physician and hospital services for a fixed monthly fee. Under the Public Health Service Act of 1973, if an HMO is offered in a geographical area in which employees reside, the employer is required to offer them the option of joining the HMO and must contribute to the HMO that same amount it spends on employees in the company health insurance plan.

Two factors, among many, that have caused change in compensation and benefits are unions and the tax structure. Following the end of World War II union pressure to add fringe benefits played a large role in the rapid development of fringe benefits in the 50s and 60s. Another influence has been the tax advantages of benefits. For the employer, some benefits represent an immediate tax deduction but a deferred cash flow. Many benefits are advantageous to the employee from a tax standpoint in that they are bought with untaxed dollars rather than with 20 to 30 percent fewer aftertax dollars. In addition, a cost saving is obtained merely through purchasing coverage on a group basis rather than an individual basis. Thus, there are a number of clear economic reasons for allocating a steadily increasing proportion of the compensation and benefits mix to benefits.

There may well also be more subtle and less well recognized social reasons for the popularity of benefits. For one thing, it may reflect changing life-styles and the need structure that result from increasing affluence. As basic physiological needs are increasingly met for larger and larger proportions of our population, there may logically be increasing emphasis on the security represented by such benefits as pensions, medical insurance, and life insurance. Further, although benefits are often thought of as satisfying lower-level physiological and security needs, many fringe benefits, including some of the ones receiving increased attention, might be said to serve higher level needs. These include educational benefits, increased vacation and holiday time, and such perquisites as the use of golf courses and tennis courts.

Significantly, however, none of these reasons for the increasing popularity of fringe benefits seem to be inconsistent with the notion that a flexible approach to compensation and benefits may be an ideal approach to the design of an effective strategy for human resources management in the

1980s. Such an approach maximizes each individual's opportunity to play a meaningful role in determining the rewards for his or her efforts; and such an approach provides each individual with the opportunity to maximize the utility of his or her total package of rewards, as perceived by the individual.

We foresee an increasing emphasis on the use of all forms of compensation to motivate rather than to placate or merely maintain. As we become more knowledgeable about the motivational consequences of pay and pay practices, it seems likely that we will take greater pains to ensure that the organization gets motivational value out of each compensation dollar spent.

This means that we will have to develop performance appraisals that will be perceived as both valid and fair. We will also have to relate such performance appraisals to changes in compensation.

One trend that began in the 1970s is the marked de-emphasis of stock-related plans that award stock (or options) to an executive on a final basis, and the increased emphasis on plans (such as performance shares) that award stock contingent on the achievement of specific objectives. This trend reflects a change in thinking at the highest executive levels about how to get the greatest motivational value out of compensation dollars.

Deferred compensation is often financially advantageous to the organization in terms of both tax treatment and cash flows. Because of the differing tax rates that face an individual during the working years versus retirement years, deferred compensation often looks more attractive than immediate compensation. With increasing affluence, this trade-off should become desirable to more and more people. In addition, as more and more organizations move toward flexible or "cafeteria" compensation, one alternative likely to be requested by employees will be deferred compensation.

The most significant trend over the next 30 years will be the increasing adoption of the contingency-based reward system. Changes in the work force and increasing knowledge about human behavior will require organizations to rethink reward systems. Companies will need to plan a cost-effective combination of extrinsic and intrinsic rewards.

SUMMARY

This chapter has emphasized the role of the reward system as a key subsystem of human resources management. Like organizational climate, the reward system is a crucial element of the work environment. The total reward system consists of both intrinsic aspects (supplied by the work itself) and extrinsic aspects (supplied by the organization). These extrinsic rewards have both financial and nonfinancial elements.

It is important that the reward system be viewed as equitable. That is, each individual in the organization should believe that the rewards he or she receives in relation to effort and contribution are fair as compared to the rewards others receive in relation to their effort and contribution.

Because money is a satisfier of both lower-level and higher-level needs in our culture, it could serve as the ideal universal reward. As many managers have pointed out, money could suffice as the only element in an organization's reward system—if the organization could afford it. However, making money the only element in the reward system is unlikely to be cost-effective. In most organizations, the effective use of nonfinancial rewards can substantially reduce the cost of the reward system.

The intrinsic reward system consists of those elements of the work itself that provide a sense of achievement, responsibility, challenge, control, and participation—the rewards that may be obtained by the individual through his or her performance of the work.

The financial reward system is made up of two primary components—compensation and benefits (in various forms). Among the forms of compensation described were salary, hourly wages, piece rates, sales commission or bonus, productivity bonus, plantwide productivity plans, profit sharing, stock options, and performance shares.

Among the benefits discussed were the statutory benefits of social security, unemployment compensation, and workers' compensation, as well as the privately funded benefits of pensions, life insurance, medical insurance, disability insurance, supplementary unemployment benefits, vacations, holidays, sick leave and other paid leave, bonuses, educational benefits, perquisites, and suggestion or service awards.

The operant conditioning theory of Skinner, the expectancy theory of Vroom, and the path–goal theory of Lawler were all shown to lead to the conclusion that there must be a critical linkage between performance and reward if a reward system is to be effective in motivating human performance.

Because of the inadequacy of the economic, social, and self-actualizing models of the person, a contingency model is required as the basis for an effective reward system.

KEY CONCEPTS

Financial rewards	Expectancy theory
Nonfinancial rewards	Equity theory
Flexible compensation	Scanlon plans
Extrinsic rewards	Fringe benefits
Intrinsic rewards	

NOTES

1. "GMAD: Jekyll or Hyde?" *Ward's Auto World,* April 1972, p. 29.
2. E. E. Lawler III, *Pay and Organizational Effectiveness: A Psychological View* (New York: McGraw-Hill, 1971); J. S. Adams, "Toward an Understanding of Inequity," *Journal of Abnormal and Social Psychology,* June 1972.
3. Ibid. See also E. Ghiselli, *Explorations in Managerial Talent* (Pacific Palisades, Ca.: Goodyear, 1971).
4. Edward E. Lawler, "Merit Pay—Fact or Fiction," *Management Review.* April 1981, pp. 50–52.
5. Larry L. Cummings, "Strategies for Improving Human Productivity," *Personnel Administrator,* June 1975.
6. B. F. Skinner, *Science and Human Behavior* (New York: Macmillan, 1953). See also David K. Hart and William G. Scott, "The Optimal Image of Man for Systems Theory," *Academy of Management Journal,* December 1972.
7. V. Vroom, *Work and Motivation* (New York: Wiley, 1964); and L. W. Porter and E. E. Lawler, III, *Managerial Attitudes and Performance* (Homewood, Ill.: Irwin, 1968). See also Orlando Behling and Chester Schriesheim, *Organizational Behavior* (Boston: Allyn and Bacon, 1976), pp. 85–87.
8. J. S. Adams, "Toward an Understanding of Inequity," *Journal of Abnormal and Social Psychology,* June 1972.
9. Lawler, *Pay and Organizational Effectiveness,* op. cit.
10. Cited in Lawrence Stessin, "Keep Your Eyes Off My Paycheck," *The New York Times,* June 13, 1976, p. F1.
11. *Ibid.* See also R. L. Opshal and M. D. Dunnette, "The Role of Financial Compensation in Industrial Motivation," *Psychological Bulletin,* August 1966; F. J. Roethlisberger and W. H. Dickson, *Management and the Worker* (Cambridge, Mass.: Harvard University Press, 1939); W. F. Whyte, *Money and Motivation* (New York: Harper, 1955); and B. M. Bass, W. P. Hurder, and N. Ellis, "Assessing Human Performance under Stress," unpublished technical report cited in Lawler, *Pay and Organizational Effectiveness.*
12. J. W. Atkinson and W. R. Reitman, "Performance as a Function of Motive Strength and Expectancy of Goal Attainment," *Journal of Abnormal and Social Psychology,* November 1956; C. L. Hulin and M. R. Blood, "Job Enlargement, Individual Differences, and Worker Responses," *Psychological Bulletin,* January 1968; C. J. French, "Correlates of Success in Retail Selling," *American Journal of Sociology,* 1960; E. E. Lawler, III, *Motivation in Work Organizations* (Belmont, Ca.: Brooks/Cole, 1973); and John P. Campbell and Robert D. Pritchard, "Motivation Theory in Industrial and Organizational Psychology," in Marvin D. Dunnette (Ed.), *Handbook of Industrial and Organizational Psychology* (Chicago: Rand McNally, 1976).
13. U.S. General Accounting Office, *Productivity-Sharing Programs: Can They Contribute to Productivity Improvement?* (Washington, D.C.: U.S. Government Printing Office, March 3, 1981).
14. Chamber of Commerce of the United States, *Employee Benefits 1981* (Washington, D.C.: U.S. Government Printing Office, 1981).

REVIEW AND DISCUSSION QUESTIONS

1. Write a five-page library research report summarizing and synthesizing what has been written in major *business* journals in the last three years on the topic "motivation of employees."
2. Visit the personnel director of a local company and discuss with him or her the firm's reward system—intrinsic and extrinsic, financial and nonfinancial.
3. Obtain a copy of a local area wage survey from the library or a local firm. Report to the class on the research methods used by the survey and the results.
4. If you were earning $300 a week and a flexible compensation plan allowed you complete freedom to choose, how would you divide up your compensation among different forms of wages and benefits?
5. Compare your answer to question 4 with the answers of your classmates. What explains the differences?
6. Write a five-page research paper discussing why it is important for employees to see a direct relationship between their performance and the rewards they receive.
7. A prominent consultant has stated that by the year 2000 practically all large organizations will have flexible compensation plans. Do you agree or disagree? Why?
8. What are some of the reasons for *not* adopting a flexible compensation program?
9. What is the objective of compensation and benefits, i.e., why do organizations pay wages and benefits?
10. Explain how conservation of both nonfinancial and financial aspects of a reward system is required for a systems approach to rewarding employees and increasing productivity.

BIBLIOGRAPHY

Anderson, Brian. "Executive Privilege." *Canadian Business*, April 1980.
Brody, Michael. "Pacesetting Contract—What's Good for General Motors May Not be Good for the Country." *Barron's*, September 24, 1979.
Burke, Paul E. "TRASOPS: The Beautiful Benefit." *Personnel Journal*, March 1978, 136–138.
Burns, John E. "Fundamentals of Compensation." *Industrial Management*, September–October 1979, 27–30.
Business Week. "How to Size Up Your Company Fringe Benefits." May 12, 1980.
Doyel, Hoyt W., and John P. McMillen. "Low-Cost Benefit Suggestions." *Personnel Administrator*, May 1980, 54–57.
Feeney, Edward J. "Conventional Compensation: A Hindrance to Productivity." *Cost and Management* 53 (5), September–October 1980, 44–46.
Field, Robert L., and Gary A. Vogt. "Ways to Pay Your Key People Well." *Personnel Administrator*, May 1979, 37–40.

Flamion, Allen. "The Dollars and Sense of Motivation." *Personnel Journal*, January 1980, 51–52, 61.
Foegen, J. H. "The Next Employees' Benefit—Grand Paternity Leave?" *Human Resource Management*, Fall 1980, 24.
Foltz, Roy G. "Benefit Plan Communication." *Personnel Administrator*. November 1980, 16.
Genders, P. "Mobilizing the Pension Package." *Personnel*, May–June 1980, 46.
Hills, Frederick S. "The Pay-for-Performance Dilemma." *Personnel*, September–October 1979, 23–31.
Jackson, L. H., and M. G. Mindell. "Motivating the New Breed." *Personnel*, March–April 1980, 53.
Kearney, William J. "Pay-for-Performance? Not Always." *MSU Business Topics*, Spring 1979, 5–15.
Levenson, Mark. "Minimum Wage Controversy." *Dun's Review*, October 1980, 32–35.
Lindsey, F. D. "Employees' Benefits Hit New Highs." *Nation's Business*, October 1980.
Litras, Thomas S. "The Battle Over Retirement Policies and Practices." *Personnel Journal* 58, February 1979, 102–110.
Lorber, Lawrence. "Job Segregation and Wage Discrimination Under Title VII and the Equal Pay Act." *Personnel Administrator*, May 1980, 31–34.
McCaffery, Robert M. "Employee Benefits: Beyond the Fringe." *Personnel Administrator*, May 1981, 26–66.
Meyer, P. "Executive Compensation: Planning For New Directions." *Personnel Administrator* 25, May 1980, 22, 27–28.
Miller, Ernest C. "Pay-for-Performance." *Personnel*, July–August 1979, 4–11.
Miller, J. J. "Trends and Practices in Employee Benefits." *Personnel Administrator*, May 1980, 48–57.
Paine, Thomas H. "Trends in Benefits and Deferred Compensation." *Compensation Review* 11 (4), Fourth Quarter 1979, 9–21.
Perham, John. "Spotlight on Pay and Perks." *Dun's Review*, April 1979, 88–94.
Piamonte, John S. "In Praise of Monetary Motivation." *Personnel Journal*, September 1979.
Schulhof, Robert J. "Five Years with a Scanlon Plan." *Personnel Administrator*, June 1979, 55–62, 92.
Shea, J. H. "Cautions about Cafeteria-Style Benefit Plans." *Personnel Journal*, January 1981, 37–38, 59.
Smith, Charles A. "Lump Sum Increases—A Creditable Change Strategy." *Personnel*, July–August 1979, 55–62, 92.
Steers, Richard M., and Lyman W. Porter. "Money and Motivation." In *Motivation and Work Behavior*, 2nd ed. New York: McGraw-Hill, 1979.
Szilagyi, Andrew D. "Money Talks—Is Anyone Listening?" *Industrial Management* 21 (6), November–December 1980, 21–24.
Thomsen, David J. "Compensation Trends in 1981." *Personnel Journal*, January 1981, 22.
Thomsen, David J. "Compensation & Benefits." *Personnel Journal* 59, March 1980, 177.
"Why Fringes Have Lost Some of Their Allure." *U.S. News and World Report*, January 1981, 66.
Wegener, E. "Does Competitive Pay Discriminate?" *Personnel Administrator*, May 1980.
Zippo, Mary. "Roundup: Employee Benefits Update." *Personnel*, May–June 1980, 39.

Administering the Compensation Program

CHAPTER OUTLINE

Developing the Compensation Strategy

Governmental Influences on Compensation

Legal Constraints on Compensation Policy
The Comparable Worth Issue □ The Civil Rights Act of 1964

Impact Of Labor Market Conditions

Impact of a Union

Procedure for Developing the Compensation System
Compensation and Benefits Surveys □ Relating Survey Data to the Reward System

Job Evaluation
Ranking □ Classification □ Point Method □ Factor-comparison

Executive Compensation

Implementing a Flexible System

Administration of Compensation and Benefits
Performance Appraisal □ Salary Review □ Maintaining the System

OBJECTIVES

1. Develop the compensation strategy for a familiar organization.
2. Design a flexible reward system for a particular organization.
3. Discuss fully the cafeteria approach to compensation and benefits.
4. Identify benchmark jobs and conduct a compensation and benefit survey.
5. Relate the data from a compensation and benefit survey to an organization's reward system.
6. Use a point, factor-comparison, ranking, or classification system to write and evaluate a job description.
7. Discuss fully the various steps of the compensation determination process.
8. Describe the impact of unions, the government, and the labor market on compensation and benefits.
9. Describe the role of human resource specialists in updating the reward system.

SPOTLIGHT:
Walton E. Burdick

Walton E. Burdick, IBM Vice President, Personnel, joined the company in Endicott, N.Y., in 1955. He subsequently held personnel positions in Dayton, N.J., New York City, and Greencastle, Ind. In 1962, he became Administrative Assistant to the IBM Director of Personnel, corporate headquarters; in 1963, Manager of Personnel Planning, and the following year was advanced to Manager of Personnel Programs and Services. In 1965, he became Director of Personnel Relations, corporate headquarters; in 1967, Director of Personnel, IBM World Trade Corporation; in 1969, Director of Personnel, Data Processing Group. Becoming IBM Director of Personnel Plans and Programs in 1970, he was elected a vice president in 1972. He was appointed Assistant Group Executive, Finance and Planning, General Business Group, in 1977. He was named IBM Vice President, Personnel, in 1980.

Mr. Burdick holds a B.S. degree in industrial and labor relations from Cornell University. He is a member of the Industrial and Labor Relations School's Advisory Council at Cornell University, Cornell's University Council, and the National Board of Junior Achievement.

Comments by Walton Burdick

The proper administration of reward systems has the potential for improving productivity in the 1980s. IBM has long recognized the significant role its reward system plays in motivating employees to achieve their maximum productivity. Several objectives guide the administration:

1. To maintain competitive pay rates based on a relevant marketplace, enabling the company to attract the very best candidates and to maintain low attrition rates
2. To administer compensation based on merit, ensuring that employees can directly influence their pay by their performance
3. To provide adequate management training and communications channels in order to assure equitable administration of the reward system

and enhanced employee understanding.

The first objective, competitive pay, is assured through extensive surveys of benchmark jobs in the relevant marketplace, development of salary structures, and establishment of pay objectives. Exempt surveys are national in scope, while nonexempt surveys are conducted locally. All IBM employees are salaried.

Relevance is the key to the survey process and receives appropriate focus by IBM to ensure that competing companies for employees or business are represented in the survey of the marketplace. IBM uses historical labor rate data and economic forecasts to project outside rate movement and to develop range structures based on these anticipated rates. Thus, the system is predictive. IBM's pay objective is to exceed on the average the salaries of those with similar skills in the relevant marketplace.

The second objective, merit pay, is achieved through internal equity, performance measurement, and equitable administration of pay increases based on performance. Internal equity is achieved through job evaluation. IBM uses an evaluation plan based on a factor point method of nine factors. Once the relative values of all jobs have been determined, employees are classified according to their duties and responsibilities.

Performance measurement in IBM is achieved through a highly interactive system known as Performance Planning Counseling and Evaluation. Measurement goals and objectives are determined jointly between employees and their managers, and formally documented in a performance plan. Over the appraisal period, there is on-going communication between manager and employee regarding goal revisions and counseling. A formal evaluation is then based on the employee's performance over that period. To ensure equity, an additional level of management review is necessary. Top-performing employees can expect to be paid a considerably higher salary than lower performers in positions of similar value. Employees are thus motivated to achieve their maximum productivity.

To assure equitable administration, IBM uses merit pay guides that take into consideration the value of each employee's job, the position in the salary range, and the individual's performance. These guides ensure that employees receive individual consideration based on their performance. IBM merit pay guides cause significant merit pay differentials to be established over time.

The third objective in IBM's reward system is adequate management training and open communication channels. These are achieved through initial training of each new manager, follow-up annual training, and an atmosphere that encourages employees to raise questions and voice concerns to their managers. Communication and education are key components of a successful reward system. Over the past several years, IBM has concentrated on improving employee and management understanding of the compensation system by emphasizing communication. The results of this strategy have been manifested in the highest levels ever of employee pay satisfaction as measured by opinion surveys.

In order to compete effectively in an increasingly competitive marketplace, relevant marketplace/performance-based pay systems, in-depth management training, and excellent employee communications are essential.

Probably no single function of HR management in the 1980s offers more opportunity to improve productivity than the administration of the reward system. This is true because the reward system has a more direct causal impact on productivity than any other management system or process. Furthermore, in the past, many organizations have not emphasized getting the maximum motivational impact from the rewards offered. The decade of the 1980s will, therefore, be a truly revolutionary time in America with regard to administration of compensation and benefits. We are already witnessing this development, dramatically illustrated by recent changes at General Motors, America's largest corporation, described below.

GM Cuts in White-Collar Pay and Benefits are Deep, But Workers Don't Seem to Mind

By Amanda Bennett
Staff Reporter of *The Wall Street Journal*
DETROIT—The salaries and benefits General Motors Corp. offered once were so rich that the company was known as "Generous Motors." Now, though, the No. 1 auto maker is turning the tables.

For the first time, GM is digging into the pay and benefits of its salaried workers, matching and even exceeding the kinds of concessions it obtained from union workers during contract negotiations earlier this month.

Since the beginning of the year, GM has taken away 10 paid holidays from its salaried employees and has rolled back the cost of living allowances. It also froze COLA [Cost of Living Adjustment] payments for 10 months. On top of that, GM has made a wide variety of cuts in its health-insurance programs, making employees kick in more for their own policies and offering lower levels of coverage for certain kinds of care, for instance.

Unilateral Move

To these workers, who have no union, "Generous Motors is reminding us subtly that these benefits were given easily and are just as easily taken away," says a computer expert, a mid-level employee. GM didn't have to negotiate the removal of the benefits from white-collar workers, the way it did with the United Auto Workers union.

Surprisingly, however, although the cuts in white-collar workers' compensation were deeper than for blue-collar workers, their objections were less profound. Unionized workers approved the contract calling for concessions by a very narrow 52% margin, and there was a great deal of internal hostility to the program among the dissenters in the union. Among white-collar workers, by contrast, "I don't hear any grumbling," says an engineer, a long-time GM worker. "We may not like it, but we recognize reality around here."

The GM move may presage similar cuts elsewhere, in both blue- and white-collar workers' benefits, because GM always has been a force in setting the nation's compensation levels. One big target is health benefits, where many have tinkered but few have actually cut. Many organizations, for example, are trying to find ways of providing health benefits to their employees more cheaply. But GM is one of the first major companies directly to reduce the coverage provided to workers.

With more attention focused overall on the cost of health care and other employee benefits, GM's cuts in white-collar compensation will "definitely have an impact," says Thomas G. Patzua, a senior vice president at Johnson & Higgins, a New York employee-benefit consulting firm.

Already another auto company, Chrysler Corp., has announced its intentions to try to follow suit in a big way. Recently, Chrysler began offering Michigan-area doctors discounts of up to $2,000 on Chrysler cars in exchange for a 10% break on medical bills for Chrysler employees.

The reason for the attention to benefits among auto companies is that such benefits are "clearly a large portion of the total costs" of a company, says Claude Kordus, a partner at Hewitt Associates, a compensation-consulting company in Long Beach, Calif. According to one survey, benefits rose to 41% of pay by 1980, from 25% in 1959. "Benefits have been escalating faster than pay by a wide margin," Mr. Kordus says.

Many GM employees say they aren't concerned about such cuts because they aren't directly visible. "If I looked at my pay stub and it was less, it would bother me," says Mr. Crawford. Others say they are happy to contribute something to help the ailing auto industry. GM, they feel, is hurting from the three-year-long sales slump just the same as other auto companies. "When the hard times come, we all have to contribute," says a 25-year GM veteran. "We're taking our lumps."

Yet others are bound by a heightened sense of work ethic in this time of trouble. "We had too much vacation," says an engineer. It was "frustrating getting the job done." Adds a marketing man, "Sure, I'm upset. The thing that bothers me is we haven't done enough to cut back."

Source: *The Wall St. Journal,* April 20, 1982. Reprinted by permission of The Wall Street Journal, © Dow Jones & Company, Inc. 1982. All Rights Reserved.

DEVELOPING THE COMPENSATION STRATEGY

As we have seen in the previous chapter, an effective reward system built on the contingency model must match the organization's history, traditions, managerial climate, formal policies, structure, and so on. Furthermore, an effective *compensation strategy* requires the reward system to be fitted to the different tasks (that is, job descriptions) and to the degree of skill and experience required in the job, the behaviors and attitudes required, the measurability of performance, and the opportunities for intrinsic rewards.

A contingency-based reward system should be adjusted to individuals who are grouped by similar needs. Some individuals will be motivated primarily by the lower-level physiological and safety needs; others will be motivated primarily by social needs; and still others will be motivated primarily by ego needs—they will seek opportunities for achievement or creativity, for development, for recognition, and so on. A few individuals may be motivated primarily by self-actualization needs, and will seek opportunities for taking on new and different responsibilities. Finally, individuals vary greatly in the degree to which they seek intrinsic rewards, extrinsic rewards, or a combination of the two. All of our evidence about human behavior indicates that a contingency-based reward system is necessary for the effective management of human resources in the 1980s. As we have seen, the motivational structure of people today is more complex than was that of people in earlier periods. In the long run, therefore, it will be a wise investment of time to design a reward system of *flexible compensation* that incorporates the adaptability of a contingency model.

In many organizations the kind of information needed to design a contingent reward system is not presently available. But this does not mean that such a system cannot be designed. Rather, it means that we must begin the design by obtaining more information about the organization, the jobs, and the individuals in order to have the data necessary to construct the reward system. The required tools, such as survey research techniques, are available in standardized form.

This need to gather more data means that HR managers who are involved in the design of reward systems will take on more of a research role than they did in the past. Such managers play different roles in the following sequence:

1. *Researcher*, determining the needs and constraints for a reward system within a particular organization, including both the degree and the direction of the flexibility desired
2. *Planner*, designing a many-faceted reward system that will accommodate as many of the needs and constraints identified in the research as possible
3. *Implementer and manager*, both introducing the new reward system and making it effective in terms of the many requirements previously discussed—communication, understanding, tie between performance and reward, accurate appraisal, equitable internal relationships, and so on

Thus, for jobs that appear to afford little opportunity for intrinsic reward and for individuals (regardless of job) who appear to be motivated primarily by extrinsic reward, the reward system should emphasize *extrinsic rewards* tied directly and proportionately to effective performance. This will necessitate, among other things, a valid and objective appraisal system, differential pay for differential performance, and public recognition of effective performance. For situations in which individuals say that they are motivated by opportunities for *intrinsic rewards* such as exploration, learning, achievement, and mastery, the reward system should certainly offer adequate and equitable pay. But for motivational purposes it might also enhance and spotlight the intrinsic rewards of the job through such means as job enrichment, participation in decision making, and increased feedback on performance.

There are a number of different influences on the organization's compensation strategy. Among these are the prevailing wages in the industry or the geographic area; governmental influence; union leaders' attitudes toward job evaluation, collective bargaining, the firm's profitability (i.e., ability to pay), the appraisal of individual performance, and the organization's overall objectives.

GOVERNMENTAL INFLUENCES ON COMPENSATION

One factor that should receive more detailed attention is the impact of governmental influence on compensation. We have already mentioned in Chapter 14 that the Employee Retirement Income Security Act of 1974 (ERISA) has exerted a major influence on privately funded pension plans. The most fundamental governmental influence on compensation, however, is that of the Fair Labor Standards Act of 1938, as amended most recently in 1977. This act sets minimum wages paid to employees "engaged in commerce or in the production of goods for commerce." Because the operational definition of the expression "engaged in interstate commerce" has been expanded over the years, the Fair Labor Standards Act applies to the vast majority of jobs in this country. Under the most recent revision, a mini-

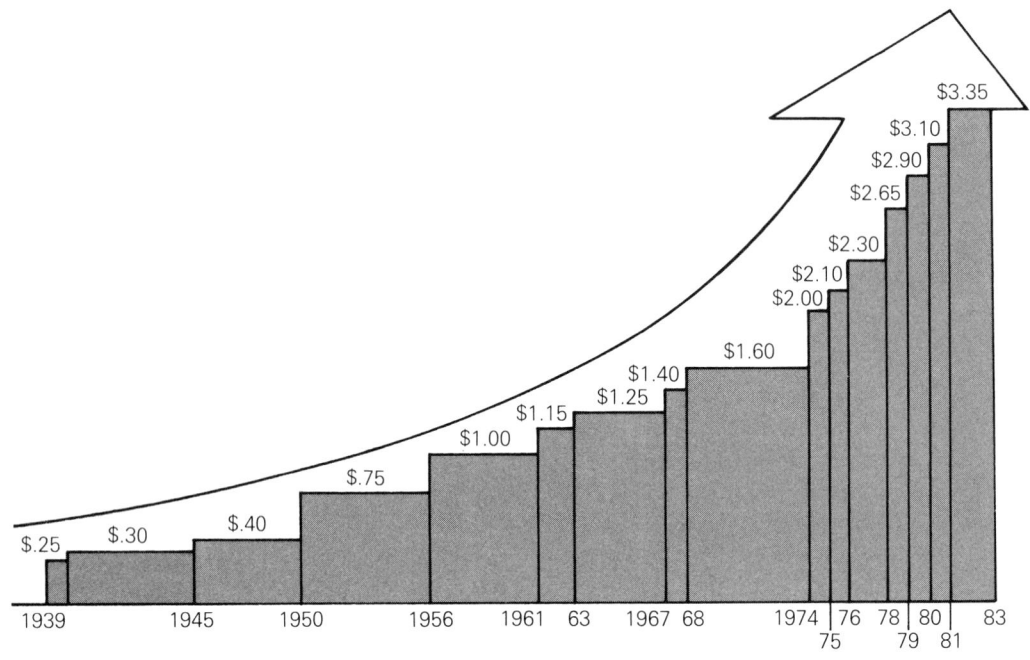

EXHIBIT 15-1
Rise of the minimum wage, 1938–1983.
Source: U.S. Department of Labor.

mum wage of $3.35 per hour must be paid to all workers covered by the act (see Exhibit 15-1).

For detailed current data, readers should consult the most recent bulletin of the Wage and Hour Public Contracts Division, U.S. Department of Labor.

The impact of the minimum wage law is not limited to its direct influence on the lowest wages paid. It also exerts indirect influence on the total wage structure by making it necessary to raise the pay of all job grades in order to maintain prevailing internal relationships.

Thus, each time an amendment to the Fair Labor Standards Act has raised the minimum wage, the entire wage structure of the country has been affected. Furthermore, there is little doubt that the act has had a direct influence on the rate of unemployment. Each time the minimum allowable wage is raised, it inevitably becomes uneconomic to utilize the services of certain marginally employable people. The result is to increase the rolls of the unemployed, thus creating a social cost that must be balanced against the social gain of raising wages.

The Fair Labor Standards Act also has an impact on compensation practice through its encouragement of guaranteed annual wage plans. If a union–management agreement guarantees pay for no less than 1,840 hours of employment per year (and provides that a higher limit will not be exceeded), the act exempts companies from paying overtime within certain limits. The net effect of this provision is to encourage guaranteed annual wage plans.

Other federal legislation prohibits discrimination in pay practices on the basis of sex, race, or age. The Equal Pay Act of 1963, an amendment to the Fair Labor Standards Act, provides that "no employer . . . shall discriminate . . . between employees on the basis of sex by paying wages . . . at a rate less than the rate at which he pays wages to employees of the opposite sex . . . for equal work on jobs the performance of which requires equal skill, effort, and responsibility, and which are performed under similar working conditions." The Civil Rights Act of 1964 requires that employers act affirmatively to ensure that there is no discrimination in either employment or pay on the basis of race, creed, color, or national origin. Finally, the Age Discrimination in Employment Act of 1967 added age to the prohibited bases of discrimination.

Another important governmental influence on compensation is Presidential Directives such as occasional wage freezes and the affirmative action requirement administered by the Office of Federal Contract Compliance.

LEGAL CONSTRAINTS ON COMPENSATION POLICY

Although the Equal Pay Act of 1963 prohibits sex-based compensation discrimination, there are, however, four legal defenses for unequal payments. Unequal payments can be based on (1) a seniority system, (2) a merit system, (3) a system that measures amount or quality of production, or (4) any factor other than sex.

To establish a *prima facie* case (i.e., a case where the burden of proof is placed upon the employer), the plaintiff—whether the individual employee or the EEOC—has the burden of proving not only a disparity in wages between males and females but also that the disparity exists in substantially equal jobs requiring equal skill, effort, and responsibility and performed under similar working conditions. To avoid liability the employer must justify the wage differentials by proving the existence of one of the four exceptions to the legislation.

The Comparable Worth Issue

Courts have consistently denied reimbursement for lost wages and promotions under the Equal Pay Act for sex-based wage discrimination claims made on a *comparable worth* basis:

> We agree that the Equal Pay Act does not authorize courts to equalize wages merely because they find that two substantially different jobs are worth the same monetarily to the employer and therefore should be paid the same wages. However, there is evidence that Congress intended that

> jobs of the same or closely related character should be compared in applying the equal pay for equal work standard.
>
> *Hodgson v. Miller Brewing Company*, 457 F. 2d 221, 227 (7th Cir., 1972)

The legislative history of the Equal Pay Act makes it clear that Congress rejected the comparable work theory because of (1) its fear that businesses would be subjected to massive, costly job re-evaluations, (2) the various interpretations that could arise as to what jobs are comparable, and (3) the desire to limit the involvement of the Secretary of Labor and courts in job evaluation.

The Civil Rights Act of 1964

Section 703(a)(1) of Title VII makes it unlawful "to discriminate against any individual with respect to his compensation, terms, conditions or privileges of employment, because of such individual's . . . sex . . ."

While *wage discrimination* solely on the basis of sex is illegal, the law recognizes several exceptions whereby differentiations do not violate the act. These exceptions closely resemble the first three defenses under the Equal Pay Act:

> Notwithstanding any other provision of this Title, it shall not be an unlawful employment practice for an employer to apply different standards of compensation, or different terms, conditions or privileges of employment pursuant to a bona fide seniority or merit system or a system which measures earnings by quantity or quality of production or to employees who work in different locations, provided that such differences are not the result of an intention to discriminate because of . . . sex . . .

IMPACT OF LABOR MARKET CONDITIONS

Wage determination is a complex process in which many different pressures and forces collide to produce the wage structure. (The term *wage structure* simply refers to the categorization of jobs into a series of job grades and to the relationships of compensation ranges for the grades.) It is not a neat process in which the "true value" of each job and its pay are determined objectively and scientifically. Moreover, the process is further complicated by the prevailing labor market conditions. Suppose, for example, that a severe shortage of computer programmers and engineers drives the prevailing wage for such jobs to an amount double the wage indicated by a company's job evaluation. The company will simply be unable to hire people with these skills unless it violates the job evaluation plan and pays something approaching the market rate.

Thus, internal compensation relationships and structures are sometimes violated or compromised in order to obtain critically short skills. As long as this is recognized as a practical accommodation to reality, a limited number of exceptions to the firm's compensation structure should cause no alarm.

On the contrary, if employees are given a straightforward explanation of the reason for the exceptions, the vast majority will accept the logic of accommodating to reality. On the other hand, some firms have gotten into serious difficulties by trying to disguise the fact that the system was being violated. Attempts to pretend that the out-of-structure wage can be justified by redefining responsibilities, for example, have a very high probability of being discovered and thus endangering the perceived validity of the total system. Honesty and a realistic assessment of the evaluation system are advisable. If the system is described as a nonscientific effort to juggle as many conflicting determinants as possible in order to come up with what will be recognized as an internally equitable set of relationships, few employees will have difficulty in accommodating to occasional job market irregularities. On the other hand, if the internal structure is advertised as "scientifically accurate and precise," any deviations will be seen immediately as an indication of basic management dishonesty or as a defeat of the system.

IMPACT OF A UNION

The union may be the most important single external influence on compensation and benefit determination. If the firm is unionized, it can be safely said that a major thrust of the union's efforts will relate to compensation and benefits. Depending on the union–employer relationship, the union's impact may range from advisory influence to virtual control.

Where compensation and benefits are determined by employer–union collective bargaining, the role of compensation and benefit surveys and of job evaluation varies greatly, depending upon the attitude of the union. Some unions use comparisons within the industry, among industries, or within their geographic area to determine their demands, and base a major part of their negotiating strategy on obtaining equality. Other unions disdain this "follower" role and simply concentrate on seeking "more" in terms of higher compensation, new benefits, or higher benefit levels.

Furthermore, some unions cooperate closely with management in designing and administering job evaluations in order to establish appropriate internal relationships within the salary structure. Other unions disdain job evaluation as a management tool to destroy traditional internal relationships among jobs. Where there is a union, its objectives, traditions, and expectations become additional constraints that must be taken into account in designing the organization's compensation strategy.

PROCEDURE FOR DEVELOPING THE COMPENSATION SYSTEM

1. Establish compensation objectives regarding type (extrinsic or intrinsic, financial or nonfinancial) and balance of rewards, and define competitive strategy within industry.

2. Conduct compensation and benefits surveys.
3. Relate survey data to the existing reward system.

Compensation and Benefit Surveys

Once the objectives have been established, the next step is to obtain the needed data for planning purposes. Sometimes these data are available from published industry or area surveys. The results of a survey of top executive compensation are shown in Exhibit 15–2.

Some industry associations conduct annual *compensation and benefits* surveys for their members. In some localities the Chamber of Commerce or another employer group conducts an annual compensation and benefits survey to provide such data. Often, however, no such survey will exist or specific data needs may not be satisfied by the survey. In such instances the organization must conduct its own compensation and benefits survey or employ a consultant to do so.

Fundamentally, the process is simple and straightforward. The first step in conducting a compensation survey is to determine a series of *benchmark jobs.* These are jobs that have been carefully and completely defined and described in the organization, and that are believed to exist in similar form in the other organizations participating in the survey. Thus, benchmark jobs provide basic reference points for comparing equivalent jobs in different organizations. After data have been obtained for a series of benchmark jobs, other jobs within the organization can be fitted in between the wage structure of the benchmark jobs, using the internal job evaluation process.

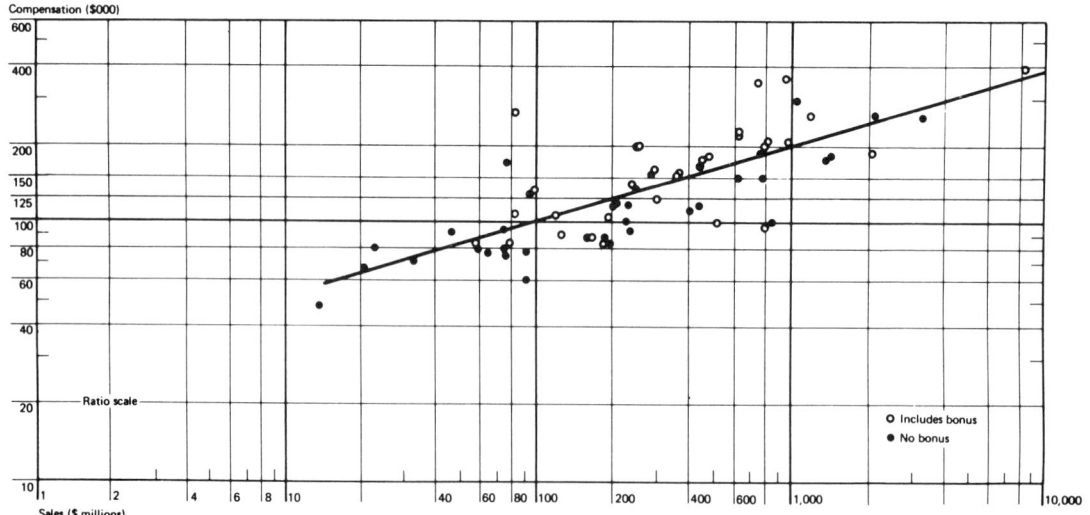

EXHIBIT 15–2
The compensation of top executives as a function of company sales.
Source: Conference Board, *Top Executive Compensation,* 1972.

ADMINISTERING THE COMPENSATION PROGRAM

Depending on the constraints, compensation and benefits surveys may be conducted by personal interview, by telephone, or by mail. In any case, a questionnaire will be used that provides a brief job description and specification for each benchmark job. Space is provided for recording minimum, maximum, mean, and median salaries paid for that job by the company being surveyed. In the case of surveys conducted by mail, it is often helpful to follow up receipt of the survey data with a telephone call to discuss unclear details and to confirm the assumed similarity of benchmark jobs, as well as to clear up any other ambiguities.

Relating Survey Data to the Reward System

Once the compensation survey data have been obtained, it is helpful to display them graphically for each benchmark job, showing the minimum pay, the maximum pay, and the median pay for each benchmark job covered in the survey, as well as the relationship between the different benchmark jobs. Such a graph is illustrated in Exhibit 15–3.

The benchmark jobs can then be used to determine a series of job

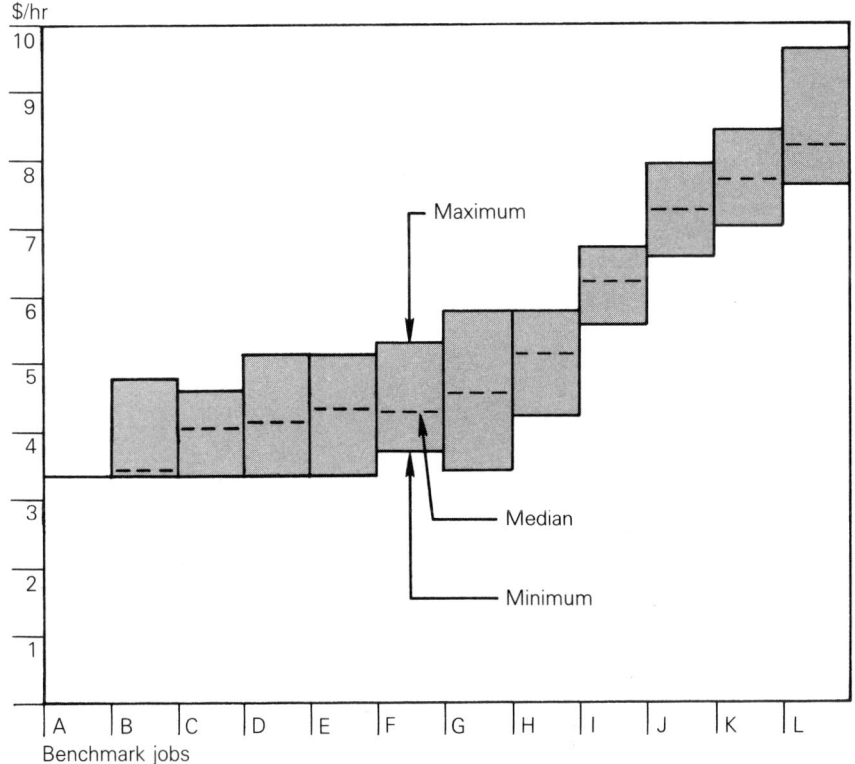

EXHIBIT 15–3
Survey data for benchmark jobs.

grades or steps and an appropriate salary midpoint and range for each grade. Depending on its objectives and strategy, the organization may wish to set its salary midpoints for each grade at the average (median) of surveyed firms, at 10 percent higher than the average, at 10 percent lower than the average, or perhaps at the average of some subcategory of the total survey.

The maximum will typically be set at a standard percentage above the midpoint, perhaps 10 percent, while the *minimum* is then determined by *deducting* this figure from the midpoint salary. Note in Exhibit 15–4 that the payroll ranges overlap. What results is a logical hierarchy of wages in which the more demanding and responsible job pays more. As employees improve their performance in a particular job, their pay can rise within the range for that job grade. Employees that reach the top of their grade, however, can only increase their pay by being promoted to a higher grade.

Sometimes a wage structure (particularly one negotiated with a union)

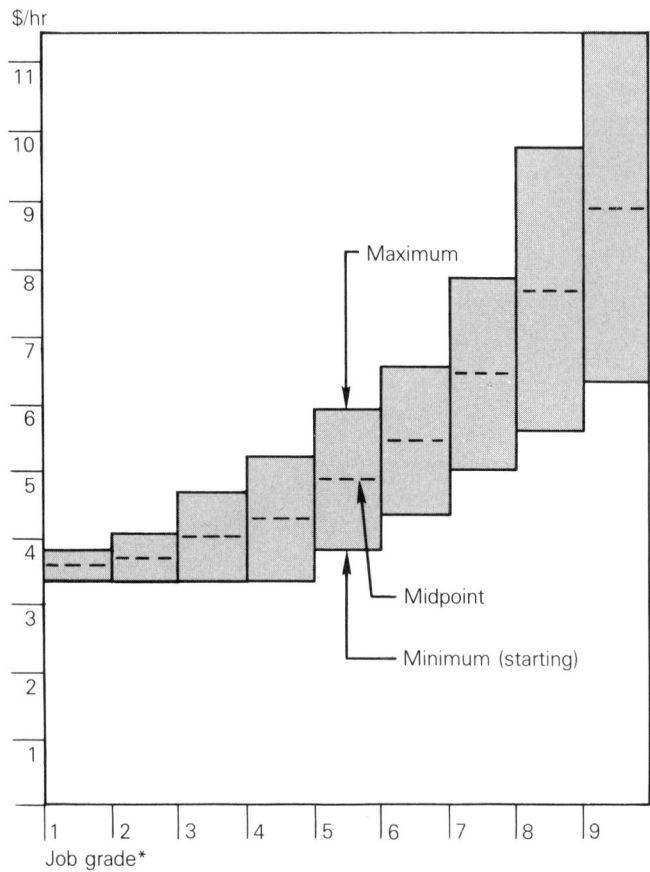

EXHIBIT 15–4
Wage structure.

may specify only one specific wage for each grade level rather than a range of wages.

Whatever the strategy, once the midpoint of the salary range for each benchmark job has been determined, and once the benchmark jobs have been arrayed along a continuum of job grades, then any job in the organization may be related to this wage structure. The appropriate salary minimum, maximum, and midpoint for that job may be determined by using a job evaluation system to compare it with the benchmark jobs. The same evaluation system is used to evaluate all of the jobs in the organization. Each job grade represents a *range* of evaluation points, and each job is assigned a grade based on its relative number of evaluation points. Once a grade is assigned to a job, that job has automatically been assigned a salary minimum and midpoint, as shown in Exhibit 15–4.

The benefits component should also be determined in relation to the compensation and benefits survey, although usually on a less mathematical basis. Determination of the mix of benefits, the level of each benefit offered, and the funding arrangements will usually be done by evaluating the organization's unique situation and its employees' needs in light of the survey data, rather than by attempting to translate the survey data directly into equivalent practice.

JOB EVALUATION

A major task in developing a wage structure is determining the relative worth of each job. This task of determining the relative worth of jobs is called *job evaluation*.

The objective of job evaluation is to ensure that internal relationships among the pay of various jobs are appropriate in light of the factors considered important *by the members of the given organization*. These factors typically include the effort, training, and experience required; the difficulty, responsibility, and hazards of the job; the value or contribution of the job to the organization; and the organization's traditions of internal job relationships. Thus, the objective of job evaluation is to ensure internal equity *in the eyes of the members of the organization*, not to ensure equity in terms of some "objective" standard external to the organization. Although such a task is impossible as a practical reality, managers have sometimes thought, and textbooks have implied, that an objective standard of equity was the goal of job evaluation. Job evaluation is still very much an art and by no means a science. Managers lose sight of this fact at their peril.

We have said that the job evaluation reflects *internal* standards of equity and traditional relationships. We have also said that once benchmark jobs are identified, the compensation and benefits survey determines industry or geographic standards for each benchmark job in order to create a wage structure based on the benchmark jobs. It should be pointed out that this process may have laid the groundwork for a serious inconsistency.

Implicit in the process of compensation determination discussed above is the assumption that internal job evaluation will create the same relationships among benchmark jobs that are found in the outside firms participating in the survey. Obviously this may or may not be the case. If we are lucky, our internal relationships will turn out to be rather close to the relationships determined by the survey. However, it is certainly possible that due to unique traditions or internal circumstances, some of our benchmark jobs are felt to be worth relatively more than our external surveys say they are worth in other organizations.

There is no standard method for dealing with this dilemma, but it is important to recognize at this point that if such practical problems arise, the only solution is to make a pragmatic judgment. Of course, the external data may help change internal perceptions. The four basic methods of job evaluation are (1) ranking, (2) classification, (3) the point method, and (4) factor-comparison. Each of these methods begins with a job description (discussed in Chapter 5). Since the job description process usually begins with having incumbents fill out a job description questionnaire and job specification sheet, care must be used in working with the resulting data to control for the natural human tendency to slant or "fudge" the data to overdescribe the difficulty and requirements of the job.

Ranking

The *ranking method* is perhaps the simplest method of job evaluation. The various jobs to be evaluated are ranked in relation to each other on a total basis. There is no attempt to determine the significant factors in the jobs or to evaluate the jobs in terms of their subelements. Rather, only a single overall judgment is made regarding the relative worth of each job in relation to the others.

This is, in fact, the most common method of job evaluation in smaller organizations, in which, perhaps, two secretaries, a typist, and a file clerk must be evaluated. In a small organization in which relatively few jobs are involved and all of the people participating in the evaluation are intimately familiar with the details of all the jobs, this is perhaps a very effective method of evaluation.

However, this method very quickly breaks down when larger groups are involved and when there is less knowledge of each of the jobs. Since there are no written guidelines for evaluation, it is obviously important that the ranking of all the jobs be done by the same individual or group so that the subjective basis for ranking can be consistent. Even under the best of conditions, there is always the danger that the individuals doing the ranking may have imperfect knowledge of the jobs or be subject to bias. To some extent this can be overcome by the use of job descriptions.

Classification

The *classification method* of job evaluation is by far the most common method used in civil service systems. In this method before any jobs are examined, an a priori assumption is made regarding the number of pay grades to be included in the final structure. Then, following the perusal of many job descriptions, a description is written for each grade or "class" of jobs in the structure.

These descriptions cover such items as the education required, the skill required, job responsibility, and other factors that are pertinent to a particular class of jobs. Thus, a particular job class or grade may be described as requiring a high school education, moderate finger dexterity, light physical exertion (as specifically described), and a moderately high level of judgment.

Once a description of each of the job grades has been written, the descriptions of the jobs to be evaluated are examined. Jobs are classified into the grade or level that has the most closely corresponding description.

Although appearing to be somewhat less "scientific" than the point or factor-comparison methods, in many situations this method may be just as accurate. Furthermore, this method is relatively easy to understand and therefore appears to be straightforward and "legitimate." Thus, in many organizations it may be easier for employees to accept this method as being "honest."

Point Method

By far the most common method of job evaluation is the point method. This procedure usually examines four or more job factors common to the jobs being evaluated and rates each job on a numerical scale in relation to each factor. Thus, points are accumulated for each factor on the basis of the relative degree to which the job is seen as possessing that factor.

For example, if the factor to be evaluated were "education," grade school or less might be scaled as one point; two years of high school as two points; high school graduation, three points; two years of college, four points; four years of college, five points; master's degree, six points; and Ph.D., seven points. A factor such as "responsibility" might scale several different levels of dollar responsibility, in terms of the value of production or the cost of errors.

The number of factors used may vary from as few as 2 to as many as 30, although several research studies have shown statistically that 4 or 5 factors seem to be about as accurate a basis for distinguishing jobs as a higher number. As can be imagined, the factors used vary widely among different organizations and industries. The more common factors in use include education, responsibility (for production, equipment, budget, persons, or safety), skill, experience, outside contacts, supervision, job conditions, physical effort, mental effort, and creativity.

Whatever the factors in a particular system, the total points for each job are determined by summing the points assigned for each factor. Each job can then be related to other jobs on the basis of their respective total point scores.

Furthermore, the point score can be related to the structure of job grades and wage ranges previously discussed by assigning a job grade to each range of points. Exhibit 15–5 illustrates point evaluation in a typical point system.

EXHIBIT 15–5
Points assigned to factor degrees and range for grades.

Factors	1st degree	2d degree	3d degree	4th degree	5th degree	6th degree	7th degree
Training							
1. Education	15	30	45	60	75	100	
2. Experience	20	40	60	80	100	125	150
Initiative							
3. Complexity of duties	15	30	45	60	75	100	
4. Supervision received	5	10	20	40	60		
Responsibility							
5. Errors	5	10	20	40	60	80	
6. Contacts with others	5	10	20	40	60	80	
7. Confidential data	5	10	15	20	25		
Job conditions							
8. Mental or visual demand	5	10	15	20	25		
9. Working conditions	5	10	15	20	25		
Supervision							
10. Character of supervision	5	10	20	40	60	80	
11. Scope of supervision	5	10	20	40	60	80	100

Score range	Grades		Score range	Grades
100 and under	1		311–340	9
101–130	2		341–370	10
131–160	3		371–400	11
161–190	4		401–430	12
191–220	5		431–460	13
221–250	6		461–490	14
251–280	7		491–520	15
281–310	8		521–550	16

EXHIBIT 15–5, *continued*

Job Rating Specifications
(clerical, technical, supervisory)

COMPTROLLER   Class _____

Code no. __B–01__
Dept. __Accounting__
Grade __15__
Total points __500__

Factors	Substantiating data	Deg.	Pts.
Education	Broad knowledge of general, cost, and payroll accounting theory and practice, budgetary control, and finance. Familiar with business organization and administration, office management and economics, foreign exchange. Equivalent to college education in business administration.	4	60
Experience	Over seven and up to eight years.	6	125
Complexity of duties	Wide variety of budgetary control, accounting, and office management duties and responsibilities, involving general knowledge of related company policies and procedures. Duties require considerable judgment in devising new methods and procedures, modifying standard practices to meet new conditions, making decisions guided by precedent and based on company policies.	4	60
Supervision Received	Under general direction of Treasurer as to policies and general objectives. Rarely refer specific problems to superior for other than policy decisions.	4	40
Errors	Probably error in judgment or supervision may result in incorrect financial data, costs, or inventory information. Considerable accuracy and responsibility involved.	4	40
Contacts with others	Contacts with various company officers, subsidiary companies, and branches, requiring considerable tact and diplomacy to obtain results through influencing others.	4	40
Confidential data	Regularly work with confidential corporate financial data such as balance sheet, profit and loss statements, costs, etc. Disclosure may be detrimental to the company's interests.	4	20
Mental or visual demand	Supervisory and contact duties involve normal mental and visual attention most of the time.	2	10
Working conditions	Usual office working conditions.	1	5
For supervisory positions only			
Character of supervision	General supervision of accounting, payroll, billing, and general office services, with responsibility for results in terms of costs, methods, and personnel.	4	40
Scope of supervision	Responsible for supervising 62 persons, including 9 subordinate supervisors.	5	60
Remarks			

Source: Glenn T. Fischbach, Chap. 12.3 from *Handbook of Wage and Salary Administration* by Milton Rock. Copyright © 1972 by McGraw-Hill, Inc. Used with permission of the McGraw-Hill Book Company.

Factor-comparison

The factor-comparison method is very similar to the point method, except that it does not evaluate each of the factors on a numerical scale. While it may use the same factors as those used in the point method, the factor-comparison method, rather than assigning points, *ranks* benchmark jobs in relation to each other on *each factor* at the outset of the process. It is important to include in this group only jobs that are widely believed to be accurately paid.

Following the ranking of the benchmark jobs on each of the factors, a fairly complex mathematical procedure is utilized to determine how much of the present rate of pay of the jobs is accounted for by each of the separate factors, that is, the weights of the factors. After this has been determined, the remaining jobs to be evaluated are then ranked on each of the factors in relation to the benchmark jobs. When the dollar values of the ranked positions on each factor have been determined, these values are summed to arrive at the dollar value of the total job. The factor-comparison method is not as widely used as the point method, principally because it is much more complicated and takes more time to learn and apply. Moreover, the fact that the method is hard to understand may lead to lack of trust in its application.

EXECUTIVE COMPENSATION

The pay of executives has special fascination for many people although it is only a special category within the general topic of compensation. First, the base salaries of executives are higher than those of others. Second, executives frequently have supplemental compensation plans that can dramatically increase their total compensation. A top executive at Mobil Oil or Revlon may earn $1,000,000 or more on top of his or her base salary. Often, executives also receive special perquisites as well. Middle-level executives in the private sector frequently earn base salaries of $50,000 to $100,000. The chief executive officer of a Fortune 100 corporation can expect a salary in excess of $250,000. Exhibit 15–6 highlights the pay of industry's 10 highest-paid executives during 1983. Notice how the bonuses and stock options dramatically increase the total amounts.

Much of this additional compensation is in the form of a deferred bonus distributed over several future periods. The purpose of such deferred compensation is both to reduce income taxes and to tie the executive to the organization by making it very expensive to leave ("the golden handcuffs").

IMPLEMENTING A FLEXIBLE SYSTEM

The mechanics of operating a flexible compensation system are a bit more complex than the principle, but well within our capabilities in the age of computers. Until only recently, the number and complexity of the compu-

EXHIBIT 15–6
Industry's ten highest-paid executives in 1983.

Executive/Firm	Salary & Bonus	Benefits	Contingent	Stock Gains	Total
Frederick W. Smith, Federal Express	413,590	704	—	51,129,969	51,544,263
Charles Lazarus, Toys 'R' Us	1,430,616	12,292	45,400	42,359,753	43,848,061
Ronald G. Assaf, Sensormatic Electronics	249,712	33,276	7,826	6,994,715	7,285,529
Steven J. Ross, Warner Communications	2,301,497	95,741	1,283,835	—	3,681,073
George L. Shinn, First Boston	2,000,000	73,876	369,170	1,089,757	3,532,803
Richard K. Eamer, National Medical Enterprises	675,183	117,436	—	2,652,099	3,444,718
John P. Laborde, Tidewater	708,161	4,956	32,041	2,468,372	3,213,530
David J. Mahoney, Norton Simon	887,917	351,577	611,121	1,145,421	2,996,036
Thomas V. Jones, Northrop	1,181,414	351,626	1,377,595	—	2,910,635
Harrington Drake, Dun & Bradstreet	750,000	74,897	19,567	1,701,170	2,545,634

Source: Based on data in *Forbes,* June 6, 1983.

tations involved made cafeteria compensation impractical. At present, however, the computer permits the employer to compute the dollar cost equivalents of an array of possible compensation options to employees participating in the flexible compensation system. Typically, options and equivalents would be computed for some or all of the following:

- ☐ Immediate cash
- ☐ Deferred cash
- ☐ Retirement plan
- ☐ Company stock investment plan
- ☐ Mutual fund investment plan
- ☐ Medical insurance (perhaps with two or three levels of coverage as options)
- ☐ Long-term disability insurance
- ☐ Life insurance

☐ Vacation time
☐ Perhaps some local individualized options

Although it is theoretically possible to compute dollar equivalents for the various forms of compensation and then to let each individual have complete freedom in selecting the mix, this is unlikely to happen in the near future for a number of reasons. One is a sense of corporate responsibility for making sure than an individual does not select so unwisely as to imperil self and family. Perhaps more important, significant tax considerations make it impractical to have some benefits totally optional. What is more likely to happen is that the company will specify a certain minimum percentage of compensation to be taken in cash and in each other area, and will then allow optional selection of incremental amounts.

Thomas H. Paine, an authority on compensation, has recommended a four-step procedure for implementing flexible compensation:

1. Establish management policy regarding the role flexibility is to play.
2. Design a balanced program encompassing both basic nonoptional benefits and flexible supplements.
3. Provide an opportunity for employees to be involved in the design of the program.
4. Establish an efficient and responsible administrative system.

The administrative system should include some controls to assist employees in avoiding serious mistakes in choices. For example, Paine recommends that after employees make their choices a computer printout be reported back to them for their review and approval before the choices become final.[1] Many companies do issue the employee a benefits statement at the moment of hire and updated versions thereafter (see Exhibit 15–7).

EXHIBIT 15–7
A benefits statement.

YOUR PROTECTION TODAY AND SECURITY TOMORROW

I. COMPREHENSIVE MEDICAL EXPENSE BENEFITS FOR YOU AND YOUR INSURED DEPENDENTS

EMERGENCY ACCIDENT
100% of the first $50 of Covered Medical Expenses Incurred for treatment of a non-occupational injury in a hospital's outpatient facilities and/or physician's office when treatment begins within 24 hours after the injury.
After satisfying a deductible of $100 per person, the Plan pays:

FIRST $2000 OF COVERED MEDICAL EXPENSES
100% of the first $2,000 of Covered Medical Expenses Incurred during each confinement in a hospital as an In-patient, and 80% of all other Covered Medical Expenses.

OVER $2,000 OF COVERED MEDICAL EXPENSES
80% of Covered Medical Expenses in excess of $2000 Incurred by an Insured during a calendar year.

COVERED MEDICAL EXPENSES INCLUDE:
• Hospital room and board, except charges for private room accommodations in excess of the average semi-private rate plus 10 per day.
• Other hospital services and supplies.
• Physician's and surgeon's fees in or out of the hospital.
• Fees for registered or licensed practical nurse.
• Extraction of Impacted teeth.
• Anesthesia and its administration.
• Diagnostic x-ray and laboratory services.
• Drugs and medicines prescribed by a physician and dispensed by pharmacist or physician.
• Maternity care and nursery charges.
• Ambulance service.
• Crutches, canes, casts, splints, trusses, and braces.

MAXIMUM BENEFIT
$10,000 lifetime maximum benefit payable for each Insured with automatic reinstatement each year up to 5

II. SICKNESS AND DISABILITY BENEFITS WHEN YOU ARE UNABLE TO WORK

SICK LEAVE BENEFIT
The Company has a liberal sick leave policy under which salary payments for work absences due to sickness or accident are considered on a case-by-case basis depending upon your length of service and other pertinent circumstances.

ACCIDENT AND SICKNESS BENEFIT
$50.00 for each work day missed up to 8 weeks if you become disabled and are under the care of a physician who certifies that you are unable to work. Benefits begin the 1st work day missed if your disability is caused by an accident, or you are sick in the hospital, and on the 6th work day if your sickness does not require hospitalization.

ACCIDENTAL DISMEMBERMENT BENEFIT
$36,000 for accidental loss of two limbs, or sight of both eyes, or one eye and one limb (one half this amount for loss of one limb or one eye).

SOCIAL SECURITY DISABILITY BENEFIT
After 5 months of total disability and for as long as total disability continues, or age 65, you will be eligible to receive a monthly benefit dependent upon your earnings history and family status. Your estimated *maximum family benefit* is $710 and is determined as follows:
$393 for you.
$125 for each dependent child, plus
$192 for your wife while caring for your dependent child,
OR
$350 for your wife or dependent husband at age 62, without a dependent child.

LONG TERM DISABILITY BENEFIT
$800 per month after 6 months of total disability for as long as your disability continues, or age 65. This monthly benefit includes disability income to which you may be entitled from Workmen's Compensation, the Accident and Sickness Plan, and Social Security benefits relating to you.

III. SURVIVORS' BENEFITS

LUMP SUM BENEFITS

$ 36,000 Basic Life Insurance
$ 15,000 Supplemental Life Insurance
$ 22,000 Employee Savings Plan (Market Value)
$ 255 Social Security
       Additional Accident Benefits
$ 36,000 Accidental Death Insurance
$100,000 Business Travel Accident Insurance
$209,255 TOTAL

MONTHLY BENEFITS

Social Security Benefit
Your surviving family will be eligible to receive a monthly benefit dependent upon your earnings history and family status. Your estimated *maximum family benefit* is $525 and is determined as follows:
$150 for each dependent child, plus $375 for your wife or husband while caring for your dependent child, OR:
$281 for your wife or dependent husband at age 60, without a dependent child.

Pension Plan Benefit
Your surviving spouse, unless you have elected otherwise, will be entitled to a lifetime monthly benefit if you have satisfied the eligibility requirements of the Pension Plan and are age 55 or older. The monthly benefit will be 100% of your accrued pension benefit or, if you have selected the 50% Provisional Payee Option, 50% of your accrued pension benefit after an actuarial adjustment.

IV. RETIREMENT BENEFITS FOR YOUR FUTURE

NORMAL RETIREMENT BENEFIT
Assuming you continue to work until your normal retirement date of 06/30/84, you will receive the following estimated monthly benefit under the terms of the Social Security Act and Pension Plan as of January 1:
$515 from the Pension Plan
$322 from Social Security
$837 TOTAL

In addition,
$161 is the estimated monthly Social Security benefit to your wife or dependent husband at age 65.

VESTED BENEFIT
After 10 years of service, you become vested under the Pension Plan. Vested means that you are entitled to a monthly benefit at age 65 if you terminate employment before retiring. The monthly amount of your accrued pension benefit is $435
X You are vested   __ You will be vested

OTHER RETIREMENT BENEFITS
- Medical coverage which supplements your Medicare coverage is provided by the Company for you and your eligible spouse at no cost to you.
- A portion of your life insurance coverage will be continued at no cost to you provided you enrolled at the time you first became eligible and continued your coverage until retirement under the Pension Plan.
- The total value of your Employee Savings Plan Account is payable in a single distribution or monthly installments.

V. THE VALUE OF YOUR BENEFITS

Using your January 1 base salary and not taking into consideration any increase, the estimated cost of your benefits for the current year is as follows:
$2,100 Is the amount you contribute, including $900 for Social Security.
$3,700 Is the amount the Company contributes, including for Social Security.
$5,800 Is the total cost of your benefits.

The Company's portion of the cost for your benefits includes contributions, where applicable, to the Pension Plan and the Employee Savings Plan, for Social Security, vacations, holidays, and the insurance plans.

Not included, but very much a part of the total employee benefit program, is the cost for such items as: Workmen's Compensation, Sick Leave, Educational Assistance, Physical Examination, Jury Duty Pay, Unemployment Insurance, and other time off from work for which you are paid.

Source: MSA Human Resource System, reprinted by permission of MSA, Inc., Atlanta, Ga.

The value of involving employees in the design of the flexible compensation program is both motivational (it gives employees an opportunity to participate in an important organizational decision) and functional (a broad cross-section of employees will reflect the needs and desires of the total employee group).

ADMINISTRATION OF COMPENSATION AND BENEFITS

The administration of compensation and benefits has three major facets:

1. The performance appraisal of individuals
2. Annual salary review for each individual
3. Maintenance of the compensation and benefit system through surveys and internal reviews

Performance Appraisal

The wage structure developed for an organization determines a number of job grades or levels. Unless each grade specifies only a single wage level (as is sometimes the case in union-negotiated plans), each of these job grades has a minimum and maximum salary. The job evaluation system determines the minimum- and maximum-salary range that may be paid to an employee assigned to that job.

Although the job evaluation system determines the range within which an individual holding a particular job may be paid, it does not in any way determine what specific salary within that range the individual should receive. Depending on the design of the particular system, the individual's compensation within the range for his or her job grade is determined by some combination of seniority (that is, time spent in the job) and individual performance.

A few organizations have compensation systems that provide for automatic progression from the entry level all the way to maximum pay for the job grade on a seniority basis (contingent on minimally acceptable performance). The more common practice is to base advancement within the range on individual performance or to provide advancement to the midpoint of the range on the basis of seniority, with advancement beyond the midpoint determined solely by individual performance.

In the majority of compensation systems, some form of performance appraisal is a major determinant of the individual's specific salary within the range determined for his or her position. Performance appraisal is in itself a highly technical procedure and a major responsibility of every line manager. For this reason, a separate chapter devoted to performance appraisal (Chapter 13) has discussed commonly used alternative approaches and the manager's critical role.

Salary Review

Following the completion of performance appraisals, line managers must perform a *salary review* of each subordinate (usually annually), in order to determine what increments to award or recommend. In many organizations, one portion of the employee's salary increase is determined by his or her manager on the basis of performance, while another portion of the increase is determined by such matters as the cost of living and changes in the structure of the compensation system. Therefore, the manager often determines salary-increase recommendations in conjunction with a member of the human resource management staff, who provides input on the organizationwide portions of the salary increase.

Generally, salary increases are determined by several factors, although the weight given to each factor may vary widely from organization to organization or from time to time:

1. Changes in the cost of living as measured by the Bureau of Labor Statistics of the Department of Labor
2. Adjustments occasioned by modifications in the wage structure as a result of changing jobs in the organization or changing relationships between jobs
3. Adjustments upward of the whole structure as a result of compensation and benefits surveys
4. Seniority or step adjustments
5. Adjustments related to the individual's performance appraisal ("merit")
6. Profitability of the company (ability to pay)

Although currently a practice in few organizations, we believe that from a motivational standpoint, it is important to make explicit the determinants of the salary increase for each individual (particularly the portion of the increase that is based on individual performance). This is often deliberately avoided in order to "avoid hurting people's feelings," but this omission is a breach of effective human resource management. One example of a system for explicitly tying merit increases to individual performances is shown in Exhibit 15–8.

In a recent article, Dr. Nathan B. Winstanley, Compensation Research Manager at Xerox Corp., has suggested the following 10 requisites for successful administration of a merit pay plan:[2]

1. *Trust and belief in management.* If this condition does not exist, there will be much less acceptance of subjective performance ratings and the merit increase practice itself.
2. *Valid job evaluation.* Once salary ranges are properly aligned with skill and responsibility, merit pay can be added for individual performance. Without job evaluation, overall salary relationships can

EXHIBIT 15–8
Merit increase guidelines.

Performance Rating	Approx. Portion of Work Force (%)	Discretionary Increase Range (%)
Outstanding	10	10–12
Consistently exceeds standards	30	7–10
Consistently meets standards	50	5–7
Sometimes meets standards— Marginal Employee	8	0–5
Unsatisfactory	2	0

become distorted; merit increases will then be used for correcting these relationships rather than for performance alone.

3. *Agreed-on tasks/criteria.* When these are discussed at the beginning of the rating period there are fewer errors of omission and commission later. Thus, there are no surprises at the time of feedback—and ideally there never should be.

4. *Job-specific, results-oriented criteria.* Performance criteria which are not specific to the job and its unique tasks are often irrelevant and conflict-prone and will certainly increase any potential legal exposure. Since this is a pay-for-performance program such criteria must emphasize results achieved (not talents employed) as much as possible.

5. *Accurate performance appraisals.* This is the bottom line in any pay-for-performance program. There is merit in merit increases only to the extent they vary with true performance.

6. *Appropriate administrative practices.* These include percent increases which, on average and in the absence of a general increase, bear some perceptible and acceptable relationship to changes in the cost of living from year to year. (Based on some of the research, one might even characterize this concept as a cultural norm.) From an incentive or motivational point of view, an appropriate reward schedule is also important. Unfortunately, such schedules are determined more by administrative than behavioral considerations. Annual reviews, for example, frequently lag behind achievement by months and thereby diminish the relationship between the accomplishment and its reward. Just the

opposite has been known to occur on the manager/executive level where time spans are in excess of a year. A twelve-month increase for them may amount to a "progress payment"; hardly pay-for-performance.
7. *Skilled feedback.* How well managers conduct the performance/salary increase reviews with subordinates can affect attitudes toward the appraisal and the increase. Day-to-day working relationships can also be enhanced or diminished as a consequence of this interview. Specific knowledge and skills are required to handle an interview of this nature.
8. *Trained managers.* Since most managers are not born with the talent discussed above—nor do they necessarily acquire it with experience—managers must be formally trained and periodically audited in the exercise of this critical skill. This is a critical skill because in many U.S. companies this particular interview is the only time the employee receives a formal and documented progress report. (It is also critical because these documents can be subpoenaed.)
9. *Maintenance and information systems.* These are necessary to make certain that the merit program is administered when and as intended within and between component organizations; they also provide a data base for later research.
10. *Follow-up research.* Identifying and minimizing bias and leniency is a must. In addition, periodic attitude surveys provide an objective measure of how well different groups of employees regard both their appraisals and merit increases; these become the basis for change and improvement.[2]

Dr. Winstanley concludes that:

If an organization is currently using a merit system, it might first make a quality check by: a) quickly ascertaining the extent to which the system conforms to the 10 requirements described above and b) asking employees what they think via an attitude survey. This last step is the ultimate criterion—for there is just no sense in awarding increases and not knowing *objectively* how they are received.

Maintaining the System

The third major function in the administration of compensation and benefits is *compensation system maintenance* through surveys and internal reviews. Compensation and benefit-surveys have already been discussed in the context of developing a wage structure. Benchmark jobs are identified, and the salaries paid to equivalent jobs by competing firms in the industry or the geographic area are determined through surveys.

For most organizations, the best practice will be to take advantage of all published surveys that may be relevant, to study and compare these

```
SALARY AND PERFORMANCE                          GATEWAY ENERGY LTD                                              PAGE 14
REVIEWS****                                A DIVISION OF WORLDWIDE ENERGY                                       07/01/82

                                            SALARY AND PERFORMANCE REVIEWS

    L1 EMPL. NO.      ******************* SALARY REVIEWS *******************    *********** PERFORMANCE REVIEWS ****
    EMPLOYEE NAME     DATE     AMOUNT    PCT CHNG   REASON            JOB CODE   DATE      RATING  SUPERVISOR   JOB CODE

    03    10375
    ANDERSON, ALFRED  06/01/82  $1,438.37   10.00   COST OF LIVING    MGR-036    06/01/82    41    J SMITH      MGR-036
                      06/01/81  $1,307.61   10.00   COST OF LIVING    MGR-036    06/01/81    38    J SMITH      MGR-036
                      06/01/80  $1,188.74   10.00   COST OF LIVING    MGR-036    05/01/79    38    J SMITH      MGR-036
                      06/01/79  $1,080.67   10.00   COST OF LIVING    MGR-036    06/01/79    20    B GREENE     MGR-036
                      06/01/78  $1,408.70   15.00   MERIT             MGR-036    06/01/78    20    B GREENE     MGR-036
                      06/01/77  $   854.37  10.00   COST OF LIVING    SPV-138    06/01/77    20    D BUNTON     SPV-138
                      06/01/76  $   705.44   9.00   COST OF LIVING    SPV-138    06/01/76    32    D BUNTON     SPV-138
                      06/01/75  $   839.81  12.00   PROMOTION         SPV-138    06/01/75    32    D BUNTON     SPV-138
                      06/01/74  $   518.40   8.00   COST OF LIVING    CLK-522    06/01/74    32    F FISHER     CLK-522
                      06/01/73  $   480.00   8.00   COST OF LIVING    CLK-522    06/01/73    32    F FISHER     CLK-522
                      NEXT SALARY REVIEW 06/01/83                                NEXT PERFORMANCE REVIEW 06/01/83

    03    10445
    ENDISON, ALMA LOUISE 01/01/82 $  500.00  5.70   LONGEVITY         SEC-002    01/01/82    15    14411        SEC-002
                      01/01/81  $   432.81   5.17   COST OF LIVING    SEC-002    01/01/81    15    14411        SEC-002
                      01/01/80  $   423.50   5.34   PROMOTION         SEC-003    01/01/80    15    13900        SEC-003
                      01/01/79  $   390.00   5.17   UNION CONTRACT    SEC-003    01/01/79    15    13900        SEC-003
                      01/01/78  $   365.28   5.01   RECLASSIFICATION  SEC-003    01/01/78    15    13900        SEC-003
                      01/01/77  $   350.00   5.12   MERIT             SEC-004    01/01/77     6    63227        SEC-004
                      01/01/76  $   325.00   5.00   DEMOTION          SEC-003    01/01/76     6    63227        SEC-003
                      01/01/75  $   300.00   4.83   COST OF LIVING    SEC-003    01/01/75     4    63227        SEC-003
                      01/01/74  $   300.00   5.08   COST OF LIVING    SEC-004    01/01/74     4    63227        SEC-004
                      01/01/73  $   300.00   5.35   COST OF LIVING    SEC-004    01/01/73     1    63227        SEC-004
                      NEXT SALARY REVIEW 01/01/83                                NEXT PERFORMANCE REVIEW 01/01/83

    03    10764
    STATON, DAVID B.  09/01/81  $5,000.00   25.00   UNION CONTRACT    MGR-023    09/01/81    17    98421        MGR-023
                      09/01/80  $2,800.00   12.60   PROMOTION         MGR-023    09/01/80    16    98421        MGR-023
                      09/01/79  $2,400.00   12.10   COST OF LIVING    MGR-023    09/01/79    16    98421        MGR-023
                      09/01/78  $1,800.00    9.98   COST OF LIVING    MGR-023    09/01/78    16    98421        MGR-023
                      NEXT SALARY REVIEW 09/01/82                                NEXT PERFORMANCE REVIEW 09/01/82

    03    20032
    TARLINGTON, JOHN H. 03/01/82 $2,000.37  37.09   MERIT             FIN-001    02/26/82    11    74820        FIN-001
                      03/01/81  $   500.00  10.22   COST OF LIVING    FIN-001
                      NEXT SALARY REVIEW 03/01/83                                NEXT PERFORMANCE REVIEW 03/01/83

    03    34254
    WADE, HERBERT H.  NEXT SALARY REVIEW 09/01/83                        09/01/81     44    14375        ACT-019
                                                                                 NEXT PERFORMANCE REVIEW 09/01/82
```

EXHIBIT 15–9
A salary and performance review report.
Source: Reprinted with permission from MSA, Inc., Atlanta, Ga.

surveys carefully, and then to conduct their own survey to supplement the published surveys.

In any case, it is probably desirable for most organizations to conduct such a review at least annually, and many organizations will have reviews in progress constantly. (See Exhibit 15–9.) The annual survey does not in itself imply a change in the organization's wage structure; it only provides a basis for decision making. Data will also be available regarding changes in the cost of living and in the organization's profitability.

Following comparison of the survey data with the organization's wage structure, a basic policy decision at the highest level (with the advice of the human resources department) must be made about changes in the organization's compensation in response to job market changes reflected in the surveys.

Need for Internal Review Internal reviews must also be conducted constantly to keep job evaluations up-to-date. Although it is important to provide a system for automatically rewriting job descriptions and re-evaluating jobs each time a job is changed, many smaller changes that occur constantly tend to be overlooked. Therefore, it is vital that a periodic audit of each job description and job evaluation be conducted to make certain that each continues to be up-to-date.

In addition, it is necessary to review the entire wage structure periodically to make sure that it is sound and appropriately related to the mix of jobs. For example, over time the necessary number of job grades may change. Or the relationship between grades may need to be changed. These things can be determined only by comparing the results of internal job evaluation reviews with the results of compensation and benefits surveys.

From a motivational standpoint it is extremely important for an organization to constantly review its total system of compensation and benefits. Only through such review is it possible to maintain a system that the employees view as "equitable" and that serves as a motivating device.

Role of the Specialist The process of maintaining the compensation and benefits system is a major piece of work in an organization of any considerable size. Thus, most organizations of more than a few employees will have at least one specialist in compensation and benefits within the human resources department. Larger organizations will have sizable departments of compensation and benefit specialists.

It is the specific assignment of these departments to keep the compensation and benefits system up-to-date through the reviews that have been discussed. In addition, they often advise and assist line managers in matters that concern the compensation and benefits system.

A final part of the internal review that can be highly valuable for management is the periodic involvement of the entire work force in a review of the reward system. One way of achieving this is through an annual questionnaire to all employees asking for their opinions on various facets of the nonfinancial and financial reward systems.

For example, questions might be asked regarding the perceived equity of the general level of wages, the wage structure, performance evaluations, and the relationship of individual pay to individual performance. Additional questions might be asked about the adequacy of the benefits provided or about the adequacy of the optional forms of compensation in a flexible compensation system.

Another procedure is to use groups of employees to review the compensation and benefits system. A very effective approach is to have an employee committee review and discuss the results of an organizationwide questionnaire survey, with an assignment to recommend changes to top management.

SUMMARY

In order to effectively motivate a wide range of employees it is important that a reward system be flexible so that the specifics of the system can vary from individual to individual and situation to situation, contingent on the individual (needs, attitudes, intrinsic versus extrinsic motivation), the task (intrinsic versus extrinsic rewards, measurability), and the organization (climate, history).

In light of our current knowledge regarding human behavior, it is clear that only a contingency-based reward system that takes into account differences among individuals, tasks, and organizations can provide an adequate basis for the motivation of individuals. As an illustration of a contingent reward system, the flexible compensation or "cafeteria" approach was described. This appears to be the best means of providing a maximum degree of individual tailoring in the reward system. From a motivational standpoint, the cafeteria approach also has the advantage of giving the individual additional control over aspects of the work that are personally important.

Also discussed was the role of the compensation and benefits specialist in planning and implementing compensation strategy. Among the specific responsibilities of compensation and benefits specialists are the various steps of the compensation determination process, including the writing of job descriptions, job evaluation, conducting compensation and benefits surveys, developing a wage structure for the organization, and constantly updating the total reward system.

We have described procedures for conducting compensation and benefits surveys using benchwork jobs, and have discussed the determination of a wage structure using the survey data along with job evaluation results for the benchwork job. Four methods of job evaluation were described and differentiated—ranking, classification, the point method, and factor-comparison.

Regular (usually annual) salary reviews that emphasize the direct tie between performance and pay increase play a vital role in using the compensation system to motivate performance instead of merely maintaining the employees.

KEY CONCEPTS

Compensation strategy

Flexible compensation

Comparable worth

Wage structure

Wage discrimination

Compensation and benefits surveys

Benchmark job

Job evaluation

Ranking

Classification

Point method

Factor-comparison

Salary reviews

Compensation system maintenance

NOTES

1. Thomas H. Paine, "Flexible Compensation Can Work!" *Financial Executive*, February 1974.
2. Nathan B. Winstanley, "Are Merit Increases Really Effective?" *Personnel Administrator*, April 1982, pp. 37–38. Reprinted from the April, 1982 issue of *Personnel Administrator*, copyright, 1982, The American Society for Personnel Administration, 606 North Washington Street, Alexandria, VA 22314, $30 per year.

REVIEW AND DISCUSSION QUESTIONS

1. Obtain from the library a textbook on job evaluation that contains a complete point plan. Using the plan, do a complete evaluation of a job familiar to you.
2. Evaluate the same job using a classification plan from the same or a different textbook.
3. Write a library research report on "maintaining a compensation and benefits system."
4. Visit the compensation manager of a local firm, and discuss with him or her the organization's procedure for job evaluation. Report your findings to the class.

5. Visit the same firm's benefits manager to obtain information on the firm's fringe benefits program. Report these findings to the class.
6. Write a five-page report on *your* views of the role of the human resource staff regarding the compensation and benefits program.
7. Describe the difference between the point method and the ranking method of job evaluation.
8. What is a wage and salary survey? How is one conducted?
9. Why is there usually overlap between the wage ranges of adjoining job grades in a wage structure?

BIBLIOGRAPHY

Brennan, E. James. "The Problem with Salary Ranges (and a Realistic Solution)." *Personnel Journal* 59, March 1980, 187–191.

Brinks, James T. "Is There Merit in Merit Increases?" *Personnel Administrator*, May 1980, 59–64.

Casey, J. F. "A Salary Administration Program for Today's Economy." *Advanced Management Journal*, Summer 1980.

Claypool, J. C. "The Annual Employee Earnings and Benefits Letter." *Personnel Journal*, July 1980.

Ewing, Larry E. "Employee Benefits Communications in the Decade Ahead." *Pension World*, February 1980, 60–66.

Fleuter, Douglas L. "A Different Approach to Merit Increases." *Personnel Journal*, April 1979, 225–226, 262.

Greene, Robert J. "Thoughts on Compensation Management in the 80s and 90s." *Personnel Administrator*, May 1980, 27–28.

Kendall, Edward L., and Philip R. Matheny. "Current Issues in Salary Administration." *Personnel Administrator*, August 1978, 34–41.

Lawler, Edward E. "Merit Pay—Fact or Fiction," *Management Review*, April 1981, 50–52.

Runzheimer, Rufus E., Jr. "Factoring Living-Cost Differentials into Salary Levels." *Personnel*, January–February 1979, 68–78.

Wolfe, Michael N., and Charles W. Candland. "Impact of the Minimum Wage on Compression." *Personnel Administrator*, May 1979, 24–28, 40.

PART IV CASE STUDIES

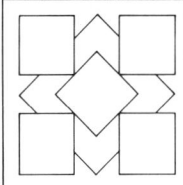

CASE STUDY:
A Matter of Money

How would you utilize a salary increase budget of $5,000 (7.5 percent of total payroll) to reward the employees in Table A? You do not have to spend the full budget, but under no circumstances may you exceed it. In your opinion, all of these individuals were properly paid in relationship to their relative performance and seniority one year (12 months) ago, when you last adjusted their compensation. The rate of inflation last year was 6.5 percent.

TABLE A
A Matter of Money

Name	Present Salary ($)	Title	Salary Grade	Years in Department	Performance	Personal Circumstances
John Mason	15,000	Analyst	6	5	Acceptable. Has missed several important deadlines, but this may not have been his fault.	Married. Large family dependent on him as sole support.
G. W. Jones	13,000	Analyst	6	2	Outstanding. Sometimes a bit "pushy" in making requests and suggestions about the department.	Single. No dependents. Has no pressing need for money. Reported to lead a rather "wild" life outside the office.
Jane Boston	12,000	Junior analyst	5	8	Consistently an excellent performer, though she has not been assigned the full range of duties of an analyst. Dependable. Often initiates improvements in work methods.	Married. Husband is a successful architect. Children in high school.

TABLE A, *continued*

Name	Present Salary ($)	Title	Salary Grade	Years in Department	Performance	Personal Circumstances
Ralph Schmidt	16,000	Senior analyst	7	15	Acceptable. Few original contributions recently. Seems to be a "plodder." Content to get by with minimum performance and participation.	Married. Financially pressed because he has two children in college (one plans to go on to medical school).
Hillary Johnson	11,000	Junior analyst	5	6	Acceptable volume, but continues to make costly mistakes. Has repeatedly been warned about this over the last years.	Single. Has a dependent mother who is chronically ill.

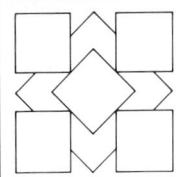

CASE STUDY:
Delta Corporation

Bill Joiner studied carefully the draft of performance objectives he had just received in the mail from one of his new sales representatives, Ralph Stone. He pondered what steps he should take next and wondered just what approach he should take in reviewing the objectives with Stone.

Bill Joiner was the Florida district sales manager for Delta Corporation, a national distributor of construction tools and equipment. Joiner's primary responsibility was the supervision of a seven-member field sales force covering the state of Florida.

Stone had just joined Delta two months earlier. This would therefore be the first time that Joiner would go through a cycle of the MBO program with him. At Delta, subordinates drafted new objectives and reviewed them with their superiors every six months.

Bill remembered that the company had stressed the importance of mutual understanding and agreement between the subordinate and the superior as the keystone of the MBO program. He wondered what action he should take in response to Ralph Stone's first attempt at drafting objectives (see Figure A).

FIGURE A
Management by objectives work sheet.

Name: Ralph Stone Title: Field Sales Representative	Department: Florida District Sales Supervisor: Wm. Joiner
Objectives	**Target Date for Completion**
1. To significantly increase the market share of the Delta product line in my territory.	Continuing
2. To develop additional contacts within my present customers' organizations as well as prospect for new business with firms that we do not now service.	Daily
3. To strengthen my knowledge of the Delta product line.	As soon as possible
4. To achieve a total sales volume of $326,000 for all products this quarter.	June 30
5. To improve customer relations.	Continuing
6. To develop my management potential by completing at least one evening course this year at Florida Atlantic University.	December 31

CASE STUDY:
Marco, Incorporated

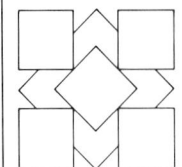

> **Statement of Grievance**
> UNITED STEELWORKERS OF AMERICA, AFL–CIO—LOCAL 319
>
> The undersigned party, having been designated to represent
> *Henry K. Moore* (United Steelworkers of America, AFL–CIO)
> in accordance with the ratified contract between Marco, Inc. and Local 319, USW, states the grievant's claim as follows:
>
> *The company has demonstrated intolerable bias against Henry K. Moore in the completion of his employee appraisal form dated August 3, 1983.*
>
> *James E. Krupp*
> Union Steward
> 8/20/83
> date

Source: This case was prepared by Robin A. Cherry under the supervision of Professor D. S. Bolon for the sole purpose of providing material for class discussion rather than to illustrate either effective or ineffective handling of an administrative situation.

Although not a direct result of the pending grievance, a five member review board has been established for the purpose of determining what, if any, changes are to be made to Marco Inc.'s performance appraisal system.

The board consists of the following members.

1. Mr. John Perkins, Compensation Manager
   52 years old
   with Marco 20 years, 12 years in present position
2. Miss Mary Jenkins, Associate Personnel Representative
   27 years old
   with Marco 5 years, 2 years in present position
3. Mr. Thomas Fisher, Production Manager–Carbon Steel Products
   43 years old
   with Marco 25 years, 6 years in present position
4. Mrs. Ralph James, Management Development Assistant
   40 years old
   with Marco 5 years, 4 years in present position
5. Mr. Jack Williams, VP Finance
   57 years old
   with Marco 15 years, 10 years in present position

The remainder of the case represents the materials presented to the board for aid in the evaluation of Marco's performance appraisal system.

Marco's History

Marco, Inc. began in 1900 as a small midwestern steel company. Marco has grown extensively in size over the past 83 years to become the nation's third largest steel company. As of 1983 net income was $198,300,000; net sales were $4,357,300,000; and net assets totaled $2,480,000.

Although known as a steel company, Marco has strived to diversify into other areas (mainly due to the failing state of the steel industry). 1983 operations are represented in Exhibit A. Marco's operational areas include domestic and international operations.

Marco takes pride in its operations and strives to run all functions by "The Marco Idea." This company policy is one of responding to the needs of others. It also means fair treatment for everyone, whether employee, customer, shareholder, or community.

Company recruiting literature depicts Marco's performance appraisal policy by stating:

> There is nothing haphazard about individual development at Marco. Our management appraisal program ensures that *all* members of the management team know how they are performing and in what direction their careers are heading. Your performance will be evaluated in relation to the Position Guide, which describes your exact job responsibilities and how you should relate to other members of your department and other units, and in light of annual objectives which are established by both you and your supervisor. *Each year* the appraisal will be formally discussed with you and you'll be given the opportunity to assist in the preparation of a personal development plan which will help you to improve the level of your performance.

Introductory Remarks to the Board

Introductory remarks are presented to the review board by two members of Marco's Human Resources department. Mr. Allan G. Hay, Management Development Manager, feels that Marco's present appraisal system *needs improvement and updating*, and thus he argues for that viewpoint. On the other hand, Mr. Gary Taggart, Associate Personnel Representative, feels Marco's system *adequately fulfills* the company's present needs in respect to performance evaluations.

Hay: The purpose of a performance appraisal is to allow the superior and subordinate to discover areas of the subordinate's work performance that deserve attention—either as an accomplishment or a development need. This process must be one of two-way communication where either participant is equally free to present performance-related subjects of concern.

EXHIBIT A

Area	People	Facilities
1. oil field equipment & production	4496	103
2. fabricated metal products	6884	72
3. industrial products & services	5824	25
4. financial services	480	16
5. carbon steel products	26,453	3
6. specialty steel products	5163	3
7. mining & raw materials	1531	20

With such a base in mind, our present appraisal system is confining. The best appraisal form is a blank sheet of paper. Marco's forms hinder effective communication by tending to restrict conversation to only those topics on the form. With effective training, our supervisors could conduct performance counseling sessions that will still cover the main points outlined in our present system and yet allow for the freedom to deal with additional, possibly even new, areas of concern. Who knows how many vital issues may now go unattended simply because we fail to allow employees to express these matters?

Marco's performance appraisal format has only been changed three times in the past thirty years, with the most recent change occurring five years ago. We need a system that is current and thus able to meet our present organizational needs. I submit that our company's needs have changed in the past five years, and so must our performance appraisal system.

Taggart: I feel Mr. Hay is being a bit of an idealist in respect to the performance appraisal function here at Marco. Our present program serves our organizational needs well. Marco needs feedback on employee performance from both superiors and subordinates in order to accomplish company functions such as giving merit increases, identifying promotion potential, developing employees, and correcting unsatisfactory performance. Our system allows

FIGURE A

Non-exempt Appraisal Form.

Directions: Please complete the section entitled Employee Self Appraisal. Return the completed form to your supervisor who will, upon completing his section, meet with you to review the form and establish your personal development plan.

EMPLOYEE SELF APPRAISAL

Name   Title   Dept.
Date

Please rate your work performance in the areas listed below according to the following scale.

NI Needs Improvement: performance meets minimum acceptable standards in most instances, but improvement is necessary in some cases.
G   Good: performance of most duties is adequate, meets most standards in an acceptable manner. Some improvement may be necessary.
VG Very Good: performs all duties and responsibilities in a comprehensive manner. Little need for improvement to be considered fully adequate for the job.
O   Outstanding: performs all duties and responsibilities in a thoroughly comprehensive manner. Efficiently uses time, manpower, and equipment in carrying out assignments.
S   Superior: all duties and responsibilities are conducted in a thoughtful and judicious manner with little or no need for direction, resulting in outstanding contributions on a continuing basis.

NI   G   VG   O   S

1. Job Skills
2. Knowledge
3. Quality of Work
4. Quantity of Work
5. Attitude
6. Please indicate your future expectations in relation to your work performance and career path.

7. Please indicate steps you are currently taking in order to reach the goals listed in question 6.

FIGURE A, *continued*

SUPERVISOR RATING

Date

Please rate the employee's job performance in the following areas (use the same rating scale as used in the Employee Self Appraisal).

	NI	G	VG	O	S

1. Job Skills
2. Knowledge
3. Quality of Work
4. Quantity of Work
5. Attitude
6. Please indicate recommendations for improving the employee's work performance.

7. Please identify areas where this employee demonstrates potential for increased responsibility.

DEVELOPMENT PLAN

Target Dates   Objectives, Goals

Supervisor's Signature
Supervisor's Title
Department
Division
Date

Marco to achieve these goals, and with sufficient employee participation through self appraisals.

Our appraisal forms serve to direct discussion, thereby ensuring that certain topics are discussed. The forms are too broad to seriously restrict conversation. By transferring to a free written appraisal form we may achieve increased employee involvement, but will guarantee increased costs as the program implementation time will rise. Also, we already encounter difficulties in scheduling and maintaining a constant year between successive appraisal counseling sessions. Mr. Hay's proposal is likely to compound this problem since each appraisal under his system will involve more preparation and probably more time.

I feel Marco has a fine performance appraisal system that functions well and needs little alteration.

Marco's Present Performance Appraisal System

Marco, Inc.'s present performance appraisal system is a complete program designed for the entire corporation; however, there are *variations* of the basic format within each company division. Appraisals are conducted annually, and are used as a foundation for promotions, pay increases, and merit increases.

The system is divided into *two* segments—one for the non-exempt employees and another for the exempt employees.

The non-exempt appraisal system begins with the appraisee completing a self appraisal form which equals one fourth of the entire appraisal form. (Figure A represents the *non-exempt* performance appraisal form.) The form is then returned to the superior who completes the part desig-

FIGURE B
Exempt Appraisal Form.

Employee   Title
Supervisor   Title
Department
Division
Date

   Please comment on the ability and performance of the employee in each of the following areas. Also, suggest appropriate short and long range goals for each.

Functional Skills:

Managerial Skills:

Communication Skills:

Interpersonal Skills:

Career Potential:

DEVELOPMENT PLAN

Target Dates   Objectives, Goals

Supervisor's Signature
Date

Source: This case was prepared by Robin A. Cherry under the supervision of Professor D. S. Bolon.

nated as the supervisor rating section. After completing these two steps, the subordinate and superior meet for a counseling session. During this confrontation the two parties review the partially completed appraisal form. They discuss topics designated on the form and evaluate the appraisee's potential and possible career paths. Finally, the two agree to a development plan for the subordinate which covers goals and target accomplishment dates for the upcoming year. Although the appraisee doesn't sign the form to indicate agreement or disagreement, nor place comments on the form, the participants are free to alter the form's contents at any time during the counseling session.

The exempt appraisal system differs in two respects. The appraisee is not involved in a self appraisal, rather the superior completes the entire form. (Figure B represents the *exempt* performance appraisal form.) Secondly, the scope of the form's topics are much broader than the non-exempt appraisal form. Upon completion of the first half of the form by the superior, a counseling session is conducted between the subordinate and supervisor that follows the same format as the non-exempt session.

Performance Appraisal Counseling Training

In order to obtain the most effective performance appraisals, all supervisors administering appraisals attend a three hour training session to instruct them in effective counseling. The training session consists of an introductory lecture outlining important points for successful counseling sessions. This information is followed by mock counseling sessions. Here the trainees are involved in a role playing capacity which also involves role reversal.

The following outline highlights the introductory material presented to the trainees.

1. Discussion should begin with the subordinate's objectives—this places emphasis in the proper place.
2. Generate two-way communication—this provides for a relaxed free flow of ideas.
3. When speaking:
   a) draw answers from subordinate by using open-ended questions
   b) stimulate thinking, rather than giving answers
   c) guide discussion to relevant issues—use appraisal form as an outline
   d) give positive suggestions, not criticism—this will prevent alienation of subordinate
   e) make discussion performance-, not personality-, oriented
4. Learn to be a good listener.
   a) concentrate on subordinate's statements
   b) ask questions when unclear on statements
   c) repeat important points to ensure correct interpretation of statements
5. Explore a variety of solutions to problems—finding the solution which is most acceptable to both you and your subordinate will increase the commitment to achieving that solution.

After receiving the above guidelines, the trainees are paired and given sample appraisal forms. One trainee assumes the supervisor position and the other the subordinate position. A counseling session is then acted out. Following this, roles are reversed and the procedure is repeated with a different sample appraisal form.

Finally, the group reunites and discusses the role playing. At this time final comments and questions are fielded.

The training program is conducted by *two* human resources representatives who serve in this capacity on a full-time basis. They conduct sessions once a week and appraising supervisors must attend at least one training session and are free to participate in a maximum of four sessions per year.

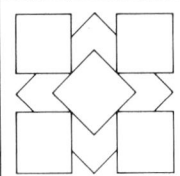

CASE STUDY:
The Old Order Changeth

The Bygone Daze Company has been in a quiet rut for the past several decades. It manufactures a traditional product that has been on the market for 35 years, and there has never been a problem in sales. As a matter of fact, the company has continually refused to accept orders from new customers. It has had a stock statement on such occasions: "All of our output is committed, and we do not plan to increase production." Over the years, the company has not realized a lot of money, nor has it lost any.

The plant is nonunion, and the 800 members of the corporate family have worked side by side—from the top office down to the shipping department—without the question of pay ever becoming a major issue. This was because when employees were hired, they reached an agreement with the personnel officer on the amount of their salary or hourly rate. Notices of increases, which rarely occur, are made by the immediate supervisor to individuals in private.

Since employment is steady, the company is considered to be a good place to work and in this regard has a preferred status. Although the employees are for the most part content in their assignments, the overall attitude throughout the company is one of almost smug indifference.

The compensation program is quite simple. Executives, supervisors, and staff personnel receive a flat salary. Production workers are paid at an hourly rate. Since output is stable, there is overtime only at year-end when inventory is taken. Employees who assist in this work, after hours, receive time and a half.

At Christmastime, each employee from the president down to the janitor receives ten shares of company stock. The stock is traded over the counter and traditionally falls in the $3½ bid and $4 asked range. No dividends have ever been declared.

Two months ago, the president and founder of the Bygone Daze Company passed away. The tradition and philosophy he established had always been rigidly adhered to. This accounted for the company's policy of limited output—just enough to assure a satisfactory return—and a family of employees who never needed to fear the wolf at the door.

The successor management feels that the time has arrived for Bygone Daze to turn over a new leaf. It plans to expand facilities, to take on new business, and to consider product line additions. The company has already signed long-term contracts with several new customers. This will assure a market for the expanded production. A new advertising and promotion campaign is in the planning stage. A major loan to cover the associated costs has been successfully negotiated, and a liberal line of bank credit has been established. Expansion of the physical plant is already in the drawing board stage, and Methods Analysts, Inc., an industrial engineering firm, is working on new systems and procedures for the production and office areas.

The major long-term concern of the new management is the impact of the company expansion on the "corporate family," which will include newly hired personnel. The new management is aware of the need for a revamping of the company's compensation system, and it is also concerned about the need for employee motivation. It has come up with a three-phase program, kept confidential of course, that summarizes its objectives:

1. Increase output through better personnel cooperation.
2. Establish a corporate pay system that is fair to all (the top executive, supervisors, office and plant employees).
3. Keep the union out.

You have been asked to suggest a new compensation program that will help the new management carry out its three major objectives. That is, you are to suggest:

1. How the company should go about establishing a pay system that is fair to all.
2. What employee motivation may be necessary in order to increase output.
3. How a climate may be established that will tend to discourage unionization of the employees.

Source: Charles A. Meloy, Associate Professor, Saint Peter's College, Jersey City, New Jersey.

V
Employee Relations

Labor–Management Relations

CHAPTER OUTLINE

Nature of Labor–Management Relations
Why Workers Join Unions ☐ Historical Developments ☐ Union Structure

Legal Framework for Labor–Management Relations
Wagner Act of 1935 (National Labor Relations Act) ☐ Taft-Hartley Act ☐ Landrum-Griffin Act

The Unionization Process
Organizing Drive ☐ Authorization Cards ☐ Recognition or Petition ☐ NLRB Election ☐ Certification or Rejection

Impact of Labor–Management Relations on the HR System
Decision Making ☐ Human Resource Policies and Practices ☐ Modifications in the Work Environment

OBJECTIVES

1. Explain why workers join unions and the implications of such a decision for human resource management.
2. Explain the development and structure of labor unions in this country.
3. Discuss the legal framework in terms of its impact on union–management relations.
4. Outline the process in which unions go about organizing workers.
5. Describe and explain the impact of labor–management relations on the human resource system.

SPOTLIGHT:
Helen G. Hoffman

Helen G. Hoffman, Esq., is a professor of labor and employment law at Florida Atlantic University. She is an active labor arbitrator for the American Arbitration Association and Conciliation Service. She was an attorney on the Staff of the National Labor Relations Board (NLRB) representing both unions and management.

Comments by Helen Hoffman

The past 30 years, an explosion in legislation protecting employees has altered the reasons many employees join unions. Now only about one fourth of American workers in private and public employment join unions. Unions originally grew in strength through the aid of social legislation and the NLRB, which helped unions organize and retain representation of employees. The NLRB is now being more conservative in its opinions, balancing the needs of both employer and employee. Recent decisions, however, have strengthened the guarantees of the union members, so that a union member can be assured of representation in the processing of grievances and participation in union affairs. Indeed, some unions today are even investing union pension funds to create jobs for members in industries that are experiencing cutback problems, or using their funds to help purchase plants that management is abandoning as unprofitable.

Courts and the NLRB recognize the problems management has in a changing technocracy with foreign labor competition. Through contract interpretation, the courts and the NLRB have expanded the concept of management rights, allowing more latitude in plant changes without forcing contract renegotiation.

Thus, statutes written from the late 1930s to the 50s to cope with industrial relations problems have adapted to the ever-changing balance between labor and management and to the general economic climate and changing technocracy.

Together, unions and management seek to meet tomorrow's needs through a legal process that has proven its flexibility in adapting to change.

Probably no single factor has influenced the management of human resources more than organized labor. A *labor union* is an organization of workers formed to further the social and economic interests of its members. The rights of workers to organize and to bargain collectively have been well established in the United States since the Wagner Act was passed in 1935. Through the collective bargaining process, unions have established patterns of labor–management relations not only in the companies unionized but also in those firms attempting to maintain nonunion status.

In this chapter, we will examine several major aspects of labor relations including the legal framework, how unions organize employees, and the impact of unions on the human resource system. In order to gain additional insights into labor–management relations, we will look briefly at why workers join unions, the status of the American labor movement, and how unions are structured.

In the next chapter, we shall examine the collective bargaining process and see that it encompasses a wide variety of issues related to such areas as compensation, retirement, fringe benefits, discipline, layoffs, promotions, and work scheduling. It should be noted that the process of collective bargaining does not give rise to these issues. They are related to the human resource system and exist even in the absence of unionization. However, if the workers are not represented by a union, management deals with problems that arise on an individual basis—or, at least, unilaterally. With the arrival of unionization, *collective bargaining* provides the vehicle by which management and representatives of the workers attempt to reach collective agreement on solving, and avoiding, problems related to wages, hours, and other conditions of employment. As we shall see in this chapter, the union, though often viewed as a party outside the organization, is very much a part of the human resource system and has a significant impact on human resource policies and practices. (See Exhibit 16–1)

EXHIBIT 16–1
A union organizer handing out a union leaflet at a plant in Mississippi. Photo: Jim Bennight.

NATURE OF LABOR–MANAGEMENT RELATIONS

As illustrated in Exhibit 16–2, about 20 million U.S. workers hold union membership. However, with the number of nonagricultural employees increasing more rapidly than union membership, union membership as a percent of the work force has declined (see Exhibit 16–3).

Changes in demand for new products and services, technological advances, and the growth in the service sector of the economy have affected the "penetration rate" of unions in the various industries. For example, in the private sector of the economy, the Service Employees Union has increased their membership 61 percent during a 10-year period, and the Communications Workers membership increased over 42 percent. The big increase in union membership, however, has been in the public sector where, as an example, unionization among state and county employees increased 180 percent between 1968 and 1978.[1]

However, with about one out of every five workers belonging to organized labor, unions are still a formidable factor, and no manager can act effectively without an understanding of unions and their impact on the human resource system. Perhaps a logical starting point is to ask this basic question: Why do workers join unions?

Why Workers Join Unions

The question of why workers join unions has been researched, discussed, and written about by numerous scholars.[2] The fact is that there are almost as many reasons for joining a union as there are union members. At the

EXHIBIT 16–2
Membership of national unions, 1930–1984.

Source: Based on U.S. Department of Labor, Bureau of Labor Statistics, *Directory of National Unions and Employee Associations, 1979*, 1980, p. 58; updated with *Statistical Abstract of the U.S., 1982–83*, U.S. Department of Commerce, Bureau of the Census, pp. 408–409; U.S. Department of Labor basic data.

EXHIBIT 16-3
Union membership as a percent of total labor force and of employees in nonagricultural establishments, 1930–1984.

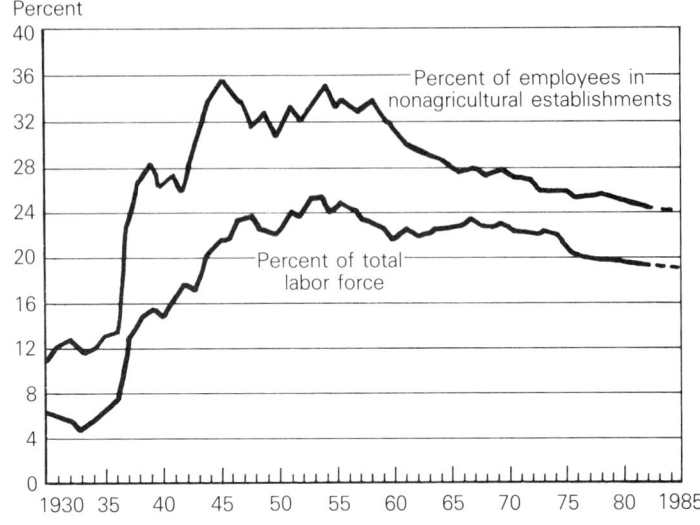

Source: Based on U.S. Department of Labor, Bureau of Labor Statistics, *Directory of National Unions and Employee Associations, 1979,* 1980, p. 60; updated with *Statistical Abstract of the U.S., 1982–83,* U.S. Department of Commerce, Bureau of the Census, pp. 408–409; U.S. Department of Labor basic data.

same time, certain common elements seem to run through these six reasons, allowing some degree of categorization:

1. *Economic reasons.* Higher wages, increased benefits, shorter hours, and improved working conditions are certainly important reasons for joining a union. Whether or not unionization actually produces these results has been debated by labor economists. What is important, however, is that workers *perceive* the unions as increasing their share of the economic package. During inflationary times, workers see their paychecks eroding in terms of purchasing power. At the same time, management becomes more cost-conscious and seeks ways to reduce costs. The natural reaction of the individual worker is to seek out the strength of numbers offered by unionization in order to bargain more effectively with the employer.

2. *Job security.* One basic human need is security. In the work environment, employees find themselves in a dependent relationship on their bosses and on what they probably view as impersonal organizations. They want to feel that they will have some cushion against economic fluctuations and resulting cutbacks. They want to know that their jobs will exist in the future and that they will be protected against unfair or arbitrary treatment. With the growth of technological change, however, workers feel especially vulnerable to job loss. For example, several thousand robots are now being utilized in manufacturing, with continued growth expected for the use of robotics in the near future.

3. *Social reasons.* Men and women are social beings. Therefore, workers have a strong need to be accepted by their peers, to belong, and to go along with others. A union meets this need by offering affiliation with peers having common interests. Some unions offer attractive benefits, such as

group auto insurance and union-owned recreation facilities. Peer pressure may also cause workers to join unions. A case in point would be the worker who is socially ostracized or even harassed by union members until he or she finally joins. As an interviewee in one study remarked, "They approached you, kept after you, hounded you. To get them off my back, I joined."

4. *Recognition.* Some employees have found that the union structure offers them an opportunity to gain recognition not available to them in the business organization. For example, a worker with little education may serve on a shop committee or even be elected to a position of influence, such as steward or officer in the local.

5. *Participation.* Many workers, especially at higher levels and in white-collar-type occupations, have explained their union membership in terms of their desire to obtain a voice in decisions that affect them in their working environment. For example, we find schoolteachers organizing to demand a say in textbook selection, class size, and student discipline. To other workers who feel lost in our large, complex, industrial society, the union is viewed as a last hope that they will be able to influence their destiny.

6. *Compulsion.* Aside from social pressure to join a union, some workers become union members simply because the employment contract requires them to do so. In fact, three-fourths of all labor contracts in the United States have union shop clauses that require new employees to join the union as a condition of employment after having served a probationary period.

We can see, therefore, that the reasons why employees join a union cannot be reduced to any single, uncomplicated statement. Aside from the case of compulsion, it would appear that unions serve a broad network of employee needs. To the extent that people cannot find opportunities to satisfy those needs in the workplace, they tend to form unions. In fact, some writers have gone so far as to say that the existence of a union is an indictment of management's failure to provide opportunities for need satisfaction at all levels of the organization.

Historical Developments

The following brief survey of historical developments will provide some insight into the problems facing labor unions. It will also furnish the necessary background for our later discussions of union structure and collective bargaining.

Early Efforts to Organize Craftsmen, such as shoemakers and carpenters, banded together as early as 1791, primarily to protest the existing wage rates. Generally, these organizations were weak and survived for only a short time. A forerunner of the union business agent[3] grew out of the need to check on shops to see whether they were adhering to the union wage scale. Employers attempted to destroy the effectiveness of unions, however, through such tactics as hiring nonunion workers and getting the courts to declare the union illegal.

During the middle and late 1800s, the labor movement concentrated on efforts to unify labor groups and to promote social and political reform. A brief-lived organization called the National Labor Union was formed in 1866 to bring together in one body many of the unions and social reform organizations. The rioting and bloodshed that characterized the 1860s and 1870s caused this period to be referred to as the "era of upheaval." In fact, the early period of labor relations in this country is an often-repeated story of inter- and intraunion squabbles, frequent bloody clashes between unions and management, and labor political activity.

In 1869 the Noble Order of the Knights of Labor was founded. Its broad goal was to replace a competitive society by a cooperative one that would give workers the opportunity to enjoy fully the wealth they created. The Knights of Labor relied on political methods and education rather than collective bargaining to promote equal pay for equal work for women, an eight-hour day, the establishment of cooperatives, and public ownership of utilities. Failure to reconcile the interests of its skilled and unskilled workers led to the downfall of the Knights of Labor and the birth of the American Federation of Labor (AFL).

Since the AFL In 1886 a group of craft unions (a *craft union* includes workers of one skill or occupation, e.g., carpenters) formed the American Federation of Labor with a philosophy of "pure and simple unionism." Its main goals were higher wages and improved working conditions. The program of the AFL leaders was, therefore, pragmatic. They were out to improve the conditions of the workers they represented, and they represented skilled workers or workers whose strategic position enabled them to command employer recognition. Most AFL leaders considered it impossible to organize a large industrial company. Some leaders, however, felt that all employees working at a facility, whether skilled or unskilled, should be members of the same union.

The AFL's failure to organize mass-production industries gave impetus to a movement to issue industrial union charters in the mass-production industries. (An *industrial union* includes all occupations within an industry, such as assemblers, machinists, and die makers in the auto industry.) The issue of organizing all workers along industrial lines was heatedly debated at the 1935 AFL convention and led to the formation of a rival group, the Congress of Industrial Organizations (CIO). The CIO's push for industrial unionism in large, mass-production industries such as steel, rubber, and automobiles met with an enthusiastic response from workers. In fact, the CIO grew to such an extent that by the end of 1937, its total membership was estimated at approximately 2 million as compared to the AFL's 3 million.[4]

In the early 1950s, leaders of these two rival organizations realized that organized labor could be strengthened if they joined forces. Efforts were made to limit raiding of members in a nonraiding pact that minimized attempts by one union to gain members, not by organizing the unorganized, but by attacking another union and pirating their members. In 1955, the AFL and the CIO merged. Today, about four out of every five labor unions are affiliated with the AFL–CIO. We shall see in the next section on union structure that the AFL–CIO is not a labor union but a federation—a "union" of unions.

Although we may at first think of unions in terms of factory and service workers, the unionization of white-collar workers such as office employees has been growing over the past few decades. In addition, professionals, representing a large portion of the middle class, have increasingly unionized due to repeated economic squeezes. Examples include actors, airline pilots, newspaper reporters, engineers, teachers, college professors, government administrators, nurses, medical interns, and law-enforcement officers.

With this brief background on the historical development of labor unions, let us consider the structure of labor unions.

Union Structure

A knowledge of union structure is essential to dealing with unions. To begin with, there are about 80,000 local unions in this country, most of which are associated with national unions. We should point out that in our discussion of unions, we include "employee associations" that bargain with employers but do not call themselves "unions." A number of professional associations, such as the National Education Association (NEA), as well as state and local government employee groups fit into this category.

The entire union structure consists of about 208 national and international organizations. Exhibit 16–4 lists the unions having 100,000 or more members. Approximately 75 percent of all union members belong to a union affiliated with the AFL–CIO. The largest of these affiliated unions are the United Auto Workers (1,357,000 members) and the United Steelworkers of America (1,238,000 members). In 1981, thirteen years after withdrawing from the AFL–CIO, the United Auto Workers rejoined the federation. The two largest bargaining organizations, the International Brotherhood of Teamsters (1,891,000) and the National Education Association (1,684,000) are independent of the AFL–CIO.

The structure of the AFL–CIO is shown in Exhibit 16–5. As noted previously, the AFL–CIO is not a labor union. It is a loosely knit federation of affiliated national, international, and independent local unions. The AFL–CIO provides a wide variety of services to its union affiliates, such as mediating disputes among unions, providing advice and assistance on organizing activities, conducting training for union leaders, supplying information and economic and legal assistance, and lobbying at all governmental levels.

The National (or International) Union[5] Most national unions are headed by a president, a secretary-treasurer, and one or more vice presidents. The

EXHIBIT 16-4
National unions and employee associations reporting 100,000 members or more.

Organization	Members (in thousands)	Organization	Members (in thousands)
Unions:		Government (NAGE)	200
Teamsters	1,891	Transportation Union	190
Automobile Workers (UAW)	1,357	Iron Workers	184
United Food and Commercial	1,300		
Steelworkers	1,238	Railway Clerks	180
State, County (AFSCME)	1,098	Fire Fighters	178
Electrical (IBEW)	1,041	Painters	164
Carpenters	784	Oil, Chemicals	154
Machinists	754	Electrical (UE) (Ind.)	162
Service Employees (SEIV)	650	Bakery, Confectionery, Tobacco	161
Laborers	608	Sheet Metal	161
Communications Workers	551	Transit Union	161
Teachers	551	Rubber	151
Clothing and Textile Workers	455	Boilermakers	145
Operating Engineers	423	Transport Workers	130
		Printing and Graphic	122
Hotel and Restaurant	400	Woodworkers	112
Plumbers	352	Office	107
Ladies' Garments (ILGWU)	323	Maintenance of Way	102
Musicians	299		
Paperworkers	275	Associations:	
Government (AFGE)	255	National Education Association	1,684
Postal Workers	251	Nurses' Association	180
Mine Workers	245	Classified School Employees	150
Electrical (IUE)	233	Police	140
Letter Carriers	230	California's Assembly of	
Retail, Wholesale	215	Governmental Employees (AGE)	105

Source: U.S. Department of Labor, Bureau of Labor Statistics, *Directory of National Unions and Employee Associations, 1979,* 1980, p. 62; updated with *Statistical Abstract of the U.S., 1982–83,* U.S. Department of Commerce, Bureau of the Census, p. 409, and unpublished union data.

officers are selected either by a convention or by referendum. A convention is the supreme governing body of most unions. The national or parent union regulates the administration of all its local union affiliates.

The national union usually has a large staff of paid professionals, such as attorneys, economists, research specialists, and public relations personnel. The national union typically negotiates a master agreement or a contract with a national firm, such as the UAW contract with the Ford Motor Company, which becomes binding on all locals dealing with that firm. The local must also receive prior approval from the national union for any strike activity. The national union helps locals in many ways, such as providing training for local union leaders, assisting locals in negotiating local contracts, setting up strike funds, and organizing new members.

The Local Union The structure of the entire labor movement is founded on the local union. It is at this level that the manager comes into day-to-day

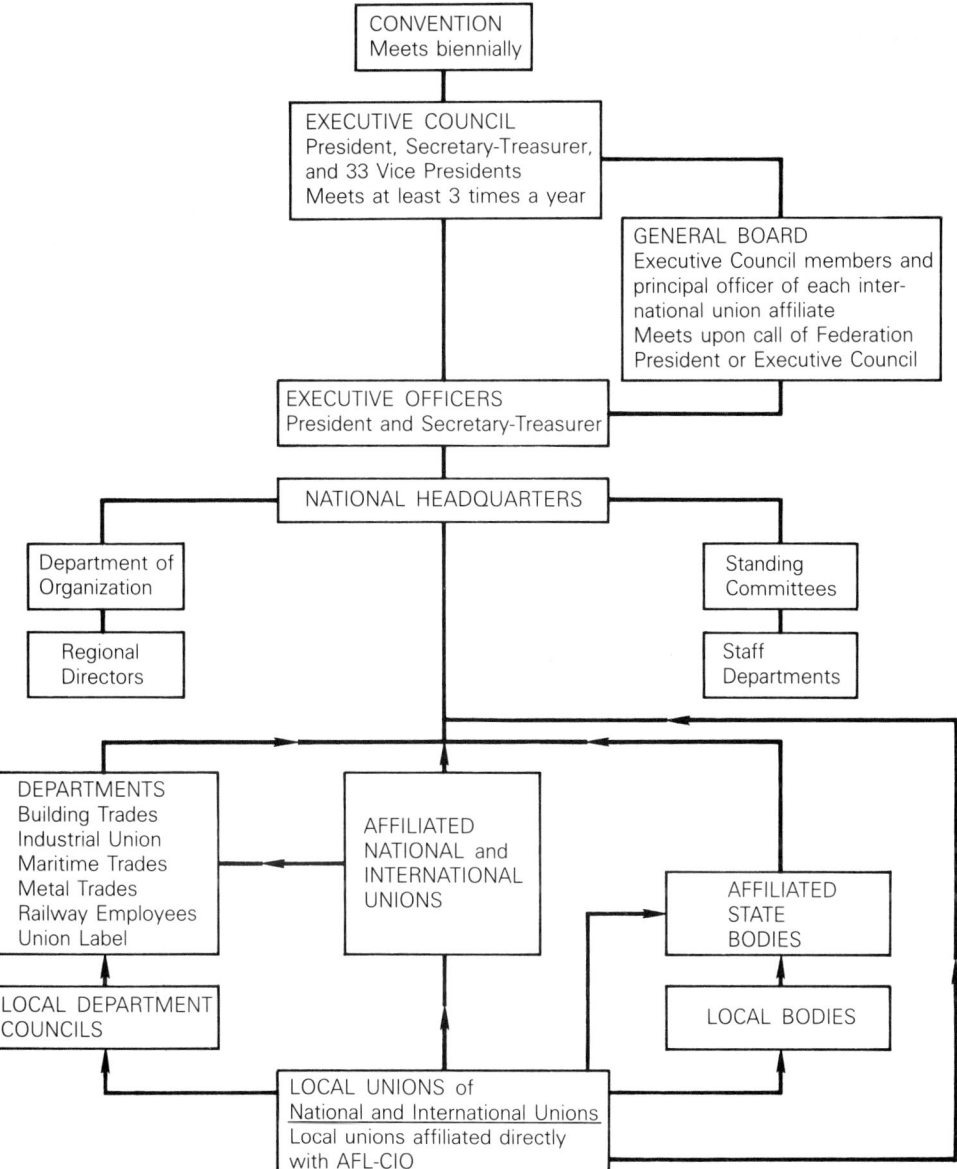

EXHIBIT 16–5
Structure of the AFL–CIO.

contact with the union. The local has direct control over the rank-and-file worker. The functions of the local are carried out by officials elected directly by the members.

The jurisdiction and the size of locals differ. In most cases the local has jurisdiction over a single plant, and its size depends on the plant size.

EXHIBIT 16-6
Organization of a typical local union.

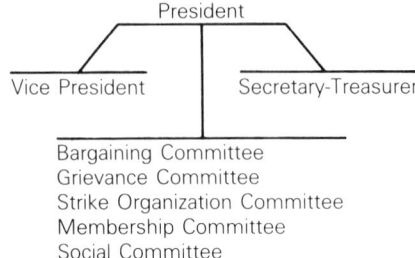

Some locals have as few as 10 to 50 members. Local 600 of the UAW, on the other hand, at one time consisted of more than 40,000 members employed at the River Rouge complex of the Ford Motor Company. Craft union locals usually have jurisdiction over their craft in a geographic area. For example, all carpenters in the city of Grand Rapids are organized under one local.

The larger local unions may have one or more full-time officers, such as a president or a business agent. The international representative from the parent union is likely to be quite important in a union without a full-time officer. More commonly, local officials have full-time jobs in addition to their union duties. This is especially true for shop stewards who are workers elected to represent employees in a plant or department. Therefore, shop stewards are key people in the relationship between the union and its members and between the union and management. As can be seen in Exhibit 16-6, a typical local union consists of a very simple organization, usually having committees, with considerable power residing in the local president.

THE LEGAL FRAMEWORK FOR LABOR–MANAGEMENT RELATIONS

The legal environment for the collective bargaining process in the United States has been formulated primarily by two federal laws: the *Taft-Hartley Act* of 1947, which amended the *Wagner Act* of 1935, and the *Landrum-Griffin Act* of 1959. In addition, important decisions of courts or labor agencies such as the *National Labor Relations Board (NLRB)* play an important part in establishing the legal framework for union–management relations. For example, the NLRB's interpretation of the Wagner Act and the Taft-Hartley Act largely determines the practical application of these laws.

The executive branch of government also serves as a source of labor laws. To illustrate, in 1962 President John F. Kennedy issued Executive Order No. 10988, which provided a measure of protection for federal employees to engage in collective bargaining. Several states followed this precedent, influencing the growth of public employee unions on the state level.

Most laws and regulations affecting labor relations are quite complicated, and the human resource manager would be best advised to seek an expert for assistance with specific problems. The following general survey, however, will give the reader a basic understanding of the legal framework within which collective bargaining must operate.

Wagner Act of 1935 (National Labor Relations Act)

The basic statute governing union–management relations is the Wagner Act of 1935 as amended by the *Taft-Hartley Act of 1947*. This act guarantees the right of covered workers to bargain collectively concerning wages and working conditions, and further regulates the union–management relationship by prohibiting certain "unfair labor practices." The act also established the National Labor Relations Board, which administers most of its provisions. The NLRB has two major functions: procedural administration relating to the start-up of unions, and watchdog against unfair labor practices.

To begin with, the NLRB *administers the procedure by which unions become the certified collective bargaining agents for a group of workers.* To see how this procedure works, consider the case of a union attempting to organize the ABC Company, a nonunion firm. According to the Wagner Act, the union organizers can attempt to get the workers to sign authorization cards. Thirty percent of the employees must sign such cards before the union can petition the NLRB to hold a representation election. When the petition for an election has been made, the employees are made aware of this fact by the NLRB, which posts Form 666, shown in Exhibit 16–7. This form briefly describes the employees' rights and states that an election may be held.

EXHIBIT 16–7
NLRB Form 666—notice to employees.

The other main function of the NLRB is to prevent labor or management from committing unfair labor practices. The five prohibited unfair labor practices for management are:

1. To interfere with, restrain, or coerce employees in the exercise of their rights to self-organization
2. To dominate or interfere in the affairs of the union
3. To discriminate in regard to hire, tenure, or any condition of employment for the purpose of encouraging or discouraging union membership
4. To discriminate against or discharge an employee because he or she had filed charges or given testimony under the act
5. To refuse to bargain with chosen representatives of the employees

Taft-Hartley Act

Provisions of the Taft-Hartley Act amended the Wagner Act to include unfair practices by unions. The six prohibitions are:

1. Coercing employees in the exercise of their rights or in the selection of a collective bargaining representative
2. Causing an employer under a union shop agreement to discriminate against employees who were denied admission to the union or were expelled from the union for certain reasons
3. Engaging in certain types of strikes and boycotts
4. Charging excessive or discriminatory initiation fees to employees covered by a union shop agreement
5. Causing an employer to pay money or other things of value for services not performed
6. Refusing to bargain collectively

The Taft-Hartley Act also allows the president of the United States to seek an injunction for a period of 80 days against strikes and lockouts affecting the nation's health and welfare. Between 1947 and 1980, the act's national emergency provisions were invoked by the president 35 times. The act also created the Federal Mediation and Conciliation Service, which has as one of its functions the attempt to resolve the dispute during the injunction's 80-day "cooling off period."

A controversial part of the Taft-Hartley Law is Section 14.b, which allows states to pass right-to-work laws that prohibit union shops. A *union shop* refers to a provision in the labor contract that states that employees must join a union after some initial period of employment (usually 30–60 days) as a condition of continuing their employment. Twenty states have chosen to exercise this option and have laws that limit the power of unions to impose membership on employees. While there are philosophical arguments for and against right-to-work laws, the unions have primarily opposed them on the argument that since all workers in an organization benefit from union gains, all workers should contribute to the financial support of the union.

Landrum-Griffin Act

Also known as the Labor–Management Reporting and Disclosure Act of 1959, the Landrum-Griffin Act has two basic aims: (1) to set minimum standards of democratic procedure, responsibility, and honesty in the conduct of union internal affairs; and (2) to clarify several parts of the Taft-Hartley Act. Accordingly, the act requires employers to file reports on their financial relationship with union leaders and on any payments to persons made for the purpose of influencing employees in the exercise of their rights. The Landrum-Griffin Act's passage resulted from the congressional investigation conducted by the McClellan Committee from 1957 through 1959, which produced 58 volumes of testimony, over half of which were devoted to evidence of racketeering and corruption in the Teamsters' Union. A major objective of the act, therefore, was to eliminate crime, racketeering, and corruption in the labor unions. To accomplish this, the act has several provisions designed to reduce conflicts of interest and transactions through which unscrupulous union officials and employers might reap financial gains at the expense of employees. For example, unions cannot make direct or indirect loans to union officers that result in a total indebtedness of more than $2,000. The word *indirect* is included in the provision to avoid such "back-door" deals as loans made by a local union to an individual who, in turn, reloans it to a union officer.

The Landrum-Griffin Act also spells out the rights of union members, the responsibilities of union officers, and the safeguards on the union funds. The amendments to the Taft-Hartley Act contained in the Landrum-Griffin Act include provisions that tighten the ban on secondary boycotts and prohibit "hot cargo" agreements (agreements in which the employer agrees not to discipline employees for refusing to handle nonunion products, which are termed *hot cargo*).

Thus, we can see that the collective bargaining process does not take place in a vacuum. It is very much influenced by public opinion as reflected in the legal environment. The human resource manager, though not necessarily expected to be a union expert, must have knowledge of unions and their operation, and of basic laws regarding union–management relations. In particular, they need to understand the union process.

THE UNIONIZATION PROCESS

It is during the union drive that emotions are likely to run high. Union organizers try to get workers' votes with promises of higher wages, better working conditions, and more power in dealing with management. In response, management counters by attempting to convince employees that

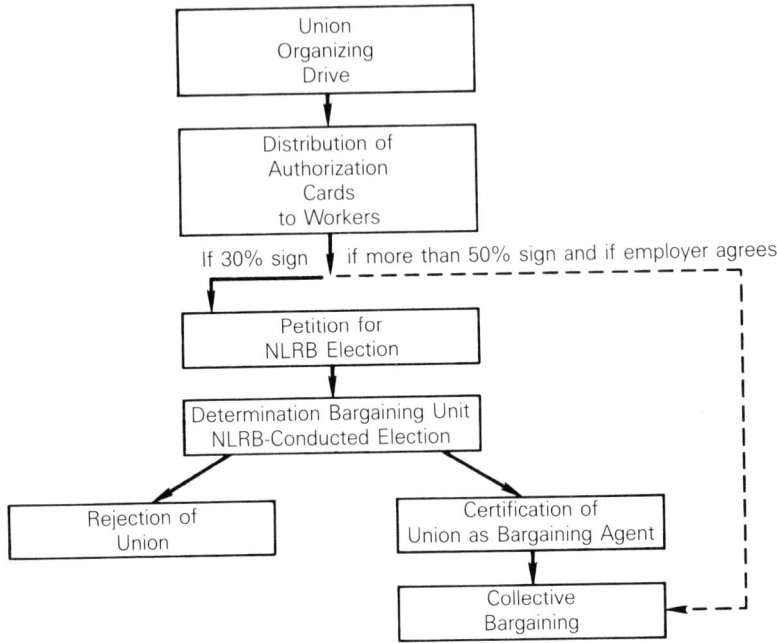

EXHIBIT 16-8
Unionization process.

they are better off without "outside influences" attempting to control their destiny. In the previous section we have seen that the NLRB is responsible for administering the procedure by which the union becomes the collective bargaining agent for a group of workers. The following overview of the unionization process will familiarize you with how unions go about organizing workers. The sequence of events in the unionization process generally occurs as shown in Exhibit 16-8.

Organizing Drive

The initiative for unionizing employees in an organization may come from the union or the workers themselves. In some cases, employees are dissatisfied and invite a union to start a unionization drive. Frequently, organizing is the result of a union's desire to grow by adding new membership. If other firms in the industry or geographic area are already unionized, the union may wish to organize a firm in order to avoid giving the nonunionized any competitive advantage.

Whatever the source for initiating the drive, the beginning phase of the drive is likely to be relatively secret in order to minimize the chances of management starting a counterattack. Workers may be contacted at their homes, at recreation events such as softball games, or by pro-union workers on the job such as during coffee breaks. Management usually learns about the union through rumors or during the "handbilling stage." Just as a firm

> A difficult job for unions is to sell people on the value of trade unionism. "We have to educate people, to help them understand that unions are not just strikes and confrontation," says union spokesman, Hubert Coker.
>
> For example, in one small southern town, "the AFL–CIO sponsors a free social-service center to assist workers and the elderly in lining up government benefits and provide counseling in legal matters, alcoholism, drug abuse and other problems. The soft-sell approach seems to work. Says the center's director, "People will come in here and say, 'I've heard about unions but I never knew they did this sort of thing.'"

Source: Excerpted from the copyrighted article "Unions Still Find South a Tough Row to Hoe," *U.S. News and World Report,* June 21, 1982.

would advertise to sell its products or services, the union during the handbilling stage attempts to create interest among the workers to "buy" the union. Various types of handbills such as brochures, letters, or circulars are placed under windshield wipers, circulated through the company's mail system, or sent to the employees' homes. (See Exhibit 16–9.)

Authorization Cards

As the union drive develops momentum, each worker will receive from the union an authorization card (see Exhibit 16–10). When signed by the employee, the card indicates a desire to vote on having a union. It does not always mean the employee will vote for the union but that he or she is interested in having the opportunity to vote. It is not unusual for employees to sign an authorization card and then vote against the union—probably a way for a dissatisfied employee who is not pro-union to get management's attention. As one employee put it:

> Sure, I signed the card but I don't think I'd vote for the union. A lot of us don't want to join a union but at the same time, we feel that the boys at corporate staff don't much care what's going on down here. . . . Maybe now we'll get their attention.

The union's aim is to get 30 percent of the employees to sign authorization cards and then to get a majority vote of those voting in the election.

Recognition or Petition

If the union is successful in obtaining signed authorization cards from over 50 percent of the employees, and if the organization does not contest union recognition, the union may directly demand that the employer deal with the union as the sole representative of the employees. When the union recognition is contested, which is the usual case, the NLRB becomes involved. The NLRB investigator, after determining if 30 percent or more employees have signed authorization cards, will determine the *bargaining unit,* the workforce actually represented by the union. The bargaining unit may

The U.S. Government Protects Your Right to Join a Union

The federal government guarantees you the right to organize a union. And just so no one can try to tell you differently, here are the actual words from the law:

"Section 7. Employees shall have the right to self-organization, to form, join, or assist labor organizations, to bargain collectively through representation of their own choosing, and to engage in other concerted activities for the purposes of collective bargaining . . . and shall have the right to refrain from any or all such activities . . ."

Further, this law protects you in exercising your rights by making it illegal for an employer to interfere. Here's the actual words of the law:

"Section 8. (a) It shall be an unfair labor practice for an employer—(1) to interfere with, restrain or coerce employees in the exercise of the rights guaranteed in section 7; . . . and (3) by discrimination in regard to hire or tenure of employment, to encourage or discourage membership in any labor organization . . ."

What this means in simple language is that the United States Government itself guarantees you the right to help organize, to join, and to support a union of your choice. This includes such activities as signing a union card, getting others to sign cards, attend union meetings, wear union buttons, pass out union literature, and talk union to other workers as long as it doesn't interfere with work.

It also means that employers break the law if they question workers or even try to find out how workers feel, who signed cards, which ones are pushing the union, who attend meetings, or any other interference with your right to freely choose a union.

Employers cannot promise raises, promotions, or other benefits in an attempt to influence workers and they also cannot take away or threaten to take away any of your benefits because of union activity.

You cannot be penalized in any way because of union activity or support. You cannot have your over-time cut, be transferred to a less desirable job, suspended, or discharged. If any employer does any of these things because of your union activity or support, the law says the worker must be reinstated to his former job without loss of seniority, and the employer must pay him for all lost wages plus interest.

So stand up for your rights. Remember: Uncle Sam stands behind you! It's the law!

United Food & Commercial Workers International Union, AFL-CIO

EXHIBIT 16–9
A union handbill.

PROFESSIONAL & HEALTH CARE DIVISION
United Food & Commercial Workers International Union
Affiliated with AFL-CIO-CLC
AUTHORIZATION FOR REPRESENTATION

I hereby authorize the United Food & Commercial Workers International Union, AFL-CIO-CLC, or its chartered Local Union(s) to represent me for the purpose of collective bargaining.

(Print Name) (Date)

(Signature) (Home Phone)

(Home Address) (City) (State) (Zip)

(Employer's Name) (Address)

(Hire Date) (Type Work Performed) (Department)

(Hourly Rate) (Day Off) (Shift) Full Time ____ Part-Time ____

Would you participate in an organizing committee? Yes ____ No ____

PRINTED IN U.S.A.

EXHIBIT 16-10
Union authorization card.

be based on job level, such as all hourly employees in the organization, or type of skill, such as all carpenters or full-time teachers in the organization.

NLRB Election

When the NLRB determines that a particular bargaining unit is appropriate, an election will be held. Since the outcome of the vote may very well be influenced by what is considered to be the appropriate bargaining unit, management may challenge the nature of the unit, thus necessitating a separate NLRB ruling. For example, in a union drive to organize a small manufacturing firm, the management wanted to include a group of technicians who were known to be against joining a union. The NLRB, feeling that the technicians not only did not share the community of interests of the other workers but also historically were not included in similar situations, ruled to exclude them.

Certification or Rejection

In looking at the record over the years, the union typically is successful in winning more than half of the elections held. However, in more recent years, the union has been winning only about 45 percent of the NLRB-conducted representative elections as compared to a 60-percent win-rate in

1965.[6] If a majority of the workers in the bargaining unit vote for the union, it is certified and must be recognized by the company as the bargaining agent for the workers. The certified union must then represent *all* employees in the bargaining unit. If the union loses the election, a subsequent election cannot be held for at least another year.[7]

THE IMPACT OF LABOR–MANAGEMENT RELATIONS ON THE HR SYSTEM

As suggested in our discussion of the legal framework for collective bargaining, an organization drive by the union requires substantial preparation on the part of management. For example, someone needs to advise management on what legally can and cannot be done during the campaign. If the firm has a centralized human resource department, this job is typically given to that department. Efforts must be undertaken to protect the company's rights and to see that the union is not guilty of unfair labor practices. Data may also have to be gathered for NLRB hearings. A smaller firm may utilize the services of a consultant or labor attorney. Exhibit 16–11 illustrates some guidelines given to university administrators during an organization drive in the university system of Florida.

It is during this initial stage of unionization that great care must be taken by management to minimize conflict that could jeopardize the collective bargaining at a later date. We have seen in the previous section on the legal framework for labor–management relations that laws exist prohibiting both the union and management from unfair labor practices. For example, it is illegal for either party to threaten employees. Since it is also illegal to discharge employees for pro-union activity, management must be certain to document terminations for poor performance during the union campaign to avoid charges of an "unfair" labor practice.

In some cases it has taken many years for the wounds to heal following especially bitter relations between the company and the union during an organization drive. Once the union is certified, unionization continues to have considerable impact on the human resource system in at least three areas: decision making, HR policies and practices, and work environment.

Decision Making

One of the first areas to be affected by unionization is decision making. The mere existence of a union is likely to mean that all management decisions are subject to closer scrutiny and challenge. Whereas even in the absence of a union, progressive managers are interested in employee participation and attitudes, unionization gives the worker a formal method for challenging decisions viewed as within the realm of collective bargaining. Certain decisions once made unilaterally by management, such as those regarding work standards or the subcontracting of work, are now subject to collective bargaining.

EXHIBIT 16–11
Example of guidelines given to university administrators during an organization drive.

Some Dos: What University Administrators Clearly May Do

University administrators in the SUS clearly may do any or all of the following:*

Tell employees they are *free* to form, join and participate in a union or *to refrain* from doing so without prejudicing their status as State employees.

Communicate to employees orally or in writing reasons for selecting the *"no agent"* option in any collective bargaining election, provided such communications are consistent with the *don'ts* hereinafter listed.

Convene meetings of employees during working hours (until the 24-hour period preceding an election) to discuss unionization for collective bargaining.

Explain to employees the dues and fees required for union membership, provided that in discussing the dues or fees which any given union requires, accurate figures taken from that union's own publications are referenced.

Provide employees with *accurate* factual data about the unions seeking their support, including affiliations with other state, national or international labor organizations, the salaries of union officials, and strike statistics (in connection with any discussion of strikes, mention should be made of the fact that strikes by public employees are prohibited by both the Florida Constitution and the Public Employees Relations Act and the possible consequences of violating the anti-strike law should be detailed).

Remind employees that signing "union authorization cards" does *not* require them to vote for any union in a subsequent collective bargaining election.

Rebut inaccurate, distorted or misleading union communications with the facts.

Relate past experiences of administrators with particular unions at institutions where an agent has been elected.

Tell employees that proposed union benefits do not occur automatically but must be negotiated—and that the BOR is not required to agree to any proposal or make any concession, provided that it is not stated or implied that the BOR will refuse to bargain any proper subject in good faith.

Some Don'ts: What University Administrators May Not Do

University administrators in the SUS may *not* do any of the following:

Promise or grant employees pay increases, promotions, benefits or special favors for not joining a union, opposing unionism or voting against a union. All personnel actions must be made in accordance with existing BOR rules and regulations and taken without regard to the employees' membership or participation in a union, or support for its activities.

Threaten loss of jobs, reduction of income, discontinuance of privileges or benefits presently enjoyed, or otherwise threaten reprisal or force by the use of intimidating language which may influence employees in the exercise of their right to form, join or assist a union or to refrain from doing so; threaten or actually discharge, discipline, transfer, promote or lay employees off because of membership in or activities on behalf of a union; or threaten, *through a third party,* any of the foregoing acts of interference.

Spy on or have a representative spy on or even openly attend union meetings (parking across the street from the place of meeting in order to watch employees entering the meeting has been held to be illegal); or conduct themselves in a way that would indicate to employees that they are being watched to determine whether or not they are participating in union activities.

Discriminate against employees actively supporting the union by intentionally assigning undesirable work to them; transfer employees prejudicially because of union affiliation or active support; or generally engage in any partiality favoring non-union employees over employees active on behalf of the union.

Discipline or penalize employees actively supporting a union for an infraction which non-union employees are permitted to commit without being likewise disciplined.

Make any work assignment for the purpose of causing employees active on behalf of a union to quit their jobs or to give up their union membership.

Intentionally assign work or transfer employees so that those active on behalf of the union are segregated from those it is believed are not interested in supporting a union.

---

*For purposes of this listing, the term *administrators* includes presidents, vice presidents, provosts and deans, together with those persons assisting presidents, vice presidents, provosts and deans in the discharge of their duties, and also includes other university personnel discharging administrative responsibilities.

Lack of contract knowledge on the part of supervisors frequently results in time-consuming and costly grievances. To remedy this, some companies have centralized certain human resource decisions and put them in the hands of higher levels of management or trained labor specialists. The unfortunate result has been a further downgrading of the first-line supervisor.

Human Resource Policies and Practices

A second area strongly affected by unionization is human resource policies and practices, which are more likely to become formalized. This comes about in several ways. The labor contract itself, as well as written statements resulting from handling grievances, formalizes matters related to wages, hours, and the conditions of employment. There is also a tendency on the part of managers to start putting in writing all actions and decisions affecting workers in an effort to protect themselves from later union charges of contract violations. This formalization is illustrated by Exhibit 16–12, which reproduces a page of contract statements dealing with lunch periods and overtime.

Often the union demands industry uniformity that may not be appropriate for a particular company. Similarly, a by-product of unionization is the introduction of "outsiders" into the human resource system. For example, one or more professional union officials who are not employees of the firm, such as the business agent or the international representative, may be

EXHIBIT 16–12
Sample page from a "typical" labor agreement.

7.8 Lunch Period Within Five Hours

(a) A lunch period, without pay, of not less than thirty minutes will be allowed employees within their first five hours worked on any shift. Employees who are assigned by Local Management to work beyond their first five hours without a lunch period will be paid one and one-half their regular straight time rate for all time worked beyond the first five hours until they have a lunch period.

(b) This Section will not apply to an employee working on a shift which includes a paid lunch period regardless of whether an actual lunch period is provided.

ARTICLE 8   OVERTIME

8.1 Definition of Regular Straight Time Hourly Rate

The regular straight time hourly rate means an employee's straight time hourly base rate plus his incentive pay and applicable shift premium.

8.2 Hours Worked in Excess of Eight (8)

The Local Management will pay an employee one and one-half times his regular straight time hourly rate for all hours he is required to work over eight (8) a day.

8.3 Hours Worked in Excess of Twelve (12)

The Local Management will pay an employee two times his regular straight time hourly rate for all hours he is required to work over twelve (12) a day.

8.4 Exceptions to Daily Overtime

When an employee is permitted by Local Management to change from one shift to another at his own request, and the new shift starts within the same twenty-four (24) hour period as his preceding shift, overtime provided under Sections 8.2 and 8.3 will not be paid. However, the starting time of the new shift will start a new twenty-four (24) hour period for the purpose of determining overtime.

New employees will become eligible to share in the impartial distribution of overtime after they complete their probationary period of employment. New employees will not be allowed to claim overtime after completing this probationary period to make up for overtime which was worked before they were on the seniority roster.

(c) If it is shown that Management was in error in the distribution of overtime during the two weeks immediately preceding the date of the review of the Foreman's record with the grievance committeeman and that an employee did not properly share in available overtime during such period, Local Management will make an adjustment in future overtime schedules within 60 calendar days after the error has been reported in writing by the committeeman to Management or at the end of the 60 day period compensate the employee for the earnings he would have earned had he been given his proper overtime opportunity.

(d) The Union will cooperate with the Local Management in fulfilling the overtime manhours to meet overtime schedules.

ARTICLE 9   WAGES (Hourly Employees)

The provisions of this Article 9 apply only to hourly employees in the production and maintenance units. Salaries of employees in the salaried units are covered by the provisions of Article 3 (Salaries) of Appendix B of this Agreement.

9.1 1968 Cooperative Can Industry Agreement and Manual

(a) The parties have agreed on the principles and the basic procedures of a cooperative program for describing and classifying hourly jobs covered by this Agreement and for the development and application of related administrative procedures.

These principles and procedures have been incorporated in an Agreement called the 1968 Cooperative Can Industry Agreement and Manual, hereinafter referred to as the Manual. The 1968 Cooperative Can Industry Agreement and involved in contract negotiations and later administration of grievance resolution. Smaller firms will have to rely more on attorneys or labor relations experts. In the event of an impasse in the collective bargaining process, such as inability to agree on a new contract, a third party will be brought in as a mediator or arbitrator.

Finally, it is often argued that as a result of unionization, management loses a great deal of flexibility in formulating and carrying out human resource policies. For example, management's discretion is reduced by union demands that policies relating to pay, promotion, discipline, transfers, and so on, be written into the contract. On the other hand, such contractual provisions ensure that all workers are treated alike.

Modifications in the Work Environment

Initially, collective bargaining may place management and the union in adversary roles. The union may attempt to dramatize every company mistake; management may try to undermine the union by showing the workers that the union is unnecessary. Needless to say, such a climate is detrimental to productivity. Take, for example, the need for a change in the work assignment. If the union and management are engaged in a power struggle, the union will try to protect the status quo and resist any changes. As a result

EXHIBIT 16–13
Example of union–management cooperation.

UAW-FORD EMPLOYE INVOLVEMENT
A Work Force Concept for Now and the Future

What it is . . .

Employe Involvement (EI) is the sum of many parts.

- It's a process in which local Unions and local Managements work together to jointly create a work climate where employes can achieve work satisfaction by directing their ingenuity, imagination, and creativity toward improving their work and the overall work environment.
- It's a means of providing employes the opportunity to actively identify and resolve problems related to their work.
- It's part sound management, part Union-Management cooperation, part human relations, part employe awareness, part communications . . . and basically good business.
- It's a Management and Union style that promotes all of this.
- And in a very real sense, Employe Involvement is a three-way partnership—a recognition by employes, the Union, and Management that their common interests can be served best when there is common effort.

"It's a matter of trust on both sides. Employe Involvement will make each employe more responsive to plant problems and fellow employes' problems."

Local Union President

Source: EI UAW–Ford, *Employee Involvement—A Handbook*, the UAW–Ford National Joint Committee on Employe Involvement, April 1980, pp. 1.

we find meatcutters refusing to handle precut and prepackaged meats, requirements that union electricians stand by to replace burned-out lightbulbs, and the use of operating engineers merely to push buttons.

There is a need, therefore, for management to recognize that its own actions and attitudes have an impact on union behavior. Furthermore, management should recognize that unions can, and do, make a contribution to cost reduction and productivity improvements. This has been dramatically demonstrated in such cases as the Kaiser Steel Corporation and numerous Scanlon plan agreements whereby the company and the union cooperate to reduce plant costs and to increase efficiency. The important thing, therefore, is for unions and management to work *jointly* toward replacing conflict with cooperation in the work environment. Exhibit 16–13 describes an "Employee Involvement" program existing between the United Auto Workers and the Ford Motor Company. The cooperative program has been used to work toward solving problems relating to such things as drug abuse, absenteeism, safety, and other work-related problems.

SUMMARY

Probably no single factor has influenced the management of human resources more than organized labor. Through collective bargaining, management and representatives of the employees try to reach an agreement in solving, and avoiding, problems related to wages, hours, and other conditions of employment. It is essentially a social process for balancing the social pressures of two groups that have a mutual interest in the human resource system.

We have examined some of the reasons why workers join unions. To provide you with insight into union operations and into interactions of unions with the organization, we have briefly surveyed the historical course of union development as well as the structure of unions. Our discussion of labor laws and regulations should give you a basic understanding of the legal environment in which collective bargaining must operate.

You have also seen that an organization drive by a union requires substantial preparedness on the part of management. Once the union is certified, unionization continues to have considerable impact on the human resource system in at least three major areas: decision making, human resource policies and practices, and the work environment.

KEY CONCEPTS

Labor union	NLRB
AFL–CIO	Bargaining unit
Wagner Act	Unionization process
Taft-Hartley Act	

NOTES

1. U.S. Department of Labor, Bureau of Labor Statistics, *Directory of National Unions and Employee Associations, 1979*. Washington, D.C.: U.S. Government Printing Office, 1980, pp. 55–66.
2. For example, see Albert Rees, *The Economics of Trade Unions* (Chicago: University of Chicago Press, 1967), pp. 94–96; Seymour Martin Lipset and William Schneider, "Organized Labor and the Public: A Troubled Union," *Public Opinion*, August/September 1981, pp. 52–56.
3. A business agent is generally a full-time paid employee or official of a local union whose duties include day-to-day dealings with employers and workers, adjustment of grievances, enforcement of agreements, and similar activities.
4. Martin Estey, *The Unions* (New York: Harcourt, Brace, 1969), p. 25.
5. Unions are called "international" in the United States because they have locals in Canada.
6. "Unions on the Run," *U.S. News & World Report*, September 14, 1981, p. 61.
7. For a discussion of some complexities involved in certifying (and decertifying) a union, see Mark Z. Sappir "The Employer's Obligation Not to Bargain When the Issue of Decertification is Present," *Personnel Administrator*, February 1982, pp. 41–45.

REVIEW AND DISCUSSION QUESTIONS

1. A number of writers and experts suggest that "unions have outlived their usefulness in those progressive companies where enlightened management treats employees like human beings." Discuss.
2. What factors cause workers to join unions? Does the existence of a union mean that management has failed to provide for the satisfaction of employee needs?
3. Briefly trace the highlights of the labor movement in this country. In what ways have the early developments in the movement influenced labor relations as it exists today?
4. Speak to an officer of a local union in your area. Find out what the national union does for the local. Discuss the major problems faced by that local union.

5. Explain how a union becomes "certified" as a bargaining agent for a group of workers.
6. What is an unfair labor practice? Do unfair labor practices pertain more to management or to the union?
7. Assume you are a union organizer for a large national union. Develop a list of arguments you would use to convince white-collar employees to join the union.
8. What can management do to counter an organizing drive by a union?
9. Discuss how the unionization of a large department store would affect human resource management in that store?
10. What is the major legislation regulating labor–management relations in the private sector?

BIBLIOGRAPHY

Batt, William L., Jr., and Edgar Weinberg. "Labor–Management Cooperation Today." *Harvard Business Review* 56, January–February 1978, 96–104.

Boyce, Timothy J. *Fair Representation, The NLRB, and the Courts.* (Philadelphia: University of Pennsylvania, The Wharton School, Labor Relations and Public Policy Series, No. 18, 1978.

Chamot, Denis. "Professional Employees Turn to Unions." *Harvard Business Review* 54, May–June 1976, 119–127.

Fulmer, William E. "Step by Step Through a Union Campaign." *Harvard Business Review* 59, July–August 1981, 94–102.

Getman, J. G., S. B. Goldberg, and J. B. Herman. *Union Representation Elections: Law and Reality.* New York: Russell Sage Foundation, 1976.

Guyan, Janet. "UAW's Failure to Organize GM Facility Leaves a Residue of Red Faces and Ill Will." *Wall Street Journal*, February 24, 1981, 48.

Imberman, Woodruff. "How Expensive Is an NLRB Election?" *MSU Business Topics* 23, Summer 1975, 13–18.

Maxey, Charles. "Organizational Consequences of Collective Bargaining." *Proceedings of the Thirty-Second Annual Meeting*, Industrial Relations Research Association, Atlanta, Ga., 1979, 94–113.

Pestillo, Peter J. "Can Unions Meet the Needs of a 'New' Work Force?" *Monthly Labor Review* 102, February 1979, 33–34.

Rose, Joseph B. "What Factors Influence Union Representation Elections?" *Monthly Labor Review* 95, October 1972, 49–51.

Sloane, Arthur A., and Fred Witney. *Labor Relations*, 4th ed. Englewood Cliffs, N.J.: Prentice-Hall, 1982.

Swann, James P., Jr. "Misrepresentation in Labor Union Elections." *Personnel Journal* 59, November 1980, 925–926ff.

Taylor, Benjamin J., and Fred Witney. *Labor Relations Law*, 4th ed. Englewood Cliffs, N.J.: Prentice-Hall, 1982.

Tomkiewicz, Joseph, and Otto Brenner. "Union Attitudes and the 'Manager of the Future.'" *Personnel Administrator* 24, October 1979, 67–70, 72.

Collective Bargaining

CHAPTER OUTLINE

Structure and Strategy of Bargaining Relationships
Bargaining Structures ☐ Bargaining Strategy

Negotiating the Contract
Preparing for Negotiations ☐ Bargaining Sessions ☐ Bargaining Issues ☐ Impasse Resolution ☐ Ratifying the Agreement

Administering the Contract
Grievance Procedure: Description and Operation ☐ A Positive Approach to Grievances

Current Developments
Concessionary Bargaining ☐ Labor–Management Cooperation Programs ☐ Computer Systems

OBJECTIVES

1. Describe the collective bargaining process in terms of contract negotiations and administration.
2. Discuss the structure and types of bargaining relationships.
3. Discuss the typical bargaining issues involved in contract negotiations.
4. Recommend ways of overcoming impasses in negotiations.
5. Identify and describe a grievance procedure.
6. Formulate a series of steps for a positive, problem-solving approach to handling grievances.

SPOTLIGHT:
William B. Allen

William B. Allen is Manager of Employee Relations at the Solid State Division of RCA Corporation. He has been a professional in the human resource field for many years and also serves as an adjunct professor of personnel/industrial relations at a local university. He received a B.S. degree in economics from St. Michael's College.

Comments by William Allen

Anyone undertaking a study of management–labor relations in the United States must first clearly understand the dramatic changes that have taken place recently and appreciate the significance of such changes.

For several decades, American industry dominated not only domestic but world markets. As a result of this condition, companies, particularly those in highly unionized basic industries such as autos and steel, were able to easily pass increased costs along to consumers. This resulted in not only unrealistically high wages, but also proliferation of inefficient work practices. The emergence of foreign competition during the 1970s and early 1980s resulted in a drastic confrontation between unions with high expectations and companies that could no longer pass on the costs of overly generous and noncompetitive contract settlements.

Then, more suddenly than almost anyone thought possible, it occurred—the combination of the severest recession since the Great Depression, government deregulation, and intense world competition started a reversal of the automatic acceleration in wages and benefits that had become a fixture of the U.S. economy in the postwar period. What had been set in motion is a clear pattern of wage deceleration, along with the first real retreat on restrictive work rules, and greater worker participation in corporate decision making.

The requirements for American industry to become competitive and able to operate in world markets call for a "new order" of cooperation and understanding of the common good by both management and labor. This will not necessarily come easy, since it requires modification of behavior among large groups of people and abandonment of traditional adversarial relationships. There are numerous examples of cases where change has taken place. There are also somewhat inexplicable cases (e.g., in the steel industry) where workers have refused to accept any concessions despite a dire economic situation and wage rates out of line not only with foreign competition, but with most of American industry.

Here at RCA Solid State Division we were able to renegotiate starting rates and progression periods that were out of line with the rest of our industry. This agreement "grandfathered" current active employees and will significantly reduce future costs without impacting current active employees.

The future will belong to those organizations whose managers and workers can forge this type of cooperative relationship.

COLLECTIVE BARGAINING

From bloodshed and rioting through labor legislation and union–management cooperation—the times have changed, and along with them the way in which the voice of labor and management is heard.

Once a union has been certified as the exclusive bargaining agent for a group of employees, management is required by law to bargain collectively with the union over matters related to wages, hours, and other conditions of employment. The purpose of such *collective bargaining* is to reach agreement on a contract that both parties can "live with" for a stated period of time. Thus, collective bargaining involves the joint determination by employees and management of problems and issues pertaining to the human resource system.

The collective bargaining process consists primarily of two phases: contract negotiation and contract administration. The *negotiation phase* entails the joint determination of the terms of the labor agreement under which both parties must operate. The *administration phase* encompasses the joint efforts for carrying out and applying the terms already agreed upon. As we shall see, the *grievance process* is the focal point for administration of the labor agreement. It is important to note that collective bargaining is an ongoing process. It is not a relationship that ends after the agreement is reached. In addition, it is a rather complex relationship which, because of its dynamic characteristics, varies somewhat in each situation. Thus, before examining how contracts are negotiated and administered, let us briefly consider the structure and types of bargaining relationships.

A 19th-century "sewing room" where foremen had awesome power.

STRUCTURE AND STRATEGY OF BARGAINING RELATIONSHIPS

The most recent data suggest that there are about 178,000 collective bargaining agreements in existence in the United States. Surprisingly, over 60 percent of these agreements involved 10 large unions. In fact, one union, the International Brotherhood of Teamsters, negotiated 35,000 of these agreements.[1] While the large number of existing agreements represents a diverse array of bargaining patterns, it is possible to categorize the many ways in which bargaining relationships are structured into several groups.

Bargaining Structures

While most bargaining agreements take place between a single employer and a single union, there are four basic *bargaining structures* for conducting negotiations:

Type 1. A single union negotiates with a single employer.
Type 2. Several unions negotiate simultaneously with a single employer.
Type 3. A single union negotiates with more than one employer.
Type 4. Several unions negotiate with several employers (usually an employers' association).

There are variations to the above basic structures. For example, if a single employer (type 1) has plants or warehouses at different locations throughout the country, one master agreement with a single union may cover all employees. Certain issues, however, may be left to local negotiations. Thus, we find in the auto industry a basic agreement between General Motors and the United Auto Workers (UAW) that covers all unionized employees at all GM plants. In addition, a supplemental agreement is negotiated between each plant and a local chapter of the UAW.

A single employer with diverse activities may negotiate agreements with more than one union. In fact, coordinated bargaining (type 2), which involves more than one national or international union bargaining as a united front with one employer, occurs with growing frequency in the public and private sector.[2]

In multiple-employer bargaining two or more employers join together to bargain with one or more unions. In the type-3 structure we find a large union negotiating with several employers, usually through an employers' association. For example, the International Woodworkers of America negotiates with the Western States Wood Products Employers' Association, which represents such companies as Crown Zellerback Corporation and Weyerhaeuser Corporation. A type-4 structure, in which several unions negotiate with several employers, is common in several industries, including construction, where all unionized contractors in a given geographic area may bargain with a number of different craft unions through their building trades council.

There have been many attempts to categorize the different *types* of *bargaining relationships* that develop between union and management. For example, Benjamin Selekman has described nine such relationships.[3] A few, such as collusion and racketeering, are less common today than they were. The following four suggest the variety of possible relationships:

1. *Containment-aggression.* Management aggressively tries to curtail the union and keep it in check, while the union attempts to usurp management's rights.
2. *Power.* Each party attempts to get every possible advantage from the other, as permitted by the economic situation.
3. *Accommodation.* Tolerance and compromise are practiced by both parties; extreme displays of power are avoided.
4. *Cooperation.* While resembling accommodation, cooperation is also characterized by mutual concern about the total work environment, such as technological change and productivity.

Bargaining Strategy

Walton and McKersie take an approach to bargaining that focuses, not on the *relationship* between the parties, but rather on the *strategy* of the bargaining.[4] They identify the most common bargaining pattern as *distributive bargaining*, which assumes that management and labor have conflicting goals and are trying to get a bigger piece of a given pie. As a result, each party develops a type of "horse-trading" strategy. Another pattern is *integrative bargaining*, in which the goals of labor and management are not seen as conflicting and, as a result, both parties try to develop mutually acceptable solutions to problem areas. The integrative approach may involve the use of special committees for joint research and fact finding to solve difficult problems. Examples of this integrative bargaining have included changes in pension and benefit plans, union action to control wildcat strikes, and improvements in the grievance procedure. Both management and the union stand to gain if these issues are mutually resolved.

The issues involved seem to be an important determinant of whether an integrative or distributive strategy develops. Some issues, such as safety, drug and alcohol abuse, and productivity improvement, are likely to result in gains for both management and the union. Thus an integrative type of bargaining may be followed. On the other hand, since wages, benefits, and subcontracting are more of a win–lose situation, a distributive strategy will probably be followed.[5]

NEGOTIATING THE CONTRACT

The more spectacular aspects of labor relations are evident during contract negotiations. At such times, public attention is focused on strikes, pickets, union demands, and employer rejections. Behind the scenes, however, both union and management work hard to prepare for negotiations and to develop proposals for handling the problems that will arise in carrying out the agreements negotiated.

The procedures used in negotiating a contract depend on the situation, since there is no one best way. However, there are several common aspects of contract negotiation, which we shall discuss here. These include preparation, bargaining sessions, bargaining issues, impasse resolutions, and ratification.

Preparing for Negotiations

The amount of preparation depends on the resources available for research and the bargaining requirements of the parties. For example, if the U.S. Steel Corporation is to negotiate with the United Steelworkers, its preparation will be extensive and carefully researched. On the other hand, a small machine shop may do very little preparation for negotiating with a local of the Machinists Union. Exhibit 17–1 illustrates a management plan for negotiations for a large company.

If the parties have already negotiated one or more agreements, the timing of the negotiations may be prescribed by the existing contract. Typically, advance notice must be given 60 days before the contract expires if changes are to be sought in a new agreement.

In preparing for negotiations, management can obtain considerable necessary information from company records. Data regarding grievances, overtime, layoffs, disciplinary action, transfers, and promotions will be useful in formulating a bargaining strategy. A review of the existing agreement will suggest clauses that need to be modified or dropped. Line managers should be polled to get their ideas on contract changes. Because of their close contact with union members, first-line supervisors are in an ideal position to know what complaints the union is likely to voice and what changes in the contract will be sought.

It is important that management formulate their objectives and an appropriate bargaining strategy for the forthcoming negotiations. Use of a "Strategy Format Form" such as illustrated in Exhibit 17–2 will assist the management negotiating team in establishing both a priority for demands or contract changes and for each demand: (1) The lowest acceptable offer; (2) the expected final agreement; and (3) the initial demand. To illustrate with a simple example, management may feel the need for extending the term of the contract from one year to two years. Accordingly, it may be given a number-one demand priority, with a 2-year contract becoming the "lowest acceptable offer," 3-year term the "expectation," and 4-year term the "initial demand." While management is preparing for negotiation, the union is busy with its preparations.

Typically the union submits a list of its proposals to the company. An important part of management's job is to price every union demand and company's counterproposal. While it is often difficult to determine a cost

EXHIBIT 17–1
Management plan for negotiations.

	8 to 12 Months Before Contract Expires	4 to 8 Months	1 to 4 Months Prior to Commencement of Negotiations	During Negotiations	Postnegotiations
Local unit management	1. Assigns responsibilities for community surveys estimating union demands and employee attitude. 2. Assesses the total corporate community and union compensation/benefit plans. 3. Assesses union/employee motivation and goals for impending negotiations.	1. Develops with division management, corporate E.R., and corporate insurance to project alternate benefit proposals that are to be designed and costed. 2. Continues all steps in the planning process.	1. Secures division approval of strategy, negotiating plans, and cost estimates.	1. Continues negotiations, clears significant cost variances from plan with division management. 2. Integrates benefit negotiations with all other items. 3. Secures agreement in accord with plan. 4. Agrees with union on method and expense to inform employees of new contract terms.	1. Evaluates previous negotiations against plan within 30 days. 2. Assigns responsibilities for the planning process so as to integrate with the division's plans. 3. Identifies tentative objectives for next contract. 4. Completes wage/benefit adjustment form.
Division headquarters management	1. Assures local unit is preparing for negotiations. 2. Plans through annual financial plan to project impact of inventory buildup, possible settlement costs, etc. 3. Identifies internal responsibilities and relationships (corporate, law, E.R., insurance, benefits, etc.). 4. Keeps corporate employee relations informed.	1. Coordinates the development of strategy and negotiating plan, consulting with corporate employee relations and benefits. 2. Develops with local management, corporate E.R., and insurance to project alternative benefit proposals that are to be designed and costed. 3. Makes broad judgment on impact on company of expected proposals in relation to division and corporate	1. Approves negotiating plan strategy. 2. Clears benefit and corporate policy variances from plan with corporate employee relations. 3. Communicates progress to senior management and corporate employee relations. 4. Approves cost variances from plan. 5. Identifies strike issues.	1. Provides in addition to those points in "1 to 4 months" column, identification of "end" position and supports local negotiators in maintaining such position.	1. Evaluates all aspects of the previous negotiations within 45 days. 2. Identifies and communicates all long-range needs to executive management and corporate employee relations. 3. Integrates planning process in the division growth plan.

561

EXHIBIT 17-1, continued

	8 to 12 Months Before Contract Expires	4 to 8 Months	1 to 4 Months Prior to Commencement of Negotiations	During Negotiations	Postnegotiations
		goals, strategy, and plans. 4. Evaluates plans to control costs and deviations from plan/strategy.			
Corporate employee relations	1. Advises division and local management of union's national position on economics, benefits, and other issues. 2. Counsels on any anticipated conflict with corporate policy, other divisions, etc. 3. Provides available historical information pertinent to planning.	1. Assists division, local management, and corporate insurance in projecting and preparing alternate benefit proposals that are to be designed and costed. 2. Keeps division and local unit informed of any external developments having impact on its planning.	1. Consults with division on strategy and plans; available for on the scene assistance or to consult with international union officers; recommends corporate point of view on issues. 2. Approves all variances from corporate personnel policy and benefit plan proposals. 3. Assures that all issues are resolved at the required levels.	1. Provides same as "1 to 4 months" column. 2. Identifies to division management potential problems having corporate impact; if necessary, advises corporate management of unresolved major issues.	1. Counsels with unions and/or unit management on negotiating experiences and/or evaluation of new contract. 2. Informs other units of results. 3. Initiates needed objectives for study policy change or corporate decision.

Source: Audrey Freedman, *Managing Labor Relations* (New York: The Conference Board, 1979), p. 24.

for many items, careful attention to costs keeps both parties aware of the relative importance to be placed on each proposal. Quantifying demands also lends objectivity to arguments on issues.

Bargaining Sessions

In many cases, the general pattern of the contract will have been determined before the actual bargaining takes place. This is especially true of any wage adjustments sought by the union, as well as the general content of the contract. The union may simply present the employer with a copy of a contract either recently negotiated in the industry or by the same union in

EXHIBIT 17–2
Strategy Format Form.

Item Demanded	Demand Priority	Highly Confidential Lowest Acceptable Offer	Expectation	Initial Demand

Source: Lawrence A. Klatt and Thomas T. Urban, *KUBSIM: A Simulation in Collective Bargaining*, 2nd ed., Columbus, Ohio: Grid Publishing, Inc., 1981, p. 33. Copyright ©1984 John Wiley & Sons, Inc.

another industry. Even given the existence of a general pattern, however, the actual bargaining between the parties will be modified to fit the needs and peculiarities of the firm involved.

The membership of the bargaining teams will depend on many factors, including the bargaining structure (one union–one employer; multiple employers, and so on). Typically, the union bargaining team consists of the officers of the local union, several shop stewards or committee members, and a representative from the national union. Management teams tend to be smaller and usually consist of the head of the human resource department, the labor-relations director (if one exists), and two to four line managers such as the head of manufacturing or the plant managers. While most firms utilize labor attorneys for legal advice during negotiations, they are seldom active members of the negotiating team. The authority of the management team is in most cases limited by guidelines established by the top management of the company.[6]

The first meeting between labor and management negotiation teams usually establishes the ground rules, procedures, and schedules for future meetings. At the initial meeting the union will often formally present its specific proposals for contract changes. The particular approach to bargaining used by labor or management may follow one or two distinct formats: the *step-by-step approach* or the *total approach*. In the step-by-step approach, each item is treated as a separate issue and is discussed and agreed upon before the negotiators move on to the next item. In the total approach, nothing is considered settled until everything is agreed upon. From a system perspective, this approach is preferred since most issues are interrelated and their impact on the total organization cannot be evaluated in isolation. In most cases, a combination of the two approaches is used.

Observing an effective labor negotiator in action will suggest that negotiating is very much an art. Exhibit 17–3 lists a number of helpful suggestions, or "bargaining homilies," that the novice negotiator might consider.

EXHIBIT 17-3
Bargaining homilies.

> Be sure that you have set *clear objectives* on every bargaining item and that you understand on what ground the objectives were established.
>
> *Do not hurry.*
>
> When in doubt, *caucus*.
>
> Be *well prepared* with firm data support for clearly identified objectives.
>
> Always strive to keep some flexibility in your position—don't get yourself out on a limb.
>
> Do not concern yourself with only what the other party says and does—*find out why*. Remember that economic motivation is not the only explanation for the other party's conduct and actions.
>
> Respect the importance of *face saving* for the other party.
>
> Constantly be alert to the *real intents* of the other party—with respect not only to goals, but also to priorities.
>
> Be a good *listener*.
>
> Build a reputation for being *fair* but *firm*.
>
> Learn to control your *emotions*—don't panic. Use emotions as a tool, not an obstacle.
>
> Be sure as you make each bargaining move that you know its *relationship* to all other moves.
>
> *Measure each move* against your *objectives*.
>
> Pay close attention to the *wording* of every clause negotiated; words and phrases are often the source of grievances.
>
> Remember that collective bargaining negotiations are by their very nature part of a *compromise* process. There is no such thing as having all the pie.
>
> Learn to *understand* people and their personalities—it may mean a payoff during negotiations.
>
> Consider the *impact* of *present negotiations* on negotiations in *future* years.

Source: Reed C. Richardson, *Collective Bargaining by Objectives: A Positive Approach,* © 1977, p. 150. Reprinted by permission of Prentice-Hall, Inc., Englewood Cliffs, New Jersey.

Bargaining Issues

The collective bargaining agreement is usually a rather lengthy contract that may be drawn up in final form by an attorney. The agreement, or contract, sets forth the basic rules and standards that govern the relationship between the employer and the employees for the duration of the agreement. Negotiations may involve an almost unlimited number of *bargaining issues*, as suggested by Exhibit 17-4, which contains a table of contents from a contract negotiated between a large multiplant employer and a large international union. All bargaining issues may also be grouped into the general categories of union security and also management rights; wages, hours, and working conditions; employee security; and administration.

Union Security and Management Rights A union tries to protect its position by negotiating a union security clause. The union will push for a *union*

EXHIBIT 17-4
Union contract between multi-plant employer and international union.

Article Number	Table of Contents	Page Number
I.	Union recognition	6
II.	Union security	6
III.	Working conditions	9
IV.	Discrimination coercion	9
V.	Working hours: straight time—overtime	10
VI.	Wage rate	18
VII.	Holidays	26
VIII.	Continuity of service—service credits	29
IX.	Vacations	32
X.	Transfers	41
XI.	Reduction or increase in forces	45
XII.	Union and local representatives and stewards	47
XIII.	Grievance procedure	51
XIV.	Strikes and lockouts	54
XV.	Arbitration	55
XVI.	Posting	57
XVII.	Notification and publicity	58
XVIII.	Financial support	58
XIX.	Lists of hirings, layoffs, and transfers	58
XX.	Traveling time and expenses	59
XXI.	Local understandings	60
XXII.	Plant closings—termination pay	60
XXIII.	Military pay differential	63
XXIV.	Jury duty	64
XXV.	Absence for death in family	64
XXVI.	Responsibility of the parties	64
XXVII.	Issues of general application	65
XXVIII.	Employment security	66
XXIX.	Duration of agreement	66
XXX.	Modification and termination	67
XXXI.	Notices	68

shop, one in which all employees are required to join within a specified time after hiring, and to remain members as a condition of employment. A variation is the *modified union shop,* which exempts certain employee groups from having to join. Substantially less security is afforded the union by an *agency shop clause,* in which employees pay a fixed monthly amount to the union but are not required to join it. Other union security issues may include the checkoff of union dues and the definition of the bargaining unit. (Checkoff refers to the company's withholding of union dues, which are then forwarded directly to the union.)

Many agreements do not contain management rights provisions on the assumption that all rights not specifically bargained away belong to management. Some companies prefer to insert specific areas of action and decision that remain the exclusive prerogative of management, such as the right to discipline for cause and the right to determine the uses for company assets.

Wages, Hours, and Working Conditions These issues provoke perhaps the most debate during negotiations, and typically result in the most extensive provisions in the labor agreement. Besides hours of work and direct compensation, discussion will focus on many subissues, such as cost-of-living adjustments, shift differentials, overtime pay, and wash-up time. Some items related to sanitary working conditions and safety devices and practices, which were once included in negotiations, are not now discussed since they are required of all covered employers under the Occupational Safety and Health Act (OSHA) of 1970. However, the union may still desire to include these legally required items as added protection for the workers. At the same time, some managements feel that adding legally required working conditions will help to define the limits of management's responsibilities.

Employee Security The employee is interested in fair treatment and a guarantee of continuity of employment. Unions, therefore, will push for seniority as the determining factor in layoffs, recalls, and promotions. Management takes the position that efficiency will suffer unless it has the right to make such decisions on the basis of ability and performance.

Due process, or the handling of grievances, is another issue under the heading of employee security. There is a need to define what is to be regarded as a grievance and to outline how employee complaints will be handled.

Administration The category of administration covers issues related to the machinery established to enforce the terms of the agreement and to put due process into effect. Examples include the payment for time spent by stewards involved in handling grievances and the selection and duties of arbitrators.

The duration of the contract and the provisions for renewal are other administrative issues. As might be expected, management pushes for longer contracts in an effort to minimize conflict. Most contracts are in effect for a two- or three-year period.

Impasse Resolution

For bargaining issues to be satisfactorily negotiated, an agreement must be reached within the limits that the union and the employer find acceptable. The area within these two limits has been called the *bargaining zone*. As seen in Exhibit 17–5, the solution sought by one party exceeds the tolerance limit of the other party, resulting in a solution outside the bargaining zone. A collective bargaining impasse will occur if the first party refuses to change its demands enough to bring it within the bargaining zone or if the second party refuses to change its tolerance level to accommodate the demands of the first party. In order to achieve an *impasse resolution*, three things may occur: strike or lockout, conciliation or mediation, or arbitration.

EXHIBIT 17–5
The tolerance limits that determine the bargaining.
Source: From R. Stagner and H. Rosen, *Psychology of Union–Management Relations*. Copyright © 1965 by Wadsworth Publishing Company, Inc. Reprinted by permission of the publisher, Brooks/Cole Publishing Company, Monterey, California.

Strike or Lockout A *strike* is the refusal of a group of employees to perform their jobs. Union leaders may seek a strike authorization from the workers to strengthen their position if an impasse develops. Therefore, a strike vote by the rank-and-file does not necessarily mean that they desire a strike or will go out on strike. More commonly, the strike vote is taken to strengthen the bargaining position of the union negotiators. Sometimes the mere threat to exercise this strike option is sufficient to win concessions from management. Exhibit 17–6 shows the issues involved in strikes. One can see that, by far, the majority of strikes occur over wage issues during negotiations.

A *lockout* is management's version of a strike; it is the refusal to allow employees to work. Although the lockout is rarely used today, it does give the employer a psychological advantage when it is perceived by the union as a show of economic strength. Since many states now permit locked-out

Major Issue	Total
All stoppages	5,506
General wage	3,135
Supplemental benefits	78
Wage adjustments	141
Hours of work	15
Other contract matters	276
Union organization and security	252
Job security	211
Plant administration	1,002
Other working conditions	137
Interunion or intraunion matters	246
Not reported	13

EXHIBIT 17–6
Issues involved in work stoppages.

Source: U.S. Department of Labor, Bureau of Labor Statistics, *Work Stoppages, 1977 and First Nine Months of 1978* (Washington, D.C.: Government Printing Office, 1979), p. 7.

employees to claim unemployment benefits, the impact of the lockout has diminished.

Conciliation or Mediation   A conciliator or mediator can be very useful when a breakdown occurs during negotiations. In conciliation, a neutral third party tries to bring the two conflicting parties together again. He or she attempts to get management or the union to settle their differences themselves by getting each to see the other's point of view.

Mediation goes a step further than conciliation by offering suggestions in addition to those proposed by management and the union. Mediation, like conciliation, is not compulsory. By offering some new alternatives, however, the mediator gives the conflicting parties the opportunity to retreat from impasse without loss of face.

The Federal Mediation and Conciliation Service (FMCS) was established by the U.S. Congress to assist unions and managements in reaching agreements and avoiding work stoppages. Sometimes the union and management will agree to bring in an outsider, such as a university professor or a local public official.

Arbitration   In mediation, a solution can only be recommended, at which time either or both parties may reject it. In *arbitration*, both parties agree beforehand to abide by the arbitrator's decision. This means that the arbitrator, in a sense, performs the role of a judge who hears both sides of the issue and then makes a decision. In the public sector, employees are commonly forbidden by law to strike and are required to submit to compulsory arbitration if an impasse cannot be resolved. In the public sector, it is also common that arbitration is not "binding" but rather "advisory" to the public officials.

As you can see, arbitration, like mediation, introduces an "outside" party into the human resource system. In fact, with arbitration, decisions that directly affect the management of human resources are made by an outside party. This means that management must take care in selecting an arbitrator. At the same time, the arbitrator must be acceptable to the union. Labor attorneys and professors teaching in the area of human resource management frequently serve as arbitrators. The American Arbitration Association, a private organization, and the Federal Mediation and Conciliation Service (FMCS), a federal agency, supply lists of experienced arbitrators. It should be noted that arbitration is seldom used in the private sector as a means of resolving an impasse during contract negotiations. As we shall see, it is primarily a process to resolve a grievance when all else has failed.

Ratifying the Agreement

In the past, when the bargaining team consisting of management and union representatives agreed on the terms of a new contract, the job of negotiating was essentially completed. The rank-and-file membership, with few exceptions, would ratify, or approve, it. This has not been the case for the last several years, however, as an increasing number of the union members have rejected the negotiated agreement presented to them by their leaders.

Since the president or chief executive officer of the company is kept up-to-date on the progress of labor negotiations, it is probably easier for the management negotiating team to get approval. The union negotiating team, however, must return to the membership and get a majority of those voting to ratify the contract. In the last decade, in about one out of 10 instances, union members have rejected the negotiated contract.

If the union members reject the proposed contract, a new round of negotiations must begin. That is why it is important for the union leaders to do an effective job of "selling" the contract to the members. Of course, not getting ratification may be part of the union's negotiating strategy to demonstrate unity among rank-and-file. The union negotiating team can then return to the bargaining table with renewed confidence and push for a higher settlement.

ADMINISTERING THE CONTRACT

The final settlement and signing of the contract does not mean that the collective bargaining process is completed until the contract runs out. As we noted at the beginning of this chapter, the collective bargaining process involves the joint determination by employees and management of problems related to the human resource system. In a sense, the contract sets the framework for labor relations in the firm. During the course of the contract period, however, problems develop related to its application and interpretation.

Regardless of the time and effort put into writing the contract, things will come up in which there are differences of opinion regarding its intent. For example, the contract may have a clause dealing with the allocation of overtime. Management may take the position that the day-shift employees have the right to overtime under certain circumstances. A group of workers on the night shift may feel that they have priority for work not completed. Or problems may develop because unanticipated issues or events arise. For example, during an "emergency," management may direct certain workers to do tasks outside their job description. Did the company violate the agreement provision specifying that employees would perform only jobs falling within their job description? As these two examples suggest, nearly every provision in the labor agreement can be the basis for day-to-day problems that must be resolved. Much of the attitude and general nature of the problem-solving efforts involved in contract administration is greatly influenced by the work climate existing in the given human resource system. It is vital, therefore, to remember that the day-to-day dealing with the union and employees is part of the collective bargaining process, which, in turn, is part of a much broader human resource system with its overall goals and policies.

Thus, we can see that negotiations comprise only a part of the collective bargaining process. It is the *grievance procedure* that provides the mechanism for continuing the process during the life of the contract. Consequently, the company should negotiate a grievance procedure which can be used to settle problems quickly and fairly while allowing management to retain the flexibility necessary to maintain stable and efficient operations.

Grievance Procedure: Description and Operation

The *grievance procedure* provides an orderly system through which management and the union can determine whether or not the contract has been violated. As already suggested, however, the grievance procedure serves other purposes. For one thing, it provides for interpretation of contract provisions. Similarly, the grievance procedure permits management and the union to meet regularly and to get a better understanding of each other's problems. In this sense, it also serves as a communication channel from the rank-and-file to top management. Often overlooked, and of great significance, is the fact that the grievance procedure is frequently a vehicle for continued collective bargaining. For example, if the union can get management to make an exception to settle a grievance, that exception may be made the basis for a union demand in the next contract negotiation. Provisions in the contract under which grievances frequently seem to develop also suggest areas for consideration and possible renegotiation at the next contract talks.

There are different types of grievance procedures. To be effective, a grievance procedure should be designed to promptly deal with and resolve the different kinds of problems that might arise under the agreement. It should also clearly define the method of taking an appeal from one step to the next. The employees, as well as management and the union, should understand the exact process to be followed. Ideally, the contract should contain a no-strike clause whereby all disputes involving the application or interpretation of the agreement will be settled via the grievance procedure and without strikes or other interruptions to operations.

Exhibit 17–7 shows a typical grievance procedure for a larger company from the time the grievance is filed until it is settled by arbitration. Such a procedure may operate as follows:

Step 1. A discussion takes place between the immediate supervisor and the employee and/or the shop steward. A grievance form may be filled out and submitted to the immediate supervisor, who writes an answer explaining his or her rationale. Many firms attempt to keep this initial step very informal by not requiring anything in writing.

Step 2. If the grievance is not settled, the employee can take the second step. The complaint would be put in writing if it was not already done in step 1. Then the employee, together with the steward or the shop grievance committee, discusses the griev-

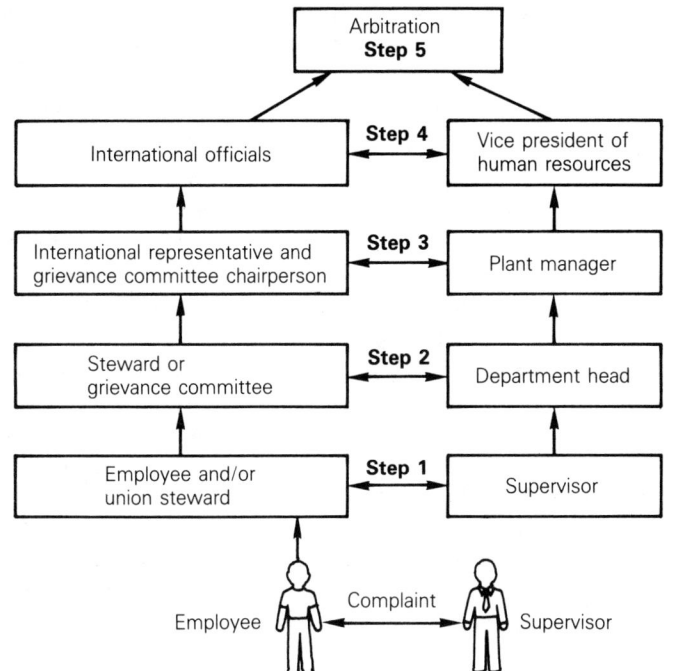

EXHIBIT 17-7
The grievance procedure for a large company.

ance with the appropriate department head. If the issue is not resolved, it continues to step 3.

Step 3. The plant manager, with advice and assistance from the human resource department, confers with the chairperson of the shop grievance committee and the international representative.

Step 4. If the grievance is still unsettled, high-ranking union officials from the international will meet with the corporate vice president for human resources in an attempt to resolve the dispute.

Step 5. In the event that the parties fail to reach an agreement, the issue is submitted to an independent *arbitrator*, who renders a binding decision. About 99 percent of all grievances are resolved before going to arbitration.[7]

A Positive Approach to Grievances

An unfortunate side effect of the grievance procedure is that it can develop into a win–lose game played by the union and the supervisors. For example, the first-line supervisor may become more concerned about maintaining a good record of "winning" grievances than about working out equitable solutions to the problems or complaints of workers. Similarly, the "loser" in a grievance case may seek redress or retaliation in other ways. Thus we find supervisors who "lost" suddenly carrying out certain rules to the letter when these rules apply to those who filed the grievance. Or, if the union lost, work slowdowns or acts of sabotage may occur. Such problems have led some critics to attack the grievance procedure as leading to lower morale and defensive behavior.

On the other hand, if management adopts a positive, problem-solving approach to handling grievances, the difficulties suggested above can be minimized or avoided, and the grievance procedure will contribute to reaching organizational goals. The firm sincerely interested in viewing the grievance procedure as a means for obtaining a better climate of labor relations may well consider the following five points.

1. Effective grievance handling does not begin with the filing of a grievance. It begins back at the bargaining table. As we have seen, negotiations constitute the beginning of the collective bargaining process, whereas the grievance procedure provides the vehicle for continuing the process during the contract life. As a result, if the contract is ambiguous or one-sided, it will invite later grievances. If the union has been misled or deceived by management during negotiations, the company can expect the union to seek redress for political purposes via the grievance procedure. Thus management's attitude at the bargaining table will provide the setting for later union–management relations.

2. The number and kinds of grievances are an indicator of problem areas in the human resource system. Periodically an analysis should be made to pinpoint problem areas either in the contract or in supervision. As illustrated by Exhibit 17–8, most of the grievances filed deal with disciplinary cases, application of the seniority system, and management rights. Furthermore, it is estimated that of the thousands of cases arbitrated nationally each year, more than one of every four involves a discipline issue.[8] Unresolved grievances work to the detriment of harmonious labor relations. In fact, some firms have found that contract negotiations had to cease until joint committees were able to resolve satisfactorily the *backlog* of grievances.

3. It is important to keep in mind that a grievance is a very important matter to the employee. This means that every employee complaint should be taken seriously. Even if the employee complaint has no merit, management should make every effort to hear the employee out and to determine the source of the grievance. Since it is easier to get to the core of the matter with oral investigation, most managers find it advantageous to discuss the employee complaint in an informal manner to the extent possible rather than rely on an escalating and legalistic exchange of written documents.

4. First-line supervisors, who are responsible for the day-to-day administration of the labor agreement, are the heart of a positive approach to grievance resolution. Frequently, however, while the human resources department is thoroughly familiar with the contract, the supervisors have only a vague familiarity with its provisions or application. Far too often, supervisors are merely given a copy of the new contract and told to "read it over

EXHIBIT 17–8
Issues in cases in which arbitrators selected from Federal Mediation and Conciliation Service panels made awards in one 12-month period.

Specific Issues*	Frequency of Occurrence
Discharge and disciplinary actions	1,226
Incentive rates or standards	77
Job evaluation	387
Seniority†	646
Overtime‡	363
Union officers—superseniority and union business	21
Strike or lockout issues	18
Vacations and vacation pay	132
Holidays and holiday pay	101
Scheduling of work	182
Reporting, call-in, and call-back pay	77
Health and welfare	51
Pensions	21
Other fringe benefits	92
Scope of agreement§	211
Working conditions, including safety	48
Arbitrability of grievance	261
Miscellaneous	237

*Compilations based on the number of arbitration awards for which data were available; that is, 3,414 of the 3,432 awards. Some awards involved more than one issue.
†Includes promotion and upgrading (137), layoff, bumping, recall (327), transfer (96), and other matters (86).
‡Includes pay (172), distribution of overtime (172), and compulsory overtime (19).
§Includes subcontracting (92), jurisdictional disputes (17), foreman, supervision, and so on (61), mergers, consolidations, accretion, other plants (11).
Source: Adapted from James Power, "Improving Arbitration: Roles of Parties and Agencies," *Monthly Labor Review*, November 1975, pp. 15–22.

carefully." There is a critical need to have supervisors receive proper guidance and instruction on interpreting the contract as well as current and past practices in the company's work rules. Supervisors need to know what the company's attitude toward grievance resolutions is, how to handle grievances, and when to seek advice from the human resource department or an immediate superior.

5. Management has a responsibility to impress on supervisors the necessity for taking adequate time from their busy schedules to dispose of grievances satisfactorily. Grievance handling must be viewed as a part of the supervisor's job rather than as an interruption of it. At the same time, higher-echelon management must evaluate each grievance on its own merits and avoid "rubber-stamping" the decision of the manager at the previous step in the grievance machinery, especially if that manager was in error.

CURRENT DEVELOPMENTS

Labor relations is a dynamic field that is responsive to economic and societal changes. Three developments in collective bargaining that have taken place in recent years are likely to continue in the future. These include concessionary bargaining, labor–management cooperation, and use of computer systems.

Concessionary Bargaining

A survey conducted in 1982 of top executives in 600 large corporations revealed that 26 percent of the unionized companies had recently obtained wage and benefit concessions from their unions.[9] A combination of a severe recession and intense world competition has resulted in rising unemployment, plant closings, and bankruptcies. This has set in motion an emerging pattern of wage deceleration and an easing of restrictive work rules. In exchange for such "concessions," management has frequently conceded to union demands for greater worker participation in corporate decision making.

To illustrate, in 1981 the Chrysler Corporation negotiated wage cuts from the United Auto Workers. To obtain this concession, Chrysler gave the UAW a seat on its Board of Directors as well as future profit sharing when the financial position of the company improves.[10] Ford and General Motors followed by winning concessions from the UAW in the areas of wage reductions and work rules. For example, Ford agreed in contracts with several key parts plants, not to purchase the parts elsewhere if workers cut production costs.[11] Firms in all industries are being successful in getting the union to reduce relief time and to change seniority practices to gain more flexibility in transferring and assigning workers within a plant.

Labor–Management Cooperation Programs

While labor–management cooperation may take many different forms, basically it involves labor and management working together to increase the productivity of the organization. For example, the Golden State Paper Company and the United Paperworkers and the Operating Engineers negotiated a 10-year plan in which productivity bonuses are paid on the basis of the tonnage of newsprint produced in years in which no strikes occurred.[12] In the previous chapter, we have discussed the UAW/Ford Motor Co. "Employee Involvement" program.

In 1982, the United Steelworkers of America reported that they were experimenting in 13 basic steel plants with a new program called "Labor–Management Participation Teams" (LMPTs). According to the union, the program is aimed at improving a worker's job security by increasing worker involvement in problem solving at the shop-floor level. Consisting of several union members and supervisors who serve on a "participation team" in each department of a plant, the team usually meets on a weekly basis during working hours to discuss and solve problems not handled by traditional labor–management relations. Thus, workers actively work at resolving such things as working conditions, production bottlenecks, safety issues, absenteeism, incentive pay, and product quality. The United Steelworkers claims that the LMPT approach has already saved millions of dollars and numerous jobs.[13]

It should be noted that while attempts at union–management cooperation go back many years, it is still regarded as being experimental. Some union leaders feel that cooperation on the shop floor will destroy the union's adversary role at the bargaining table. Some managers question the ability of the union to discard old attitudes and work habits. However, the record of accomplishments is a strong indication that more programs of labor–management cooperation will be introduced at future bargaining tables.

Computer Systems

The use of computer systems among union and management is having an impact on labor relations, especially in the area of contract negotiations. For example, several large unions such as the United Steelworkers, the International Association of Machinists, and the United Auto Workers have developed sophisticated information systems for use in contract negotiations. Facts and figures regarding various contracts within the industry are stored in the computer. This information becomes very valuable in substantiating demands during negotiations. Similarly, questions regarding costs can usually be answered in a few seconds if initial data is correct.

In order to keep up with the growing sophistication of large unions at the bargaining table, the human resource specialists are also finding it necessary to utilize computers and information systems. Data regarding absenteeism, payroll costs, productivity, arbitration cases, benefits, employee data, and so on are needed upon request. Using LAIRS (Labor Agreement Information Retrieval System), the labor specialist today has access to thousands of documents including court decisions, articles, and research reports pertaining to labor relations.

SUMMARY

Collective bargaining provides the vehicle by which management and representatives of the workers try to reach collective agreement in solving, and avoiding, problems related to wages, hours, and other conditions of employment. It is essentially a social process for balancing the social pressures of two groups that have a mutual interest in the human resource system.

The collective bargaining process consists primarily of two related phases: contract negotiation and contract administration. To provide some familiarization with the negotiation phase, we have discussed five of the more important aspects of contract negotiation: (1) preparing for negotiations, (2) bargaining sessions, (3) bargaining issues, (4) impasse resolution, and (5) ratifying the agreement.

Contract administration encompasses the joint efforts of management and the union in carrying out and applying the provisions of the labor agreement. Central to this process is the grievance procedure, which provides an orderly system through which management and the union can resolve disputes. Much of the attitude and the general nature of the problem-solving efforts involved in contract administration is greatly influenced by the work climate existing in the human resource system. It is vital, therefore, to remember that management's day-to-day dealings with the union and employees are part of the collective bargaining process, which, in turn, is part of the much broader human resource system.

Three recent developments in labor relations include concessionary bargaining, labor–management cooperation programs, and greater usage of computer programs.

KEY CONCEPTS

Collective bargaining

Bargaining structure

Bargaining relationships

Bargaining issues

Impasse resolution

Bargaining zone

Strike

Grievance procedure

Mediation

Arbitration

REVIEW AND DISCUSSION QUESTIONS

1. Show how the collective bargaining process is influenced by public opinion.
2. Compare and contrast Selekman's categorization of bargaining relationships with Walton and McKersie's strategy approach.
3. What issues are usually covered in a labor agreement?
4. With regard to contract negotiations, define and distinguish among conciliation, mediation, and arbitration.
5. What purposes are served by the grievance procedure? Is the principle of a grievance procedure primarily applicable to unionized employees, or would it apply equally well in a nonunion organization?
6. Discuss the proper role of the first-line supervisor in contract administration.
7. How can the first-line supervisor be made more effective in handling employee grievances?
8. What criteria would you suggest for evaluating the collective bargaining process in a specific organization?

9. Explain what is meant by labor–management cooperation programs. Give examples.
10. Visit the human resource department of a large, unionized organization. How are they utilizing computers in their dealings with the union?

NOTES

1. U.S. Department of Labor, Bureau of Labor Statistics, *Directory of National Unions and Employee Associations, 1979* (Washington, D.C.: Government Printing Office, 1980), p. 74.
2. Abraham Cohen, "Union Rationale and Objectives of Coordinated Bargaining," *Labor Law Journal* 27, February 1976, pp. 75–83.
3. Benjamin M. Selekman, "Varieties of Labor Relations," *Harvard Business Review* 27, March 1949, pp. 177–185. Also see Thomas A. Kochan, "Toward a Behavioral Model of Management under Collective Bargaining," Working Paper, Alfred P. Sloan School of Management, M.I.T., November 1980.
4. Richard E. Walton and Robert B. McKersie, *A Behavioral Theory of Labor Negotiations* (New York: McGraw-Hill, 1965).
5. For an interesting discussion of an optimal labor relations strategy, see John R. Arthur and Warren C. Ogden, "Here's How to Formulate a Labor Relations Policy," *Personnel Administrator*, February 1982, pp. 35–38.
6. Audrey Freedman, *Managing Labor Relations* (New York: Conference Board, 1979), p. 30.
7. For an excellent discussion of arbitration, see Harold W. Davey, *Contemporary Collective Bargaining*, 4th ed. (Englewood Cliffs, N.J.: Prentice-Hall, 1982), pp. 185–225.
8. *Ibid.*, p. 188.
9. "Concessionary Bargaining: Will the New Cooperation Last?" *Business Week*, June 14, 1982, pp. 66–81.
10. "Pleas for Wage Relief Flood into the UAW," *Business Week*, February 16, 1981, p. 27.
11. *Business Week*, "Concessionary Bargaining," p. 69.
12. *Monthly Labor Review* 98, May 1975, p. 70.
13. "Basic Steel Industry's Revival May Depend on LMPT's," *Steelabor* 47(6), June 1982, p. 6.

BIBLIOGRAPHY

Beal, Edwin F., and James Begin. *The Practice of Collecting Bargaining*, 6th ed. Homewood, Ill.: Richard D. Irwin, 1982.

Bloom, Gordon F., and Herbert R. Northrup. *Economics of Labor Relations*, 9th ed. Homewood, Ill.: Richard D. Irwin, 1981.

Crawford, Vincent P. "On Compulsory Arbitration Schemes." *Journal of Political Economy* 87(No. 1), 1979, 131–159.

Davey, Harold W. *Contemporary Collective Bargaining*, 4th ed. Englewood Cliffs, N.J.: Prentice-Hall, 1982.

Fleming, Robben W. *Labor Arbitration Process*. Urbana, Ill.: University of Illinois Press, 1965.

Marshall, Howard O., and Natalie J. Marshall. *Collective Bargaining*. New York: Random House, 1971.

Mueller, Stephan J., and A. Howard Myers. *Labor Law and Legislation*, 4th ed. Cincinnati: South-Western Publishing, 1974.

National Industrial Conference Board. "White-Collar Unionization." *Studies in Personnel Policy*, No. 220, 1970.

Power, James. "Improving Arbitration: Roles of Parties and Agencies." *Monthly Labor Review*, Spring 1975.

Rees, Albert. *The Economics of Trade Unions*. Chicago: University of Chicago Press, 1962.

Richardson, Reed C. *Collective Bargaining by Objectives*. Englewood Cliffs, N.J.: Prentice-Hall, 1977.

Ruben, George. "Industrial Relations in 1980 Influenced by Inflation and Recession." *Monthly Labor Review*, January 1981, 15–20.

Sayles, Leonard R., and George Strauss. *The Local Union*, 2nd ed. New York: Harcourt Brace, 1967.

Scheiman, Martin F. *Evidence and Proof in Arbitration*. New York: Cornell University, 1981.

Selekman, Benjamin M. "Varieties of Labor Relations." *Harvard Business Review* 27, March 1949, 177–185.

Sherskin, Michael J., and W. Randy Boxx. "Building Positive Union–Management Relations." *Personnel Journal*, June 1975.

Sloane, Arthur A., and Fred Witney. *Labor Relations*, 4th ed. Englewood Cliffs, N.J.: Prentice-Hall, 1982.

Stagner, Ross, and Njalman Rosen. *Psychology of Union–Management Relations*. Belmont, Ca.: Wadsworth, 1965.

Stevens, Carl M. *Strategy and Collective Bargaining Negotiations*. New York: McGraw-Hill, 1963.

Taylor, George W., and Fred Witney. *Labor Relations Law*. 4th ed. Englewood Cliffs, N.J.: Prentice-Hall, 1982.

U.S. Department of Labor, Bureau of Labor Statistics. *A Brief History of the American Labor Movement*. Washington, D.C.: U.S. Government Printing Office, 1970.

U.S. Department of Labor, Bureau of Labor Statistics. *Directory of National Unions and Employee Associations, 1979*. Washington, D.C.: U.S. Government Printing Office, 1980.

Walton, Richard E., and Robert B. McKersie. *A Behavioral Theory of Labor Negotiations*. New York: McGraw-Hill, 1965.

Yoder, Dale, and Herbert G. Heneman, eds. *ASPA Handbook of Personnel and Industrial Relations*. Washington, D.C.: The Bureau of National Affairs, 1976.

Quality of Work Life and Employee Maintenance

CHAPTER OUTLINE

QWL—What and Why

Specific Issues in QWL

QWL and Maintenance Concepts

Implementation of Employee Maintenance and Service Programs

Safety □ Medical and Health □ Legal, Financial, and Consumer Services □ Pensions and Retirement Services □ Transportation □ Food □ Recreation □ Career Counseling and Outplacement □ Policy Manual Development □ P/HR Diagnostic, Planning, and Controlling Reports □ P/HR Employee Information Reports

QWL and Productivity

OBJECTIVES

1. Define the quality of work life.
2. Identify at least 10 specific issues in QWL.
3. Describe a program for implementation of employee maintenance and service programs.
4. Describe the impact of QWL changes on productivity.

SPOTLIGHT:
Ronald Assaf

Ronald Assaf was born in Akron, Ohio, where he attended public schools and the University of Akron. He began his business career in 1955 as a management trainee for Kroger Company, a retail food chain. He spent the next 12 years with Kroger in various management capacities in the Akron/Cleveland area. In 1967, with two partners, he founded Sensormatic Electronics Corporation for the purpose of developing a product for use by retail stores to protect shoplifting. He served as Executive Vice President until 1971, when he was elected Chairman of the Board. In June, 1974, he was appointed President and Chief Executive Officer of the company as well. He continues to hold these positions today.

In June, 1974, when he assumed the CEO responsibilities, his company had revenues of $6.7 million, income of slightly over $500,000, a net worth of $465,000, and employed 214 people. By comparison, for the last fiscal year, which ended May 31, 1983, Sensormatic had increased its revenues to $86 million, showed record net profits of $23 million —46 times the 1974 level—and had a net worth of approximately $160 million. Sensormatic currently employs 1,200 people and has an 80-percent market share of the electronic article surveillance industry, with slightly over 70 percent worldwide.

Mr. Assaf is a member of several professional organizations: a Director of North Carolina National Bank, Florida, a member of South Florida Association for Corporate Growth, American Electronics Association, American Management Association's President's Club, and the Electronic Manufacturers' Association. He is also active in many civic organizations as Vice President of the Florida Atlantic University Foundation Board, member of the Board of Regents of the College of Boca Raton, member of the Senior Advisory Board for Junior Achievement of South Florida.

Comments by Ronald Assaf

Sensormatic is a very rapidly growing company, and a cornerstone of our strategy for exceptional growth and profitability is confidence in our human resources. We expect Sensormatic employees at all levels to be highly motivated and self-reliant. We are a lean organization, and we have to expect top performance from our people at all times with a minimum of supervision.

We feel that it is consistent with this approach to place a great deal of emphasis on employee maintenance programs to promote good physical health, as well as mental well-being. We cannot afford to have people out sick or worrying about nonwork problems any more than is absolutely necessary. Thus, we feel it is a good investment for the company to have a very progressive program to create a high-quality work-life environment.

Among the important elements of this program are:

- Life insurance for employees
- Major medical insurance for employees and dependents
- Hospitalization and health insurance for employees and dependents
- Dental insurance for employees and dependents
- Long-term and short-term disability insurance
- Vacations and holidays
- Paid sick/personal time off
- Retirement plan based entirely on company contributions (of company stock, and other investments)
- Tuition reimbursement
- Stock purchase plan (which allows employees to purchase company stock at a discount of 15 percent below the market price with no brokerage fees)
- Sports leagues and after-work recreation funded by the company
- Employee assistance programs for drug or alcohol problems and for other personal or family problems requiring professional counseling
- Wellness programs to improve employees' health and to allow early detection of potentially serious medical problems
- Safety and health programs to insure maximum protection of employee safety and health on the job

All of our fringe benefit programs for employees as well as medical insurance for dependents are entirely paid for by the company, and in 1982 these costs exceeded $6,500 per employee. As a growth company, we have found it highly cost-effective to fund certain of our benefits such as retirement plans primarily with company stock rather than with cash, although the plan portfolio also includes other investments.

In summary, we feel that through careful planning to minimize the cash drain of fringe benefits and careful cost control over the programs, we have achieved a situation in which our expenditures on employee maintenance are a prudent investment. This investment pays handsome returns in the form of a motivated, committed workforce in good health with a high *esprit de corps.*

Emphasis on employee maintenance and a high-quality work environment are key elements in our strategy for exceptional growth and financial performance.

> *Question:* When I quit my job my boss called me "drifter," and I would like to know how many times an average person changes jobs in a lifetime.
>
> *Answer:* Americans switch jobs about 10 times and move an average of about 13 times before giving up the ghost. In fact, last year [1981] 2.5 million persons enrolled in courses to learn new professions. According to sociologists, people are not so much chasing the buck but instead looking for the more elusive rewards of peace of mind and a better quality of life.[1]

The P/HR manager is the one person in a company who has as his or her main responsibility the development of the best possible work environment. Like income taxes, the complexity and turbulence of the modern world produce such stress on people that they seek ways to avoid them. People are realizing that work takes up a major portion of time and their lives, and they do not want to suffer while performing. Quality of life includes as a major portion quality of work life (QWL).

QWL—WHAT AND WHY

QWL has a nice sounding ring to it like "the American Dream," but what is it really? In a broad-gauge article, Richard E. Walton proposed eight criteria for measuring QWL:[2] (1) adequate, fair compensation, (2) safe, healthful working conditions, (3) opportunity to develop human capacities, (4) opportunity for career growth, (5) social integration in the work force, (6) constitutionalism in the work organization, (7) work and quality of life, and (8) social relevance.

Adequate and Fair Compensation Different people have different ideas of what constitutes "adequate." Fair compensation, however, may be measured in terms of external rates, internal compensation structure, and, to some extent, in terms of fairness to stockholders.

Safe and Healthful Working Conditions Unions have fought long and hard for safer working conditions. Often, companies also recognize that safe and healthful working conditions are a matter of enlightened self-interest as well as a legal and humanitarian requirement. Sometimes, however, for various reasons, companies have resisted efforts to make the workplace more safe and healthful. This probably reflects a false sense of economy, rather than either a humane outlook or a rational cost–benefit analysis. Industries lose approximately 49 working days per year per 100 employees because of occupational illness. The industries that lose the greatest number of days to work-related injury or illness are: newspapers, lumber and wood products, meat packing, railroad equipment, and truck transportation. Those that have the least number of days lost are communications, chemical products, aircraft, electrical equipment, and petroleum refining.[3]

Opportunity to Use and Develop Human Capacities Traditionally, work became subdivided on the assumption that specialization, and the learning curve, led to higher productivity. QWL is improved, however, to the extent that the worker can exercise more control over his or her work, and the degree to which the job embraces an *entire* meaningful task, not just a segment of one.

Opportunity for Career Growth Jobs in operations or in the office can be learned within a week to a year. Most blue-collar and clerical workers, therefore, reach a peak in earnings early in their careers except for the inclusion of across-the-board increases. Educational requirements pose a barrier to promotion for most such workers.

Professionals such as engineers or programmers peak somewhat later. Obsolescence provides additional discouragement. Managers also reach a plateau because fewer can be promoted on the approach to the top of the hierarchy.

Social Integration in the Work Force Walton, in the article referred to earlier, states that a satisfying identity and self-esteem are influenced by five characteristics of the work place: freedom from prejudice, egalitarianism (the absence of status symbols), upward mobility, supportive work groups and community of feelings, and interpersonal openness.

Constitutionalism in the Work Organization QWL includes constitutional protection for employees on such matters as privacy, free speech (dissent without fear of reprisal), equity, and due process. As with all factors in QWL, there is an optimum degree of *constitutionalism*. Beyond this, QWL is damaged. If constitutionalism increases to the point where every action by management is challenged and lengthy procedures are followed, workers lose satisfaction in getting their jobs done. The focus shifts to beating the company instead of working as part of it. The company may, as a result, also suffer, fall behind competitors, go out of business, thereby bringing QWL down to zero. In some industries, such as mining, labor unions have played a vital role in bringing protection to the worker from arbitrary and capricious actions by management.

Work and Quality of Life For the employee, it is desirable to have work-life mesh with total life. That is, working hours (overtime), business travel, transfers, and vacations should not be such as to strain family relationships.

Social Relevance of Work The corporation, by acting in a socially responsible way, enhances the feelings of the workers about their jobs. The production of napalm, the pollution of the environment, or other activities under attack by the public and government may cause workers to depreciate the value of their work and to lower self-esteem.

SPECIFIC ISSUES IN QWL

Who is responsible for QWL? The unions believe that they are contributing most by dragging management, kicking and screaming, into improved working conditions. The United Mine Workers' gains in the 1930s and 1940s are a good example of the union's struggle to improve safety, health, working conditions, and pay.

Corporate management, on the other hand, can point to improved physical surroundings, benefit plans, and improved compensation plans as signs of leadership in QWL.

The P/HR manager's task is to identify the QWL issues that extend beyond maintenance functions and prepare to lead the way in the 1980s. A discussion of 11 major QWL issues for the 1980s follows.

Pay and Stability of Employment Good wages still rank high on employees' expectations. Inflation, increased taxation because of "bracket creep" and Social Security taxes, and rising property and sales taxes are having tremendous impact on the disposable income of workers. New forms of compensation may be sought to by-pass some of these factors, or legislation may be sought either to shift the burden or to reduce government expenditures.

Good wages without stability of employment mean poor income. Companies must improve planning to anticipate changes in demand rather than reacting to them with sudden shifts up and down in employment. The P/HR manager must develop plans and policies that can be sold to top management to accomplish this.

Occupational Stress Productivity can enhance QWL for those workers who find satisfaction in being highly productive in society. At the same time, QWL can be decreased when enforced levels of productivity become dysfunctional as stress is created through speedup and long hours. Stress is determined by the nature of the work, the physical work environment, the time spent at work without renewal (burnout), the characteristics of the worker, and his or her match to the job. Stress is any factor that disturbs a person's psychological or biological equilibrium or harmony. Exhibit 18–1 shows that while some stress is helpful in bringing about motivation (eustress), results may also be the harmful loss of adequacy and security (distress).

Pressures that produce stress may be organizationally derived or self-imposed. Symptoms of distress include irritability, hyperexcitation or depression, unstable behavior, fatigue, stuttering, trembling, psychosomatic pains, heavy smoking, and drug abuse. The P/HR activities should include identification, prevention, and treatment of this rapidly increasing problem.

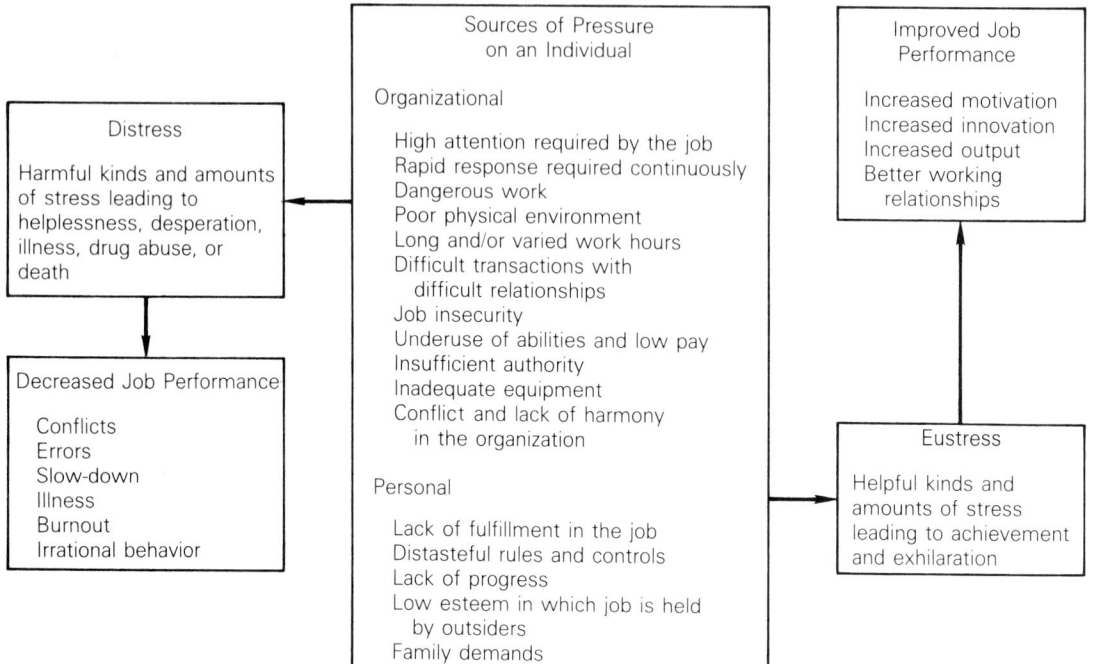

EXHIBIT 18–1
Stress and performance.

Usually, treatment is handled by the company's health maintenance office in the P/HR organization.

Corporate Wellness Programs Corporate health care is becoming increasingly proactive, teaching employees to take care of themselves before serious health problems develop. The growing trend of companies offering employee health promotion programs at the worksite has made "wellness" the latest business buzzword. Effective health promotion programs in such areas as smoking cessation, hypertension control, and other forms of cardiovascular risk-reduction have long-term positive economic impact well worth the relatively minimal expenditures involved. Businesses willing to devote resources to health promotion can expect to gradually reduce absenteeism, hospitalization, disability, excessive job turnover, and premature death.

Responses range from the simplest of approaches, such as comprehensive health-screening, to more ambitious programs with fitness trails or weight-lifting equipment. In the end, all employee health-promotion schemes are geared toward one thing—prevention. With annual U.S. medical costs exceeding $245 billion, a good share of which belongs to industry, it's no wonder American businesses are working to head off steadily mount-

EXHIBIT 18-2
Examples of corporate "wellness" programs.

Source: Metropolitan Life Insurance Company.

ing health-care costs. (See Exhibit 18-2.) To be of value to the employee, a program must combine relaxation, exercise, and diet, with active participation by the individual as well as support by the company. The wellness triad developed by Karl Albrecht is shown in Exhibit 18-3.

Alternative Work Schedules The five-day, 40-hour work-week has been the standard work week in American industry since 1940. In the past decade, industry and government have been concerned with *alternative work schedules* to accommodate employees and changing social conditions. Possibili-

EXHIBIT 18–3
The factors of relaxation, exercise, and diet form a synergistic wellness triad.

	Enhances This Factor:		
	Relaxation	Exercise	Diet
This Factor: Relaxation	Calmer attitude makes living more enjoyable; relaxation and recreation get higher priority.	Changes time priority; makes it easier to make time for exercise.	Reduces anxiety-related eating; increased body awareness and relaxation reduce over-eating at meals.
Exercise	Improved physical condition enables the body to consume stress chemicals; makes relaxation skills easier to learn and maintain.	Improved physical condition raises energy level; makes more exercise easier and enjoyable.	Regular exercise burns calories, promotes gradual weight loss, increases metabolic level, reduces appetite.
Diet	Reducing consumption of alcohol, tobacco, and caffeine makes parasympathetic relaxation response easier.	High-quality diet increases energy level; exercise becomes easier as weight decreases.	Good eating habits become easier to maintain over time.

Source: From the book, *Stress and the Manager* by Karl Albrecht. © 1979 by Prentice-Hall, Inc. Published by Prentice-Hall, Inc., Englewood Cliffs, NJ 07632.

ties considered have been (1) work at home,[4] (2) flexitime, (3) staggered hours, (4) four-day, 40-hour week, (5) reduced work-week, and (6) part-time employment.

Work at home, or flexiplace, offers advantages to workers with home scheduling problems (children or invalid relations), workers who are handicapped, or workers who work best on their own. It also benefits employers because it reduces office needs and overhead costs. The computer industry especially lends itself to electronic work-at-home situations. Disadvantages include start-and-stop in response to family demands, isolation from fellow professionals, and negative effect on development of skills and promotability.

Flexitime usually is developed around certain minimum core hours during which workers must work. This permits workers to vary starting times, quitting times, and lunch periods to suit personal and recreational needs. Often a community-wide approach, staggered hours are used mostly in high automobile traffic areas so that workers may avoid heavy traffic in arriving to and leaving work. The reduced work week such as the 36-hour work-week with full pay has been a popular goal of unions. Finally, part-time work is of growing interest as more wives enter the labor market, and as husbands and wives both contribute to income. Part-time work may allow more attention to children and to combined recreation.

> **Different Forms of Flexitime, from Least to Most Flexible**
>
> *Flexitour:* Employees choose a starting and quitting time, stick with that schedule for a period, and work eight hours a day.
> *Gliding time:* Employees may vary their starting and quitting time daily, but they must still work eight hours, or another company-set length, every day.
> *Variable day:* As long as employees work the number of hours required by the end of the week or month, they can vary the number of hours they work each day.
> *Maxiflex:* Employees may vary their daily hours and don't have to be present for a "core" time on all days.

The two most common proposals for change in work schedules are adoption of a shortened work week, typically a four-day week, and adoption of a work schedule with variable starting and quitting times (flexitime). The compressed work week (four days or even three days) has received relatively more attention in the United States, and flexitime has received relatively more attention in Western Europe.

In concluding a research study examining employee attitudes toward alternative work schedules, Mahoney has concluded that:

> The research evidence generally supports the proposition that employees view with favor changes from the traditional five–forty work schedule to flex-time and four–forty work schedules; both flex-time and the four–forty schedule are preferred to the five–forty work schedule. Except for persons already working a four–forty schedule, approximately equal proportions prefer each of the newer work schedules. Persons working the four–forty schedule in this study express an overwhelming preference for that schedule, a finding that may be company specific. Clearly, however, change to a nontraditional work schedule would be viewed as a benefit by persons in this study. The relative benefit associated with different work schedules varies among individuals, some preferring one schedule and others preferring another. Preferences do not appear to be related to job satisfaction; rather, they appear to be a function of individual orientations towards leisure. The work schedule which offers the individual improved leisure time is preferred.[5]

Worker Participation and Control of Work Unions have recently emphasized worker participation as a means of improving QWL. Worker participation means that management must usually change its style to bring workers into the creative and decision processes. Workers obtain more control over their jobs, feel that they are using their skills to make a real contribution to the success of their company, and bring about opportunities for better pay.

You will recall from the last chapter the successful cooperation between Ford Motor Company management and the UAW in their Employee Involvement (EI) program (see Exhibit 16–12 for a description of EI at Ford).

EMPLOYEE RELATIONS

The process of actually launching this EI program at a Ford plant is shown in Exhibit 18–4. In 1979, Ford and the UAW initiated an Employee Involvement program, under which local unions and plant management form

> Even if in its early stages, UAW–Ford Employee Involvement (EI) is producing valuable results for employees, local unions, local managements and, in the final analysis, for customers. Employees who are involved in EI projects say they feel a greater sense of job satisfaction, self-esteem, belonging, pride in workmanship, and contribution. Local union representatives and management personnel report that EI contributes to improved attitudes and communication, better relations, fewer grievances, fewer complaints, and improved employee morale and job performance. Additionally, locations are reporting that employees are contributing very importantly to better product quality, first-time capability, improved work environment, better relations between employees and supervisors, and to other improvements in the work place. In other words, they are saying that "EI works!"

Source: Donald F. Ephlin and Peter J. Pestillo, *Employee Involvement . . . It Works,* issued by the UAW–Ford National Joint Committee on Employment Involvement, 1980.

EXHIBIT 18–4
Ford's Employment Involvement Program in action.

Dearborn Engine Plant and UAW Local 600

The Dearborn Engine Plant's joint steering committee was formed in March 1980. A pilot project was selected and employe volunteers were chosen by lottery in April. Problem-solving training started in May and the first employe problem-solving group presentation to the joint steering committee was made in June. Following are some examples of the problems addressed—and the fixes implemented—at this location:

Problem: *Excessive scrap and tool breakage on cylinder head milling machines caused by broken timing belts.*
Solution: Install limit switch to automatically stop the head feed when timing belts break.
Payoff: Reduced scrap and tool breakage . . . improved quality and reduced tool cost.

Problem: *Lack of information about EI activities for employes not participating in problem-solving groups.*
Solution: Install bulletin boards in the plant for posting of EI information. Devote part of the plant newspaper to EI news.
Payoff: Better communication . . . better informed employes.

Indianapolis Plant and UAW Local 1111

The Indianapolis Plant was among the first locations in the Company to initiate an EI project. Discussions and meetings began in mid-1978 and EI was formally launched in December 1979 with the establishment of a joint steering committee. The first employe problem-solving group started functioning in January 1980. Here are some of the results of problem-solving activities at Indianapolis:

Problem: *Off-center drilled and pinned steering gear valves from B&K centering machines.*
Solution: Alter heat treating specifications to reduce hard stock, modify grind and length of drills, and rebuild major machine components.
Payoff: Sustained increase in first-run valve production capability and improved product quality . . . purchase of centering retest machine placed on hold.

Problem: *Layout of work area required employes to hand carry parts from work station to opposite side of washer to load conveyor.*
Solution: Extend conveyor line adjacent to work stations.
Payoff: Improved working conditions . . . made job easier.

Source: EI UAW–Ford, Employee Involvement—A Handbook, The UAW–Ford National Joint Committee on Employee Involvement, April 1980, pp. 2, 3.

problem-solving committees to make jobs more productive and satisfying for workers. These committees are prohibited from making changes in the UAW's local or national agreements, but the cooperative attitude that comes to the fore in this process can affect bargaining over local practices.

Recognition Recognition of the employee as a person rather than a unit of labor increases QWL and reduces alienation of the worker toward the company. Worker participation represents a major step in recognition of the importance of the worker to the company's success.

Recognition for a particular task or for accomplishments over a period of time may be given in many forms—as a news item in a paper; congratulations at a meeting of employees; a plaque or trophy; a change of title; addition of subordinates and responsibilities; time off; a vacation trip; election to an exclusive group of executives; key to the executives' washroom; larger, better-located, or refurnished office; or membership in a country club, among others.

A manager who gives such recognition on a regular basis according to the contingency model of reward provides reassurance to employees that each is an individual, not a machine.

> For decades the steel industry has operated basically as an autocratic industrial institution. Simply put—workers were hired to do exactly as ordered by their foreman. No questions, no back-talk. A good worker was one who showed up on time, every day, did as he was told and did not complain. Thus, a steelworker learned quickly that he was just a check number, hired to labor, with no right to use his experience, mind, or fulfill his desire to participate.
>
> A worker was stripped of dignity and pride. A worker wanted to believe in our system of democracy, but was puzzled by the absence of industrial democracy in the workplace for the major part of his life span. This workplace dissatisfaction has been compounded today by the growing fear of more layoffs and plant shutdowns—a combination that has resulted in workers being alienated from their company with no real concern or interest in production or product quality.
>
> The problem has become more acute due to the fact that steelworkers hired in the last two decades are a part of the new generation with changing cultural attitudes, who want more out of life than a paying job that robs them of their self-identity. They are demanding a job that gives satisfaction for personal input, and a feeling of having contributed something more than just their guts and sweat in the work process.[6]

Source: Sam Camens, Asst. to the President of the United Steelworkers of America, in a statement on "Labor–Management Participation Teams in the Basic Steel Industry," before the U.S. House of Representatives, Subcommittee on Oversight and Investigation, April 23, 1982.

Relations between Worker and Supervisor Good leadership usually implies good relations between worker and supervisor as discussed in Chapter 8, Motivation and Leadership for Productivity. The old heavy-handed authoritarian style of leadership tends to lower QWL in the modern workplace, whose workers are more highly educated.

Grievance Procedures and Due Process The ability of the worker to seek fair treatment from the company without jeopardizing employment has been a major gain. Both union and nonunion workers are usually granted grievance opportunities and due process protection from arbitrary sanctions by management. Note that managers and CEOs are not that well protected—it is not uncommon for a CEO to suddenly "resign" for "personal reasons."

Adequacy of Resources The institutionalization of long-range and short-range planning, as well as MBO, has led to greater matching of resources to stated objectives. It is less likely that a manager will be asked to establish worldwide sales and then be given a $5,000 annual budget. MBO, in particular, relates required resources to objectives.

Seniority and Merit in Employment For operating (shop) employees and unionized employees, seniority is perceived as the basis for advancement, perquisites, and layoffs. At the professional and managerial levels, merit (i.e., individual performance) is perceived as the fair basis for such personnel actions. In between, the clerical, supervisory, and subprofessional occupations may pose a problem for a company. Inappropriate treatment means lower QWL and possibly new unionization.

Limitations on Subcontracting Limitations on subcontracting reassure workers that employment is apt to be stable. Often subcontracting is an indication that the company is uncertain about its future. In addition, the less the subcontracting, the greater the opportunities for the employees. At the same time, management must continue to inform employees that subcontracting for peak periods means that workers will not have to be hired and laid off with each business cycle.

QWL AND MAINTENANCE CONCEPTS

The primary objective of the P/HR function is improving productivity through providing a motivating QWL. Earlier in the chapter we suggested criteria for a proactive approach in which the P/HR manager can actively advise and support line management in its day-to-day activities. This represents a proactive approach to HR management.

There is also a wide range of maintenance functions that are the responsibility of the P/HR manager. The principal objective of these maintenance functions is to build QWL. At the same time, some of these may improve productivity by reducing absenteeism, sick leave, alienation, or loss of valuable employees. These maintenance activities include traditional fringe benefits such as health insurance and pensions (these are discussed

QUALITY OF WORK LIFE AND EMPLOYEE MAINTENANCE

in detail in Chapter 14). They also include safety programs, suggestion systems, counseling programs, employee assistance programs, and workplace conveniences, among many others. The variety of such services is astonishing, as indicated in Exhibit 18–5.

EXHIBIT 18–5
P/HR services.

Medical and health

First-aid stations
Sick room
Nurse
Medical office/department
First-aid specialist
Doctor
Social worker
Psychologist
Psychiatrist
Dentist
Cardiopulmonary resuscitation

Blood bank
Physical exams
Blood-pressure checks
Alcohol and drug abuse programs
Vaccination/inoculation
Counseling for mental health
Eye exams
Quit-smoking program
Stress-reduction program
Weight-control program

Safety

OSHA

Safety training programs

Legal and financial services

Notary public
Credit union
Paychecks deposited in employee's bank
Paycheck cashing privileges at local bank
Scholarships/grants for employees' children

Financial counseling
Emergency loans
Legal advice
Income tax assistance
Savings incentive plans

Consumer services

Discounts on company products/services
Discounts on other companies' products/services

Consumer information programs/materials
Company store

Pensions and retirement services

Social Security
Company pension plans

ERISA

Transportation

Parking lot/garage
Carpool-formation assistance
Vanpool

Shuttlebus from outlying area to workplace
Subsidies for use of public transportation

Food

Vending machines
Subsidized cafeteria

Snack/sandwich counter
Dining room

Recreation

Outdoor playfields
Showers, lockers for sports
Conditioning facilities (exercise room, sauna, etc.)
Indoor sports facilities (gym, swimming pool, etc.)

Recreation park
Sports teams
Social interest groups

Career counseling and outplacement

Policy manual development

P/HR diagnostic, planning, and controlling reports

HR computer system

P/HR employee information reports

(HR computer reports to update employees on benefits status, sick leave, etc.)

IMPLEMENTATION OF EMPLOYEE MAINTENANCE AND SERVICE PROGRAMS

Implementing employee maintenance and service programs in medium to large companies will be a manager or a single specialist, who is responsible for each activity. Exhibit 18–6 shows typical reporting relationships. We will discuss the implementation of only a few of these services.

Safety

Safety and health at the workplace are both governed by OSHA regulations. In addition, general physical and mental health maintenance is programmed by many employers. General standards issued by OSHA cover several categories: (1) occupational health and environmental controls (sanitation, color codes, means of egress, walking and working surfaces); (2) hazardous substances and equipment; (3) protective services (equipment, medical, fire); (4) handling, storage, usage, guarding of materials and equipment; and (5) power tools, equipment using compressed gas and compressed air. In the past, OSHA conducted surprise inspections, and failure to meet standards resulted in citations and fines. More recently, emphasis has shifted to programs to encourage voluntary compliance. Inspectors must now give advance notice of their visits.

Need for Safety Legislation More than 80 million Americans spend their days on the job. Together, they are perhaps our most valuable national resource. Yet, until the recent past, no uniform and comprehensive provisions existed for their protection against workplace safety and health hazards.

In 1970, Congress considered annual figures such as these:

- Job-related accidents accounted for more than 14,000 worker deaths.
- Nearly 2.5 million workers were disabled.
- Ten times as many man-days were lost from job-related disabilities as from strikes.
- Estimated new cases of occupational diseases totaled 300,000.

In terms of lost production and wages, medical expenses, and disability compensation, the burden on the nation's commerce was staggering. Human cost was beyond calculation. Therefore, the Occupational Safety and Health Act of 1970 was passed by a bipartisan Congress *"to assure so far*

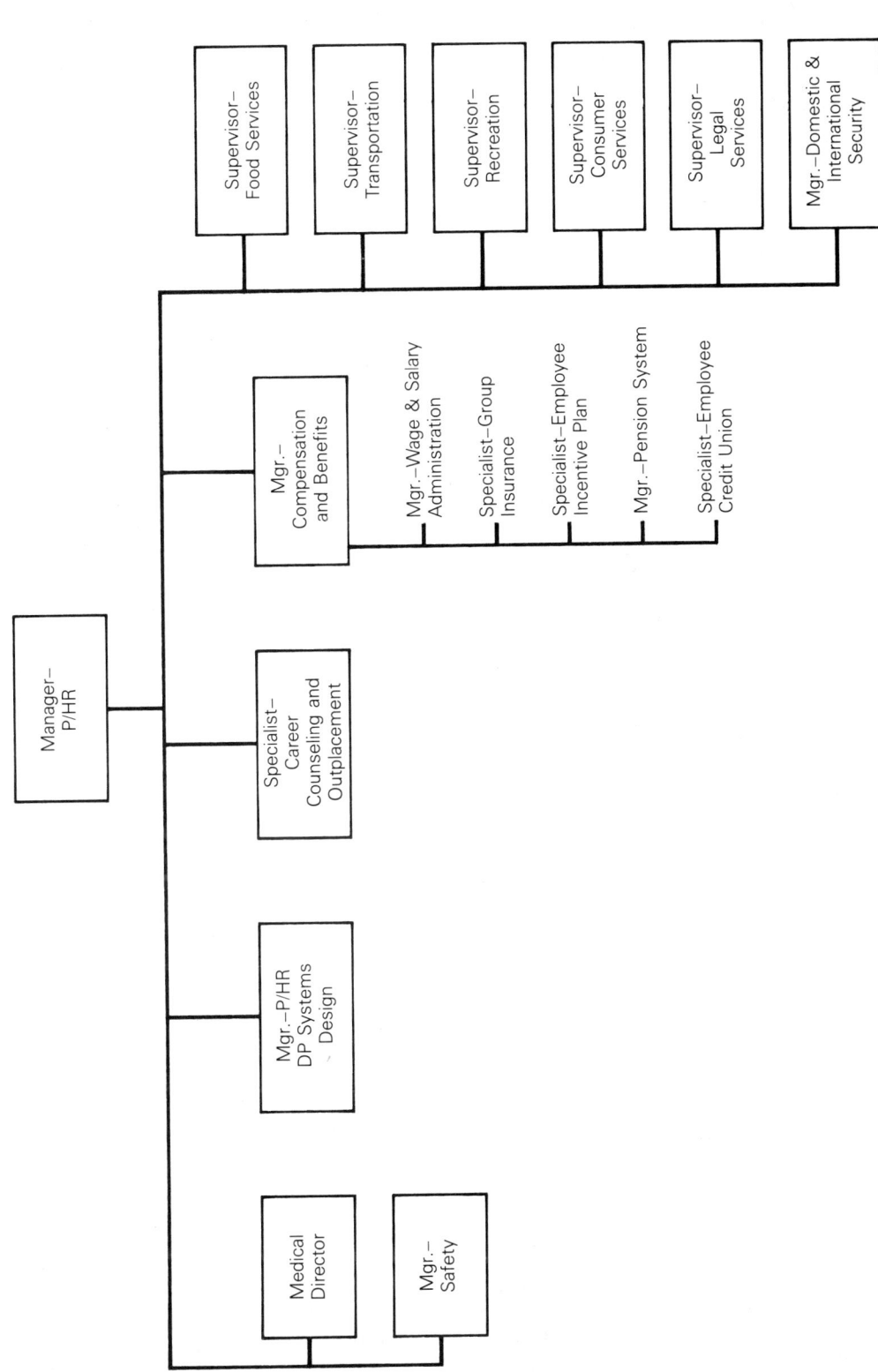

EXHIBIT 18-6
Partial organization chart showing placement of maintenance and service activities.

as possible every working man and woman in the Nation safe and healthful working conditions and to preserve our human resources."

OSHA's Purpose Under the provisions of the act, the Occupational Safety and Health Administration (OSHA) was created within the Department of Labor to:

- Encourage employers and employees to reduce hazards in the workplace and to improve existing safety and health programs or implement new ones
- Establish "separate but dependent responsibilities and rights" for employers and employees for the achievement of better safety and health conditions
- Establish reporting and recordkeeping procedures to monitor job-related injuries and illnesses
- Develop mandatory job safety and health standards and enforce them effectively
- Encourage the states to assume the fullest responsibility for establishing and administering their own occupational safety and health programs, which must be "at least as effective as" the federal program.

While OSHA continually reviews and redefines specific standards and practices, its basic purposes remain constant. OSHA strives to implement its Congressional mandate fully and firmly with fairness to all concerned. In all of its procedures, from standards development through implementation and enforcement, OSHA guarantees employers and employees the right to be fully informed, to participate actively, and to appeal its actions.

Standards The general duty clause of the Occupational Safety and Health Act states that each employer "shall furnish to each of his employees employment and a place of employment which are free from recognized hazards that are causing or are likely to cause death or serious physical harm to his employees."

In carrying out its duties under the act, OSHA is responsible for promulgating legally enforceable standards.

Employers may make application to OSHA for a variance from a standard or regulation if they lack the means to readily comply with it, or if they can prove that their facilities or methods of operation provide employee protection that is "at least as effective as" that required by OSHA.

Safety Administration OSHA defines specific responsibilities and rights for both employers and employees. One employer responsibility is to maintain a record of all occupational illnesses and injuries connected with his or her business. On forms OSHA-200, OSHA-101, and OSHA-102, all injuries that fall in the following categories must be recorded.

1. Death (regardless of length of time between injury and death)
2. One or more lost workdays
3. Restriction of work or motion
4. Loss of consciousness
5. Transfer to another job
6. Medical treatment other than first aid

Exhibit 18–7 shows Form OSHA-200, a log of occupational injuries and illnesses.

The safety program is usually administered by a safety manager or a safety specialist, who identifies areas of safety concern for the particular company and works with managers to identify specific hazards on a continuing basis, develops safety training programs, and develops safety policies. The safety manager in large companies must take a view of safety that transcends the mere meeting specific requirements. He or she should structure the entire program on the basis of hazard recognition, hazard analysis, hazard control, and then interface this system with medical treatment. Exhibit 18–8 shows such a program in more detail. The symptom that tells us that something is wrong with the safety system is the occurrence of an unsafe act, an unsafe condition, and an accident.

In addition, the safety specialist must keep up to date on OSHA regulations in the *Federal Register*, and insure that proper OSHA records are maintained by the HR data base manager. A computer-based HR information system permits easy development and transmission of reports to OSHA and other governmental agencies. In the event of an accident, the accident report is also used for worker's compensation evaluation. Exhibit 18–9 shows just such an accident report.

Medical and Health

The health and medical manager provides technical medical advice to the safety manager and provides a range of services from preventive health care to emergency medical treatment. Such services may consist of:

- Pre-employment screening physical exams
- Periodic physical exams
- Checks for blood pressure, diabetes, eye problems
- First aid/CPR training programs
- Vaccinations
- Quit-smoking and weight-control programs
- Counseling for mental health, alcoholism and drug abuse, and stress
- Blood bank
- First aid and emergency treatment, medications
- Reports on health problems that affect worker's compensation benefits

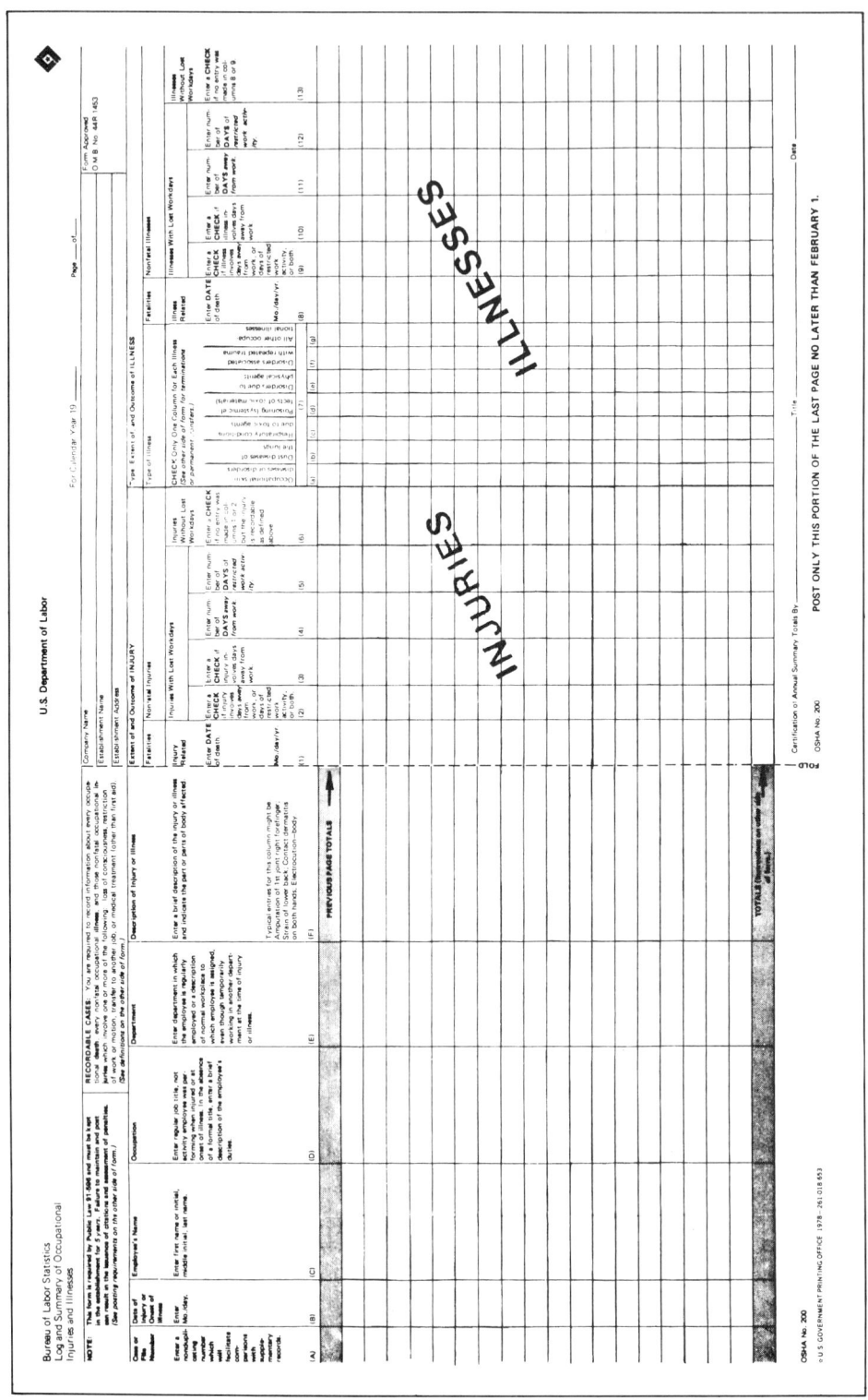

EXHIBIT 18–7 Log of occupational injuries and illnesses, Form OSHA-200.

EXHIBIT 18–8
The three aspects of safety.

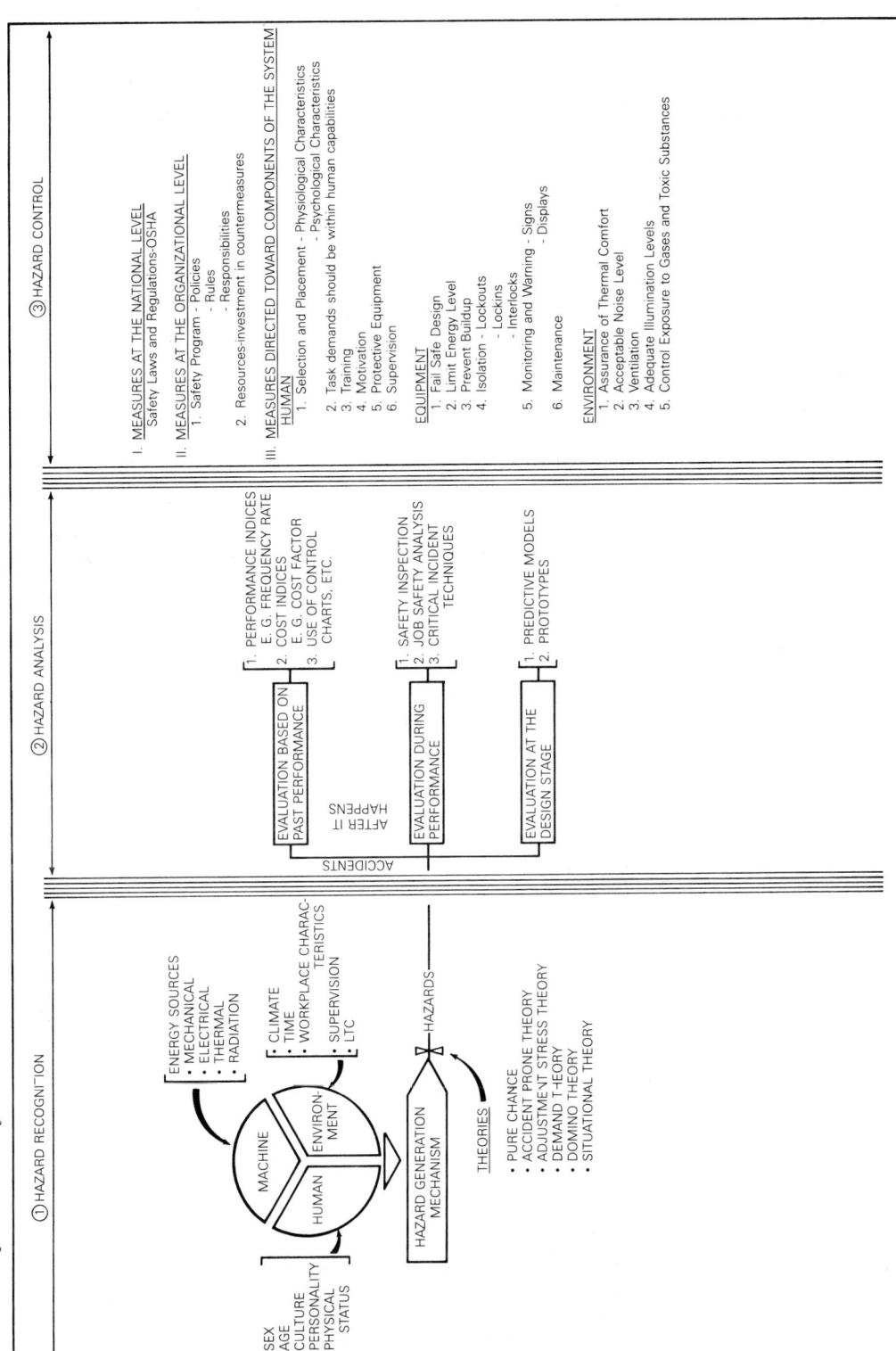

Source: Mahmoud A. Ayoub, "The Problems of Occupational Safety," *Industrial Engineering*, April 1975, p. 17. From Andrew R. Hale and Richard M. Hale, *A Review of Industrial Research Literature*, Committee on Safety and Health at Work Research Paper, London: HMSO, 1972.

OSHA No. 101
Case or File No. _____

Form approved
OMB No. 44R 1453

Supplementary Record of Occupational Injuries and Illnesses

EMPLOYER
1. Name _____
2. Mail address _____
   (No. and street)   (City or town)   (State)
3. Location, if different from mail address _____

INJURED OR ILL EMPLOYEE
4. Name _____ Social Security No. _____
   (First name)   (Middle name)   (Last name)
5. Home address _____
   (No. and street)   (City or town)   (State)
6. Age _____   7. Sex: Male _____ Female _____ (Check one)
8. Occupation _____
   (Enter regular job title, *not* the specific activity he was performing at time of injury.)
9. Department _____
   (Enter name of department or division in which the injured person is regularly employed, even though he may have been temporarily working in another department at the time of injury.)

THE ACCIDENT OR EXPOSURE TO OCCUPATIONAL ILLNESS
10. Place of accident or exposure _____
    (No. and street)   (City or town)   (State)
    If accident or exposure occurred on employer's premises, give address of plant or establishment in which it occurred. Do not indicate department or division within the plant or establishment. If accident occurred outside employer's premises at an identifiable address, give that address. If it occurred on a public highway or at any other place which cannot be identified by number and street, please provide place references locating the place of injury as accurately as possible.
11. Was place of accident or exposure on employer's premises? _____ (Yes or No)
12. What was the employee doing when injured? _____
    (Be specific. If he was using tools or equipment or handling material, name them and tell what he was doing with them.)
13. How did the accident occur? _____
    (Describe fully the events which resulted in the injury or occupational illness. Tell what happened and how it happened. Name any objects or substances involved and tell how they were involved. Give full details on all factors which led or contributed to the accident. Use separate sheet for additional space.)

OCCUPATIONAL INJURY OR OCCUPATIONAL ILLNESS
14. Describe the injury or illness in detail and indicate the part of body affected. _____
    (e.g.: amputation of right index finger at second joint; fracture of ribs; lead poisoning; dermatitis of left hand, etc.)
15. Name the object or substance which directly injured the employee. (For example, the machine or thing he struck against or which struck him; the vapor or poison he inhaled or swallowed; the chemical or radiation which irritated his skin; or in cases of strains, hernias, etc., the thing he was lifting, pulling, etc.)
16. Date of injury or initial diagnosis of occupational illness _____
    (Date)
17. Did employee die? _____ (Yes or No)

OTHER
18. Name and address of physician _____
19. If hospitalized, name and address of hospital _____

Date of report _____ Prepared by _____
Official position _____

EXHIBIT 18-9
Detailed OSHA report, Form OSHA-101.

EXHIBIT 18-10
Work-injury ratios by age.[1]

Age	Percent Employment Distribution[2]	Percent Work Injury Distribution	Work-Injury Ratio[3]
16-17	3.2	1.9	.59[4]
18-19	5.3	6.8	1.28
20-24	15.2	21.0	1.38
16-24	23.7	29.7	1.25
25-34	26.4	30.3	1.15
35-44	18.7	16.7	.89
45-54	17.6	13.6	.77
55-64	11.4	8.8	.77
65-	2.2	0.9	.41[4]

[1]Based on current cases in 26 states; includes illnesses.
[2]Industry employment source CPS data, 1977.
[3]The ratio computation is column 3 divided by column 2.
[4]Because of the relatively small magnitudes associated with one or both components in these ratios, the relative errors for these age groups would be larger than those for the other age groups.
Source: Norman Root, "Injuries at Work Are Fewer among Older Employees," *Monthly Labor Review,* March 1981, p. 31. Reprinted by permission.

Small companies may have a dispensary with a full-time nurse on duty. Larger companies have a well-equipped diagnostic facility with a physician full-time on the premises. Also, even small companies may employ a psychologist or psychiatrist on a part-time basis for counseling and mental health services. Of course, companies often provide extensive health insurance plans as a part of their total compensation and benefits package (see Chapter 14 for a detailed discussion of benefits). Moreover, under Title XIII of the Public Health Service Act of 1973, if a health maintenance organization (HMO) is offered in a geographical area in which employees of a company reside, the company is *required* to offer employees in the covered area the option of either continuing with the company health plan or joining the HMO and having the company contribute to it the same amount it now spends on employees in the company health plan.

In effect, it gives the employee the choice of staying with the company program or going with the HMO, in which case at least part of the HMO cost will be paid by the company (most HMOs would cost more than the company coverage).

Legal, Financial, and Consumer Services

The legal services for employees are likely to be supplied by the company's legal department. The P/HR manager must develop a policy and program approved by top management so that the legal department can allocate people to this activity. A major service traditionally provided is defense of an employee being sued for performing an act in the course of performing his job. At the top executive level, such suits are more frequent. Today, unions may also provide legal services for the members.

Financial services such as credit unions and emergency loans are usually the responsibility of a financial administrator rather than the P/HR department. Credit unions facilitate saving by the automatic withholding of a designated portion of an employee's wage or salary. The credit union also usually pays a little higher interest rate than banks. The P/HR department generally plans for, and initiates, financial services, obtains approval, and monitors the implementation.

By far the most common consumer service arranged for by P/HR is the discount on the purchase of company products.

Pensions and Retirement Services

There are three major types of pensions—legislated, company, and individual. Social Security is a legislated pension. The Social Security Act passed in 1935 was designed to supplement income of retired people, age 65 and older, by providing old-age, survivors', disability, and retirement benefits. It has gone through substantial changes, and people are relying increasingly on it for a major portion of their post-retirement income. Contributions, made through payroll deductions that are also matched by the employer, have not been able to keep up with outgoing payments in the last few decades, however, so that the fund keeps facing crises (see Exhibit 18–11). In 1983, Congress enacted legislation making major changes in Social Security to put it on a financially sound basis by simultaneously raising social security taxes and lowering benefits.

Combined Social Security and income tax deductions now reduce the employee's takehome pay by a significant amount. Whereas the accounting department programs the payroll deductions, it is the P/HR manager who

EXHIBIT 18–11A
The impact of new 1983 law on workers.

	Maximum Taxable Wage Base	Tax Rate on Wage Earner and Employer		Maximum Tax Each Year	
		Old Law	New Law	Old Law	New Law
1982	$32,400	6.70%	6.70%	$2,170.80	$2,170.80
1983	$35,700	6.70%	6.70%	$2,391.90	$2,391.90
1984	$37,500	6.70%	7.00%	$2,512.50	$2,625.00*
1985	$40,500	7.05%	7.05%	$2,855.25	$2,855.25
1986	$43,800	7.15%	7.15%	$3,131.70	$3,131.70
1987	$46,800	7.15%	7.15%	$3,346.20	$3,346.20
1988	$50,100	7.15%	7.51%	$3,582.15	$3,762.51
1989	$53,400	7.15%	7.51%	$3,818.10	$4,010.34
1990	$57,000	7.65%	7.65%	$4,360.50	$4,360.50

*Subject to a credit equal to 0.3% of wages.

EXHIBIT 18-11B
Dollar by dollar, the tax amount.

Earnings	$15,000	$20,000	$25,000	$30,000	$40,000
1983	$1,005	$1,340	$1,675	$2,010	$2,392*
1984	$1,050	$1,400	$1,750	$2,100	$2,625*
1985	$1,058	$1,410	$1,763	$2,115	$2,820
1986–87	$1,073	$1,430	$1,788	$2,145	$2,860
1988–89	$1,127	$1,502	$1,878	$2,253	$3,004
1990	$1,148	$1,530	$1,913	$2,295	$3,060

*Maximum for year based on maximum taxable wage base.
Note: Totals do not include refunded tax credit in 1984.
James Hildren, Robert A. Barr, Richard C. DeLouise, "Social Security to the Rescue—What It Means to You," *U.S. News & World Report,* April 4, 1983, pp. 23–25.

must consider the *impact* of these deductions in developing compensation plans.

Company pension plans are initiated voluntarily by companies who wish to supplement their employees' Social Security pensions.

Pension Plans Get More Flexible

When Robert B. Young, Jr. took over in 1980 as president of Lockheed Engineering & Management Services Co. (LEMSCO), he wanted to cut the cost of the company's pension plan, high by U.S. industry standards. He also needed a recruiting tool for engineers, computer programmers, and other technically skilled workers. Young's solution to both problems is a new retirement plan that guarantees immediate vesting and portability of pension contributions in place of a plan that required a worker to stay at LEMSCO at least 10 years to earn a pension. The LEMSCO plan may set a competitive standard for the aerospace industry, and it typifies the approach other employers may take as pressures increase for faster vesting for the 50 million workers covered by private pension plans.

Traditional pension plans have been unsuitable for employees of government contractors, says Young, who after 25 years in the aerospace industry had no vested pension benefits himself until 1980. This is because government contracts run from three to five years, forcing the 2 million employees of contractors to change employers frequently—and change pension plans long before their 10-year vesting date.

LEMSCO avoids this by vesting workers as soon as they join its new plan, after two years of service. Lockheed makes contributions ranging from 2% to 5% of pay, depending on seniority. When they leave, employees can roll over this money and the interest it has earned into another retirement vehicle. Previously, says Young, "if we lost our contract, most of our people would have nothing. Now they will get something."

Source: Reprinted from the November 8, 1982 issue of *Business Week* by special permission, © 1982 by McGraw-Hill, Inc.

The increase in Social Security benefits must also be considered by the P/HR manager in developing a company pension system. He or she must ask if the company should have a pension plan while keeping in mind that company pensions are useful in attracting and holding good employees because, unlike Social Security, benefits may be lost if an employee quits.

The Employee Retirement Income Security Act (ERISA) of 1974 was passed to regulate company pension plans or to protect long-term employees from loss of benefits. Now an employer who develops a private plan must give minimum vesting rights. (Vesting means that an employee receives benefits from the plan if he or she has contributed for a certain number of years regardless of whether he or she stays longer.) Under ERISA an employer must provide full vesting of pension rights after 10 years of service. Many companies with pension systems that did not meet ERISA requirements simply abolished their pension plans. The ERISA legislation also provides the basis for tax-favored Individual Retirement Accounts (IRAs), which are individually funded retirement plans.

The result of ERISA has been to protect many employees' pensions from the impact of dismissal, quitting, and mergers. The impact of a merger is a problem for the P/HR manager, who must make recommendations to management if the acquired company has no pension system, a better pension system, or a significantly different pension system.

One other weakness of company pensions is that many are not fully funded to pay off all their liabilities to former employees. The tremendous variation among companies in unfunded vested benefits in 1978 is evident:

Company	Unfunded Vested Benefits As Percent of Net Worth
Bendix	37.2
LTV	100.7
Lockheed	157.0
Westinghouse Electric	30.3

Finally, Individual Retirement Accounts (IRAs) may be offered through the company. For example, the company may arrange for payroll deductions to be paid to an insurance company. These deductions are not taxable as income until the employee receives an annuity in retirement, when his or her income will presumably be lower. Compound interest also accumulates on the principal before taxes so that the fund grows faster than direct personal investment.

Transportation

Transportation services may include a company bus that transports employees located in a particular area or development to and from work. Much more common is a shuttle running between two plants in the same city or nearby cities. Companies also have car pools whereby an employee may sign out a car for a long trip or an in-town errand. In addition, P/HR may provide in-plant vehicles for transporting visitors and workers around very large plants. Finally, the company may provide parking lots and designated parking spaces for employees and visitors. In crowded cities, such spaces represent a considerable enhancement in working conditions.

Food

Food services in the plant provide direct benefits to both the company and the employees. They may vary from a lunch room set aside with vending machines to a full-fledged cafeteria. For the company, it means that employees are less apt to return late from lunch. Fewer "brown bag" lunches also improve on sanitary conditions and appearance. The employees usually gain by being able to eat a leisurely lunch at low prices. Both company and workers may gain from lunchtime socializing, which may deal with business.

Recreation

The P/HR manager must give careful consideration to recreation facilities and activities. In some situations, employees may believe that the company is intruding on their personal lives. In other companies, however, employees may welcome such activities as building a company "family" (group cohesion). The services may be passive whereby playing fields, tennis courts, or a pool may be provided for those who desire them. At the other extreme, the company may organize teams to play other company teams, prepare fitness programs, encourage workers to participate, and donate trophies.

Career Counseling and Outplacement

Career assistance services should be supported by trained counselors. Line managers generally have a perspective that is limited to the line of progression they themselves are in. Further, they have little time for outplacement. (This topic has been covered in detail in Chapter 12.)

Policy Manual Development

In many small- to medium-size companies, the task of developing and maintaining the company policy manual is usually assigned to the P/HR manager. The manual communicates the philosophy of the company by explicitly stating company procedures and ranges of behavior for various situations. A company manual may be subdivided into such sections as Organization, Administration, Personnel, Operations and Planning, Finance, and Legal.

Policies are expressions of management's desires, and the P/HR manager is an advisor and interpreter. When a P/HR manager has carefully written out a policy desired by management, he or she must circulate it for formal approval by appropriate managers. Approved policies are inserted in a notebook, copies of which are filed with managers throughout the company. Updating is accomplished by circulating updated pages to managers recorded as having copies of the policy manual.

P/HR Diagnostic, Planning, and Controlling Reports

The HR computer system (or software system) makes possible a wide variety of reports for management. If the data base management system has been well designed and implemented, information may be quickly retrieved to help diagnose problems, and perform planning and control of the HR system. Diagnosis may be accomplished by obtaining trends, comparisons of current activities with objectives or industry standards, or classification of data to show differences among groups of people or situations. Such diagnosis may uncover deficiencies in the QWL.

As examples, consider the following:

1. Absenteeism is increasing slowly. Further data retrieval and classification show that, except for one department, absenteeism is actually stable throughout the company.

2. Company sales are projected to increase by 25 percent over the next three years. A computer-planning program that matches personnel to tasks and overhead shows that HR requirements will only increase by 5 percent, however, over the same period.

3. The number of days of sick leave being taken each year has increased per employee. Investigation determined that employees viewed sick leave as time to be taken off for personal business if it were not used up by the end of the year. The company, therefore, reversed its policies to allow a portion of sick leave to be carried over from year to year. It also clarified its policy on sick leave.

P/HR Employee Information Reports

A service supplied by most personnel departments that has grown increasingly important in recent years is a reporting of status to employees. The status of pension benefits, payroll and deductions, profit-sharing, sick leave days due, education and training summaries, seniority, and a personnel skills/job qualifications profile may be reported to each employee periodically.

QWL AND PRODUCTIVITY

Increased QWL may often be achieved at very little cost. For example, a revision to the compensation plan to achieve greater internal fairness may be a small one-time cost. Improved safety rules and some protective devices such as safety glasses in the plant may be introduced at negligible cost.

Worker recognition by the supervisors, awards and plaques for jobs well done, and news stories are low-cost items. Such actions may encourage workers to spend less time griping and more time trying to do a better job. In the case of safety improvements, lost time due to injuries also may be reduced. As a result of many such additions to QWL, output can be increased at low cost so that productivity (output/input) increases.

Unfortunately, continual increases in QWL eventually lead to decreasing productivity. For example, if wages and benefits are increased sufficiently, the unit cost of a product increases while worker output no longer increases. In other words, there is an optimum value of QWL, as measured by some index representing all the factors making up QWL, which produces a maximum productivity (Exhibit 18–12).

We do not imply that improved quality of work life leads to job satisfaction and then improved job performance. The idea that satisfaction "causes" improved performance has long been dismissed. (You may remember the distinction made by Herzberg between hygiene factors and motivators in Chapter 8.) In such research, however, performance has been narrowly defined as quantity of output or quality of craftsmanship. If performance is expanded to mean "good citizenship," job satisfaction appears to be strongly related to citizenship.[5] Good citizenship consists of such behavior as helping co-workers with a job-related problem, accepting orders with enthusiasm, promoting a positive team spirit, and accepting temporary unfavorable work conditions without complaint.

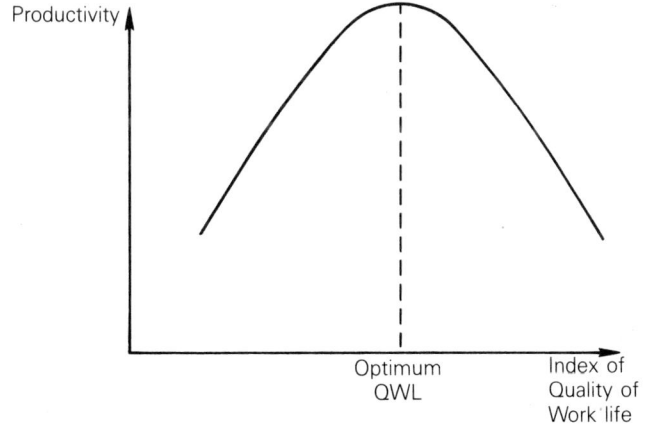

EXHIBIT 18–12
Productivity and quality of work life.

SUMMARY

The P/HR department has broadened its activities greatly in recent years. Overall, HR management is concerned with productivity and quality of work life (QWL). QWL action may be approached proactively to achieve motivation of workers. Management may also enhance QWL of employees by enhancing "fringe" benefits. These approaches are both included in a broad philosophical overview proposed by Richard E. Walton:

- Adequate and fair compensation
- Safe and healthy working conditions
- Opportunity to use and develop human capacities
- Future opportunity for continued growth and security
- Social integration in the work organization
- Constitutionalism in the work organization
- Work and the quality of life
- The social relevance of work life

The maintenance services that support QWL are:

- Medical, health, and safety
- Legal and financial services
- Consumer services
- Pensions and retirement services
- Transportation
- Food
- Recreation
- Career counseling and outplacement
- Policy manual development
- Diagnostic, planning, and controlling reports for P/HR employee information reports

Most companies do not measure productivity changes against expenditures for improved QWL. Because so many other factors influence productivity, this may be impossible to do. The enlightened organization should attempt it, however. Companies with a low index of QWL may well achieve higher productivity by increasing QWL.

KEY CONCEPTS

QWL	Alternative work schedules
Quality of life	Employee maintenance
Constitutionalism in the work place	OSHA
	HMO
Occupational stress	Outplacement
Wellness program	

REVIEW AND DISCUSSION QUESTIONS

1. Discuss QWL in relation to productivity.
2. Make a list of all factors that you can think of that could produce stress on the job.
3. Discuss how occupational stress, alternative work schedules, and corporate wellness programs are related to each other and to productivity.
4. (a) Sketch a rectangle and label the bottom side "Time," going from 6 A.M. to 10 P.M. Show an alternative work schedule, first, by shading portions of the rectangle for a required core time of 10 A.M. to 2 P.M., and, then, by indicating two possibilities for an individual who likes to start work early and quit early. (b) Discuss the practicality of allowing some employees to work half-time at home and half-time at the office.
5. Merit is used as the basis for advancement in the office. Why should it be used or not used as the basis for pay in the shop as a factor in QWL?
6. The cost of administering OSHA is very large in terms of expense both to the government and to employees. Discuss whether from a cost–benefit view you believe OSHA is justified.
7. Develop, in general terms, a pension plan that would be fair to employees and employers. Take into account such ideas as security, worker mobility, employer cost, etc.
8. Give the pros and cons of having the I.R.S. tax employees for maintenance and service program benefits that they receive.
9. Give the pros and cons of having an executive dining room.
10. Describe the kinds of employee information reports that you believe are cost-effective.

NOTES

1. "Tropic Magazine," *Miami Herald*, July 11, 1982, pp. 1–2.
2. Richard E. Walton, "Quality of Working Life: What Is It?" *Sloan Management Review*, Fall 1973.
3. "Interview with Thorne Auchter, Administrator, Occupational Safety and Health Administration," *U.S. News and World Report*, July 19, 1982, p. 71.
4. Fritz K. Pious, Jr., "Working at Home Appeals to Few; Unions and Others Foresee Problems," *World of Work Report*, May 1, 1982, p. 1.
5. Thomas A. Mahoney, "The Rearranged Work Week." © 1978 by the Regents of the University of California. Reprinted from *California Management Review*, volume XX, no. 4, p. 39, by permission of the Regents.
6. Thomas S. Bateman and Dennis W. Organ, "Job Satisfaction and the Good Soldier: The Relation between Affect and Employee 'Citizenship,'" *Academy of Management Journal*, December 1983, pp. 587–595.

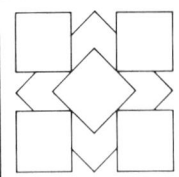

CASE STUDY:
How Much Better Must a Junior Employee Be to Win a Bid over a Senior Man?

What Happened:

When personnel director Bob Nelson arrived and saw the two men impatiently pacing in front of his office, he mentally groaned: "*Not* before my morning coffee!"

Then he said: "I know, I know. Sam, here, feels he should have won that bid on the flaker operator job. But our plant manager, Jim Mayer, put up a convincing case for promoting the junior man."

"He may have convinced you," the steward replied, "but not us. We're here to give the company a chance to correct its mistake. Otherwise, we're going to fight this right through arbitration."

"Okay, let's go over it. We put up the job for bids. If two men are eligible, the senior man gets the job—provided abilities are relatively equal. Sam is the senior man, but he got turned down."

The personnel director then enumerated the manager's reasons:

1. The manager asked six foremen to evaluate the two men and to consider eight criteria: Mechanical aptitude, ability to follow written instructions, ability to keep written records, judgment, initiative and attitude, health, responsibility, seniority.
2. When the scores were in, every one of the six said that Ralph had the edge over Sam.
3. Also, Ralph had worked three months on the flaker job—so he even had experience.

"None of that proves Sam can't handle the job. The junior man may be a little better—but that doesn't give him the right to promotion over a senior man," persisted the steward.

Source: The newsletter *Employee Relations in Action*, (New York: Business Research Publications, Inc., 1973). Reprinted by permission.

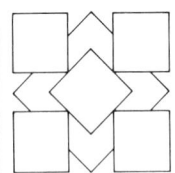

CASE STUDY:
Can You Bar Employees from Discussing Their Salaries among Themselves?

The Problem:

"I'm getting a measly $435 a month," Eunice Gilmer lamented to a co-worker. "The personnel director, Mrs. Bickley, promised I'd get a raise as soon as I proved my worth. I'm still waiting." She also talked to another employee—who agreed they were underpaid.

Eunice became so resentful that she reminded Mrs. Bickley of her "promise." The personnel executive denied making such a commitment. Later that day,

Eunice's co-worker asked for a raise and was turned down too.

The personnel chief learned that Eunice was voicing salary dissatisfaction with co-workers. She reminded her that the company forbade employees to discuss their salaries with each other—and fired Eunice for violating this rule.

Eunice then haled the employer before the National Labor Relations Board on unfair labor practice charges. The company insisted:

- ☐ Eunice violated our rule that employees keep salaries confidential from co-workers.
- ☐ The ban helps us prevent jealousy and resentment by employees who earn less because they have less skill or seniority.
- ☐ We haven't violated the National Labor Relations Act. We haven't interfered with employee efforts to organize a union or bargain collectively.

Eunice replied stoutly: "We need not organize a union to get N.L.R.B. protection. It's enough if a few employees act together to improve conditions."

Source: The newsletter *White-Collar Management* (New York: Business Research Publications, 1981). Reprinted by permission.

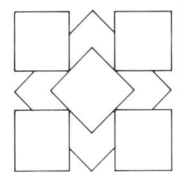

CASE STUDY:
Certified Health Delivery Systems (A)

Certified Health Delivery Systems (CHDS) is a medium-sized health care organization located in the midwestern United States. CHDS provides part-time, intermittent skilled nursing and rehabilitative services to homebound individuals at their place of residence. The organization provides nursing care, physical and occupational therapy, speech therapy, hospice care and the services of medical social workers and nutritionists. These services are provided under the guidance of the patient's own physician.

CHDS is operated as a non-profit organization and employs a field staff of 30 registered nurses, 1 nutritionist, and 32 other non-professionals. A support staff of 25 is maintained in the home office (see Exhibits A and B for the organizational charts). The professional staff works out of seven field offices which cover a radius of 125 miles. The field offices report directly to the director of professional services who is based in the home office. For 1979, CHDS had a total operating budget of approximately two million dollars.

Background

CHDS had never had a formalized labor relations program to deal with unions or employee grievances. It had always been the feeling of the home office staff that the employees of CHDS were professionals and thus would be adverse to any overtures by unions. The employees of a similar organization had recently voted in a union (Federated Nurses), but this home health agency was located in a large metropolitan area and it was felt that different environmental factors were at work there. Thus,

611

the management of CHDS was astonished when they received notice from the National Labor Relations Board (NLRB) in September of 1979 indicating that the Federated Nurses (FN) had filed a petition demanding recognition as the exclusive bargaining agent for all the registered nurses employed by CHDS.

After reviewing the situation, the Director of Professional Services reached the conclusion that the impetus for the recognition petition derived from a dispute over mileage reimbursement paid to the nurses. It had been the practice for each nurse to provide her own transportation when she traveled to and from the homes of patients and she would be reimbursed at a rate of 17¢ per mile traveled. On the average, each nurse would travel 30 miles a day, five days a week. Early in March of 1979, the staff made a formal request for a raise in mileage reimbursement. This request was given to the Executive Director of CHDS who indicated that the matter would be considered by the finance committee of the board of directors. Spurred by this request, the Executive Director had a series of meetings with the nursing supervisors concerning salary adjustments for certain job classifications, redesigning of jobs, and improvements in fringe benefits. During these discussions several alternative plans were drawn up for discussion. In May these alternatives were presented to the board of directors for consideration. The board decided, in light of a projected operating deficit for the current fiscal year of $30,000, to reject all of these proposals. After the results of this meeting were made known, the nurses complained to the Director of Professional Services that they were becoming frustrated and dissatisfied with a number of factors. They considered management to be unresponsive to their problems, the gasoline crisis was causing rising fuel prices and long lines and they felt that their patient load was being slowly increased. They pleaded with her to present their case to the board for an increase in the mileage rates to at least 25¢ a mile. In June this request was denied by the board. They cited the fact that the organization was still operating in the red and that other similar agencies in the area were only paying 16¢ per mile. At the July board meeting the Director of Professional Services again expressed her concern over the high level of agitation being caused among the staff over this issue. The board voted to table her request until the September meeting. They stated for the record that they would consider increasing the mileage reimbursement rate provided that the organization is out of the red and that productivity is increased.

At this point the Director of Professional Services, who was enrolled in a survey course in Management/Labor relations at a local university as a part of her MBA work, became increasingly concerned over the volume of complaints from the professional staff. She feared a union representation petition or even the possibility of a strike by the nurses. However, she was frustrated in her attempts to alleviate this situation due to the absence of the Executive Director who was on a three week vacation in Europe. When the Executive Director returned in late July she was able to convince him of the seriousness of the situation. He then informed the board who called an emergency meeting in mid-August. At this meeting an increase in the mileage rate to 20¢ was approved, retroactive for one week.

The Organizing Campaign

Upon receipt of the representation petition, the Director of Professional Services was placed in charge of the campaign to keep the union out. She was assisted in this task by the attorney who was on retainer to CHDS. The first issue faced was the determination of the appropriate bargaining unit. FN wanted to include in the unit only registered nurses and the nutritionist. CHDS wanted to include all the field employees in the unit. There were two reasons why management wanted the larger unit. First, they felt that if the union did win, it would be desirable to have only one contract and one union to deal with. But of more importance, it was felt that the support for the union was much weaker in the lower levels of staff personnel (non-professional) and that the inclusion of these individuals would greatly weaken the union's chances of winning the election. After a lengthy hearing, the NLRB decided that the appropriate unit would be only the registered nurses and the nutritionist. The NLRB further ordered that due to the geographical distances involved, that the election would be conducted by a mail ballot. The election was to be held two weeks after the date of the hearing and the voters were to be allowed two weeks to mail in their ballots (all campaigning was to be stopped when the ballots were mailed out). CHDS's campaign was based on a strategy of mail out literature and a series of meetings with the employees in the field. Exhibit C contains a representative sample of the letters mailed by CHDS to eligible voters in the unit. In scheduling the meetings in the field, the Director of Professional Services was careful to try to bring together the field offices in such a way that she would match one office that seemed to be leaning toward the union with one that seemed to have a majority sympathy against the union. This strategy seemed to be somewhat successful as those who were against the union were willing to voice their opposition and thus enable much of the anti-union statements to come from co-workers rather than directly from management, allowing the management representative to take a somewhat passive role.

The union relied on a campaign of union literature mailed to the employees, personal contact with each employee in the unit, and small meetings in the homes of pro-union nurses employed by CHDS. Their major appeals were based on two points:

1. Poor wages and working conditions at CHDS
2. The failure of management to listen to the complaints of the employees

The union lost the election by a wide margin. Of thirty-one eligible voters, 20 voted no representation, 8 voted for the union, 2 abstained and one ballot was voided due to technical violations.

The day after the election results were certified by the NLRB, the union filed an unfair labor practice charge seeking to have the election results thrown out. They charged that the management had engaged in coercion, intimidation and threats against those who voted against the union. They cited the group meetings with the nurses in the field offices and the mail out literature as proof of these charges.

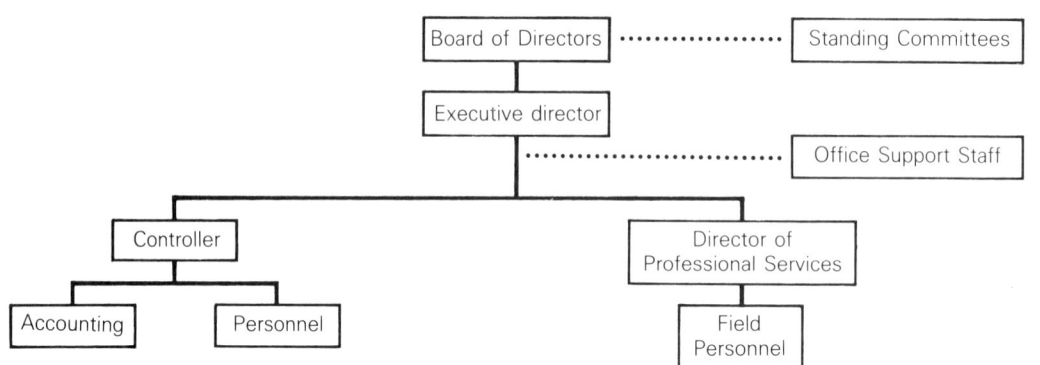

EXHIBIT A
Organizational chart—Certified Health Delivery Systems.

EXHIBIT B
Field office personnel—Certified Health Delivery Systems.

Office Number	Registered Nurses	Nutritionist	Other
1	9	0	8
2	5	0	6
3	2	0	3
4	4	0	3
5	2	0	3
6	2	0	2
7	6	1	7
Total	30	1	32

Note: Each office also contracts out services when needed.

EXHIBIT C
Campaign letters—Certified Health Delivery Systems

October 26, 1979

Dear Fellow Employee:

This is the first of a number of leaflets planned to provide you with accurate information so that you can make an informed decision about your future and about the Certified Health Delivery Systems.

I am sure all of you are aware that a union has been trying to organize the registered nurses at Certified Health Delivery Systems for some time. We believe that you should have a right to vote in secret whether or not you want a union. At the same time we believe that you should have all of the information necessary to make an informed decision when you vote.

We have recently received notification from the National Labor Relations Board that an agency of the United States Government is directing a mail election. The election will be held sometime in November. As soon as we are informed of the exact date, we will let you know. Between now and then you will have to decide for yourself whether you are better off with or without a union. Your decision will affect your future. I am deeply concerned about you making the right decision. I want to make my position very clear to you. I am strongly opposed to a union representing any of our employees, be they registered nurses, licensed vocational nurses or anyone else.

I have been asked whether we would have to agree to what the union asks if it should win the election. While we would, of course, negotiate in good faith with the union, we would not be able to agree to anything that is improper or unreasonable for Certified Health Delivery Systems.

I have also been asked whether, if the union won, the end result would be more or less in wages and benefits. The answer is simple. Everything is negotiable. This means that you could end up with higher wages than you have been receiving in the past, the same amount, or less. The same thing would be true of fringe benefits, such as health insurance.

It is unfortunate that unions very often make inflated promises to employees during the pre-election period. Promises are easy to make when you don't have to deliver on them.

Unions sometimes strike to force a company to do some things which it wouldn't agree to do voluntarily. You all know the hardships that can occur during a strike; you read about it in the newspapers every day. What you may not know is that a company can lawfully, permanently replace employees who engage in an economic strike. A company's only obligation to employees who wish to return to work is to place striking employees on a preferential hiring list and to hire from this list if and when openings occur.

The union will ask you to vote for it and suggest that if you want to change your mind, you can vote it out any time want to. The fact is, it is much easier to bring in a union than to get rid of one.

What do you know about this union? Have you read its Constitution? Have you read its Bylaws? Do you know if this union is affiliated with any larger union, such as the Teamsters? As a union member, you would be bound to follow every rule in this Constitution. Have you learned what it costs to join the union? Do you know what the monthly dues, assessments and fines of the union are?

Lastly, I would like to talk to you about our philosophy. We are a professional organization offering professional services to a very large community. We consider each of you professionals with tremendous responsibility and we expect you to exercise your independent judgement with every patient with whom you have contact. We do not believe that this type of relationship can be enhanced through unionization.

All of us want better things in life for ourselves and our families. I believe that at Certified Health Delivery Systems this can be achieved without a union. Sharing the rewards of our profession is a fundamental principle which unites us all.

I will be talking with you in the very near future and providing you with additional material to think about. I am sure you will agree after considering all the facts that you are better off without a union. If you have any questions, please feel free to come and discuss them with me. Thank you.

Sincerely,

Mary Bunting, Director
Professional Services

November 1, 1979

Dear Fellow Employee:

Enclosed with this letter is a bill you might receive if you became a member of a union.

This bill is an obligation you could assume if you vote to place yourself under the control of the union. Part of the bill is for the monthly dues you would have to pay.

Part of the bill is for fines that could be levied against you by the union for failure to attend union meetings—or refusing to march in picket lines—or simply as "discipline" for not following union orders.

These are a few of the ways the union takes a large part of your pay check. If the union gets in, you could receive a monthly bill from it for the rest of your working life.

You may want to think about this and decide to invest your money differently.

Mary Bunting, Director
Professional Services

....

BILL

Federated Nurses

Ms. Jane Doe, R.N.
Certified Health Delivery Systems

UNION BANK ACCOUNT (no money-back guarantee if we don't deliver on our promises)

DUES	$ _____
Initiation Fee	_____
Fines	?
Strike Fund Assessment	?
Other Special Assessments	_____
TOTAL PAYMENT DUE AFTER JOINING	UNLIMITED

November 5, 1979

Dear Fellow Employee:

I wrote to you recently about union fines. They are used, as you know, by unions to punish members for violating union-made rules. The following are actual cases in which union members have been fined by their unions:

REASONS	AMOUNT OF FINE
A union member attended church instead of a union meeting	$ 5.00
A union member refused to walk a picket line (per month)	50.00
A union member exceeded union-set production quotas.................................	100.00
A union member refused to comply with order of union business agent	300.00
A union member filed unfair labor practice charges against the union.....................	450.00
A union member informed the company that a fellow employee union member had violated company rule	500.00
A union member made derogatory remarks about the union and its officials...............	1,000.00
A union member refused to join a strike	2,000.00
A union member returned to work during a strike	3,651.28

Why put yourself in a position where this could happen to you?

Mary Bunting, Director
Professional Services

November 8, 1979

(letter individually addressed to all nurses and nutritionists eligible to vote in the union election)

In the next few days you will be asked to decide whether you wish to be represented by a union. Before you make a final decision, I would like to share a few thoughts with you.

Certified Health Delivery Systems is a small, nonprofit community agency and by its very nature is different from most other types of organizations. We have very limited control over our revenue, we have a policy and tradition of providing care to all patients regardless of ability to pay, and in order to provide services throughout our service area we have numerous relatively small offices as opposed to a single, more efficient office.

The point I would like for you to consider is that a union is usually chosen for the purpose of making major changes, particularly economic changes. Our resources, as with our sources of revenue, are limited and thus the amount of money available to the Board of Directors for salaries and other related costs is similarly limited. Our financial situation varies from year to year. For example, during the first three months of this year the agency had a net loss of $31,420. This loss has since been reduced to slightly over $14,000. A new and very important factor affecting our financial situation is the cost limitation being imposed by Medicare on all home health agencies. Our limitation will begin effective January 1, 1980. As you can see, the flexibility to make economic changes is extremely limited. Therefore, the benefit that the union offers may prove to be illusionary. Their ability to bargain and make changes is necessarily limited to the resources of the CHDS. Yet, you will continue to pay union dues.

Questions concerning our financial status have been asked during recent meetings. I would like to point out that we post a complete financial statement each month. If you have not done so in the past, please review these statements as they contain complete and detailed information concerning our financial status. If you have any questions, please contact Mary or myself for additional information.

Finally, I urge you to vote in any manner that will serve your interest best. I sincerely believe you should vote against union representation, but above all, please consider the facts and vote!

Sincerely,

William R. Graves
Executive Director

November 7, 1979

Dear Fellow Employee:

I felt you might be interested in some news items that have appeared in the past on the front page of the New York Times:

UNION ORDERS 8,500 TO PARADE OR PAY

Approximately 8,500 union painters, decorators and paperhangers have been ordered to participate in next Monday's Labor Day parade here or be subject to fines.

The members of District Council 9 of the Painters, Decorators and Paperhangers Union have been told that the council designated the occasion as a mandatory picketing day in accordance with its bylaws and that any member who failed to report for a place in the parade would be fined. The members of the union were informed of the decision by postcard. The message from the council prescribed the parade uniform for its members.

What happens to members who refuse to parade? Is a fine imposed? The following Letter to the Editor of the New York Daily News illustrates one person's experience.

ONE WORKER'S UNION

My union gave us notice to march in the Labor Day parade. I had to refuse because I had to attend my grandfather's birthday celebration, so I was fined $30. When I objected to the fine, my employer had to suspend me for two weeks' layoff for insubordination to union officials. I was fined another $20 for objecting to that. I then managed to get hold of a restricted mimeographed copy of our union bylaws. It stated that fines of union members become the property of union officials, so our union officials have managed to make a profit of about $3,000 for their Labor Day efforts. Nice, maybe, for a down payment on a girlfriend's apartment?

Need any more be said? When you vote *NO UNION*—you vote *NO FINES*.

Mary Bunting, Director
Professional Services

Source: This case was prepared by John Chaney and Alicia Quiroz as a basis for class discussion rather than to illustrate either effective or ineffective handling of an administrative situation. Copyright © 1980 by John Chaney and Alicia Quiroz

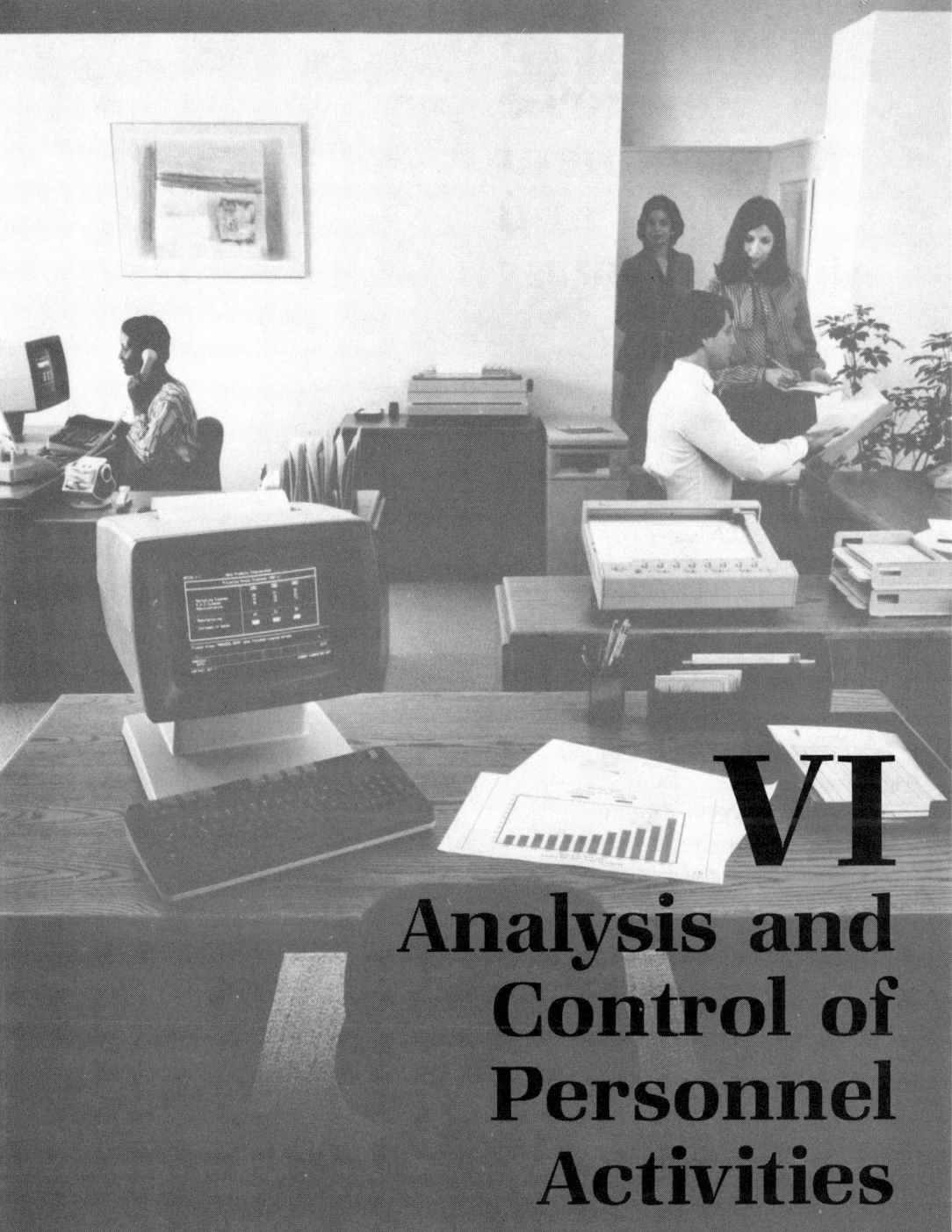

VI
Analysis and Control of Personnel Activities

The Human Resource Management System and the Computer

19

CHAPTER OUTLINE

What *Is* a System?

Environment and Subsystems

Advantages of the Systems Perspective
Clearer Thinking about Human Resource Management □ Combination of All Other Approaches □ Facilitation of the Manager's Job

Dimensions of a System: Operations and Information

Developing and Installing the HR Management System
Design Phase □ Implementation Phase □ Operational Phase □ Maintenance Phase

The Computer-Based HR Information System
Manual HR Information Systems □ Computerized Files and Data Processing Systems □ Data Base Management System (DBMS) □ Security, Privacy, and Protection against Threats

Role of the Computer in Modern HR Management Systems

OBJECTIVES

1. Define a system and the systems approach
2. Prepare a block diagram of HR management operations and information flow
3. Describe the major steps in developng a HR management system
4. Describe the general nature of the HR data base management system
5. Distinguish between privacy and security in a computerized HR management system

SPOTLIGHT:
Sidney H. Simon

Sidney H. Simon is Corporate Vice President and Product Manager at Tesseract Corporation. He formerly was Manager of Personnel Information and Benefits Administration, Bechtel Power Corporation in San Francisco, Ca. Mr. Simon received a B.S. in Industrial Engineering from Pennsylvania State University and an M.S. in Management Science from West Coast University. After graduation from Pennsylvania State, he was employed by TRW as a programmer/analyst. Mr. Simon became associated with human resource systems initially from a data processing perspective. His career path has remained basically in the data processing area related to human resource management through systems analysis, project management, and management roles.

Mr. Simon has a broad background in systems work based on employment with TRW Systems, Equity Funding Corporation, System Development Corporation, and Bechtel. In addition, he is the founder of the Association of Human Resource Professionals, a professional society serving the needs of people interested in the many aspects of human resource systems.

Comments by Sidney Simon

My philosophy has been to support all aspects of business with computer systems to help people do their jobs better. The personnel department has, in general, been the last major corporate function to utilize computers and other forms of automation. What is important is that most companies, regardless of size and business type, realize that managing today's labor force is already a complex issue and becoming more so. With labor costs continually escalating, management's requirements for accurate and timely work force information are becoming more critical to a company's operation. The personnel department is constantly being requested to provide the needed work force status and planning information, and it must be able to respond in a reasonable time frame.

To be responsive to managers' requests, personnel needs some type of automated system. Whatever name it is called—personnel data system, human resource system, HRIS, employee data system, and so forth—its basic purpose will be the same: effective and efficient management of the company's greatest asset, its people. Obtaining, installing, and operating a human resource management system is not a simple job. Although all such systems may do the same basic job, satisfying the same basic objectives and goals, there are many differences in the manner in which they are designed, constructed, and operated. Personnel's real requirements and operating environment must be clearly understood and defined before any automated system can be selected and implemented.

Defining personnel's information needs is not an easy task because they are constantly changing. This is due to many issues over which personnel has little control, such as management changes, reorganizations, and new legislation/regulations. Today's human resource management systems must be designed and developed to meet tomorrow's needs. This is a real challenge in which personnel must be willing to participate.

Personnel must be more than just involved in the process of obtaining and implementing a human resource management system—*Personnel must be committed.* Personnel representatives should be permanently assigned to a project team responsible for defining the needs, evaluating alternatives for implementing a solution, and implementing the accepted solution. In some instances, personnel should manage the project team assembled for this purpose. A lack of leadership from personnel will result in either no system being implemented or in a system that does not satisfy the needs of the organization when installed. Personnel's human resource management system representatives must also insure that all other personnel-related issues are not overlooked.

The automated human resource management system is really only a portion of the total personnel system. The automated components must be well integrated with the other personnel system functions, such as policy, procedures, communications, and organization structures. These other personnel functions can have a major effect on the automated features and must be addressed on a continuing basis.

This chapter is concerned with those issues noted above. A conceptual approach is presented to insure that all items are covered in a logical manner. Application of the principles must be tailored to the particular personnel organization and its operating environment.

Every day we hear about new kinds of systems or old ideas expanded into systems. We read about home heating systems, plumbing systems, sewage systems, airline systems, home computer systems, and ecological systems. No longer do we buy cameras, shelves, or razors; we buy photographic systems, shelving systems, and shaving systems. In these modern times, we have all adopted the "systems perspective." In this chapter, we will amplify on how we can take a systems view of HR management with computerized processing of information.

In the past, some scholars have studied HR management in terms of the functional or process view by describing the activities performed. Other scholars focused on the behavioral aspects of HR management. One viewed HR management as diagnosis of problems and their solutions. Others have viewed it as an information flow and decision process.

The systems view integrates and combines all approaches and knowledge about HR management. For this reason, it is important for us to understand the nature of systems and how they work. In addition, modern computer technology makes it important for us to understand computer-based information systems as an aid to HR management.[1]

WHAT *IS* A SYSTEM?

The concept of *system* has been defined and used by many scientists and scholars in such diverse fields as physics, sociology, psychology, mathematics, cybernetics, and management.[2] Systems have evolved in businesses over time as business and its environment have grown larger and more complex. We have, therefore, progressed from talking about individuals, pieces of equipment, and other parts of a company to talking about mixed groups of elements that are combined to work toward clearly specified mutual objectives.

A system is, simply, a group of people and things *working together* to achieve some *common set of goals*. A system is basically a *processor* of inputs designed to achieve specified outputs. In Exhibit 19–1, several examples of systems and their characteristics are given to clarify the system concept.

From Exhibit 19–1, we note that the HR management system acts upon, or *processes*, employees to transform them into more productive, and perhaps more fulfilled, people. The system also produces reports for managers and the government. Exhibit 19–2 amplifies this important system.

The HR management system (HRMS) is an unusual, if not unique, system. Exhibit 19–3 shows how the HRMS processes an employee in terms of assigning work, training the employee, appraising and compensating the employee, and administering the employee's benefits. In Exhibit 19–3a,

EXHIBIT 19-1
Some systems and their basic characteristics.

System	Basic Goals	Elements	Inputs	Outputs
Manufacturing company	Produce goods at a profit	Managers Professionals, operative employees Equipment Facilities	Materials Energy (light, power) Information	Products Information
University	Improve education of people Conduct research and disseminate results	Faculty, administration, support people Buildings Equipment Books	Students Information Energy	Educated students Research Community services
Bank	Store money for customers Provide loans, trust services, checking services, and credit	People, buildings, machines, money	Money, information, energy	Money, services, information
HR management system	Acquire, develop, and maintain a highly productive work force Improve employee satisfaction	All company managers Personnel specialists Equipment Facilities	Candidates for jobs All employees Retirees Information Energy	Productive employees More satisfied employees Reports required by management and the government

manager A is an element of the system that processes another employee. In Exhibit 19-3b, the HR management system processes manager A in his or her role as an *input* to the system that acts upon manager A. That is, the system appraises, compensates, etc., manager A in his or her role as an input.

From the above discussion, we see that we may describe a system by simply describing:

1. System goals
2. Elements and their behavior
3. System structure, or the relationships among the parts
4. System processes, or the activities that go on to achieve common goals and information flow
5. Inputs and outputs of the system

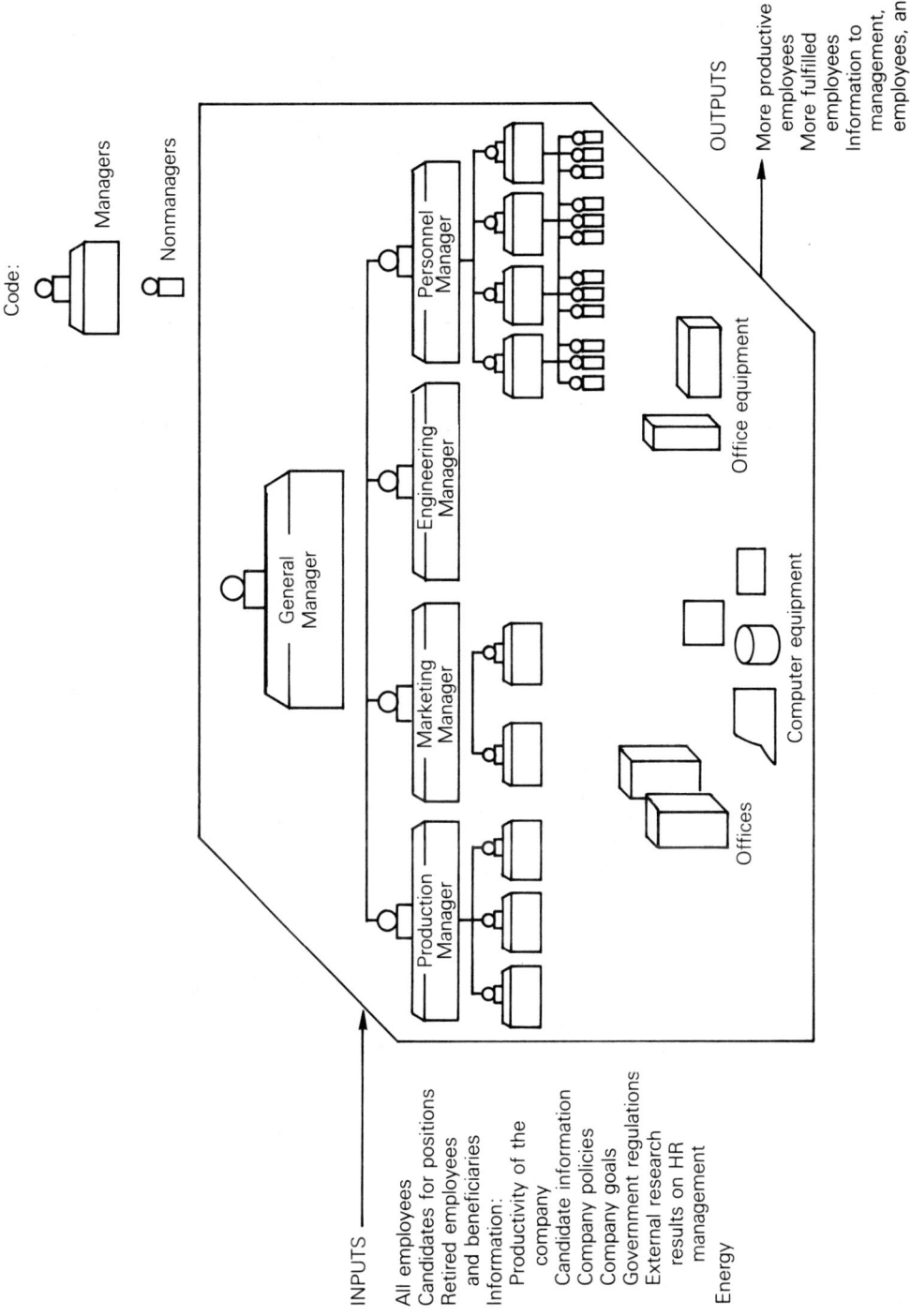

EXHIBIT 19–2
Human resource management system.

EXHIBIT 19–3
Dual role of the manager as system element and as system input in the HR management system (HRMS).

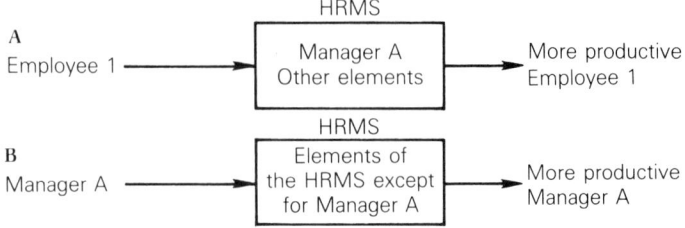

ENVIRONMENT AND SUBSYSTEMS

Where do inputs come from and outputs go to? The answer is the environment. Anything that is not a part of the system is "outside" the system. For example, if we focus on a particular business as a system, the environment consists of competitors, the economic system, the legal system, the social system, and, in fact, everything in the world outside of the particular business. Inputs are not necessarily controllable—in the form of information, people, energy, and physical things (raw materials to floods to bombs), they

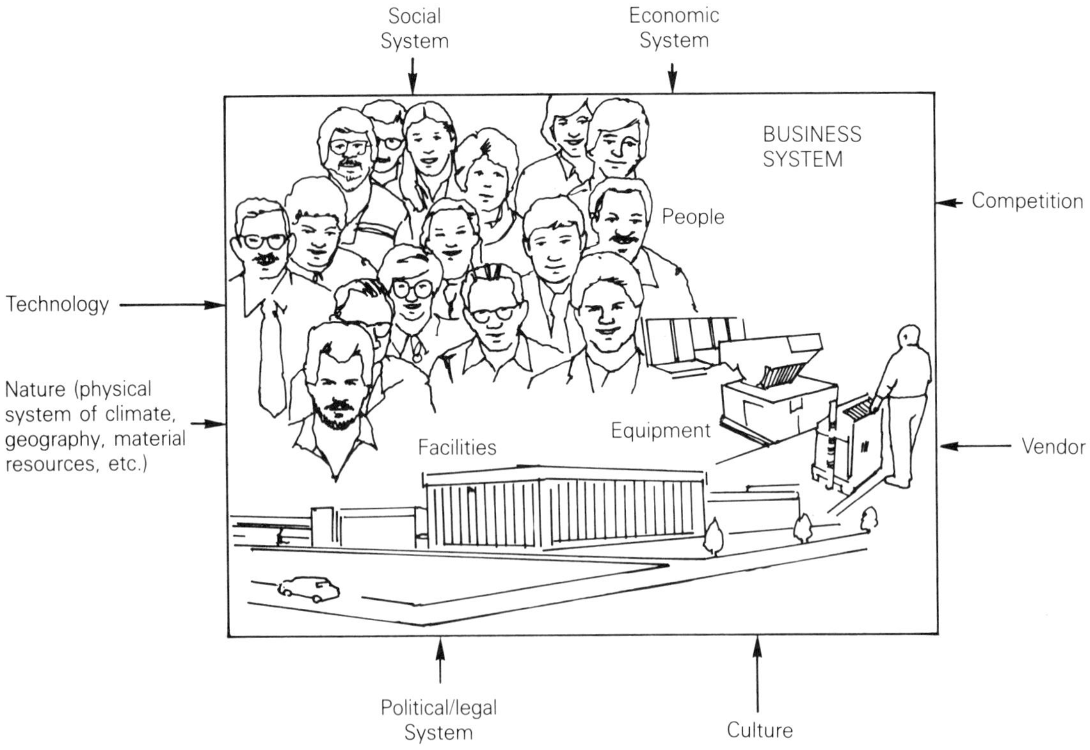

EXHIBIT 19–4
Environment of a business.

may intrude into the system. At the same time, the company may be acting in a way that influences the environment by turning out products and services, lobbying for changes in the law, adding to technology, or polluting or cleaning the environment. (See Exhibit 19–4.)

The systems that we are most familiar with interact with their environments because of inputs and outputs. For this reason, we say they are *open* systems.

We have seen what is outside of our system by looking out, and, lo, we have found the "environment." What do we see when we turn inward? In the case of the HR management system, we see that it is composed of a number of "smaller" systems called *subsystems*. For example, we can identify a recruiting and selection subsystem or a training and development subsystem, among others. On the other hand, the HR management system is a subsystem of the business system itself.

Which is a system and which is a subsystem? Whatever is our main focus of attention is viewed as *the* system, and smaller systems within *the* system are called *subsystems*.

ADVANTAGES OF THE SYSTEMS PERSPECTIVE

Clearer Thinking about Human Resource Management

If we take the time to write down, or "document," the description of the HR management system, our thinking about the system in a particular company will be made much clearer. First, in the *systems approach*, we will have to spell out the objectives of the system. This will lead to better planning and less confusion about responsibilities. Also, allocation of resources may be made appropriately depending upon the scope and mix of objectives of the system.

Second, the systems approach requires that we define both structure and relationships among the elements of the system. In the case of people as elements, we must decide what people will do and how they should relate to each other to carry out the personnel activities. This reduces overlapping duties, conflict, gaps in the processing, and failure to make decisions. It also leads to more effective and efficient ways of carrying out personnel activities.

Third, the systems approach focuses on the flow and sequencing of work by the system. That is, we look at what must be done, how it must be done, who must do it, and when it must be done. This requires development of an information subsystem to provide integration and coordination of such system activities. The supporting information subsystem is made up of interpersonal communication procedures, man–machine communication, intergroup-information flow, computer data processing, and recognition of human (internal) processing characteristics.

Fourth, the systems approach can deal rationally with conflicting objectives and allocation of limited resources. For example, suppose that management establishes as goals: (1) low pay, (2) high worker satisfaction, and (3) high productivity. These goals may conflict with each other in complex ways. In the systems approach, "tradeoffs" in degree of achievement of the objectives are made in order that the system, over all, will function best. Thus, "not-so-low" pay, a "medium" level of worker satisfaction and only "fairly high" productivity may be the best balance for the long-range profitability of the company.

Similarly, in the allocation of resources among personnel, marketing, production, and finance/accounting, the systems approach will lead the business as a whole toward functioning at its full potential. In the past, allocation of resources has often been based on attempts to optimize the individual subsystems, thereby neglecting potential tradeoffs in performance among systems. The result has been low total system performance.

Fifth, and finally, the systems approach emphasizes system control. The most common type of such control is feedback control (Exhibit 19–5). In feedback control, the output, or system performance, is compared with the input goal. If there is a variance, the system takes corrective action. (Chapter 17 discusses control at length.)

For example, suppose the input goal for the travel budget for the personnel department is $2,000 per month. The accounting department accumulates charges for January, prepares a report, and sends a copy to the personnel department. The charges appear as $2,600. Upon receiving this feedback of a variance of $400, the personnel manager requires that all travel requests with estimated expenses detailed be sent to her for review. Her secretary maintains a cumulative estimate for the month. Further, the personnel manager may then prepare a plan for annual travel based upon requests by her subordinates at the beginning of the year.

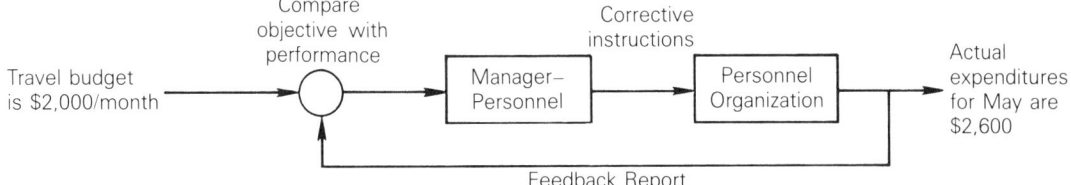

EXHIBIT 19–5
Feedback for control of a system.

Combination of All Other Approaches

The systems approach has sometimes been misunderstood as being a quantitative, mechanistic, and limited approach to the study of management (and hence HR management). Nothing could be further from the truth—at every step of the application of the systems concept, *all* of human knowledge is applicable as it combines all methods of studying problems. Social psychology, management process and practice, decision theory, information and communication theory, and cost–benefit analysis are some of the major disciplines that are combined in the design of systems.

The increasing complexity of our world, the nature of our productive institutions and of human resource management in particular can no longer be handled by such one-dimensional approaches as the organizational behavior approach or the process approach. There are just too many complex, conflicting goals, too many complex and sophisticated elements in a system, too many possible complicated and sophisticated relationships among system elements, structure, processes, and information flow. There are also too many complex, complicated, subtle relationships among systems and their environments to be treated by other than the systems approach.

Facilitation of the Manager's Job

The systems approach means that the manager looks at system objectives and tasks first and then coordinates subsystems and elements. It is easier to look at the big picture and to subdivide tasks as in the systems approach than to try to juggle many small tasks without an integrating framework. In HR management, we adopt a systems approach by first establishing a few overall objectives. We then ask, what major tasks must we carry out to achieve these objectives? How should we organize to achieve the tasks and system objectives? How should we relate the organizational subgroups (subsystems) so that they will be mutually supportive?[3]

Without a systems approach, management would be attacking many separate problems and trying to optimize the solution in each case. Such attempted optimization for many tasks with conflicting objectives will lead to poor total management of human resources. The result? The synergy from a systems approach is lost.

DIMENSIONS OF A SYSTEM: OPERATIONS AND INFORMATION

We noted earlier that systems are processors of inputs. Therefore, to design or describe a system, we must identify the operations performed. In a simple system where operations are performed sequentially, we could list the operations. In many systems, however, parallel operations are carried out. This requires a network schematic, or *block diagram*. Because block diagrams are often easier to read than narratives or lists, they are generally used for operating diagrams. Our model for Part II of this book is essentially a simplified block diagram of the human resource management process.

Operations cannot be performed in a vacuum; information must be transmitted from one stage to the next. In other words, associated with an operating system is an *information system*. A complete information system flow diagram can convey a fairly complete picture of the relationships among workers. An information flowchart that shows only information received by managers and the flow among managers is called a *management information system (MIS)*. The MIS deals with managerial planning, controlling, and decision making, and the nature and structure of management reports.

It should be pointed out that the broadest term for transmission of information is called communication, a process discussed in detail in Chapter 10. In very small firms with only a half-dozen employees, practically all communication is informal. Only as the firm grows is there a need for *formal* types of communications such as reports, forms, procedures, and so on. The result is an information system in addition to informal, interpersonal communication.

DEVELOPING AND INSTALLING THE HR MANAGEMENT SYSTEM

When a company is just starting up, it is desirable to plan for the HR management system. A personnel staff specialist may be assigned to lead such a project to determine the structure, responsibilities, and roles of managers and personnel specialists. Policies and procedures will need to be established. Flow of information, forms, and reports will have to be specified. The resulting description is called the *design* of the HR management. After the system has been designed, it then must be implemented by staffing the personnel department, installing offices and equipment, and disseminating the forms, policies, and procedures.

There are other times when the HR management system, or a major part of it, must be redesigned. When the company merges with another company or expands to such an extent that the old "system" can no longer be patched up by easily made changes, a major rethinking is required. If major new social legislation appears on the scene over a period of a few years, a new look at the system may be appropriate. Finally, technological change may indicate the need to throw out the old and to devise a new HR management system. For example, the development of the computer, the development of data base management systems, and the development of low-cost data and video communication systems are currently causing redesign of a part or all of HR management systems.

The HR management system consists of the following structures, elements, and processes in two categories:

Management	Personnel Organization
Managers	Personnel specialists
Office facilities	Office facilities
Furniture and equipment	Furniture and equipment
Responsibilities and roles	Responsibilities and roles
Positions in the organizational structure	Positions in the organizational structure
Information flow	Information flow
Policies, procedures, forms	

The design or redesign of the HR management system may affect all of these items.

The development and installation of a HR management system follows the four steps typical of all types of system development: (1) design, (2) implementation, (3) operation, and (4) maintenance. The study of this approach to system development and installation is particularly relevant today as more and more companies automate their HR information systems. We will discuss the development of the HR management system first and focus on the special nature of its information subsystem. Four phases are involved: design, implementation, operational, and maintenance.

Design Phase

Objectives and Scope The design of any system starts with "needs-research." We must identify problems in HR management as well as desired objectives. We must also determine the philosophical approach to the treatment of people within the company and the scope of activities to be included in the HR system. Some of the answers may be found in the corporate strategy, but others may require new management decisions. Let us look at a few specific examples of objectives and scope problems.

1. *Lean or heavily staffed organization:* General Electric Company has a large central staff organization providing research and counsel on management, the various functional areas, and personnel management. Fuqua, on the other hand, is a large diversified company that maintains a very lean corporate management of about 30 people in its Atlanta headquarters. A lean staff means that the size of the personnel department will likely be small.
2. *Capital-intensive or labor-intensive:* In a Japanese machine tool plant where robots are used, there are more tour guides than workers. In contrast, thousands of people may be employed at U.S. auto plants. In the latter case, the HR management activities will be very extensive.
3. *Few high-quality workers vs. many less-skilled workers:* The HR management system will be shaped by objectives falling between these extremes.
4. *Multiple plants, warehouses, and offices:* Whether the personnel department should be centralized and small or large in scope or whether it should be decentralized is a question to be answered. In fact, a centralized staff along with decentralized personnel departments at the other plants is most common.
5. *Scope of organization development and training programs:* Some companies have few or no training programs, while other companies such as General Electric and Westinghouse spend millions of dollars annually on training and development.
6. *Subcontracting of services vs. in-house activities:* We may wish to subcontract training and some benefits programs or to hire con-

sultants for special tasks such as compensation system development. Such outside services mean a leaner personnel department.
7. *Company expansion rate:* In a rapidly expanding company, the HR management system should be designed to keep ahead of the expansion in number of employees.
8. *Emphasis on personnel activities:* Some managements that focus primarily on short-term costs may have the objective of keeping the personnel department to an absolute minimum. Other companies that focus on the potential of human resources for profit may consider large expenditures on HR management to be an investment that will produce much larger gains.

These, and many other decisions on objectives and scope affect the design of the system.

Required Outputs and Inputs The outputs of the system—the specific objectives that the system must achieve—must be defined. Outputs of the HR management system consist of:

1. Productivity of employees
2. Satisfaction of employees
3. Development (improvement) of workers and the organization
4. Reports that permit planning and controlling of the system
5. Reports required by the government
6. Reports and information published for use by the employees, the industry, or the public

Similarly, inputs to the HR management system must be determined. Some examples of inputs are:

Input	Source
Notification of violation of EEO laws	EEOC
Candidate availability	Person seeking employment
Application to take a company training program	Employee
Direct labor costs	Accounting
Absenteeism	Time cards and time clerks
Workers' attitudes	Attitude survey results
Industry wage rates	Trade associations

Conceptual and Detailed Designs The next step in system design after the establishment of needs, objectives, scope, outputs, and inputs is to block out the general nature of the system. This "general design" is called the *conceptual design.* By analogy, if you were designing a home, you would first sketch out the general shape, dimensions, and arrangement of rooms. When you found an arrangement that you liked, you would have an architect draw up detailed plans.

For the HR management system, the conceptual design includes the system performance requirements, subsystems required to fulfill performance requirements, and an outline of data storage and the information subsystem. The result is a conception of the total HR management system for the company. Exhibit 19–8 shows part of the conceptual design for a complete HR management system. The other remaining portion of the conceptual design is the organization structure or responsibility chart presented in Exhibit 1–10. Part II of this text amplifies on all of the subsystems shown in Exhibit 19–6.

The detailed design of the HR management system consists of such items as policies, detailed procedures, position guides, forms and records employed by the various subsystems, the computer system (if utilized), and facilities and equipment required.

Implementation Phase

When the detailed design has been completed and documented, the HR management system may be implemented. In this phase, workers are hired or reassigned to staff the personnel department, offices and equipment are provided, the computer is installed, and computer software programs are prepared or purchased. The system is tested and debugged. In other words, the HR management system design is converted to an operating system.

Operational Phase

The operational phase is simply the on-going continued operation of the system to achieve system objectives until the system is terminated or replaced.

Maintenance Phase

The maintenance phase runs parallel to the operational phase. Maintenance consists of modifying the system because of changes in such factors as:

1. The organization itself
2. Government policies, regulations, and legislation
3. Economic conditions that impact such HR management subsystems as recruiting or compensation
4. Industry and competitive conditions that may also affect recruitment and compensation
5. New technology that may affect training, recruitment, and the HR management information system

Maintenance is applied by changing such system components or activities as:

1. Policy statements
2. Reports received by a manager who replaces an incumbent manager

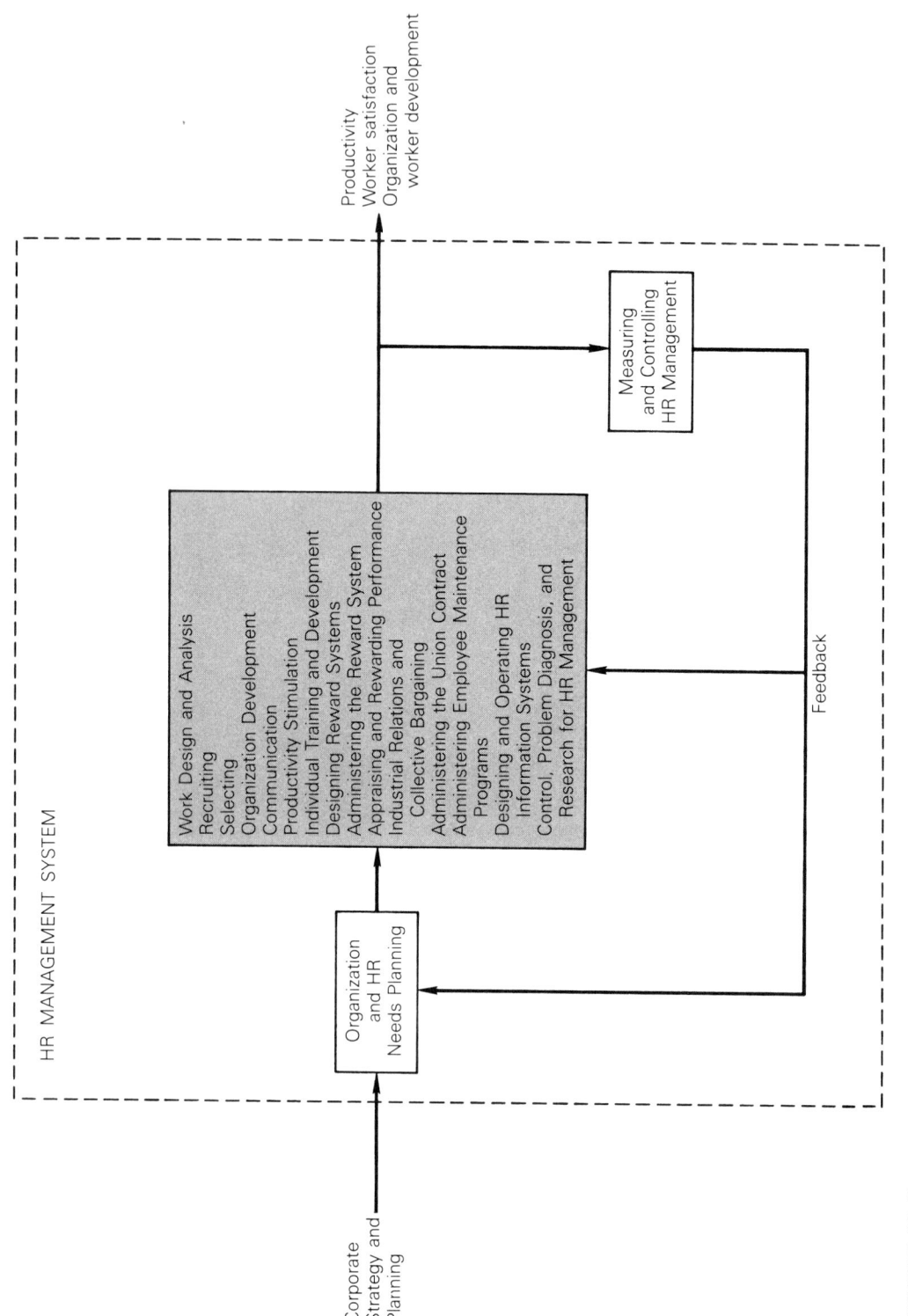

EXHIBIT 19-6
The HR management system.

3. Forms
4. Operating subsystems, processes, and procedures
5. Computer hardware configurations
6. Computer programs
7. System controls and security needs
8. Organization and staffing

COMPUTER-BASED HR MANAGEMENT INFORMATION SYSTEM

The HR management information system is a system designed to link together the people and equipment carrying out the operations of the system. It may be described as the flow and storage of data and information. To visualize the system, think of all reports and forms that enter the HR management system; think of the flow, transformation, and generation of forms or reports within the system; and think of all the forms and reports flowing out from the system.

Specifically, consider the application form of a candidate for employment. This form is received by the recruiter. It is then filed with others. The form is retrieved from the file when the personnel department receives a job specification and authorization of a position. The application form is then reproduced and copies are sent to managers responsible for hiring. This flow of information is only a small part of the entire flow of information in a HR information system.

Three kinds of HR management information commonly found in companies today are (1) manual systems with manually operated files, which are found in very small companies and in backward larger companies; (2) computerized files and computerized data processing, which are found in most progressive companies; and (3) fully computerized systems with data base management systems (DBMS), toward which a few of the largest, most progressive companies are working. We will now discuss each of these three types of HR management information.

Manual HR Information Systems

The manual system consists of a set of forms and manual files. The manual file consists of a set of records. A record likely consists of a manila folder for each employee with the employee's employment history, appraisals, and salary maintained in the personnel department. A set of records that duplicates the compensation and benefit information may be maintained in the payroll section. Further duplication of an employee's records may exist in the files of the employee's manager.

Manual entries on forms and typing of changes on the records often fall behind so that the records are not accurate or up-to-date. Such systems also suffer from lack of procedures to keep duplicated information in different files consistent with each other. As organizations grow larger, the manual systems tend to break down under the burden of manual processing.

The increasing complication of benefits plans, OSHA and ERISA, compensation plans, tax deductions, vacation plans, and so forth have turned manual systems into a nightmare. Further stretching their capacities is the need for tracking job candidates, employees in training programs, and promotion of employees for EEO compliance.

Computerized Files and Data Processing Systems

Computerized systems may be based on either (1) replacing clerical work by a computer, in essence, using the same procedures as for the manual system except that computations, clerical processing, and some reporting are done more quickly and accurately; or (2) a set of data processing software modules that are linked to each other and to a central employee data system in some way. We will now outline this second type of computerized system.

We may identify four principal data storage and processing modules needed for an automated HR information system. As shown in Exhibit 19–7, these modules are the employee data system, the position system, the compensation system, and the budgets system. The employee data system stores and retrieves current data on all present employees. This includes such data as name, address, Social Security number, date of birth, sex, race or ethnic origin as required by the EEOC, education, skills, appraisals, and compensation rate.

EXHIBIT 19–7
Computer-based human resource information system.

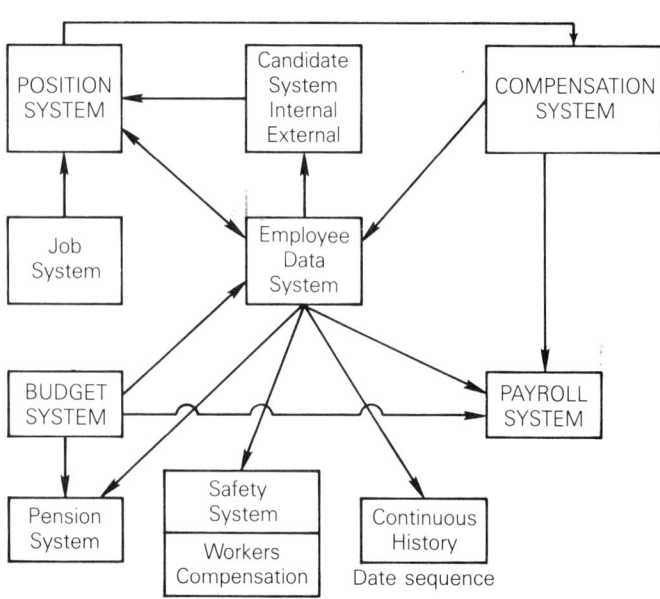

The position system lists all positions and their attributes. Inputs from the job system and candidate system provide this system with job data and data concerning the position incumbents, candidates, or position vacancies.

The compensation system maintains data on wage and salary structure, compensation of incumbents in positions, and provides such information to the payroll system and to the employee data system.

The budgets system stores data on budgets and makes this data available to the payroll system, the pension system, and employee data system for control of these systems.

Basically, such automated HR management information systems consist of linked data bases with "application programs" that store, manipulate, and retrieve data and provide reports. These system modules, as found in commercial software systems, tend to be independent so that we may start with the employee data system or the payroll system and add on one module at a time. The computer software application program provided by a leading company in the human resource management field is shown in Exhibit 19–8. Note the optional modules that may be added on to the basic modules.

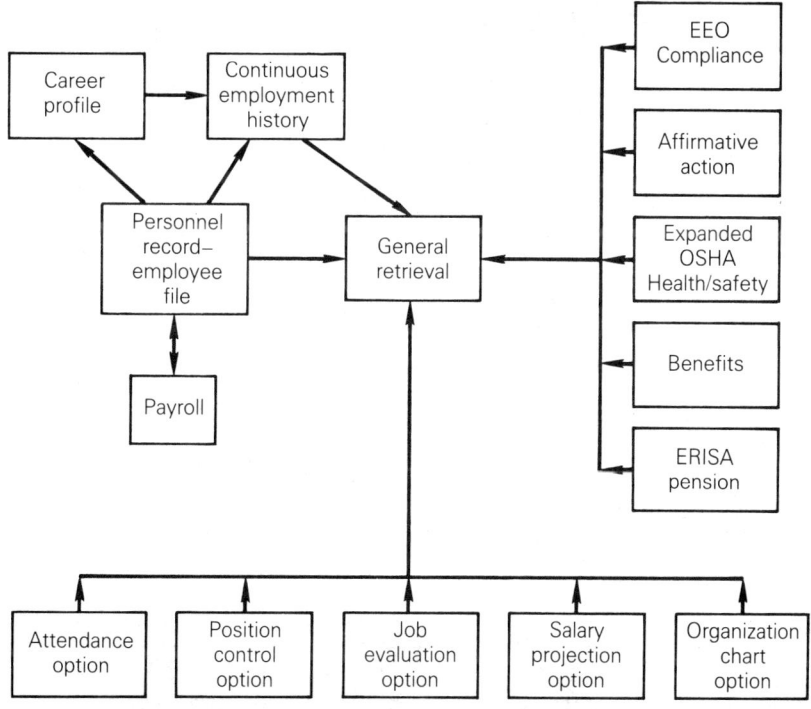

EXHIBIT 19–8
Computer software application program of human resource information. (Courtesy of InSci)

Insurance Premiums

This premium statement summarizes the costs of coverage for employee and employer by insurance plan.

```
                        ABC COMPANY
                      PERSONNEL SYSTEM
                  INSURANCE PREMIUM STATEMENT

REPORT: BENADM2                               DATE: 01/13/77
-----------------------------------------------------------------
                                   EMPLOYEE    COMPANY    COVERAGE
            INSURANCE TYPE         PREMIUM     PREMIUM    AMOUNT
-----------------------------------------------------------------
(1)  NON-CONTRIBUTORY LIFE            .00     1,043.80    1535000
(2)  NON-CONTRIBUTORY AD,D            .00        76.75    1535000
(3)  BASIC CONTRIBUTORY LIFE       537.25     1,043.80    1535000
(4)  BASIC CONTRIBUTORY AD,D        76.75         .00     1535000
(7)  DEPENDENT LIFE                130.95         .00     1535000
(8)  LONG TERM DISABILITY          729.12         .00       76750
(9)  MAJOR MEDICAL- EMPLOYEE       241.53     1,149.45          0
```

Insurance Participants

This detailed list of participants provides an audit trail of coverage by employee.

```
                          ABC COMPANY
                       PERSONNEL SYSTEM
                     INSURANCE PARTICIPANTS

REPORT: BENADM1                                       DATE: 01/13/77
--------------------------------------------------------------------------
                                       COV  EFFECTIVE  EMPLOYEE  COMPANY
   EMPLOYEE NAME    SO.SEC.NO. SEX BIRTH DATE TYPE DATE PREMIUM  PREMIUM  COVERAGE
--------------------------------------------------------------------------
BAUER, ELAINE L.   100-22-6124  F  42 SEP 12  BL1         6.65    12.92   19000
                                              BL2          .95      .00   19000
                                              DL1         1.35      .00   19000
                                              LTD         9.02      .00     950
                                              L1           .00    12.92   19000
                                              L2           .00      .95   19000
                                              MME         2.49    11.85       0
BAUER, JOAN O.     100-82-9740  F  47 APR 26  BL1         4.20     8.16   12000
                                              BL2          .60      .00   12000
                                              DL1         1.35      .00   12000
                                              LTD         5.70      .00     600
                                              L1           .00     8.16   12000
                                              L2           .00      .60   12000
                                              MME         2.49    11.85       0
BAUER, REBECCA E.  100-19-6019  F  38 NOV 07  BL1         8.75    17.00   25000
                                              BL2         1.25      .00   25000
                                              DL1         1.35      .00   25000
                                              LTD        11.88      .00    1250
                                              L1           .00    17.00   25000
                                              L2           .00     1.25   25000
                                              MME         2.49    11.85       0
BLACK, GLORIA L.   100-44-1908  F  48 JUL 21  BL1         5.25    10.20   15000
                                              BL2          .75      .00   15000
                                              DL1         1.35      .00   15000
                                              LTD         7.13      .00     750
                                              L1           .00    10.20   15000
                                              L2           .00      .75   15000
                                              MME         2.49    11.85       0
BLACK, JENNY E.    100-24-3596  F  40 NOV 11  BL1         6.65    12.92   19000
                                              BL2          .95      .00   19000
                                              DL1         1.35      .00   19000
                                              LTD         9.02      .00     950
                                              L1           .00    12.92   19000
                                              L2           .00      .95   19000
                                              MME         2.49    11.85       0
BLACK, MARK A.     100-34-6311  M  22 MAY 14  BL1         6.65    12.92   19000
                                              BL2          .95      .00   19000
                                              DL1         1.35      .00   19000
                                              LTD         9.02      .00     950
                                              L1           .00    12.92   19000
                                              L2           .00      .95   19000
                                              MME         2.49    11.85       0
BLUE, GLORIA L.    100-26-9801  F  41 DEC 05  BL1         6.65    12.92   19000
                                              BL2          .95      .00   19000
                                              DL1         1.35      .00   19000
                                              LTD         9.02      .00     950
                                              L1           .00    12.92   19000

         B E N E F I T   A D M I N I S T R A T I O N    BY  T Y M S H A R E
```

Terminal Inquiry

Here the user makes an inquiry at the terminal for a summary of insurance coverage for all full-time employees, broken down by sex.

```
>SUM CNT.S_S_N OVER MALES OVER FEMALES
>ACROSS COV_CODE
>IF STATUS IS 'F'
>END

           COV_CODE
           BL1   BL2   DL1   LTD   L1    L2   MMC   MME   MMF   MMS   SL1   SL2
           ---   ---   ---   ---   ---   --- ---   ---   ---   ---   ---   ---
S_S_N COUNT 73   78    45    86   198   198   15    85    31    23    39    37
MALES       31   30    18    33    61    61    3    20    18     8    19    17
FEMALES     42   48    27    53   137   137   12    65    13    15    20    20
```

TYMSHARE

©TYMSHARE INC. 1977, Litho in U.S.A.   PERS® is a registered trademark of Tymshare, Inc.

EXHIBIT 19–9
Benefits reports in hard-copy form.

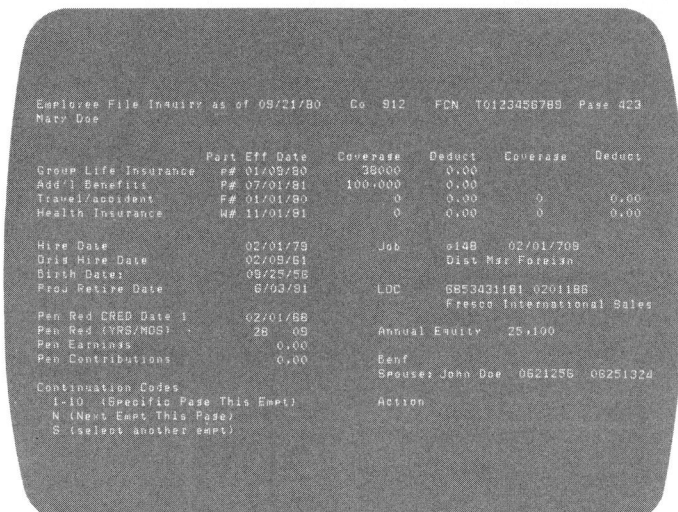

EXHIBIT 19–10
Video display of HR information.
(Courtesy of InSci)

The outputs of these computer-based systems may be hard copy (printed form) as shown in Exhibit 19–9 or in video form as depicted in Exhibit 19–10.

Data Base Management System (DBMS)

Some disadvantages of simply automating clerical processes or of using computerized modules arise because of redundancy and lack of integration of all HR data into a single current data base. In manual systems, for example, the employee's name and Social Security number may appear in the payroll file, the manager's file, the personnel inventory file, and the benefits file. This represents considerable duplication of data. In addition, every time a name is added or dropped, all of the files carrying the name should be corrected instantly. It is apparent that such maintenance of files is unlikely. In addition, such systems are often tied to a particular computer processing language so that changes in data structure or change to another language requires a lot of expensive programming.

In this section, we will present a type of integrated system of data that, combined with a computer system, will produce information based on the latest data. Other advantages will become evident as we explain such a *Data Base Management System (DBMS)*. In order to explain the DBMS, we will first have to outline the general nature of a computer system.

Computer System A computer system consists of:

1. Hardware: if you kick it, you'll hurt your toe
2. Software: instructions telling the computer what to do
3. People: to do those things that the particular hardware and software in use can't do

The computer system may be compared with a manual system as follows:

	Manual System	Computer System
Input	Documents, voice reports, etc.	Tape readers, terminals
Data Processor	Human	Central processing unit (CPU)
Storage or memory	File cabinets, rotary files, notebooks, human memory	Magnetic tapes, magnetic discs, etc.
Outputs	Documents, typed reports, drawings, voice reports, etc.	Computer printout sheets, video displays, magnetic tapes, microfilms, etc.

The principal computer hardware components of interest to us are:

1. The central processing unit (CPU), which adds, subtracts, and compares. It also controls the sequencing required for giving instructions.
2. The main memory, which is very closely related to, and sometimes considered a part of, the CPU. It stores the data being manipulated and the programs for the manipulation. It is somewhat limited in size.
3. Secondary storage, which is a mass storage system from which data may be taken and entered in primary storage. Data may be stored directly in secondary storage or it may be entered as the output from the computer.
4. Input and output devices, such as video terminals, allow us to enter data into main or secondary memory.

Exhibit 19–11 shows schematically the components of the computer with optional input and output devices. Exhibit 19–12 presents a photo of a computer system with interactive video terminals for inputs and outputs.

Integrated P/HR Data Base We now visualize a very simple but powerful concept for providing all the reports we will need for human resource management in an *integrated P/HR data base*. First, we enter every item of P/HR management data in the secondary storage (data base) only once. We then prepare a set of computer programs to select and relate data elements in any form we wish. No longer do we have to list names and attributes of workers half a dozen times. Once stored, any authorized person may call for a combination in the form of a record. Exhibit 19–13 shows, on the right, a representation of the data base, and on the left, a list of programs. We may envision sweeping the list of computer programs across the data base and

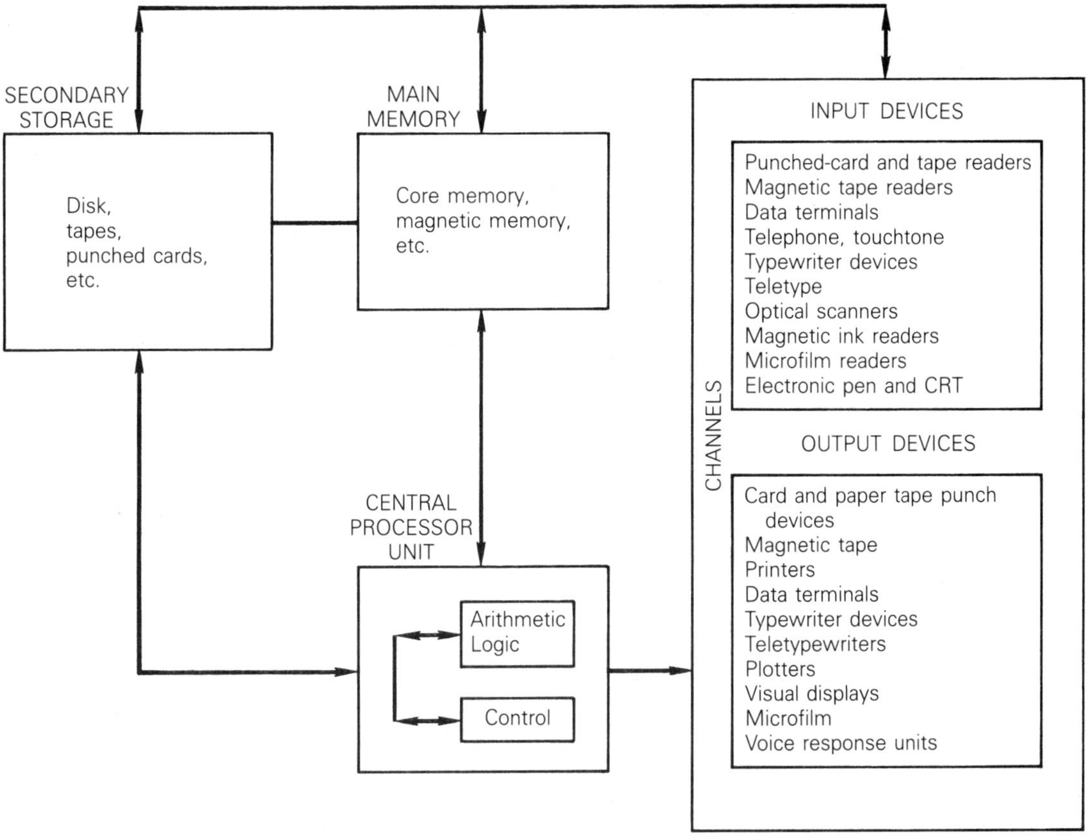

```
                                              ┌─────────────────────────────────┐
                                              │         INPUT DEVICES           │
┌──────────┐         ┌──────────┐              │  ┌───────────────────────────┐  │
│SECONDARY │         │  MAIN    │              │  │ Punched-card and tape readers │
│ STORAGE  │         │  MEMORY  │              │  │ Magnetic tape readers     │  │
│          │         │          │              │  │ Data terminals            │  │
│ Disk,    │         │Core memory,             │  │ Telephone, touchtone      │  │
│ tapes,   │         │magnetic memory,         │  │ Typewriter devices        │  │
│ punched  │         │ etc.     │              │  │ Teletype                  │  │
│ cards,   │         │          │              │  │ Optical scanners          │  │
│ etc.     │         │          │              │  │ Magnetic ink readers      │  │
│          │         │          │              │  │ Microfilm readers         │  │
│          │         │          │              │  │ Electronic pen and CRT    │  │
└──────────┘         └──────────┘              │  └───────────────────────────┘  │
                                               CHANNELS  OUTPUT DEVICES         
                                              │  ┌───────────────────────────┐  │
                         CENTRAL              │  │ Card and paper tape punch │  │
                        PROCESSOR             │  │   devices                 │  │
                          UNIT                │  │ Magnetic tape             │  │
                      ┌─────────────┐         │  │ Printers                  │  │
                      │ Arithmetic  │         │  │ Data terminals            │  │
                      │   Logic     │         │  │ Typewriter devices        │  │
                      ├─────────────┤         │  │ Teletypewriters           │  │
                      │  Control    │         │  │ Plotters                  │  │
                      └─────────────┘         │  │ Visual displays           │  │
                                              │  │ Microfilm                 │  │
                                              │  │ Voice response units      │  │
                                              │  └───────────────────────────┘  │
                                              └─────────────────────────────────┘
```

EXHIBIT 19-11
Computer components.

EXHIBIT 19-12
In-use terminals with video displays. (The Harris 1670; courtesy of Harris Corporation)

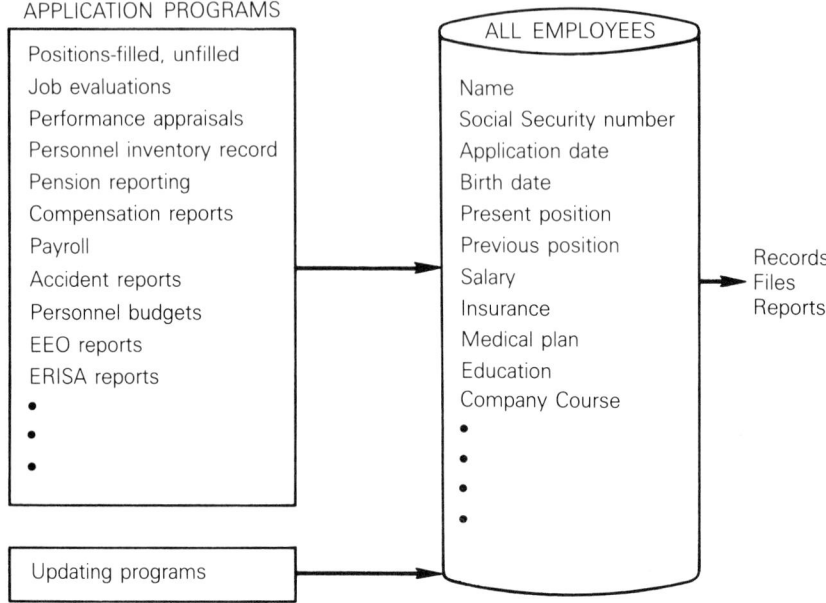

EXHIBIT 19-13
Computer programs applied to an integrated data base.

producing any desired report. The report may be a standard one or one specially constructed by a new program added to the program list.

A more complete listing of all data required for HR management is provided by Exhibit 19-14. From such data, the computer may construct all kinds of regular and special reports for management.

EXHIBIT 19-14
Human resource data base.

Personal Data
Name
Pay number and Social Security number
Sex
Date of birth
Marital status
Minority group classification

Recruiting Data
Date of recruiting contract
Responsible recruiter or interviewer
Source of candidate referral (newspaper ad, employment agency, resume, etc.)
Date of referral of candidate or application to interested managers
Names of supervisors or managers referred to
Date of interview(s)
Date of offer of employment or signoff
Test scores and interviewer ratings
Reasons for selection/rejection of candidate
Date added to payroll
Number of jobs open for which candidate was potentially qualified
Number of other applicants for same open job or jobs

Educational Data
College degrees, high school diploma, level of educational attainment
Field of degree
Date of degree
Schools or institutes attended
Special employer-sponsored courses completed
Professional licenses held

Compensation/Work Assignment Data
Exempt/nonexempt or hourly/salaried classification
Current salary or pay rate
Bonus or commission participation
Date and amount of next forecast salary/pay increase
Previous pay rates and dates effective
Previous dollar and percent increase and dates of increase
Organizational reporting level
Position title
Supervisor/individual contributor status
Job code
Hours worked
Premium time hours worked

Performance Evaluation/Promotability Data
Personal interests

EXHIBIT 19–14, *continued*

Work preferences
Geographical preferences (for multiplant operations)
Rank value of contribution in current work group
Special nominations and awards
Appraisal reports
Date of last appraisal
Growth potential as rated by manager
Previous promotions considered for, and dates of consideration
Date of demotion
Reason for demotion
Date of last internal transfer
Dates considered for apprenticeship or other special training
Reasons for elimination from consideration for apprenticeship or other special training
Dates of, type, and reason for disciplinary action
Productivity/quality measures
Absenteeism record
Tardiness record
Suggestions submitted (usually to a formal suggestion plan)
Cost reductions submitted
Grievances filed

Work Experience Data
Names and locations of previous employers
Prior employment chronology
Military service
Job skills possessed
Product line experience
Managerial or supervisory experience
Foreign language spoken, written, read
Publications authored
Special skills or hobbies of potential value to the business
Patents held
Elective governmental positions
Security clearances held

Length of Service/Layoff Data
Date hired by employer (actual or adjusted for lost service)
Seniority date (if different from date of hire)
Date of layoff
Last pay rate
Recall status

Association Data
Memberships in professional, technical, or trade associations and dates
Positions as officer of associations and dates

Union Membership Data
Union membership/representation status
Controlling union contract
Union officer status
Dues checkoff status

Location/Contact Data
Home address
City and state
Zip code
Home Phone
Present component and work assignment
Geographic location of work assignment
Office phone
Emergency notification

Benefit Plan Data
Medical and/or life insurance plan participation
Pension plan participation
Savings plan participation
Pay for time not worked (vacation, illness, lost-time accidents, personal time off, death in family, jury duty, military reserve duty, etc.)
Tuition refund plan participation
Etc.

Separation from Payroll Data
Date of removal from payroll
Reason for leaving
Forwarding address
Name and address of new employer
Amount of pay increase obtained with new employer
Eligibility for rehire

Safety/Accident Data
Noise level (in decibels) in work area
Exposure to noxious fumes, chemicals, heat, or cold on job
Record of injury (date of accident, date reported, nature of injury, cause of injury, record of medical attention given, name of attending physician)
Classification of injury (disabling or nondisabling, days of work lost, lost time charged)
Physical limitations resulting from injury
Workmen's compensation claim data

Open Jobs or Positions Data
Job request control number
Job title
Position or job code
Educational requirements
Experience requirements
Permissible salary range
Date by which position must be filled

Work Environment Data
Average educational level of co-workers
Average salary of co-workers
Number of job openings in component
Percent employees terminating employment (for some standard period)
Accident frequency and severity rates for position or component
Relative frequency of job changes in component
Manager's or supervisor's years of supervisory experience
Selection or inheritance of employee by present manager
Relative frequency of manager's or supervisor's disciplinary action
Manager's or supervisor's tendency toward strict or lenient rating of employees
Amount of overtime worked in component
Percent of employees dissatisfied with work, pay, supervisor, etc. in component

Position/Job History Data
Job or position ID number
Job or position code
Date job or position established
Permanent/temporary classification of job
Identity of past incumbents in job
Dates of change in job incumbents
Dates of vacancies in positions
Type of change involved for each person leaving position (newly hired, lateral transfer, promotion from another position)
If a promotion, identity of position promoted from
Location of job in organization structure
Manager or supervisor to whom position reports

Labor Market Data
Analysis of local manpower availability
Unemployment levels by skill, occupation, age, sex, etc.
Predicted future manpower needs
Identification of scarce and surplus manpower pools
Wage and salary, shift differentials, etc.

Source: Adapted from Glen A. Bassett, "PAIR Records and Information Systems," *ASPA Handbook of Personnel and Industrial Relations,* Washington, D.C.: The Bureau of National Affairs, Inc., 1979.

DBMS Objectives for HR Management The objectives of a HR DBMS are to:

1. Provide instant access to the latest changes in the data underlying the HR management system
2. Eliminate redundancy of data by structuring them so that they are suitable for all HR computer application programs
3. Permit multiple concurrent updating of information for retrieval
4. Allow for growth of the system through added data and programs
5. Be independent of any particular software language
6. Reduce maintenance of application programs and provide for on-line maintenance of the data base
7. Provide security for the data base
8. Prevent invasion of privacy for specified data

Definition and Description of the DBMS The DBMS is essentially a computer-based system that will structure, store, update, revise, and retrieve data while maintaining security (defense against threats) and privacy. The DBMS has seven basic components as depicted in Exhibit 19–15 and listed below:

1. *The data base administrator*, who is responsible for the data base schema (organization), integrity, and relations with users
2. *The schema*, which describes the nature of logical and physical relationships among records in the data base

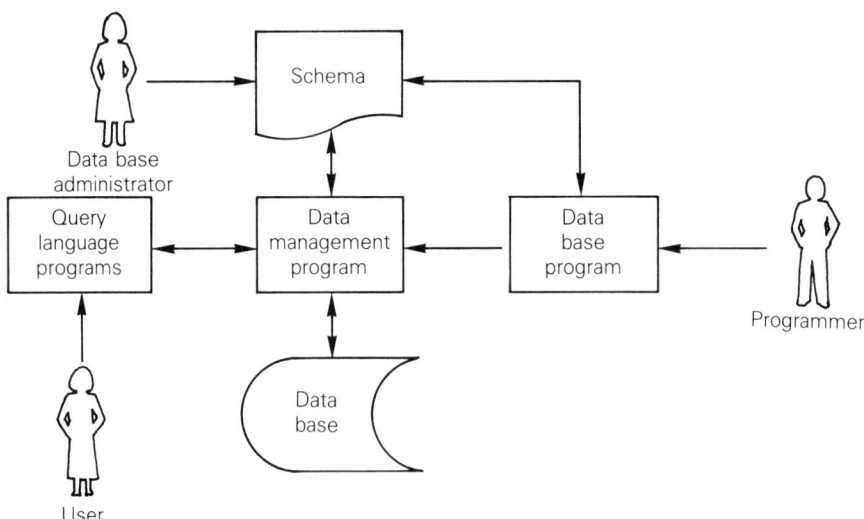

EXHIBIT 19–15
Data base management system components. *Source:* Robert G. Murdick, *MIS: Concepts and Design,* ©1980, p. 473. Reprinted by permission of Prentice-Hall, Inc., Englewood Cliffs, N.J.

3. *The data management program*, which creates all physical records in the data base and controls all subsequent record input and output activities of the data base
4. *Query language programs*, which permit managers to ask questions and receive answers by querying the data base in ordinary language
5. *The data base*, which contains the physical records
6. *The programmer*, who serves as a user interface to the data base system
7. *Data base programs*, which the programmer uses to derive information from data in the data base; these are "application programs."

Data Base System The data base shown in Exhibit 19–15 is actually an important subsystem of the DBMS. Besides serving its central function of storing data, it also interfaces with transactions that occur in the HR system (see Exhibit 19–16). For example, when an employee's salary is raised or when an employee completes a training program, these data are entered in the data base. The data base system also interfaces with the reporting system at its output end.

In addition, the data base system contains both a duplicate data base and a capability to recreate the data base from a history of transactions.

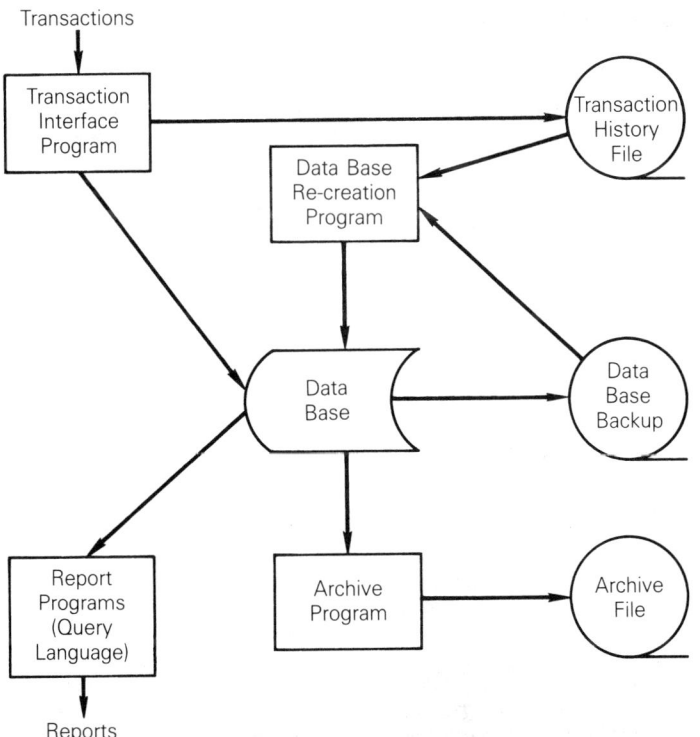

EXHIBIT 19–16

Data base system with support subsystems. *Source:* Robert G. Murdick, *MIS: Concepts and Designs,* © 1980, p. 490. Reprinted by permission of Prentice-Hall, Inc., Englewood Cliffs, N.J.

These backup files are usually stored on mass storage devices such as magnetic tape and located in a protected area remote from the regular computer system.

Finally, the data base maintains archives of old data so that the data base may be limited to data currently of interest.

Security, Privacy, and Protection against Threats

In human resource management, it is vital to have complete, accurate data and history of all employees and retirees. Also, it is important to protect the privacy of certain data. Security and privacy are closely related. We, therefore, define security and privacy and give a summary table for protection of data.

Data security means protection of data against (1) accidental destruction or modification by forces of nature (such as flood, fire, and lightning) or by people; (2) intentional destruction or modification by unauthorized people; and (3) accidental or intentional disclosure to unauthorized people.

Data privacy means that organizations or individuals have the right to restrict or influence disclosure and dissemination of information about themselves.

EXHIBIT 19–17
Protection of programs and master files.

Computer System Elements	Hazards		
	Loss	Defects	Disclosure
Hardware	Conscientious preventive maintenance.		Hardware encoding of key information. Protection against electronic eavesdropping or intrusion into remote access systems.
Software	Careful program design, testing and maintenance to: 1, Ensure appropriate response to hardware malfunctions. 2. Limit entry of erroneous input data. 3. Detect and eliminate program bugs. 4. Minimize operator errors.		Passwords, etc., to prevent outside access to programs and files of remote access systems. Passwords, etc., to limit access to critical programs and files by in-house personnel. Software encoding or other concealment of key information.
Personnel	Proper training and qualification of personnel for key job positions.		Pre-employment screening of personnel.
Procedures	Adequate supervision and scheduling of work assignments.		
	Systematic copying of program and master files. Controls over storage and use of programs and master files. Separation of programming, data control, computer operation, and librarian functions. Complete contingency plan, including loss prevention measures and provision for back-up facilities.	Controls over data input and output, programs and master files. Controls over program changes.	Limited access to key areas. Special supervision of key processing. Careful disposal of printout, cards, tape, etc. Good internal access control and supervision of personal belongings. Controls over access to and use of programs, master files, and the computer.
Facilities	Design and location of building to minimize exposure to fire, flooding, smoke, structural collapse, riot, sabotage, and vandalism. Safe storage facilities for programs, master files and documentation. Off-site storage facilities.	Good control of environment—air-conditioned room for prime power, and freedom from dirt contamination—to minimize hardware errors.	Building design to permit adequate access control, and to minimize opportunities for intrusion.

Source: Robert V. Jacobson, "Providing Data Security," *Automation,* June 1970, p. 88. Copyright, Penton/IPC Inc., June 1970.

In Exhibit 19–17, methods of protection against hazards associated with various components of the computer system are tabulated. The hazards covered are (1) loss of data due to negligence, theft, or physical damage; (2) defects, or errors due to lack of control or environmental contamination of computer hardware; and (3) disclosure, or unauthorized access to data.

Privacy promises from Chase Manhattan

Employees:

- May see any "individually identifiable" information in their personnel files except for that about future planning.
- Will have sensitive information—such as medical files—kept separate from personnel files.
- Must give prior O.K. for release of any data to outsiders except to confirm employment dates.
- Will be told the reason for any information collected about them.
- Will have nothing in their files irrelevant to "job-related decisions."
- Will have any customer relationship with the bank kept separate from the employee relationship.
- Are assured that files are open only to Chase personnel with a "need to know."

Customers:

- Will be the primary source of any information collected about them.
- Will be told what outside sources are tapped for data.
- Will not have their names and addresses sold to outsiders.
- Can block disclosure of information to outsiders unless in response to a subpoena or credit inquiry.
- Will be told of subpoenas for personal information before it is turned over, unless a court prohibits it.
- Will have all discussions of their banking relationship confined to bank employees "directly concerned."
- Will have the opportunity to verify all information and correct inaccuracies.

Data: Chase policies adopted 11/23/81

Source: Reprinted from the January 11, 1982, issue of *Business Week* by special permission. © 1982 by McGraw-Hill, Inc.

ROLE OF THE COMPUTER IN MODERN HR MANAGEMENT SYSTEMS

The development of computer capabilities and decrease in cost have put computers within the reach of practically all companies. Multiplication operations have gone from 2,000 per second in 1952 to over 2 million per second. In the same period, the cost of 100,000 multiplications on an IBM computer has declined from $1.26 to less than one-half cent. Minicomputers/word processors with access to usefully large memory disks and high-speed printers sell for under $5,000. Video terminals are beginning to appear more frequently on managers' desks.

From the manager's viewpoint, the computer is simple. It stores and retrieves large amounts of data in almost any form. It processes numbers and words in many ways and yields outputs in many usable forms and media. It also "reasons" in many ways. In addition, people at great distances from the computer and from each other can communicate and work together with the computer. The major drawback, at present, is that preparing instructions, or programs, for the computer is still expensive. This is changing, however.

We still have to record data, but by recording it once in the computer, we never need to write it again. No longer do we have to copy data from form to form, from several forms or reports to make another report, or store duplicate records within the personnel department and in offices of managers. Once data are correctly entered in the computer, any authorized person at any nearby or remote location may call forth the data in video form, printed form, or graphic form.

The computer thus aids management in making decisions, in planning, and in controlling. The computer makes possible the preparation of the many reports on human resources that are required by the government. The computer requires that we look at the HR information system as a whole and not simply as the automation of old manual paperwork procedures.

The extent to which the computer is employed in the various HR subsystems is suggested by Exhibit 19–18. The software programs now in use or planned to be put in effect within one year, based on a sample of 181 respondents from manufacturing, financial, and commercial companies, are shown according to the number of employees in personnel work. It is apparent that for large personnel organizations and, hence, large companies, computer programs for data storage and information processing are widely used.

EXHIBIT 19–18
Survey of human resource software programs in use or planned for implementation within one year.

Software Programs	Number of Employees in Personnel		5 or less		6–15		16–25		26–50		51–74		Over 75	
			Now (%)	Plan	Now (%)	Plan	Now (%)	Plan	Now (%)	Plan	Now (%)	Plan	Now (%)	Plan
Employee identification data			36.3	27.2	53.3	26.0	71.4	14.2	82.3	8.8	81.8	9.0	98.0	0.0
Payroll			54.5	9.0	69.5	13.0	89.2	0.0	85.2	5.8	81.8	9.0	96.0	1.9
Position control			9.0	27.2	17.4	26.1	35.7	25.0	26.4	38.2	54.5	36.3	56.8	21.5
Job identification			9.0	27.2	39.1	19.6	57.1	21.4	58.8	17.6	54.5	27.2	74.5	5.8
Job evaluation			27.2	9.0	17.4	23.9	28.5	28.5	47.0	17.6	36.3	36.3	50.9	9.8
Benefits			54.5	27.2	60.8	21.7	60.7	32.1	76.4	8.8	54.5	36.3	80.3	13.7
Pension			36.3	27.2	65.5	17.4	57.1	25.0	76.4	8.8	72.7	18.1	84.3	9.8
ERISA			36.3	0.0	32.6	10.8	28.5	25.0	47.0	14.7	45.4	18.1	54.9	9.8
EEO			36.3	18.1	54.3	17.4	64.2	17.8	79.4	14.7	81.8	9.0	82.3	9.8
Safety			9.0	18.1	6.5	13.0	17.8	14.2	17.6	5.8	36.3	27.2	29.4	23.5
Workers compensation			36.3	9.0	6.5	10.8	10.7	28.5	17.6	8.8	9.0	18.1	33.3	7.8
Manpower planning/manning/back-up tables			0.0	18.1	21.7	28.2	3.5	28.5	17.6	47.0	9.0	45.4	31.3	31.3
Training and development			18.1	0.0	15.2	23.9	10.7	28.5	29.4	35.2	27.2	45.4	45.0	45.0
Staffing search			0.0	9.0	17.4	26.1	7.1	28.5	29.4	41.1	45.4	27.2	39.2	27.4
Compensation administration			9.0	27.2	54.3	26.1	64.2	21.4	88.2	11.7	72.7	18.1	80.3	7.8
Grievance data			0.0	9.0	4.3	6.5	3.5	10.7	2.9	17.6	0.0	18.1	13.7	15.6
Attitude survey			0.0	18.1	6.5	8.6	3.5	10.7	17.6	0.0	9.0	27.2	23.5	11.7
Performance appraisal/promotability			0.0	9.0	28.2	23.9	25.0	35.7	5.0	26.4	45.4	27.2	56.8	21.5
Continuous employee history			18.1	36.3	52.1	28.2	28.5	32.1	67.6	26.4	63.6	27.2	70.5	19.6
Report generator			0.0	27.2	41.3	21.7	35.7	7.1	67.6	14.7	63.6	27.2	78.4	13.7

Source: Unpublished study by Fred Schuster, 1982.

SUMMARY

The world we live in has grown more complex. Technology rushes ahead faster than most of us can comprehend it. Organizations must deal with large intricate problems in compressed time spans. The only method for integrating the activities of people, equipment, and facilities to achieve desired ends in our modern, turbulent environment is through a systems approach. The systems approach brings together knowledge from sciences for integrated planning and control. It requires definition of the systems of concern: the system objectives, the components, the structure of the system, the relationships among components, the required inputs, and the required outputs.

In the past, HR management has been presented independently as an organizational behavior problem, in a process or descriptive manner, and from a diagnostic, situational approach. The systems approach includes all of these and more. Most importantly it adds the HR information system to the operating system to complete the total system.

The HR management system is an open system, that is, it interacts with many elements and systems external to itself. In fact, the HR management system is a *sub*system of the business it is in. In turn, the HR management system is made up of subsystems that are studied in this text.

Within the structure of the plans, the HR management system must be modified or constructed for the first time. There are four phases to such a project: the design phase, both conceptual and detailed, the implementation phase, the operational phase, and the maintenance phase. It is extremely important that complete documentation be maintained during this process. The documentation consists of flowcharts, tables, narratives, diagrams, and analyses.

The HR management information system links together the system elements during operations and provides management reports for planning, control, and problem solving. The three levels of sophistication, from lowest to highest, are (1) the manual, document-based system, (2) computer-based automation of individual subsystems, and (3) the total, computer-based, data base management system (DBMS).

The use of computers in HR management systems is sweeping through businesses like a tidal wave. The computer serves three basic purposes: data storage, data processing, and data retrieval and presentation. In sophisticated HR management, the computer has either replaced or automated record keeping in benefits and personnel inventory systems. At the other extreme, the computer system has become a vital decision support system and, in the middle, it has become an integral part of daily operations in compensation, training, recruiting, and placement.

In addition, the computer is a powerful tool for management control, diagnosis of human resource problems, and research for the solution of human resource problems. The following chapter deals with these latter three topics.

KEY CONCEPTS

System

Systems approach

Information system

Conceptual design

Data Base Management System (DBMS)

Integrated P/HR data base

Data security

Data privacy

REVIEW AND DISCUSSION QUESTIONS

1. Define "system" and relate the definition to the human resource management system.
2. What are the advantages of the systems approach to: (a) T & D? (b) Appraisal? (c) Union relations?
3. (a) Distinguish between an operations flowchart and an information flowchart. (b) Draw a single block diagram flowchart that combines both operations and information for T & D.
4. What are the four phases in the development of a computerized P/HR management system?
5. Compare the components of a manual HR management system with a computerized system by setting up a table covering inputs, elements, data base, data processing, and outputs.
6. Relate each chapter of this book to the blocks of the computer-based HR information system in Exhibit 19–9.
7. Distinguish between a completely integrated HR data base and a distributed data base typically found in manual HR management systems.
8. A decision support system (DSS) may be defined as a computer system with a terminal such that a manager may interact easily with the computer to obtain information useful in making decisions. The DSS user must be able to "converse" with the computer in a language convenient for the user to obtain data from the data bank and manipulate it in models of his/her own construction or those in a model bank.
   On the basis of this definition, give three possible applications of a DSS in P/HR management.
9. How could lack of privacy of HR data harm employees? Give reasons for and against privacy laws and policies with respect to HR management.
10. From Exhibit 19–18, what effect does number of employees have on management's use of HR software programs?
11. What are the support subsystems of a data base system?

NOTES

1. Rochelle O'Hara, "A Survey of Change: Information Processing and Human Resources," *Training and Development Journal*, May 1983.
2. For examples of definitions, see Robert G. Murdick, *MIS: Concepts and Design* (Englewood Cliffs, N.J.: Prentice-Hall, 1980), p. 503; and David O. Ellis and Fred J. Ludwig, *Systems Philosophy* (Englewood Cliffs, N.J.: Prentice-Hall, 1962).
3. Mary Ann Van Glinow, "The Design of a Career-Oriented Human Resource System," *Academy of Management Review*, January 1983.

BIBLIOGRAPHY

Cascio, Wayne F., and Elias M. Awad. *Human Resources Management: An Information Systems Approach.* Reston, Va.: Reston Publishing, 1981.

Chen, Kuang-Chian. "A Conceptual Structure of Corporate Strategic Planning Information Systems." *Managerial Planning*, September–October 1977.

Connor, Patrick E., and Boris W. Becker. "Values and the Organization: Suggestions for Research." *Academy of Management Journal*, September 1975.

Flowers, Vincent S., and Bernard A. Coda. "Human Resource Planning: Foundation for a Model." *Personnel*, January–February 1974.

French, Wendell L. *The Personnel Management Process*, 5th ed. Boston: Houghton Mifflin, 1982.

Gehrman, Douglas B. "Techniques of Planning in Employee Relations." *Personnel Journal*, November 1979.

Hofer, Charles W., and Dan Schendel. *Strategy Formulation: Analytical Concepts.* St. Paul, Minn.: West, 1978.

Lee, Sang M., and Cary D. Thorp, Jr., Eds. *Personnel Management: A Computer-Based System.* New York: Petrocelli Books, 1978.

Meals, Donald W., and John W. Rogers, Jr. "Matching Human Resources to Strategies." *Planning Review*, September–October 1980.

Murdick, Robert G. *MIS: Concepts and Design.* Englewood Cliffs, N.J.: Prentice-Hall, 1980.

Murdick, Robert G., and Fred Schuster. "Computerized Information Support for the Human Resource Function." *Human Resource Planning* 6 (1), 1983.

Ramsey, Jackson E. "A Framework for the Interaction of Corporate Value Objectives, Corporate Performance Objectives, and Corporate Strategy." *Journal of Economics and Business*, Spring–Summer 1976.

Rowland, Kendrith M., and Scott L. Summers. "Human Resource Planning: A Second Look." *Personnel Administrator*, December 1981.

Schendel, Dan E., and Charles W. Hofer, Eds. *Strategic Management.* Boston: Little, Brown, 1979.

Schoderbek, Charles G., Peter P. Schoderbek, and Asterios G. Kefalas. *Management Systems: Conceptual Considerations.* Dallas: Business Publications, 1980.

Senn, James A. *Information Systems in Management*, 2nd ed. Belmont, Ca.: Wadsworth, 1982.

Tetz, Frank F. "System for Managing Human Resources." *Journal of Systems Management*, October 1974.

Thompson, Arthur A., and A. J. Strickland III. *Strategy Formulation and Implementation.* Dallas: Business Publications, 1980.

Human Resource Management Control, Problem Diagnosis, and Research

CHAPTER OUTLINE

Systems View of HR Control
Meaning of Control □ Framework for Control of Human Resources □ Desirable Characteristics of Control Systems □ Impact of Control Systems on Organizational Performance

Types of Control Systems
Control of Input: Getting It Right the First Time □ Feedback Control: Getting Back on the Right Track □ Control of the Process: Keeping on the Right Track

Systems View of Organizational Control
Role of the Manager □ Role of the Personnel Department

Developing the HR Control System
Identifying System and Subsystems to Be Controlled □ Identifying Type of Control System to Be Used □ Identifying Criteria for Effectiveness of the HR System □ Identifying or Developing Criterion Measures □ Developing a Management Information System

Diagnosis
Basis for the Diagnostic Approach to HR Management □ An Application

Human Resource Research
What Is Research? □ Why Do HR Research? □ Who Does HR Research? □ What the HR Manager Needs to Know about Research □ Principal Research Techniques for HR Management □ Typical Applications of Research to HR Problems

OBJECTIVES

1. Explain the nature of control and control systems.
2. Explain the role of the P/HR department in the control of HR activities.
3. Describe the development of a HR control system.
4. Explain the diagnostic approach to HR management.
5. Explain the need for research in P/HR activities.
6. Identify a wide range of applications of research to P/HR activities.

SPOTLIGHT:
Alan L. Collins

A lan L. Collins is currently involved in human resource administration with Inland Steel Company. In his current position, he is responsible for assisting with personnel research, human resource planning, and management education programs. He interviews and evaluates employees with supervisory potential, provides management development, and reviews results with area executives. Prior to assuming the above responsibilities, he administered recruitment, staffing, and personnel programs for Inland.

Mr. Collins received his B.S. degree in Management and an M.S. degree in Industrial Relations from the Krannert School of Management at Purdue University. Mr. Collins has taught courses in Personnel, Human Resource Management, and Supervision at Purdue University–Calumet and at Calumet College. He has also served as a keynote speaker and seminar leader at conferences on personnel for various professional societies.

Comments by Alan L. Collins

Inland Steel Company, the nation's seventh largest steel manufacturer, has traditionally had very strong programs designed to attract and develop college graduates for technical and managerial responsibilities. However, the practical application of personnel research techniques has recently enabled Inland to make key decisions involving the retention of these new college graduates.

From 1977 to 1981, Inland experienced a steady increase in turnover of these graduates to levels that concerned company officials. The utilization of practical personnel research enabled Inland to dig deeper into this problem, review the pertinent facts, and prepare suggested solutions. A review of the relevant data drawn from the personnel research study specifically disclosed that:

1. The average annual number of voluntary resignations at Inland during 1979–1980, though lower than the

overall industry average, increased by 108 percent over this same average for the previous five years (1973–1978).
2. There was an increase in those leaving due to the availability of greater career opportunities in the job market. Personnel data revealed that while, in 1976–1979, this reason accounted for over half of all reasons for leaving, the figure jumped to over 70 percent of all reasons in 1980.
3. Turnover was highest among newly hired employees. A total of 52 percent of all terminating employees had less than 3 years of experience and over 69 percent had less than 4 years of service.

As a result of the above personnel research findings, a number of programs were proposed and implemented. They included:

1. *A plantwide career guidance program.* This program was initiated to provide employees, especially new hires, the opportunity: (a) to gain a better understanding of their interests and abilities and how these match available jobs at Inland, and (b) to identify jobs or career areas that they should consider for transfer.
2. *Improved selection procedures.* Job specifications for college recruited positions were developed to identify the specific qualifications needed for these jobs and to help recruiters more effectively match employees with these initial job assignments.

The implementation of these and similar programs helped Inland actually decrease its turnover by 5 percent in 1982, which saved the company over $56,000 in employee replacement costs.

There is the story of two barefoot boys sitting by a stream in the country on a summer day. One boy kept wiggling his toes until finally the other one asked him why he kept wiggling his toes. The first boy replied, "To keep the elephants away." The other said, "But there aren't any elephants within a thousand miles of here." The first replied, "You see, it works!"

Control systems work something like wiggling your toes to keep the problems away. When they don't keep the problems away, we have to diagnose the situation to find out what problem is causing the out-of-control situation. We then must do some sort of research to help us find possible solutions to our problem. In this chapter we will provide a brief introduction to control concepts and then explain the process of control, diagnosis, and research in human resource management. The systems view is essential to any development of control and diagnosis.

SYSTEMS VIEW OF HR CONTROL

Meaning of Control

Control has been used to mean many things: to regulate, guide, coordinate, align performance with a standard, restrain, and screen input or output. For a HR systems approach, however, we define control more rigorously. *Control* means bringing within limits or maintaining (1) the performance of an individual or a group, *or* (2) the characteristics of an individual or group, *or* (3) the characteristics or value of a variable (such as individual, group, or process attributes) within prescribed limits.

Most commonly in practice, the control process consists of measuring performance and output so that objectives are accomplished as planned. Controlling is closely related to planning because plans provide control objectives and controlling ensures that plans are properly implemented. The control process keeps managers informed as to whether activities are going according to plan so that managers may take any required corrective action. Frequently, simply formalizing and communicating the comparison between actual and planned performance challenges the manager to determine the causes of problems and to take corrective action.

In order to control, standards or objectives must be established, performance must be compared with standards, and prompt remedial action must be taken when results deviate significantly from objectives. One of the major challenges in developing control systems for human resources is the development of measuring systems. Measuring or assessing human and organizational performance is a complex and difficult task, as we shall see.

Control of organizations has been studied from two perspectives: (1) the behavior of individuals and (2) outputs that result from behavior.[1] Our view of human resource management suggests that we take a broader and more complete view, namely the systems view. As we shall see, the systems view includes structure, relationships among individuals and groups (subsystems), process, types of control systems and their impact, etc.

The fact that *people* control all other components of the business such as facilities, equipment, financial resources, and information systems makes control of the human resource system most important. Control is made difficult because behavior is not completely predictable (human error, for example), because equipment and information systems breakdowns are not completely predictable, and because external factors (illness, misinformation, fire, weather, sabotage, etc.) may intrude to affect the functioning of the human resource system.

This chapter deals primarily with the design and operation of the HR control system. That is, we focus on the development of such a system in business in terms of objectives, process, and structure. We treat the system in terms of modifying inputs, processes, and outputs as opposed to focusing on behavior modification. We consider the process for bringing the system back under control through problem diagnosis and research. The *implementation* of the control system extends to getting people to modify their behavior as discussed throughout the previous chapters of this book.

Framework for Control of Human Resources

Because human resources control all outputs of the business, it follows that we may control each level of the business in terms of goals, effectiveness, and efficiency:

Total company: Measure key performance areas such as profitability, market position, productivity, personnel development, employee attitudes, and so on.

Subsystems: Measure organizational performance against objectives.

Individuals: Measure performance against standards and objectives.

The subsystems of particular interest to us in this chapter are the HR subsystem, the corporate personnel subsystem, and the personnel organizations (subsystems) established below the corporate level at the division and business levels. Exhibit 20–1 shows how the personnel subsystems are

EXHIBIT 20–1
System outputs to be controlled for control of human resources.

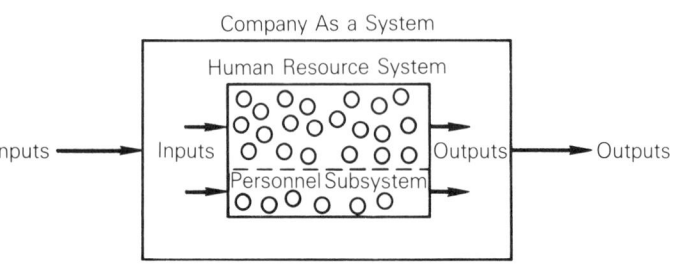

part of the human resource subsystem, which, in turn, is a part of the total company system.

Desirable Characteristics of Control Systems

Both line managers and the human resource department have major responsibilities for the measurement and control of performance.

A system of performance measurement and evaluation should be:

1. Related to company goals
2. Based on plans
3. Based on standards of measurement
4. Readily understandable by everyone
5. Limited to key points and events
6. Objective and quantitative whenever possible
7. Able to detect variances and problems quickly
8. Economical
9. Able to modify organizational behavior for preventive and corrective purposes
10. Able to increase motivation and discourage dysfunctional response to control

Impact of Control Systems on Organizational Performance

Basically, control systems should result in increased organizational effectiveness and efficiency. They do this by providing clear and challenging standards and relating the reward system and the control system. A control system can affect the *direction, intensity,* and *duration* of the group's work efforts if the control system (1) is expressed in operational terms for the group and the individual, (2) is such that the group or individuals can significantly affect the outcomes being measured, and (3) identifies variables that can be clearly measured. Some of the desirable characteristics of control systems listed previously will tend to produce a positive response to a control system.

Alternately, acceptance of a control system may be passive within certain limits and have no effect on performance. Finally, control systems may actually *reduce* effectiveness and efficiency. For example, if the objectives of the control conflict with goals or norms of the individuals in the group, open or covert resistance may develop. Speedup of an assembly line or policies that don't make sense to the individuals who are affected illustrate this point. Other instances that may reduce organizational performance include very tight controls where supervision is close, frequent detailed reports are required, formal paperwork is required for trivial approvals, or resources are too limited to permit good performance.

The impact of formal control systems on HR system performance is very complex. The chapters on leadership, motivation, and the reward system provide more amplification.

658 ANALYSIS AND CONTROL OF PERSONNEL ACTIVITIES

TYPES OF CONTROL SYSTEMS

Controlling is a *dynamic* activity because both the long-range and the short-range objectives of a company *change with time*. As a result of the actions of competitors or new technical developments, for example, short-range objectives may change from month to month. In addition, managers and employees change as human resources are hired, promoted, demoted, or fired. Keeping performance on target with established goals in a dynamic environment requires considerable managerial skill. This process, called *maintaining dynamic equilibrium*, is a balancing act in which changes occur continually. Let us see how it is done.

Control may be accomplished by modifying inputs to a system, modifying the system process, and screening outputs. In addition, the feeding back of information about performance to earlier stages of the system in various combinations with these control methods leads to a number of conceptual schemes for controlling organizations. We shall start with an explanation of a simple scheme and proceed to describe more complex control systems.

Control of Inputs: Getting It Right the First Time

If a system is perfectly designed and constructed (next to impossible), then we may control the output by varying the inputs. Thus, we get the correct output automatically the first time, without having to find errors and then correct them. Proper design includes:

1. Establishing the correct formal work system
   A. Issuing policies that will guide people toward desired action
   B. Establishing long-range and short-range plans to explain who does what, when, and where
2. Staffing the system with right number, mix, and quality of workers
3. Maintaining the organization by T & D
4. Supplying the right mix of human resources, equipment, plant and facilities, and financial resources

Let us demonstrate input-control with a very simple example. Exhibit 20–2 shows a staffing group in the P/HR department. Note that results are

EXHIBIT 20–2
Input control in an open-loop system.

not measured and corrective action is, therefore, not taken. Because there is no information feedback, this is called an *open-loop system*.

If the system operates properly, new employees added to the payroll will be of the correct number, quality, and mix of skills and will arrive at the right time. This ideal condition is not likely to be achieved by merely controlling inputs, however. Further, we will rarely know whether the inputs or system should be changed because such insight will occur only when outputs become noticeably poor—that is, when it is already too late.

Sometimes, such an input-controlled system may be used for reasons other than ignorance. For example, suppose the T & D group in the P/HR department processes a group of managers through a course in ethics. The output of behavior change or improved organizational effectiveness would be difficult to define and measure.

Feedback Control: Getting Back on the Right Track

In *feedback control*, we wait until we see what happens and then feed back information to see whether what happened matched our input plan. For feedback control, we must first set standards of performance or specific objectives to be accomplished in a given time. We observe the difference (variance, as the accountants say) and then use some technique to modify the organization's behavior and functioning.[2]

Exhibit 20–3 illustrates feedback control for a maintenance crew. The system consists of the crew foreman and maintenance workers. The system objective is to repair at least 15 machines per day on the average. We find, however, that only 13 machines per day are being repaired. This measurement is fed back in a report that compares it with the desired number. The variance of two machines per day is information that causes the crew foreman to take corrective action. Such action could be (1) revising the design of the maintenance system (structures, procedures, obtaining more resources

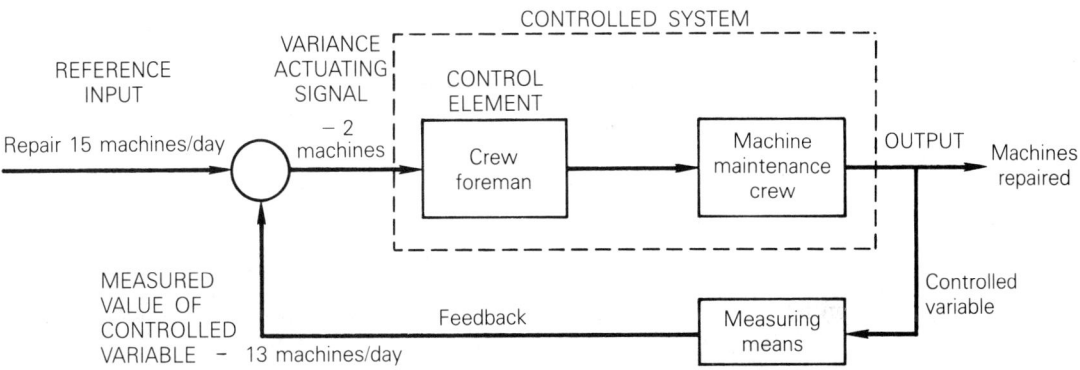

EXHIBIT 20–3
Feedback control.

or equipment, etc.), (2) modifying behavior of the crew through training, leadership, incentives, etc., or (3) a combination of the two.

An important consideration is the amount of deviation that is permitted before corrective action is taken.

If the organization were to be controlled to correct for every little deviation from standard, it would be jerked this way and that. It would be difficult to sustain a well-directed thrust toward the main goals. As an illustration, suppose that a turnover standard were set at 2 percent. If turnover for a three-month period hits 2.3 percent, should management come charging out of its firehouse with engines clanging? No. We would probably set limits, such as 1.5 percent to 2.5 percent. If turnover exceeds these limits in either direction, it is *exceptional.* Management then takes notice only of exceptions so that it is said to "manage by exception."

A common form of feedback control is to *sample* the output. Work sampling is employed, for example, to observe a work group at random times. Conclusions may be drawn, such as "Workers spend 22 percent of their time operating calculating machines and 5 percent of their time at the coffee machine." This information is fed back and compared with standards in plans or with industry data. The organization's behavior is then modified, if necessary, by the methods described in the preceding chapters.

Control of the Process: Keeping on the Right Track

Besides controlling the inputs alone or controlling inputs and processes by feedback control, we may control by *anticipating* deviations from objectives and correcting before they occur. This is sometimes called *steering control.* If you are driving an automobile, you do not wait until you are off the road before making a correction; you anticipate what will happen if you come to a curve in the road and change direction to match the curve.

In an organization, we steer by controlling the organization *at the time the processes are performed* in *anticipation* of changes required to meet fixed or *changing* objectives. This means that we must add a forecasting activity to our system diagram. And, just to be safe, steering systems usually have feedback control as well.

To maintain steering control on a current basis, companies employ three methods: day-to-day monitoring, coordination, and self-control.

Monitoring the Day-to-Day Processes Suppose we look at a specific group, the materials handling section in a company. The function of this group is to move heavy equipment, desks, files, and even portable walls from one point in the plant to another. In order to maintain close control, one large company uses the single-job plan. Instead of giving a group of the handlers a batch of jobs at the beginning of the day, the supervisor gives the group one job and requires the group to report back, with the time spent filled in on a form. Thus the supervisor can monitor each job and can quickly determine whether the group is falling behind the daily work plan.

This real-time monitoring process, as it is called, may be used for many work groups requiring rather close supervision, such as work groups doing clerical jobs in accounting or insurance offices. Of course, such supervision may be very costly in terms of decreased motivation. This is the sort of judgment that makes managing human resources a difficult challenge.

Coordinating Coordinating consists of keeping all members of the organization synchronized by gearing their jobs together. A mob is not coordinated. A crack Marine rifle drill team is a coordinated group.

In order to coordinate a group, companies use a variety of techniques that interconnect jobs and the timing of activities. Examples of these techniques are listed in Exhibit 20–4.

Self-Control As we have seen in Chapter 5, people may be motivated through job enrichment. Giving individuals control over their own work is one means of enriching jobs. An organization as a whole may exercise great control over its work as it progresses through self-control. Instead of feeding information about problems up the line and having correctional directives flow down, the organization is given information, adequate time, and higher-level support to solve its own problems.

A very crude but clear illustration of this is the Zero Defects programs that some companies have instituted. Zero Defects means doing the job right the first time. When Avandale Mills in Alabama instituted ZD, more than 50 significant improvements in yard and fabric quality, efficiency, and waste reduction occurred in just six months. Communicating the nature, the number, and the cause of defects to workers allowed them to correct and improve their methods.

EXHIBIT 20–4
Techniques for coordination.

Oral Techniques	Written Techniques
Regular staff meetings	Statements of company objectives and philosophy
Problem-review meetings	
General organization and information meetings	Organization charts
	Documented plans
Conferences or technical meetings	Operating and policy manuals
Committee meetings	Program instructions, "work packages," work orders
Task-force meetings	
Manager–subordinate daily interviews	Memos, reports, letters, bulletins
The grapevine	Minutes of meetings
	Engineering and manufacturing drawings
	Specifications

MBO and Control Systems   MBO is a "partial" self-control system because objectives are set jointly by the manager and the subordinate. Also, the manager monitors progress at periodic intervals by comparing progress with the mutually agreed-upon objectives. There are usually substantial time periods such as one to six months between feedback of results to the manager. In between feedback times, the subordinate controls his or her own work. Because of the time delays in feedback to management, MBO does not generally represent a good feedback control system by itself. A formal reporting system of progress reports can alleviate this problem, however.

MBO objectives set for managers should be congruent with organizational system outputs. Individual contributors, in turn, should have objectives that fit in with broader system objectives. Controlling the many parts of the business system does not necessarily result in total system control, however. For this reason the concept of Key Result Areas was developed to measure performance of the business as a whole. Personnel is one of these key areas.

SYSTEMS VIEW OF ORGANIZATIONAL CONTROL

The leadership activities, interpersonal communications among employees, and the formal system of reports are the superficial evidence of a control system. Such activities, however, do point out that information flow is the critical feature in a control system. In this section we will discuss the underlying concepts required to design a meaningful and effective control system for managing human resources.

Role of the Manager

Each manager leads and controls an organization subsystem, that is, the group of people who report to him or her. The degree to which a manager exercises either direct or indirect control depends upon the manager's style, the people in the organization, and the situation. The manager is held *accountable* for the performance of the organization. Thus, the manager has a vital interest in the control procedure.

Control, like other management functions, arises from the need to obtain the best use of scarce resources and to attain the goals of the organization. Although the idea of control may arouse opposition from individuals who like to carry out their work without interference, some degree of control is necessary for the orderly and efficient management of any group of people. The good manager also makes the target for control "results," not the restriction of people.

Role of the Human Resource Department

The HR department performs six major activities in controlling organizational components:

1. Screening candidates for employment
2. Conducting T & D activities for managers and nonmanagers
3. Developing reward systems
4. Developing indicants and disseminating measurements of these to management
5. Advising on or participating in labor relations activities
6. Developing and administering formal company-to-employee communications systems

The HR department influences the design of the control system by advising managers, formulating policies and procedures for approval of managers, and supplying statistical and other monitoring information.

DEVELOPING THE HR CONTROL SYSTEM

We will now give the operational procedure required for establishing a HR control system. As discussed earlier in connection with Exhibit 20–1, such control must be related to outputs at five system and subsystem levels:

1. Total business
2. HR system
3. Organization subsystems
4. P/HR management system
5. P/HR management subsystems

If we control human resources properly, then we will have controlled the total business. Therefore, one approach to controlling HR is to make sure that total company goals are achieved. (We discussed these company goals in the form of Key Result Areas earlier.)

Second, we may control the HR system directly by controlling inputs, processes, and outputs.

Third, if we control the organizational subsystems such as production, marketing, accounting, and so on, we will have controlled (plausibly) the HR system.

Finally, if the P/HR management system and its subsystems are doing their jobs, the HR system will be under control.

Identifying System and Subsystems to Be Controlled

The first step in developing a control system is to clearly identify the system and subsystems to be controlled. Because control of human resources results in control of the total business, the system at the top of our hierarchy of systems is the total business. The total business consists of employees, facilities, equipment, and money. In some cases, we might define on-site consultants or sole customers or vendors as parts of the system.

The human resource system is defined by listing all people that we consider to be in the system.

The organizational subsystems vary in scope from divisions of worldwide corporations to a small quality-control group. In addition to these administrative subsystems, there may be systems that cut across the organization's structure such as the capital budgeting system, the new product development system, the productivity improvement system, and so forth. All such systems should be identified for control purposes.

The HR department as a whole constitutes a special organization subsystem of interest. In addition, it also consists of subsystems that must be controlled.

The inputs for each system should be identified. Similarly, the output variables and system objectives should be identified.

Identifying Type of Control System to Be Used

Most control systems in business are simple feedback systems. That is, the manager who is the controller of a system receives reports of system performance and then takes corrective action. The introduction of computers has reduced considerably the delay time for such reports.

For feedback systems, standards, or referent values, must be established for input variables. Limits must then be established for deviations of output from standard. When the performance of a subsystem falls outside the established limits, a report is fed back to the manager.

Process control systems are also fairly commonly used for controlling some human resource activities. One tool for predicting organizational output so that control may be exercised concurrently with the work is the *rolling forecast.* Consider a three-week rolling forecast of physical output per worker-hour. We start with a forecast of this index for each week of the year. At the start of each week, we forecast again for the three weeks ahead. As we forecast, we plan corrections that will bring annual output into line with the total for the year. In Exhibit 20–5, an example of a three-week rolling forecast made at the beginning of week 4 is shown. Adjustments are planned by the manager so that actual output to date *plus* the three-week forecast of output *plus* the remainder of the annual plan will give the total output originally planned.

Identifying the Criteria for Effectiveness of the HR System

At this stage we simply identify criteria that could indicate if the HR system is operating effectively and efficiently. Once again we should refer to our hierarchy of systems that places the total business system at the top. What criteria signify that the business is functioning well? The answer to this

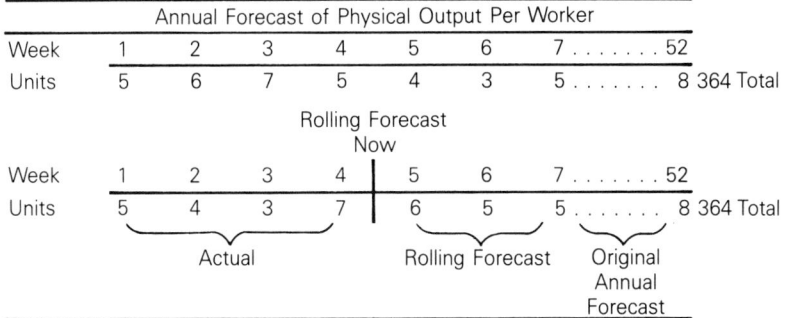

EXHIBIT 20-5
A three-week rolling forecast for process control.

depends on what kind of stakeholder you are. We rank three groups for which criteria should be identified:

Group	Criterion
Owners	Profit
Workers	Worker satisfaction
Society	Varies according to the particular segment of society

At the lower levels, we have placed managers of operating systems. Criteria for each system will vary, but productivity is a common one. Productivity combines utilization of resources with amount and quality of output. Between inputs and outputs, there may also be *intervening variables* with their own criteria.

The identification of criteria for measuring the effectiveness of the personnel department is of particular interest to us. Some criteria might be:

1. Recruitment of "quality" employees
2. Maintenance of the work force
3. Development of the work force
4. Worker motivation
5. Quality of counsel to management on labor relations
6. Low cost of personnel services

Once again, organizational goals serve as the basic criteria, and these goals will be somewhat different from company to company.

J. Barton Cunningham states that there are no generally accepted conceptualizations prescribing the best criteria for measuring organizational

Approach	Criteria
1. Rational goal	Goal achievement
2. Systems resource	Efficient distribution of resources among subsystems
3. Managerial process	Capability and productivity of planning, controlling, decision making for goal-related tasks
4. Organizational development	Organization's ability to work as a team and fit the needs of its members
5. Bargaining	Ability of the system manager to obtain resources
6. Structural, functional	Durability and flexibility of the organizational structure to respond to diversity and change of events
7. Functional	Usefulness of the system to its client groups

effectiveness. His review of research leads to seven approaches, all of which may be used simultaneously:[3]

A comparison between evaluation criteria from 17 models and the 10 most important criteria as perceived by managers may be made by examining Exhibits 20–6 and 20–7.

From the above discussion, it is apparent that identifying criteria is one not-so-easy task, but developing practical criterion measures is an even more difficult task.

EXHIBIT 20–6
Frequency of occurrence of evaluation criteria in 17 models of organizational effectiveness.

Evaluation Criteria	No. of Times Mentioned (N = 17)
Adaptability–flexibility	10
Productivity	6
Satisfaction	5
Profitability	3
Resource acquisition	3
Absence of strain	2
Control over environment	2
Development	2
Efficiency	2
Employee retention	2
Growth	2
Integration	2
Open communications	2
Survival	2
All other criteria	1

Source: Richard M. Steers, Organizational Effectiveness: A Behavioral View, Santa Monica, Ca.: Goodyear, 1977, p. 46.

EXHIBIT 20–7
Ten most important criterion measures as perceived by the three managerial groups.

	Levels of Management					
	Top Management		Middle Management		Lower Management	
Rank	Criteria	Value	Criteria	Value	Criteria	Value
1	Productivity	5.2	Communication	5.7	Leadership	5.6
2	Leadership	5.1	Motivation	5.3	Motivation	5.5
3	Motivation	4.9	Leadership	5.3	Communication	5.3
4	Planning	4.8	Productivity	5.1	Job satisfaction	4.9
5	Job satisfaction	4.7	Planning	3.9	Productivity	3.8
6	Communication	3.9	Coordination	3.9	Planning	3.7
7	Coordination	3.5	Cooperation	3.6	Lack of conflict	2.9
8	Reliability	3.2	Job satisfaction	2.3	Personnel	2.9
9	Cooperation	3.1	Reliability	2.2	Coordination	2.3
10	Lack of conflict	2.4	Lack of conflict	2.1	Cooperation	2.1

Source: Mahmoud A. Wahba and Harris Jack Shapiro, "Managerial Assessment of Organizational Components," *Academy of Management Journal,* June 1973, p. 281.

Identifying or Developing Criterion Measures

The fundamental requirements for a control system are standards and limits, measurement of performance and/or process, and information flow of measurement results to managers and individual workers. Practically speaking, we must have scales that most often are in numerical form. Some things such as number of physical units of output can easily be measured. Other criteria such as worker satisfaction may have to be measured by the development of *indexes* or measured indirectly by measuring *indicants* such as tardiness and turnover. Some common practical measures are described next.

Work Performance When we think of measuring company performance we usually think in terms of daily units of output, product quality, profits, or increases in assets. For an organizational subsystem such as marketing, we may think of sales volume per salesperson, cost per sale, or salesperson turnover.

The difficulty in measuring performance, however, develops because performance consists of two inseparable components, quantity and quality. In a very real sense, quantity and quality represent two conflicting goals in terms of the limited time and cost available. For example, given a certain amount of money and time to produce widgets, we can only produce so many widgets without sacrificing quality. Assuming properly trained workers, we can only increase the number of units produced beyond a certain level by sacrificing some quality, or produce higher quality units by reducing the number produced. Thus, more quantity and higher quality require more time and/or cost. The point is that performance, which consists of both quantity and quality, is interrelated with the funds and time available. We can see then that controlling is a process that requires a delicate balance among certain "givens" if organizational objectives are to be met.

Statistical Measures Various types of statistics are commonly used to compare the organization's performance to some criteria. This is usually done by collecting certain data, such as the number of people absent or costs per worker, and then analyzing these data by the use of ratios and other comparative methods.

Exhibit 20–8 lists some indexes that are used in measuring the effectiveness or efficiency of organizational performance. It is important to keep in mind that ratios or statistics in themselves never evaluate anything. For example, let us consider turnover, which may be defined as:

$$\frac{\text{Number of people who leave in a month}}{\text{Number of people employed at midmonth}} \times 100$$

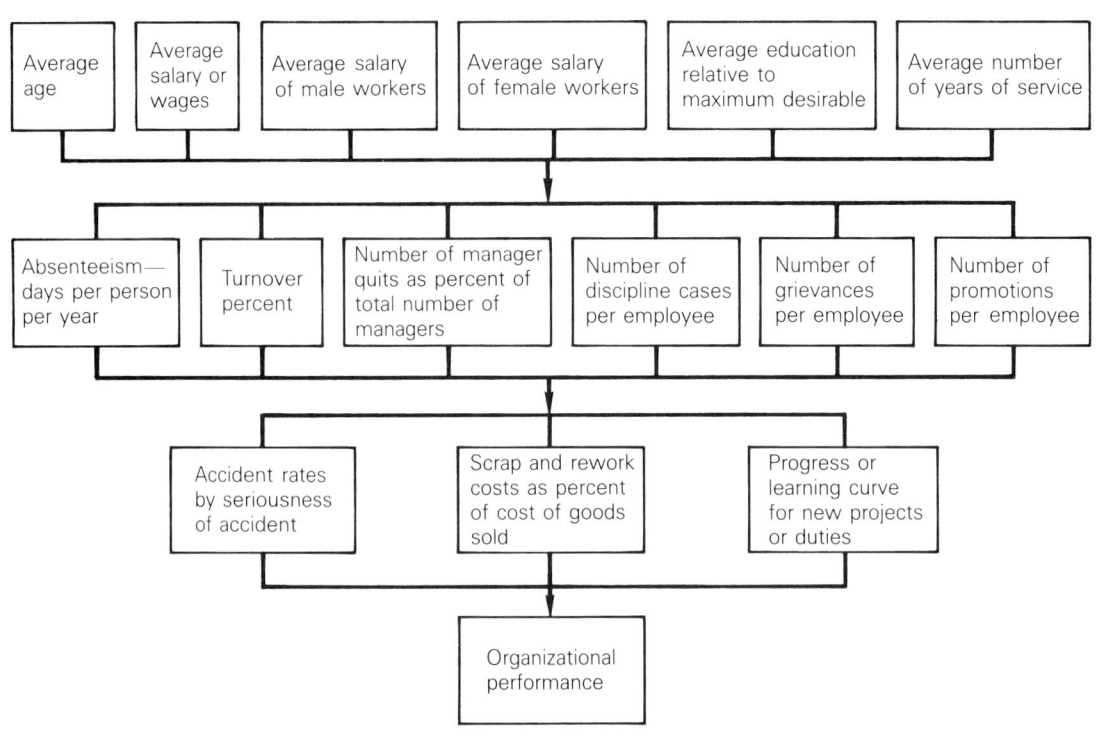

EXHIBIT 20–8
A. Indexes for comparison in measuring organizational performance.

EXHIBIT 20-8, continued
B. Indexes used to measure organizational performance.

*Effectiveness measures**

1. Physical output per worker-hour
2. Physical output per year for a specific organization
3. Physical output per manager
4. Payroll costs per unit of physical output
5. Number of promotions divided by the number of employees
6. Reduction in the number of grievances filed
7. Employee attitude ratings of company work conditions

Ineffectiveness measures

1. Scrap loss per organization unit
2. Accidents per organization (number and seriousness)
3. Lost time due to accidents
4. Number of grievances lost in arbitration
5. Employee turnover
6. Lost time due to tardiness
7. Sabotage incidents per organization unit
8. Average days of sickness per employee

Efficiency measures

1. Dollar value of cost reductions per employee
2. Number of contracts or customers served on schedule and within budgeted costs
3. Increase in dollars of sales per employee

Intervening variables in organizational performance

1. Average age of workers, managers, and nonmanagers
2. Employee job satisfaction as measured by attitude surveys
3. Length of service of employees by class of work
4. Employment distribution by sex, race, ethnic group, and manager/nonmanager
5. Salary and wage structure ratios
6. Number of employees enrolled in educational programs
7. Amount company spends per year on education and training per employee
8. Number of patents per employee
9. Number of days of leave granted per employee
10. Number of work-days spent at professional meetings per employee
11. Quit rate

*A survey of literature on effectiveness models is given by Richard M. Steers, "Problems in the Measurement of Organizational Effectiveness," *Administrative Science Quarterly,* December 1975. Most of these models do not provide direct quantitative indexes. See also Exhibit 20-6.

If the firm's turnover rate is computed to be 5 percent, is this good or bad? This cannot really be answered without looking at the turnover rates of similar companies in the area or at some industry turnover average through comparative analysis. We would also want to look at our own rate for past periods through historical analysis. If our rate were 5 percent versus 10 percent for the industry, this might suggest that employees who may not be contributing to organizational effectiveness are being retained. Therefore, no turnover at all may well be as bad as "excessive" turnover.

In Exhibit 20-8B, we have listed organizational performance indexes in more detail and have indicated whether they are effectiveness or efficiency indexes.

Intervening Variables Good organizational performance is highly dependent upon an organization's cohesiveness and upon the quality, motivation, and technical competence of its members. *Causal variables* are inputs to the human resource system that provide these factors. Between the inputs and the outputs of the organization, these are characteristics of the organization in action. These are called *intervening variables*. Rensis Likert, former director of the Institute for Social Research at the University of Michigan, has made a long and extensive study of the measurement of intervening variables.[4]

Attitude questionnaires have been developed and used by a number of companies to measure the characteristics of an organization in action. Perhaps the most sophisticated use of attitude questionnaires has been made by Likert, who incorporates survey feedback methodology in his design for a human control system. Likert's approach is particularly relevant for us because it applies the feedback control methodology we have already discussed to the control of human resources.

Likert's methodology consists essentially of measuring attitudes longitudinally in an organization on a recurring basis, utilizing a highly refined and validated questionnaire. The results of these surveys are fed back to top management, within the framework of Likert's model incorporating systems 1, 2, 3, and 4. This enables the executives to take corrective action with regard to human resources. Thus, Likert's model closely matches the general model for feedback control systems detailed earlier.

Exhibit 20–9 shows Likert's conception of the relationships among input, intervening, and output variables. In this exhibit, system 1 represents an "Exploitive Authoritative" management system, system 2 represents a "Benevolent Authoritative" system, and system 4 represents a "Participative Group." Arrows 1 through 4 indicate how causal variables in the Likert model lead to the associated intervening variables. If the intervening variables are measured and found to be at the favorable end of the scale used, then, as arrows 1 and 2 indicate, the output variables will be favorable. On the other hand, arrows 3 and 4 indicate that intervening variables in authoritative systems lead to undesirable performance or organizational characteristics.

Likert's methodology is the first explicit application of this general model to human resources. Exhibit 20–10 shows a sample of the Likert Survey Questionnaire and indicates the scaling technique that characterizes his methodology. Exhibit 20–11 shows a sample of items from another questionnaire form.

The Likert model is quite extensive and rich in its implications. We have brought it up only to show input/output concepts that are of interest to management for controlling the organization. For a full treatment of the model, the reader should refer to Likert's book, *The Human Organization*.

Net Change in Valuation of Human Resources Another approach to measuring organizational effectiveness is to evaluate the human resources in

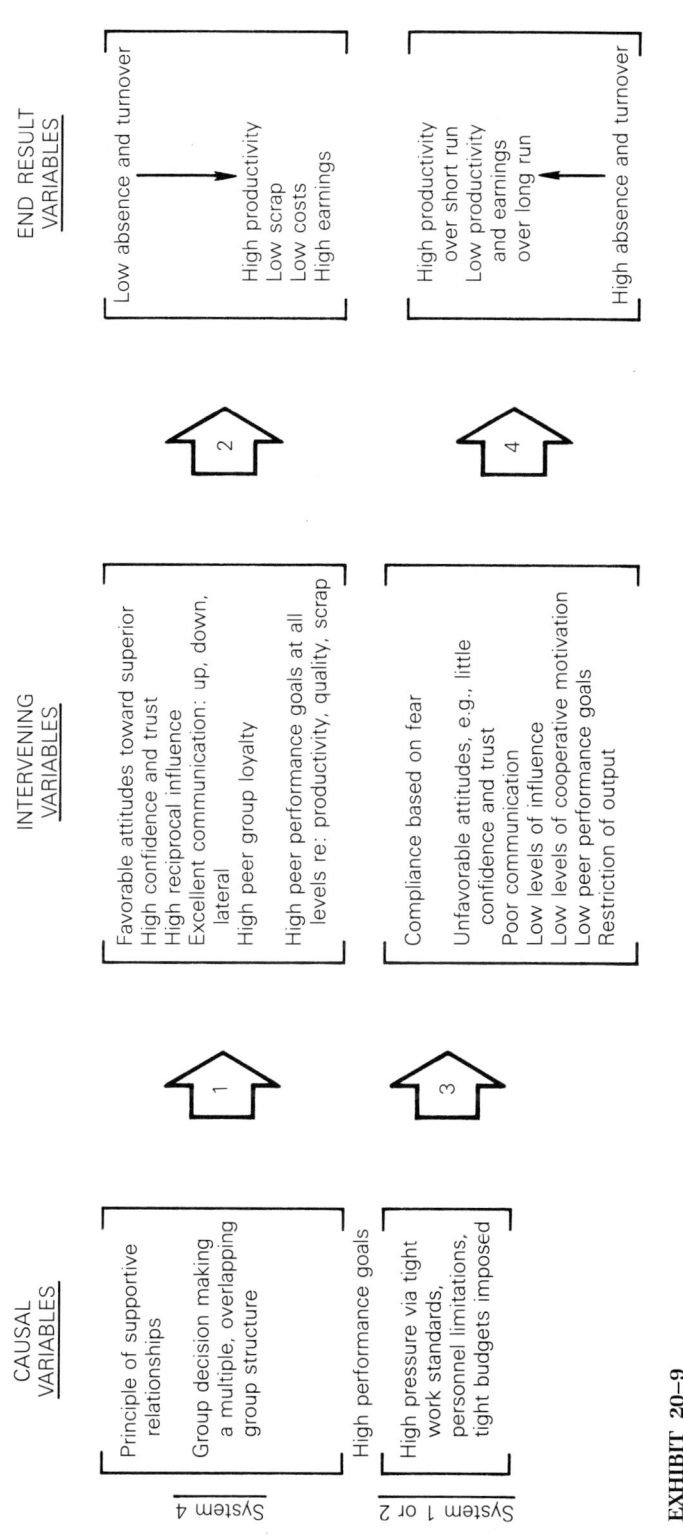

EXHIBIT 20–9
Simplified diagram of relationships among variables for System 1 or 2 and System 4 operation.

Source: Adapted from Rensis Likert, *The Human Organization: Its Management and Value* (New York: McGraw-Hill, 1967), p. 137. Copyright © 1967 McGraw-Hill Book Company. Reproduced with permission.

671

EXHIBIT 20–10
Likert Survey Questionnaire Excerpt.

Instructions:
1. On the lines below each organizational variable (item), please place an *n* at the point which, *in your experience*, describes your organization at the present time (*n* = now). Treat each item as a continuous variable from the extreme at one end to that at the other.
2. In addition, if you have been in your organization one or more years, please also place a *p* on each line at the point which, *in your experience*, describes your organization as it was one to two years ago (*p* = previously).
3. If you were not in your organization one or more years ago, please check here _____ and answer as of the present time, i.e., answer only with an *n*.

Organizational variable					Item no.
1. Leadership processes used a. Extent to which superiors have confidence and trust in *subordinates*	Have no confidence and trust in subordinates	Have condescending confidence and trust, such as master has in servant	Substantial but not complete confidence and trust; still wish to keep control of decisions	Complete confidence and trust in all matters	1
b. Extent to which subordinates, in turn, have confidence and trust in *superiors*	Have no confidence and trust in superiors	Have subservient confidence and trust, such as servant has to master	Substantial but not complete confidence and trust	Complete confidence and trust	2
c. Extent to which superiors display supportive behavior toward others	Display no supportive behavior or virtually none	Display supportive behavior in condescending manner and situations only	Display supportive behavior quite generally	Display supportive behavior fully and in all situations	3
d. Extent to which superiors behave so that subordinates feel free to discuss important things about their jobs with their immediate superior	Subordinates feel completely free to discuss things about the job with their superior	Subordinates feel rather free to discuss things about the job with their superior	Subordinates do not feel very free to discuss things about the job with their superior	Subordinates do not feel at all free to discuss things about the job with their superior	4
e. Extent to which immediate superior in solving job problems generally tries to get subordinates' ideas and opinions and make constructive use of them	Always gets ideas and opinions and always tries to make constructive use of them	Usually gets ideas and opinions and usually tries to make constructive use of them	Sometimes gets ideas and opinions of subordinates in solving job problems	Seldom gets ideas and opinions of subordinates in solving job problems	5

2. Character of motivational forces a. Underlying motives tapped	Physical security, economic needs, and some use of the desire for status	Economic needs and moderate use of ego motives, e.g., desire for status, affiliation, and achievement	Economic needs and considerable use of ego and other major motives, e.g., desire for new experiences	Full use of economic, ego, and other major motives, as, for example, motivational forces arising from group goals	6

Source: Rensis Likert, *The Human Organization: Its Management and Value* (New York: McGraw-Hill, 1967). Reproduced with the permission of the Estate of Rensis Likert.

EXHIBIT 20–11
Some items from an attitude survey form.

How much attention has your immediate manager given to helping you with your personal career plans?
  There has been no need for such a discussion so far. ☐ 0
  He has helped me considerably in developing my own personal career plans. ☐ 1
  Although my manager has never formally discussed career planning with me, he has nevertheless given me all the opportunity for development and advancement that I could ask for. ☐ 2
  He has discussed the subject with me, but has helped me only a little. ☐ 3
  I need this kind of help, but haven't gotten it from my manager. ☐ 4

To what extent have you been given sufficient information about ways to qualify yourself for promotional opportunities?
  I have no interest in this kind of information. ☐ 0
  I've received full and sufficient information—all I need. ☐ 1
  I've received quite a bit of information. ☐ 2
  I've received some information but need quite a bit more. ☐ 3
  I've received nowhere near enough information. ☐ 4

Within this operation, is the right amount of emphasis placed on developing the abilities of people so they will be ready for upgrade or promotion, as contrasted with going out and looking for people who are already fully qualified?
  Too much emphasis is put on searching out people who are already fully qualified. ☐ 1
  About the right emphasis is placed on both factors. ☐ 2
  Too much emphasis is put on trying to develop people who are already in the operation. ☐ 3

The promotion policy here places the *most* emphasis on:
  I don't know. ☐ 0
  Performance on the present job. ☐ 1
  Qualifications and background for the new job. ☐ 2
  Length of service. ☐ 3

Knowing or being known by the right people. ☐ 4
Other. ☐ 5

Do you know what you need to do in order to qualify yourself for upgrade or promotion?
  I have no interest in qualifying for a promotion. ☐ 0
  I'm quite certain I know exactly how to qualify myself for upgrade or promotion. ☐ 1
  I believe I know fairly well how to qualify myself for upgrade or promotion. ☐ 2
  I don't think I know very well how to qualify myself for upgrade or promotion. ☐ 3
  I don't know at all how to qualify myself for upgrade or promotion. ☐ 4

To what extent is your opportunity to advance out of your current job limited by a lack of formal training or education?
  Without further formal training or education, I can't advance beyond where I am now. ☐ 1
  Without further formal training or education I may advance just a little, but I'll never get a chance at any real promotions. ☐ 2
  Even without further formal training or education, there is still a fair chance that I can advance and be promoted. ☐ 3
  I believe I can continue to advance easily with only a minimum of added formal training or education (in-house courses, for instance). ☐ 4
  I believe that there is no limit on my opportunity to advance or be promoted, regardless of whether I ever take any further formal training or education or not. ☐ 5

How long have you been in your present job assignment—that is, doing the same type of work? (Being upgraded, downgraded, or transferred to another type of work would be a change in job assignment.)
  Less than 6 months. ☐ 1
  7 to 18 months. ☐ 2
  19 months but less than 3 years. ☐ 3
  3 to 5 years. ☐ 4
  More than 5 years. ☐ 5

terms of dollars and cents, or *human resource accounting*. This concept, proposed by Rensis Likert, was put into practice by Robert L. Woodruff, Jr., Vice President–Human Resources for the R. G. Barry Corporation. According to Woodruff, investments in human resources are made in group processes and team development. The R. G. Barry Corporation started with an outlay-cost approach consisting of:

- Recruiting outlay costs
- Acquisition costs of bringing a new person into the company
- Formal training costs
- Familiarization costs
- Investment building experience costs (the development of a capability beyond the normal expected)
- Development costs associated with specific technical skills

The first pro forma balance sheet developed by the company to combine financial and human resources is given in Exhibit 20–12. The change in the value of "net investments in human resources" may be considered to provide a measure of total organizational performance. The same concepts could be carried down through the hierarchy of organization components to measure the smallest formal groups in the company.

Although human resource accounting has fallen out of style, it is still a useful guide to change in value of the organization.

Variance of Performance from Objectives A method that has received increasing attention in recent years is the management by objectives approach. In this case, the factor measured is the variance of the performance from the objective. Exhibit 20–13 shows an application of MBO to an organizational group. Accordingly, all goals and activities of any work group are divided into three categories: problem-solving objectives, innovative goals, and routine chores. At the individual level, employees then work with their supervisor to set quantitative and qualitative goals for each work unit and activity.

George Odiorne suggests three other approaches to evaluating human resource programs. These involve comparing your organizational performance with external standards as follows:

1. Audit your organization by comparing your programs with those of other companies, especially the successful ones.
2. Have an outside authority, such as a consultant, audit your organization.
3. Have a staff department, such as the human resource department, set up all policies, procedures, and rules regarding human resource management. The internal auditor, along with his or her regular duties of checking revenues and expense procedures, audits the degree of compliance with these standards. This method is useful in ensuring compliance with legal requirements such as EEO and union contracts.

EXHIBIT 20-12
The total concept.

R. G. BARRY CORPORATION AND SUBSIDIARIES
Pro Forma Balance Sheet
(financial and human resource accounting)

Assets

	1969 Financial and human resource	1969 Financial only
Total current assets	$10,003,628	$10,003,628
Net property, plant and equipment	1,770,717	1,770,717
Excess of purchase price of subsidiaries over net assets acquired	1,188,704	1,188,704
Net investments in human resources	986,094	—
Other assets	106,783	106,783
	$14,055,926	$13,069,832

Liabilities and stockholders' equity

Total current liabilities	$ 5,715,708	$ 5,715,708
Long-term debt, excluding current installments	1,935,500	1,935,500
Deferred compensation	62,380	62,380
Deferred federal income taxes as a result of appropriation for human resources	493,047	—
Stockholders' equity:		
Capital stock	879,116	879,116
Additional capital in excess of par value	1,736,253	1,736,253
Retained earnings:		
Financial	2,740,875	2,740,875
Appropriation for human resources	493,047	—
Total stockholders' equity	5,849,291	5,356,244
	$14,055,926	$13,069,832

Statement of Income

	1969 Financial and human resource	1969 Financial only
Net sales	$25,310,588	$25,310,588
Cost of sales	16,275,876	16,275,876
Gross profit	9,034,712	9,034,712
Selling, general, and administrative expenses	6,737,313	6,737,313
Operating income	2,297,399	2,297,399
Other deductions, net	953,177	953,177
Income before federal income taxes	1,344,222	1,344,222
Human resource expenses applicable to future periods	173,569	—
Adjusted income before federal income taxes	1,517,791	1,344,222
Federal income taxes	730,785	644,000
Net income	$ 787,006	$ 700,222

Source: R. L. Woodruff, Jr., "Human Resource Accounting," *Canadian Chartered Accountant,* September 1970, p. 159. Reprinted with permission from CA magazine, published by The Canadian Institute of Chartered Accountants, Toronto, Canada.

Developing a Management Information System

Results of measurements must be communicated to managers. This must be done on a selective basis, however, or managers would spend all their time reading detailed reports with minor problems. Managers should re-

EXHIBIT 20-13
A bank's performance appraisal form for its corporate planning office.

```
Performance Appraisal

Name _____                    Date _____
                                               Date _____
                                               Date _____
                                               Date _____

PERFORMANCE MEASURES

1. Not Adequate. Not fully up to stand-   2. Fully Adequate. Performance meas-   3. Above Expectancy. Performance    4. Exceptional Performance is unusual
   ard development or other action           ure satisfactory to all standards.     consistently exceeds standards.     and clearly of superior quality. Con-
   needed.                                                                          Contribution is above expectancy    tribution is unique and is easily and
                                                                                    overall.                            generally identified and accepted as
                                                                                                                        such.
```

Accountabilities and Measurements	Performance Value

I. Has the Corporate Planning Office provided the CEO with adequate assistance in:
   a. The formulation of long-range policies, plans, and goals?
   b. Have existing corporate planning manuals been updated on a timely basis?
II. Have strategic planning needs been adequately defined?
III. Has the office provided adequate assistance to the CEO in the establishment of:
   a. Environmental assumptions?
   b. High performance standards?
IV. In connection with corporate performance standards, has the office adequately maintained a profile of our 22 competitive banks?
V. Has the coordination of long-range plans been:
   a. Effective?
   b. Timely?
VI. Were the objectives of the annual Planned Growth Conference adequately met?
VII. Have policies, plans, and goals relative to corporate development (product extension as well as mergers and acquisitions) been adequately defined?	

Source: James K. Brown and Rochelle O'Connor, *Planning and the Corporate Director* (New York: Conference Board, 1974), p. 54.

ceive *exception reports* when performance exceeds established limits about the standard. Management should also receive brief summary reports to study trends and actual total system performance. In addition, managers should be able to obtain detailed data, if needed, to help solve particular problems. As noted in Chapter 19, modern computer-based DBMS make such a management information system possible for control of the HR system.

DIAGNOSIS

While it is easy to say that control is achieved by keeping some HR variables within desired limits, it is not so easily done. First, we need to find the *problem* that produces such a symptom, and then must solve the problem by identifying both its cause and ways to remove it. The process of finding the problem and its cause from analysis of symptoms is called *diagnosis*. The science of treating diseases and their causes is called *pathology* in the medical field. Both of the above terms could appropriately be applied to the treatment of HR systems. The diagnostic approach consists, then, of:

1. Identifying symptoms of malfunctioning HR systems from the data provided by control systems
2. Diagnosing the problem and its causes by data gathering and analysis of the HR system

3. Treating the pathology to remove the causes of the malfunctioning of the HR system

A more detailed look at the diagnostic approach to managing human resources is given in Exhibit 20–14. An illustration of the process is provided by Exhibit 20–15.

Basis for the Diagnostic Approach to HR Management

The diagnostic approach starts with the assumption that the HR system is in place and functioning reasonably well. In real life, however, good things do not continue. Changes in the environment, changes in the work force, changes in working conditions or procedures, or changes in leadership produce changes in output of the total HR system and some subsystems. It is even possible that changes in the output of various subsystems counteract each other so that the total HR outputs do not noticeably change. Diagnosis is, in nontechnical language, "trouble-shooting" guided by theory or a model.

An Application

We have discussed a general model of the diagnostic approach (shown in Exhibit 20–14). We will now show a more complex example of diagnosis. We

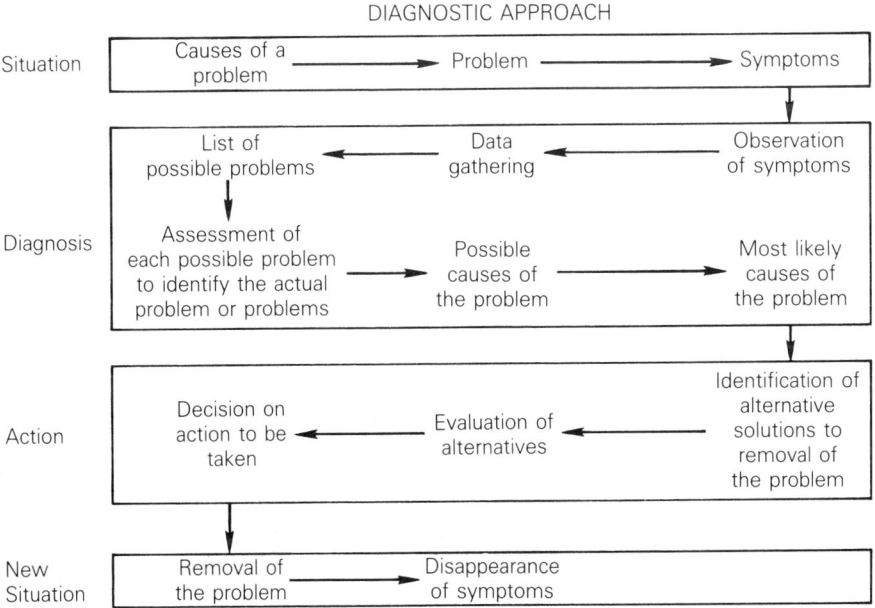

EXHIBIT 20–14

EXHIBIT 20-15
Example of diagnostic approach.

1. *Observation of symptoms*
   A. Customers complain that twisted strand cables are failing and breaking.
   B. Output of cables fluctuates and varies from standard.

2. *Data gathering*
   A. Number of feet of cable manufactured meets schedule.
   B. Fluctuations appear in the Quality Control group's output.
   C. Test equipment and QC procedures have remained unchanged.
   D. QC group consists of long-term employees previously highly satisfied with their jobs.

3. *List of possible problems*
   A. Production equipment is wearing out and not producing according to specs.
   B. New production employees are not adequately trained.
   C. QC group has become dissatisfied over some recent, unknown incident.
   D. Some physical change in QC employees is preventing them from performing the fine inspection work.

4. *Assessment of each possible problem*
   After data are gathered on each possible problem it appears that the QC employees are unable to see defects in the cable as well as they could in the past. As a result, defective cable is slipping past them to customers.

5. *Possible causes of the problem*
   A. Inadequate lighting
   B. Too rapid production and QC
   C. Physical change in employees caused by age

6. *Most likely cause*
   Employees are all now in their mid forties so that most have become far-sighted and cannot see tiny flaws in the cable.

7. *Alternative solutions*
   A. Transfer all QC employees to other work and bring in younger workers.
   B. Buy all the QC employees bifocal glasses.

8. *Decision*
   Buy all QC employees bifocal glasses.

will trace the causes of system malfunctioning that have led to symptoms such as:

1. Lack of care for company property
2. Hostility toward the company
3. Sabotage
4. Psychological withdrawal from organizational activities (apathy)
5. High frequency of dispensary visits

For these symptoms, we gather data about the employees, their work history, and possible immediate or direct causes that could produce these symptoms. It turns out that immediate causes are:

1. Absenteeism
2. Turnover
3. Poor mental health
4. Dissatisfaction with jobs

You may have noticed that these causes are actually symptoms themselves and not malfunctioning systems. We must, therefore, continue our diagno-

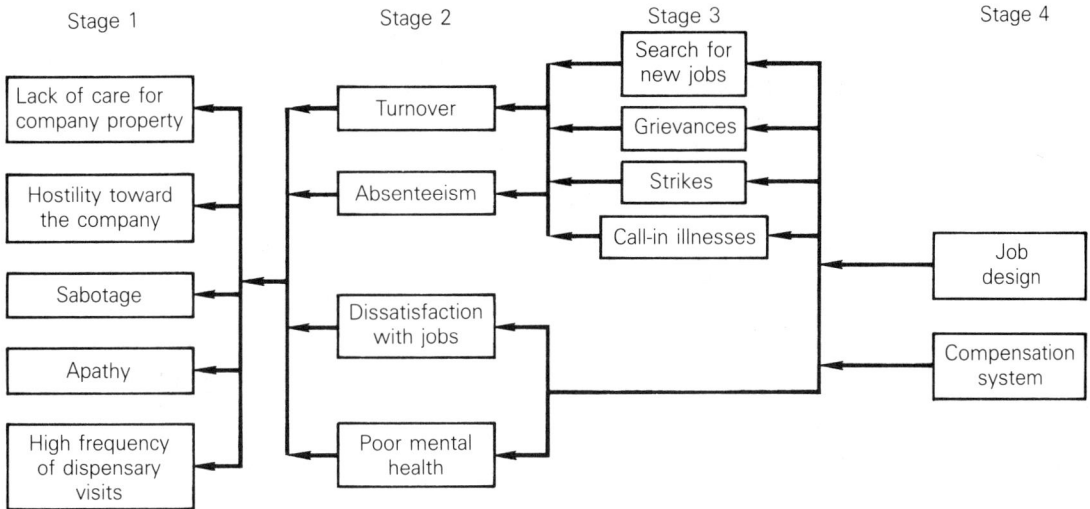

EXHIBIT 20–16
Diagnosis to identify malfunctioning HR systems.

sis. Exhibit 20–16 shows that we next identify the apparent causes of turnover and absenteeism as searches for new jobs by employees, grievances, strikes, and call-in illness. Again, these are symptoms. We note from data gathered that these symptoms may be traced to job design and the compensation system. We also note that other symptoms—job dissatisfaction and poor mental health can be traced to the same systems. These two systems are apparently the malfunctioning systems. The causes of the malfunctioning and appropriate corrective action must finally be determined. To carry out this last step, we must analyze the functioning of healthy systems as described in Chapters 5, 13, 14, and 15. Either or both of the systems, job design and compensation, may be the culprit leading to our initial set of symptoms. Note that possible symptoms at each stage may be determined from outputs of the HR management control reports.

HUMAN RESOURCE RESEARCH

What Is Research?

Diagnosis is a form of research in that it attempts to answer a question, namely "What are possible causes of the apparent symptoms or variances?" *Research* is a systematic approach to solving problems based upon a hypothesis (or model), explanatory principles, and the gathering of empirical data. Research is distinct from common-sense methods of problem solving because these are based upon specific experiences and relatively incomplete and biased data. For example, suppose that a company were faced with a rapid increase in turnover in one of its departments. A common-sense approach might have us looking at the characteristics of the manager and perhaps attributing the cause to him or her. In research, we would use a diagnostic model to trace the symptoms back to possible causes such as changes in the nature of the work, compensation for comparable work in other companies, new unliked employees, changes in the manager's behavior, and so on. Data would be gathered and analyzed utilizing statistical and other scientific techniques. The conclusion might be quite different from the common-sense approach.

Research may fall between the extremes of basic research and applied research. Basic research seeks new knowledge regardless of application. For examples, theories of motivation or the relationship among employee benefits, salary, and turnover would be subjects for basic research. Applied research is an investigation to solve a particular problem within a company. For example, what should company ABC spend on T & D to maximize profits? Only a few large companies conduct basic research.

Data for research may be primary or secondary. If a company conducts an attitude survey or an experiment, it is generating primary data. Secondary data are those obtained from research carried out by others and usually available in publications. Companies keep much data useful for research in their computerized data bases. On the other hand, company personnel researchers often require data from external sources (to be discussed later in this chapter).

The cost of research can vary widely. Therefore, the personnel researcher should prepare a proposal for management approval before undertaking research. In some cases, the human resource information system can manipulate, classify, and analyze data quite economically. In other cases, very expensive research projects are required to be specially designed for an important problem.

Why Do HR Research?

Human Resource research is useful for solving and preventing all types of problems. It is, in a sense, the most generalized form of control because it guides us toward achieving basic objectives. Human Resource research, by telling us what we *should* be doing, assists in setting objectives and plans that form the basis of control. When things do go wrong, research is much more likely to lead us to correct solutions than common sense alone. In addition, results from research may be more generalized and will, therefore, apply to future situations.

Who Does HR Research?

In the very large companies, there may be a corporate staff group that conducts basic research in personnel problems of general interest to the company. At lower levels of large companies and in medium-size companies, there sometimes is a personnel researcher who works on special problems

> **Research vs. Common Sense**
>
> It has been assumed for years, from common sense, that turnover is dysfunctional because it is expensive to replace employees. A study of a real organization showed that the savings over a 5-year period produced by replacing a top-pay employee earning $10.45/hour with an entry level employee at $5.82/hour amounted to $50,000. The savings consisted of salary, recovered pension, and return on recovered savings.
> For a 15% turnover rate in a 30-person organization, a savings of $389,000/year would be achieved!

Source: Dan R. Dalton and William D. Todor, "Turnover: A Lucrative Hard Dollar Phenomenon," *Academy of Management Review,* April 1982.

of interest to management. In most companies, however, the individual responsible for a functional area such as T & D or compensation does his or her own research.

Fortunately, doing your own research is greatly aided by data from the research of many external organizations. For example, universities and consulting companies do much research that is published and readily available. The U.S. Bureau of Labor Statistics reports on its research in its monthly publication. A number of professional associations such as The Conference Board, Bureau of National Affairs, American Compensation Association, and the American Management Association provide a continuing source of valuable data and research. For a list of associations, organizations, and publications important to researchers and managers in the human resource field, see Appendices A and B at the end of this chapter.

What the HR Manager Needs to Know about Research

The modern manager of human resources does not have to be a trained researcher, but he or she must have a general knowledge about research. The manager should know what research is and what its limitations are. He or she must have a general idea of the general methods or techniques of research. The HR manager must have some knowledge of data bases and computer facilities available for research. The purpose of having such knowledge is to put the manager in a good position to suggest or evaluate proposals for research put forth by members of the personnel section. We will therefore introduce the principal research techniques in terms of what they are like and what they do.

Principal Research Techniques for HR Management

There are six commonly used research techniques for inquiry into human resource problems. The first is simply a systematic search of literature to find either relevant data or previous research by others that will solve the problem. One approach is to go through bibliographies, abstract services, and directories in the library to search for publications of interest. Another approach is to start with an article on the topic and trace its bibliography to other articles and their bibliographies.[5]

Perhaps the most common type of HR research is simply historical research. The researcher gathers data already in company records and analyzes it. For example, the careers of employees who completed certain company T & D programs could be compared with careers of employees with comparable backgrounds who did not take the program. The results would indicate whether the T & D program is worth retaining.

Sample survey methods, if properly designed statistically, permit estimating an average and variability of a large number of people or their characteristics at a low cost. For instance, we might wish to determine how many of our 3,000 employees do not have proper lighting for their work. One way of determining this would be to use a light meter to measure the lighting at each employee's work station. Alternatively, a probability sample of, say, 100 employees could be used to estimate the proportion of the 3,000 employees with proper lighting.

Experimental design is another research method that may provide valuable data for human resource management. This method is used to determine if certain "treatments" lead to different results. For example, one group of employees could be selected to work the regular five-day, 40-hour week. Another group properly selected could be put on a four-day, 40-hour week; another group could be put on a flexitime basis. The object would be to determine if these different "treatments" resulted in a significant difference in productivity.

Correlation and regression analysis, relatively simple techniques, provide the HR management with information about the association and likely causal effects between two variables. As an example, we might use such methods to see if there is a relationship between favorable worker attitudes toward their jobs and amount of company-sponsored T & D courses taken.

A much more complex set of research methods involves multivariate analysis. This is a statistical method that simultaneously analyzes two or more variables in a sample of observations. In one form, it permits measuring the association between two or more *sets* (or groups) of variables.

Typical Applications of Research to HR Problems

The kinds of control and problem areas where research may help in HR management are abundant. Examples of such topics and one of the research techniques that might be used, depending on how the problem is stated, include:

1. *Legal environment*
   A. Closing a plant—Library research
   B. Sexual harassment—Library research
2. *Organization and HR planning requirements*
   A. Forecasting HR needs—Correlation of manpower with sales
   B. Attrition forecast—Historical studies

3. *Work design*
   A. Physical work arrangement—Experimental design
   B. Fatigue as a function of task variety—Correlation
   C. Job rotation variables associated with worker satisfaction variables—Multivariate analysis
   D. Impact of the computer on absenteeism and productivity—Multivariate analysis
4. *Recruiting*
   A. Labor markets—Literature (library) research
   B. Sources of candidates—Probability sample survey
5. *Selection*
   A. Effectiveness of interviewing—Historical studies
   B. Test validation—Correlation
   C. Disadvantaged workers vs. productivity over time—Correlation
6. *Productivity, leadership, and motivation*
   A. Effectiveness of leadership styles for various organizational components—Multivariate analysis
   B. Effects of wage increases on productivity—Correlation
7. *Organization development*
   A. Attitudes of managers before and after OD program—Experimental design
   B. Change in productivity vs. hours of OD effort—Regression analysis
8. *Communicating*
   A. Change in attitude with new communication format—Multivariate analysis
   B. Productivity and efficiency change with quality circles—Multivariate analysis
9. *Individual T & D*
   A. Career progress vs. T & D hours in a variety of courses—Multivariate analysis
   B. Effectiveness of various T & D courses—Experimental design
10. *Career development*
    A. Counseling available vs. counseling demand—Historical records
    B. Effectiveness of counseling—Historical records
11. *The reward system*
    A. Comparison of rewards with those of other companies—Multivariate analysis
    B. Cost trend of reward system—Historical study
12. *Administering the reward system*
    A. Compensation vs. turnover—Regression
    B. Cost of benefits—Historical study
13. *Appraisal and reward*
    A. Legal problems and constraints under EEO—Library research
    B. Appraisals vs. rewards—Correlation and regression

14. *Labor–management relations*
    A. Number of grievances by department—Historical study
    B. Cost of administering the union contract—Historical study
15. *Employee maintenance*
    A. Cost of employee maintenance programs—Historical study
    B. Attitudes of employee toward cafeteria—Sample survey
16. *Control system*
    A. Methods of control vs. attitudes of employees—Multivariate analysis (or library research on other company studies)
    B. Control limits vs. number of problems requiring investigation—Sample survey

SUMMARY

Control of HR systems means bringing within limits or maintaining performance or attributes of individuals or groups within prescribed limits. The HR system and its subsystems control all the systems in the business so that control of the HR system is very important. Such control requires the establishment of standards, development of measures of effectiveness and efficiency, information systems, and implementation processes. It also requires diagnosis of problems when systems exceed control limits and research to develop control standards and solve control problems.

Control systems should be (1) based on company goals and plans, (2) clearly expressed standards, (3) key tasks and events, (4) objective and quantitative whenever possible, (5) able to inform managers and workers of variances from standards quickly, and (6) economical. The personnel department is responsible for advising management on the construction of HR control systems and their impact on the organization. Company managers are accountable for the actual design, implementation, and operation of the HR control systems.

Control may be accomplished by (1) modifying system inputs, (2) modifying the system process, (3) screening outputs.

A very important concept is feedback of information about output of a system or subsystem to an individual worker or manager responsible for such output. This permits the worker/manager to correct the inputs, the system design, or the system processing to bring output within the established limits about the standard. A feedback system is called a closed loop system whereas a system without feedback control is called an open loop system.

Control of the system process with feedback means that there is a delay because action is not taken until a significant deviation has taken place. With steering control of the process, however, the output of the system is *predicted* so that corrective action may be taken *before* the deviation from standard occurs.

MBO, or management by objectives, is a well established method for controlling individual workers and managers. It depends, usually, on feedback after three to six months of activity so that it is more of a long-term control system than day-to-day monitoring, coordinating, and self-control.

Control of HR takes place at the various administrative levels: total company, division, business or profit center, functional, and functional subsystem. Of particular interest to us is control of the personnel department functional system and its subsystems.

The first step in developing the HR control system is to develop system descriptions and operating flowcharts for all systems as we have done in the previous chapters for the personnel department subsystems. The inputs, the processes, and the outputs are thus clearly defined.

The second step is to decide what kind of control system is suitable for each subsystem and the total HR system. That is, is a simple feedback control, process steering control, or a combination appropriate? Is MBO, the slow feedback control, adequate?

The third step is to identify criteria that can be used as the basis for measuring how well a particular HR subsystem is performing. Such criteria must be established by viewing organizational performance through the eyes of stakeholders such as the company owners, workers, and societal groups.

Criteria may be derived from approaches suggested by researchers, models developed by researchers, and criteria proposed by managers. Most criteria cannot be directly scaled for measurement. Instead, various indexes or other indirect or partial criterion measures must be developed.

Fourth, we develop the criterion measures such as:

1. Statistical measures
2. Attitude surveys for measuring intervening variables within the organization
3. Net change in accounting valuation of human resources
4. Quantitative objectives, partial objectives, or Key Result Areas

Finally, we develop a management information system. Such a system determines the information needs of managers, captures data required to produce reports for monitoring and feedback, and includes a reporting structure appropriate for each level of management. Such a report structure provides summary reports, exception reports, and the opportunity for managers' inquiries to be answered promptly and accurately.

When systems malfunction or their environment changes, symptoms of problems appear. Diagnosis is the search for the underlying problems and the specific causes of the problems. A model of the HR system and principles describing its functions are required for systematic diagnosis. When the control report tells us that certain variables have exceeded their control limits, we have symptoms with which to start. We then work backward through the model to diagnose the root problems.

Research is the systematic search for answers to questions (solutions to a problem) utilizing scientific methods, techniques, and principles. HR research can be used to establish control systems, to help prevent the HR activities from going out of control, and to help solve problems when activities have gone out of control. Common methods and techniques utilized in the vast number of possible human resource control and problem areas are:

1. Literature, or library, searches
2. Historical record studies
3. Probability sample survey methods
4. Design of experiments
5. Correlation and regression
6. Multivariate analysis

The HR manager does not need to have any skill in personally employing these techniques. It is important that he or she have a knowledge of what each of these can do to aid in solving problems. Also, because the HR manager must evaluate proposals, or even make proposals, to do research in the personnel area, the manager must have a general feeling for the complexity, cost, and time involved in carrying out various types of research.

KEY CONCEPTS

Control

Feedback control

Steering control

Intervening variables

Indicants

Human resource accounting

Diagnosis

Research

NOTES

1. William G. Ouchi, "The Transmission of Control through Organizational Hierarchy," *Academy of Management Journal*, June 1978, p. 174.
2. Charles G. Schoderbek, Peter P. Schoderbek, and Asterios G. Kefalas, *Management Systems: Conceptual Considerations* (Dallas: Irwin-Dorsey Limited, 1980).
3. J. Barton Cunningham, "Approaches to the Evaluation of Organizational Effectiveness," *Academy of Management Review*, June 1970.
4. Rensis Likert, *The Human Organization: Its Management and Value* (New York: McGraw-Hill, 1967).
5. For a concise but complete guide to library research, see Robert G. Murdick and Donald R. Cooper, *Business Research: Concepts and Guides* (New York: Wiley, 1982), pp. 139–151.

REVIEW AND DISCUSSION QUESTIONS

1. Define "control" and show how the definition covers the various meanings of control found in the literature.
2. What are the two perspectives for studying control of organizations?
3. Discuss the role of the P/HR in the three-level framework for control of human resources.
4. A company wishes to control "quality" of people hired. Propose a control system that matches the list of desirable characteristics of a control system as given in the text.
5. Discuss the following table as to whether you agree with the items in the cells and state your reasoning for agreement or disagreement.

	Rewards	Punishment
Tight control	Effective control	Ineffective control?
Loose control	Effective if objectives are made specific and clear	Ineffective control?

6. Assume that you are writing a policy and procedure for vacation applications. Everybody cannot go on vacation at the same time nor can certain key people. However, it is desirable to try to give as many people as possible a choice of vacation time. Prepare both a brief policy and a procedure for approval of vacation times.
7. Management wishes to reduce or eliminate the practice of employees utilizing sick leave for vacation time. As P/HR manager, devise a control system to help management accomplish this purpose.
8. "All P/HR reports are control reports for management." Discuss.
9. Management wishes to identify the most competent and effective employees early in their careers and to reward them promptly by salary increases and promotions. Develop a control system to be implemented by P/HR that will help management accomplish this objective.
10. Criteria for measuring organizational effectiveness should be judged in terms of relevance, freedom from bias, reliability, and availability. Explain what each of these four terms means to you.
11. In the Likert model, give a hypothetical scenario of a high-pressure situation and trace the intervening variables and end results specific to your scenario.
12. Discuss the pros and cons of the human resource accounting model.
13. (a) What is the diagnostic approach to HR management? (b) Give an example of applications of the model in Exhibit 20–14 starting with "observation of symptoms" that employees are taking long coffee breaks, arriving late, and rushing out of work at the stroke of 5 P.M., quitting time.

14. List five problems for which research by the P/HR could be cost-justified.
15. "Students majoring in P/HR management should be required to take a course in research." Discuss.

BIBLIOGRAPHY

Cameron, Kim. "Measuring Organizational Effectiveness in Institutions of Higher Education." *Administrative Science Quarterly*, December 1978.
Connolly, Terry, Edward J. Conlon, and Stuart J. Deutch. "Organizational Effectiveness: A Multiple Constituency Approach." *Academy of Management Journal*, April 1980.
Cunningham, J. Barton. "Approaches to the Evaluation of Organizational Effectiveness." *Academy of Management Review*, July 1977.
Cutler, Paul. *Problem Solving in Clinical Medicine: From Data to Diagnosis.* Baltimore: Williams and Wilkins, 1979.
DeWitt, Frank. "A Technique for Measuring Management Productivity." *Management Review*, June 1970.
Ferguson, Charles R. *Measuring Corporate Strategy.* Homewood, Ill.: Irwin, 1974.
"General Electric Company," BC260R2. Cambridge, Mass.: Harvard Business School Intercollegiate Case Clearing House, 1970.
Glueck, William F. *Personnel: A Diagnostic Approach*, rev. by George T. Milkovitch. Plano, Tex.: Business Publications, 1982.
Jauch, R., and Skigen, M. "Human Resource Accounting: A Critical Evaluation." *Management Accounting*, May 1974.
Jones, D. M. C. "Accounting for Human Assets." *Management Decision*, Summer 1973.
Kepner, Charles H., and Benjamin B. Tregoe. *The Rational Manager.* New York: McGraw-Hill, 1965.
Lawler, Edward E. III, and John Grant Rhodes. *Information Control in Organizations.* Pacific Palisades, Ca.: Goodyear, 1976. See Chap. 9, "Measuring the Human Organization."
Likert, Rensis. *The Human Organization: Its Management and Value.* New York: McGraw-Hill, 1967.
Likert, Rensis. "Human Organizational Measurements: Key to Financial Success," *Michigan Business Review*, May 1971.
Likert, Rensis. "Human Resource Accounting: Building and Assessing Productive Organizations." *Personnel*, May–June 1973.
Mock, Theodore J., and Hugh D. Grove. *Measurement, Accounting, and Organizational Information.* New York: Wiley, 1979.
Murdick, Robert G. *MIS: Concepts and Design,* Englewood Cliffs, N.J.: Prentice-Hall, 1980.
Murdick, Robert G., and Donald R. Cooper. *Business Research.* New York: Wiley, 1982.
Newman, William H. *Constructive Control.* Englewood Cliffs, N.J.: Prentice-Hall, 1975.
Nutt, Paul C. "Calling Out and Calling Off the Dogs: Managerial Diagnosis in Public Service Organizations." *Academy of Management Review*, April 1979.

Ouchi, William G., and Mary Ann Maguire. "Organizational Control: Two Functions." *Administrative Science Quarterly*, December 1975.

Paine, Frank T., and William Naumes. *Strategy and Policy Formation.* Philadelphia: Saunders, 1974.

Pugh, D. S. "The Measurement of Organization Structures." *Organizational Dynamics*, Spring 1973.

Safiuddin, Mohammed. "Systems Analysis," Part 2, *Machine Design*, January 25, 1973.

Schoderbek, Charles G., Peter P. Schoderbek, and Asterios G. Kefalas. *Management Systems: Conceptual Considerations.* Dallas: Irwin-Dorsey Limited, 1980.

Schuster, Fred E. "The Human Resources Index: A Tool for Evaluating and Controlling the Management of Human Resources." *Personnel Administrator*, October 1982.

Steers, Richard M. *Organizational Effectiveness: A Behavioral View.* Santa Monica, Ca.: Goodyear, 1977.

Steers, Richard M. "Problems in the Measurement of Organizational Effectiveness." *Administrative Science Quarterly*, December 1975.

Stokes, Paul M. *A Total Systems Approach to Management Control.* New York: American Management Association, 1968.

Thierauf, Robert J. *Management Auditing: A Questionnaire Approach.* New York: AMACOM, 1980.

Wahba, Mahmoud A., and Harris Jack Shapiro. "Managerial Assessment of Organizational Components." *Academy of Management Journal*, June 1973.

Wallace, Marc J., Jr. "Methodology, Research Practice, and Progress in Personnel and Industrial Relations." *Academy of Management Review* 8 (1), 1983.

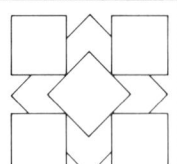

CASE STUDY:
Fast Food—Slow Control

MEMORANDUM

TO: Ms. Donna Gulin, Director of Human Resource Services
FROM: Dave Minter, President

Our financial control system tells us that we have problems involving people performance. By the time we get the word, identify the problem, and take corrective action, however, a lot of money has gone down the drain.

I read something about "key result areas" recently. Could you identify key performance areas for our personnel, develop standards and methods of measurement, and propose a program for the implementation of control?

Donna Gulin recently received her MBA from Florida Atlantic University. Although she had had several years of business experience, this was her first executive position—Director of Human Resource Services for the Hercules Hamburger Company. She had held this position only three months when she received the above memo.

Hercules Hamburger Company was a fast-food chain of 30 outlets in southeast Florida. The outlets were owned and managed by the company. The problem areas were personnel turnover, the tendency of managers to let the outlets get run-down in appearance, occasional failures to keep equipment and premises clean, and occasional failure of order-takers to be courteous and prompt in servicing customers.

In addition, it appeared that managers who obtained good locations tended to drift rather than build up business the way managers did at poorer locations. Managers did not always identify with the company objectives of growth and dynamism.

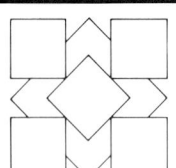

CASE STUDY:
Improving a Computerized HR Information System

In 1979, Airco comprised eight major divisions of approximately 12,000 employees, half salaried. The corporate payroll department paid almost 80 percent of the salaried employees and about 20 percent of the hourly employees.

With few exceptions, each division had a payroll office for its hourly employees. Each office had its own unique standards and procedures which caused problems for the corporate payroll and employee benefits departments. These payroll systems were supported by their own computer systems, using different data collection, edit checking and reporting procedures. The differences caused inconsistent, late and sometimes just plain wrong information when it reached the corporate employee benefits department.

Airco faced four major problems. First, manual procedures did not keep pace with the company's current and divisional requirements. Second, the divisions had difficulty in providing timely and accurate data to the corporate departments. Third, the divisions also had a need for information from the corporate departments. And fourth, the multiplicity of payroll offices, systems and procedures was in itself a significant problem.

The company addressed these problems with three objectives in mind: improve the quality of data; reduce the number of payroll offices and improve the timeliness of the data for corporate departments and divisions.

During a feasibility study, corporate and division representatives from industrial relations, payroll and data processing were interviewed as to their departments' needs. The investigations produced three alternative approaches.

The first alternative was to keep the system intact. Maintain a centralized salary payroll, attempt to improve the existing corporate benefits system, and improve the accuracy of the benefits files by comparing their information with the division's.

In essence, this alternative was a holding pattern and only minimally addressed the three objectives of the project. It would, however, improve data quality by comparing and highlighting inconsistencies between the systems.

The second alternative maintained the decentralized approach, but also recommended that we install one common package at corporate payroll and at the payroll offices with similar computers.

Airco would have one vendor with several versions of the package located in the payroll offices. In addition, we would identify and audit the use of standard editing requirements, thereby achieving commonality in data problem.

Under the third alternative we would change our basic way of doing the payroll. We would have one package and it would be a centralized system. All payrolls would be converted onto the corporate payroll. This approach, however, also recommended that file maintenance be done locally. We would make use of additional minicomputers and existing computer hardware to allow remote locations to enter the information locally, have it edited, and passed to the corporate system. We would also use computers to produce remote checks and various reports.

Source: Richard J. Balicki, "Teamwork Makes the System Fit." Reprinted from *Infosystems,* August 1983. Copyright Hitchcock Publishing Company.

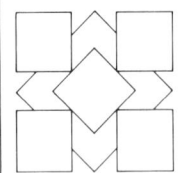

CASE STUDY:
A Problem of Research Methodology

Caroline Spiller had just been hired by Midwestern Bank, Inc., comprised of 10 individual banks throughout the state. She was given the title of Systems Researcher in the Human Resource Department at headquarters with the idea that she would assist the Manager of Human Resources, Della Ornston, on special assignments. Spiller had just been graduated from a college of business, where she had studied such topics as operations management, statistical methods, research methodology, and computer systems.

One of the problems that supervisors and executives at the bank found was affecting operations adversely was the fact that new employees were often confused about what the bank's policies and procedures were. Even the more experienced employees were upset with contradictory information they would get concerning their performance.

Spiller was assigned to clarify the problem to be researched. As her first attempt, she prepared the following:

The Statement of the Problem

This research proposes to determine how sources of feedback influence employee satisfaction and performance in the work setting.

The Subproblems

1. *The first subproblem.* The first subproblem is to determine what are the sources of feedback that influence employee satisfaction and performance.
2. *The second subproblem.* The second subproblem consists of determining the relative importance an individual attaches to a source of information.
3. *The third subproblem.* The third subproblem consists of measuring satisfaction and performance variations in the work setting when various sources of feedback are employed.

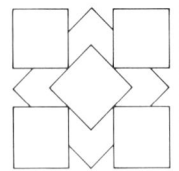

CASE STUDY:
Computer and Telecommunications Technology, Inc.

Computer and Telecommunications Technology, Inc. (C & TT) is a high-tech company that employs 2,000 people at its single plant site in Houston, Texas. It was founded in 1978 by two brothers, Jim and Fred Ure. Initially it produced components for computers and telecommunications hardware, but it quickly expanded into production of systems involving both computers and communication equipment.

In January 1985, approximately one third of its work force was in research and

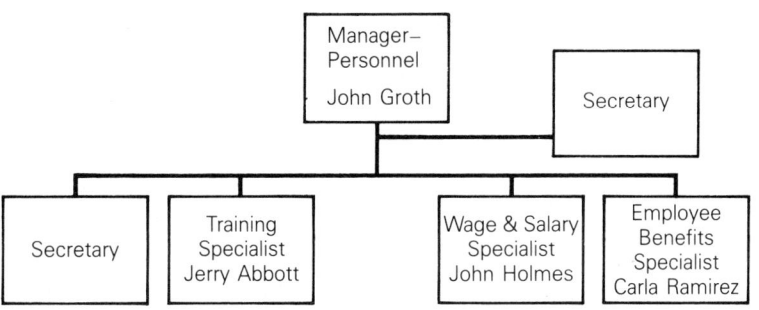

EXHIBIT A
Personnel Department in January 1985.

engineering, one third in manufacturing, and the rest in marketing, support services, and administration. The personnel department consisted of six employees as shown in Exhibit A. John Groth and the line managers carried out the recruiting activities for the company.

Records of all employees were kept on McBee key-sort cards. Additional correspondence and forms relating to employees were kept in individual manila folders in file cabinets in the personnel department. Current salary data were kept by personnel, payroll, and individual section managers. The section managers throughout the plant also maintained files on their subordinates for review of salaries, promotions, and training needs.

The employee benefits specialist, Carla Ramirez, had anticipated the growth of needed records. She had also been assigned EEO record-keeping and reporting tasks. She had, therefore, established a record-keeping system employing punched computer cards in 1980. By borrowing time on a minicomputer in the accounting department, she was barely able to keep up with her responsibilities. Often her reports were late because the computer was in use when she needed it.

John Groth was aware of the problems for the personnel department created by the rapid growth of C & TT, the need to attract very high-quality creative people, and the need to develop a high QWL. He had had numerous discussions with the president, Jim Ure, on this subject. In view of the company's intention to set up a 500-employee plant in Los Angeles by July 1987, the problems of expanding and upgrading personnel services had become urgent. Groth, therefore, wrote a memo to Ure to emphasize the need for action (Exhibit B). He shortly thereafter received a comprehensive reply from Jim Ure (Exhibit C).

EXHIBIT B

C & TT, Inc.
INTEROFFICE MEMO

TO: Jim Ure
FROM: John Groth
February 8, 1985

Jim, I would like to summarize the personnel department situation and my proposals for the future following our discussions over the past year.

We have the following problems at present, which will get worse as we expand at Houston and open the L.A. plant:

1. Recruiting and interviewing is taking so much of my time that I do not have time to supervise my department well.
2. Jerry Abbott is so wrapped up in the details of running classes that he cannot put together a good T & D program and keep records updated.
3. Our benefits program will soon break down under the weight of number of employees and new government reporting requirements.
4. We have no one to design and analyze jobs. Holmes is tied up in one crisis after another as the managers bring out new position titles to ratchet up salaries of key employees.

I propose that we adopt the following actions immediately as a means of looking forward and heading off crises:

1. Hire one recruiting specialist
2. Hire an assistant and a secretary for Jerry Abbott in T & D
3. Hire an assistant and typist for Holmes in Wage and Salary administration
4. Establish a records room for employee benefits records, hire a clerk to assist Ramirez, and provide her with a PC (personal computer).

After you have considered this proposal, I would like to get together with you and nail down your decisions.

EXHIBIT C

C & TT, Inc.
INTEROFFICE MEMO

TO: John Groth
FROM: Jim Ure
February 22, 1985

I have given your memo of 2/8 a lot of thought, along with other problems posed by our rapid growth and further anticipated growth. It seems to me that Personnel can make our business more effective and contribute profit by

1. Providing research on human resource activities that will increase productivity and QWL
2. Providing a human resource management information system that will (a) give managers information for decisions affecting their people, and (b) supply regular concise reports on indicators of human resource activities, status, and trends for planning and control purposes
3. Establishing and maintaining an integrated HR data base to aid us in carrying out service programs such as T & D, employee benefits, promotions and transfers, and EEO tracking

As I envision this, Personnel would require a minicomputer and about 3–5 terminals. Perhaps this system could operate independently of other management information systems within the company except for accessing by Payroll. As a start, I suggest that you hire a systems analyst immediately to develop a proposal and possibly head up future development of the system. (Check with Don in the MIS section.)

At the same time, would you please determine from our managers the type of HR information they want, including detail and frequency? Would you then prepare a proposed set of HR reports? Also, could you suggest a number of research projects Personnel could perform to help us solve some of our current problems?

Let's get together at 1:30 P.M., March 21, to see how we stand on this. I'll see you at lunch tomorrow in case you have any immediate questions.

APPENDIX A
Important Organizations in Personnel Management

AFL–CIO
815 16th Street, N.W.
Washington, DC 20006

American Arbitration Association
140 W. 51st Street
New York, NY 10020

American Center for Quality of Work Life
3301 New Mexico Avenue, N.W.
Washington, DC 20016

American Compensation Association
P. O. Box 1176
Scottsdale, AZ 85252

American Management Association (AMA)
135 West 50th Street
New York, NY 10020

American Productivity Center
123 N. Post Oak Lane
Houston, TX 77024

American Society for Personnel Administration (ASPA)
30 Park Drive
Berea, OH 44017

American Society for Training and Development (ASTD)
Suite 305
600 Maryland Avenue, S.W.
Washington, DC 20024

Bureau of Industrial Relations
University of Michigan
Ann Arbor, MI 48104

APPENDIX A

Bureau of Labor Statistics (BLS)
U.S. Department of Labor
3rd Street & Constitution Avenue, N.W.
Washington, DC 20210

Bureau of National Affairs (BNA)
1231 25th Street, N.W.
Washington, DC 20037

U.S. Department of Labor
3rd Street & Constitution Avenue, N.W.
Washington, DC 20210

Equal Employment Opportunity Commission (EEOC)
2401 E Street, N.W.
Washington, DC 20566

Human Resource Planning Society
P. O. Box 2553, Grand Central Station
New York, NY 10017

International Association for Personnel Women
150 W. 52nd Street
New York, NY 10019

International Personnel Management Association (IPMA)
1850 K Street, N.W., Suite 870
Washington, DC 20006

Labor/Management Mediation Service
1620 I Street, N.W., Suite 616
Washington, DC 20006

National Association for the Advancement of Colored People (NAACP)
1790 Broadway
New York, NY 10019

National Association of Manufacturers (NAM)
1776 F Street
Washington, DC 20006

National Association of Temporary Services
1001 Connecticut Avenue, N.W.
Suite 932
Washington, DC 20036

National Safety Council
444 N. Michigan Avenue
Chicago, IL 60611

National Safety Management Society
6060 Duke Street
Alexandria, VA 22304

Occupational Health Institute
150 N. Walker Drive
Chicago, IL 60606

Occupational Safety and Health Administration (OSHA)
200 Constitution Avenue, N.W.
Washington, DC 20210

Office of Federal Contract Compliance (OFCC)
200 Constitution Avenue, N.W.
Washington, DC 20210

Office of Productivity and Technology
Bureau of Labor Statistics
U.S. Department of Labor
441 G Street, N.W.
Washington, DC 20001

Pension Benefit Guaranty Corporation
P. O. Box 7119
Washington, DC 20044

U.S. Chamber of Commerce
1615 H Street, N.W.
Washington, DC 20062

Work in America Institute
700 White Plains Road
Scarsdale, NY 10583

APPENDIX B
Important Periodicals for Management of Human Resources

Academy of Management Review	Quarterly; Academy of Management, c/o Dennis Ray, P. O. Box K2, Mississippi State, MS 39762
Bureau of National Affairs	Weekly; Bureau of National Affairs, Inc. 1231 25th Street, N.W., Washington, DC 20037
Business Week	Weekly; 1221 Avenue of the Americas, New York, NY 10020
Compensation Review	Quarterly; American Management Association, 135 West 50th Street, New York, NY 10020
Dun's Review	Monthly; P. O. Box 3088, Grand Central Station, New York, NY 10017
Fortune Magazine	Monthly; Time Inc., 514 N. Fairbanks St., Chicago, IL 60611
Harvard Business Review	Bi-monthly; Graduate School of Business Administration, Soldiers Field, Boston, MA 02163
Human Relations	Monthly; Plenum Publishing Corp., 227 W. 17th Street, New York, NY 10011
Human Resource Planning	Quarterly; Human Resource Planning Society, P. O. Box 2553, Grand Central Station, New York, NY 10163
Industry Week	Monthly; Penton Publishing Co., Penton Bldg., Cleveland, OH 44113
Industrial Engineering	Monthly; American Institute of Industrial Engineering, 25 Technology Park/Atlanta, Norcross, GA 30092

IMPORTANT PERIODICALS FOR MANAGEMENT OF HUMAN RESOURCES

Industrial Management	Six times/year; Institute of Industrial Engineers, 25 Technology Park/Atlanta, Norcross, GA 30092
Journal of Human Resources	Quarterly; Journal Division, The University of Wisconsin Press, 114 North Murray Street, Madison, WI 53715
Journal of Safety Research	Quarterly; National Safety Council, 444 N. Michigan Avenue, Chicago, IL 60611
Labor Law Journal (The)	Monthly; Commerce Clearing House, Inc., 4025 W. Peterson Avenue, Chicago, IL 60646
Monthly Labor Review	Monthly; Superintendent of Documents, U.S. Government Printing Office, Washington, DC 20402
Organizational Dynamics	Quarterly; AMACOM, 135 W. 50th Street, New York, NY 10020
Personnel	Bi-monthly; American Management Association, 135 West 50th Street, New York, NY 10020
Personnel Administrator	Monthly; American Society for Personnel Administration, 30 Park Drive, Berea, OH 44107
Personnel Journal	Monthly; The Personnel Journal, Inc., 1311 Olympic Blvd., Santa Monica, CA 90404
Personnel Psychology	Quarterly; Personnel Psychology, Inc., 3121 Cheek Road, Box 6965, College Station, Durham, NC 27708
Public Personnel Management	Quarterly; 1850 K Street, N.W., Washington, DC 20006
Quality Circle Quarterly	Quarterly; International Association of Quality Circles, P. O. Box 30635, Midwest City, OK 73140
Training Development Journal	Monthly; American Society for Training and Development, Box 5307, Madison, WI 53705
Wall Street Journal	Daily; Dow Jones-Irwin, Inc., 1818 Ridge Road, Homewood, IL 60430

GLOSSARY

Action Research Model: A specific strategy (consisting of a series of steps) designed to achieve an effective organizational development program.

Affirmative action: Positive actions taken by employers to eliminate job discrimination and to ensure equal employment opportunity.

AFL–CIO (American Federation of Labor and Congress of Industrial Organizations, 1955): A unified focal point of most labor unions that represents about 77 percent of the union members in the United States.

Alternative work schedules: Alternative core and optional days and/or hours that make up a work week.

Andragogy: The teaching of adults, as opposed to pedagogy, the teaching of children.

Appraisal: The measurement and evaluation of an individual's performance against established standards of performance.

Appraisal interview: A private communication between manager and subordinate concerning the evaluation of how well the employee has met the demands of his or her job.

Aptitude tests: Devices that measure one's ability to learn specific jobs.

Arbitration: The method of settling a labor dispute in which a neutral third party hears the case and issues a decision.

ASPA (American Society for Personnel Administration): A professional society devoted to improving and maintaining standards of excellence in the field of P/HR; members include both professionals and students in college chapters.

Aspiration: A life-goal that an individual sets for himself or herself.

Assessment centers: Facilities that undertake the evaluation of job candidates or of present employees for the purpose of promotion.

Attitudes: Predispositions to evaluate or respond to some object or aspect of the world in a favorable or unfavorable manner.

Attitude survey: A means to uncover employee perceptions of their organization; the method used to obtain this information is often a questionnaire or interview.

Bargaining unit: The group of employees actually represented by the union.
Bargaining zone: The negotiation area between the employer's tolerance limit and the union's tolerance limit.
Behavioral interventions: Specific techniques designed to affect the behavior of individuals and groups in order to obtain organizational change.
Behavioral learning theory: A theory based on conditioning through stimulus response or response–stimulus and reinforcement by rewards and/or punishment.
Benchmark job: A job within an organization whose duties and responsibilities are similar to and highly identifiable with jobs in other organizations within the relevant labor market.
Broadcast communications: A communication system that links all the workers in the organization to the ideas and concepts of management; most of this system is usually nonpersonal, such as company bulletins and newsletters.

Career development: Programs and activities that help individuals plan their future careers to achieve their maximum self-development.
Career management: An attempt by the individual to plan future work activities by matching his or her abilities with the needs of the organization.
Career path: The progression of jobs that forms one's career.
Career planning: A personnel activity that attempts to connect an individual's desires for the future with the needs of the organization.
Career stages: An individual's career movement through four stages: exploration, establishment, midcareer, and disengagement.
Central tendency error: A rater bias in which too many ratees are assigned an average score.
Change agent: An individual who attempts to bring about constructive change within the organization, group, or individual, usually through a psychological approach; synonyms are interventionist or consultant.
Classification: A job evaluation method involving the breakdown of positions into grades based on criteria such as education, job responsibility, and skill required.
Closed shop: A provision for a union under which management agrees to hire only union members; thus, in order to be considered for employment, one must be a union member. The closed shop is illegal in most circumstances.
Cognitive learning theory: A theory stating that people recognize the relationship between signs in their environment and their desired goals.
Collective bargaining: The negotiation between management and a formal representative of the employees on the terms of employment for all workers in a bargaining unit.
Comparable worth: A notion grounded in the belief that men's jobs are not necessarily inherently of more value than women's jobs.
Compensation and benefits surveys: A means of obtaining information concerning a company's existing compensation program for comparative and planning purposes.
Compensation strategy: The goals, objectives, and policies of a reward system that are designed to match an organization's history, traditions, managerial climate, structure, and tasks.

Compensation system maintenance: A process of continually reviewing the compensation program through the use of surveys and internal reviews.

Concessionary bargaining: The voluntary yielding of disputable issues for the sake of negotiation.

Conceptual design: The phase of project management in which a system is conceptualized in general or approximate form for evaluation before the detailed design is started.

Concurrent validity: A predictor of the future success of the applicants that is developed by measuring the test scores of job applicants against the test scores of current employees.

Constitutionalism in the workplace: Concepts of employee rights including privacy, dissent without punishment, equity, and due process.

Construct validity: A criterion of proof that a test does, in fact, measure a particular trait and that the trait is critical for job performance.

Content validity: A criterion of proof that a relationship exists between the content of a test or selection procedure and the job in question.

Craft unions: Formal organizations that include all workers who have a common skill or occupation.

Criterion-related validity: An estimate of the extent to which there exists a relationship between test scores and measures of job performance.

Cooperative T & D: A program that consists of combined on-the-job and off-the-job training provided by the company in cooperation with a school.

Culture: The concepts, attitudes, habits, and skills of a given group of people in a specific environment.

Data base: The integrated collection of organized data of an organization.

Data base schema: The logical and physical relationship that links the data stored by an organization.

Data privacy: The right of individuals or organizations to restrict the dissemination of information about themselves.

Data security: The physical protection of data against acts of nature and people as well as protection against modification by, or disclosure to, unauthorized people.

DBMS (Data Base Management System): A computer-based system that will control the definition, creation, retrieval, updating, and revision of the data base.

Development: In learning theory, a person-oriented process that focuses on improving the conceptual, decision-making and interpersonal skills of the individual.

Diagnosis: The search for underlying problems of a system that is malfunctioning.

DOT (Dictionary of Occupational Titles): A U.S. Department of Labor publication giving approximately 30,000 concise job descriptions.

Due process: The right of an accused person to have established legal and administrative procedures followed so that fairness is achieved; part of constitutionalism in the workplace.

Education: Individual-related learning that broadens the range of responses of the individual to life situations.

EEO (Equal Employment Opportunity): Those personnel practices, directives, and laws covered by Title VII of the Civil Rights Act of 1964 and the Equal Employment Opportunity Act of 1972 dealing with prevention of discrimination in the workplace because of sex, race, religion, national origin, or other protected status.

Effectiveness: The degree to which objectives are achieved.

Efficiency: The ratio of output to input of a person or organization performing a task.

Emergent behavior: Group behavior that "emerges" in the workplace because it is created by the group members to meet members' needs; goes beyond behavior required to perform the assigned worker.

Employee Involvement (EI) Program: A joint problem-solving process whereby unions and management establish joint committees to make jobs more productive as well as more satisfying for the workers.

Employee maintenance: Those personnel benefits given to improve the quality of work-life without regard for specific compensation for work performed; as opposed to compensation, in which benefits such as vacation or life insurance given on the basis of job.

Employee Retirement Income Security Act (ERISA): Legislation designed to protect employees against inadequately funded pension plans through the regulation of pension plans by employers.

Employment agency: A placement service that attempts to match unemployed individuals with job openings.

Employment tests: Devices that assess the probable match between job candidates and job requirements.

Equal Employment Opportunity (EEO): Principle underlying laws that are designed to provide equal treatment and employment opportunities and to prohibit any discrimination based on race, religion, national origin, sex, and age.

Equity theory: A theory of work motivation based on the idea that people compare their input/output ratio and their resulting rewards with other people doing comparable work or having comparable backgrounds.

ERISA: See Employee Retirement Income Security Act.

Executive order: A presidential order applying to government contractors that is designed to promote access to jobs that, in the past, have been unavailable to members of certain protected groups.

Expectancy model: The theory important to job design, that focuses on matching individuals' goals to organizational goals.

Expectancy theory: A model that explains and predicts how much energy or effort an individual is likely to exert based upon his or her perceptions of expectancies and outcomes.

External recruitment: Searching for a candidate outside of the firm to fill a position within the firm.

Extrinsic rewards: Those rewards external to the job itself, such as compensation, promotion, vacation, and fringe benefits; distinct from intrinsic rewards.

Factor comparison: A form of job evaluation that allocates a part of each job's wage to the key factors of the job; the result is a relative evaluation of the organization's job.

Fair employment practices: Anti-discrimination laws that promote equal employment opportunities for protected groups.

Fair Labor Standards Act (1938): Legislation requiring that most employers pay minimum wages and compensate overtime for time over 40 hours per week.

Feedback control: Control that is achieved by comparing (feeding back) the outputs of a system with desired input criteria and having the error produce a change in system functioning.

Financial rewards: Those rewards that are of monetary value, such as wages and benefits.

Flexible compensation: A system that provides each individual a number of options as to the form and timing of his or her total compensation package.

Flexitime: A work schedule whereby employees work eight hours a day but choose a starting and quitting time that holds for an extended number of weeks.

Formal communication: An exchange of information and meaning between two or more people through structured organizational channels; distinct from informal communication.

Formal organization: A group of people whose activities are consciously coordinated toward a common objective or objectives; distinct from informal organization.

Fractional flow model: A means for estimating the number of workers in types of positions based upon the flow (change) from positions of an earlier period.

Fringe benefits: Any rewards provided to an employee in addition to wage or salary; typical benefits include retirement plans, stock options, health and medical plans, paid vacations, and other time off.

Gliding time: A work schedule whereby employees may vary their starting and quitting times daily but still work the standard numbers of hours per day.

Grapevine: An informal communication system that arises spontaneously from social interaction of people in an organization.

Grievance: A complaint, usually filed by an employee, that a condition of the labor agreement has been violated by the management.

Group cohesion: The strength with which individuals are bound together in a group.

Halo error: A rating error that occurs when a rater tends to give an employee similar ratings on all facets of job performance because of a general overall impression.

Herzberg's two-factor theory: Motivation based on "hygiene" of maintenance needs and motivating needs of people.

HMO (health maintenance organization): A form of health maintenance where the insurer provides a medical staff and facilities and the emphasis is prevention of illness.

Hot cargo: A term given to nonunion products that union employees refuse to handle.

Hourly wages: Payment for work on the basis of a set rate or wage for each hour actually worked.

Human resource accounting: A method for valuing and including human resources in an accounting balance sheet.

Human resource management: All activities of both line managers and personnel staff that deal with people in association with a workplace.

Impasse resolution: An agreement reached on a bargaining issue within the limits that both the union and the employer find acceptable.

Informal communication: An unofficial flow of information between people in an organization; distinct from the formal communication system.

Informal organization: Spontaneously formed groups of people who interact regularly for some identifiable purpose; distinct from formal organization.

Instrumentality: When used in expectancy theories of motivation, the individual's perception that achievement of an intermediate goal will lead to a subsequent related goal, it is usually expressed as a probability.

Interest tests: Devices that measure an applicant's interest in a particular job.

Internal recruitment: Choosing a candidate from within the firm to fill a job opening.

Interpersonal communication: A process by which one person transmits ideas, concepts, images, or sentiment to another; this exchange usually occurs at the individual level.

Intervening variables: Variables that are intermediate to causal (input) variables and output variables of an organization.

Intrinsic rewards: Feelings of satisfaction people obtain directly from their own activities such as achievement, recognition and competence; distinct from extrinsic rewards.

Job: A group of positions that are identical or similar with respect to their major job tasks.

Job analysis: The systematic collection, organization, and evaluation of information about jobs in an organization.

Job characteristics model: A model that relates task characteristics to job dimensions.

Job description: A written detailed statement of the purposes, task elements, responsibilities, tools employed for a specific job, and conditions under which the job is performed.

Job enlargement: Adding more tasks to a job in order to increase the number of job tasks.

Job enrichment: Adding more responsibilities, autonomy, and control to a job.

Job evaluation: A comparison of jobs by the use of formal and systematic procedures to determine their relative worth within the organization.

Job sharing: A scheduling tactic that allows two or more workers to do the same job by working different hours, days, or weeks; the total hours worked by all shares usually are equal to the hours worked by one full-time employee.

Knowledge workers: Employees such as professionals and technicians whose work mainly involves conceptual skill.

Labor market: A geographical area in which the availability of people looking for work and the availability of job openings interact to determine the price of labor.

Labor union: An organization of workers formed to protect their mutual interests with the legal authority to negotiate with the employer.

Laboratory training: The creation of an experimental laboratory situation in which people are brought together in groups to interact in an unstructured environment.

LCI (Learner-Controlled Instruction): Method of teaching in which the learner proceeds at his or her own pace in the learning process.

Leniency error: A rating error that occurs when an individual is rated higher than his or her performance justifies.

Local union: The base structure of the entire labor movement whereby the manager comes into direct contact with the union, and the local union has direct control over the rank-and-file worker.

Management by objectives (MBO): A systematic, formal goal setting and review, conducted jointly by managers and subordinates, throughout various levels in an organization; the emphasis is placed on measuring people according to how well they reach agreed-upon objectives.

Managerial Grid: A specific methodology for team building that consists of a series of carefully planned individual and group exercises designed to develop awareness of managerial style, interpersonal competence, and group effectiveness.

Maslow's need hierarchy: An ordering of human needs from basic physiological through social and self-actualization needs for the purpose of explaining motivation.

Maxiflex: A work schedule whereby employees may vary their daily work hours and don't have to be present for a "core" (common) time on all days.

MBO: See management by objectives.

Mediation: An attempt on the part of a third party to assist union and management negotiations in reaching a voluntary agreement.

MPDQ (Management Position Description Questionnaire): A structure for developing an inventory of activities for a manager.

Need hierarchy: A concept formulated by Abraham Maslow to describe human motivation. Human needs are described as proceeding up a hierarchy from the lowest-level physiological needs to the highest-level self-actualization needs.

NLRA (National Labor Relations Act of 1935, also known as the Wagner Act): Legislation providing that employees could either join or not join unions for the purpose of their own aid, protection, and negotiation with employers.

NLRB (National Labor Relations Board): A governmental agency created to prevent unfair labor practices and to hold union elections.

Nonbehavioral interventions: Specific techniques of a more structured nature that are designed to achieve organizational change; these techniques may involve changes in the organizational structure, work design, technology, or compensation system.

Nonfinancial rewards: Those rewards other than monetary ones such as recognition, praise, and title promotion.

Norms: Standards of behavior set by an individual reference group.

Occupational Safety Health Act (OSHA): Legislation designed to protect the health and safety of employees in the workplace.

Occupational stress: A condition brought about by a person's reaction to the work environment that adversely affects his or her mental and physical health and work performance.

Off-the-job training: Leaves of absence to attend school, after-hours T & D at schools, seminars away from work, and correspondence courses.

Operant conditioning: Proposed by B. F. Skinner, a learning theory stating that behavior results from environmental inputs rather than initiation by the individual.

Organization development (OD): An intervention strategy that uses group processes to focus on the whole organization in order to bring about planned change.

Outplacement: The activity maintained by a company to help employees leaving the company find another suitable position.

PAQ (Position Analysis Questionnaire): A method for analyzing jobs quantitatively; developed at Purdue University.

Path–goal model: A theory of leadership–motivation that is based on two hypotheses: The leader's function is a supportive supplemental activity and the motivational impact of the behavior of the leader is determined by the situation.

Path–goal theory: A theory of human motivation formulated by Porter and Lawler; see path–goal model.

Performance tests: The measure of how much the job candidate already knows about the job or how well he or she is able to do it.

Personality tests: Devices that attempt to measure the different traits or characteristics of the personality.

P/HR management: The management of recruiting, staffing, training, developing, rewarding, utilizing, and maintaining workers in an organization.

Piece rate: A compensation program in which payment is based on the number of items completed; most commonly used for manual workers in a manufacturing facility.

Placement tests: The assignment of employees to positions ensuring that job demands are met as well as the individual's needs.

Point method: A form of job evaluation that assesses the relative importance of the job's key factors in order to arrive at the relative worth of jobs.

Polygraph tests: Devices that measure certain physiological changes caused by stress.

Position: A set of tasks sufficient to justify the employment of a worker.

Position description (Position Guide): A written summary of the objectives, responsibilities, and relationships for a position.

Posting: A method of publicizing job openings within the firm.

Productivity: The quantity and quality of output of an individual or an organization relative to the input resources.

Productivity bonuses: A type of incentive system that provides employees with additional compensation when they surpass stated productivity goals.

Quality circle (QC): About 6 to 12 workers doing related work who meet regularly to identify, analyze, and solve product quality and production problems.

QWL (quality of work life): The extent to which employees are able to satisfy their important individual needs in their work environment.

Ranking: A method of performance evaluation in which ratees are ranked according to relevant performance dimensions.
Recruitment: The practice of generating capable applicants to apply for employment.
Rehabilitation training: Training experience oriented to the special skills and attitudes required by some people to become or remain useful.
Reliability: The characteristic of a test assuring that the results will be consistent each time the individual takes the test.
Requisition: A request to fill a specific or anticipated job vacancy. It should contain information that describes the position to be filled, duties to be performed, and the experience and qualifications required of the candidate for the job.
Reverse discrimination: In an attempt to enforce affirmative action practices, preferential treatment given to minorities and females, with accompanying discrimination against the white male.
Rewarding: Compensating employees for their performance.
Role model: An individual with similar job duties and responsibilities whose performance can serve as an example to be emulated.

Salary: A compensation program that provides regular, periodic payments, with the amount of payment unaffected by the number of units produced or hours actually worked.
Salary reviews: An annual evaluation of an employee's salary in order to determine what increments to award or recommend.
Sentiments: A combination of attitudes and emotions used as a basis for action or judgment.
Similarity error: A rating error in which the rater gives higher marks to subordinates whose background and attitudes are similar to the rater's own than to those who do not share such characteristics.
Situational theory: As applied to leadership theory, an approach stating that the effectiveness of a leader depends upon situational factors such as the nature of the group members and leader–member relationship, task structure, and the position power of the leader.
Socialization: A process by which people adapt or conform to the common needs of a social group or organization.
Staffing: Filling positions within the organization, which includes practices such as recruitment, selection, and training.
Steering control: Continuous anticipation of outputs to provide adjustments to inputs before output errors result.
Strategic plan: A documentation of the major milestones, allocation of resources, assignment of responsibilities, and timing of actions required to achieve strategic (long-range and integrated) objectives.
Structured interview (patterned interview): Based upon the type of job and its specifications, a predetermined list of questions that are asked of all job candidates.
System: The set of elements or parts that are interrelated to work together toward common goals by acting on inputs to produce desired goals (primarily).

Team building: An application of the general technique of lab training to actual working groups usually comprised of peers and a superior.

Uniform Guidelines: A framework used to determine if federal laws on discrimination are being adhered to by an employer; developed in response to the several, often conflicting guidelines the federal agencies were issuing.

Union: An organization of workers, acting collectively, attempting to protect and promote their mutual interests through collective bargaining. See labor union.

Union shop: A provision that states that an employer may hire a nonunion worker but once hired, must become a union member within a specified period of time.

Upward communication: A flow of information and ideas from a lower level to a higher level within an organizational structure.

Valence: A concept used in expectancy theories of motivation, the strength of a person's desire to achieve a specific goal.

Validity: The extent to which a selection technique (usually a test) measures what it is supposed to measure.

Value: A concept about what is fundamentally good or desirable that an individual holds onto as a guide through life.

Vesting: A provision in retirement plans that gives workers rights to a pension after a specified number of years of service; the employee is entitled to a pension payout even if the employee quits before retirement.

Vestibule training: Training in a simulated environment such as a training job shop that provides the worker with the skills required on the job.

Vroom-Yetton model: A guide for choosing leadership style that depends on identifying the rationality of a decision, commitment of the group to implement the decision, and the time required to make the decision.

Wage structure: A system of pay grades and classifications that defines the pay program of an organization.

Wagner Act of 1935 (National Labor Relations Act): Legislation that gives an employee the right to become a union member, free from employer pressure.

Weighted application blanks: Job application forms designed to determine which items on the blank correlate more with actual job success; these items, in turn, are weighted more heavily than the others in the employee selection process.

Wellness programs: All company-sponsored programs to diagnose and maintain the health of its employees through prevention of illness.

Work analysis: The process studying the characteristics of a work system that includes the process of redefining jobs in terms of tasks and behaviors, as well as education, skills, relationships, and responsibilities required.

Work breakdown structure (WBS): The division of a major project or task into a hierarchy of tasks for the purposes of planning and control.

Work design: A broad term for the process of defining tasks and jobs to achieve both organizational and employee goals.

Work ethic: The belief that work is a central part of life and a desirable goal providing satisfaction.

Work simplification: The process of redesigning work to simplify it further.

WPSS (Work Performance Survey System): The highly developed and tested system for structuring task statements, preparing a survey questionnaire, and analyzing the resulting data with a computer program.

NAME INDEX

Adams, J. S., 459, 467, 468, 481
Albrecht, K., 587, 588
Albright, L., 224
Alpin, J. C., 385, 401
Altinus, C., 21, 42
Alverson, G. F., 372
Aquilano, N. J., 166
Argyris, C., 78, 91
Arthur, J. R., 577
Arvey, R. D., 224
Atkinson, J. W., 246, 262, 481
Auchter, T., 609
Ayoub, M. A., 599

Bacon, P. C., 290, 294
Badawy, M. K., 92
Balicki, R. J., 691
Barnard, C. I., 252, 266
Barnes, L. B., 288, 291, 294
Barr, R. A., 603
Bass, B. M., 250, 253, 265, 266, 319, 330, 481
Bassett, G. A., 643
Bateman, T. S., 609
Beckhard, R., 271, 294
Behling, O., 481
Belt, J. A., 224
Bennett, A., 487
Bennis, W. G., 290, 330
Blake, R. R., 287, 288, 291, 294
Blood, M. R., 481
Bolon, D. S., 518, 522
Borman, W., 217, 224
Bowman, E. H., 125
Bray, D. N., 224

Breaugh, J. A., 194
Brown, G. D., 71
Brown, J. K., 676
Brown, M. A., 92
Bullock, D. H., 343, 372
Burdetsky, B., 145

Campbell, D., 400
Campbell, J. P., 286, 294, 481
Canter, R. R., 164
Carlisle, H. M., 256, 264, 266
Carrell, M. R., 381
Carroll, S. J., 224
Carter, J. O., 396
Cascio, W. F., 224
Chaney, J., 612
Chapman, J. B., 72
Chartier, R., 92
Cherry, R. A., 518, 522
Cohen, A., 577
Coons, A. E., 266
Cooper, D. R., 686
Cooper, K. C., 224
Crow, A., 347
Crow, L. D., 347
Cummings, L. L., 423, 447, 462, 481
Cunningham, J. B., 665, 686
Cureton, B., 372
Cureton, J., 372
Curley, J., 193

Dalton, D. R., 681
Dalton, G. W., 276, 294
D'Aprix, R., 309

Davey, H. W., 577
Davis, L. E., 139, 164
DeCotis, T. A., 428, 447
DeLouise, R. C., 603
Dewey, J., 346, 372
Dickson, W. J., 294, 481
Digman, L. A., 342, 372
Dodge, R., 261
Downey, H. K., 447
Downs, C. W., 431, 434, 435, 447
Drabek, T. E., 92
Drucker, P. F., 413, 419, 422, 423, 447
DuBois, N. F., 372
Dunnette, M. D., 217, 224, 225, 286, 294, 447, 481
Dyer, L., 382

Eddy, W. B., 274
Ellis, D. O., 651
Ellis, N., 481
Ephin, D. F., 590
Estey, M., 551
Ettkin, L., 72
Evans, V. M., 193

Fee, F. X., 396
Field, H. S., 437, 448
Ferry, D. L., 141, 142, 164, 167
Fiedler, F. E., 255, 256, 266
Fine, S. A., 225
Fischbach, G. T., 501
Floersch, R. E., 31
Foltz, R. G., 330
Frank, L. L., 291, 294

Freedman, A., 562, 577
French, C. J., 481
French, J. R. P., 414, 423, 447
Freshley, D. I., 330
Futrell, C., 468

Gael, S., 157, 160, 164
Gagné, R. M., 348
Gallese, L., 224
Gatza, J., 423, 447
Georgoff, D. M., 351, 372
Gerster, D. K., 385
Ghiselli, E., 481
Giblin, E. J., 31
Gilbert, T. F., 372
Gilbreth, F., 137
Gilbreth, L., 137
Ginsburg, L. R., 398
Glueck, W. E., 192
Gorlin, H., 223, 400
Greiner, L. E., 275, 276, 288, 291, 294
Greller, M. M., 330
Griffin, R. W., 164
Grix, J. J., 328, 330
Gutteridge, T., 382

Hackman, J. R., 139, 140, 142, 164, 291, 294
Hale, A. R., 599
Hale, R. M., 599
Hall, D. T., 380, 400
Hall, J., 330
Hanley, J., 260
Hargis, K., 367
Harper, S. F., 414, 447
Harris, O. J., Jr., 330
Hart, K. K., 265, 481
Hass, J. E., 92
Hayes, M. A., 330
Hedges, J. N., 42
Hellriegel, D., 447
Heneman, H. G., Jr., 193, 220n, 428, 447
Herman, S., 289
Herold, D. M., 330
Herzberg, F., 244, 245, 246, 262, 291, 294, 467, 607
Hildren, J., 603
Hite, S., 42
Hoffman, J., 164
Holden, P. B., 224
Holley, W. H., Jr., 72, 437, 448
Hollmann, R. W., 447
Holt, C. C., 125

Horton, N. R., 42
House, R. J., 266, 286, 294
Howard, A., 224
Huck, J. R., 224
Hulin, C. L., 481
Hull, C. L., 348
Hurder, W. P., 481
Huse, E. F., 290
Huseman, R. C., 330, 342

Jacobson, R. V., 646
Janger, A. R., 28
Jerdee, T. H., 72
Johnson, L. S., 23

Kahn, R. L., 164, 251, 266
Katz, D., 92, 251, 266
Katzman, M. S., 145
Kay, E., 414, 423, 447
Kefalas, A. G., 686
Khumawala, B. M., 125
Kiefer, C., 82
Kiggundu, M. N., 164
Kimberly, J. R., 290
Kindall, A. F., 413, 423, 429, 431, 446, 447
Klatt, L. A., 92, 563
Klubeck, S., 319, 330
Kluckholn, C. K., 92
Kochan, T. A., 577
Kondrasuk, J. N., 431, 447
Kornhauser, A., 414, 446
Kotter, J. P., 97
Kurtz, D. L., 92
Kuzmits, F. E., 381

Lashutka, S., 272
Lawler, E. E., 247, 248, 265, 461, 466, 468, 481
Lawrence, P. R., 276, 280, 294
Lazer, R. T., 447
Leaf, T. L., 72
Leavitt, H. J., 275, 277, 294
Ledvinka, J., 66, 67, 72
Lee, H. C., 328, 330
Lee, J. A., 244, 246, 265
Lee, W. B., 125
Levine, E. L., 224
Levinson, Daniel J., 393
Lewin, K., 275, 294
Likert, R., 413, 414, 447, 670, 671, 673, 674, 686
Lindeman, E. C., 349, 372
Lindroth, J., 193
Linscott, J., 144

Lipsett, S. M., 551
Locher, A. H., 429, 431, 432, 434, 447
Logue, C. M., 330
London, M., 388, 396
Lorsch, J. W., 280, 294
Lowell, J., 458
Ludwig, F. J., 651
Luft, J., 322, 330

Mager, R. F., 361, 372
Mahoney, T. A., 589, 609
Main, J., 23, 372
Margulies, N., 291, 294
Martin, N. H., 92
Maslow, A. H., 85, 243, 244, 246, 262, 265
Mausner, B., 265
Mayo, E., 91
McClelland, D. C., 246, 247, 262, 265
McGregor, D., 85, 92, 271, 294, 413, 414, 422, 423, 447
McKay, N., 272
McKersie, R. B., 559, 577
Mellor, E. F., 42
Meloy, C. A., 525
Meyer, H. E., 24, 42
Meyer, H. H., 414, 423, 447
Miller, E. C., 224
Miner, J. B., 224
Miner, M. G., 224
Miron, D., 265
Mitchell, T. R., 92, 266
Mobley, W. H., 439, 448
Modigliani, F., 125
Moffatt, T. L., 215
Moorhead, G., 164
Mortensen, C. D., 330
Moscinski, P., 431, 434, 435, 447
Mouton, J. S., 287, 288, 291, 294
Murdick, R. G., 37, 125, 330, 351, 372, 644, 645, 651, 686
Murphy, B. P., 372
Murray, H. A., 92
Murray, S., 430
Muth, J. F., 125

Nash, A. N., 224
Nichols, J. M., 286, 294
Nielson, W. R., 290, 294
Nunke, B., 187, 188

O'Connor, R., 676
Odiorne, G. S., 431, 447, 674

NAME INDEX

Ogden, W. C., 577
O'Hara, R., 651
Oldham, G. R., 139, 140, 142, 164
Opshal, R. L., 481
Organ, D. W., 609
Ornati, O. S., 31
Ouchi, W. G., 686

Paine, T. H., 504, 513
Parker, T. C., 217, 224
Patten, T. H., Jr., 50, 71, 289, 290, 294
Paul, W. J., 291, 294
Pavlov, I., 348
Perry, W. E., 394
Pestillo, P. J., 590
Piaget, J., 348
Pious, F. K., Jr., 609
Pondy, L. R., 330
Porter, L. W., 244, 246, 247, 248, 265, 466, 481
Power, J., 573
Pritchard, R. D., 481
Puch, F. L., 224
Puda, E., 224

Quiroz, A., 612

Raia, A. P., 290, 294
Rees, A., 551
Reitman, W. R., 481
Richardson, E., 19, 22, 42
Richardson, R. C., 564
Riesel, V., 42
Robertson, K., 291, 294
Rock, M., 501
Roethlisberger, F., 294, 481
Rome, P., 224
Root, N., 601
Rosen, B., 72
Rosen, H., 567
Rosenzweig, M., 224
Ross, J. E., 330
Rudnitsky, H., 193

Sappir, M. Z., 551
Schneider, W., 551
Schoderbek, C. G., 686
Schoderbek, P. P., 686
Schrank, R., 22, 42
Schriesheim, C., 481
Schuster, F., 413, 429, 431, 446, 447, 648
Schuster, F. E., 281, 292
Schwab, D. P., 423, 428, 447
Schwartz, I. R., 400
Scott, W. G., 92, 265, 481
Selekman, B. M., 559, 577
Shannon, C. E., 330
Shapiro, H. J., 667
Silbey, V., 224
Simon, H. A., 125
Skinner, B. F., 249, 262, 265, 348, 466, 481
Sloan, S. B., 372
Slocum, J. W., Jr., 447
Snyderman, D. B., 265
Sparks, C. P., 224
Stagner, R., 567
Staley, R. K., 372
Starling, G., 42
Steers, R. M., 246, 265, 666, 669
Steinzor, B., 319
Stessin, L., 481
Stewart, R., 159, 161, 164
Stogdill, R. M., 266
Stone, C. H., 224
Stroh, P., 82
Stumpf, S. A., 388, 396
Sutermeister, R. A., 265

Taft, R., 422, 447
Tate, L. E., 290, 294
Taylor, F. W., 137, 236
Taylor, J. C., 139, 164
Teel, K. S., 429, 431, 432, 434, 435, 447, 448
Tersine, R., 21, 42
Thomas, J. M., 330

Thorn, I. M., 396
Thorndike, E. L., 348
Todor, W. D., 681
Tolman, E. C., 348
Toth, E. R., Jr., 94
Tracey, W. R., 372
Travers, R. M. W., 372
Tucker, D., 224
Tuthill, M., 68

Urban, T. T., 563

Van Cleve, R. R., 42
Van de Ven, A. H., 141, 142, 164
Van Glinow, M. A., 651
Vroom, V. H., 247, 248, 257, 265, 266, 466, 481

Wahba, M. A., 667
Walker, J. W., 193, 383
Walker, W. B., 414, 447
Walton, R. E., 559, 577, 583, 584, 609
Wanous, J. G., 194
Wanous, J. P., 194
Watson, J. B., 348
Weaver, W., 330
Weidenbaum, M. L., 72
Welsh, A., 164
Wernimont, P. F., 193
Whisler, T., 414, 447
White, L. P., 286
Whyte, W. F., 481
Wikstrom, W. S., 447
Wilhelm, S. J., 193
Winstanley, N. B., 507, 509, 513
Woodruff, R. L., Jr., 674, 675
Wooten, K. C., 286

Yetton, P. W., 266
Yoder, D., 193, 220n

Zenger, J. H., 367
Zoglin, R., 13, 42
Zuboff, S., 143, 164

SUBJECT INDEX

AAP. *See* Affirmative action programs
ACA. *See* American Compensation Association
Adverse impact, 61
Affirmative action programs (AAP):
  development of, 56–58, 59
  purpose of, 50, 55–56
  recruitment, effect on, 177, 178–79
  reverse discrimination, 58, 60
  selection process, effect on, 218
  See also Equal Employment Opportunity laws
AFL-CIO. *See* American Federation of Labor–Congress of Industrial Organizations
Age Discrimination in Employment Act, 12, 51–52, 54, 176, 491
Alcoholism, 10, 11
Allen, William B., 555–56
Alternative Work Patterns (AWP), 144–45
Alternative work schedules, 587–89
American Arbitration Association, 568, 695

American Assembly Seminar, 19, 25
American Center for Quality of Work Life, 695
American Compensation Association (ACA), 38, 695
American Federation of Labor–Congress of Industrial Organizations (AFL-CIO), 534–35, 537, 695
American Management Association, 4, 695
American Productivity Center, 19, 20, 695
American Society for Personnel Administration (ASPA), 37, 219, 695
American Society for Training and Development, 38, 695
Andragogy, 348–49, 350
Application blanks, 203–6, 207
Appraisal. *See* Performance appraisal
Apprenticeship Act of 1937, 359
Aptitude tests, 208
Arbitration, 568
Assaf, Ronald, 581–82
ASPA. *See* American Society for Personnel Administration
Assessment centers, 217, 342

Attitude surveys, 309–11
AWP. *See* Alternative Work Patterns

Back-pay decisions, 69
Bakke v. *Regents of the University of California* (1978), 60
Barron, Howard P., 47–48
Behaviorally anchored rating scales (BARS), 425, 427–28
Behaviorist theories, 347–48
Benchmark jobs, 494–97
Benefits:
  costs of, 474–76
  cuts in, 487–88
  popularity of, 478
  privately funded, 477–78
  statutory, 64–65, 476–77
  See also Compensation; Reward systems
Benson, Louis P., 377–78
Berra, Robert L., 409–10
Burdick, Walton E., 485–86
Bureau of Industrial Relations, 695
Bureau of Labor Statistics, 696
Bureau of National Affairs, 696
Business planning, 104, 105, 106–9

Career, definition of, 380
Career crisis, 392, 393
Career development:
  definition of, 380
  evaluation and feedback, 399
  framework for, 395, 396, 397
  job assignments, 397
  training experiences, 397–99
Career management:
  advantages of, 379–80
  definition of, 380
  functions of, 381–82
  human resource planning, relation to, 382, 383, 384
  organization-centered approach, 378
  responsibility for, 384
Career path, 380, 387–88
Career planning:
  advantages of, 385
  definition of, 380
  individual:
    career stages, 391–92
    influencing factors, 390
    planning process, 392–93
  organizational:
    career paths, 387–88
    identifying employees, 386–87
    individual plans, 389–90
    responsibility for, 388–89
  prevalence of, 387
  responsibility for, 384–85
Career stages, 391–92
Chamber of Commerce, U.S., 697
Change agents, 297
CIO. *See* American Federation of Labor–Congress of Industrial Organizations
Civil Rights Act of 1964, Title VII, 50–51, 54, 61, 62, 175–76, 491, 492
Classical conditioning, 348
Cognitive learning theory, 348
Collective bargaining, 17–18
  bargaining relationships, 559
  bargaining strategies, 559, 560, 563
  bargaining structures, 558
  computers, effects of, 575
  concessionary bargaining, 574
  contract administration, 569–73
  contract negotiations, 559–60
  bargaining sessions, 562–63, 564
  impasse resolution, 566–68
  issues, 564–66
  preparations for, 560–62
  ratification, 568–69
  definition of, 530
  governmental regulations regarding, 65–66, 538–41
  grievance procedures, 570–73
  labor-management cooperation programs, 574–75
  purpose of, 557
Collins, Alan L., 653–54
Communication:
  in appraisal and regulation, 303
  broadcast system, 312
  in coordination of activities, 302
  discussion plans, 325–26
  formal systems, 303, 304, 305–7, 309–11
  importance of, 301–2
  improvement of, 324–29
  informal systems, 303, 304, 312–20
  information, nature of, 315–16
  interpersonal:
    barriers to, 319–20
    definition of, 314–15
    listening, 318–19
    objectives of, 315
    patterns for, 313–14
    personal filters, 317
    physical aspects, 319
    power in, 318
    psychological aspects, 317–19
    selective perception, 317
    semantic aspects, 319
    source credibility, 318
    time aspects, 319
    verbal and nonverbal communication, 318
  Japanese management style, 302
  leadership, relation to, 302–3
  line managers, role of, 304–5
  manager-subordinate, 322–24
  messages, nature of, 316–17
  models of, 320–22
  in problem solving and innovating, 302
  program for, 324–25
  trust, role of, 325
Communication formats:
  attitude surveys, 309–11
  bulletin boards and posters, 306
  bulletins, 305
  communication audits, 307, 309
  employee handbooks, 305
  face-to-face, 308–9
  grievance procedures, 311
  job postings, 306
  Labor Relations Audit, 299
  newsletters, 306
  official reports, 306
  open forums, 307
  orientation programs, 305, 323
  policy manuals, 306
  special-purpose programs, 307
  staff and committee meetings, 307
  suggestion systems, 309
  video, 306
Comparable worth issue, 491–92
Compensation:
  bonuses, 470, 471, 472–73
  deferred, 479
  executive, 502, 503
  flexible, 14, 456–57, 459–62, 470, 478–79, 488, 502–5, 507
  governmental regulations regarding, 64–65, 489–92
  hourly wages, 469–70
  objectivity in, 15
  performance, relation to, 443–44
  piece rates, 471
  plantwide productivity plans, 472
  profit-sharing plans, 473
  quality of work life, part of, 583
  salary, 469
  sales commissions, 470
  Scanlon plan, 472
  stock-related supplemental plans, 473–74
  See also Benefits; Reward systems

SUBJECT INDEX

Compensation administration:
  benchmark jobs, 494–97
  benefit cuts, 487–88
  communication channels, 485–486
  comparable worth, 491–92
  compensation and benefit surveys, 494–95
  flexible systems, 502–5, 506
  governmental regulations regarding, 489–92
  internal standards of equity, 497–98
  job evaluation, 497–501, 502
  management training, 485–486
  merit pay, 485, 486, 507–9
  pay rates, 485, 486
  performance appraisals, 506
  program development, 488–89
  salary increases, 515, 516
  salary reviews, 507–9
  specialists in, 511
  system maintenance, 509, 510, 511–12
  unequal payments, 491
  unions, effect of, 493
  wage discrimination, 492
  wage structure, 492–93, 496–97
  work force involvement, 511–12
Competencies of management, 4
Computers:
  collective bargaining, effect on, 575
  components of, 640, 641
  Data Base Management System (DBMS), 639–40, 641, 642, 643, 644–46
  data processing systems, 636–37, 638, 639
  files, computerized, 636–37, 638, 639
  human resources management system, use in, 647–48
  impacts of, 7, 14–15
  quality of work life, used for, 606
  social interactions, effect on, 143, 144
  training and development, effects on, 347, 370

Concessionary bargaining, 574
Consensus management, 256
Constitutionalism, 584
Contingency approach, 9
Contingency models, 119
Contract negotiations. See under Collective bargaining
Control system. See Human resource control system

Data Base Management System (DBMS), 639–40, 641, 642, 643, 644–46
Davis Bacon Act of 1931, 65
DBMS. See Data Base Management System
Decision models, 119–20
Decision Support Systems (DSS), 143
Development, 346
  See also Training and development
Discrimination, 10, 11, 12
  See also Equal Employment Opportunity laws
Drug abuse, 11
DSS. See Decision Support Systems
Duty, definition of, 135–36

Education, company investments in, 24–25, 346
EEO. See Equal Employment Opportunity laws
EEOC. See Equal Employment Opportunity Commission
Employee handbooks, 305
Employee Involvement (EI) programs, 548, 589–91
Employee maintenance:
  employee information reports, 606
  financial services, 602
  food services, 605
  legal services, 601–2
  medical and health programs, 597, 601
  pensions, 602–4
  policy manual development, 605–6
  quality of work life, relation to, 592–93
  recreation facilities, 605
  responsibility for, 594, 595

retirement services, 602–4
  safety, 15–16, 594, 596–97, 598, 599, 600
  transportation, 604–5
Employee Retirement Income Security Act of 1974 (ERISA), 65, 477, 489, 604
Employee selection. See Selection
Employees. See Work force
Employment agencies, 185–86
Employment testing:
  achievement tests, 207
  aptitude tests, 208
  benefits of, 209–10
  intelligence tests, 208
  interest tests, 208
  legal issues, 210–11
  performance tests, 207
  personality tests, 209
  polygraph tests, 209
Energy shortage, 11–12
Equal Employment Opportunity Commission (EEOC), 51, 53, 61, 176, 202, 436, 696
Equal Employment Opportunity (EEO) laws:
  executive orders, 53, 54, 55
  federal, 50–52, 54, 69
  human resource planning, effect on, 113–14, 115, 117
  selection process, effect on, 218–20
  state and local, 53, 54
  See also Affirmative action programs
Equal Pay Act of 1963, 51, 54, 491, 492
Exception reports, 676
Ex-convicts, 11
Executive orders, 53, 54, 55, 56, 538

Fair Credit Reporting Act, 212
Fair employment practices. See Equal Employment Opportunity laws
Fair Labor Standards Act of 1938, 65, 489, 490
Federal Mediation and Conciliation Service (FMCS), 540, 568, 573
Federal Unemployment Tax Act of 1935, 476

FJA. *See* Functional Job Analysis
Flexiplace, 588
Flexitime, 13–14, 144–45, 588–89
FMCS. *See* Federal Mediation and Conciliation Service
Formal organization, 77–78, 87
Fractional flow models, 118–19
Functional Job Analysis (FJA), 154–55, 156–57

Gael, Sidney, 129–30
General Aptitude Test Battery (GATB), 208
Giudice, Sal J., 455–57
Governmental regulations:
  collective bargaining, 65–66, 538–41
  compensation and benefits, 64–65, 476–77, 489–92
  history of, 49–50
  job design, effect on, 145
  performance appraisal, effect on, 436–38
  recruitment, 175–77, 178–79
  safety in the workplace, 15–16, 62–64, 594, 596–97, 599, 600
  selection process, 61, 62, 217–220
  See also Affirmative action programs; Equal Employment Opportunity laws
Grayson, C. Jackson, 19
Grievance procedures, 311, 324, 570–73, 592
Griggs v. *Duke Power Company*, 217–18
Guaranteed annual wage plans, 490–91

Handicapped workers, 11, 52
Health maintenance organizations (HMOs), 478, 601
Hodgson v. *Miller Brewing Company*, 491–92
Hoffman, Helen G., 529
Homosexuality, 13
HRI. *See* Human Resources Index
HRMS. *See* Human resources management system

Human resource control system:
  characteristics of, 657
  development of, 663–70, 671, 672–73, 674–76
  diagnosis of problems, 676–79
  effectiveness of, 664–66, 667
  feedback control, 659–60
  impact of, 657
  input controls, 658–59
  measures for:
    human resource accounting, 670, 674, 675
    intervening variables, 670, 671, 672–73
    management by objectives, 674, 676
    statistical measures, 668–69
    work performance, 667–68
  process control, 660–62
  purpose of, 655–56
  responsibility for, 662–63
  subsystem control, 656–57
Human resource information system:
  computerized files, 636–37, 638, 639, 690–91
  Data Base Management System (DBMS), 639–40, 641, 642, 643, 644–46
  data processing systems, 636–37, 638, 639
  development of, 675–76
  flowchart of, 629–30
  manual, 635–36, 640
  security and privacy, 646–47
Human resource management:
  careers in, 31, 32, 33, 34–35, 36
  definition of, 5, 7
  functions of, 26, 27, 28
  future trends, 7
  goals of, 25–26
  governmental regulations, effects of, 66–68, 69, 70
  history of, 5–7
  job development, 131, 132, 133
  leadership development, 250, 251
  position description, 34–35
  professionalization in, 35–38
  subfunctions of, 9
  unionization, effects of, 546, 547, 548–50

work design, 134–35
work group classification, 89, 90
Human resource management system (HRMS):
  computers, use of, 647–48
  conceptual design, 632–33, 637
  definition of, 623, 624
  design phase, 630, 631–33
  employee processing, 623–24, 625, 626
  environment of, 626–27
  implementation phase, 633
  maintenance phase, 633, 635
  objectives of, 631–32
  operations performed, 629–30
  outputs and inputs, 632
  subsystems, 627
  systems approach to, 627–29
  See also Human resource information system
Human resource planning:
  activity plans, 104, 105, 109
  advantages of, 103
  attrition of workers, 114
  business planning, integration with, 104, 105, 106–9
  career management, relation to, 382, 383, 384
  constraints on, 117
  elements of, 102
  equal employment opportunity considerations, 113–14, 115, 117
  intermediate-range plans, 104, 105, 108
  manpower requirements:
    determination of, 109, 110, 111–14, 115
    forecasting of, 117–20
    net change in, 114, 116–17
  manpower supply forecasting, 120–22, 123
  operating plans, 104, 105, 108
  productivity factors, 114, 116
  strategic plans, 104, 105, 106–8
Human Resource Planning Society, 696
Human resource research:
  applications of, 682–84
  problem identification, 692
  purpose of, 679–80

Human resource research, *continued*
  responsibility for, 680–81
  techniques for, 681–82
  turnover, effect on, 653–54
Human Resources Index (HRI), 281, 283, 284, 310–11

Individual Retirement Accounts (IRAs), 604
Informal organization, 76–77, 78–79, 80, 81–82, 87
Information, definition of, 315–16
Information system. *See* Human resource information system
Insurance coverages, 461
Integrated approach to management. *See* Systems approach to management
Intelligence tests, 208
Interest tests, 208
International Association for Personnel Women, 696
International Personnel Management Association, 696
Interviews:
  employment, 213–16
  exit, 324
  job analysis, 153–54
  organization development, 279
  performance appraisal, 439, 441–42
IRAs. *See* Individual Retirement Accounts

Japanese management, 302
JDS. *See* Job Diagnostic Survey
Job, definition of, 136
Job analysis:
  approaches to, 129–30
  definition of, 131, 132
  objectives of, 149–50
  program for, 150–51, 152
  Functional Job Analysis, 154–55, 156–57
  interviews, 153–54
  management work analysis, 159–60, 161
  Position Analysis

Questionnaire, 155, 157, 158
  task inventories, 152–53
  Work Performance Survey System, 129, 130, 157, 159, 160
Job Bank, 186
Job description, 146
Job design:
  bottom-up approach, 130, 136
  class of work, 146
  classical model, 137–38, 139
  definition of, 131, 132
  documentation, 146, 147–48
  expectancy model, 138–39
  factors influencing, 141, 142, 143–45
  governmental regulations, effect of, 145
  job characteristics model, 139–40
  machines, concerns regarding, 143
  model of, 141, 142
  top down approach, 130, 136
Job development, 131, 132
Job Diagnostic Survey (JDS), 140, 141
Job elements, 135
Job evaluation:
  classification, 498–99
  objectives of, 497
  point method, 499–501
  ranking, 498
Job inventory questionnaire, 130
Job postings, 306
Job redesign, 131, 132, 161–62
Job sharing, 145
Job specification, 146, 148
Johari Window, 322
Johnson, Lyndon B., 55, 318

Kennedy, John F., 538
Knights of Labor, Noble Order of the, 534

Labor, U.S. Department of, 696
Labor/Management Mediation Service, 696
Labor-Management Participation Teams (LMPTs), 574–75
Labor-Management Relations

(Taft-Hartley) Act of 1947, 66, 538, 540–41
Labor-Management Reporting and Disclosure (Landrum-Griffin) Act of 1959, 66, 538, 541
Labor markets, 174
Labor Relations Audit, 299
Labor unions. *See* Unions
Landrum-Griffin Act. *See* Labor-Management Reporting and Disclosure Act of 1959
LCI. *See* Learner-controlled instruction
Leadership:
  authority, 252–53
  communication, relation to, 302–3
  definition of, 250–52
  leader-follower relationship, 263–64
  organization characteristics, effect of, 264
  personality traits for, 263
  power, 252
  quality circles, 259, 260, 261, 262
  tasks, relation to, 264
Leadership theory:
  application of, 251, 259
  leadership styles, 254–55, 261
  path-goal theory, 258
  situational theories, 255–57, 261
  trait theories, 253–54, 261
  two-dimensional theory, 255
  Vroom-Yetton model, 257–58, 259, 261
Learner-controlled instruction (LCI), 360
Learning curves, 114, 116
Learning theories, 347–49, 350
Leaves of absence, 14
Line managers, 5, 33, 68, 304–5, 342, 389
LMPTs. *See* Labor-Management Participation Teams
Lockouts, 567–68

Machaver, William V., 299–300
Management by Objectives (MBO), 288–90, 419, 422–23, 424–25, 426–27, 429, 431, 438–39, 440,

Management by Objectives, *continued*
441–42, 517, 662, 674, 676
Management information system (MIS), 629–30
Management Position Description Questionnaire (MPDQ), 159
Management resource planning, (MRP), 228–30
Management training, 336, 485, 486
Managerial grid, 287–88
Managerial groups, 87–88
Manpower inventories, 112
MBO. *See* Management by Objectives
McGeddy, Donna, 75
Medical and health programs, 597, 601
Merit pay, 485, 486, 507–9
Message, definition of, 316–17
Meyer, Mary Coeli, 235–38
Midlife crisis, 392, 393
Military Selective Service Act of 1967, amended, 176
Minimum wage laws, 65, 489–90
MIS. *See* Management information system
Money as reward, 463
Motion economy, 137, 138
Motivation:
 definition of, 242
 psychological contract, 237
 quality circles, 259, 260, 261, 262
 sources of, 133, 236–37
Motivation theory:
 application of, 242, 421
 equity theory, 467–68
 expectancy model, 247–49, 261, 466
 need for achievement, 246–47, 261
 need hierarchy theory, 243–44, 245, 261
 operant conditioning, 236, 249–50, 261, 348, 466
 two-factor theory, 244–46, 261
MPDQ. *See* Management Position Description Questionnaire

MRP. *See* Management resource planning
Myart v. Motorola, 211

National Association for the Advancement of Colored People (NAACP), 696
National Association of Manufacturers (NAM), 696
National Association of Temporary Services, 696
National Labor Relations (Wagner) Act of 1935, 49, 66, 530, 538, 539–40
National Labor Relations Board (NLRB), 538, 539–40, 543, 545
National Safety Council, 696
National Safety Management Society, 696
NLRB. *See* National Labor Relations Board
Norris-LaGuardia Act of 1935, 66

Obsolescence, 338
Occupation, definition of, 136
Occupational Health Institute, 696
Occupational Safety and Health Act (OSHA) of 1970, 15, 63, 64, 145, 566, 594, 596
Occupational Safety and Health Administration (OSHA), 596–97, 598, 600, 697
OD. *See* Organization development
Office of Federal Contract Compliance (OFCC), 53, 61, 62, 175, 491, 697
Office of Federal Contract Compliance Programs (OFCCP), 56, 67, 68
On-the-job training, 359
Operant conditioning, 236, 249–50, 261, 348, 466
Organization development (OD):
 action research model, 277, 278, 279–82, 283, 284
 data feedback and discussion, 280–82, 283, 284

 data gathering, 279–80, 281
 definition of, 271
 effectiveness of, 290–92
 Greiner's model, 275, 276
 intervention, 279, 282, 285–90
 laboratory training, 282, 285–86
 Leavitt's model, 275, 277
 macro approach, 271–73, 274
 management by objectives, 288–90
 managerial grid, 287–88
 objectives of, 273
 organizational diagnosis, 280
 team building, 286–87
 T-group training, 282, 285
 three-step model, 275
 traditional training, comparison with, 274
 underlying themes, 274–75
Organizational behavior:
 individual workers, 83–85
 work groups, 76–82, 86–89, 90
Organizational iceberg, 289
Orientation programs, 305, 323
OSHA. *See* Occupational Safety and Health Act of 1970; Occupational Safety and Health Administration
Otto, Kenneth L., 101–2
Overtime, 190

PAI. *See* Personnel Accreditation Institute
PAQ. *See* Position Analysis Questionnaire
Pattan, John, 335–36
Pension Benefit Guaranty Corporation, 697
Pensions, 65, 602–4
Performance appraisal:
 climate for, 435–36
 communication of results, 303, 445
 compensation, relation to, 443–44
 for compensation administration, 506
 definition of, 411
 dynamic nature of, 434–35
 evaluation of program, 436
 exempt appraisal, 522

Performance appraisal, *continued*
  governmental regulations regarding, 436–38
  implementation of program, 439, 440–45
  improvement of, 436
  interviews for, 439, 441–42
  non-exempt appraisal system, 521–22
  prevalence of programs, 429, 431
  problems with, 435
  profit performance measurement, 418–19
  raters, 412, 432, 434, 436, 523
  rewarding, relation to, 438–39, 440, 443–44, 466–68
  uses of, 411–13, 431–32, 433
Performance appraisal techniques:
  appraisal forms, 520–21, 522
  behaviorally anchored rating scales (BARS), 425, 427–28
  critical incident approach, 418, 422
  essays and checklists, 415, 418
  forced-choice, 415, 418, 421
  forced-distribution, 415, 420
  Management by Objectives (MBO), 419, 422–23, 424–25, 426–27, 429, 431, 438–39, 440, 441–42, 517
  motivation-oriented approach, 413–15
  ranking, 415, 421
  trait rating, 413–15, 416–17, 419, 432
Personality tests, 209
Personnel Accreditation Institute (PAI), 37
Personnel administration, 38
Personnel/human resource departments, 5, 29–30, 31
Personnel/human resource management. *See* Human resource management
Personnel/human resource specialists, 5, 8–9
P/HR management. *See* Human resource management

Physical examinations, 216
Piece work, 471
Placement strategy, 220–21
Policy manuals, 306, 605–6
Polygraph tests, 209
Position, definition of, 136
Position Analysis Questionnaire (PAQ), 155, 157, 158
Position description, 146, 147–48
Powell, Louis, 60
Privacy Act of 1974, 212
Productivity:
  decline in, 18–19
  definition of, 4
  factors determining, 240–41
  improvement of, 19–20
  job satisfaction, effect of, 21–22
  measurement of, 239–40
  quality of work life, relation to, 606–7
Professional and technical groups, 88
Profit-sharing plans, 473
Promotions, 15, 610
Public Health Service Act of 1973, 478, 601

Quality circles, 259, 260, 261, 262
Quality of work life (QWL), 4, 16, 133
  alternative work schedules, 587–89
  career growth, 584
  compensation, 583
  computers used for, 606
  constitutionalism, 584
  employee maintenance, relation to, 592–93
  grievance procedures, 592
  human capacity development, 584
  merit in employment, 592
  pay, 585
  productivity, relation to, 606–7
  program elements, 582
  recognition, 591
  resource adequacy, 592
  seniority, 592
  social integration of work force, 584

  social relevance of work 584–85
  stability of employment, 585
  stress, 585–86
  subcontracting limitations, 592
  wellness programs, 586–87, 588
  worker participation in control of work, 589–91
  worker-supervisor relations, 591–92
  working conditions, 583–84

Reality checks, 395
Recruitment:
  alternatives to, 190
  cost effectiveness of, 191–92
  definition of, 171–72
  evaluation of programs, 190–92
  external, 181, 182, 183, 184–189
  government regulations regarding, 175–77, 178–79
  internal, 177, 178–81
  job previews, 191
  labor markets, 174
  management resources planning, 228–30
  organizational policies, 174–75
  record keeping, 177
  responsibility for, 172
  union involvement, 174
  vacancy requisitions, 172, 173
Recruitment methods and sources:
  advertising, 182, 185
  colleges and universities, 187–88
  cooperative programs, 188
  employee referrals, 182
  employment agencies, 185–86
  high schools, 185
  internships, 188
  job posting, 180–81
  search consultants, 186
  trade and professional associations, 188–89
  "walk-in" applicants, 182
Reference checks, 212–13
Regression curves, 118

Rehabilitation, 346
Retirement, 12, 602–4
Reverse discrimination, 58, 60
Reward systems:
  cafeteria approach. See flexible compensation *below*
  contingency approach. See flexible compensation *below*
  extrinsic, 462–63, 465–66, 489
  fairness in, 459
  financial *vs* nonfinancial rewards, 458–59
  flexible compensation, 14, 456–57, 459–62, 470, 478–79, 488, 502–5, 506
  insurance coverages, 461, 478
  intrinsic, 464–66, 489
  pay decisions, 461–62
  pay secrecy, 468
  performance, relation to, 438–39, 440, 443–44, 466–68
  promotions, 15, 610
  purpose of, 458
  See also Benefits; Compensation
Rewarding, definition of, 411
Robotics, 19, 121
Rockefeller, Nelson, 318

Safety in the workplace, 15–16, 62–64, 594, 596–97, 598, 599, 600
Safety managers, 597
Scanlon plan, 472, 550
Schultz v. Wheaton Glass Company (1970), 51
Search consultants, 186
Selection:
  application blanks, 203–6, 207
  assessment centers, 217
  employment interviewing, 213–16
  employment testing, 207–11
  evaluation of processes, 221–22
  factors influencing, 200–1
  governmental regulations regarding, 61, 62, 217–20
  legally inappropriate questions, 205–6
  objectives of, 199
  objectivity in, 15

physical examinations, 216
preliminary screenings, 203
reference checks, 212–213
responsibility for, 199–200
strategies for, 220–21
validity and reliability of techniques, 201–2
Sexual harassment, 12–13, 61, 62
Simon, Sidney H., 621–22
Site locations, 11–12
Skills inventories, 180
Social Security Act of 1935, 476, 602
Spiller, Larry, 197–98
Sponsor-protege relationships, 390
Staffing. *See* Recruitment; Selection
Stress, 585–86
Strikes, 567
Subcontracting, 190
Supreme Court, U.S., 60, 218
System. *See* Human resource management system
Systems approach to management, 27, 39–41, 627–29
Systems designers, 15

T & D Grid, 351, 352
Taft-Hartley Act. *See* Labor-Management Relations Act of 1947
Task, definition of, 135
Task inventories, 152–53
Technological determinism, 137
Television. *See* Video
Temporary help, 190
T-groups, 282, 285, 358
Theory Y, 85
Time on the job, 13–14
TMS. *See* Training Mission Statement *under* Training and development
Toscano v. Ninno, 62
Toth, Edward R., Jr., 3
Training, definition of, 346
Training and development:
  apprenticeships, 355, 359
  career objectives, 349, 351, 352
  computers, effects of, 347, 370
  cooperative programs, 359

evaluation of, 364, 365, 366, 367, 368–69
facilities and times, 362–63
information systems for, 369
instructional materials, 361–62
instructors for, 360
learning theories, 347–49, 350
levels of learning, 354–55
long-range planning, 342–44
management training, 336
mandated training, 342
modification and maintenance, 363, 369
needs assessment, 336, 340–42
objectives of, 337
off-the-job training, 359
on-the-job training, 359
prevalence of programs, 337
program characteristics, 344, 346–47, 351, 353–54
recruitment of trainees, 363
responsibility for, 345
system structure, 338, 339, 340
T & D Grid, 351, 352
teaching-learning process, 360–61
teaching techniques, 355, 356–58
Training Mission Statement (TMS), 343–44
vestibule training, 359
Trend projections, 118

Unemployment insurance tax, 477
Unfair labor practice, 540
Union, definition of, 530
Union shops, 540, 564–65
Unions:
  attraction of, 531–33
  authorization cards, 543, 545
  bargaining units, 543, 545
  certification of, 545–46
  compensation administration, effect on, 493
  craft, 534
  demands of, 17
  elections for, 545
  handbilling, 542–43, 544
  history of, 533–35
  industrial, 534
  labor agreements, 548

Unions, *continued*
  local, 536–38
  management decisions, involvement in, 546, 548
  membership of, 16–17, 531, 532, 536
  national, 535–36
  organizing drives, 542–43, 611–17
  recognition of, 543, 545
  recruitment, involvement in, 174
  shop stewards, 538
  strikes, 567
  structures of, 535–38
  union-management cooperation, 549, 550
  unionization process, 541–43, 544, 545–46
  white-collar workers in, 535
  work environment modification, 549–50
  as work group, 88–89
  See also Collective bargaining; Work force
United States Employment Service (U.S.E.S.), 182, 185–86, 208, 209, 210
United Steelworkers, v. *Weber*, 60
U.S.E.S. *See* United States Employment Service

Video, 306, 357
Vietnam Era Veterans Readjustment Act of 1974, 52, 54
Vietnam War veterans, 52
Vocational Rehabilitation Act of 1973, 11, 52, 54, 176

Wage discrimination, 492
Wagner Act. *See* National Labor Relations Act of 1935
Walsh-Healey Act of 1936, 65
Watson, Debbie, 169–70
Wellness, 586–87, 588
Whistle blowing, 24
Women, 9–10, 12–13
Work, definition of, 135
Work design, 131, 132, 133–135
Work ethic, 21–22
Work force:
  compensation administration, involvement in, 511–12
  educational levels of, 20–21
  employee needs and expectations, 3, 7, 15–16, 62–64
  knowledge workers, 22, 24
  midlife career changes, 24–25
  professional identification, 24
  social integration of, 584
  underqualified workers, 25
  value systems of, 21–22
  worker characteristics, 83–86
  See also Unions
Work force planning, 9
Work groups:
  classification of, 89, 90
  emergent behavior subsystem, 79, 80, 81
  formal organization, 77–78, 87
  informal organization, 76–77, 78–79, 80, 81–82, 87
  managerial, 87–88
  professional and technical, 88
  required behavior and sentiments, 81–82
  unions, 88–89
Work in America, 19, 21–22
Work in American Institute, 697
Work modules, 144
Work Performance Survey Systems (WPSS), 129, 130, 157, 159, 160
Workers. *See* Work force
Workers' compensation laws, 63–64, 477
Working climate, 272–73, 311
WPSS. *See* Work Performance Survey System

Zero Defects programs, 661